LEONILSON

DEDICATE

-TO THE WISE MAN

-TO THVNDERS

-TO THE GAZE of THE PAINTINGS WE LOVE

-TO THE books you TOLD ME

-TO SVMMER 90

-TO THE OTHER SIDE of THE OLD STREET

-TO THE STRIPE SHIRT YOU GAVE ME

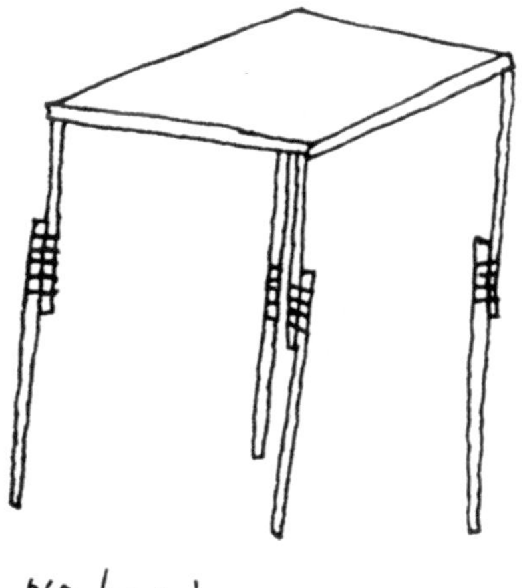

NO bombs
NO CASTLES ON SANd
NO dRVMS
IT'S ON ME

EMPTY MAN
LONE
READY

NOW AND OPPOR TUNI TIES

1. **Leonilson**
[Dedicate],
circa 1991
Permanent ink on paper
22 × 8 cm
Collection of Francisco Meirelles de Andrade,
São Paulo, Brazil
PL.1200.0/00

Distributed internationally by
KMEC Books
Artbook | D.A.P

STRATEGIC
PARTNER

Lei de
Incentivo
à Cultura
Lei Rouanet

itaú

MINISTÉRIO DA
CULTURA

GOVERNO FEDERAL
BRASIL
UNIÃO E RECONSTRUÇÃO

LEONILSON

CURATED AND EDITED BY
Adriano Pedrosa

WITH ASSISTANCE OF
Teo Teotonio

TEXTS BY
Adriano Pedrosa
Carlos Eduardo Riccioppo
Irene V. Small
Julia Bryan-Wilson
Miguel A. López
Pablo Lafuente
Teo Teotonio

MASP MUSEU DE ARTE DE SÃO PAULO ASSIS CHATEAUBRIAND

SPON SOR'S FORE WORD

Itaú Cultural

A figure of extreme relevance in contemporary visual arts, José Leonilson (1957-1993) deserves to be always revisited. His artistic production, primarily autobiographical, has brought into discussion subjects which remain central, such as gender identity, violence against minorities, and the LGBTQIA+ culture.

The exhibition *Leonilson: Now and Opportunities*, organized by the Museu de Arte de São Paulo Assis Chateaubriand (MASP), is an opportunity to bring the public once again close to the questions and reflections of an artist who dared to expose himself through an intimate language.

With a long tradition of supporting arts and culture, Itaú, through its strategic partnership with MASP, contributes to the construction of critical thinking and the promotion of citizenship, to the enlargement of the access to and the participation in cultural activities, and to the preservation and dissemination of Brazilian cultural and artistic heritage.

At Itaú Cultural (IC), Leonilson was featured in the solo exhibition *Sob o peso dos meus amores* [Under the Heavy Weight of My Loves] (2011), curated by Bitu Cassundé and Ricardo Resende. On our website (itaucultural.org.br) and YouTube Channel it is possible to see documents from the retrospective focused on the artist's work, which presented more than three hundred items.

The documentary *A paixão de JL* [JL's Passion] (2014), directed by the filmmaker Carlos Nader and produced by IC, includes tapes recorded daily during the artist's final years. They feature the documentation of his everyday life, his dreams, memories, reflections upon artistic practice and confessions about love and death. The feature film was elected best Brazilian documentary at the 2015 edition of the festival *É tudo verdade*. On Itaú Cultural Play (itauculturalplay.com.br), streaming platform dedicated to Brazilian audiovisual production, you can watch the documentary free of charge.

In the field of visual arts, Itaú Cultural organizes exhibitions in both physical and virtual spaces, as well as educationally oriented activities. In our headquarters, located at Paulista Avenue, a cultural corridor in the city of São Paulo, exhibitions featuring Claudia Andujar and Guto Lacaz are scheduled for 2024, from April to June and from August to October, respectively, in addition to a group show which takes fashion as its theme (from November 2024 to February 2025). Check out our website and social network profiles for our program and for exclusive, detailed content on the universe of culture and art.

LEO NIL SON AT MASP

Adriano Pedrosa

It is with a great sense of pride that the Museu de Arte de São Paulo Assis Chateaubriand (MASP) presents a solo exhibition dedicated to the work of Leonilson (1957–1993). *Leonilson: Now and Opportunities* is contextualized in a full year dedicated to *Queer Histories* at MASP, which also includes exhibitions devoted to Catherine Opie, Francis Bacon (1909–1992), Lia D Castro, Mário de Andrade (1893–1945), the collectives Gran Fury and Serigrafistas Queer, and the MASP Renner collection, exhibitions in the Video Room by Kang Seung Lee, Manauara Clandestina, Masi Mamani/Bartolina Xixa, Tourmaline and Ventura Profana, in addition to the large international group show *Queer Histories*.

Working with painting, drawing, objects, engraving, installation, textile, and embroidery, Leonilson is a fundamental artist in the history of Brazilian contemporary art at the end of the twentieth century. His work has an extremely particular, diaristic character, reflecting on the themes of his daily life, whether more personal or more political, in a queer dimension, although always full of poetry and beauty. The last years of his production, especially from 1989 onwards, are when the artist produces his most extraordinary works. In August 1991 he discovers that he is HIV-positive, eventually developing the associated syndrome and dying just under two years later, in May 1993. Although Leonilson was quite successful and received recognition during his lifetime in Brazil, it was only after his death that his work began to acquire more significant international visibility. A little less than two years after his death, in January 1996, an exhibition of his works opened at The Museum of Modern Art (MoMA), as part of the museum's well-known *Projects* series, *Projects 53: Oliver Herring/Leonilson*, curated by Starr Figura.

Leonilson participated in numerous exhibitions, such as the biennials of Istanbul, Paris, São Paulo, and Venice, and more recently, important solo exhibitions accompanied by catalogs were organized in New York (Americas Society, 2017), Berlin (KW Institute for Contemporary Art, 2020–21), Stockholm (Moderna Museet, 2021), Malmö (Malmö Konsthall, 2021), and Porto (Museu Serralves, 2021–22). Today, the artist's works are in the collections of major museums in Brazil, Europe and the United States, such as MASP, Pinacoteca do Estado de São Paulo, Museu de Arte Moderna do Rio de Janeiro, Museu de Arte Moderna de São Paulo, Museu Nacional de Belas Artes, and Museu de Arte Contemporânea da Universidade de São Paulo, as well as MoMA, Art Institute of Chicago, Los Angeles County Museum of Art, Tate, Centre Pompidou, Museu d'Art Contemporani de Barcelona, Museo de Arte Contemporáneo de Castilla y Léon, among others.

MASP currently possesses four works by Leonilson, and we are immensely grateful to the individuals who generously donated them to the museum in the last four years: Fernanda Feitosa and Heitor Martins, who gave us the exceptional painting

Agora e as oportunidades [Now and Opportunities] (1991) [img. 152], reproduced on the cover of this book, and Luisa Malzoni Strina, who gave us the iconic drawing *Príncipe* [Prince] (1991) [img. 170], from the important series *Os dedicados* [The Dedicated], reproduced on the back cover. Both donations were carefully chosen as extraordinary representations of the artist's paintings and drawings. Feitosa and Martins' donation, made in 2020, sparked the very beginning of this project. Strina's donation arrived at the museum shortly before the exhibition opened, and *Príncipe* is understood as a kind of emblem for "new opportunities," a counterpoint to the painting's multi-headed figure. In addition to these two works, the collection also includes a watercolor and a drawing, both untitled [imgs. 377, 378] and produced in 1980, which represent the museum's historic building itself, donated by the Bezerra Dias family and the Sociedade de Amigos do Projeto Leonilson in 2021.

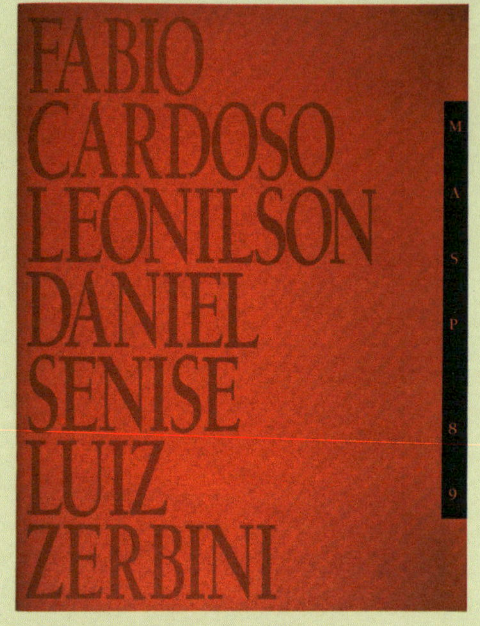

2

In this context, the MASP exhibition, which borrows its title from the only painting by Leonilson in the museum's collection, *Agora e as oportunidades*, brings together 323 works, documents and publications relating to the artist's last five years of production, from 1989 to 1993. It is worth remembering that Leonilson exhibited at the museum in 1989, in a group show alongside Daniel Senise, Fabio Cardoso and Luiz Zerbini, in the gallery on the second basement floor of MASP [imgs. 2, 3], in 2000, in the show *Brasil: psicanálise e modernismo* [Brazil: Psychoanalysis and Modernism], and in 2017, in *Histórias da sexualidade* [Histories of Sexuality]. Now with this new exhibition, we hope to offer a special opportunity for the general public to come into contact with the work of one of the most unique artists in Brazilian art, an essential figure in the international panorama of queer artists, and for specialists to also be able to review and reconsider his legacy, disseminating, multiplying and deepening the readings and understandings of his work.

Special thanks are due to the Projeto Leonilson, which cares for the artist's legacy, and particularly to Gabriela Dias and Ana Lenice Dias, who supported us with enthusiasm and generosity throughout the production process of the exhibition and this book. Our gratitude goes to the guest authors who contributed with texts to the catalog: Carlos Eduardo Riccioppo, Irene V. Small, Julia Bryan-Wilson, Miguel López and Pablo Lafuente. Many thanks to Teo Teotonio, the curatorial assistant who worked on the exhibition and its publication

2. *Fabio Cardoso, Leonilson, Daniel Senise, Luiz Zerbini,* cover of the catalog of the exhibition held at MASP in 1989

3. *Fabio Cardoso, Leonilson, Daniel Senise, Luiz Zerbini,* catalog with reproductions of the works *Desejo é um lago azul* [Desire Is a Blue Lake] (1989) [img. 52], and Oceano Atlântico [Atlantic Ocean] (*circa* 1989) (PL.2369.0/00), unknown collection

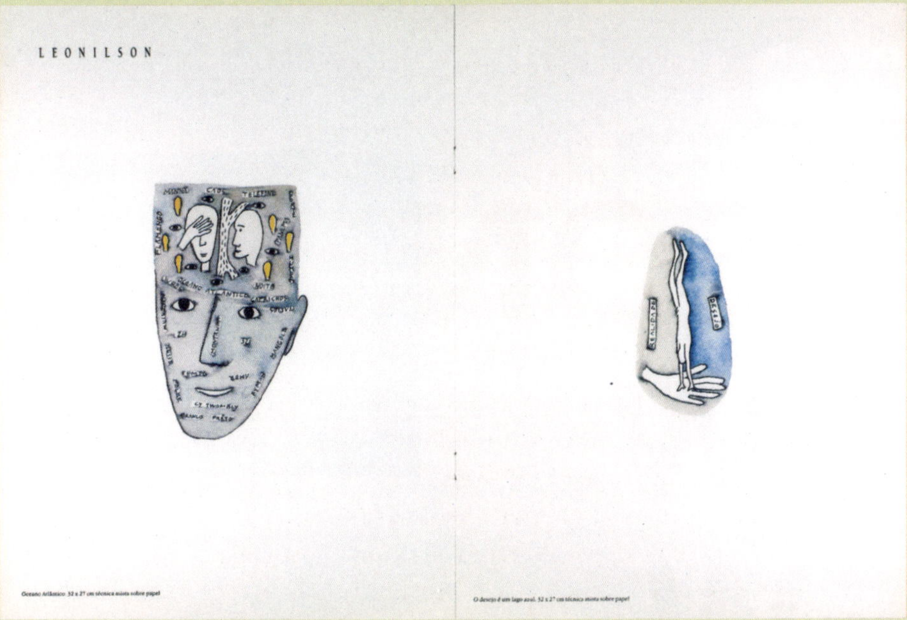

3

and who wrote a biographical note for this book, as well as to Rara Dias and Alexsandro Souza, who conceived the graphic design. We would like to extend our immense thanks to all the museum teams who work in different stages and aspects contributing to the success of the project, especially those who are most directly involved in the construction of the exhibition and this book: the Production team, coordinated by Marina Moura, Editorial, led by Carol Ribas, and Exhibition Architecture and Design, with Flora Gurgel.

Acknowledgement is due to the many collectors and institutions that generously lent works for this exhibition: Adriano Sammarone, Ana Eliza and Paulo Setubal, Andrea and José Olympio Pereira, Charlô Whately, Cristina Secaf Rebello, Daniel Senise, Eduardo Brandão and Jan Fjeld, Flávia and Guilherme Teixeira, Francisco Meirelles de Andrade, Graham Steele and Ulysses de Santi, Janka Babenco, Jassanan Amoroso Dias Pastore, Jean-Marc and Maguy Etlin, Leda Catunda, Luisa Malzoni Strina, Marcelo Secaf, Marcia and Luiz Chrysostomo, Maria Pini Piva, Mary Miranda, Patricia Levy, Paula Nazarian, Paulo A. W. Vieira, Rafael Moraes, Ricardo Bezerra and Bete Dias, Ricardo Resende and Jose Mauro Del Royo Correa (*in memoriam*), Susana and Ricardo Steinbruch, Thiago Tannous, Valdirlei Dias Nunes, Banco Itaú, Museu de Arte Moderna de São Paulo, Museu de Arte Moderna do Rio de Janeiro, Museu Nacional de Belas Artes, as well as those who chose to remain anonymous. We would also like to thank those individuals who helped us during the process of researching and locating Leonilson's works: Erica Schmatz, at Galeria Almeida & Dale, and Kiki Mazzuchelli, at Galeria Luisa Strina, both in São Paulo.

Finally, the realization of this project would not have been possible without the essential support of all the trustees and patrons of MASP, the Ministry of Culture and the Federal Government, through the Federal Law of Incentive to Culture, as well as Itaú, our strategic partner that supports us in this and all other activities throughout the year.

LEO NILSON NOW: NEW OPPOR TUNI TIES

Adriano Pedrosa

The works are all a diary. They are completely personal.

I think what we can do with art is to give a heads up to society a little. We can't change the world, but we can show some things.

Leonilson[1]

The globes and the maps; the oceans and the stars; the rivers and the lightning; the bridges and el puerto*; the Dead Sea; the mountains and the interior volcano; the island and* el desierto*; the abysses and the rocks; the towers, the ruins, and the sand castles; the forests, the trees, the fruits, and the flowers; the gold and the pearls; the brooches and the pendants; the cities and the streets; the door and the zigzag; the storms and the heart; the shots and the bombs; the wings and the anchors; the knives and the fires; the poems and the boys; the saints and the crucifixes; the clocks, the watches and the hourglass; the lampshade and the candles; the organs and the scars; the white shirt and the blue pants; the eggshells; the letters and the numbers; the circle, the square, and the rectangle; the cube, the cone and the cylinder; the temples, the bathrooms and the steam; the staircase and the mirror; crowns and scepters; desire and danger; sexuality and illusion; the liars, the traitors, and the princes; the blacks, the Jews, the homosexuals, the women, the communists, the prostitutes, the disinherited, the indigenous people, the AIDS sufferers.*

Leonilson (1957–1993) is both a central and marginal artist in the history of recent Brazilian art. Central because his importance and influence are undeniable, given the number of exhibitions and the presence of his work in museum collections in Brazil and abroad. Leonilson has also been the subject of films, plays, and countless monographs and academic dissertations.[2] But perhaps the most persuasive proof of the enormous appeal of his works is the fact that they appear on the bodies of so many individuals. The hashtag #Leonilson on Instagram reveals many tattoos with his works, such as *Favorite Game* (1990) [img. 115], posted by @ane.lie on April 12, 2019 [img. 4], among others.[3]

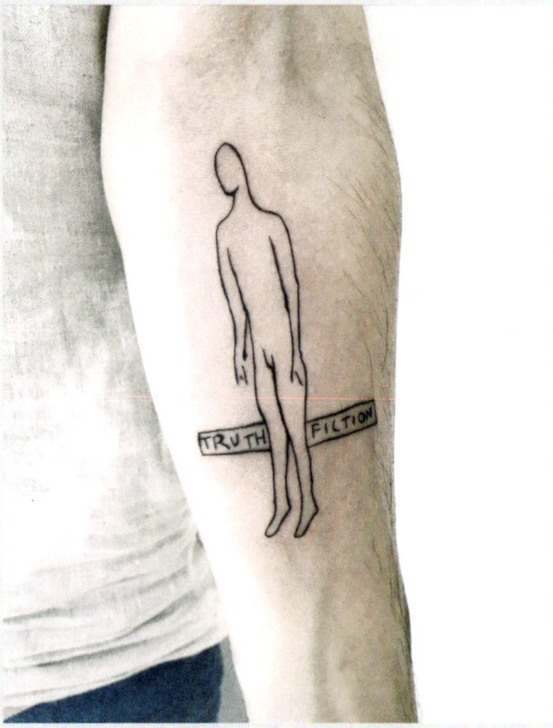

4

However, Leonilson is also marginal, an anti-hero of sorts. He doesn't seem to fit easily into the narratives of his predecessors, contemporaries, or movements in Brazilian art. His work is immensely singular, idiosyncratic, and personal, with an aesthetic, genealogy, and poetics that are very much his own, distinct from the Brazilian artists who preceded him, or even from those of his generation[4]—it is, in fact, on the margins. His most significant influences include his mother, Carmen, who embroidered at home daily, the fabric business of his father, Theodorino, as well as Arthur Bispo do Rosário (1909–1989), another marginal Brazilian artist, along with figures like the Americans Duane Michals and Eva Hesse (1936–1970), the German Blinky Palermo (1943–1977), the Swiss Paul Klee (1879–1940), as well as the Greek poet Konstantinos Kaváfis (1863–1933). Yet, above all, Leonilson is marginal because, in Brazil in the late 1980s, he was a gay man, and from mid-1991 onward, living with HIV, which led to prejudice and discrimination in a much more conservative context at the time.

In such a "completely" personal and diaristic work, the temptation towards biographism is risky. Therefore, we should avoid reading Leonilson's works and words seeking definitive and univocal interpretations. In his interviews, he himself admits contradictions or changes his mind, and even in his recordings, we sometimes recognize a fictionalized Leonilson—not coincidentally, he encoded the names of friends and lovers in his works and audio recorded tapes. In reality, it is often impossible to know if the subject represented in the work is the artist, another character, or a fictionalized version of one of these. In this context, the exhibition *Leonilson: Truth, Fiction*[5] that I organized in 2014 took as its starting point a drawing that highlighted the artist's "favorite game" between truth and fiction [img. 115]. Borrowing the epigraph from the meta-autobiography by French writer Roland Barthes (1915–1980): "everything here must be understood as said by a character in a novel."[6]

The 2014 exhibition was organized around thematic clusters. Today, ten years later, it is productive to seek another approach: the strictly chronological one. Periodizing the phases of an artist is especially challenging in the case

4. Tattoo made by Anelie Schinaider on Felipe Félix, based on Leonilson's *Favorite Game* (1990) [img. 115], published by @ane.lie in 12.4.2019

of Leonilson, who died so young—at 36, in 1993, from complications of AIDS. The artist turned 32 on March 1, 1989, and would work for another five years. This period constitutes the "late Leonilson," in which the artist increasingly developed and refined his work, achieving a truly sublime synthesis—with its characteristic almost mystical or religious features, reaching its peak in 1993 with *Instalação sobre duas figuras* [Installation on Two Figures] [imgs. 236-239], his last work, at the Capela do Morumbi in São Paulo.

Naturally, this is not a linear progression, and it is indeed problematic to talk about progress and evolution. However, between comings and goings, there is an extraordinary development in these five years, with an economy of colors, lines, gestures, compositions and brushstrokes in parallel with an intensification of the power of images, narratives, meanings and materials. Thus, this exhibition is organized chronologically, divided into five chapters, each dedicated to a year of the artist's work, with an additional sixth, which brings together the illustrations created by Leonilson for Barbara Gancia's weekly column in the *Folha de S. Paulo* newspaper between 1991 and 1993. Revisiting Leonilson now chronologically offers us new opportunities for reading, understanding and interpretation.

The title of the exhibition, *Leonilson: Now and Opportunities*, borrows the title of an essential painting by the artist in the MASP collection, the only one that actually depicts the glasses with the different minorities written on the canvas, *Agora e as oportunidades* [Now and Opportunities] (1991) [img. 5]: "blacks," "homosexuals," "Jews," "women," "crippled," "communists," reflecting a political attitude of the artist, something that is rarely seen in the rest of his work. There are also other versions of the so-called "work of minorities," as I will discuss later in this text.

*

1989 was a crucial year for Leonilson. During this period, the artist devoted himself deeply to drawing, as evidenced by the large number of them in this chapter. He was an avid and restless traveler, and the portability of paper allowed him to work away from his studio. Additionally, as is characteristic of the medium, drawing provided an opportunity for the artist to sketch compositions more quickly, offering him great freedom of experimentation. It also allowed for a reduced, intimate, and delicate scale, well-suited to the themes of a diary. Leonilson's model consisted of creating a drawing that occupied only a small part of the paper, slightly off-center. It was done in black permanent ink on paper and often received one or two additional colors in gouache or watercolor. The large blank area surrounding the figure provides

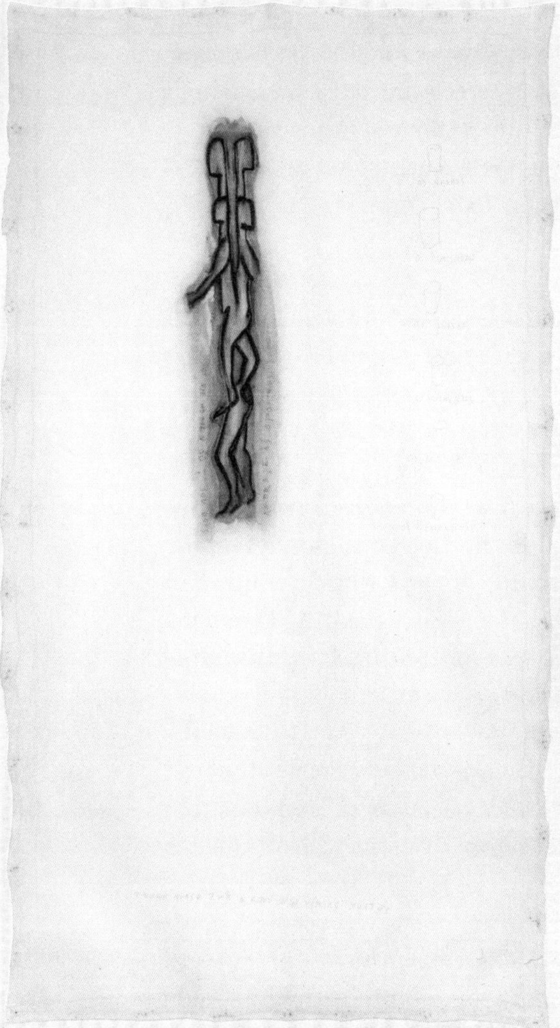

a sense of delicacy and solemnity, simplicity and preciousness to the work. A significant portion of the drawings can be divided into three types: on one hand, those with human figures, either alone or duplicated, or objects that represent subjects or evoke the relationship between them. On the other hand, there are landscapes and maps, sometimes combined. Additionally, there are seemingly abstract geometric drawings, at times associated with maps or human characters. All of these are frequently accompanied by texts in black (when they are not purely text [imgs. 104-107]), providing more clues for the construction of the narrative, even if in an elusive or cryptic manner, accentuating the great poetic and literary dimension.

Each of Leonilson's drawings deserves an essay. Here, I call attention to the theme of the double, which appears with male characters in pairs, mirrored, connected by a bridge [imgs. 58, 158] or by their sex [img. 59], within each other's heads [img. 54], holding clocks [img. 57], or represented by objects and constructions [img. 62].[7] The theme of the double is fundamental in gay imagery, and Leonilson had already approached it previously, but starting in 1989, he began to explore it in a deeper and more poetic way, becoming a leitmotif in his work and a powerful queer index of his production in the following years [imgs. 109, 110, 111, 114, 116, 144, 145]. The simple yet extraordinary *Untitled* [img. 59] deserves special mention, as it is the first time the double appears nude, with the two men embraced and their sexes connected in carnal union, marking the artist's most explicitly queer work up to that point, representing a decisive step for Leonilson in 1989.

Leonilson's drawing model is not limited to works on paper and is transposed, as a formal and processual scheme, into painting, in a kind of drawing in an expanded field. It is revealing that in the excerpt below, he seems to confuse painting and drawing, the white of the paper with the raw canvas:

5

5. Leonilson
Agora e as oportunidades
[Now and Opportunities], 1991 [img. 152]

Yes, the *canvas* has a color and there is a drawing on it, which is the work. Also, the *white of the paper*, when I leave it, is very important. That's why the drawing is small and not large. Sometimes I do want to make a large drawing, covering all of the *white paper*. It is still very important for me to use the white space. It is still very important for me to make it *raw* or else fill the canvas with a color or pattern and make a tiny drawing over it.[8]

Some canvases from 1989 are notable examples of two typologies of the drawing in the expanded field. In *O porta fortuna* [The Fortune Bearer] [img. 48], the canvas is left blank, and the figure is depicted in acrylic paint at the center of the composition, with the man extending his arms in front of a cornucopia from which fruits emerge, a harbinger of abundant, fertile, and happy times, a hope of a new phase that reappears in certain works by Leonilson as an expression of new opportunities that, however, seem to frustrate him. This is the case of works such as *Próximo futuro desejado* [Coming Desired Future] [img. 94], *Aos próximos anos* [To the Coming Years] [img. 93], and works from the series *Se você sonha com nuvens* [If You Dream With Clouds], such as *Anjos; homens* [Angels; Men] [img. 193], all from 1990. In the second typology, the artist uses a single color to cover the background before drawing or painting the figure. The most common approach is to cover the canvas with diluted acrylic paint, achieving a watercolor effect on the canvas—as in *Here Comes Your Man* [img. 49],

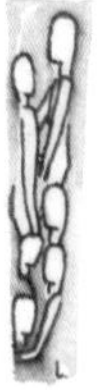

6

6. Leonilson
Atrito corporal [Body Friction], *circa* 1990

Permanent ink and watercolor on paper
23 × 30 cm
Private collection, Palma de Mallorca, Spain
PL.1257.0/00

a monochromatic green painting where the character is surrounded by words and numbers drawn in black, with "24" indicating the age of the Rio de Janeiro resident depicted in the work, and "Flamengo," the neighborhood where the artist used to stay at the home of his friend, artist Daniel Senise. The model of drawing in the expanded field would be used by Leonilson throughout the rest of his career, composing some of his most notable canvases, such as *You Don't See That* [img. 154], *The Game Is Over* [img. 179], and *Agora e as oportunidades*, all from 1991.

Another substantial theme developed in 1989 is geometry—a significant reference for an artist with a São Paulo background, given the weight of the concrete art tradition in the city. Leonilson's geometry is against the grain. On the one hand, it often contains figurative allusions and is associated with romantic and poetic inclinations, as in *Man With No Shelter* [img. 70]: a geometric figure in ochre forms a sort of abstract portrait, its text describing a passionate man "with no shelter" who "kiss[es] the stars," "walk[s] over the water," and "puts fire on [his] soul." Or the eccentric case of *Rapaz lembrando da Baía de Guanabara* [Young Man Recalling the Guanabara Bay] [img. 81], where the character's thoughts are absorbed, not by memories of the Rio de Janeiro landscape, but by geometric figures orbiting around him. Geometry is also a feature in maps, as in *Liberec* [img. 89]. The title refers to the Czech city, in a drawing that pays tribute to the young student Jan Palach (1948-1969), who set himself on fire in Prague in protest against the Russian invasion during the Prague Spring, as well as to Blinky Palermo, since it bears similarities to *Komposition mit 8 roten Rechtecken* [Composition With 8 Red Rectangles] (1964) by the German artist who also died young, at 36 years old. It's interesting to underline the connection between Jan Palach and the *Man with No Shelter*: while the former set his body on fire in political protest, the latter sets his soul on fire for love.

In 1988, some works already hinted at the use of fashion and decorative fabrics, as well as embroidery: this is the case of *Untitled* (PL.1356.0/00), *Roxo com bulbos verdes* [Purple with Green Bulbs] (PL.0998.0/00), and *Rifat* (PL.0411.0/00), which references Turkish fashion designer Rifat Ozbek, made in velvet; *Dobradura de seda com pedras* [Silk Folding With Stones] (PL.0845.0/00), in silk shantung; and three works made with fabric napkins: *Adam* (PL.0023.0/00), *Norte* [North] (PL.0409.0/00), and *Untitled* (PL.1150.0/00). In 1989, Leonilson introduced new, unconventional textile materials, such as the opulent white silk fringe in *Untitled* [img. 67], a work that flirts with minimalism both in terms of color and in its almost complete lack of interference with the material, beyond stretching or mounting it on a frame; velvet, embroidered with a heart and metal swords in *Luta de espadas sobre veludo roxo* [Sword Fight on Purple Velvet] [img. 68]; and felt, embroidered with crystal pendants, in the iconic *Voilá mon coeur* [Here Is My Heart] [img. 69].[9] These materials are associated with others from the world of sewing and reflect both family life and the deep interest in fashion of a queer man who, venturing into the realm of textiles, inserts himself into a feminine tradition.

*

In **1990**, Leonilson continued to introduce new materials from the world of sewing and fashion into his wall works, which sometimes took on a three-dimensional existence through relief, transparency, and materiality, as he had done with the silk fringe the previous year. Two materials were particularly rich for the artist. The first is guipure lace, the most noble of French laces, with which the artist created the brilliant *O singelo* [The Plain One] [img. 99]—the following year, in 1991, guipure lace of a different pattern would be used in *O apaixonado, o zig zag, 5 minutos* [The Enamored One, the Zigzag, 5 Minutes] [img. 186], *Far South; Far North* (PL.15661.0/00), and *Das estrelas e de seus olhos* [Of the Stars and of Their Eyes] (PL.1456.0/00). Here, it is worth reflecting on the artist's minimalism against the grain. He was fascinated by the austerity of minimalism, with its white, pure, silent, immaculate surfaces, free from the expressive gesture of the artist's hand. In 1981, he visited an exhibition by the American artist Robert Ryman (1930–2019) at the Centre Pompidou in Paris, with Ryman's white paintings, which Leonilson described as "something super important."[10] However, despite his attraction to minimalism, he was an artist who intensely expressed his passions and emotions in his works, his diary, far from the cold, analytical, and detached attitude of the minimalist artists of the 1960s and 1970s, such as the Americans Carl Andre (1935–2024) and Donald Judd (1928–1994). There is a significant simplicity that recalls minimalism in many of Leonilson's white works, yet the artist could not resist adding baroque elements that subvert the purity of classical minimalism, forming his own minimalism against the grain. This is evident in the silk threads [img. 67] and the white guipure lace [img. 99] —which, despite its white color, with its excessive and refined character, carries a sense of decadence—where he merely covers the frame with the material, evoking a white monochrome by Ryman. Thus, Leonilson subverts minimalism by introducing its opposites: the baroque, ornamentation, gold [img. 362], the body, scars [img. 192], passion [img. 103], and his own name [img. 191].

Another material introduced in 1990 is voile, which becomes fundamental in the late Leonilson period, extensively used by him. White voile also alludes to minimalism but with an ethereal, sensual, and sometimes religious lightness and transparency. This is evident in the sublime *O q. você desejar, o q você quiser, eu estou pronto para servi-lo* [Whatever You Desire, Whatever You Want, I Am

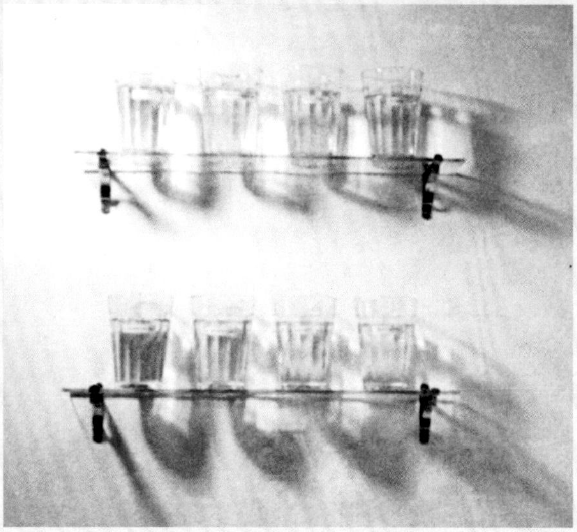

7

Here, Ready to Serve You] [img. 103], a modestly crafted ceremonial tunic with the title embroidered on its hem, evoking voluntary servitude, religious devotion, and intense passion. Another important embroidery from this year is O *dia do herói* [The Day of the Hero] [img. 125], the largest of the drawings in the expanded field, where the vast white area allows the artist to construct various small sets of figures and words around the themes of love, abandonment, loss, loneliness, and longing, creating a penetrating portrait of our "otário" [foolish] and "bobo" [silly] anti-hero.

Two extremely significant themes emerged in 1990: minorities and AIDS. This was a radical step for Leonilson, who had always developed a more personal, intimate and diaristic work, and now assumed a political, public voice, albeit in a poetic form. The works around the different minorities are quite remarkable and truly pioneering in the Brazilian context at that time; six versions of them were made, mentioning the "blacks," "Jews," "homosexuals," "women," "communists," "crippled," and at times also or alternatively the "prostitutes," "disinherited," "gypsies" and "AIDS sufferers." The first work appears in 1990 as a drawing made directly on the wall of the Escola de Artes Visuais do Parque Lage in Rio de Janeiro for an exhibition that lasted only two days[11] (PL.3073.0/00). In the same year, Leonilson made a drawing in black ink, *Untitled* [img. 101]. In 1991, came four other works: an installation with eight glasses of water in the window of the Galeria Thomas Cohn, in Rio [img. 7], reconstructed for this exhibition; a project for an unpublished catalog for the Museu de Arte Contemporânea de Campinas (PL.2245.1/03), an illustration for *Folha de S. Paulo* [img. 269], and *Agora e as oportunidades*, the only painting in the series. It is worth quoting Leonilson's substantial words about this critical moment in his career:

> **I do perceive the segregation that exists. And of course, I belong to one of these minorities, or to more than one. Several things that I speak of are subject of segregation. [...] So, I wanted to make a more public work, but this is still part of my diary. It's something I suffer and experience daily. [...] It has a far more political attitude of social concern than other works, in which I keep talking about my loves, my most intimate relationships, my most private things, and which I, rudely speaking, make for myself.**[12]

7. Leonilson
As minorias [The Minorities], [1991]

Glasses, water, and typing
on paper, on glass shelves
Private collection, São Paulo, Brazil
PL.3042.0/00

In this context, the theme of AIDS resurfaces in 1990, a year before the artist discovered that he was living with HIV. He had already mentioned the syndrome in a 1985 work: *Saque e aproveite a vantagem* [Serve and Enjoy the Advantage] [img. 358], a work made on pages of the *Jornal da Tarde* newspaper in which the headline reads "AIDS, a doença mortal que assusta o mundo" [AIDS, the deadly disease that scares the world].[13] In 1990, the theme was treated in a more forceful and poetic way, in an approach to queer themes, in drawings illustrating guidelines for safer sex. There are two sets: the first, with three drawings: *Masturbação mútua* [Mutual masturbation] [img. 116], *Voyeurismo* [Voyeurism] [img. 117] and *Fantasia* [Fantasy] [img. 118]. The second, with five, also includes *Beijo seco* [Dry Kiss] [img. 357] and *Atrito corporal* [Body Friction] [img. 6]. It is interesting to note that the scheme of what appears to be six men in friction forming a column in *Atrito corporal* resembles that of the multiple man in *Agora e as oportunidades*, which, in addition to the glasses and minorities, bears the text: "Sou um homem só, sou dois" [I am one man, I am two]. The double becomes a transfiguration of the multiple, with its orgiastic evocations.

*

In **1991**, a test on August 22 reveals to Leonilson that he is living with HIV, and this is the crucial milestone of this very difficult and prolific year—an entire exhibition could be dedicated to the works made during this period. It is sometimes difficult to distinguish whether the work was made before or after the test, which has confused certain readings and interpretations. The interview published here was conducted in March and May 1991 and mentions several works, which were therefore made before the test in August, including some that are mistakenly understood as after the fact—such as *Agora e as oportunidades*, *The Game is Over*, *C/ ela sempre por perto* [With Her Always Around][14] [img. 201] and *Perversos inocentes* [Innocent Perverts] (PL.0996.0/00). In the same way that we do not know whether, in Leonilson, we are in the territories of truth or fiction, we also do not know whether some works from 1991 were made before or after the fateful test. The fact is that the feeling of loss, hopelessness, vulnerability and fear of death ("with her always around") that we see in some works made in the first half of this year will become more acute and acquire new meaning after the diagnosis.

Leonilson produced a large number of works in this intense and painful year, especially in embroidery, and they are truly astonishing: *Leo não pode mudar o mundo* [Leo Can't Change the World] [img. 156], *Síndrome de abandono* [Abandonment Syndrome] [img. 159], *33/34* [img. 160], *It's You Deep in Me* [img. 161], *Se você sonha com nuvens* [If You Dream of Clouds] [img. 162],

Mr. One Night Stand [img. 167], *O ilha* [The Island One] [img. 183], *Pescador de pérolas* [Pearl Fisher] [img. 184], *José* [img. 191], *34 com Scars* [34 With Scars] [img. 192], A.P. [img. 362],[15] and *El desierto* [The Desert] (PL.0008.0/00). Most of them are made with white voile, but there are also works in felt, rustic silk, canvas, and linen. All have a large, untouched white, ecru, or beige background on which texts and images are embroidered in black or have gold paint on the border [img. 362], which configures the model of the drawing in the expanded field, the artist's minimalism against the grain, and lends poetic drama to the compositions and their narratives, enhanced by the vast silence of their surroundings.

In drawing, a notable series was created in 1991: *Os dedicados* [The Dedicated], thirteen works that represent the artist's passions and loves [imgs. 168-78], eleven of which are reproduced in this book[16]—two of them have their whereabouts unknown. In the series, Leonilson seeks to develop another symbology, conceiving new images beyond his lexicon[17]. Like Bispo, Leonison had a penchant for lists, and after compiling the names of figures from the worlds of art, cinema, music and fashion, as well as nightclubs in Rio and São Paulo in *São tantas as verdades* [So Many Are the Truths] (1988) (PL.0827.0/00), Leonilson now lists his loves, his muses—from the emblematic and dashing *Príncipe* [Prince] (1991) [img. 170] to one that he ironically does not even remember, but still deserves his tribute [img. 178].

In 1991, Leonilson began to create illustrations for Barbara Gancia's column in *Folha de S. Paulo*, published weekly from March 9 until two weeks before his death on May 14, 1993. In this case, we know the dates of the works, and it is revealing that shortly after his AIDS test, on September 4, a version of the work of minorities was published, now including "those with AIDS," "the undesirables," and "those with poison" [img. 269]. In the illustrations, we find a more politicized and vocal Leonilson, making harsh criticisms of violence [imgs. 252, 304], corruption [imgs. 250, 252, 255, 304], sexism [img. 304], conservatism [img. 255], consumerism and the primacy of capital [imgs. 250, 253, 258, 275, 279, 318], the anti-abortion law [img. 255], segregation and social inequality [imgs. 252, 253, 255, 258, 304], including a reference to Donald Trump [img. 252]. In the newspaper, the artist brings political criticism to his diary, once again going beyond the "completely personal."

*

In **1992**, AIDS is already the protagonist of many of Leonilson's works, although often without direct reference to the syndrome. Although the notion of "allegory of the disease" was used to identify the works created while the artist was aware that he was living with HIV, it is not so much an allegory. After all, if allegory identifies a narrative that seems to talk about one subject when in reality it talks about another, a series like *O perigoso* [The Dangerous One] [imgs. 202-208] announces the disease in an unequivocal way. The first drawing in the series, *O perigoso* [img. 202], includes the artist's own HIV-positive blood. According to Leonilson: "I have no shame. The series *O perigoso* has this title because I effectively represent a danger to other people."[18] The series poetically mixes images and words from the world of the disease and the religiosity of the "dangerous" subject—a bottle with pills, a pricked finger dripping blood, an arm receiving serum, a crucifix—with names of flowers—"lisianthius" (referring to the lisianthus), arum lilies, primrose, daisy—, the guardian angel and the fairies. *Quantos já se foram e pra que* [How Many Are Already Gone and What For] [img. 210] also refers to AIDS, and despite the painful title-question, it has exuberant colors, mixing blue and pink. It is difficult to distinguish the images on the canvas, but Antonio Gonçalves Filho identified them, probably after conversations with the artist, as the Brazilian Iguaçu Falls in the lower part and sperm in the upper left corner,[19] resounding and vigorous images that insist on celebrating life and sex, despite the disease.

Leonilson produced many self-portraits, some more oblique, concealed, abstract or uncertain, others more evident, although coded, written with his initials, his age or his name. With the awareness and inexorability of finitude, now with "her always around" in fact, the image of the body disappears, no longer finds its figuration, and the "I" is re resented minimally—a few letters, dots and numbers—in increasingly smaller, delicate, precious objects that will outlive the artist. In 1991, we find *José, 34 com Scars* and 33/34. In 1992, the reductionism of self-representation becomes radical with *Auto-retrato* [Self-Portrait] (PL.0853.0/00), *Bolsinho* [Small Pocket] [img. 229], *Saquinho* [Small Bag] [img. 230], and *El puerto* [The Harbor] [img. 231]. José Leonilson Bezerra Dias' initials or nickname—JL, JLBD or Leo—are concisely embroidered, sometimes accompanied by his age, weight and height—35 years old, 60 kilos, 179 cm. Perhaps the small pocket and the small bag are reliquaries that could carry something that remains of this body, of his memory, souvenirs, something that belonged to him but are now ultimately empty. However, the mirror covered in a green and white striped fabric brings with it only the memory of the refusal to look at it, to return his image and reflection—Leonilson did not like mirrors,[20] although curiously he dedicates a drawing to them the following year [img. 240].

*

1993 was, finally, a year of very few works: there are only twelve in the catalog raisonné, in addition to sixteen illustrations for *Folha de S. Paulo* [imgs. 330-347], the last published just two weeks before the artist's death. These illustrations have an increasingly hesitant style, and the very last one bears the expressions "não ouço, não vejo, não faço" [I don't hear, I don't see, I don't do] inscribed on it [img. 345], possibly reflecting on the imminence of his death, two weeks later. One of the paintings, *São Sebastião de cabeça para baixo* [Saint Sebastian Upside Down] [img. 243], represents the saint in agony with his feet up—it is Leonilson's second portrayal of Saint Sebastian, a gay male icon who represents martyrdom and sensuality, and who had already appeared in *Pobre Sebastião* [Poor Sebastião] [img. 153] the previous year. Both are inspired by *Sebastiane* (1976), the classic and controversial experimental film by British filmmaker Derek Jarman (1942–1994). Spoken entirely in Latin, the film tells the story of a handsome, queer soldier named Sebastian who is martyred for resisting sexual harassment from his captain.[21]

The last work, which the artist never saw finished, is the monumental *Instalação sobre duas figuras*, presented at the Capela do Morumbi in São Paulo, a few weeks before his death. Having a religious background, Leonilson composes the setting for his own mass, a moving final rite of passage, expressing the transition from life to death. There are five elements presented as unconventional garments, in voile and cotton, in white and the same orange that appears in the self-portraits-reliquaries of the previous year. The protagonist is Lazarus, who Jesus resurrected after four days, represented by a duplicated and mirrored shirt on a hanger, possibly a double self-portrait or in a amorous fusion; next to him, a long skirt also on a hanger, evoking a maternal figure [img. 238]. In front of the two, *Los delícias* [The Delicious Ones] [img. 236] represents "the dedicated," and, in the background, *Da falsa moral* [Of the False Morals] and *Do bom coração* [Of the Good Heart] represent good and evil in the final scene [img. 239].

*

More than three decades after his death, Leonilson continues to offer us new opportunities for reading, inspiration and meaning. He is the shy, sensitive and inflammable character [imgs. 51, 100], an empty man [img. 199] divided between truth and fiction [img. 115], a nonconformist loner [img. 215] with abandonment syndrome [img. 159], an accident victim [img. 164] with scars [imgs. 163, 192], one who can't change the world [imgs. 72, 73, 199], he is almost two meters tall and has been alone for several nights [img. 152], he is the man with no shelter [img. 70] who does not give up [imgs. 82, 83], he is simple [img. 99] and has fire in his hands [img. 108], he is the dangerous one [img. 202] who does not like mirrors [img. 231], but has his protective inner mountain [img. 47]. The image that remains of Leonilson, through works, exhibitions, books, films, plays and tattoos, is that of a resonant anti-hero, multiple and contradictory. There is a bit of him in many of us.

Translated from the Portuguese by Adriano Pedrosa

Adriano Pedrosa, Artistic Director, MASP

NOTES

1 "Concentrated Conversations," interview with the artist made in 1991 and reproduced in this book, pages 347 and 365.

2 The films are: *Com o oceano inteiro para nadar* [With the Whole Ocean to Swim] (1997), by Karen Harley, and *A paixão de JL* [JL's Passion] (2014), by Carlos Nader, both presented in this exhibition. The play is the monologue *Ser José Leonilson* [To Be José Leonilson] (2019), by Leonardo Moreira and Laerte Késsemos. For the monographs and academic studies on the artist, please refer to the bibliography included at the end of this volume.

3 *O criador de casos* [The Troublemaker] (1989) (PL.1264.0/00), posted by @milaink on 2.7.2018; *Inflamável* [Inflammable] (*circa* 1990) [img. 138], posted by @walkeramon on 8.7.2019; *O grande rio* (1991) [img. 157], posted by @michellbarrosss on 10.7.2017; *Oceano, aceita-me?* [Ocean, Will You Accept Me?] (1991) [img. 158], posted by @_carolinaccamargo on 15.4.2022; and *Da qualidade de ser forte* [Of the Quality of Being Strong] (1991) (PL.0659.0/00), posted by @tinicorosa em 26.10.2020, among others. The "PL." number mentioned throughout this book indicates the catalog entry established in Ana Lenice Dias and Gabriela Dias (eds.), *Leonilson: catálogo raisonné.* (São Paulo: Projeto Leonilson, 2017). Following the raisonné, attributed titles or translations appear between brackets in the captions.

4 Although Leonilson is associated with the Brazilian *Geração 80* [80s Generation], characterized by the so-called "pleasure of painting," a motto of the time, and by large colorful canvases with expressionist gestures that identified the production of young artists then, his most exceptional work emerges with another aesthetic at the end of the decade, especially from 1989 onwards, a turning point in his work and for this reason the starting point of this exhibition.

5 Adriano Pedrosa (ed.), *Leonilson: Truth, Fiction.* (São Paulo/Rio de Janeiro: Pinacoteca do Estado de São Paulo/Cobogó, 2014). The exhibition traveled to the Centro Cultural Banco do Brasil in Belo Horizonte and in Brasília in 2015.

6 "*Tout ceci doit être considéré comme dit par un personage du roman.*" Roland Barthes, "Roland Barthes par Roland Barthes." In: *Oeuvres complètes*, v. 3, 1974–1980. (Paris: Éditions du Seuil, 1975), 81.

7 The theme of the double is also explored in painting, in 1989 with *Isto é a lua, Not the Last Chance* [This Is the Moon, Not the Last Chance] [img. 55] and two *Untitled* works [imgs. 60, 61]—and in 1990 with *Jogos perigosos* [Dangerous Games] [img. 113], *Mar do Japão* [Sea of Japan] [img. 132], and two other *Untitled* works [imgs. 119, 120].

8 "Concentrated conversations," 376. Emphasis added.

9 On this work, see my essay "Voilà mon coeur", In: Lisette Lagnado (ed.), *Leonilson: são tantas as verdades [So Many Are the Truths]* (São Paulo: Projeto Leonilson, 2019).

10 "Concentrated Conversations", 334.

11 On September 29 and 30, 1990. See Carla Lencastre, "As artes sem fronteiras," *O Globo*, 29.9.1990.

12 "Concentrated Conversations," 365–368.

13 On this work, see "Concentrated Conversations," 368.

14 "Her" refers to *morte*, death, which in Portuguese is a feminine noun. For Leonilson's explanation on this work, see "Concentrated conversations", 349.

15 On A.P., see "Concentrated Conversations," 379–380. There are two other works in this series, with white voile and a gold painted hem (PL.1262.0.00 and PL.0408.0/00).

16 The location of two drawings is unknown.

17 "I tried to make this series quite different. I kept remembering the guys I had met and what they reminded me of." "Concentrated Conversations," 373.

18 Antonio Gonçalves Filho, "Leonilson expõe seu diário feito de sangue," *Folha de S. Paulo*, 18.3.1993.

19 Ibid.

20 "I never much liked to look at myself in the mirror", Lisette Lagnado, 2019, op. cit., 98.

21 On Saint Sebastian and Derek Jarman, see "Concentrated Conversations," 352.

ON DIS TANCES AND JOUR NEYS

Carlos Eduardo Riccioppo

In 1989, Leonilson made a drawing, later called *Longo caminho de um rapaz apaixonado* [Long Way of a Young Man in Love] (1989) [img. 8], in which the distance between two lovers seems to be its main subject.[1]

The horizontal surface is divided into three parts: on the left, Leonilson draws something like a log or a stake within an orange strip, inscribing the acronym "SP" (São Paulo) just above it; on the right, the same arrangement is reproduced, and the word "Rio" is inscribed. In the central area of the drawing—which should represent an intermediate space between the two points, between the two cities (São Paulo and Rio de Janeiro)—two torsos appear side by side, frontally. Each of them has a kind of pulley in the chest area. Finally, the phrase that gives the work its title— "long way of a young man in love"—has been written in the bottom of the drawing, beginning in the lefthand corner of the composition.

The two pulleys appear connected to each other; although the idea of travel or displacement appears straightaway in this drawing, what actually seems to matter is that the very interval between one place and another has little or nothing to do with the physical and objective distance between the two cities, here transfigured in the image of a mechanical device that connects the two subjects.

Such is the construction of an affective discourse, based on the metaphors of the heart as an engine—although the more obvious figure of the heart is avoided by the artist, who replaced it with the diagrammatic drawing of the two pulleys inscribed in a series of similar circular shapes. The discourse is presented in a demonstrative way, almost as if the work could be a kind of "teaching aid" for the narrative it constitutes.

Leonilson's themes revolve around a constant lamentation, a feeling of loneliness or isolation—one that is often expressed through figures, words, and phrases that reappear work after work, stating the artist's lack of power in the face of the world. In fact, his entire body of work is permeated by crystallized formulas for dealing with these feelings: images such as "ugly ducklings," little boats lost in the ocean, and words like "lonely," "needy," "nonconformist" keep appearing and reappearing in his works, often with little variation from one work to the next, so that the whole discourse presented through these images and phrases is articulated according to the same clichés.

These images, gleaned from the daily circulation of cultural signs, had been appearing in Leonilson's works since long before; and one of the transformations that the artist's work went through at the turn of the 1980s into the 1990s can be seen precisely in the appearance of these cultural signs in his drawings with large areas left entirely blank, as if they were isolated and tiny apparitions. However, concomitant with the appearance of this type of "arrangement" in Leonilson's works—moreover, one that also appeared in his paintings—the artist had these same clichés at his disposal for other types of spatial organization in his works.

In *Longo caminho de um rapaz apaixonado*, what is striking is the fact that these clichés appear articulated as if they were the terms of a *scheme*: they are required to have the same abstract existence as the elements of language or the variables and parameters of a mathematical system, and for this reason they appear to be interchangeable, typical, perhaps precisely because they intend to have a diction of universal validity.

But it is precisely through this personal vocabulary that Leonilson will seek to communicate experiences that are intended to be personal, and private, so that a kind of mismatch begins to drift over the artist's work, one between a fully sentimental discourse and a way of presenting it that constantly treats it as abstractions, generic models.

The final years of the 1980s revealed that from this mismatch would ensue in the most forceful formulations of his work. It will seem much closer to a

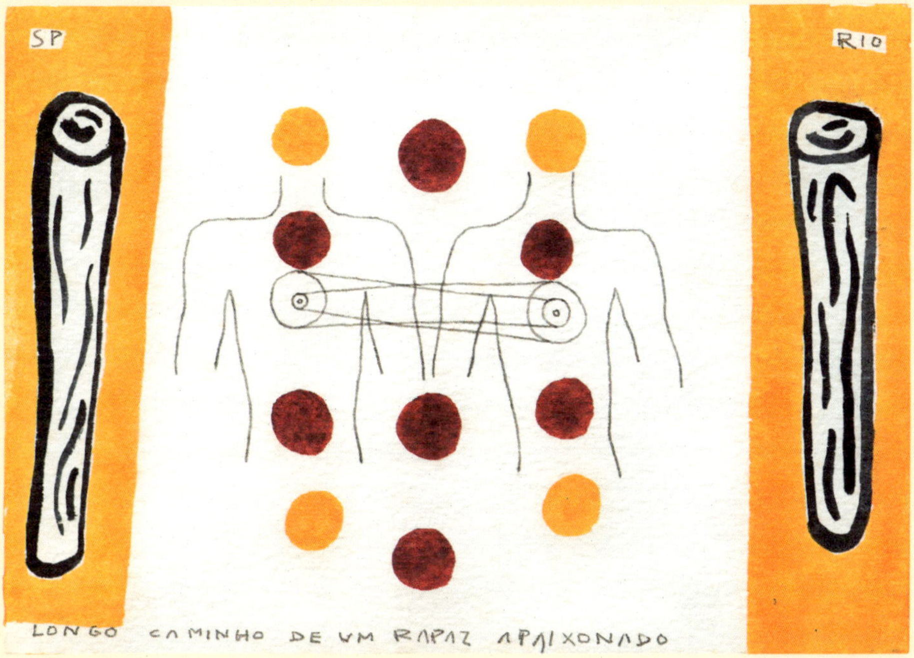

8

dramatic sense the more it bets on its capacity to infuse the small personhood of a gesture into the repetition of anodyne signs of mass culture; the more parsimonious it is in handling materials (whether this means leaving out the big gestures of painting, or simplifying the lines in drawings or prints); in its gesture of isolating simplified and immediately identifiable forms. A "dramatic sense" because, ultimately, the work seems to come up against fatality at every turn: whatever experience it seeks to organize, it will always be threatened by triviality. Because it turns out that the success of its communication only takes place in direct proportion to a process of the trivialization of the very experiences it seeks to communicate.

If *Longo caminho de um rapaz apaixonado* can perceive a form for the melancholy of the two separated lovers, and if it does so by using a worn-out vocabulary, this is a sign that the experience of distance or separation shown there can only be expressed as a constant threat of emptying and homogenization. And if the artist continues to bet on articulations like these, it is because he realizes that, on the other hand, the demotion of his experiences has a kind of bluntness that is dear to a realistic perception of matters of the heart, the private matters of the subject.

Leonilson's references to cartography, to the "scientific" representation of the human body, to the structures of scientific manuals and theorems seem to have been configured as a necessary discipline for the artist, as a kind of

8. Leonilson
[Longo caminho de um rapaz apaixonado] [Long Way of a Young Man in Love], *circa* 1989

Permanent ink, gouache, and China ink on paper
12 × 18 cm
Private collection, São Paulo, Brazil
PL.1277.0/00

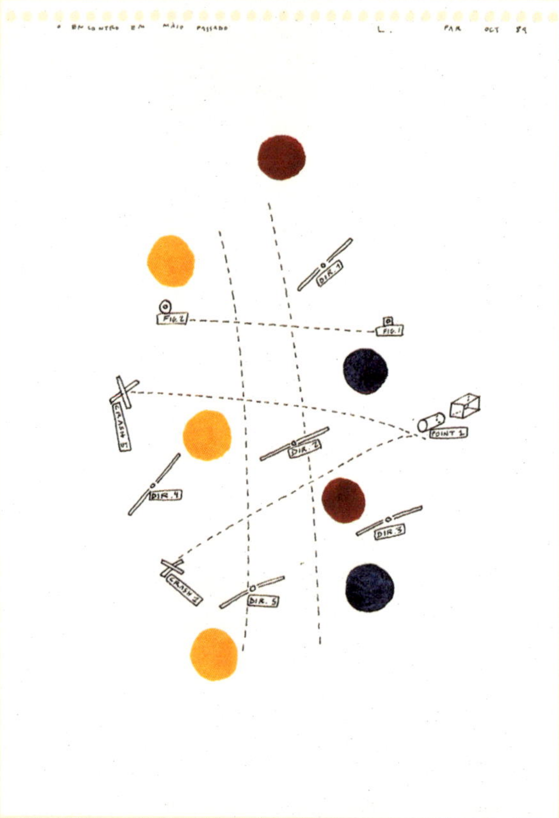

9

apprenticeship through which the work would acquire its ultimate form. From the moment the artist subjected all his material to the abstract ordering of these schematic structures, the work paradoxically saw itself as capable of repositioning Leonilson's expressive will in the midst of confronting so many indifferent signs; it was at the risk of being redundant in a kind of "cheap cosmology" that the artist bet on articulating his materials in order to make them communicate his intimate experiences. Perhaps such bet is what lays behind the common impression that the most obvious characteristic of Leonilson's work is its "fragility."

Made at the same time as *Longo caminho de um rapaz apaixonado*, in October 1989, *O encontro em maio passado* [The Encounter in Last May] [img. 9], is perhaps an even clearer example, among Leonilson's drawings, of this schematic structuring mode that the artist began to employ in a large part of his work.

It is a drawing whose elements are reduced to a few round patches of color and a series of captioned figures, repeated and numbered. Dashed lines indicate the links between these figures: crosses (captioned "Crash 1" and "Crash 5"), figures made up of a circle and two rectangles (identified as "Dir." 1 to 5), perhaps reminiscent of the image of an airplane seen from the front; figures made up of concentric circles or a circle superimposed on a square, as if they were targets (named as "Fig." 1 and 2); and a figure composed by the representation of a cylinder and a parallelepiped ("Point 1"). The title phrase, "The encounter in last May," appears in the top left corner of the drawing and, in the top right corner, the artist signs it ("L."), dates it ("OCT" and "89"), and takes note of the place where it was made ("PAR").

Everything happens as if the drawing were a kind of graphic, an illustration that would even have its *raison d'être* expressed in its "header." By making reductions to the summary structures of graphs and captions, Leonilson's drawings learn to seek a demonstrative character for the expression of intimate things. This

9. Leonilson
[O encontro em maio passado]
[The Encounter in Last May], 1989
[img. 85]

reduction of vocabulary to graphic symbols is of the same nature as the artist's use of cultural signs: both are not borrowed from a specialized vocabulary, but from their common usage. After all, they are symbols gleaned from popular science manuals and textbooks, which makes them elements that find their way into the artist's work after having been popularized by their application in the average culture. It is worth noting, however, that this type of structuring of the work in "universal" shapes responds to the artist's need to report a simple passage in the artist's life or a thought that occurred to him at some point. In this way, what seems to be the major issue in the work is the formulation of a poetic document that can be autobiographical, but which also acquires the force of a generic truth.

In the years that followed, between 1990 and 1993, the year of his death, these poetic equations had taken root: when looking at the "headings" of many of the drawings and paintings that the artist had produced at that time, one can see that all of their elements referred to the particular conditions in which one work or another was made—the inscription of the artist's name, his age, the date and place where it was made—came to appear in some of Leonilson's works (and above all in many of his embroideries) as their main characters. Many are the works that content themselves with being the exact record of the time, place, and particular conditions of the artist at the time they were produced (his weight, his age, his height) [img. 10].

In the drawings and paintings from the turn of the decade, one can already see Leonilson's attention to elements that refer to the moment the work was made as an important part of what constitutes it. In these drawings, we can also glimpse a common matrix among the stitches used in his embroidery—especially the dashed lines that indicate (as in *O encontro em maio passado*) the displacement of one figure towards another, and divide, as if mimicking the shape of maps, small territories or axes on surfaces.

One should also pay attention to the curious inscription "PAR" in the "header" of *O encontro em maio passado*. It seems that the inscription refers to the location where the work was made; possibly Paris. The drawing is one of many in which the artist inscribes this type of header, but it is above all one of many in which the names of the

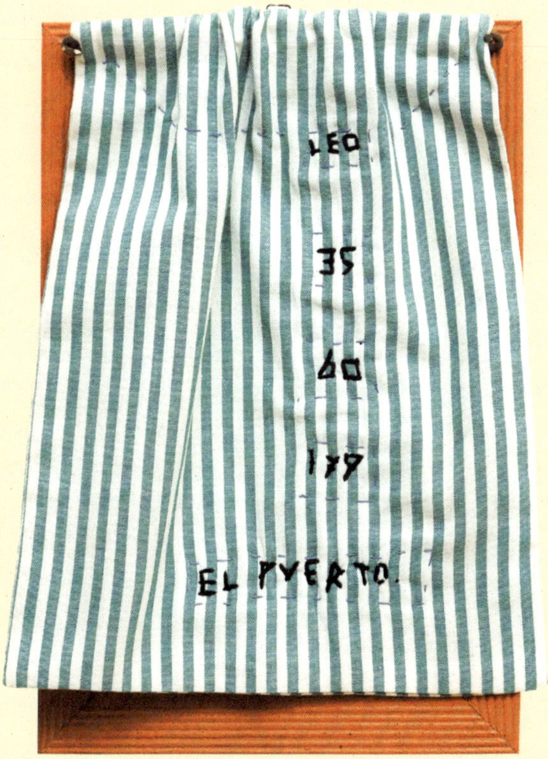

10

10. Leonilson
El puerto [The Harbor], [1992]
[img. 231]

places where they were made appear in abbreviated form, curiously the same one commonly used to designate cities in travel agencies and airports. The theme of travel in general is not the only one to show up in these works; they also allude to a series of places that share some similarities, such as the desert, the sky, or the ocean—places marked by some lack of definition, by the geographical aspect of offering little to no points of reference to a location. It is no matter of chance that Leonilson, who elected *emptiness* as a privileged theme in his work since at least the mid-1980s, would stick to places like these in his works from the end of the decade onwards. The artist seems to find in these liminal places an indeterminacy of spatial status that perhaps carries the same poetic possibilities he used to find in maps, which also appear in his recurrent use of images of abysses and groundless spaces. Perhaps Leonilson discovered that these places, once viewed as "settings" for the works, were capable of diluting geographical references, achieving an ever-undefined kind of spatial notation in the works, some sort of spatial formulation that always treats the world as a "retreat."

The fact that these works started to allude to these places was perhaps not only a thematic choice for the artist—in the end, they were open spaces available to all kinds of symbolic references, precisely because they were averse to the Cartesian principle of occupation and scrutiny. It is no coincidence that these spaces began to inhabit the imaginary of the work in a decisive way at the very moment when the artist's efforts to mark the objective place where his works were made was intensifying, by adding dates and acronyms referring to cities and countries here and there. Perhaps all of this is part of a deeper perception of the work in relation to its own time: a time when the artwork seemed to be going through a process of ultra-professionalization and institutionalization, which, in the Brazilian case, was also accompanied by the internationalization of the country's production.

The question might become clearer if we observe that such places do not appear in his work only as allusions. Inscriptions such as "PAR," which appears in *O encontro em maio passado*, if they do not confirm it, at least raise the suspicion that the artist's works were often conceived in transit, perhaps even in airports, hotels, or airplanes. Perhaps Leonilson makes a point of stating the time at which these works were produced may be due to the impossibility of deducing where they came from or were conceived: they are just regular figures used all over the world, and arrangements that could have been put together anywhere; emerging as a kind of loss of density of the place where the works were produced that is often hinted at when you notice that many of these drawings still have the size and burrs of a page torn out from the notebook that he would carry everywhere he went.

This is meant to say that the artist's references to undefined places or "non-places" find a certain correspondence in the fact that the works were made from the perspective of a subjectivity that increasingly recognized itself as referring to a private universe, evoking anything other than sensations and thoughts that would have occurred to him, as if he didn't need to pay attention to the surrounding world. And if this is, as suspected, the main evidence of the autobiographical nature of his work, it should be noted that the celebratory sense that much of the critical literature on Leonilson has attached to this autobiographical trademark over the years seems to betray the dramatic content that it carries. It is undoubtedly an autobiographical work, resembling a kind of "intimate diary," as has so often been suggested; but we must also recognize how much discontent this autobiographical character reveals: if the artist opens the 1990s with works that deal with his personal struggles and hardships, this would necessarily trigger a deep discomfort in these works, which becomes evident through the reduction of his gestures to segmented and rigid lines, the reduction of the figurative field to repeated clichés in many works, the reduction of their scale, and, above all, the reduction of the elements present in his works to only very few inscriptions.

More than a mere reference to travels and remote places, Leonilson's work is deeply marked by a certain phantasmagoria; his private existence, after all, is the only fixed point through which this body of work is organized. It is no wonder that the whole experience the work deals with is marked by relativization, by leaps between different semantic fields, and by weaves of analogical associations that tend to dematerialize everything. The idea that Leonilson's work is like a diary in which he records everyday notes corresponds, therefore, not to the successful communication of subjectivity, but rather to the reduction of each experience to the isolation of his private life. It is not surprising that the work does not need the physical location of the studio to be created, and that it takes place wherever he has the notebook at hand—somewhere, however, that doesn't bear the sign of a conquest. It is, after all, a work that activates a relationship between the loneliness and isolation it deals with, with an existence that only comes about through the constitution of a negative place for itself. If, in the years following the turn of the 1980s into the 1990s, Leonilson's work became increasingly focused on its autobiographical character, this was the result of a profound withdrawal of the work into itself, like the recognition of a lack of resourcefulness to intervene elsewhere or to deal with anything other than its own contingency.

Although the work is full of images of drifting, fluctuations, and journeys, it doesn't seem to associate these images with a heroic sense of "breaking new ground"; on the contrary, if there is anything in Leonilson's work (he was also known at the time as a "traveling artist") that derives from all these references, it is not a sense of continuous expansion, but the incessant reiteration of a certain reserve, of leading oneself into exile.

Distance had been taken as the main subject in another of his drawings, possibly made between the late 1980s and early 1990s. The title of it contained the sentence "some distances between 2 points," which appeared inside a kind of "text box". On top of this box, the artist made a picture, inside which he drew and listed five objects, which are likely: a piece of wood; something like a band saw, toothed belt, or handsaw; a sword; a wind instrument; and a ruler. On the left, Leonilson wrote the letter "A," and on the right, the letter "B," both also inside small "text boxes" attached to the central frame.

One cannot help but immediately notice the pun on the classic and oft-repeated formula that states that the shortest distance between two points is always a straight line—the drawing seems to interpose a series of examples relativizing that idea. In fact, the two points, "A" and "B," are represented there perhaps in the same way as they might appear in mathematical diagrams. Due to the demonstrative nature of the drawing, the whole series of objects (which suggest different possibilities for connecting the two points) also takes on a schematic aspect—everything must necessarily be simplified to clearly and paradoxically serve the purposes of "exposing" a feeling.

If Leonilson's drawing had long been reduced to a few traces, with contained and often segmented gestures, in *Algumas distâncias entre 2 pontos* [Some Distances Between 2 Points] (*circa* 1990) [img. 11] it becomes clear that this reduction in the use of materials and expressive procedures is associated with a faith in the "communicative vocation" of the works: it is a question of probing the digressive dimension of drawing, whose meaning is not fulfilled in its objective presentation, but always points to a narrative that remains suspended.

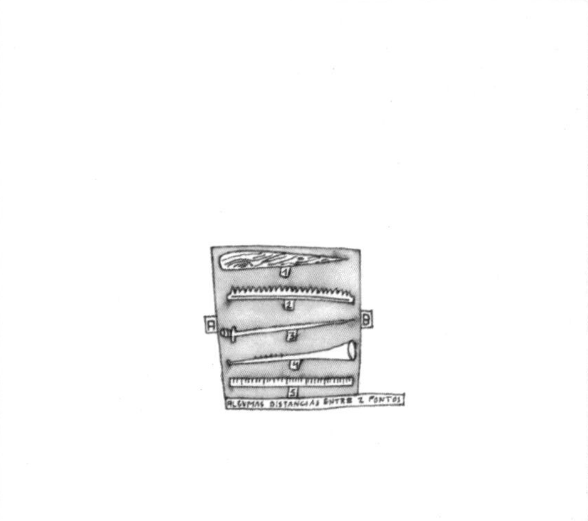

11

If Leonilson was interested from the outset in all sorts of materials that circulated in the cultural universe (advertising figures, colloquial expressions, set phrases), throughout his work he would learn to use them in order to promote a more reflective dimension of thought, in the face of which he found it important to ensure that these worn-out images retain their transparent, simplistic aspect, of immediate legibility. What these works will use of such cultural elements is precisely their unmistakable, readily identifiable composition, so that the artist will organize them into sets, as if they were ciphers or signs for the composition of "messages." These image-clichés must therefore be devoid of any elements that might threaten their clarity, which perhaps characterizes the restraint of the gesture, the "cleanliness" and "scarcity" of his works.

As in some of his paintings from the late 1980s, Leonilson mimicked maps. In many of his drawings, he reproduces a series of diagrams, giving them a demonstrative aspect. In these drawings, words and phrases play the roles of captions and titles at the same time, while their final composition evokes something of the structure of illustrated manuals.

But those numbered objects that appear in *Algumas distâncias entre 2 pontos* also try to restore a certain sensitive dimension to their interrelationship, which comes firstly from the fact that they are "technical objects" that are drawn by hand, and always drawn in a simplified way. Above all, from the material dimension that these objects give the distance between "A" and "B": the physical presence of the wood, the edge of the "saw," the sound implied by the musical instrument, the threat of the sword, and the objectification of distance in the markings of the ruler. And yet, Leonilson's work insistently points to a reduction of the materiality of things to a digressive, imaginative dimension; but what seems most decisive in the constitution of this drawing is that the digressive dimension takes on a body, and one that is the materialization of everything that is abstract, of everything that shows negative value, or, at the very least, of everything that in its nature tends not to be recognized as value in itself.

Around 1991, Leonilson produced two works: *KMS.; Horas* [KMS.; Hours] [img. 12] and *Se você sonha com nuvens* [If you Dream of Clouds] [img. 13], both with a similar cross-shaped structure. Although their supports differ—one of the works is a canvas cut out and painted, while the other is a stitched voile—the "theme" of both revolves around the idea of a distance that is marked by relativization, evoked in one case by the embroidered inscriptions "Kms." and "hours," and in the other by the inscriptions "if you dream of clouds" and "the distance between the cities," also embroidered.

Made around the same time, the two works are good examples of the constant movement of Leonilson's work, which seems to operate by varying degrees between opacity and transparency when it comes to the articulation of its

11. Leonilson
[Algumas distâncias entre 2 pontos]
[Some Distances Between 2 Points], *circa* 1991
[img. 200]

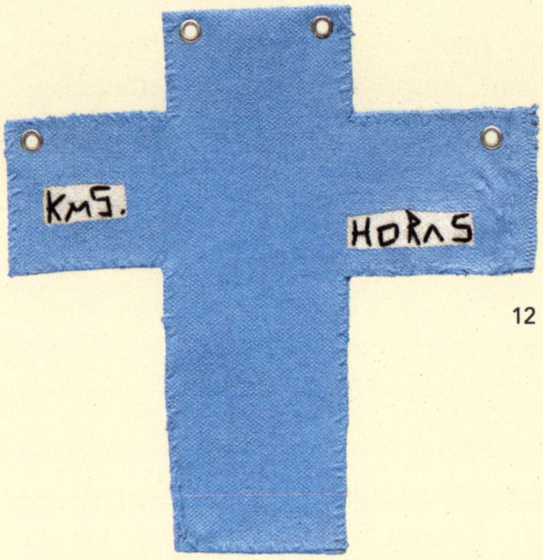

12

materials—here reduced to canvas, voile, blue paint, and sewing thread, in addition to a few words and phrases.

On the blue canvas, the inscriptions refer to measures of space (km) and time (hours) as objective ways of measuring distance, duration, and speed. On the voile, the two phrases combine, in the realization of the idea of a certain "distance between the cities," and something of a *will* (implied in the idea of "dreaming of clouds") and in an imprecise measurement, the clouds themselves being what separates one city from another.

It is worth noting how phrases like "if you dream of clouds"—constructed from a direct or first-person speech—are recurring in Leonilson's work, and share something with advertising slogans. In the case of *Se você sonha com nuvens*, the title phrase could even resemble a call or symbolic promise of freedom, figured above all in the idea of displacement—an idea that appears more immediately in the units of measurement of the other work.

However, what seems most remarkable about both works, when compared, is that the idea of displacement tends to take on a kind of *form* that qualifies them: it is the cross-shaped structure which, associated with blue in one work and with the whitish transparency in the other, seems to evoke cloud and sky at the same time, so that both allude to an aerial displacement. The allusion would be present, above all, in the evocation of those images of "seas of clouds" that can be seen from above and, furthermore, in the structural proximity of the two works to the cross-shaped form of airplanes.

The idea of "dreaming of clouds" would contain the possibility of a flight, a stroke of the mind that projects itself elsewhere. But "dreaming of clouds" can also refer to the dream of the journey itself, of leaving the place where you are and going somewhere else. Perhaps at this point both works could lead us to think about the artist's career, full of trips around the world. Still, what would be at stake in this case is not the discovery of places per se, which the artist could have visited; rather, both works seem to state a profound indifference regarding the places of departure or arrival, placing the accent in the way the interval between them emerges: the first contains no reference to specific places, but only to terms of a speed equation; the other makes use of the corporeality and a whole symbolism linked to the figure of clouds.

12. Leonilson
[KMS.; *Horas*] [KMS.; Hours],
circa 1991

Acrylic paint and
thread on cut canvas
17 × 17 cm
Private collection,
São Paulo, Brazil
PL.1119.0/00

13. Leonilson
Se você sonha com nuvens
[If You Dream of Clouds],
circa 1991 [img. 162]

Precisely because they focus on the distance between two points—and not on the points themselves—both works seem to want to constitute themselves as *topos*, as realities referring to something that, on principle, is an abstract place of thought.

At that time, the artist already had *lack* and *scarcity* as his favorite subjects, so these works dealing with *distance* are somewhat aligned with the same desire of giving a concrete aspect to a series of experiences whose common feature would be the profound absence of a bodily dimension.

In this sense, one can perhaps assume that the appearance of embroidery in Leonilson's work stems from a discovery that is internal to the work: the type of *materiality* acquired by the surfaces or supports he used at the end of the 1980s. Both the monochrome surfaces of his paintings and the vast blank areas in his drawings—which stood out for being profoundly devoid of meaning, especially in opposition to the small arrangements that appeared on them—ended up reiterating precisely their opacity; their material or concrete existence. Of course, these surfaces contrasted their opacity with the transparency of the tiny arrangements that occupied small parts of them; but the surfaces were made so gigantic in scale that the final impression was that the arrangements were floating around, as if they had a different nature than that of the surfaces—or as if they were unable to extract anything from the support, which, in turn, would only be able to remit them to their opaque material reality.

The embroideries that would intensify from that moment on added to his body of work the search to confront these experiences of *emptiness* and *distance*, as if they really had a body; or, to put it differently, as if they marked the discovery of a physical dimension to a series of experiences crossed by a profound negativity.

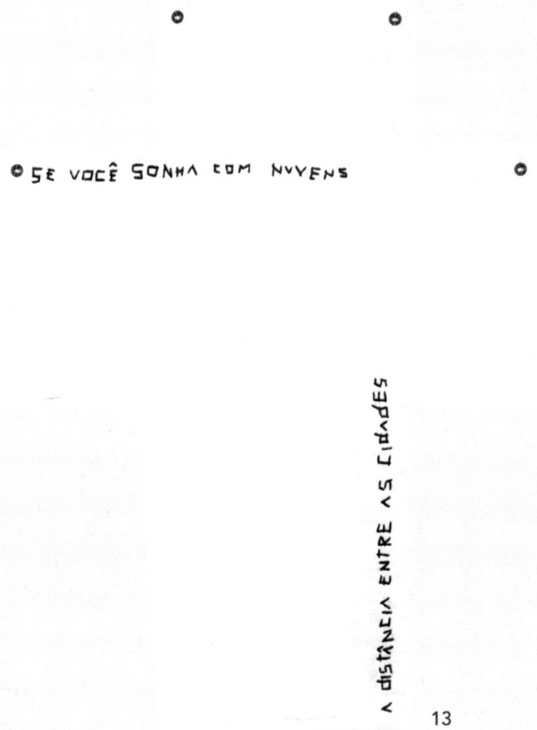

13

In *KMS.; Horas* and *Se você sonha com nuvens*, Leonilson seems to be trying to recompose a concrete dimension to the experience of *distance*, as if he were giving it the status of *form*, just as he would have done in those earlier works with the radically abstract experience of *emptiness*. The cross shape of the airplane, the white of the clouds, the units of measurement, and a loose sentence expressing are all elements that, once combined, bring these formal matrices back to a singular experience.

Made in 1990, the painting *Mar do Japão* [Sea of Japan] [img. 14] could indeed exemplify the way in which Leonilson's work ended the 1980s, announcing the final moment in the constitution of a poetics marked by the idea of scarcity that, above all, arose through the demarcation of *emptiness*, *distance*, *isolation*, and the *abyss* as the major experiences to which his work was to refer in his final three years of life.

This large-format painting features a cluster of a few figures and phrases in the central region of the canvas, while the rest of the surface is covered in green acrylic paint. The brushstrokes in the green area are apparent and outline the arrangement, establishing with it the same relationship of scale so common to the artist's drawings from the same period—the schematic, concentrated, and tiny figures shrink in relation to the anodyne surface, which expands.

The elements that make up the central composition of the painting behave as if they were, at the same time, an aerial view image, a cartographic plan, or a schematic drawing in frontal view. It is a simplified drawing of two heads, one of them white, with no references to physiognomy, and the other in profile, filled with a simplified drawing of the "world map." Both are surrounded by a yellow outline, which takes on the identity of either an indication of a cartographic location (in the section marked as "Sea of Japan"), a street or avenue (in the space between them), or a ruler or tape measure (at the top end of the composition, above the head in profile and the map).

Arranged as they are, alluding to geographical spaces that are somehow determined, these figurative elements are inserted as the representation of a plot of land. Around the arrangement, the rest of the coverage seems to evoke a large ocean, mainly due to its dark green shade and the apparent, multi-directional, watery, and dissolved brushstrokes.

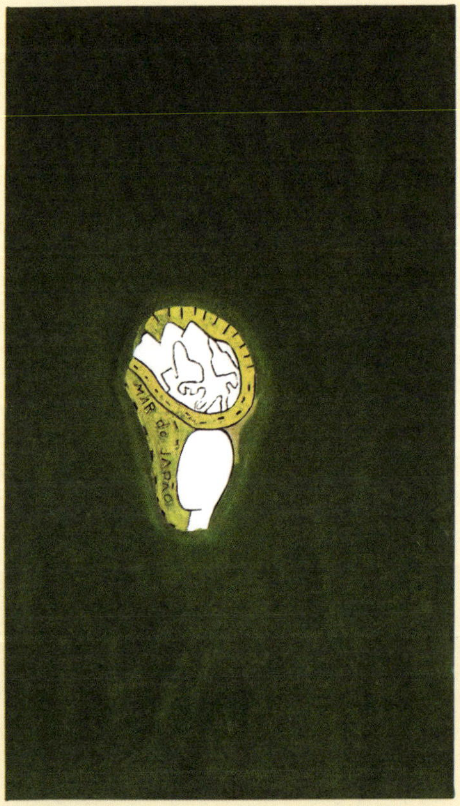

14

Since the work does not differentiate between the frontal and the aerial view, the canvas remains an empty, open spatial construction, available for accepting discourses of different kinds. And since Leonilson adopts a relationship of scale that makes such arrangements tiny in relation to the expansive surface, his painting thus suggests a cartographic perspective that offers the image of an island in the middle of the ocean, thereby demarcating an image of isolation that operates on both the material and the symbolic level.

For this reason, the work projects itself beyond its objective demarcations, making the void of references in terms of axis and scale, which operates from within the work, and also becomes a theme of the work itself. After realizing that the procedure of isolating those arrangements, which float on large surfaces, would suggest an unrestricted willingness to articulate them according to a multitude of different narratives, the artist began to speak (through phrases and captions) of isolation as his most recurring feeling.

If Leonilson tried to comment on his personal experiences in his works from then on, if he sought to restore a subjectivity that expressed itself in an autobiographical key, this attitude arose amid an experience of seclusion that became evident both in the composition of his images as well as in the captions and narratives of his works. Such is the origin of the intimacy of his oeuvre: if, on the one hand, that feeling of isolation opens up a gap to state all sorts of idiosyncrasies, on the other hand, its autobiographical resourcefulness only becomes possible because it is driven by the declaration of its insufficiency, of its inability to communicate anything beyond its own private existence, cut off from the world. Perhaps *Mar do Japão* is the redoubling of a thought about oneself, one head deriving from or unfolding the other.

Leonilson's references to ideas of travel and displacement are countless. Going back to the beginning of the 1980s, one could note the artist's decision to make a series of set designs for the theater group Asdrúbal Trouxe o Trombone, thematically focused on means of transport; or one could count, throughout the entire decade, a few hundred figures of boats, cars, planes, rivers, streets—in short, a whole series of elements that are organized under the more general theme of a world increasingly and decisively enmeshed in a dynamic of pure "circulation." However, if we were to look at the series of writings left by the artist, we would have to recognize that Leonilson showed interest in a series of themes and characters from literature that evoked the figure of the traveler, especially that of Ulysses, to whom he referred a dozen times and who may have inspired him in some works, in addition to being the main character of an unfinished book project. The artist also made a series of recordings up until 1993, in which comments about his travels were recurrent, not to mention the diaries and journals he left behind, in which are documented some brief thoughts, notes, and sketches in different places around the world, later repurposed in many of his works.

Nonetheless, it is interesting to note here not so much the recurrence of travel-related themes, but their importance for the constitution of a poetics marked, at the opposite end, by seclusion within a private universe. Perhaps this poetics does bear the mark of resignation at times, but it ultimately reveals an acute

14. Leonilson
[Mar do Japão]
[Sea of Japan], 1990
[img. 132]

perception of oneself: someone troubled by a series of attempts to restore oneself in any expressive dimension, even if this was only possible in the repeated realization of a profound retreat into one's own solitude.

Perhaps a work such as *Para o meu vizinho de sonhos* [For My Neighbor in Dreams], made around 1991 [img. 15], can offer a final example that clarifies the way in which his poetics were constituted in his last years.

It consists of a patch of orange felt, cut out and embroidered, on the upper edges of which the artist has attached two eyelets, by which the work must be suspended.

The work recalls the silhouette of a building, and the economy of the materials employed is striking: a rectangular patch of felt, the black thread of the seams, and the eyelets. Starting from the rectangular felt, the artist extracts three rectangles from the lower part (there, these "jagged cuts" suggest doors) and sews them vertically, lining them up on the left side of the piece (as if they were windows). From bottom to top, on both sides, he also cuts, up to about half of the rectangle, two strips of fabric, which are folded up and also sewn; on the upper part, aligned to the right, he embroiders the phrase "for my neighbor in dreams," finally sewing the eyelets.

It is curious to glimpse, in the economy of procedures of this work, a "constructive" horizon and perhaps, even more so, to notice how much of an inspiration from the Neo-Concrete movement the work may contain: the materials employed are candidly manifest and appear under the action of time; the use of felt, above all, leaves no room for doubt that it is a material that carries a certain weight, appearing frayed under the shaping action of the force of gravity. Above all, the work seems to refer to a visual shape—the rectangle—that loses its idealized aspect and acquires material power: it is cut out, reassembled, subjected to a certain "fall and fit." But this "constructive" aspect of the work—one which, incidentally, will be present in many of Leonilson's works—doesn't constitute a systematic or deliberate procedure; it ends up subsumed in the insistent configuration of commonplace objects (such as the building represented here), whose flatness is reiterated, as if the discourses these works carry insist on articulating themselves in the aforementioned digressive dimension.

In a work that so often reiterates the feeling of a lack of place, Leonilson also speaks of addressing how the piece presents itself as an effort to communicate, as a search for a recipient, but as one who is projected in an inaccessible intimacy—a "neighbor of dreams," to whom one only gets close to using one's imagination. Before it is able to gesture towards any "message," the work announces itself as an attempt at communication doomed to failure; on the other hand, it seems to turn the difficulty of communication into its own theme and, in doing so, is accomplished as the very image of a place that is as impossible as it is imaginary—sure enough very close to the idea of "addressing" itself without a destination.

Translated from Portuguese by Daniel Lühmann

Carlos Eduardo Riccioppo is a professor in the Fine Arts department at the Institute of Arts of the Universidade Estadual Paulista (UNESP) and the Graduate Program in the Arts at the same institution, in the Visual Arts program, where he researches theoretical, historical and cultural approaches to art. He was a History, Theory and Criticism professor in the Fine Arts department at the School of Communications and Arts of the Universidade de São Paulo (USP) between 2012 and 2017, where he completed his undergraduate, master's and doctorate degrees.

NOTES

1 This text is a new and revised version of a chapter from my Master's thesis, supervised by Prof. Sônia Salzstein, Ph.D.,—whom I thank—in the Fine Arts department at the Universidade de São Paulo (USP), in 2012, under the title *Leonilson, 1980-1990*.

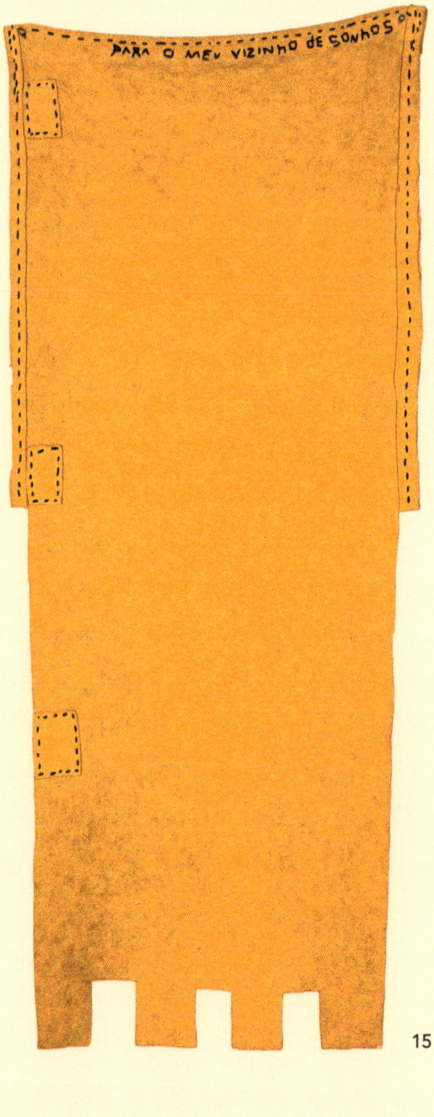

15

15. Leonilson
Para o meu vizinho de sonhos
[For My Neighbor in Dreams],
circa 1991

Thread on felt
90 × 38 cm
Collection of Eduardo Brandão and Jan Fjeld, São Paulo, Brazil
PL.0820.0/00

HANDS ON FIRE

LEONILSON WITHIN QUEER NEEDLEWORK NETWORKS

Julia Bryan-Wilson

José Leonilson's (1957–1993) painting *Homem c/ fogo nas mãos* [Man with Fire on His Hands] (*circa* 1990) [img. 16] depicts a schematically outlined human body seen in profile floating on an undifferentiated blue ground. Though this figure has no definable features, the artist's title indicates gender, so I will refer to him with male pronouns. His face is a mostly uncolored rectangle where the raw canvas shows through, though a few black smudges bleed out from the thick outline. Blazing out from his outstretched arms are hot, crimson-red flames. The canvas is unstretched, its woven matrix unraveling around its side edges, stubbornly reminding us of its textile nature.

The image relates to much of Leonilson's artistic work in that it depicts a small, simplified portrait surrounded by ample negative space that allegorically suggests larger narratives around love, transgression, and loneliness. In particular, *Homem c/ fogo nas mãos* can be read as a comment on the artist's own illness; it was around this time that Leonilson's HIV-positive status catalyzed a transition in his art because he was forced to largely abandon paint with its constantly irritating hand-washing and turn instead to the use of non-toxic materials like threads. His hands were thus fiery in several senses—made vulnerable and inflamed from an allergic reaction worsened by his disease, but also burning, that is "on fire," with creative potential for radical statements.

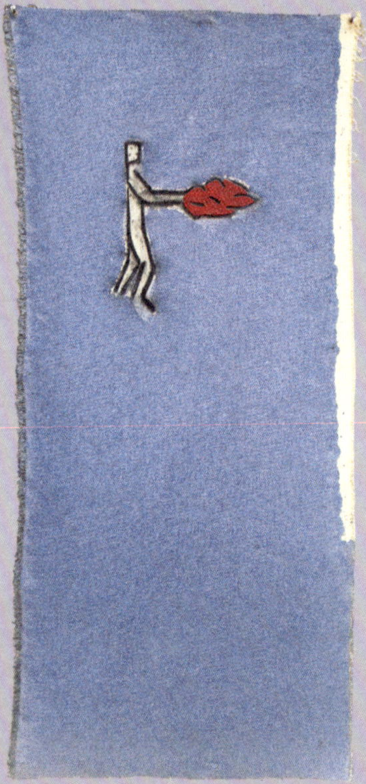
16

For example, in his stunning, pared-down piece 34 *com Scars* [34 With Scars] (1991) [img. 17], Leonilson has approached the surface of the fabric as a kind of skin. Its pale, softly buckling cloth has been interrupted by two lines, crisscrossed with somewhat crude black sutures that have been stitched with thread and appear more as homegrown, desperate attempts to close an injury than the neat, surgical precision work of a nurse or doctor working in a brightly lit hospital. The edges of the voile cloth have also been hemmed with black thread to prevent fraying and to create a visible border, along with a tiny number in the upper right—34—the artist's age when he completed the piece.

Art critic Luis Pérez-Oramas has noted that a full genealogy of Leonilson's use of textiles would have to account for the influence of Neo-Concrete artists Hélio Oiticica (1937–1980) and Lygia Clark (1920–1988) as well as a range of practices spanning high and low:

[...] the evocation of the Shaker quilts that the artist saw in New York in 1986; the Casa da Saudade, his father's textile warehouse; the memory of the School of the Sacred Heart where he learned to embroider; his allergy to pigments; and, above all, the recognition of the coincidence between the beginning of his own embroidery and Bispo's [Arthur Bispo do Rosário] exhibition, the shaping effect on his work of the moving image, and, prior to all others, his "mother embroidering at home every day."[1]

This genealogy would also need to include Leonilson's deep admiration for the soft fiber-based sculptures of post-minimalist artists such as Eva Hesse (1936–1970), whose folded sheets on the ground and hanging net-covered objects he found particularly inspiring.[2]

What is more, Leonilson's practices of embroidery are linked to a larger phenomenon of artists using needlework for political purposes, and in this essay, I outline some instances of queer activist and militant artistic work specifically related to the global AIDS crisis in which the stitch and the suture were invoked for polemical reasons. As Jenni Sorkin noted regarding Leonilson's pocket-sized

16. Leonilson
Homem c/ fogo nas mãos
[Man With Fire on His Hand],
circa 1990 [img. 108]

17. Leonilson
34 com Scars [34 With Scars],
1991 [img. 192]

34 *com Scars*, handkerchiefs "have historic and symbolic significance, having been utilized as a means of signaling desire and availability between gay men in public places."[3] The so-called "hanky code," in which squares of colored cloth were tucked into back pockets according to an elaborate sign system, was a way to flag preferences and to subtly gesture to others one's readiness for cruising—but Leonilson takes fabric out of hiding, or out of the closet, so to speak, airing it in plain sight with works that directly reference mutual masturbation, voyeurism, and, of course, AIDS.[4]

Though textile needlework is often loosely categorized as "women's work," all kinds of genders have deployed embroidery to mend clothes, embellish garments, and pass down memories. The feminized procedures of sewing have been stereotypically characterized as calming or soothing, but a needle can also prick the skin, wound, and draw blood, and I insist on this stabbing action as angry, resistant, and dissident.[5] The artists and makers I discuss might not have been known to each other within their lifetimes, yet they constitute a rich tapestry of comparisons that demonstrate the needle's simultaneously piercing and reparative function.

The stitch's ferocity is made nowhere clearer than in the black and white photograph *Silence=Death* (1989) [img. 18], taken by Andreas Sterzing of David Wojnarowicz (1954–1992) (who had been diagnosed with HIV in 1987) with his mouth sewn shut, pools of blood collecting at each little hole in his flesh and dripping down his chin. A hand holding a threaded needle appears next

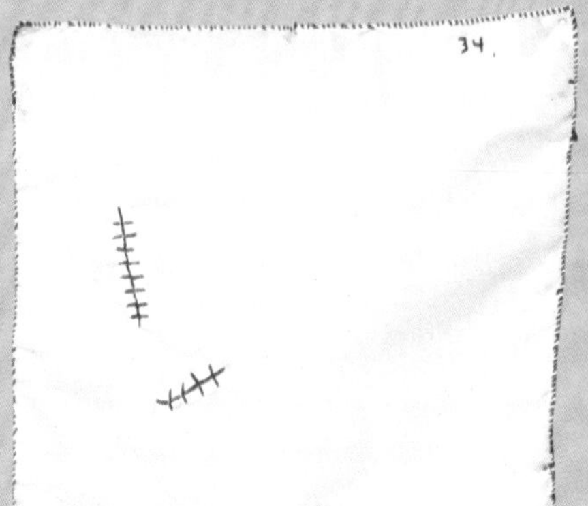

17

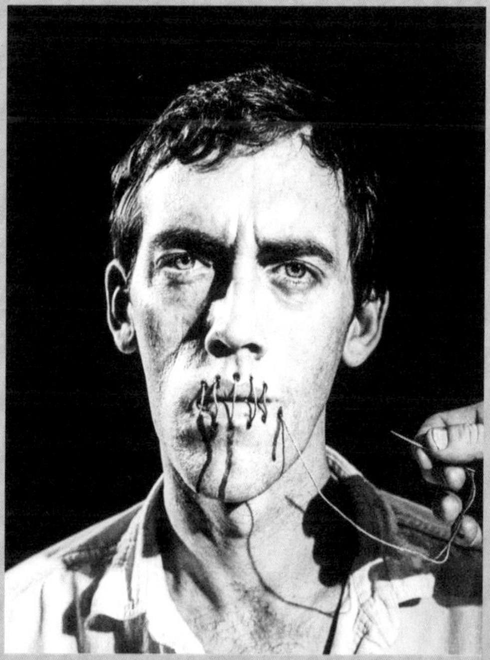

18

18. Andreas Sterzing
David Wojnarowicz (Silence=Death); New York, 1989/2014

Pigment print
61 × 47 cm
Delaware Art Museum, acquisition fund, 2020, Wilmington, United States

19

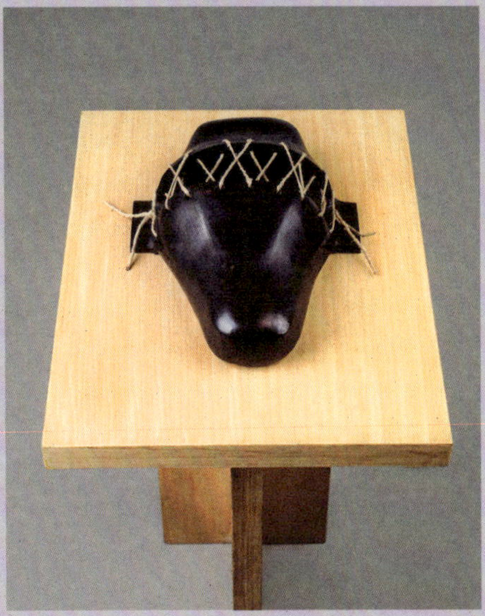

to his face, ready to continue this shocking protest act as the artist stares defiantly out at the viewer, his brow furrowed with rage and concern. Produced in a moment of the US "culture wars" in which it was highly controversial to discuss queer sexuality or the AIDS crisis, Wojnarowicz refers to the famed slogan of ACT UP as well as to his artworks that had been singled out and censored by right-wing politicians and Christian leaders.[6] His picture was staged; the artist collaborated with a theatrical cosmetic artist who meticulously glued short lengths of embroidery threads into place and used makeup to simulate puncture marks.[7] Yet Sterzing's haunting photograph depicts how artists were ready to go to extreme measures to make themselves heard amid deathly governmental neglect, and often turned to needlework—either as metaphor or as material—to do so.

A related use of the stitched face can be found in Spanish artist José Gonzalez (Pepe) Espaliú's (1955–1993) sculpture from the series *Máscara* (1989) [img. 19]. Espaliú, who died of AIDS-related causes in 1993, was interested in how discourses of disclosure and secrecy produced tension around queer artistic portraiture. His sleek bronze mask looks at once like a relic from a prehistoric cult and a contemporary fetish or BDSM accouterment.[8] Rough twine is snaked through perforations punched around the mask's eye slit, producing textural contrast. In many of his works, Espaliú played with the mask to suggest the slippage between public persona and psychological interiority; here he uses a fiber to create a further barrier between self and other, seen and unseen.

Espaliú worked across genres to create objects that were formally refined and highly aesthetic; after his diagnosis in 1990, he dove more definitively into performance. For his iconic intervention *Carrying*, from 1992, the HIV-positive artist was ferried around the town of San Sebastián in the arms of friends, his bare feet never touching the ground as flyers that read "an action in AIDS" were tossed. This tender live act makes literal the idea of mutual support and has religious symbology, given its site-specific location in a place of holy pilgrimage, the notion of the untouchable body, and widespread misinformation

19. Pepe Espaliú
Untitled, from the series *Mask*, 1989

Patinated bronze,
hemp rope and wood
32 × 25.5 × 10.5 cm
Museu D'Art Contemporani de Barcelona Collection,
MACBA Foundation, Spain

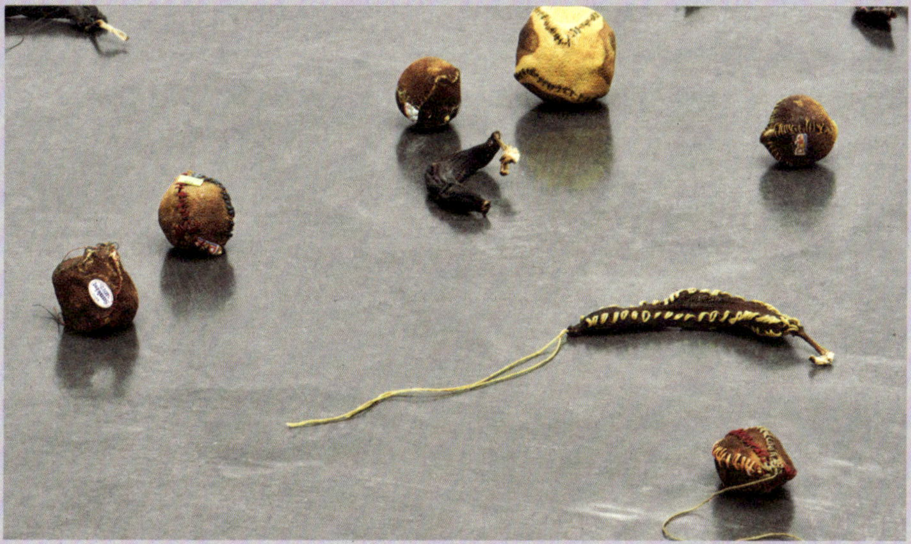

20

about the dangers of skin-to-skin means of contracting the virus. Because the carriers had to interlace their arms under Espaliú's body, their bones formed a matrix-based cradle that relates to the criss-crossed intertwining of threads that gives woven fabric its strength.

New York-based artist Zoe Leonard's series *Strange Fruit* (1992–97) [img. 20] emblematizes the notion of the textile stitch as vital for healing. Leonard, who was active in AIDS organizing efforts and in 1991 co-founded the lesbian collective fierce pussy, witnessed the deaths of dozens of friends and embarked on a project in which she sutured together nearly 300 empty fruit skins (including oranges, bananas, and avocados). Laid directly on the floor, the husks slowly decompose and dry out, shriveling and some turning back in a gesture that recalls the tradition of the memento mori painting. Leonard has commented that her obsessive act of sewing, including the occasional insertion of zippers or buttons, was in part inspired by her friend Wojnarowicz. Indeed, her series is explicitly dedicated to him: it was first titled *Strange Fruit (for David)*.[9] She utilizes consumed, eaten fruit as a surrogate for the human body and the impossibly impoverished traces that one leaves behind after one departs. Leonard's work also recalls resourceful feminist uses of sewing to create new meaning out of what has been discarded, and its durational component is in dialogue with women's time-based performance art.

Strange Fruit is in a lineage with works such as Brazilian artist Letícia Parente's (1930–1991) *Marca Registrada* [Trademark] [img. 21], a ground-breaking piece of video art from 1975 that prefigures much feminist and queer work with stitching. Parente's ten-minute piece consists of a close-up shot of the artist

20. Zoe Leonard
Strange Fruit (detail),
1992-97

Banana, orange, grapefruit, lemon, and avocado peels, thread, zippers, buttons, sinew, needles, plastic, wire, stickers, fabric, trim, wax
Variable dimensions

Philadelphia Museum of Art, purchase with funds contributed by the Dietrich Foundation and with the partial gift of the artist and the Paula Cooper Gallery, 1998, United States

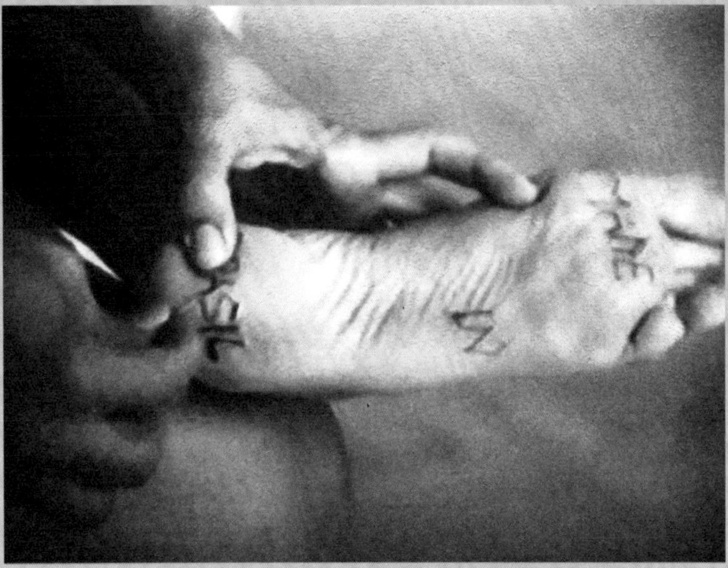

21

hand-sewing the words “Made in Brasil” with black thread onto the sole of her left foot. This action is made possible by the relative thickness of the skin on that part of the body and the artist’s dexterity with the needle, but it still registers as a violent interruption of the integrity of flesh. Created during the military dictatorship in Brazil, Parente comments on the undue, imperialist influence of U.S. politics and products across South America, knowingly stitching the phrase in English and only reserving the Portuguese for the spelling of her country.

The Egyptian-born Lebanese artist Nicolas Moufarrege (1947–1985), who moved to New York City in 1981, was a further crucial figure for queer textiles. Though he died of AIDS-related complications in 1985, at the age of 37, he made a mark on the city’s queer scene with his writing and his artwork. Moufarrege’s lushly realized tapestries combine needlepoint and painted pigment, often drawing freely from ancient religious iconography, pop art, comic books, commercial sources, and Arabic script. In this untitled work from 1983 [img. 22], a muscular, disembodied arm reaches down from the boldly patterned upper right corner, a ribbon in its hand unfurling down off the lower edge of the piece. The arm is partly outlined with a strip of red that flows down the canvas and collects like a bloody sea along with the tears shed by a classically Egyptian eye as bodily fluids mingle. Bringing together past and present with his campy coloration and his lusty depiction of masculine bodies, Moufarrege invokes many strands of art historical references and queerly entangles them.

21. Letícia Parente
Frame of ***Marca registrada***
[Trademark], 1975

Video
10’33”
Collection of André Parente,
Rio de Janeiro, Brazil

Paraguayan artist Feliciano Centurión (1962–1996), who died in Argentina of AIDS-related causes in 1996, was also skilled with embroidery as well as with crochet and knitting. In his piece *Te Quiero* [I Love You] (1993) [img. 23], Centurión has combined several textile forms by hand-stitching the Spanish language phrase on a crimson circle, bordered by the lace of a doily, and then mounting this in the center of a found, gray striped blanket. He often referred to vernacular craft and folk practices of textile making in his art, some of which depicted animal creatures he found entrancing and short, evocative text phrases. The needlework of Leonilson and Centurión was featured in the recent exhibition *Unravel: The Power and Politics of Textiles in Art* (Barbican Art Centre, 2024), demonstrating connections between their queer stitchwork and placing them in a larger genealogy of feminist and activist making.[10] Both artists embroidered onto small-scale household items like napkins and handkerchiefs, signaling the profound familiarity we all have with the fabrics of everyday life that surround us night and day.

Centurión grasped how blankets hold intimate meaning; they comfort us, warm us, and surround us when we dream. They are infused with our smells and our stories. And his use of blankets further echoes the world's largest folk art project and the most visible use of queer needlework during the global AIDS epidemic—the NAMES Project AIDS Memorial Quilt [img. 25]. Created in a crowdsourced manner by thousands of individuals mourning those who died, the AIDS Quilt was initiated in the late 1980s by activists in San Francisco, California, as a way to provide a collective outlet for grief, and it explicitly recruited the comforting, domestic associations linked to women's quilting and sewing. I have discussed in my 2017 book *Fray: Art and Textile Politics* how the Quilt is a varied and diverse arena for multiple, often contradictory statements about politics, longing, and loss.[11] With over 50 thousand individual panels, it is hard to summarize or assess the amount of textile labor and handmade care that goes into the Quilt, from expert mother quilters sewing exquisitely detailed panels for their lost sons to children stapling on favored stuffed animals in honor of aunts and uncles. But one thing is certain: the Quilt stands as a monumental emblem of the connection between AIDS, memorialization, and needlework.

Another project that likewise uses sewing to evoke losses from HIV/AIDS, but is specifically geared to commemorate trans

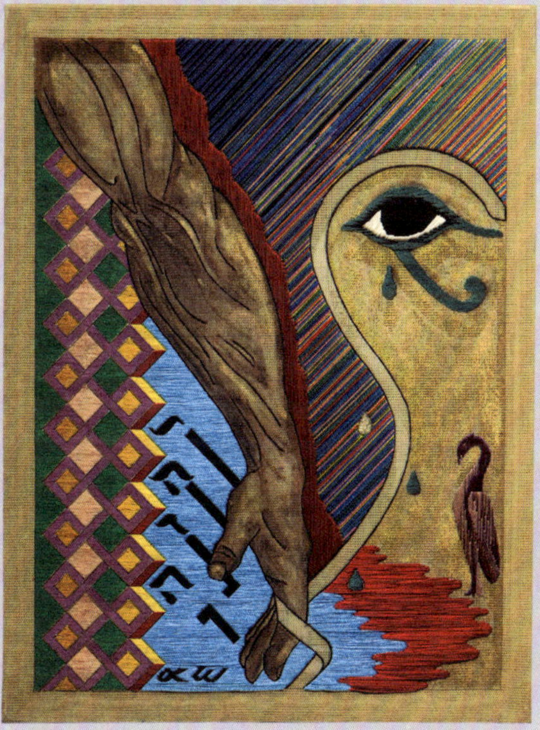

22

22. Nicolas Moufarrege
***Untitled*, 1983**

Thread and pigment
on needlepoint canvas
66 × 48 cm
Collection of Tim Cone,
Washington D.C.,
United States

and gender-non-conforming people, is the Archivo Memoria Trans México's project entitled *Hospital de Ropa* [Clothing Hospital]. Founded as a nomadic initiative in 2022 by Brandy Basurto, Emma Yesica Duvali, César González-Aguirre, Terry Holiday, Erick Molina, Samuel Nicolle, and María Ponce, the *Hospital de Ropa* endeavors to breathe life into stories of transwomen who have died of AIDS in Mexico since the 1980s. As González-Aguirre describes it, "scraps of fabric, clothes that once belonged to loved ones, costume jewelry, and other hand-me-downs formed the bulk of the materials we amassed to create imagery that dealt specifically with experiences of remembrance and grief."[12]

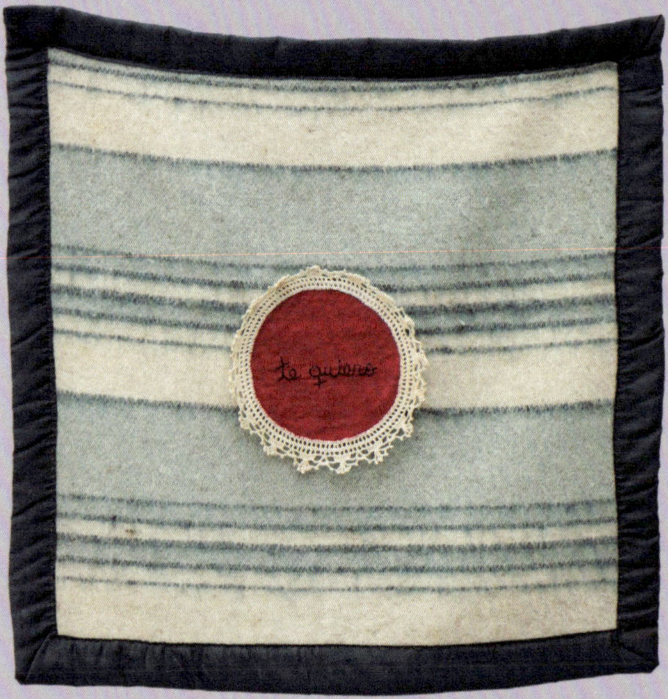
23

Leonilson's last work, from 1993, was an installation made for a chapel in São Paulo, the Capela do Morumbi, that he did not live to see fully realized. One object in this installation is a textile entitled *Lásaro* [img. 238], made from two crisp white button-down shirts sewn together and conjoined at the waist. One hangs upright on a hanger, while the other is inverted and dangles upside down, its sleeves brushing the ground. The shirts are mirror images of each other, forever attached "at the hip," as we say in English to refer to inseparable couples. Leonilson's *Lásaro* is part of a long line of art that uses paired identical objects to poetically evoke same-sex partnership and queer bonds, including Cuban-born Felix Gonzalez Torres' (1957–1996) pillowcases and clocks. (Gonzalez-Torres passed away due to complications of AIDS.).

In a recent homage, queer Korean artist Kang Seung Lee has recreated Leonilson's shirts but made them out of hemp fiber *sambe* and stitched them with antique 24K gold threads [img. 24].[13] This piece, *Untitled (Lázaro, José Leonilson, 1993)*, from 2023, has been translated into regionally-specific materials by Lee as he uses a traditional cloth for Korean garments; notably *sambe* is historically worn by mourners during funerals and for dressing the dead. On the upper right in the delicately glittering thread is embroidered lettering (spelling out "LAZARO") based on American Sign Language that refers

23. Feliciano Centurión
Te quiero [I love you], 1993

Embroidered fabric mounted on wool blanket
50 × 52 cm
Collection of Eduardo F. Constantini, Buenos Aires, Argentina

24. Kang Seung Lee
Untitled (Lazaro, José Leonilson, 1993), 2023

Sambe (hemp fiber fabric), antique 24K gold thread, coat hanger
191 × 69 × 8 cm
Courtesy of the artist and Commonwealth and Council, Los Angeles, United States and Mexico City

to another figure who died due to AIDS-related causes and is a touchstone for Lee, the Chinese-American artist Martin Wong (1946–1999). Early in his career, Wong was a costume designer for the genderqueer subcultural group The Cockettes and hence is also part of the history of queer textiles. With these tributes, Lee creates an affective archive that places him within a network of queer artists, past and present, who use needlework to hint at desire as well as those who are more straightforward about their orientations.

In 1987, queer writer and activist Néstor Perlongher (1949–1992) wrote:

In the crisis of the AIDS epidemic, it's hard to say what's more terrifying: the devastating effects the disease has on the physical body, riddled with a succession of shocking symptoms; or the other, less "physical" effects in the sphere of public opinion, which, while merely "discursive," have as much impact on the contemporary codification of the body, its passions and its actions.[14]

24

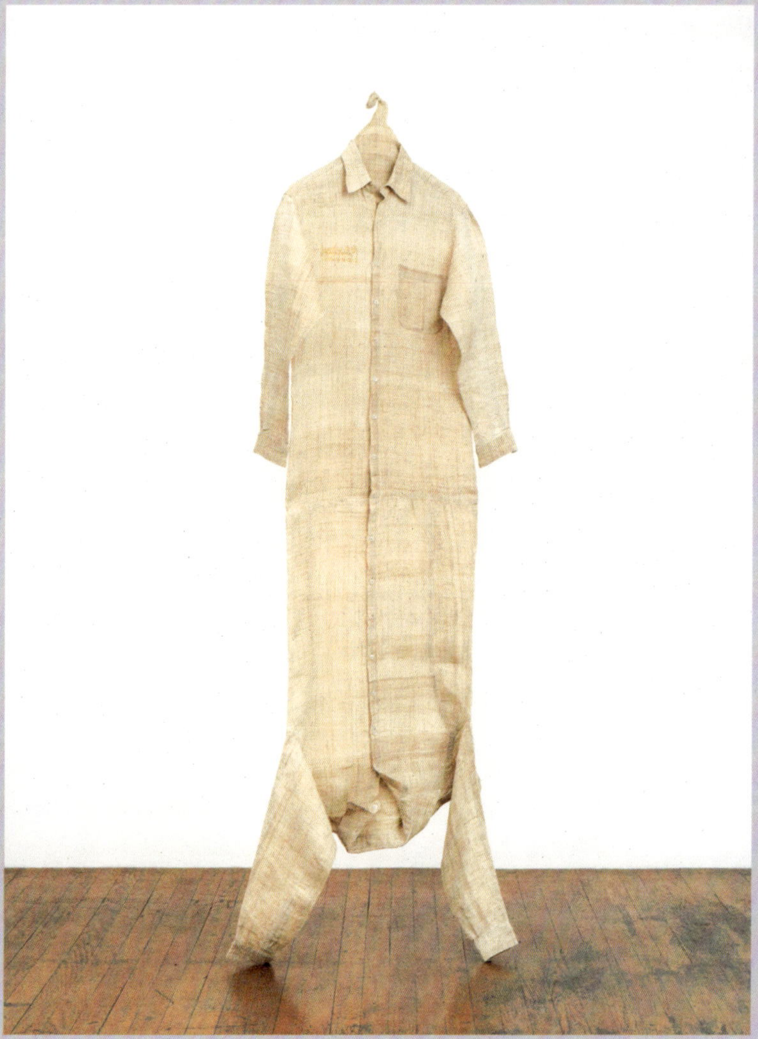

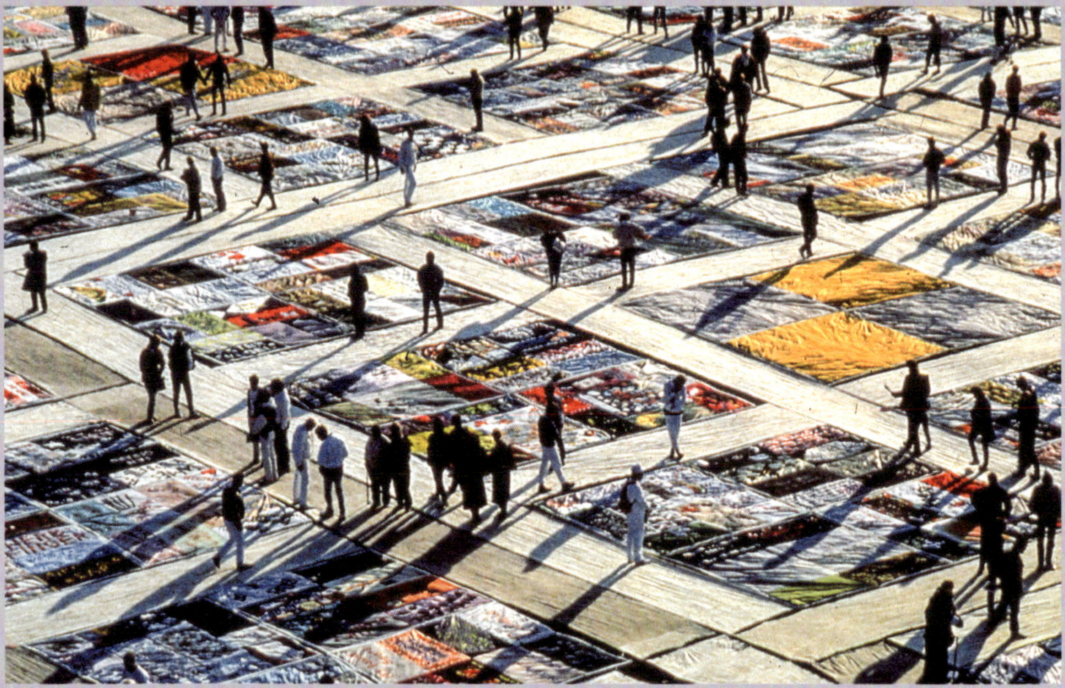

25

Perlongher, who had been born and raised in Argentina but at the time was living as a "sexual exile" in Brazil, published these words in the prominent Brazilian newspaper *Folha de S. Paulo*. Perlongher aptly diagnoses how, within the heated homophobic rhetoric of the AIDS crisis of the 1980s and 1990s, the infected queer body was posited as a grave threat to the normative public, as same-sex practices threatened to tear apart the "social fabric" of the collective body. Between 1991 and 1993, Leonilson contributed illustrations to *Folha de S. Paulo,* at times accompanying texts about public health, drawn with the artist's distinctive line.[15] Yet, his most open statements about his own vulnerable body were rendered in embroidery—as with these other artists I have written about whose hands were on fire as they urgently worked with needle and thread to repair the ruptured social fabric.

25. AIDS Memorial Quilt from the NAMES Project, Washington D.C., United States, 1989, Courtesy of National AIDS Memorial, San Francisco, California, United States

Julia Bryan-Wilson, Curator-at-Large of Modern and Contemporary Art, MASP.

NOTES

1 Luis Pérez-Oramas, "Leonilson: Parangolé-Poem." In: *José Leonilson: Empty Man* (New York: Americas Society, 2017), 111. Oramas cites an interview by Lisette Lagnado, "Interview with the artist." In: Lisette Lagnado, *Leonilson: são tantas verdades [So Many Are the Truths]* (São Paulo: Projeto Leonilson, 2019), 84.

2 Adriano Pedrosa in conversation with Leonilson, included in this volume.

3 Jenni Sorkin, "Running Stitch, Outrunning Time." In: *José Leonilson: Empty Man*, op. cit., 200.

4 Adriano Pedrosa, "Introdução." In: *Leonilson: Truth, Fiction* (São Paulo/Rio de Janeiro: Pinacoteca do Estado/ Cobogó, 2014), 21.

5 One of the most important feminist voices related to the politics of embroidery is Rozsika Parker, *The Subversive Stitch Embroidery and the Making of the Feminine* (London: Women's Press, 1984).

6 For more on the censoring of Wojnarowicz, see Richard Meyer, *Outlaw Representation: Censorship and Homosexuality in Twentieth Century American Art* (London: Oxford University Press, 2002).

7 I am grateful to Zoe Leonard for providing me with information related to this photograph.

8 BDSM refers to a range of kink practices and is an acronym usually standing for "bondage, domination, submission, and masochism."

9 See Nina Quabeck, "Intent in the Making: the Life of Zoe Leonard's *Strange Fruit*." Burlington Contemporary, May 2019. Available at https://contemporary.burlington.org.uk/journal/journal/intent-in-the-making-the-life-of-zoe-leonards-strange-fruit. Retrieved May 16, 2024.

10 Lotte Johnson, Amanda Pianatih, Wells Fray-Smith, and Diego Chocano (curators); Julia Bryan-Wilson (curatorial advisement), *Unravel: The Power and Politics of Textiles in Art* (London/Amsterdam: Barbican Art Centre/Stedelijk Museum, 2024). This exhibition catalog includes my essay "Fibre Creatures, Furry Beasts: Queer Textile Crittercism," 21–25.

11 Julia Bryan-Wilson, "Remains of the AIDS Quilt." In: *Fray: Art and Textile Politics* (Chicago: University of Chicago, 2017).

12 César González-Aguirre, "Brandy Basurto, Emma Yesica Duvali, César González-Aguirre, Terry Holiday, Erick Molina, Samuel Nicolle, and María Ponce, *Clothing Hospital*, 2022." In: David Evan Frantz, Christina Linden, and Chris E. Vargas (eds.), *Trans Hirstory in 99 Objects* (Museum of Transgender History/Hirmer, 2023), 228.

13 Kang Seung Lee has also made a video and a mixed-media work of the same title.

14 Néstor Perlongher, "Corporal Order," published in "Trends and Debates" section, *Folha de S. Paulo*, Feb. 21, 1987; reprinted in Néstor Perlongher, *Plebeian Prose* (London: Polity Press, 2019), 43.

15 Nicholas C. Morgan, "Forging a Public Sphere: José Leonilson in the *Folha de São Paulo*." *ARTMargins*, v. 9, no. 1, Feb. 2020, 7–28.

LETTER TO LEO NILSON AND HIS GOLDEN LITTLE STONES

Miguel A. López

The volcano. That's what we have inside us, something that explodes, this loads of feelings. The volcano is like when I feel full of things, ready to explode.

Leonilson (March, 1991)

All the works are objects of desire.

Leonilson (November, 1992)

Dear Leonilson,

I must confess that I have spent the last few weeks reading the conversations you had with Lisette Lagnado and Adriano Pedrosa in 1991 and 1992, shortly before your death.[1] These recordings, mainly conducted in São Paulo, in places as diverse as your studio, friends' houses, or the hospital, offer an intense and emotional testimony, in which you review your life and creative processes in the face of the uncertainty about how much time you had left due to the then lack of effective treatments available for HIV/AIDS. "I don't know if I have six months, two years or twenty years left," you told Lisette in November 1992, before adding, "So, through neither pain nor pity, my relationship with people has gotten a lot better."[2]

Through these recorded and transcribed conversations, I have traveled with you to Madrid, New York, Paris, Rio de Janeiro, and Frankfurt. I feel like I toured museums through your excited gaze upon encountering Paul Klee (1879–194), Antoni Tàpies (1923–2012), Joseph Beuys (1921–1986), Blinky Palermo (1943–1977), and Keith Haring (1958–1990), and I saw you knocking on Antonio Dias' (1944–2018) door in Milan in October 1981 to show him your drawings and seek his support in a city where you had arrived with nothing and no one. As I made this journey with you, I remembered the impact being face-to-face with your drawings had on me in 2010 when some of them were exhibited at the MUSAC museum, in León, Spain.[3] I am not sure if it was the first time I saw your works, but it probably was because they profoundly struck me. They were all small in format, and I especially recall two of them. The first one, *Sua montanha interior protetora* [Your Sheltering Inner Mountain] (1989) [img. 26], is a watercolor measuring 25.5 × 18 cm that depicts a character with open arms and exposed genitals within a mountain. At the top of the composition, rows of eyes shed tears and seem to watch over from the sky. That character was naturally you, Leonilson, and I found it touching that you drew an erupting volcano on your chest.

The second one, *Masturbação mútua* [Mutual Masturbation] (1990) [img. 27], a watercolor drawing on a 30 × 23 cm paper, is part of a series about safe sex practices in the face of the HIV/AIDS epidemic. The drawing shows two male silhouettes whose arms cross each other in the middle of the paper and whose hands then touch each other's genitals in a gesture of passion, complicity, and tenderness. The image occupies less than a quarter of the page, inviting us to get closer to see it in an act of erotic proximity and voyeurism. The curators set up your drawings in a very small white room, located at the highest point of the exhibition's design. It was as if it were the summit of a mountain that one accessed by crossing circular corridors and climbing stairs.[4] I wonder what you would have thought of that location, Leonilson, considering the significance that mountains have held for you as places of care and refuge. I appreciated that the space was so intimate and that no more than two or three people could fit in to see the work at the same time, because this encouraged me to have a personal encounter with you. Although I have been fortunate enough to see exhaustive exhibitions of your work—*Leonilson: Truth, Fiction*, in São Paulo in 2014, *Empty Man*, in New York City in 2017, and *Corpo político* [Political Body], in São Paulo in 2023[5]—I truly believe that this initial encounter with your drawings was decisive for me.

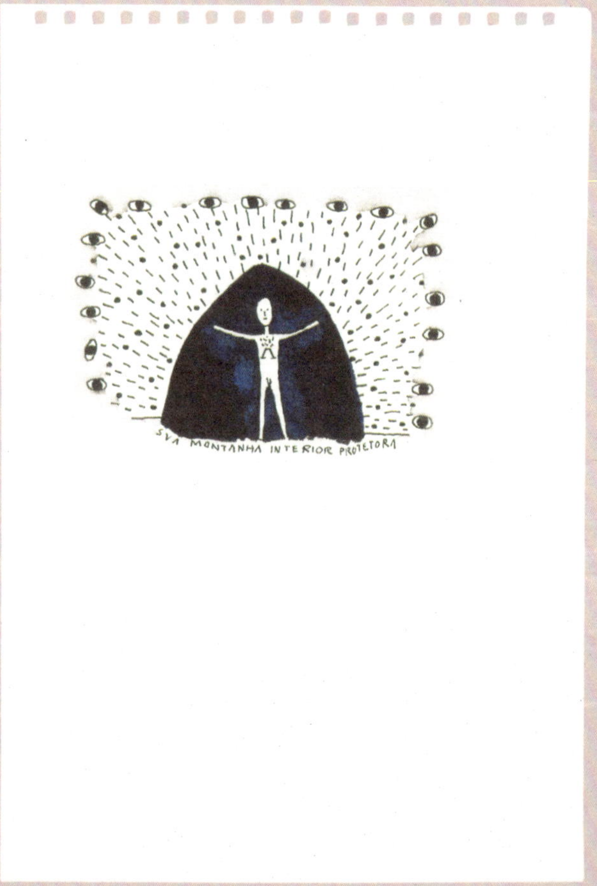

26

Reading these interviews has returned to me that initial feeling of captivation and surprise I felt when I saw your drawings almost fifteen years ago. I was moved by the way you describe your works as "letters that were never sent" or as the result of "platonic love."[6] Emotional relationships have been at the center of these interviews in such an intense way, I do not know if this is because that has always been the heart of your work, or because your illness—and the possibility of imminent death—reinforced that need to embrace love as that which gives meaning to life. I think it is more about the former, but certainly, understanding that our bodies are fragile and perishable impels us to treasure every breath of life passionately.

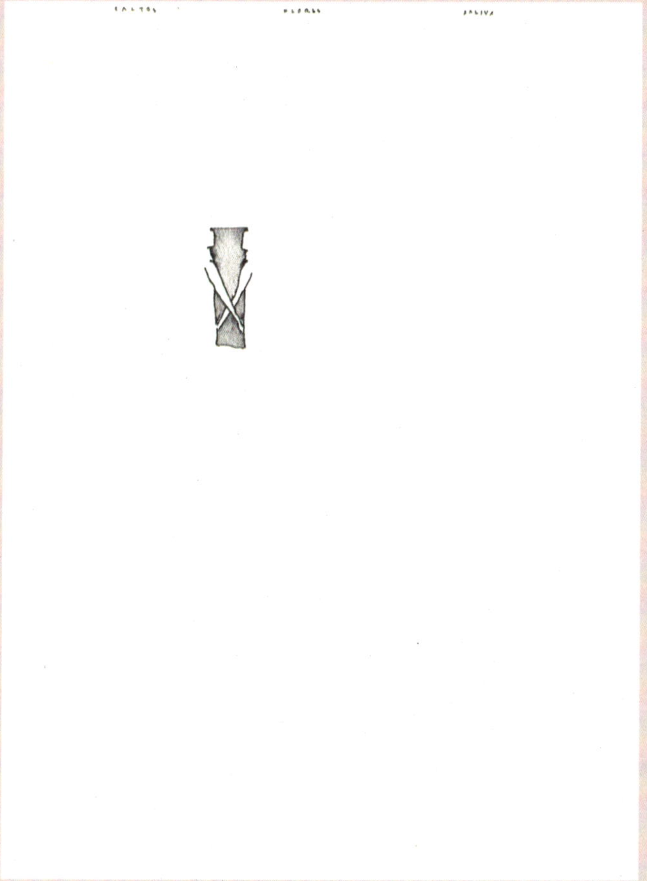

27

Although your works are self-referential, you knew those emotions were not exclusive and anyone could identify with them. "[My work] speaks of feelings. The things that I speak about are not mine. Everyone feels this, everyone goes through breakups...."[7] However, your work had a distinctive aspect. Rather than delving into affections abstractly, your pieces address the struggles of homosexual desire at the dawn of the HIV/AIDS crisis. "Things have changed, relationships have changed completely," you told Adriano in March 1991, three months before testing positive for HIV. It was not only the uncertainty that arose from confronting a disease for which there was then no clear medical knowledge or accessible treatments at the time, but also the violent onslaught of homophobic discourses and moralizing images that conservative groups were pushing in an attempt to control and domesticate non-normative forms of life. You were also aware that the diagnosis radically changed others' social perception of you:

26. Leonilson
Sua montanha interior protetora
[Your Inner Sheltering Mountain], 1989
[img. 47]

27. Leonilson
Masturbação mútua
[Mutual Masturbation], 1990
[img. 116]

I am a dangerous person in the world. No one can kiss me. I can't have sex. If I cut myself, no one can take care of my cuts, I have to go to a clinic. [...] I have something inside me that makes me dangerous. I don't need a weapon. It is enough to cut myself.[8]

In 1992, shortly after recovering from pneumonia, you made a series of seven small drawings titled *O perigoso* [The Dangerous One] [imgs. 202-8]. The first of them was a self-portrait: a circular stain, floating in the middle of the blank page, made with black ink and a drop of your HIV-positive blood. Below it, you had written "O perigoso." In the other drawings, you represented your arm receiving intravenous medicine, your finger being pricked for a blood test, five pills in a transparent glass, a crucifix, a clock portrayed as your guardian angel, and a rosary accompanied by the word "as fadas" [the fairies]. The whole set was a kind of diary: a poetic account of medical treatment and protection, where the extreme fragility of your body contrasted with the fear that society had of you due to the possibility of contagion.

You were not the only one using your own bodily fluids to elaborate on the social stigma against homosexual people. A few years earlier, the Colombian artist Wilson Díaz produced *Sementerio* [Sementery] (1986) [imgs. 28, 29], a series of eight drawings made mixing sperm and black ink. The drawings consisted of traces of semen on paper, from which Wilson painted lines and spots loaded with organic connotations in the form of abstract landscapes. The title—which combined the words "semen" and "cemetery"—although it seems to evoke the orgasmic experience (*petite mort*), alluded, in fact, to the deathly atmosphere left by the spread of HIV/AIDS in the world at a time when even the handling of corpses was uncertain. Many funeral homes refused to serve relatives of people who had died due to the syndrome. Many bodies of people with HIV were buried clandestinely.[9] By presenting an abstract scenario rather than a figurative representation of his body, Wilson seems to claim strategies of indistinction as a way of resisting surveillance systems—based on the identification and recognition of faces or bodies—of HIV-positive people. Just like you, Leonilson, Wilson used his fluids to present homosexual desire as an experience socially marked as a death sentence.

Your works manifest an urgency to exist on the sentimental plane: bearing witness to affections and naming a homosexual love that, in those years, was not common to see publicly represented in Brazil. You distanced yourself from a local art scene that you felt was generally too cerebral, intellectualized, and shaped by the theoretical discussion associated with the conceptual art of the 1970s.[10] It is significant that while rejecting the predominance of theory, you

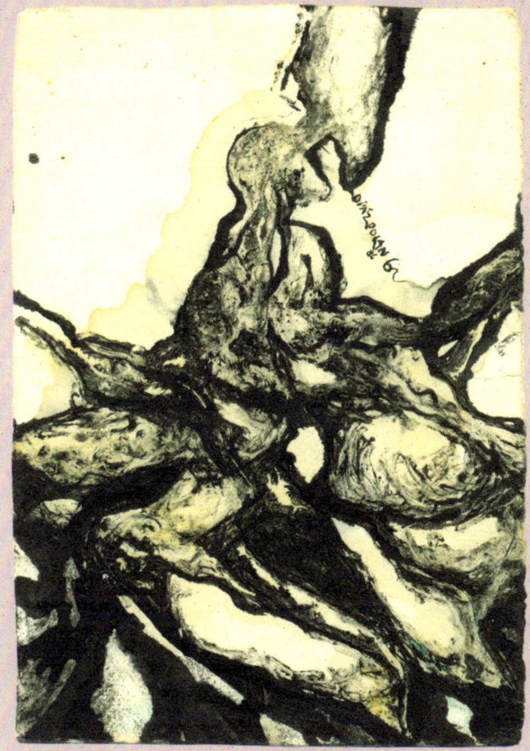

28

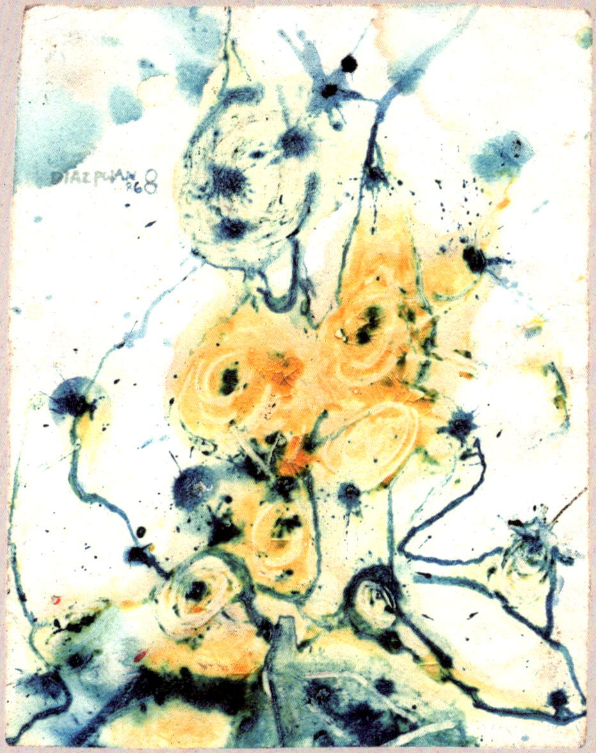

29

also felt a lack of critical support for your work, as well as that of other artists of your generation, of an accompaniment that should be able to pay attention not just to ideas, but to spirit and desire, that is, an embodied theory of the sensual and the erotic.

I didn't need an accompanying theory in order to do my work. I wanted to do what I was feeling. I fell in love with someone and made many works for that person, and that was important to me. Now, I think that this, too, can be discussed in a critical or theoretical way.[11]

For you, one of the most significant aspects of affective relationships is what they teach us. "What worries me in life are my love relationships, my relationships with people. [...] You learn how to deal with it because that's the great thing about relationships: you are learning how to deal with people, how to deal with this important thing you had," you told Adriano in March 1991.[12] What you say is almost the opposite of what society has imposed as common sense, namely, that we have so much work and that there is no time for love, or that

28. Wilson Diaz
Sementerio (nº 6)
[Sementery (nº 6)], 1986

Semen and paint on cardboard
19 × 13.5 cm
Private collection

29. Wilson Diaz
Sementerio (nº 8)
[Sementery (nº 8)], 1986

Semen and paint on cardboard
14.5 × 11.5 cm
Private collection

love is not a priority and will come when other things are resolved. In a world of overwhelming violence, where people prefer not to fall in love to avoid pain or because their end is often seen as a social failure, you surrender to love and expose it completely, recognizing your own difficulties in building and sustaining those bonds. "I'm referring to the distance that I myself establish. The barriers are put there intentionally," you said with melancholy in November 1992.[13] It is not coincidental that bridges or conduits are protagonists in your paintings and drawings, like *Jogos perigosos* [Dangerous Games] (*circa* 1990) [img. 113] or *O grande rio* [Large River] (*circa* 1991) [img. 157], in which they appear connecting male heads and torsos that are physically distanced.

Your work always returned to love (dis)enchantments as if trying to underline the complex experience of *giving ourselves* to others: not only how challenging it is *to love* and *let ourselves be loved* but also exploring all that range of loving sensations—doubt, fascination, confusion, euphoria, or alienation—felt in our bodies and how to deal with them. I think of *Longo caminho de um rapaz apaixonado* [Long Way of a Young Man in Love] (*circa* 1989) [img. 8], a small drawing (12 × 18 cm) of two male torsos, side by side, joined at the center by a pulley connecting both hearts. At the opposite ends of the image, you wrote "SP" [São Paulo] on the left and "Rio" [Rio de Janeiro] on the right, referring to the spatial separation between the characters and the frustrations associated with that. I wonder, Leonilson, if that second person you referred to in the drawing was Adriano. You have not hesitated to express your admiration for him more than once, and it is known that you two used to have long conversations over the phone that could last hours and even days. Perhaps this revelation is irrelevant. However, behind its apparent frivolity, lies a political aspect: I am not interested in a clear and stable definition of your relationship but rather in its contingent and speculative condition because it accounts for all the possibilities of building structures of affection—affections that go beyond the traditional couple figure or that reveal a desire without a center, moving simultaneously in multiple directions. Whether it is something chimerical or not, passionate love appears in your works as something that alters our frames of reference and ways of imagining the future.

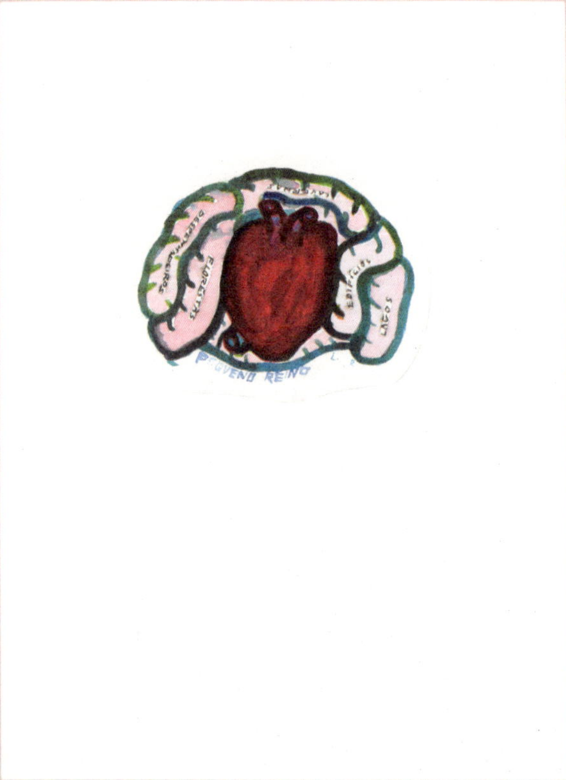

On second thought, perhaps your work is not so much concerned with

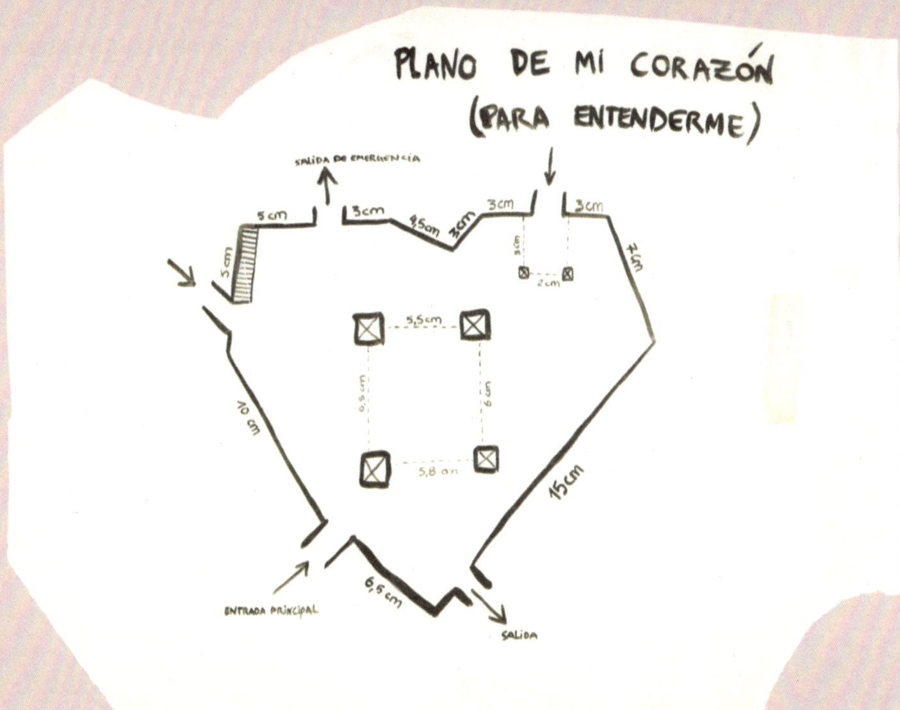

31

love as it is with the formation of desire. One of my favorite works of yours is *Pequeno reino* [Small Kingdom] (*circa* 1988) [img. 30], a small watercolor drawing on paper showing a red heart superimposed on what seems to be the silhouette of a brain. In the different lobes of the brain, you wrote words that contained geographical allusions ("lagos" [lakes], "florestas" [forests], "edifícios" [buildings], among others), as if it were a brain-cartography. In other works of yours, you had already presented human anatomy as a map. In the paintings *As ruas da cidade* [The City Streets] (*circa* 1988) [img. 42] and *O que posso fazer dentro de mim* [What I Can Do Within Me] (1991), the body's organs appear as city streets, and in *Todos os rios* [All the Rivers] (1989), you present several rivers of São Paulo erotically converging on lips painted at the center of the canvas. In fact, *Pequeno reino* reminds me of a beautiful drawing titled *Plano de mi corazón (para entenderme)* [Map of My Heart (To Understand Me)] (2001) [img. 31], by the Argentine artist Fernanda Laguna, in which she represents her heart as the architectural plan for a room. Fernanda places the measurements of the columns and interior walls of her heart (10 cm, 15 cm, 7 cm) and also draws four doors that are the entrances to the arteries. Next to each door, she writes the words "entrada" [entrance], "salida" [exit], and also creates a "salida de emergencia" [emergency exit] for what I imagine are the moments when love ends and one must fly away.[14] Much of her work consists of inventing languages to convey intense loving emotions. I think you would have loved to meet her.

30. Leonilson
[Pequeno reino]
[Small Kingdom], *circa* 1988

Watercolor on cut
paper glued on paper
32 × 24 cm
Private collection,
São Paulo, Brazil
PL.0669.0/00

31. Fernanda Laguna
Plano de mi corazón (para entenderme)
[Plan of My Heart (To Understand Me)], 2001

Marker on vegetal paper
53 × 68 cm
Los Angeles County Museum of Art,
gift Dario Werthein, 2016,
United States

But in your *Pequeno reino*, beyond the organ's allusion to a map, what fascinates me is how that heart imposes itself on the brain, obstructing it, becoming the absolute ruler of that territory. The obstruction of reason suggests a praise of frenzy and outburst, or perhaps the sheer power of a great passion. Your work evokes that ever-present possibility that arises in the encounter of two or more people: feeling sparks flying and the formation of intense connections that will let go of your old self, although it may not necessarily turn into a love relationship, or, perhaps, it will. Few people have accurately described such an experience of loss of control as Julia Kristeva has done in her 1983 book *Histories d'amour* [Tales of Love]:

> **Love is the time and space in which "I" assumes the right to be extraordinary. Sovereign yet not individual. Divisible, lost, annihilated; but also, and through imaginary fusion with the loved one, equal to the infinite space of superhuman psychism. Paranoid? I am, in love, at the zenith of subjectivity.[15]**

Kristeva traces the vertigo of *being in love*, the sensation of wildness but also loss, because in that cataclysm, one ceases to be who they are to become another. I believe your works, Leonilson, emerge precisely out of that volcanic eruption of total subjectivity mentioned by Kristeva. While you describe your works as letters that were never sent, I feel that your messages did arrive and shook many hearts in unexpected times and places. There is a reason why I am here writing you this letter thirty years after your death, wishing I had met you.

Your work also has a predictive dimension. There is something you told Adriano, when talking about your exhibition at the Luisa Strina gallery in 1989, that resonated with me. "I was preparing myself for something. With each exhibition, I'm preparing myself for something that will happen in my life."[16] While you were talking about how your work and your life matured over the years—becoming more rigorous and responsible, in your words—I also believe you were trying to say that the images you create announce something you could not have known otherwise. In one of the conversations, at a time when the illness began to weaken your body, Lisette asked you why you did not have a carpenter make wooden sculptures shaped like twisted bridges—another personal metaphor for misunderstandings in the love realm. She asked if you refused to delegate execution because that could create an authorship conflict. And you replied: "Simply because I like to do it. It's my pleasure. [...] I already said that my work is not as important as the learning. It is really important to learn from what you do."[17] I imagine your works like antennas that made your body vibrate as if it were receiving revelations.

32. Leonilson
Bom rapaz em embalagem ruim
[Good Lad in a Bad Packaging], 1991

Thread on voile, crepe, and velvet
45 × 40 cm
Private collection, São Paulo, Brazil
PL.0011.0/00

One of the most visible effects of the illness manifested in your physical strength. Shortly after learning of your diagnosis, you stopped painting. The pigments contained toxic components that affected your health, so you dedicated yourself almost exclusively to sewing and embroidering. In the 1980s, you created some pieces mixing painting, objects, and weaving, such as *Rifat* (1988), in which you placed what appear to be wire earrings on a velvet fabric, or the series of fabrics where you embroidered buttons of many colors as if it were an inventory, an alphabet, or a form of coded accounting. "With embroidery I reveal my ambiguity in my relationship to my manhood," you said, underlining how embracing tenderness and vulnerability is one of the greatest betrayals of masculinity.[18]

In contrast to previous years, the fabric pieces created between 1991 and 1993 carry a unique energy, tinged with melancholy. I would have liked to sit down with you to talk about those geometric landscapes you composed with different types of fabric. *Bom rapaz em embalagem ruim* [Good Lad in a Bad Packaging] (1991) [img. 32] or *O imperfeito* [The Imperfect] (1993), are made by joining three different materials (for example, crepe, velvet, and voile). You cut each material of various colors into rectangles and arranged them horizontally in the style of a 1960s abstract painting. When I first saw them, I thought they could be softly colored pieces in the style of Mark Rothko, but in reality, Leonilson, these textile pieces are composed of pure colors, very different from Rothko's blurred edges in which the tones fade and blend.

I actually dare to think that *Bom rapaz em embalagem ruim*, *O imperfeito*, and other similar works of yours are a secret homage to the *Stoffbilder* [fabric pictures] [img. 33] that Blinky Palermo created between 1966 and 1972: rectangular works on frames composed of monochromatic fabrics that he bought in local stores, cut horizontally, and then sewed together, usually combining three colors. Your color palette (whites; reds and browns, or yellows; violets and whites) is very close to Palermo's. And it does not surprise me that these works would have been another way for you to secretly dedicate something to someone, just as you did in the series of small drawings *Os dedicados* [The Dedicated] (1991) [imgs. 168-78], where you celebrated homoerotic desire and the affection and passion for men you had met at

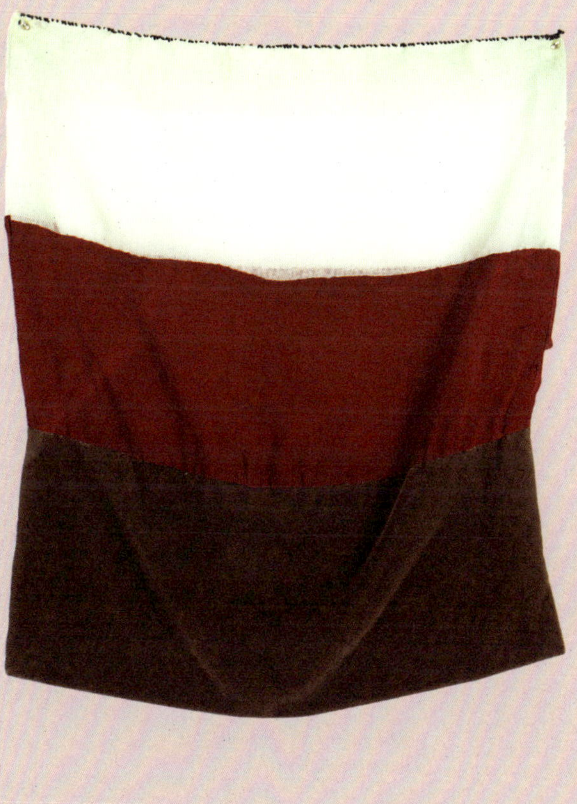

32

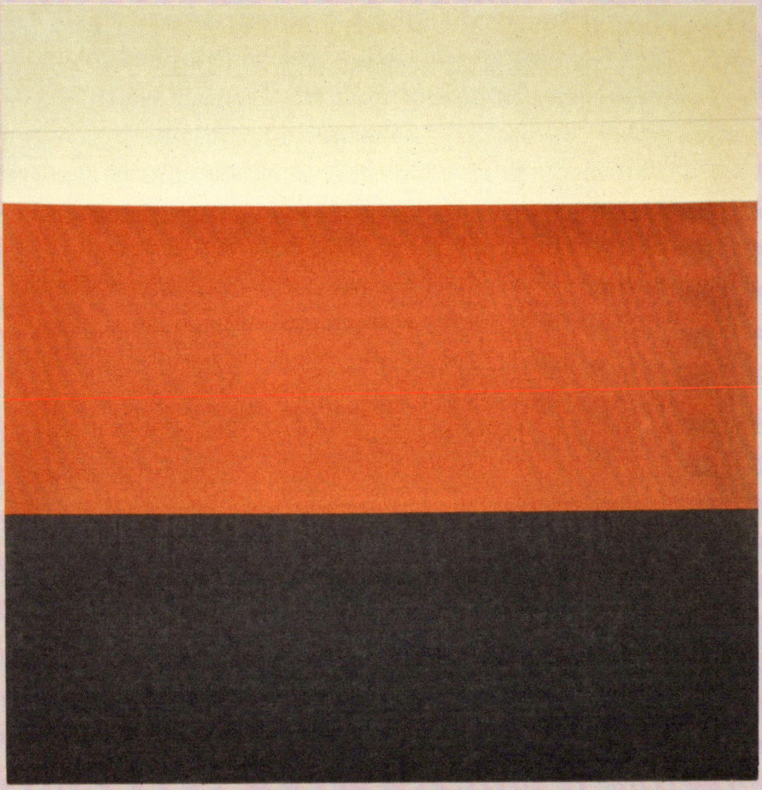

33

different times in your life. "Sometimes I had only seen a photo and dedicated a work to that person. Sometimes I fell in love with the photo. I know it's kind of crazy, but it's ok," you told Lisette, almost laughing.[19] But it does not seem so far-fetched to me. Your words invite me to consider the role of platonic loves in our lives; not so much as a record of whom we have desired but as a testimony to the many ways of desiring.

In your textiles from those years, you introduce small symbols or phrases. In one of them, from 1991, you embroidered almost invisibly at the top a phrase that made me smile: "Leo não pode mudar o mundo porque os deuses não admitem qualquer competição com eles" [Leo cannot change the world because the gods do not admit any competition with them]. In *34 com scars* [34 With Scars] (1991) [img. 192], you embroidered on the top of the textile the shape of two sutures, which you painted around with almost invisible white brushstrokes. Your age (34) was embroidered on the same cloth, to the right and in a smaller size. As if it were your own naked body, the piece immerses us in the memory of the scars and the way the body processes pain and regenerates itself.

When I see these works of yours, I cannot help but think of Feliciano Centurión, a Paraguayan artist who around the same time also received an HIV-positive

33. Blinky Palermo
Untitled, 1970

Cotton fabrics on
raw cotton canvas
200 × 200 cm
Hessisches Landesmuseum
Darmstadt, Germany

diagnosis. Based in Buenos Aires, Centurión then quitted painting on canvas to dedicate himself to embroidery, crocheting, and painting on blankets found in stores in his neighborhood. As his health weakened, and he lost strength, he began working with even smaller elements, such as napkins, pillows, or other household materials. Those were difficult times because HIV/AIDS had started to take away several artist friends from Feliciano's inner circle, like Omar Schiliro (1962–1994) and Liliana Maresca (1951–1994), who died in the same year.[20] In that scenario, he dedicated himself to embroidering a set of phrases in an affirmative exercise of opposition to death and the need to cling to time: *Estoy despierto* [I Am Awake] (1991–1993), *Que en nuestras almas no entre el terror* [Let No Terror Enter Our Souls] (1992), *Busco refugio* [I Seek Refuge] (1990–1993), *La muerte es parte intermitente de mis días* [Death Is a Recurring Part of My Days] (1990), *Estoy vivo* [I Am Alive] (1994), *Renazco a cada instante* [I Am Reborn in Every Moment] (1995), *Soy el alma que no muere* [I Am the Soul that Does Not Die] (1996), and *Me adapto a mi enfermedad* [I Adjust to My Illness] (1996) [img. 34].

Like you, Leonilson, for Feliciano, a strong influence was the memories of his mother, who was a weaver. According to researcher Francisco Lemus, "on the day of his passing, Feliciano's workshop was filled with works with hastily embroidered phrases on any fabric surface; works that slipped through his hands, revealing the private world traced between the four walls of a house and a group of friends."[21] I think you two share something profound, not only a poetic in your ways of representing the sick and pained body, but also the intuition of textiles as emotional witnesses and objects charged with a ritual and protective quality. Both of you incorporated biological information about your bodies. In *El puerto* [The Harbor] (1992) [img. 231], you embroidered your name (Leo) and below it, three numbers, one on top of the other: 35, 60, and 79.

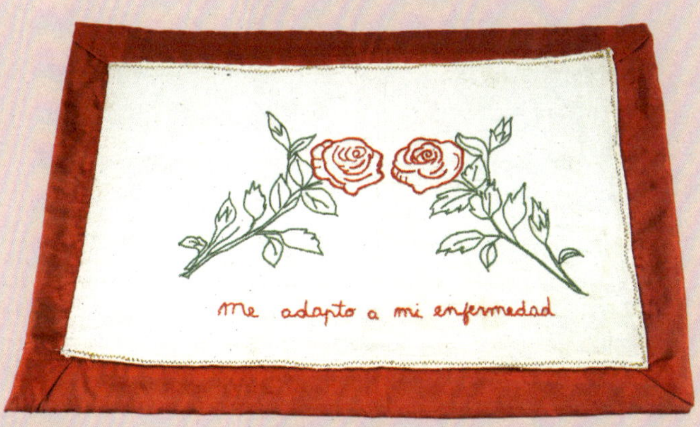

34

34. Feliciano Centurión
Me adapto a mi enfermedad [I Adjust to My Illness],
from the series *Flores del mal de amor* [Flowers of Love Sickness], 1996

Hand embroidered blanket
54 × 36.5 cm
Blanton Museum of Art, The University of Texas at Austin,
purchase with funds provided by Donald R. Mullins, Jr., 2004,
United States

These referred to your age, weight, and height, as if it were a fragment of a medical report. In the last year of his life, 1996, Feliciano created embroidered pieces in which a design of lines and colored dots converge, as if they formed a drop of blood as seen under a microscope, along with verses about the composition of his blood flow. One of them says: *mis glóbulos rojos aumentan/ glóbulos blancos me protejen/ mientras mi sangre fluye/ dejo que el amor me guíe* [my red blood cells increase/ white blood cells protect me/ as my blood flows/ I let love guide me]. Another one says: *en el silencio del descanso/ mi sangre fluye /solo tu amor en un acto de/ fé, puede salvarme* [in the silence of rest/ my blood flows/ only your love in an act of/ faith, can save me]. In both cases, the ideas of the harbor and the flow of blood refer to a journey, to an incessant movement.

In that journey, Leonilson, you carry all those passions that passed through your life and transformed it, including those people who inhabited your desires and imaginations, as well as others with whom you shared your most intimate and everyday spaces. "To love fully and deeply puts us at risk. When we love we are changed utterly," says bell hooks, reminding us that love always affects us more than we imagine or more than we want to accept.[22] It can also be a journey full of storms like that piece of yours, *Tempestades no coração* [Storms in the Heart] (1991) [img. 35], dedicated to the people who come in and out of our lives: ex-lovers turned into friends whom you portray as golden stones on a large purple canvas. The memories of those heartfelt encounters are like stones along the path, but not just any rocks—they are golden stones: precious gold that you do not want to be far from or let slip away, even if romantic ties have faded. And I believe you are also one of those golden little stones, one that I stumbled upon almost fifteen years ago, and now has returned to stay.

With love, as if my words were fire, mountains, and a bridge to reach you through the planes of time, geography, and existence.

Toronto, March 2, 2024

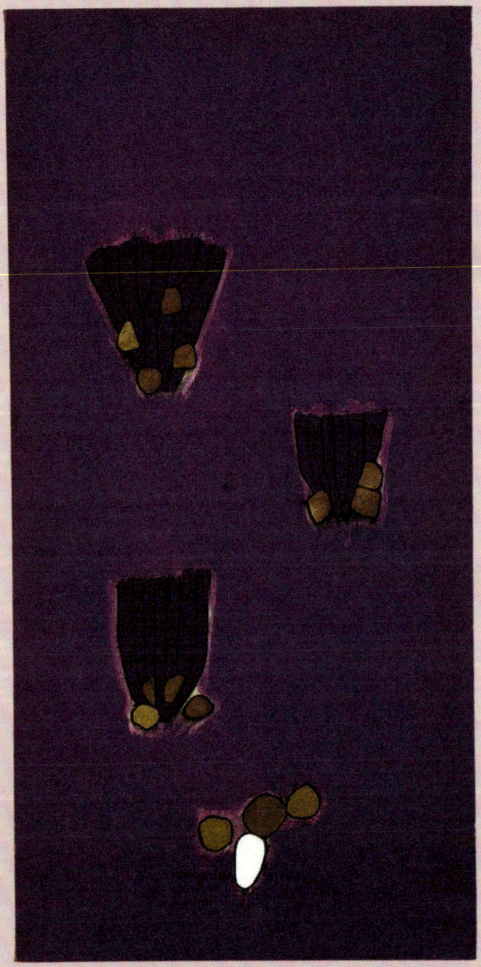

35

Translated from Spanish by Jess Oliveira

Miguel A. López is a writer and curator. In his practice, he focuses on the role of art in politics and public life, collective work and queer and feminist rewritings of history. He is a co-curator for the 2024 edition of the Toronto Biennial of Art. From 2015 to 2020, he worked as chief curator, and later co-director at TEOR/éTica, Costa Rica. In 2014, he curated the section *Deus é bicha* [God is Queer] and the presentation of Giuseppe Campuzano's Travesti Museum for the 31st Bienal de São Paulo.

NOTES

1 See Lisette Lagnado, "A dimensão da fala." In: *Leonilson: são tantas as verdades.* *[So Many Are the Truths]* (São Paulo: DBA Melhoramentos, 1998), 79–136; and Leonilson and Adriano Pedrosa, "Concentrated Conversations." In: Krist Gruijthuijsen (ed.), *Leonilson: Drawn* (1975–1993) (Berlin: Hatje Cantz Verlag, 2020), 257–309.

2 Lisette Lagnado, 1998, op. cit., 98. Leonilson died on May 28, 1993 in São Paulo, Brazil.

3 The exhibition was called *Modelos para armar. Pensar Latinoamérica desde la colección* MUSAC [Models Kits. Thinking Latin America from the MUSAC Collection] and was curated by Agustín Pérez Rubio, María Inés Rodríguez, and Octavio Zaya. It included a series of works by Leonilson recently acquired by the then-director Agustín Pérez Rubio for the MUSAC collection.

4 The exhibition design of *Modelos para armar* was carried out by the Greek artist and architect Andreas Angelidakis.

5 *Leonilson: Truth, Fiction,* curated by Adriano Pedrosa at the Pinacoteca de São Paulo from August 9 to November 9, 2014. *Empty Man*, presented at the Americas Society, curated by Cecilia Brunson, Gabriela Rangel, and Susanna V. Temkin, from September 27, 2017 to February 3, 2018. Curated by Agustín Pérez Rubio, *Corpo político* was at the Almeida & Dale gallery in São Paulo from August 5 to October 7, 2023.

6 "This could either be a painting or a letter" said Leonilson in 1988. See Lisette Lagnado, "Leonilson: símbolos coloridos," *Galeria: Revista de Arte*, no. 8, 1988, 26–29. See also Lisette Lagnado, 1998, op. cit., 87.

7 Leonilson and Adriano Pedrosa, 2020, op. cit., 274.

8 Lisette Lagnado, 1998, op. cit., 124.

9 In the mid-1990s, the artist revisited the idea and produced the installation *Sementerio* (1995–1996), this time composed of the semen of dozens of donors who provided him with 18 × 18 cm papers with their seminal remains. The work was presented in the form of a grid, evoking the arrangement of graves in a cemetery. On that occasion, the artist also left papers marked with a seal for attendees to take, ejaculate on them, and contribute to the project. Regarding Wilson Diaz's work, see: Equipo TransHisTor(ia) (María Sol Barón Pinto and Camilo Ordónez Robayo), *Con Wilson... Anotaciones, artistadas e incidentes* (Bogotá: Ministry of Culture, 2013).

10 See Leonilson and Adriano Pedrosa, 2020, op. cit., especially 231–241.

11 Ibid., 233.

12 Ibid., 274 and 277.

13 Lisette Lagnado, 1998, op. cit., 114.

14 Regarding Fernanda Laguna's work, please refer to Rosario Guiraldes (ed.), *Fernanda Laguna: The Path of the Heart* (New York: The Drawing Center, 2022).

15 Julia Kristeva, *Tales of Love*, translated by Leon S. Roudiez (New York: Columbia University Press, 1987), 5.

16 Leonilson and Adriano Pedrosa, 2020, op. cit., 280.

17 Lisette Lagnado, 1998, op. cit., 116.

18 Ibid., 116.

19 Ibid., 85.

20 Regarding the 1990s art scene in Argentina, see Francisco Lemus, "Art y vida: los años noventa en Buenos Aires." In: Francisco Lemus (ed.), *Imágenes seropositivas. Prácticas artísticas y narrativas sobre el vih en los años 80 y 90* (La Plata, EDULP, 2021), 37–66.

21 Francisco Lemus, "La mala vida," *Terremoto*, no. 20, May 2021. Available at https://terremoto.mx/revista/la-mala-vida/. Retrieved Aug. 23, 2024.

22 bell hooks, *All about Love. New Visions* (New York: Harper Collins, 2001), 187.

35. Leonilson
Tempestades no coração
[Storms in the Heart], 1991

Acrylic paint and metallic paint on canvas
150 × 76 cm
Private collection,
São Paulo, Brazil
PL.1060.0/00

NEGA
TIVE
CAPA
BILI
TY

ON *NINGUÉM* (1992)

Irene V. Small

NINGUÉM. NOBODY. NO ONE. *Ninguém*, as in: There's nobody at the door; nobody knows him. *Ninguém merece*: Nobody deserves that. But also *ninguém*, as in: nobody of significance, an individual of little consequence, a body with no name. *Ninguém* inhabits the underside of *someone*, somebody. *Somebody* entails distinctiveness, or its possibility. *Ninguém* is a placeholder, the anonymity and abstraction of a person who is no one in particular. Anybody, anyone—*alguém*—but defined through the force of negation.

Leonilson's [1957–1993] *Ninguém* [img. 36] dwells within this deliberate absence of identity. Even so, it is a work that singularizes, again and again, its materiality, context, authorship, addressee. Made in 1992, a year after the Brazilian artist learned he was HIV-positive, and a year before his death at the age of thirty-six, it consists of a small pillow, its case hand-sewn from fabric remnants. The front is a piece of machine-embroidered pink pillowcase (pink like Pepto-Bismol, Mother's Day cards, artificial Easter eggs), the back a swath of tartan extended with panels of taupe and peach cotton. Too small for bed, it seems intended for succor rather than sleep: something to clutch in the darkness, rest one's head on during the day. Despite its title, the work's

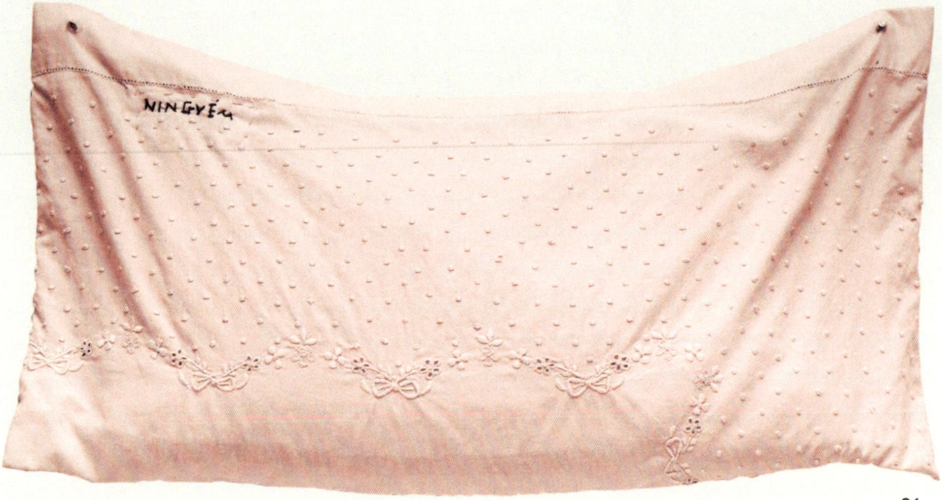

36

delicate, pieced-together construction carries the affective charge of a specific hand, a specific body. A year earlier, Leonilson had stitched his first name, JOSÉ, on a stretched rectangle of shimmering, cloudlike voile in the same position as NINGUÉM, the upper left-hand corner, as it might appear on a grade-school worksheet or a bureaucratic form [img. 37]. The substitution of one designation for the other is inextricable from the later work's corporeal allegory. Leonilson surely knew that viewers would approach it as both a reliquary and a memento mori.

Originally, the artist suspended *Ninguém* from two metal rods against a wall, the pillow's padded interior sagging gently toward the middle with all the vulnerability and opacity of a body. Stretched upward and affixed by means of incisions in the pillowcase's upper corners, the display allowed gravity itself to map the pictorial vectors of crucifixion. Leonilson's childhood was suffused with Catholicism, and even as his work veers far from faith it is replete with Christian iconography: stigmata, scars, bleeding hearts, crosses, crowns, swooning and supine bodies, miraculous touches that bridge worlds apart. The prostrate life-size figure in his painting *O que ele está fazendo* [What He Is Doing] (1986) [img. 38] is physically punctured at head, heart, and groin. There is an unmistakable echo of the claustrophobic compression of Hans Holbein's [*circa* 1497–1543] *The Body of the Dead Christ in the Tomb* (1521–22) [img. 39] and of the pockmarked skin of Christ in Matthias Grünewald's [1470–1528] Isenheim altarpiece (1512–16), which had inspired Holbein in turn. In *Ninguém*, the off-center lunette of ornamental flowers and ribbons adumbrates a shape similar to that of the prone body in *O que ele está fazendo*, only here in radical abstraction. Internal to the very process of handling and installing the work—appending it to a wall, removing it to rest, protecting it by securing its

36. Leonilson
Ninguém [Nobody],
[1992] [img. 216]

37. Leonilson
José, 1991 [img. 191]

recumbent form—is the entirety of Christ's crucifixion, deposition, and entombment. Notably, *Ninguém* offers nothing in the way of resurrection; it remains in the register of condemnation and sorrow.

Owing to its increasing material fragility, *Ninguém* is no longer hung vertically when exhibited but laid as an ordinary pillow would be, on a horizontal surface, where we peer at it from above. What it loses in bodily affect, it gains in discursivity. Now sharing the plane of handwriting, its single word approaches a salutation, while its embroidered nubs proliferate like so many ellipses across a page. In one of the first critical accounts of the artist's oeuvre written after his death, Lisette Lagnado wrote that Leonilson's work constituted an "epistolary fiction," with each piece "constructed as a letter to an intimate diary" that would inevitably be made public.[1] In this sense, *Ninguém* is equally a work of aching exposure and of bitter denouncement, resonant today not despite but because it was aimed at the artist's own time, when AIDS ravaged gay communities and the ailing body was weaponized by the Right. (The same year he created *Ninguém*, Leonilson made a drawing called *O perigoso* [The Dangerous One] [img. 202] with a single drop of his own blood.)

Leonilson was an avid traveler whose bohemian itinerancy seems ever more distant from our state of pandemic isolation and paranoia induced in 2020. He encountered Shaker embroidery at the Whitney Museum of American Art in New York; read Wittgenstein in Antonio Dias' [1944–2018] studio in Milan; sold drawings to survive in Madrid; visited the Jewish ghettos of Venice; constructed a snow volcano for a show in Munich. Along the way he fell in love with the work of Eva Hesse [1936–1970] and Blinky Palermo [1943–1977]; sewed errant maps; and imagined writing an autobiographical fiction inspired by the wandering Ulysses. And yet despite his own cosmopolitanism, Leonilson's work has been little known outside the country of his birth until relatively recently. In Brazil, however, his work is revered not only for the distinctive-

37

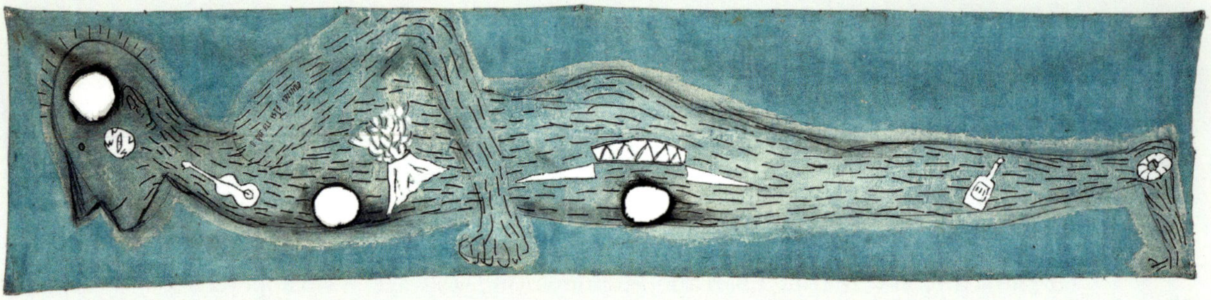

38

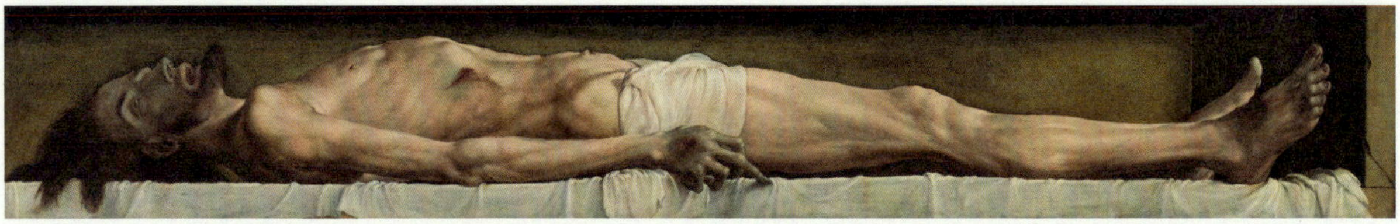

39

ness of its own poetic charge, but also for the way it charts an aesthetic constellation that includes Lygia Clark [1920–1988] and Hélio Oiticica [1937–1980]; members of his own generation, such as Leda Catunda and Daniel Senise; the fantastical constructions of the psychiatric inmate Arthur Bispo do Rosário [1909–1989]; and popular traditions from the country's northeast, where Leonilson grew up. His sensibility—caustic yet romantic and exquisitely queer—indexed a particular moment that followed Brazilian redemocratization, when exuberance about the demise of the military dictatorship mixed with cynicism about the country's ongoing political scandals and its embrace of neoliberalism.

If an epistolary work presumes distance and delay, we might recognize *Ninguém* as a dispatch to us in the present. Indeed, as Ivo Mesquita observes in a catalog essay for the artist's 2021 retrospective at KW Institute for Contemporary Art in Berlin, to revisit Leonilson's work in the midst of a global pandemic, with authoritarianism on the rise, is to see ever more clearly the force of the artist's critique of hypocrisy, social violence, and greed.[2] As Mesquita notes, Leonilson's 1993 caricature of populist sentiment—three banners proclaiming PATÉTICO, RIDÍCULO, VULGAR—applies equally to Brazil's former president Jair Bolsonaro (and former US president Donald Trump, for that matter) [img. 40]. Bolsonaro's hate-filled rhetoric is directed at precisely the "undesirables" the artist listed in two related drawings: women, Roma, Communists, the LGBTQIA+ community, Black people, people

38. Leonilson
O que ele está fazendo
[What He Is Doing], 1986

Acrylic paint, colored pencil, marker, and cutting on unstretched canvas
47 × 221 cm
Private collection,
São Paulo, Brazil
PL.0924.0/00

39. Hans Holbein, the Older
The Body of the Dead Christ in the Tomb, 1521-22

Oil on limewood
32.5 × 202 cm
Kunstmuseum Basel, Amerbach-Kabinett, 1662, Switzerland

who have developed AIDS, Jews, the disabled, the Indigenous, sex workers. Against the fascistic logic that renders such individuals *ninguém*, Leonilson's work proposes dispossession as the site of pluriversal identification. As Arthur Rimbaud [1854–1891] wrote, "Je est un autre" [I is an other].

It is inevitable that the increasing material fragility of *Ninguém* has intensified its memorial character. But perhaps the work invites, even more urgently, an apotropaic reading, one in keeping with the fabric amulets or pouches—called *bolsas de mandinga*—of Afro-Brazilian tradition, worn in proximity to the body to shield it from evil spirits and disease. Shortly after Bolsonaro was elected in 2018, a phrase began appearing in social media, posted by the "undesirables" and their allies whom the new president had made the target of his scorn. The phrase, "Ninguém solta a mão de ninguém," was used by student activists in the era of the dictatorship, when military police would cut off the electricity within classrooms ahead of a raid. It translates to "No one let go of anyone's hand," only with the palindromic intensity of *ninguém* on either end. *Ninguém*, here, is the grammar and syntax of protection and entanglement. It is also the horizon toward which we reach today: to touch an(other); to find in *ninguém* the solidarity of *we*.

But as an artist friend reminded me, another *ninguém* runs through recent Brazilian politics as well, exemplified by the response of a protester interviewed during the June 2013 demonstrations against political negligence, when the streets overflowed with demands for sweeping transformation [img. 41]. In answer to a journalist's request for their name and political affiliation, the protester said, "Take note: I am nobody." Although those uprisings—when demonstrators danced on the roof of the National Congress—seem many lifetimes ago, the phrase deflects nostalgia. As the philosophers Peter Pál Pelbart[3] and Vladimir Safatle[4] have since described it, the declaration speaks to a certain desubjectivization as the kernel of another form of politics: a radical refusal

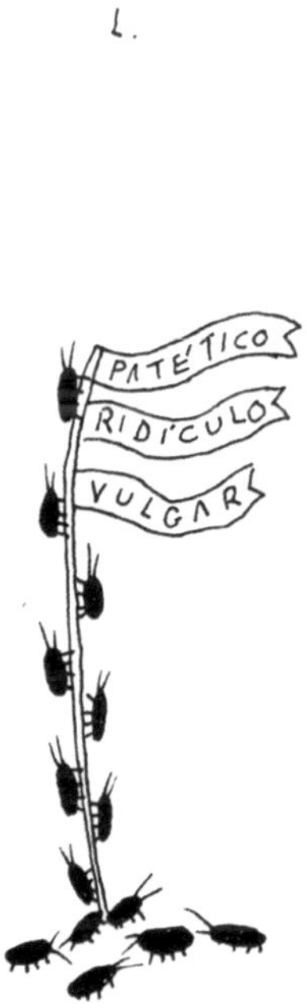

40

40. Leonilson
[Comer barata é o novo barato da cidade] [Eating Roaches Is the New Craze in Town], 1993
[img. 341]

of nomination within the existent grammar of power. (How different than the claim to be "patriots" made by the members of the right-wing mob that stormed the U.S. Capitol on January 6, 2021 and Brasília on January 8, 2023.) In this sense, *ninguém* is also a lesson of strategy in the face of excessive force. "My name is nobody," Ulysses declares to the cyclops Polyphemus before blinding him in *The Odyssey*. As the giant roars that "nobody" attacked him, Ulysses steals away.

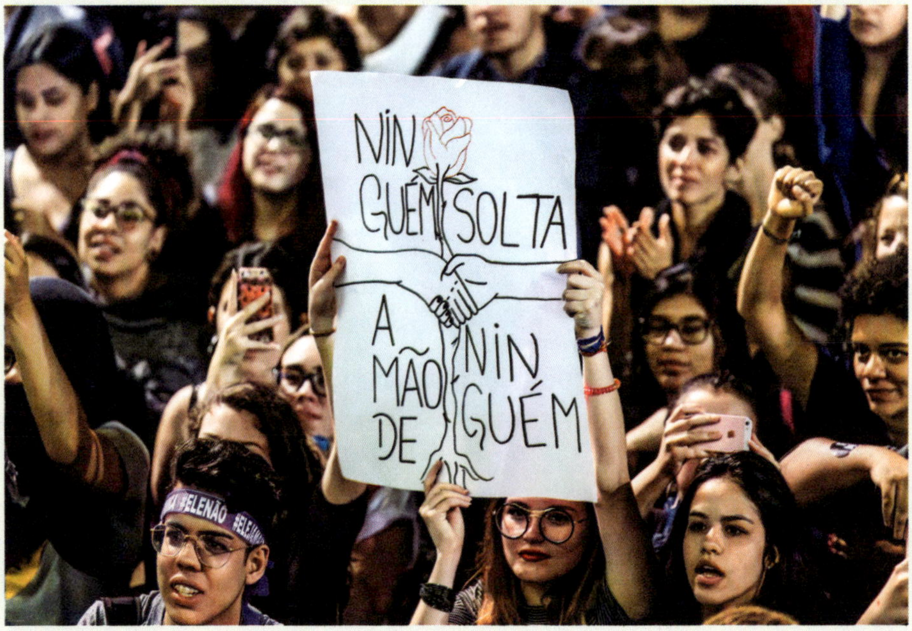

41

41. Anti-Jair Bolsonaro protesters with "Ninguém solta a mão de ninguém" (No one let go of anyone's hand) poster, São Paulo, Brazil, October 30, 2018
Courtesy of Mídia NINJA, Brazil

Irene V. Small is an associate professor of contemporary art and criticism at Princeton University. She is the author of *Hélio Oiticica: Folding the Frame* (2016) and *The Organic Line: Toward a Topology of Modernism* (2024).

Source: SMALL, Irene. "Close-up: Negative Capability." *Artforum*, v. 59, no. 5, March 2021. Revised version.

NOTES

1 Lisette Lagnado, *Leonilson: são tantas as verdades [So Many Are the Truths]* (São Paulo: Projeto Leonilson, 2019). [Editor's Note]

2 Ivo Mesquita, "Psychic Body, Visible Body, Revisited." In: Krist Gruijthuijsen (ed.), *Leonilson: Drawn* (1975-1993) (Berlin: Hatje Cantz Verlag, 2020). [Editor's Note]

3 Peter Pál Pelbart, "Anota aí: eu sou ninguém," *O Povo online*, Oct. 30, 2014. Available at https://www20.opovo.com.br/app/opovo/vidaearte/2014/10/30/noticiasjornalvidaearte,3339478/leia-artigo-do-filosofo-tradutor-e-professor-peter-pal-pelbart.shtml. Retrieved Apr. 9, 2024. [Editor's Note]

4 See Laura Luedy, Mariana Toledo Borges and Hyury Pinheiro, "'Anota aí: eu sou ninguém': entrevista com Vladimir Safatle," *Ideias*, v. 10, Nov. 2019, 1-38 and Vladimir Safatle, *Quando as ruas queimam: manifesto pela emergência* (São Paulo: n-1 edições, 2016). [Editor's Note]

GETTING CLOSER WITHOUT GETTING TOO CLOSE

SOME THOUGHTS ON APPROACHING LEONILSON'S WORK

Pablo Lafuente

I, OR A MEMORY OF IT

Writing about an artwork without knowing anything about the person who made it. That would be a bit like having sex with someone you have never met before, someone you may not be able to even identify by name. Maybe because it's too dark to see clearly, or simply because there are too many people around, and you can't tell one person from the other.

If getting to know the person before, or after, that situation is a matter of choice rather than a moral obligation—or, better, a matter of negotiation—, when it comes to writing about art, familiarity with the artist as a subject who is both a willing protagonist and a conscious author often presents itself as an epistemological demand. Such demand is perhaps more present in the visual arts than other areas of cultural production, as the consequence of a dominant historical hermeneutics in which the lives of the artists are generally considered the key to understanding their work and of an art system which ascribes cultural and financial value partly on the basis of the assigned significance of individual authorship. And it may appear more pressing today, when it is amplified in the form of an ethical and political demand, as the subject comes to be understood through a dynamic of contested identities, and first-hand experience is privileged as the source of legitimate knowledge.

Most of the existing writings and publications on Leonilson's work, which he made from approximately 1980 until his death in 1993, are posthumous, many written by people who knew him as a person as well as an artist.[1] And many attempt to explore how the artist's biography, his sexual orientation, his habits, thoughts and feelings, and his death of AIDS-related complications may have shaped both his process of art-making and the recognition his work meets today. As if his work were the unmediated expression of a subjectivity and a will, and its relevance were simply guaranteed by the way it captures an experience that was his but is also supposed to function as a symptom of a time and place. The exhibition catalogs dedicated to Leonilson's work often include pictures of the artist on his own, with friends, in his travels and moments of leisure, as if his own image, exposed in documentary detail, were meant to complete the generic faces of the figures that appear in his later work, giving a very concrete figurative conclusion to artworks that are often reductions towards abstraction. The two films dedicated to him, Karen Harley's *Com o oceano inteiro para nadar* [With the Whole Ocean to Swim] (1997) and Carlos Nader's *A paixão de JL* [JL's Passion] (2014), seem to serve as a template, as if his voice had escaped from the cassette tapes he registered between 1990 and 1993, so that he can speak to us every time we are looking his work, or thinking about, it, his voice insistently reminding us of what he was thinking when he was in the process of making it.

Thus, the absence of the person Leonilson coexists with the insistent presence of Leonilson as a historiographic and symbolic subject to whom his work immediately needs to relate, as a narrative anchor that guarantees its relevance. Or rather, Leonilson's passing in 1993 allowed for the emergence of a new subject who seems to be the only channel to access his practice, even though that subject is unlikely to coincide with the person that he was then or the person he would be today if he were alive—and who seems also different from the subject Leonilson presented through his work, the fictional construction implied in 2014 by the exhibition and catalog *Leonilson: Truth, Fiction.*[2]

But the issue here is not which subject is the true Leonilson, the potential key for the accurate reading and the guarantee for the rightful significance of his practice. The challenge is, rather, the opposite: the possibility of considering his work while avoiding the struggle between all those given subjects. How to approach Leonilson's practice without the presence of Leonilson, without having to become familiar with his name beforehand? Because, in what is perhaps the most concrete and more absolute sense of his absence, we are already having to do so.

NOT I, OR "LE MOI EST HAÏSSABLE"[3]

One of the starting quotes in Leo Bersani's (1931–2022) 1987 essay "Is the Rectum a Grave?,"[4] a founding text for queer theory and one of the earliest writings within the cultural academic context to respond to the AIDS epidemic, is Blaise Pascal's (1623–1662) rejection of the self. When Pascal, in his reunion of fragments published posthumously in 1670, deems self-loathsome, he is referring to a self that is a symbol of *amour propre*, a self as belief and confidence in one's own ability and value. For him, the fundamental problem is not the fact that the self is a fiction, an illusion of the imagination that attempts to camouflage a mere addition of diverse, shifting qualities. The problem is that the relationship that the self establishes with other selves is completely asymmetrical, as each self wants to be valued in itself; it puts itself in the center, and the only things it identifies as worthy in the others are its own qualities.

Such constructed self, for Pascal, merely operates as a passion that leads men to appear rather than be, to look at their life rather than living it—A Baudrillardian nightmare optimized by Instagram.

For Bersani, Pascal's (very) early rejection of the self as a figure of power was a useful precedent in his attempt to understand, at a time when the homosexual subject was threatened with annihilation by a new disease, how such a subject was created by a heterosexual society. With the help of a psychoanalytic framework, Bersani aimed not to preserve that given subject, but rather attempted to present a relational reading that exposed the violence and inconsistencies of a society constructed around the phallus. The rectum, then, is not a grave for the homosexual subject at the time of AIDS, but as a grave for the regime of subjectivity that characterizes Western civilization, with its modern (individual, rational) subject.

A decade earlier, shortly before the epidemic started, Guy Hocquenghem (1946–1988) had already made the case that the potential for undoing modern subjectivity resided with homosexual desire. The self rejected by Pascal, Hocquenghem writes in *Le Désir homosexuel* [Homosexual Desire] (1972), is actually a "he," a male subject built around the centrality of the phallus. A phallus that creates identity and gender difference, and that can only operate and take its central stage through the sublimation of the anus, of its ability to desire.[5] In this process, the anus has no social function except such sublimation. Its role is completely private: through the process of learning to control it, it becomes the site for the formation of the person and, consequently, of private property. Control of the anus is the precondition of taking responsibility for such property.

According to Hocquenghem, because homosexual desire is concerned with anal eroticism, it interrupts that dynamic of sublimation and, with it, the centrality of the phallus. It is a prepersonal state of desire, opposed both to reproductive sexuality and Oedipal reproduction, and therefore a risk to identity:

Homosexual desire is a group desire; it groups the anus by restoring its functions as a desiring bond, and by collectively reinvesting it against a society which has reduced it to the state of a shameful little secret. [...] To fail one's sublimation is in fact merely to conceive social relations in a different way. Possibly, when the anus recovers its desiring function and the plugging in of organs takes place subject to no rule or law, the group can then take its pleasure in an immediate relation where the sacrosanct difference between public and private, between the individual and the social, will be out of place.[6]

Grouped homosexual desire transcends the oppositions that structure society as we understand it, opening new ways for engaging and comprehending what is of value and what is common. Hocquenghem, who would die of AIDS in 1988, a year after the publication of "Is the Rectum a Grave?," is more optimistic, more daring than Bersani. Perhaps because the epidemic made a difference. Or maybe it was too difficult to be a revolutionary self in 1980s New York.

WE, OR HOW TO MAKE THINGS AVAILABLE?

Perhaps that was also the case for Leonilson in São Paulo in the late 1980s and early 1990s. Or maybe it wasn't.

A work titled *As ruas da cidade* [The City Streets] (1988) [img. 42], shows the internal organs of a human body in an unstretched canvas of a size slightly larger than an average adult human. There is a body there, but not (yet) a subject. We see the lungs, brain, heart, and intestine, all the organs in the right locations, some of them identified through their written names. It is a slightly inaccurate rendering—there is an amateur feel to it—, but we can easily tell one part from the other and their relative positions. The system is open to its outside, but through words rather than images. The sentence "são tantas as verdades" [so many are the truths], underneath the brain, above the trachea, may refer to diverse and contradictory stimuli coming from an unresolved world that feeds in too many certainties. At the bottom, below the rectum, "as ruas da cidade," the words that make up the title, suggest a process of evacuation, a flow from the inside of the system towards its outside, an act of emptying out. The pictorial language, the intentional informality of the unstretched canvas, the apparent lack of concern with finalization... they speak about an artist who knows he can afford to appear unconcerned with issues of making. Another work from the same year, also an unstretched canvas of a similar size, adopts the earlier sentence about truths as its title [img. 43] and lists a long series of artists—visual artists like Joseph Beuys (1921–1986), Cy Twombly (1928–2011) or Eva Hesse (1936–1970), choreographers like Michael Clark, actors like Gerard Depardieu, and fashion designers like Cristóbal Balenciaga (1895–1972)—, perhaps references that allow for this work to exist as it does, or maybe just mere information that passed through the artist's mind when making it. There is definitely an ambivalence, an inconsistency that doesn't want to be resolved, an act of naming that refuses to go deeper, but that still tries to create relations.

42. Leonilson
[As ruas da cidade]
[The City Streets], *circa* 1988

Acrylic paint on
unstretched canvas
200 × 95 cm
Private collection,
São Paulo, Brazil
PL.1190.0/00

43. Leonilson
São tantas as verdades
[There Are So Many Truths], [1988]

Acrylic paint, colored pencil,
semiprecious stones, and cooper
wire on unstretched canvas
200 × 106 × 2 cm
Private collection, São Paulo, Brazil
PL.0827.0/00

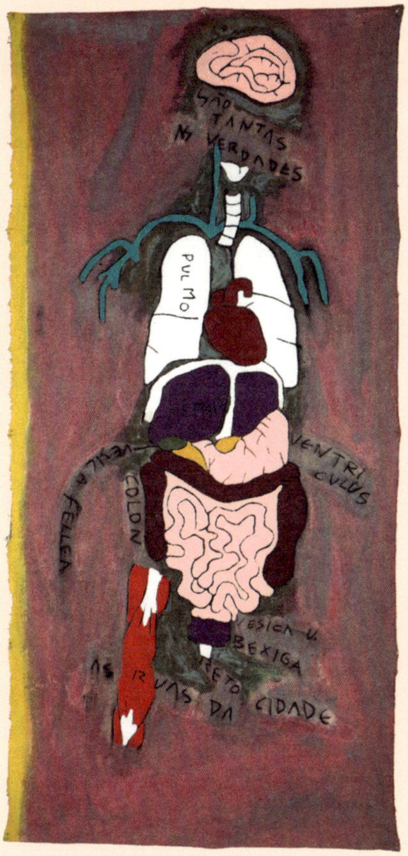

42

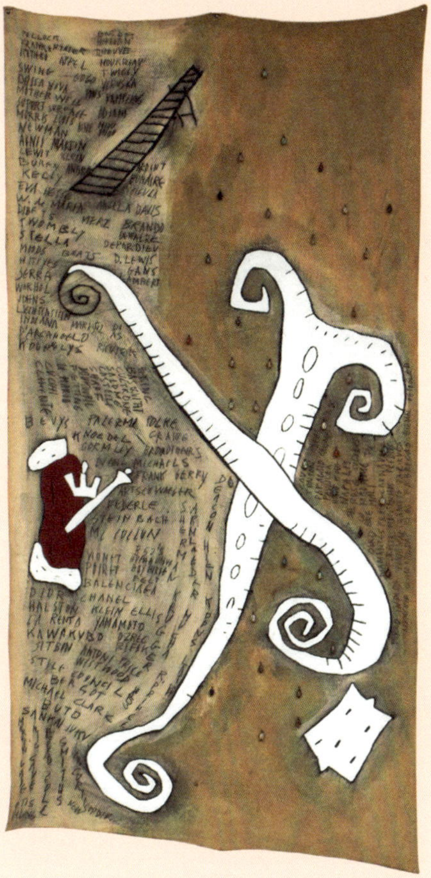

43

While the body of As *ruas da cidade* connects itself to the outside through words, the bodies of *Jogos perigosos* [Dangerous Games] (*circa* 1990) [img. 44], a smaller painting made two years later, are connected both through words and lines, countering another set of lines—a wall, a road, a trajectory—that separates the figures. Things are neater here, but not necessarily tidy. Unlike the two earlier works, the size and the economy adopted in the rendering of the figures suggest increased control through a language that echoes graphic design or comics and in which expression (be it the artist's or the figures') is not to be found. The figures are anonymous, impersonal, but somehow comforting in their defined outline. What seems to matter, rather than the figures themselves or the people they may be, is the possibilities they have of either connecting towards intimacy or drifting apart.

In that work, like in *Mentiroso* [Liar] and *Cheio, vazio* [Full, Empty], both from 1992 [imgs. 45, 46], and many others made from 1990 to 1993, there is a dissonance between what is being said (meaningful, with a certain

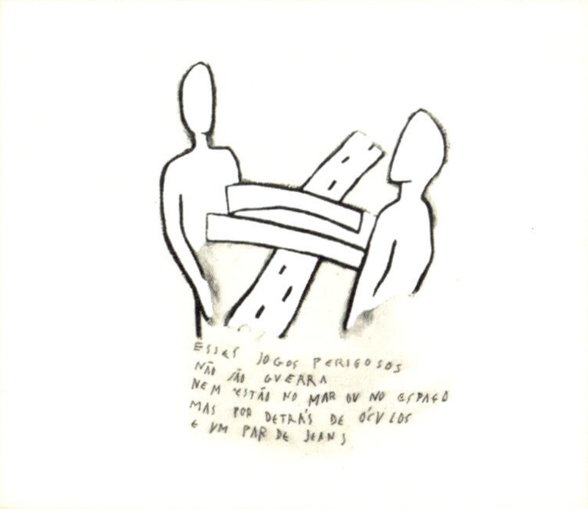

44

44. Leonilson
[Jogos perigosos]
[Dangerous Games], *circa* 1990
[img. 113]

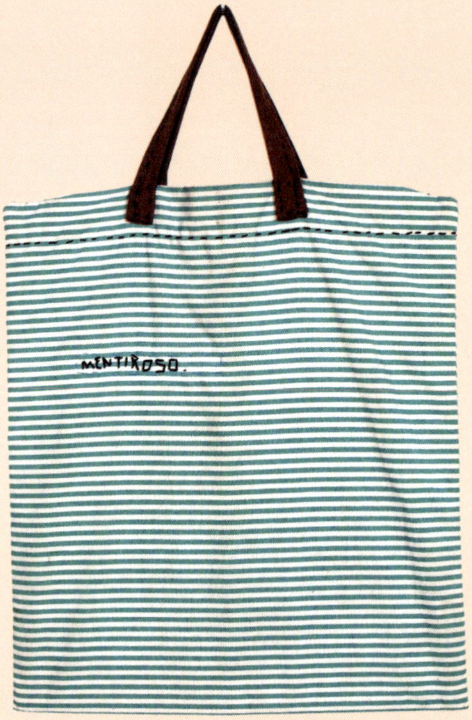

45

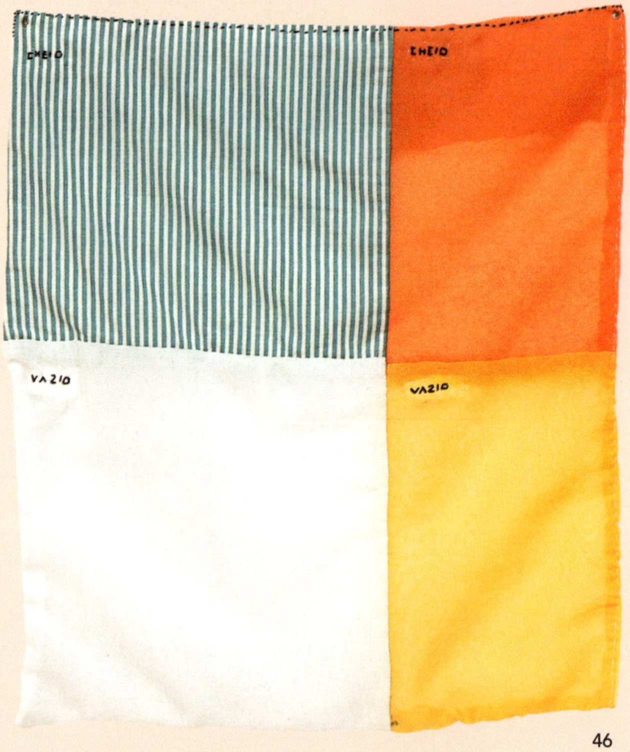

46

gravity, as if they were supposed to actually mean what it says) and the materiality of the works, the way they make themselves present (smaller, playful and simple in their colors and textures, almost inoffensive in their overall appearance). They look like things that shouldn't matter much, but that shouldn't bother anyone and could, perhaps, deserve a second look, and a bit more time. Unassuming and self-aware at the same time. Like small, personal treasures that the maker would keep close to himself. You could say that they're not invested in their own value as objects—but that would imply being naive about the processes of creation of value in art, and neither Leonilson nor us can afford to be naive about that.

In 1977, Mario Mieli (1952–1983) wrote *Elementi di critica omosessuale* [Homosexuality and Liberation: Elements of a Gay Critique] in an attempt to think of the revolutionary potential of homosexual desire towards the creation of what he called "gay communism." The book concludes with a sentence that brings that desire back to the rectum—or rather, the ass: "I keep my treasure in my arse, but then my arse is open to everyone..."[7] A radical act of giving, beyond property; an act of making available promiscuously, with no sign of guilt. Such promiscuity of homosexual desire is, for Mieli, but also for Hocquenghem,

45. Leonilson
Mentiroso [Liar], [1992]

Thread and felt on
striped cotton fabric
51 × 34 cm
Private collection,
Rio de Janeiro, Brazil
PL.1422.0/00

46. Leonilson
Cheio, vazio [Full, Empty],
1992 [img. 233]

the very mode of desire itself, the desire that has the potential to achieve a revolution. Or, as the anonymous text "Les Culs énergumènes" [The Screwball Asses] asks in 1973, "Can we maintain, then, that the day when desire has extended to incorporate non-desire (or so-called non-desire), the revolution will have been accomplished?"[8]

Can we imagine a situation in which the value of Leonilson's works comes from their potential for such availability rather than from the fact that they were made by him? Neither the earlier, larger, and messier canvases nor the later, smaller, more fragile works are available in this way today, and we can't say for sure if Leonilson ever wanted them to behave in that way—or whether he'd like them to do so were he with us today. But we can still speculate about their ability to do so—if our desire is strong enough. And perhaps then we could learn with them how to free other things up, so they behave (materially, symbolically) in ways still unknown to us.

Pablo Lafuente is the artistic director of the Museu de Arte Moderna do Rio de Janeiro since 2020. He co-curated the 31st Bienal de São Paulo and the exhibitions *A Singular Form* (Secession, Vienna, 2014), *Dja Guata Porã: Rio de Janeiro indígena* (Museu de Arte do Rio, 2017–18), and *Some May Work as Symbols: Art Made in Brazil, 1950s–70s* (Raven Row, London, 2024), among others. He also worked as an editor (*Afterall* and Afterall Books), curator (Office for Contemporary Art Norway) and professor (Central Saint Martins and Universidade Federal do Sul da Bahia).

NOTES

1 Including textual production, in the forms of essays and interviews, by Adriano Pedrosa, Eduardo Brandão, Jan Fjeld, Ivo Mesquita, Leda Catunda, and Lisette Lagnado.

2 The exhibition was curated by Adriano Pedrosa at the Pinacoteca do Estado, in São Paulo, which published the catalog that same year.

3 Blaise Pascal, "Pensées diverses II – Fragment n° 5 / 37." Available at http://www.penseesdepascal.fr/XXIV/XXIV5-moderne.php. Retrieved May 15, 2024.

4 Leo Bersani, "Is the Rectum a Grave?," *October*, v. 43, Winter 1987, reprinted in *Is the Rectum a Grave? and Other Essays* (Chicago and London: The University of Chicago Press, 2010), 3–30.

5 See Guy Hocquenghem, *Homosexual Desire* (Durham and London: Duke University Press, 1993).

6 Ibid., 111.

7 Mario Mieli, *Homosexuality and Liberation: Elements of a Gay Critique* (London: Gay Men's Press, 1980), 145.

8 Anonymous, "Les Culs énergumènes," *Recherches*, no. 12, March 1973, 226. Translation by the author.

REPRODUCTIONS OF WORKS

The captions of the works follow the format established by the artist's catalog raisonné, edited by Ana Lenice Dias and Gabriela Dias Clemente (São Paulo: Projeto Leonilson, 2017), which includes the registration number, starting with the letters "PL." Titles given by third parties are enclosed in brackets, as is the English translation. The original language of the titles varies between Portuguese, English, Spanish, and French.

1989

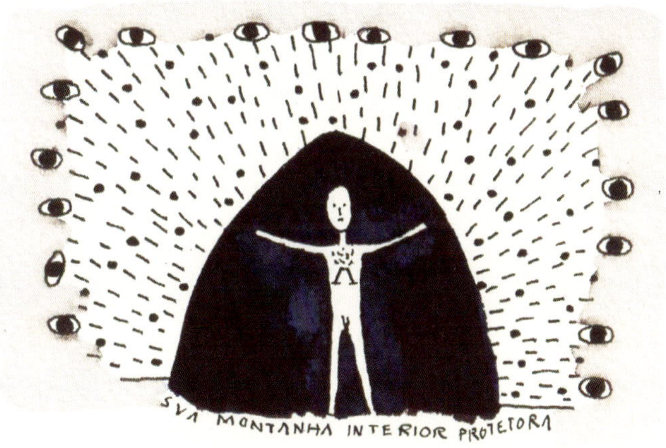

47. ***[Sua montanha interior protetora]*** [Your Inner Sheltering Mountain], 1989

Permanent ink, China ink, and watercolor on paper
25.5 × 18 cm
Museo de Arte Contemporáneo de Castilla y León, MUSAC collection, Spain
PL.1273.0/00

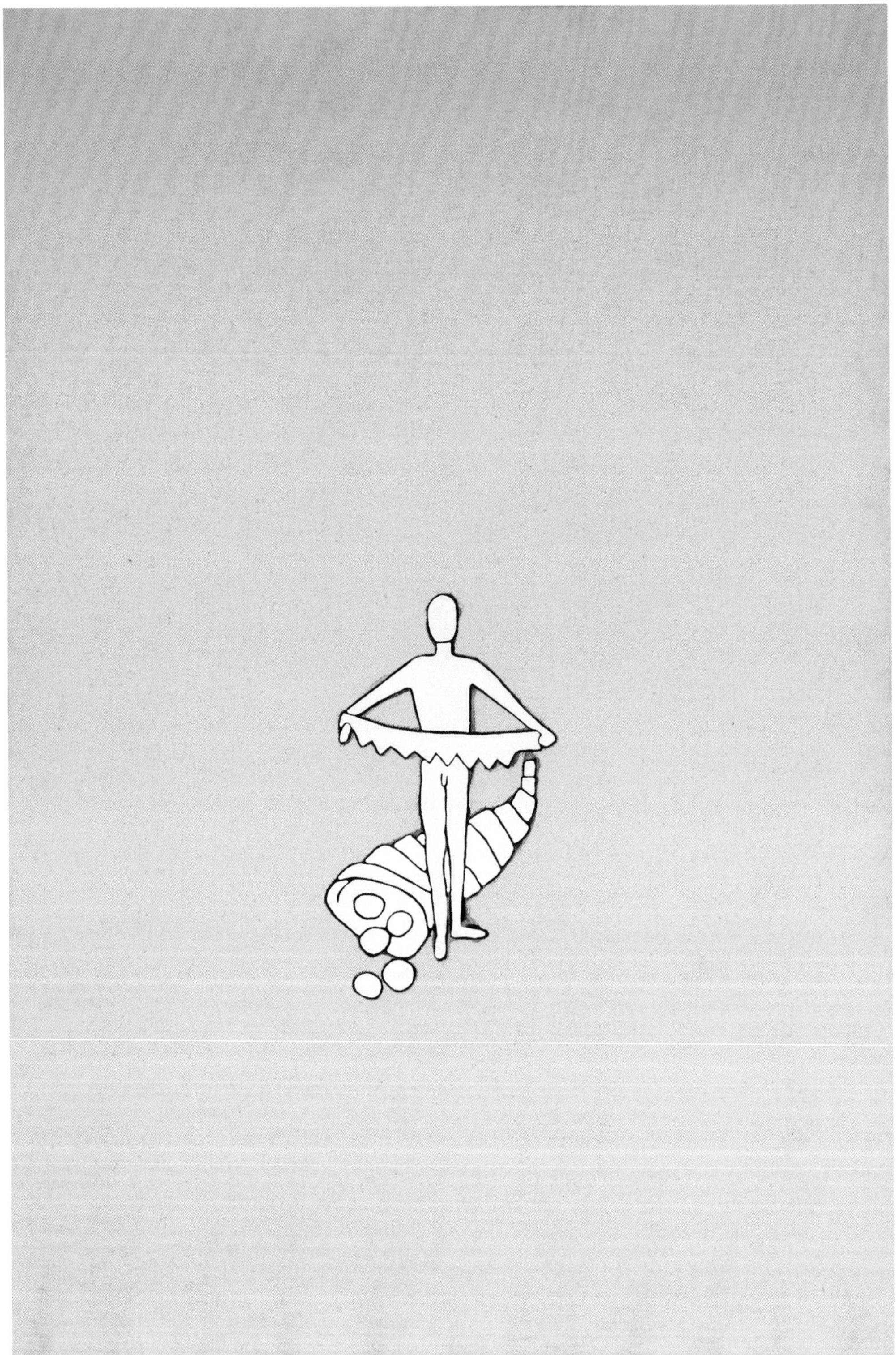

48. ***O porta fortuna***
[The Fortune Bearer], 1989

Acrylic paint on canvas
150 × 100 cm
Collection of Susana and Ricardo Steinbruch,
São Paulo, Brazil
PL.2207.0/00

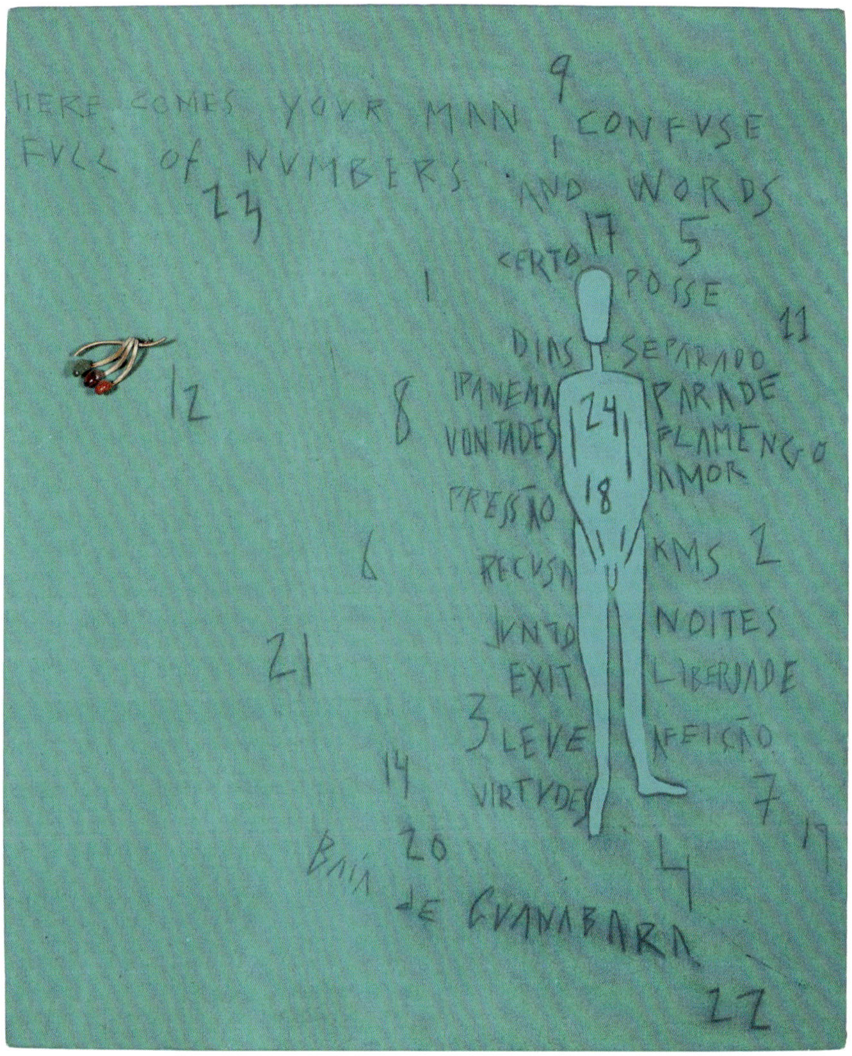

49. ***[Here Comes Your Man]***, 1989

Acrylic paint, colored pencil, and metal brooch with semiprecious stones on canvas
65.5 × 54 × 2 cm
Private collection, São Paulo, Brazil
PL.1291.0/00

50. ***[Homem com chapéu]***
[Man With Hat], 1989

Permanent ink and
watercolor on paper
40.5 × 30.5 cm
Collection of Luisa Malzoni Strina,
São Paulo, Brazil
PL.1157.0/00

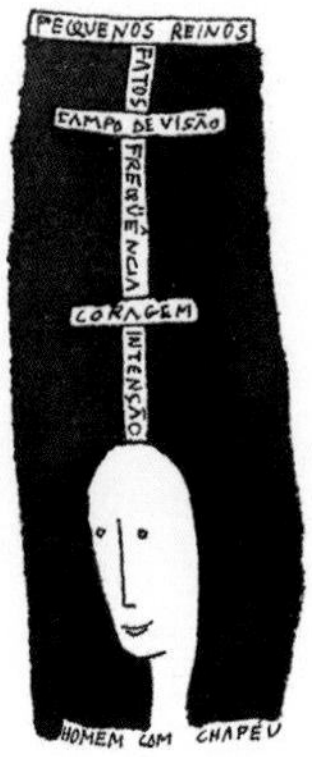

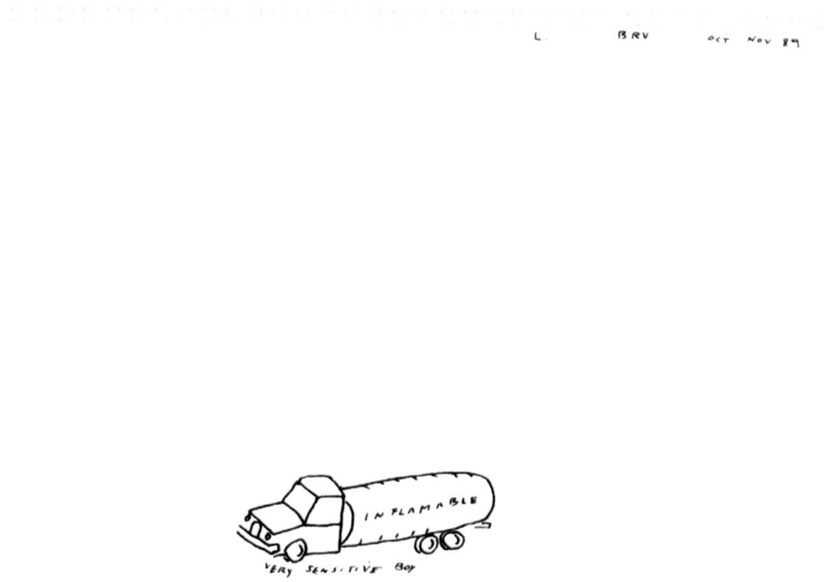

51. *[Very Sensitive Boy]*, 1989

Permanent ink on paper
30 × 21 cm
Private collection,
São Paulo, Brazil
PL.0984.0/00

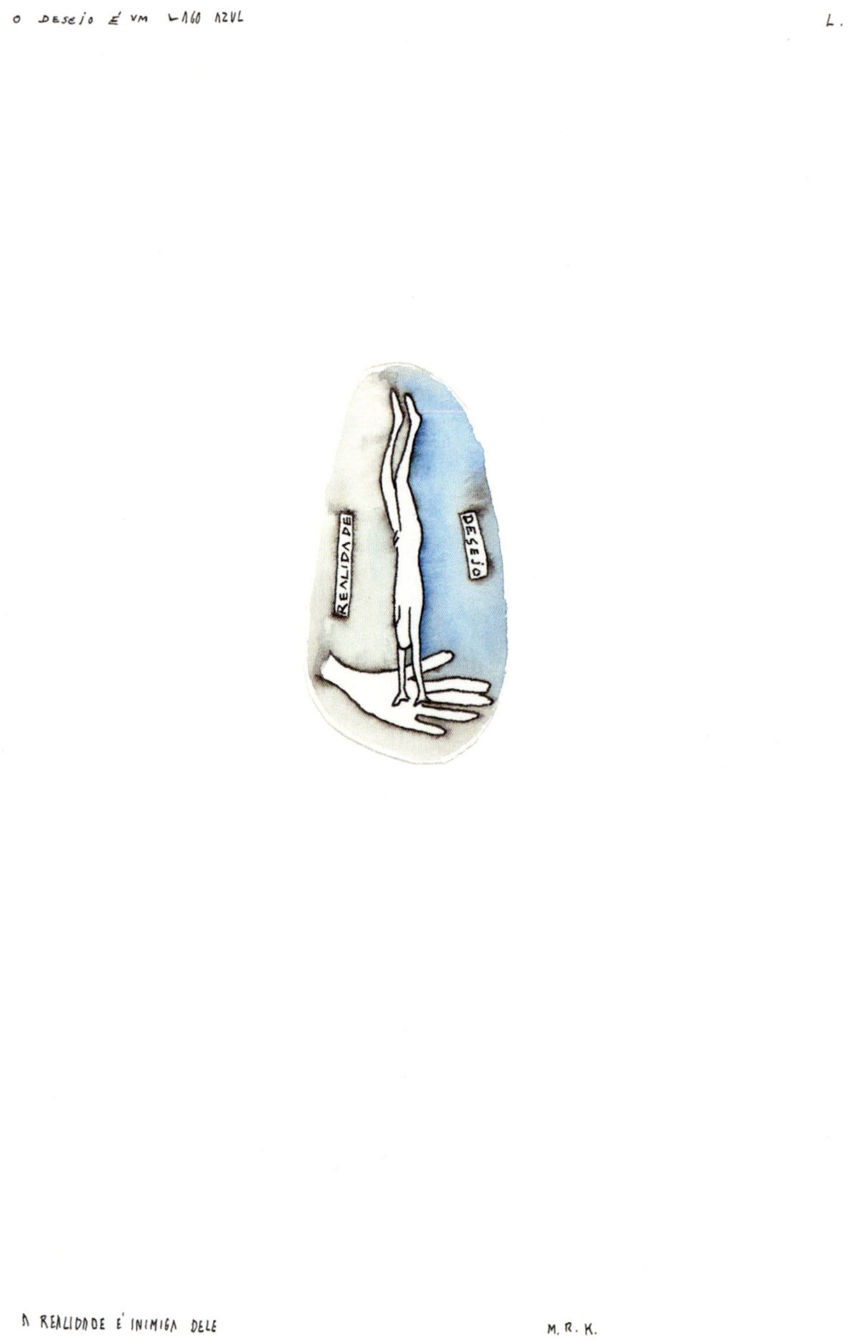

52. ***[O desejo é um lago azul]***
[Desire Is a Blue Lake], 1989

Watercolor and
permanent ink on paper
32 × 24 cm
The Museum of Modern Art,
gift Friends of Contemporary
Drawing, 1999,
New York, United States
PL.1529.0/00

53. ***[Os anéis do rapaz]***
[The Young Man's Rings], 1989

Permanent ink and
watercolor on paper
25.5 × 17.5 cm
Collection of Luisa Malzoni Strina,
São Paulo, Brazil
PL.1281.0/00

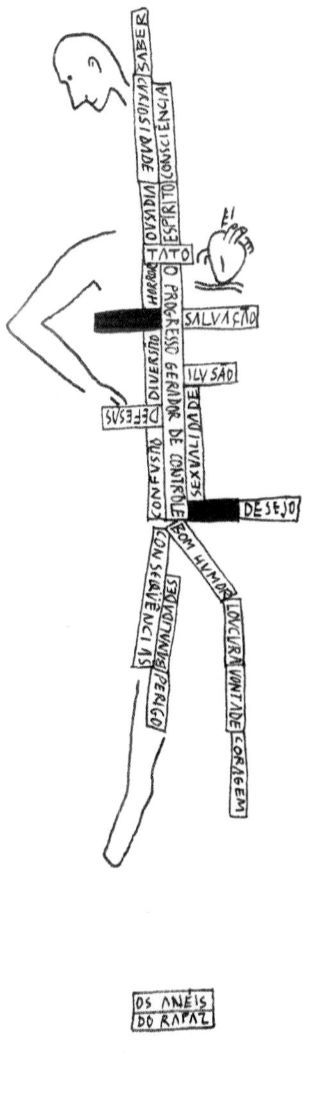

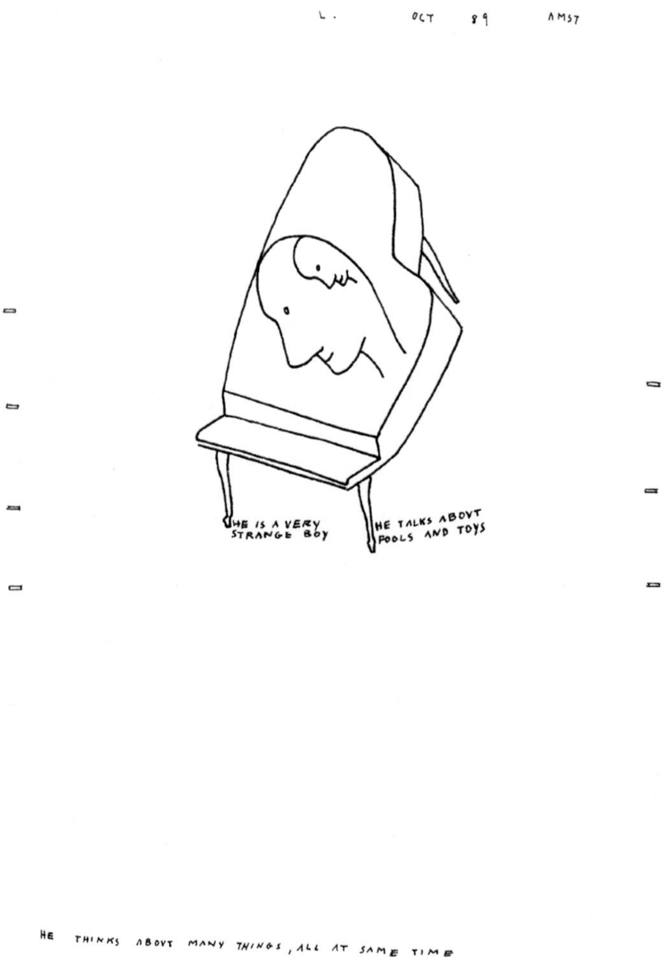

54. ***[He Thinks About Many Things, All at the Same Time]***, 1989

Permanent ink on paper
23.5 × 16.5 cm
Collection of Luisa Malzoni Strina,
São Paulo, Brazil
PL.1146.0/00

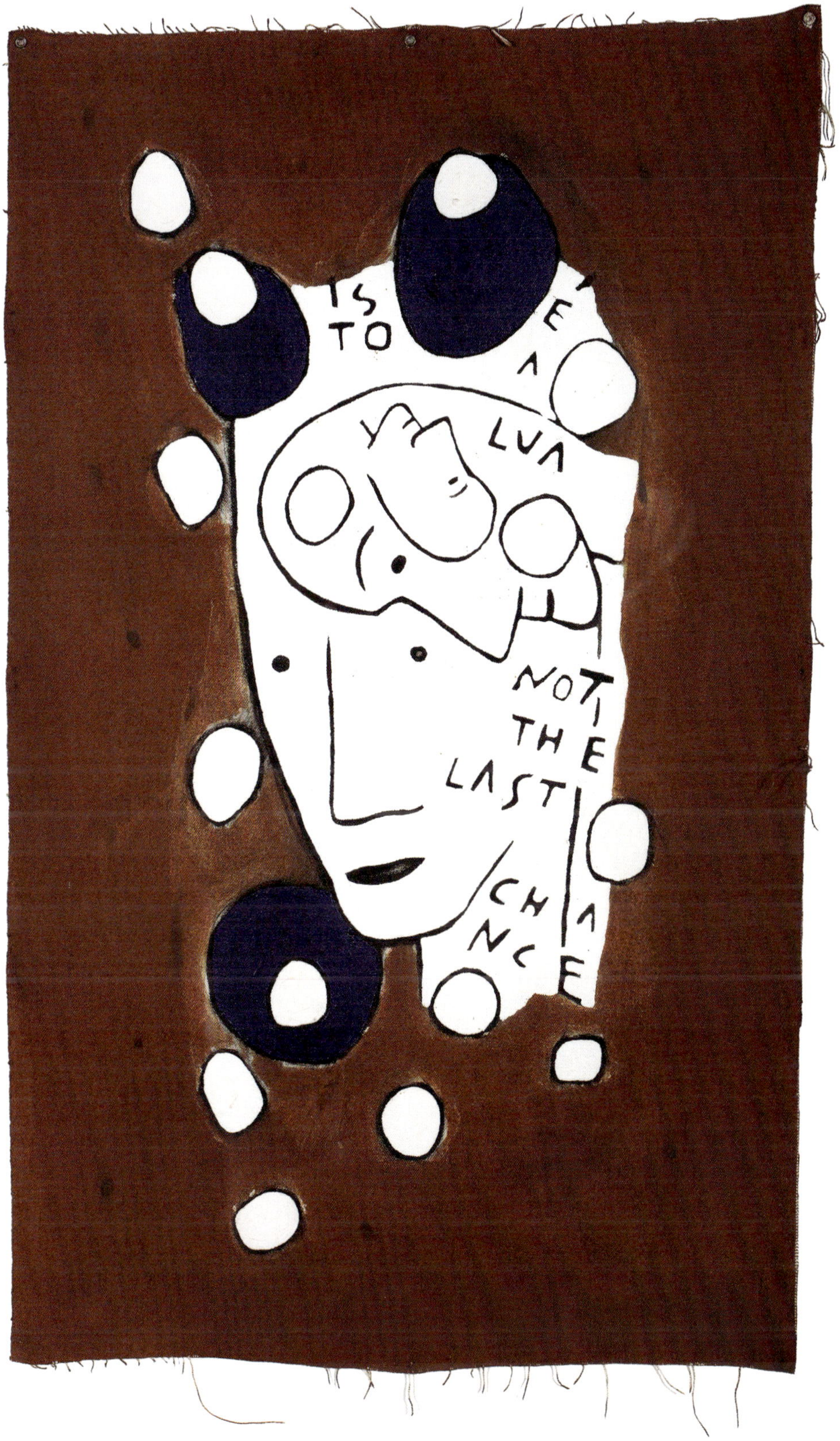

55. ***Isto é a lua, Not the Last Chance*** [This Is the Moon, Not the Last Chance], 1989

Acrylic paint on unstretched canvas
83 × 50 cm
Collection of Jardis Volpe,
São Paulo, Brazil
PL.0746.0/00

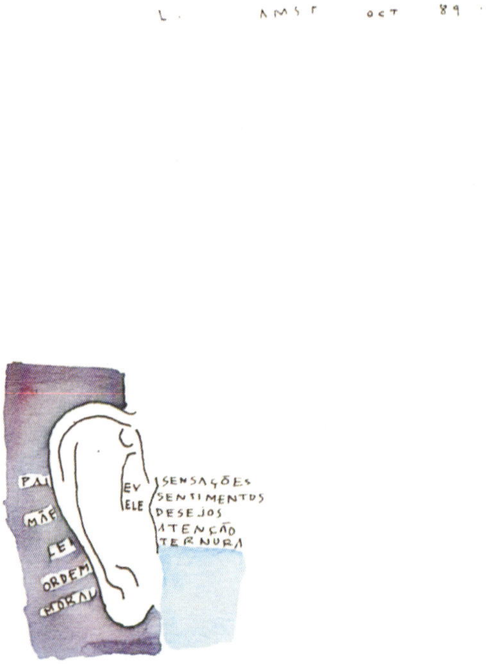

56. ***[Eu; ele]*** [Me; Him], 1989

Permanent ink and
watercolor on paper
32 × 24 cm
Collection of Marcia
and Luiz Chrysostomo,
Rio de Janeiro, Brazil
PL.1289.0/00

57. ***[Nós não temos a hora certa]***
[We Don't Have a Right Time],
circa 1989

Permanent ink and
watercolor on paper
32 × 24 cm
Private collection,
São Paulo, Brazil
PL.1201.0/00

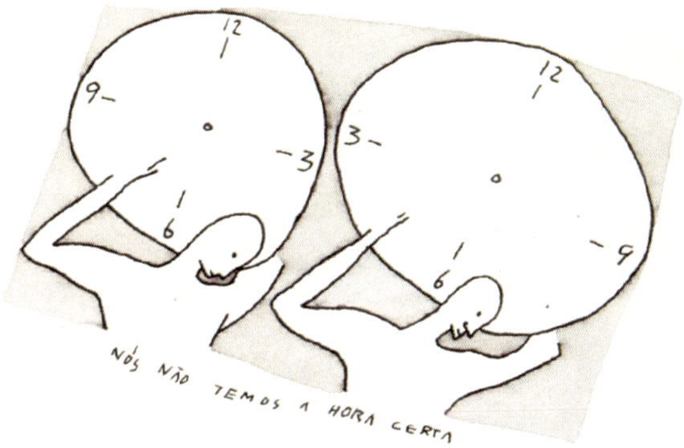

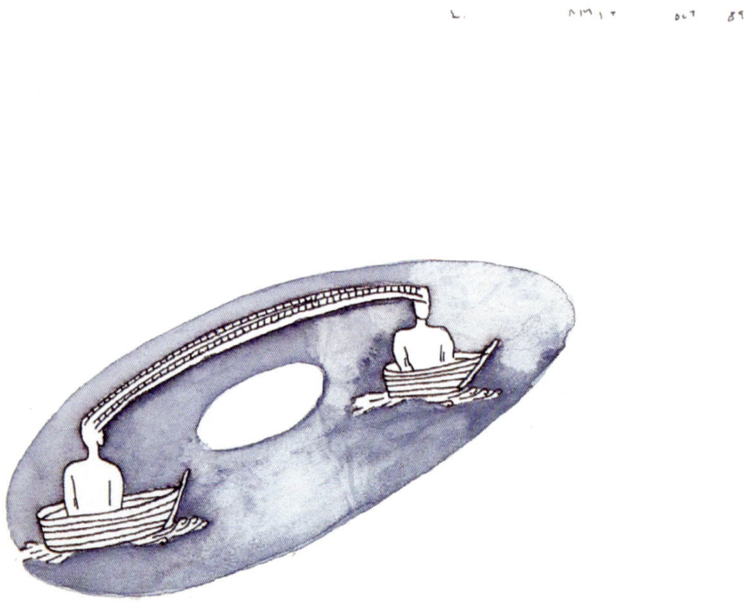

58. ***Untitled***, 1989

Permanent ink and
watercolor on paper
32 × 24 cm
Collection of Guilherme Salvatore,
São Paulo, Brazil
PL.0660.0/00

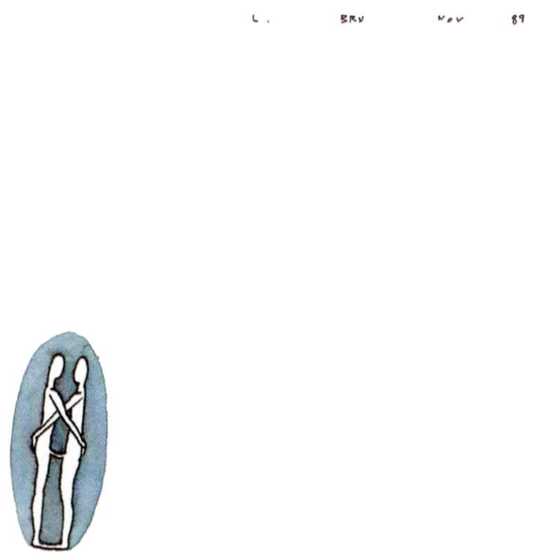

59. ***Untitled***, 1989

Permanent ink and
watercolor on paper
30 × 21 cm
Collection of Graham Steele
and Ulysses de Santi,
United States
PL.1165.0/00

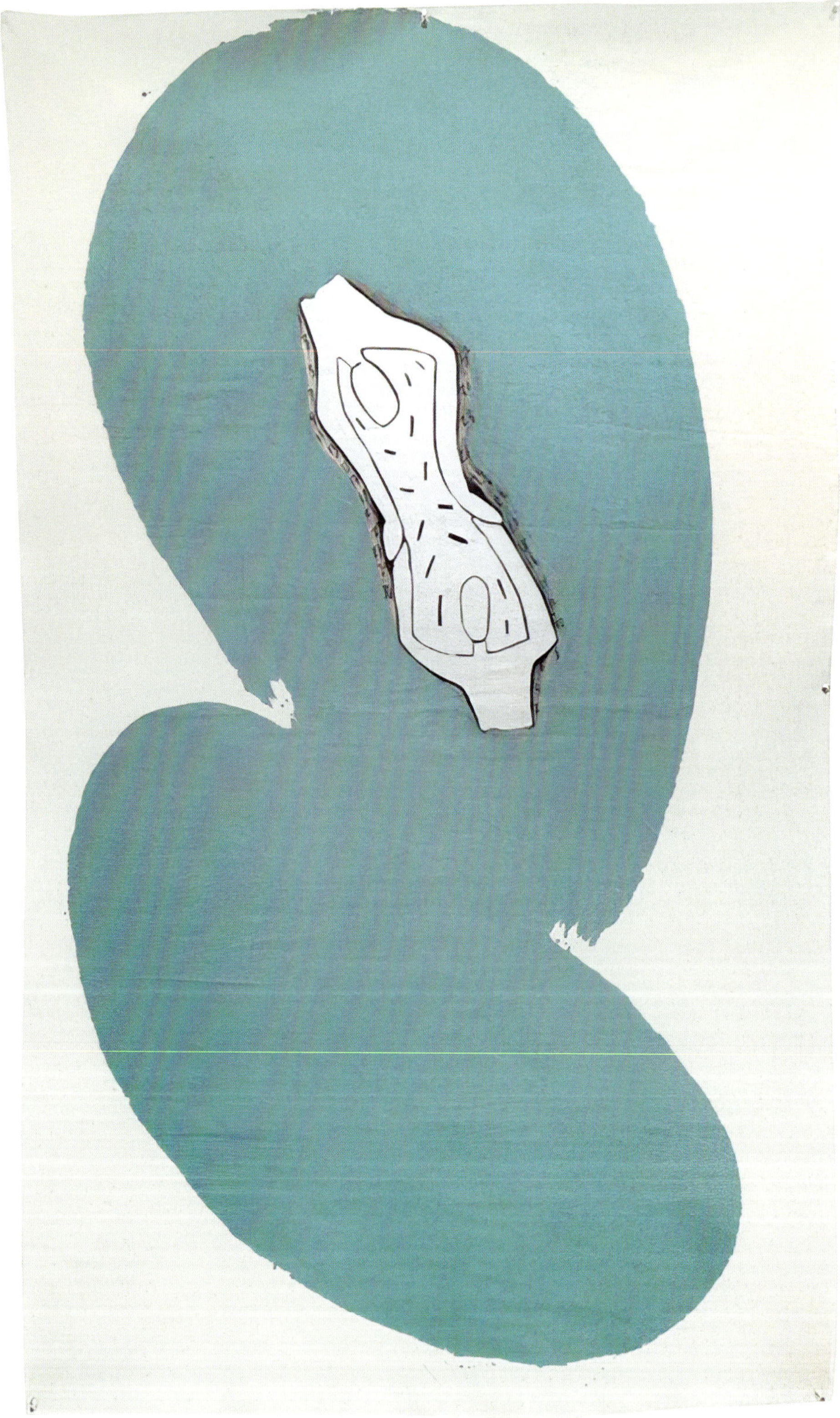

60. ***Untitled***, 1989

Acrylic paint on unstretched canvas
160 × 95 cm
Collection of Luisa Malzoni Strina,
São Paulo, Brazil
PL.0814.0/00

61. *Untitled*, 1989

Acrylic paint on canvas
143 × 100 cm
Private collection,
São Paulo, Brazil
PL.0712.0/00

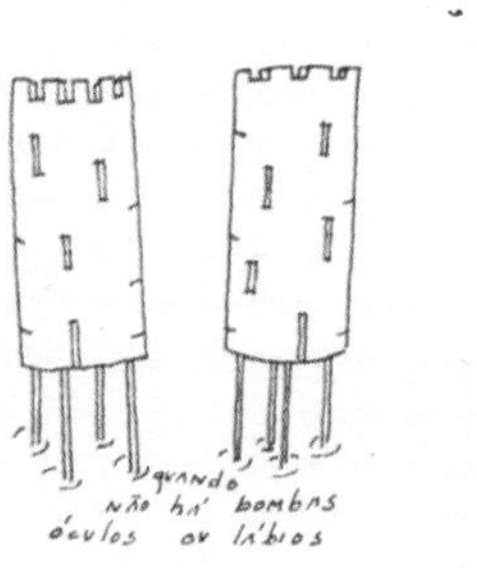

62. [***Quando não há bombas, óculos ou lábios***] [When There Are No Bombs, Eyeglasses, or Lips], *circa* 1989

Permanent ink on paper
26.5 × 33.5 cm
Private collection,
São Paulo, Brazil
PL.0999.0/00

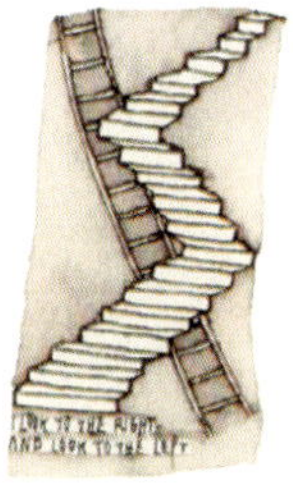

63. ***[Look to the Right and Look to the Left]***, 1989

Permanent ink and
watercolor on paper
32 × 24 cm
Private collection,
São Paulo, Brazil
PL.1278.0/00

64. ***So Many Days***, 1989

Permanent ink on paper
29 × 21 cm
Private collection,
São Paulo, Brazil
PL.0035.0/00

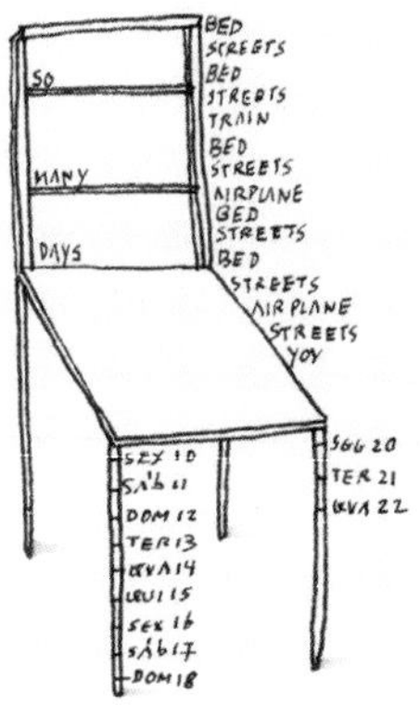

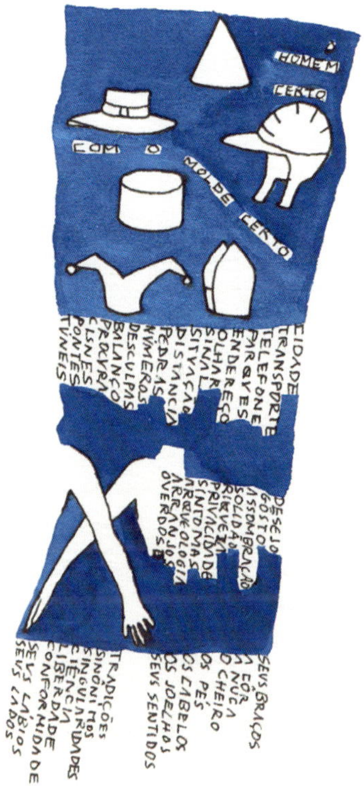

65. ***[Homem certo com molde certo]***
[Right Man With Right Mold], *circa* 1989

Permanent ink and
watercolor on paper
32 × 24 cm
Collection of Thiago Tannous,
São Paulo, Brazil
PL.1199.0/00

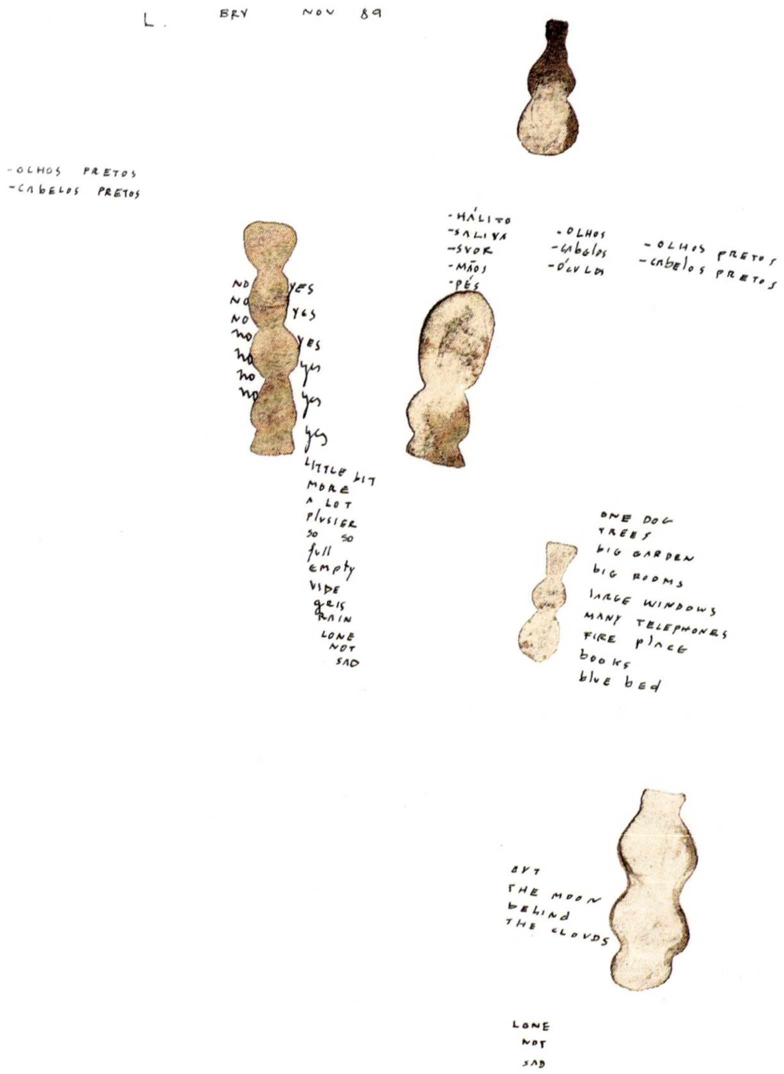

66. *[Olhos pretos; cabelos pretos]*
[Black Eyes; Black Hair], 1989

Permanent ink and
watercolor on paper
30 × 21 cm
Collection of Luisa Malzoni Strina,
São Paulo, Brazil
PL.1159.0/00

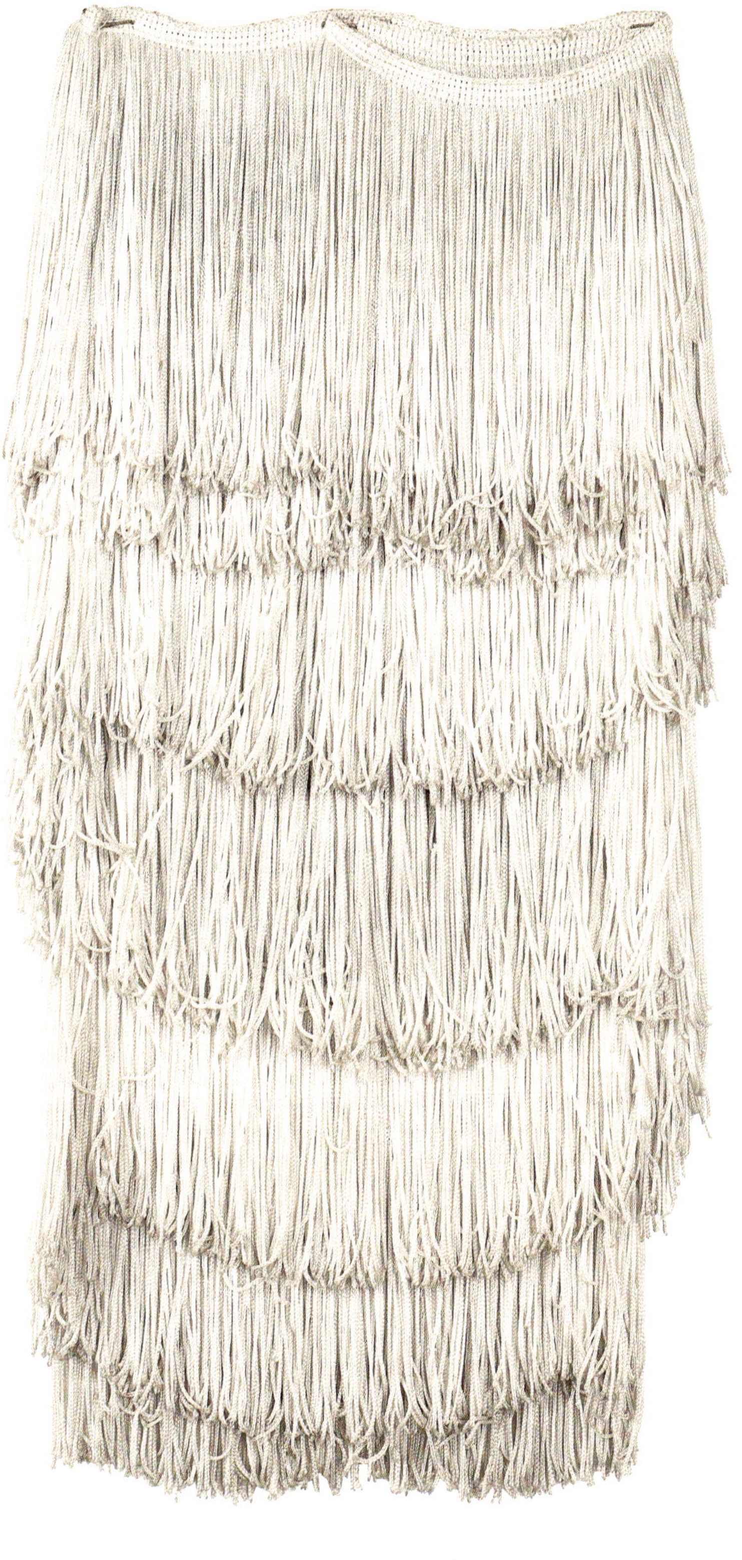

67. ***Untitled***, 1989

Silk thread fringe
on chassis
47 × 22 × 3 cm
Private collection,
São Paulo, Brazil
PL.1240.0/00

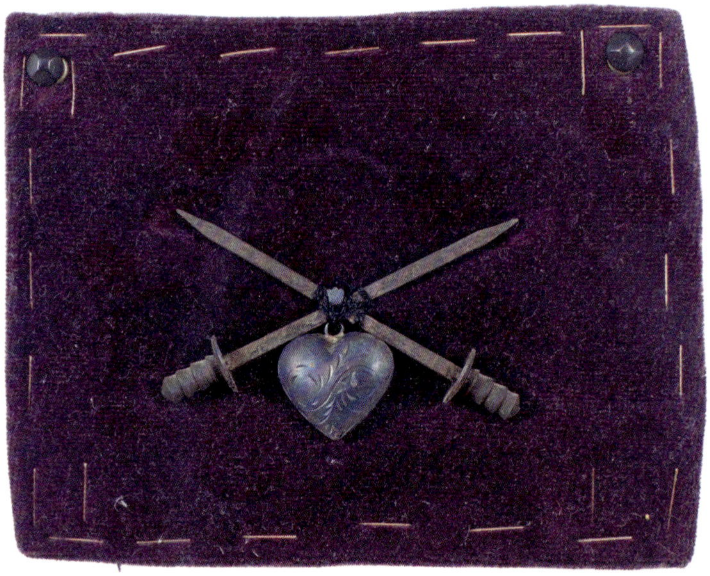

68. ***Luta de espadas sobre veludo roxo*** [Sword Fight on Purple Velvet], 1989

Miniature swords and metal heart, staple, and thread on velvet on unstretched canvas
12 × 15 × 1 cm
Collection of Luisa Malzoni Strina, São Paulo, Brazil
PL.1284.0/00

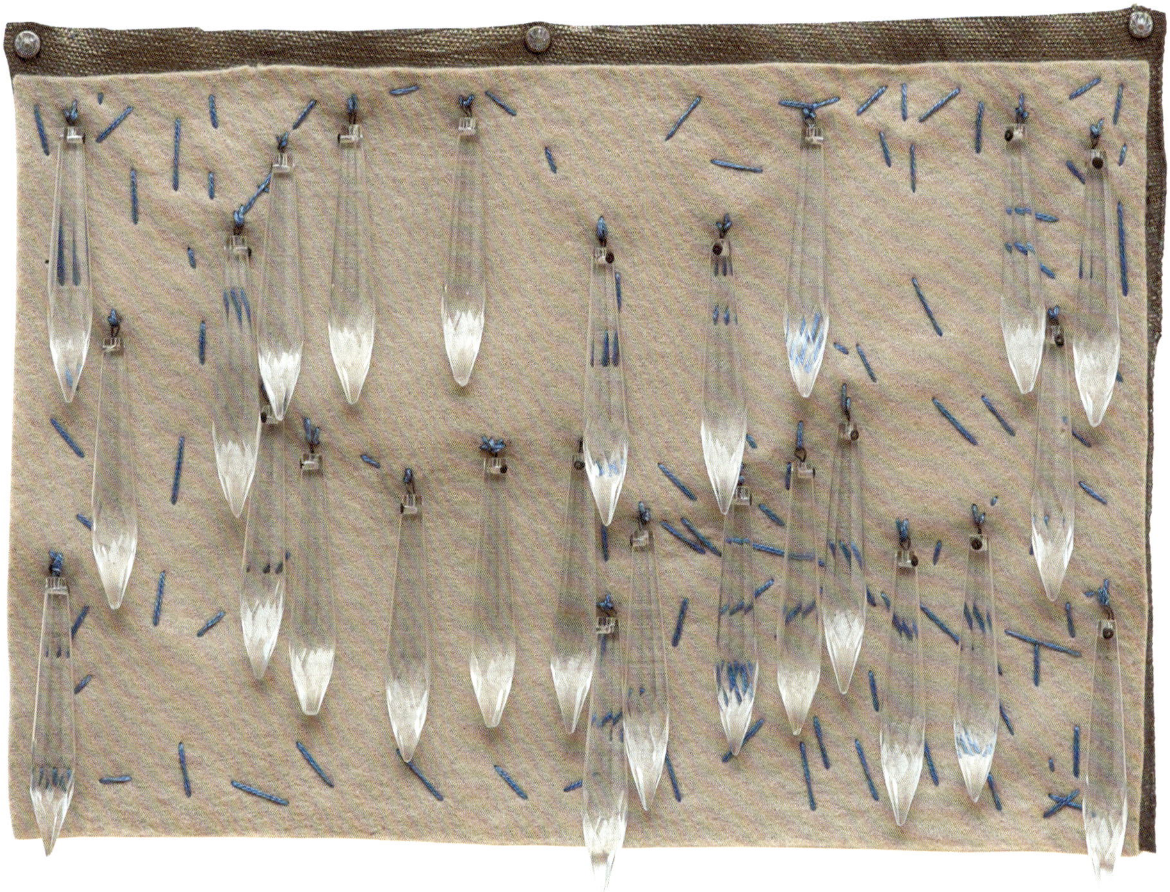

69. ***Voilà mon coeur***
[Here Is My Heart],
circa 1989

Crystals, thread, felt, and metallic
paint on unstretched canvas
22 × 30 × 2 cm
Collection of Susana and
Ricardo Steinbruch,
São Paulo, Brazil
PL.1296.0/00

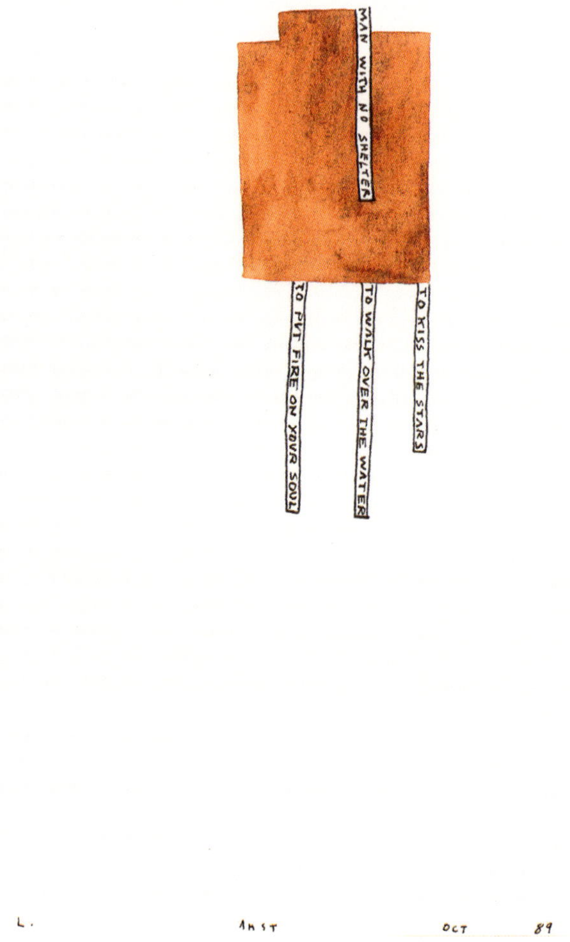

70. [***Man With No Shelter***], 1989

Permanent ink and
watercolor on paper
24 × 16.5 cm
Collection of Adriano Sammarone,
São Paulo, Brazil
PL.1275.0/00

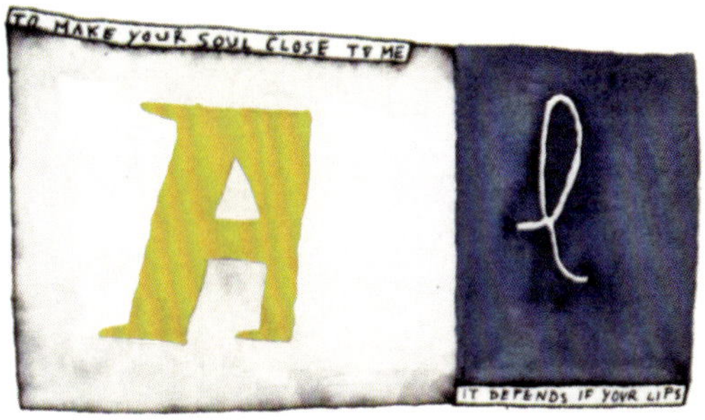

71. ***To Make Your Soul Close to Me***, 1989

Watercolor and
permanent ink on paper
32 × 24 cm
The Museum of Modern Art,
gift família Bezerra Dias/
Projeto Leonilson, 1999,
New York, United States
PL.1528.0/00

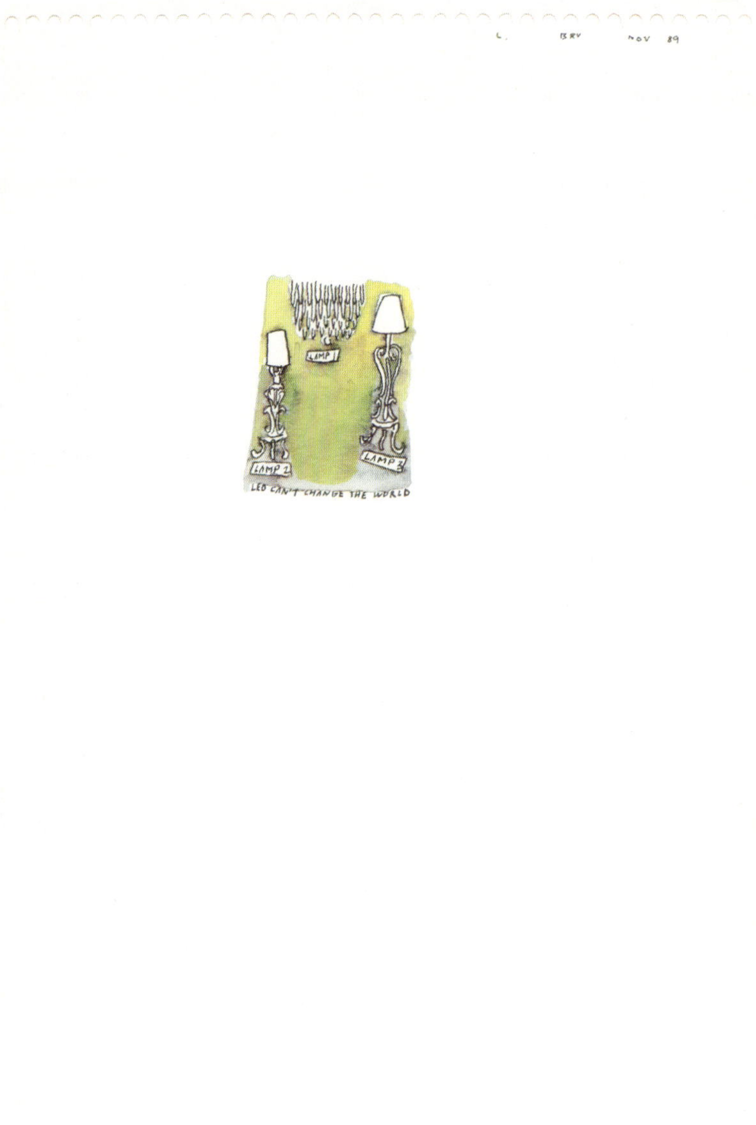

72

72. ***Leo Can't Change the World***, 1989

Permanent ink and watercolor on paper
30 × 21 cm
Private collection, São Paulo, Brazil
PL.0910.0/00

73. ***Leo não consegue mudar o mundo*** [Leo Can't Change the World], 1989

Acrylic paint and metallic paint on unstretched canvas
156 × 95 cm
Private collection, São Paulo, Brazil
PL.0615.0/00

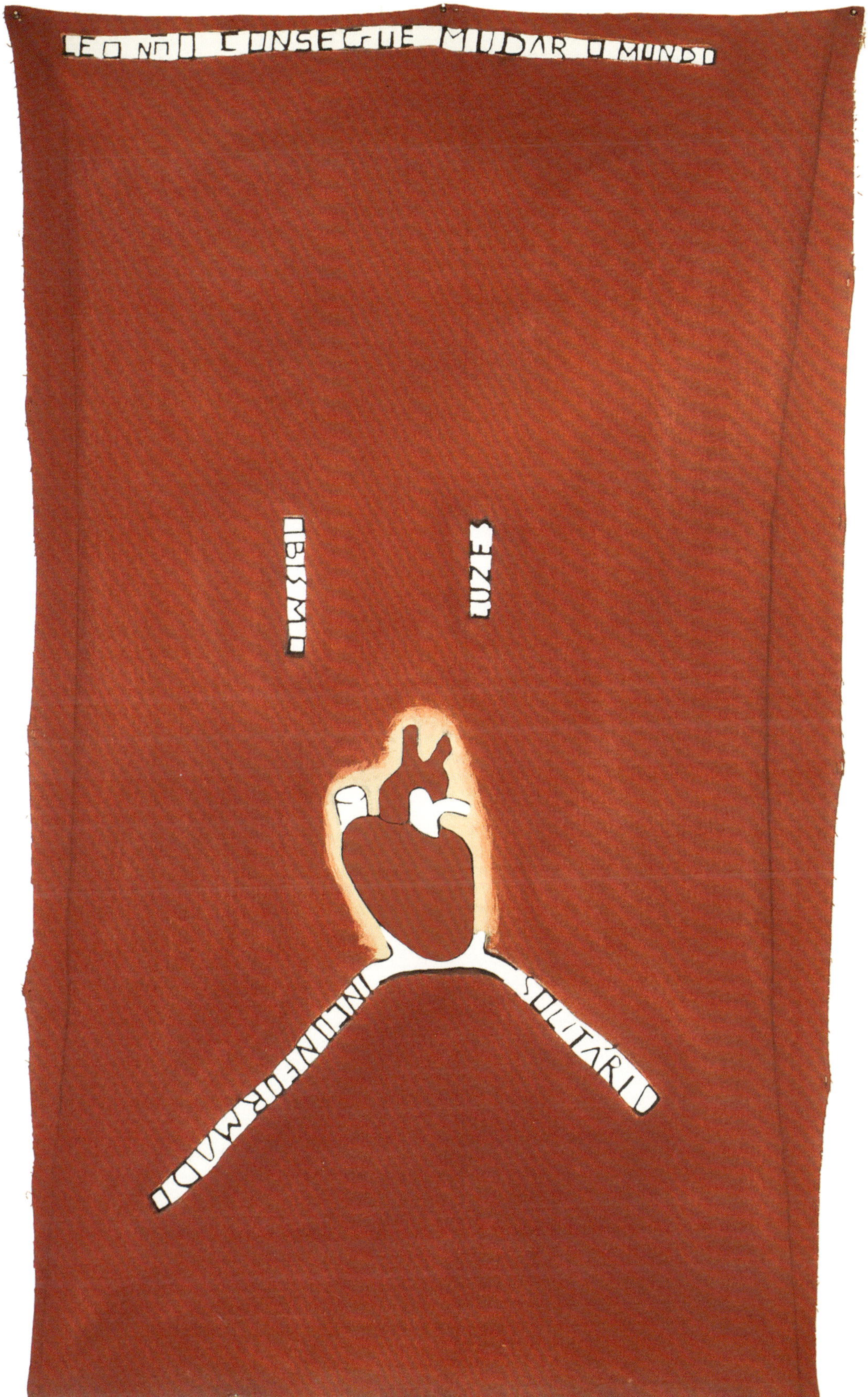

113

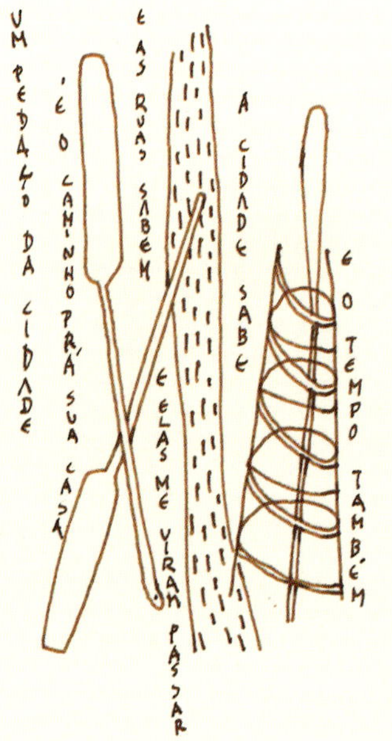

74. *A cidade sabe e o tempo também*
[The City Knows and Time Too],
circa 1989

Permanent ink on paper
34 × 24.5 cm
Museu de Arte Moderna de
São Paulo, gift Carmem Bezerra Dias
and Theodorino Torquato Dias, 1997,
Brazil
PL.1042.0/00

75. ***Os homens com suas próprias atenções***
[Men With Their Own Attentions], 1989

Watercolor and
permanent ink on paper
32 × 24 cm
The Museum of Modern Art,
gift Friends of Contemporary
Drawing, 1999,
New York, United States
PL.1530.0/00

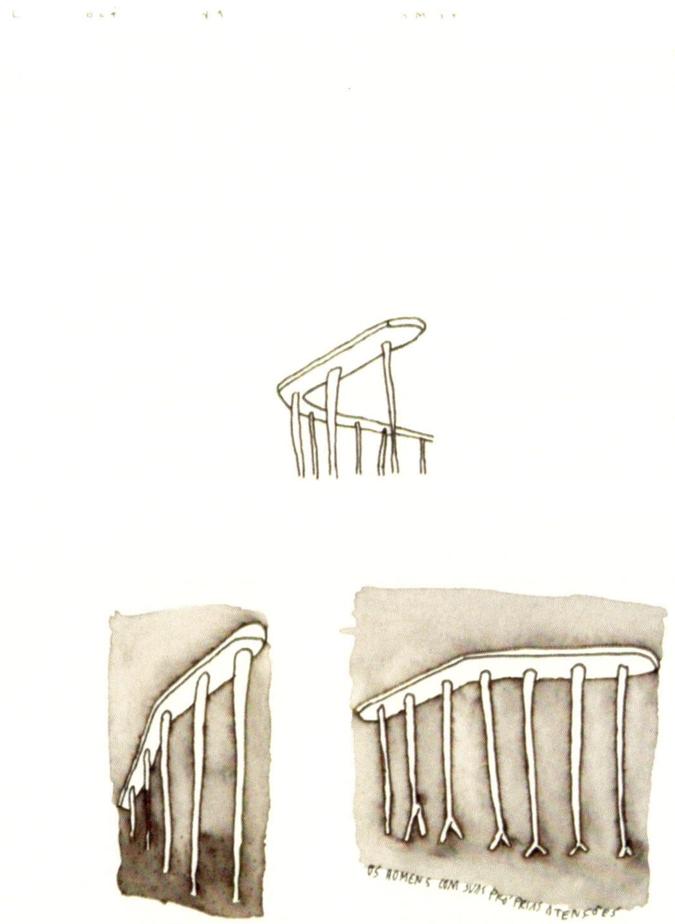

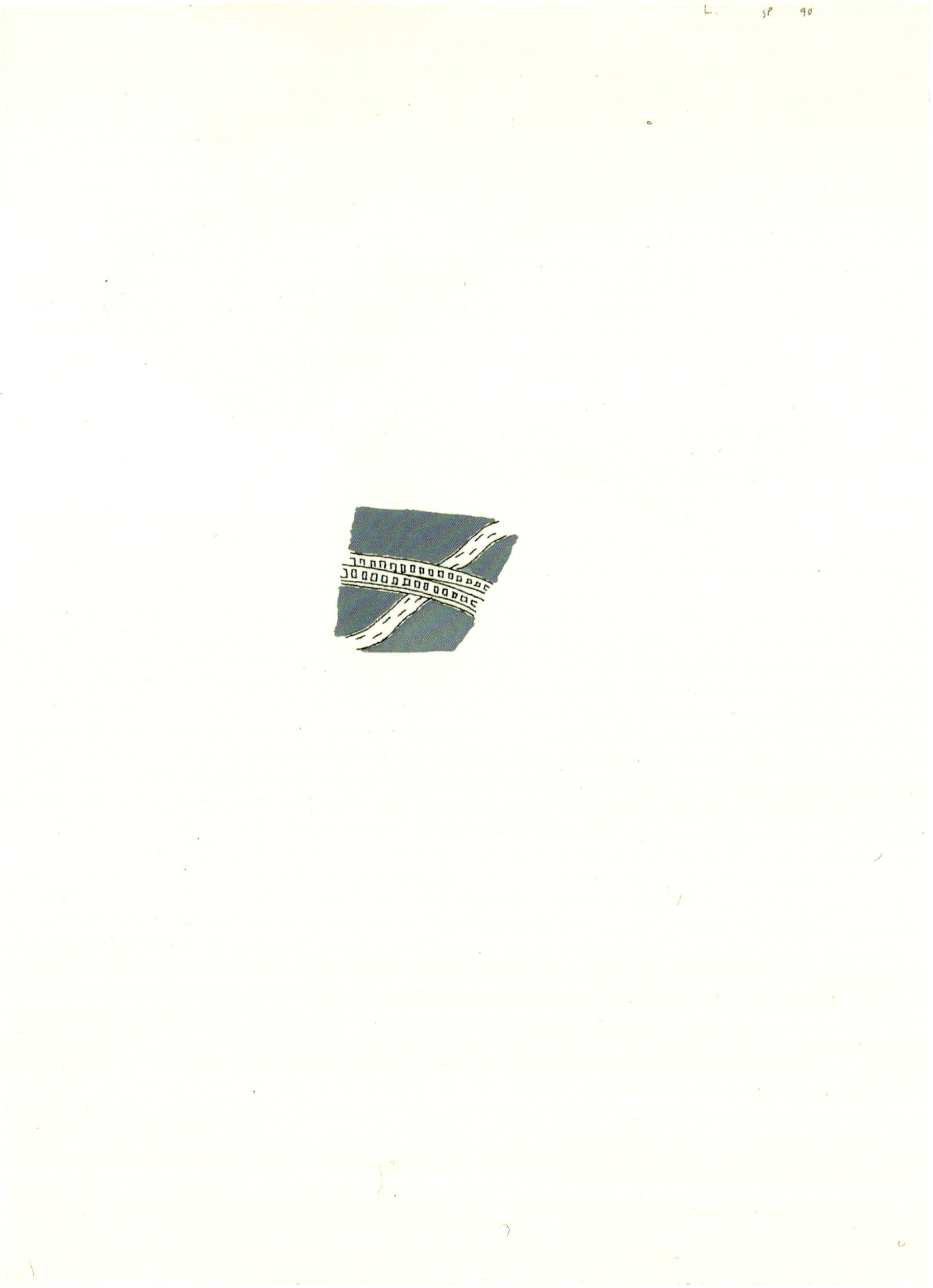

76. ***Untitled*****,**
from the series *Onde está o oceano*
[Where Is the Ocean], 1990

Permanent ink and
gouache on paper
41 × 31 cm
Collection of Daniel Senise,
Rio de Janeiro, Brazil
PL.3055.0/00

77. ***Untitled*****,**
from the series *Onde está o oceano*
[Where Is the Ocean], 1989

Permanent ink on paper
41 × 31 cm
Private collection,
São Paulo, Brazil
PL.3053.0/00

78. ***[Deserto; oceano]*** [Desert; Ocean], from the series *Onde está o oceano* [Where Is the Ocean], 1990

Permanent ink and
gouache on paper
41 × 31 cm
Private collection,
Rio de Janeiro, Brazil
PL.3054.0/00

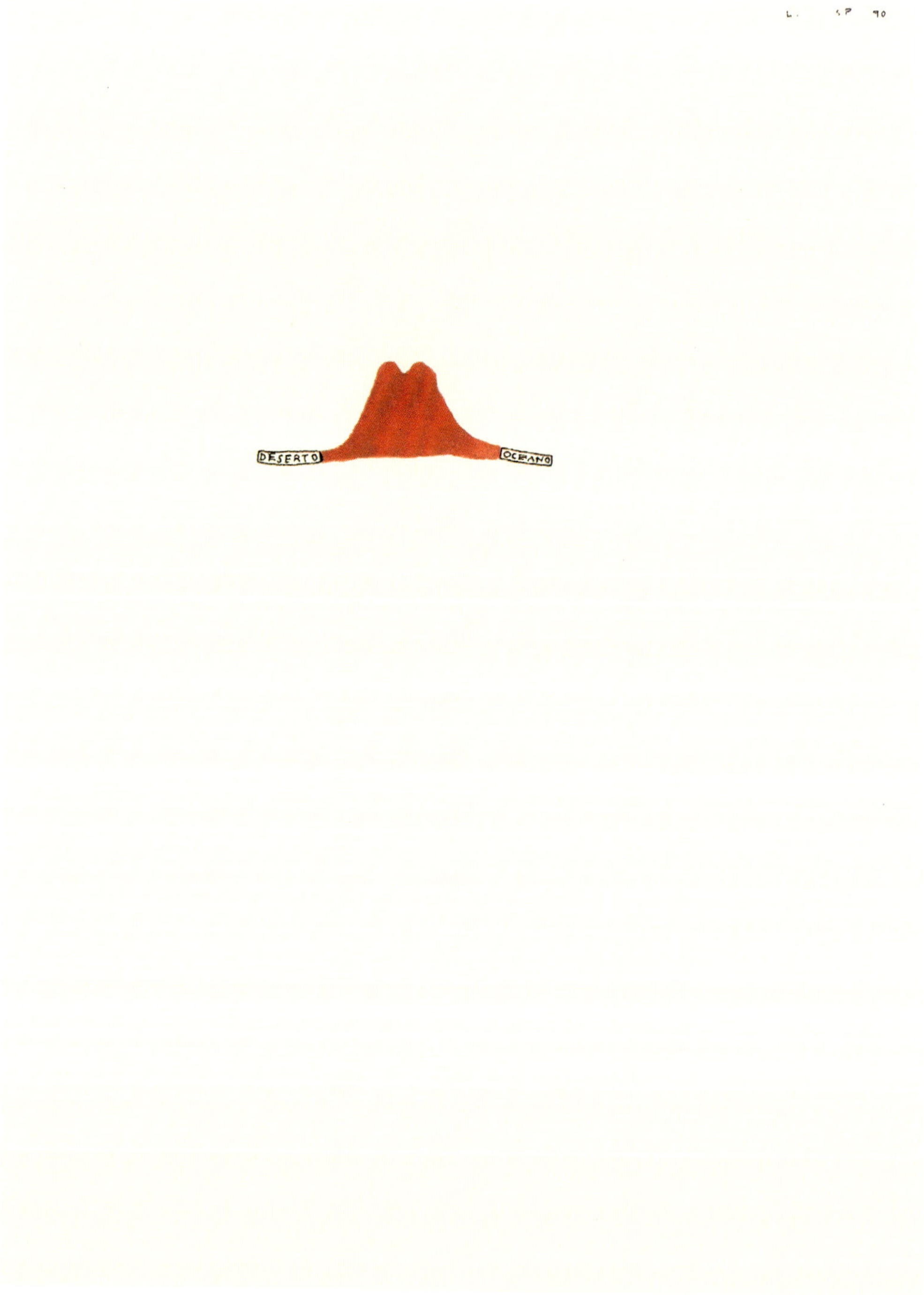

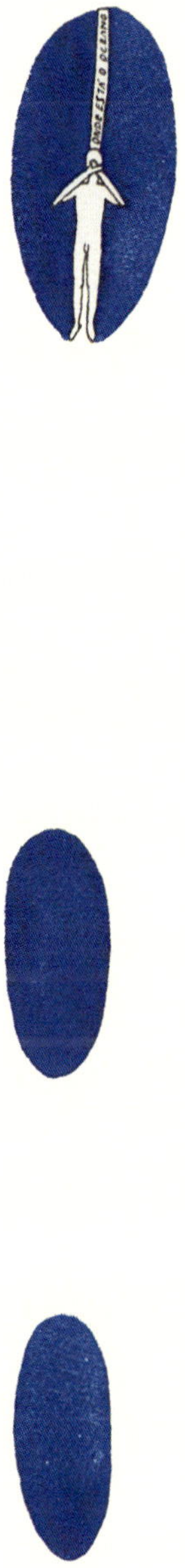

79. [*Onde está o oceano*]
[Where Is the Ocean], from
the series *Onde está o oceano*
[Where Is the Ocean], *circa* 1989

Permanent ink and
watercolor on paper
41 × 31 cm
Private collection,
Rio de Janeiro, Brazil
PL.3052.0/00

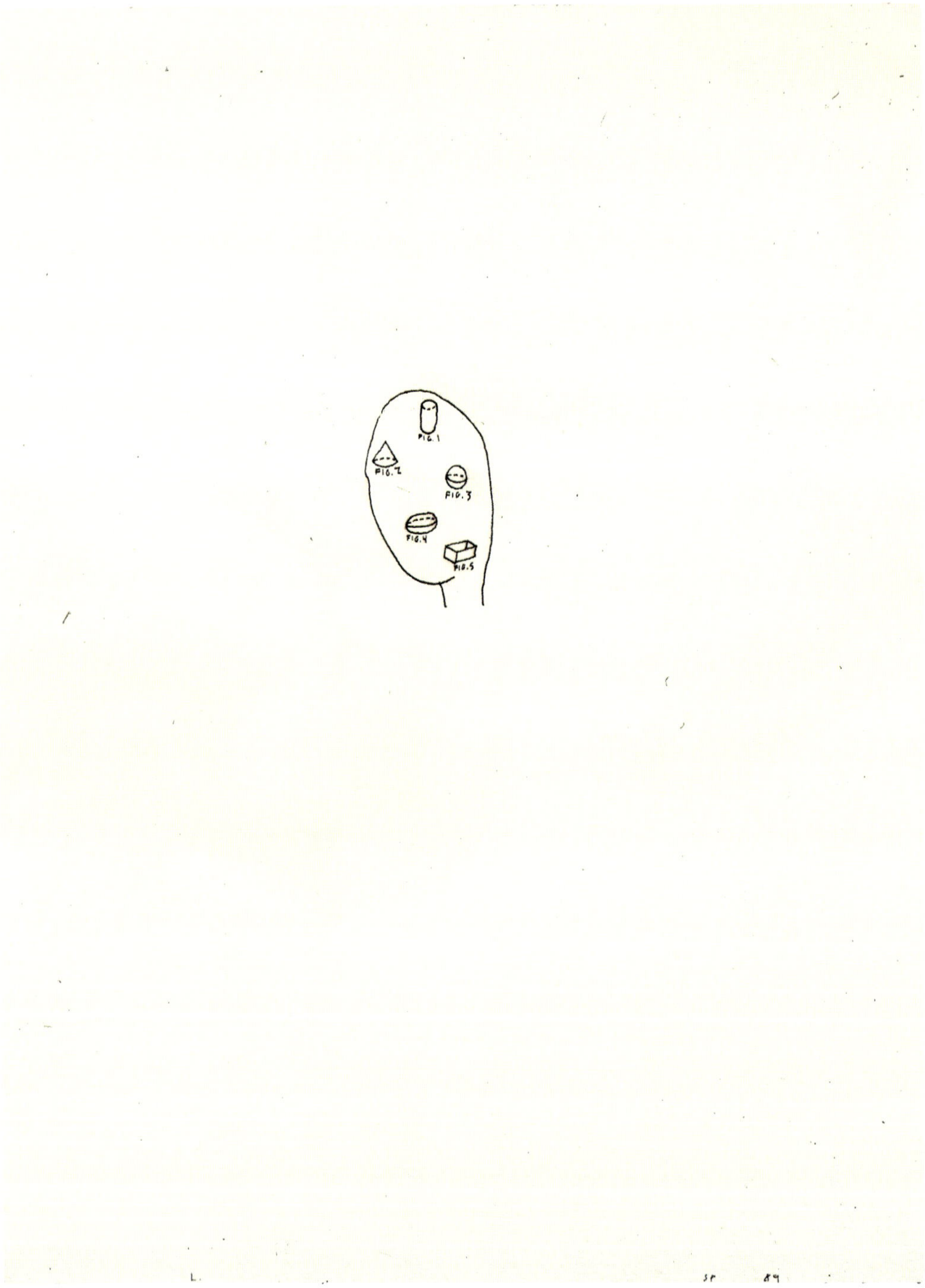

80. ***Untitled***,
from the series *Onde está o oceano*
[Where Is the Ocean], 1989

Permanent ink on paper
41 × 31 cm
Collection of Daniel Senise,
Rio de Janeiro, Brazil
PL.3056.0/00

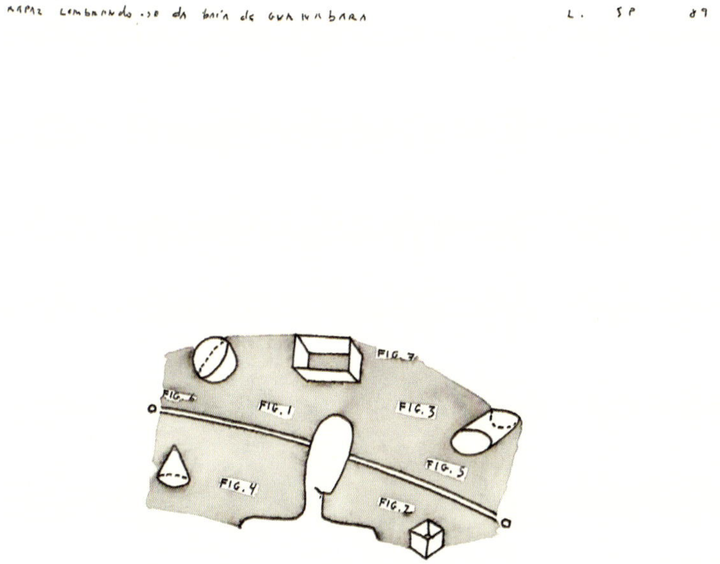

81. [***Rapaz lembrando-se da Baía de Guanabara***] [Young Man Recalling the Guanabara Bay], 1989

Permanent ink and
watercolor on paper
32 × 24 cm
Collection of Francisco Meirelles de Andrade,
São Paulo, Brazil
PL.1202.0/00

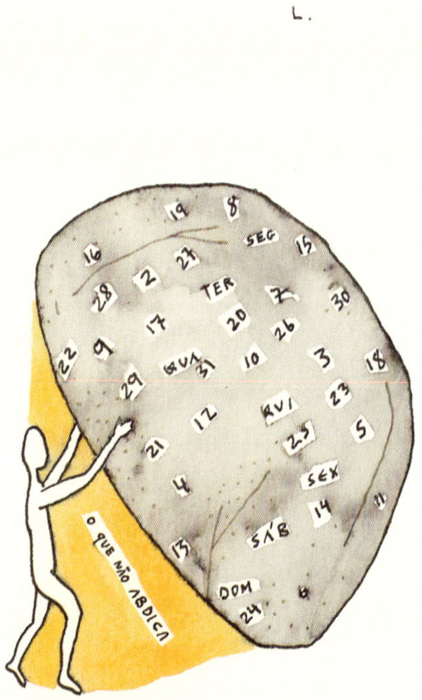

82. ***[O que não abdica]***
[He Who Does Not Resign],
circa 1989

Permanent ink and
watercolor on paper
24 × 16.5 cm
Collection of Mary Miranda,
São Paulo, Brazil
PL.0299.0/00

83. ***[O q. ñ abdica]***
[He Who Does Not Resign], 1989

Permanent ink and
watercolor on paper
41 × 31 cm
Collection of Luisa Malzoni Strina,
São Paulo, Brazil
PL.1187.0/00

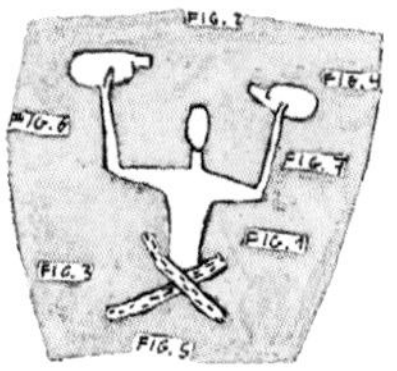

L. O q. Ñ ABDICA SP 89

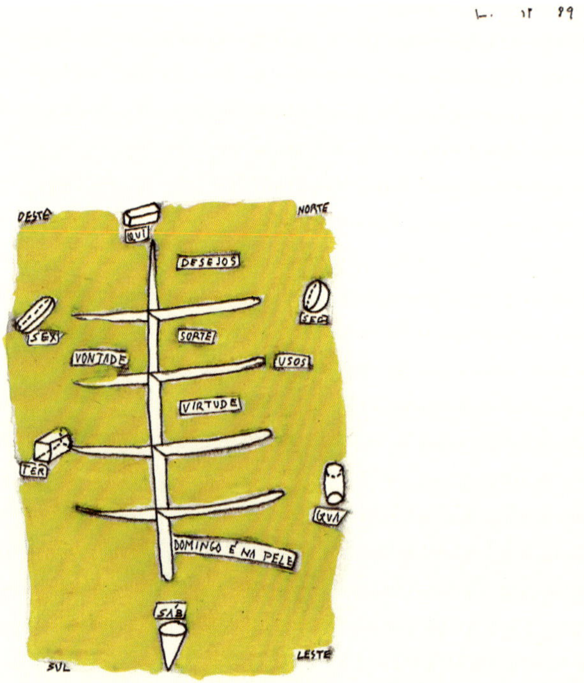

84. ***[Domingo é na pele]***
[Sunday Is on the Skin], 1989

Permanent ink and
gouache on paper
32 × 24 cm
Private collection,
São Paulo, Brazil
PL.1175.0/00

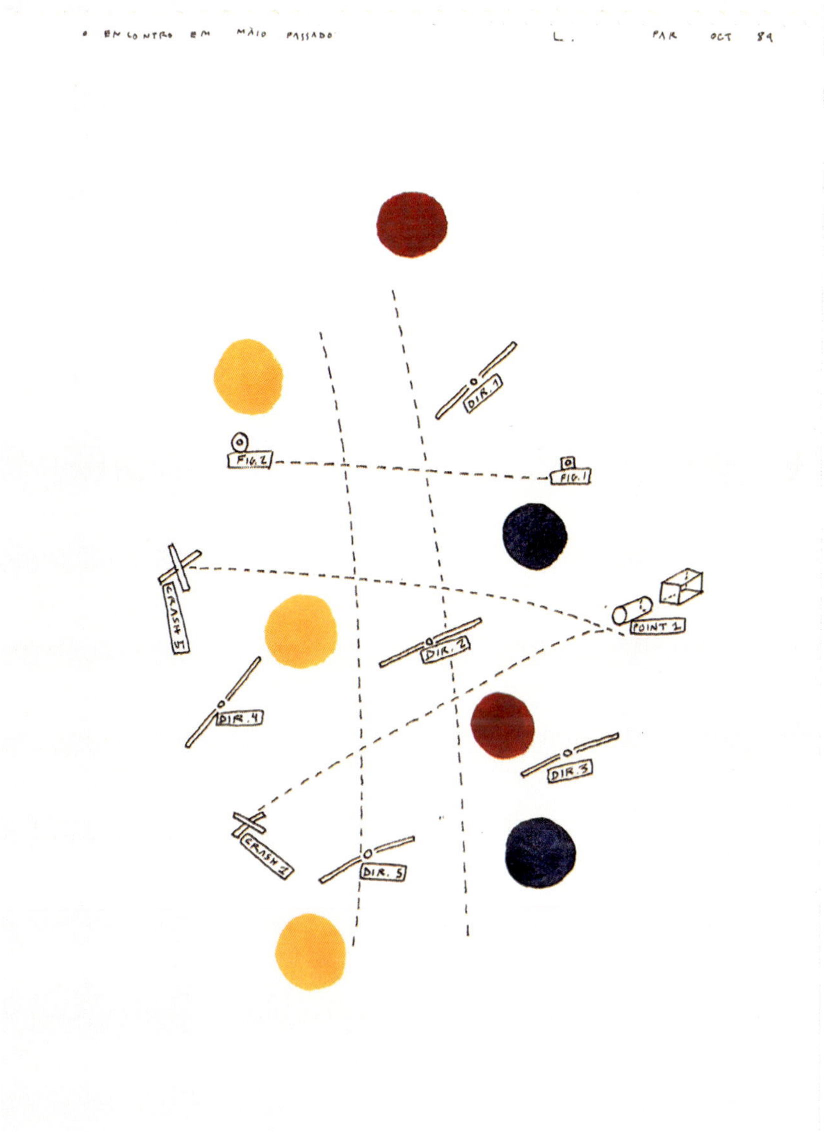

85. ***[O encontro em maio passado]***
[The Encounter in Last May], 1989

Permanent ink and gouache on paper
29.5 × 21 cm
Centre Pompidou, Musée national d’art moderne, Centre de création industrielle, purchase Sociedade Amigos do Projeto Leonilson, 2005, Paris, France
PL.0031.0/00

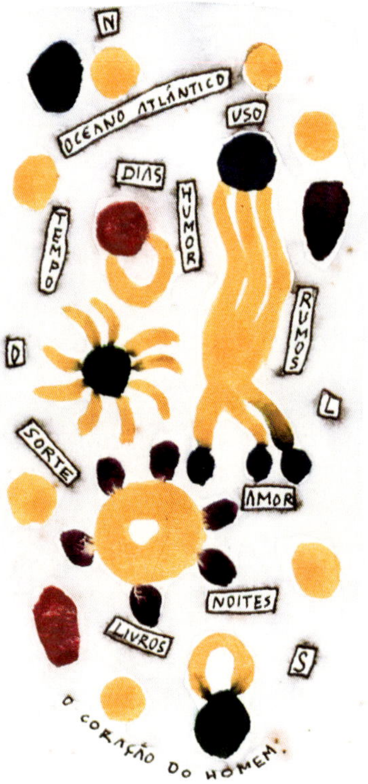

86. ***[O coração do homem]***
[Man's Heart], *circa* 1989

Watercolor and
permanent ink on paper
32 × 24 cm
Collection of Patricia Levy,
Rio de Janeiro, Brazil
PL.1323.0/00

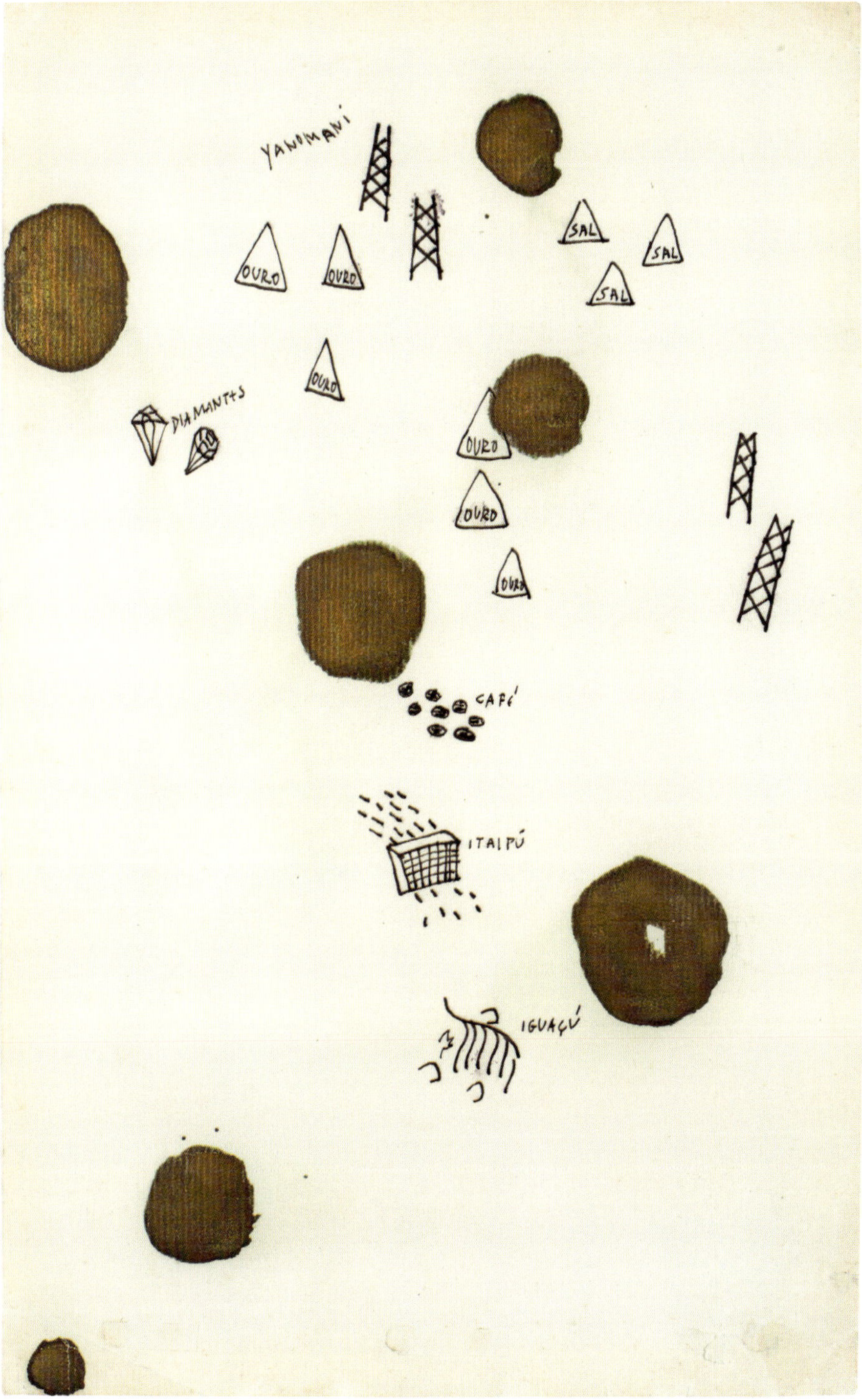

87. *Untitled*,
circa 1989

Marker and metallic paint on paper
32 × 20 cm
Private collection, São Paulo, Brazil
PL.0446.0/00

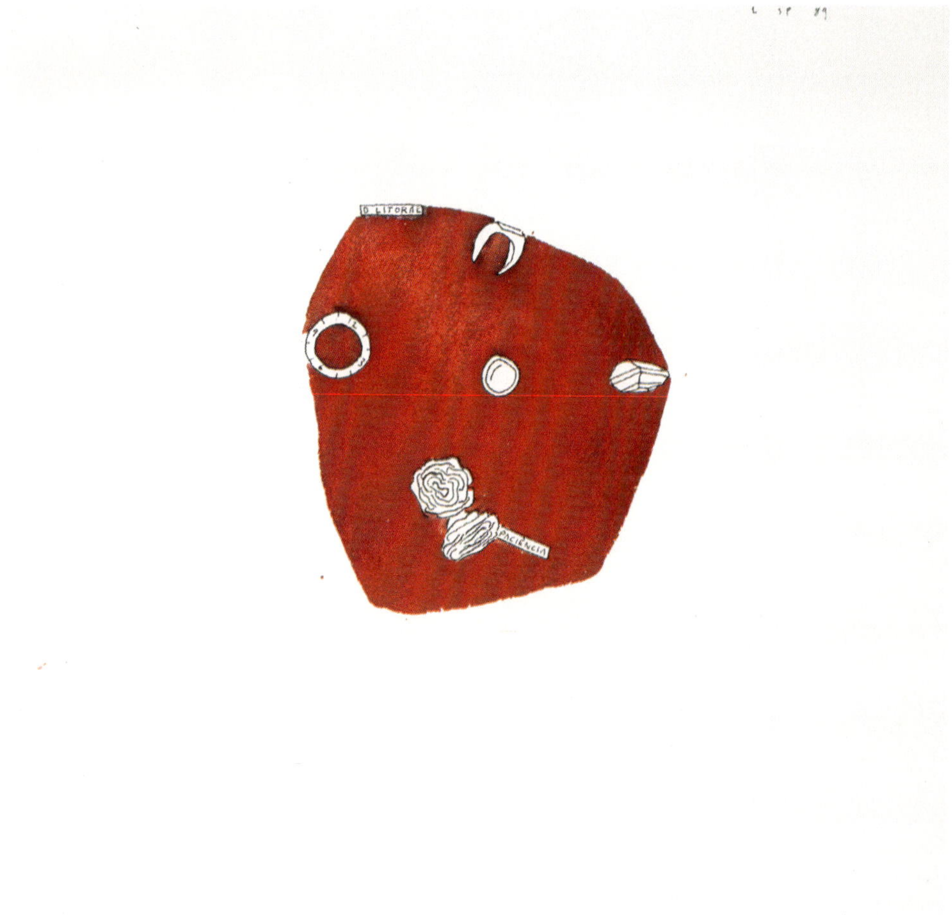

88. ***O litoral*** [The Shore], 1989

Watercolor and
China ink on paper
41 × 31 cm
Museu de Arte Moderna
do Rio de Janeiro, sponsor
White Martins, Brazil
PL.1470.0/00

89. *[Liberec]*, 1989

Permanent ink and
watercolor on paper
40.5 × 30.5 cm
Collection of Ana Eliza and Paulo Setubal,
São Paulo, Brazil
PL.1160.0/00

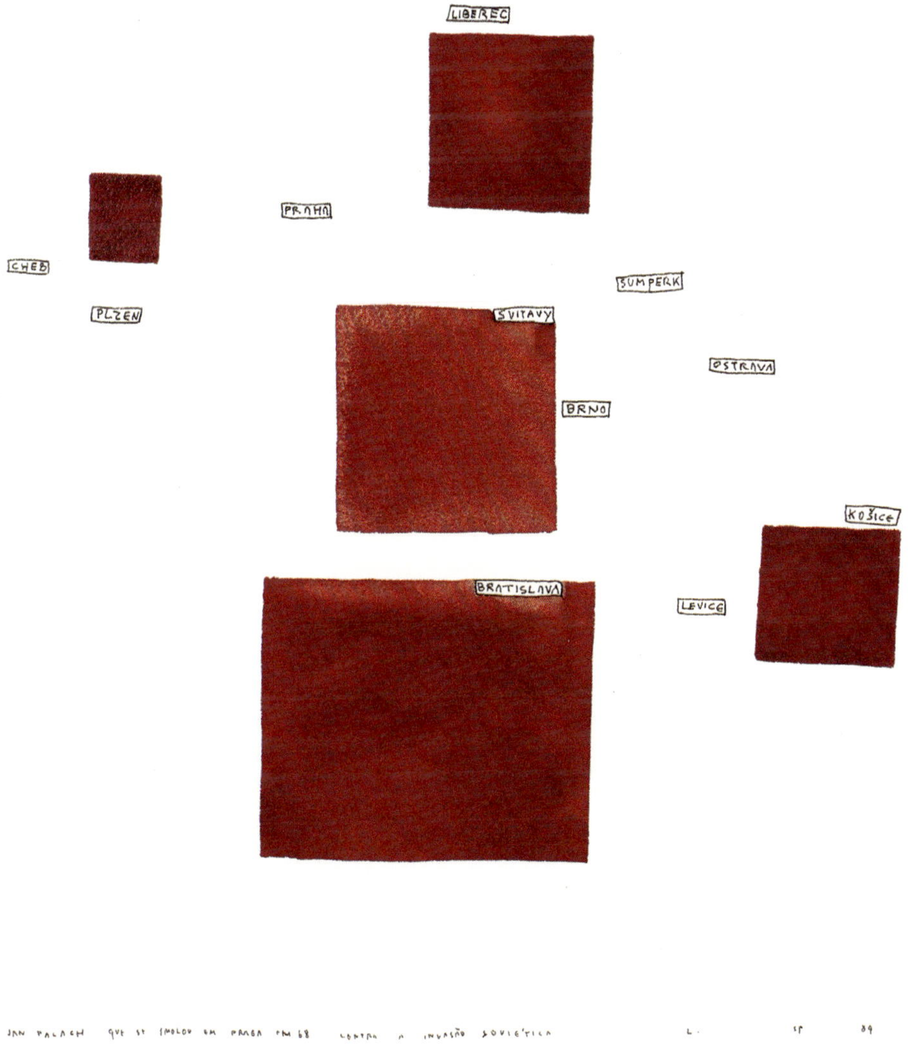

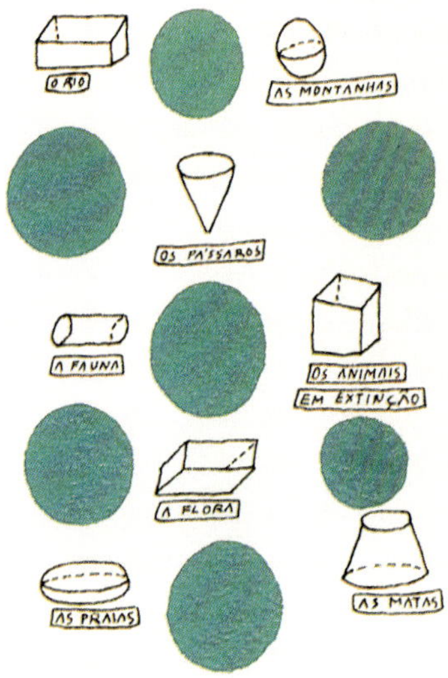

90. ***Sem título n° 1***
[Untitled #1], 1990

Watercolor and China ink on paper
31 × 23 cm
Museu de Arte Moderna
do Rio de Janeiro, sponsor
White Martins, Brazil
PL.1467.0/00

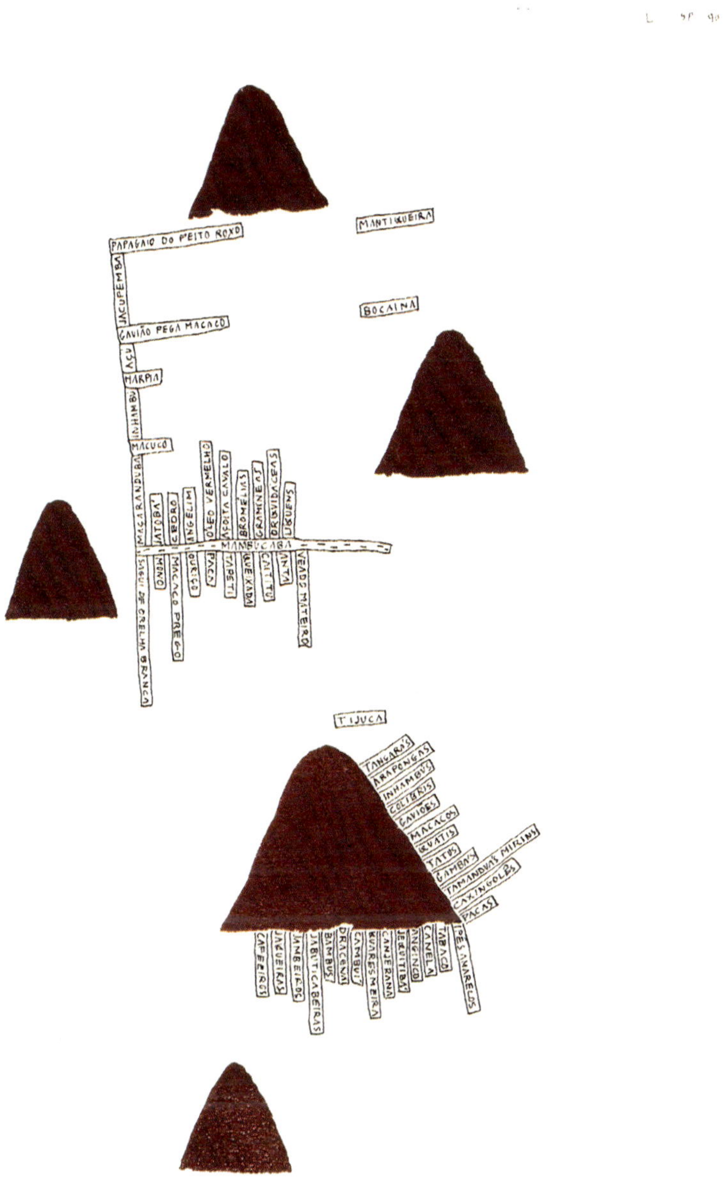

91. ***Mantiqueira***
Bocaina Tijuca**, 1990**

Watercolor and China ink on paper
41 × 31 cm
Museu de Arte Moderna
do Rio de Janeiro, sponsor
White Martins, Brazil
PL.1466.0/00

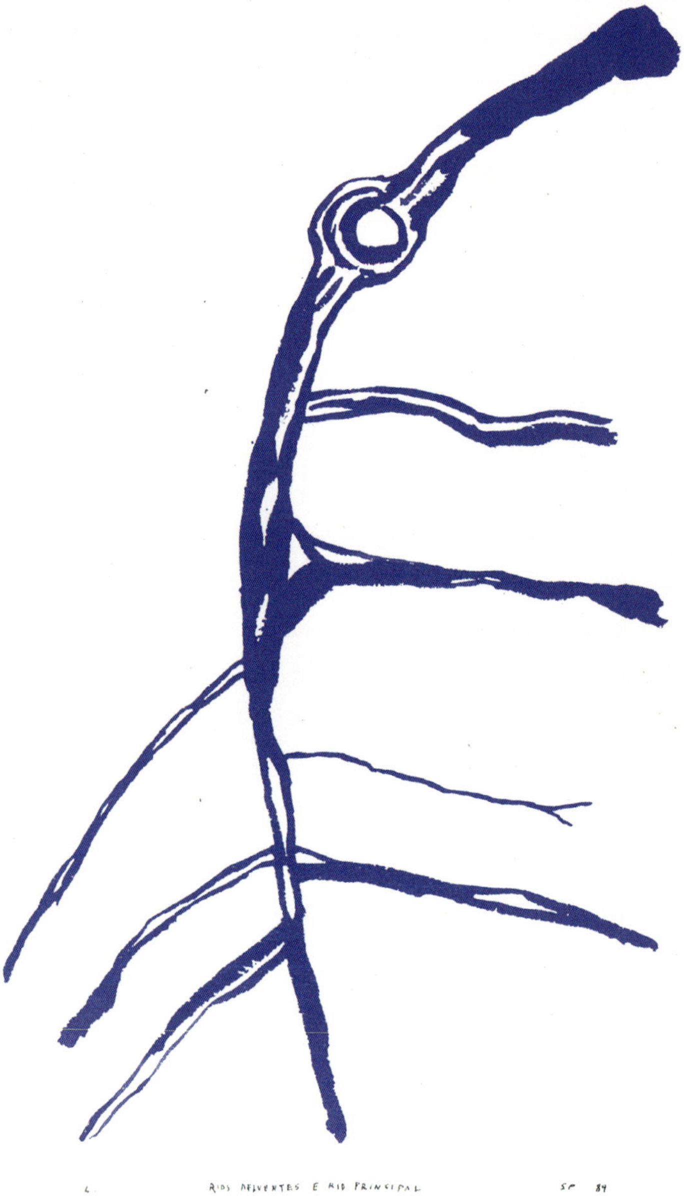

92. ***Rios afluentes e rio principal***
[Affluent Rivers and Main River], 1989

Watercolor and China ink on paper
41 × 31 cm
Museu de Arte Moderna
do Rio de Janeiro, sponsor
White Martins, Brazil
PL.1469.0/00

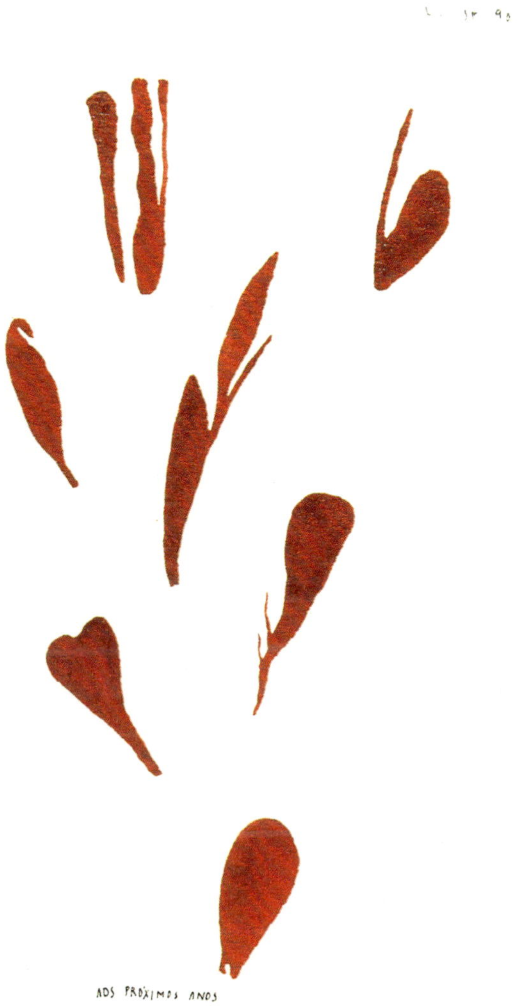

93. ***Aos próximos anos***
[To the Coming Years], 1990

Watercolor on paper
31 × 23 cm
Museu de Arte Moderna
do Rio de Janeiro, sponsor
White Martins, Brazil
PL.1471.0/00

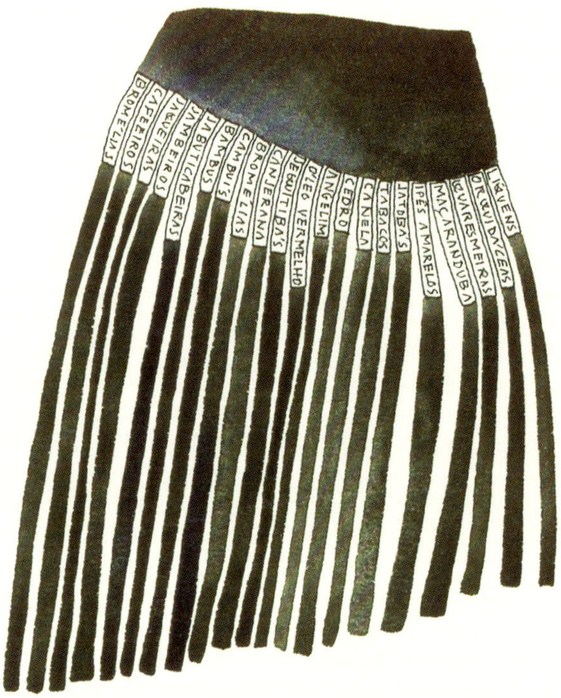

95. ***Sem título n° 4***
[Untitled #4], 1990

Watercolor and China ink on paper
31 × 23 cm
Museu de Arte Moderna
do Rio de Janeiro, sponsor
White Martins, Brazil
PL.1876.0/00

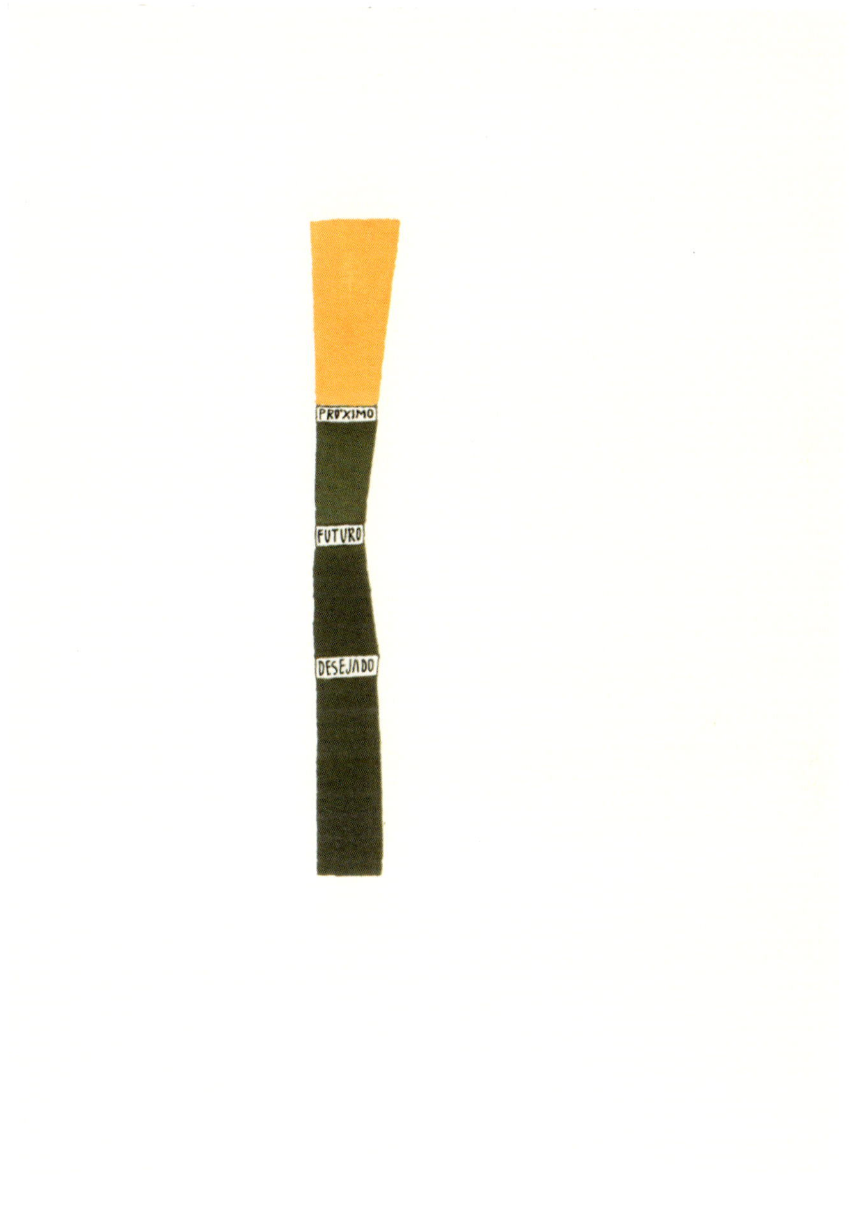

94. ***Próximo futuro desejado***
[Coming Desired Future],
circa 1990

Watercolor and China ink on paper
31 × 23 cm
Museu de Arte Moderna
do Rio de Janeiro, sponsor
White Martins, Brazil
PL.1878.0/00

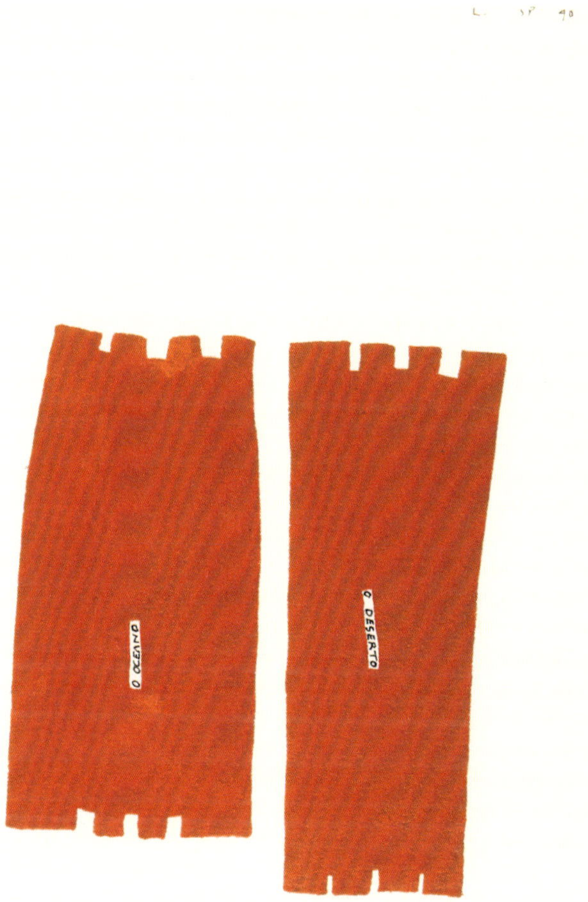

96. ***O oceano, o deserto***
[The Ocean, the Desert], 1990

Watercolor and China ink on paper
31 × 23 cm
Museu de Arte Moderna
do Rio de Janeiro, sponsor
White Martins, Brazil
PL.1879.0/00

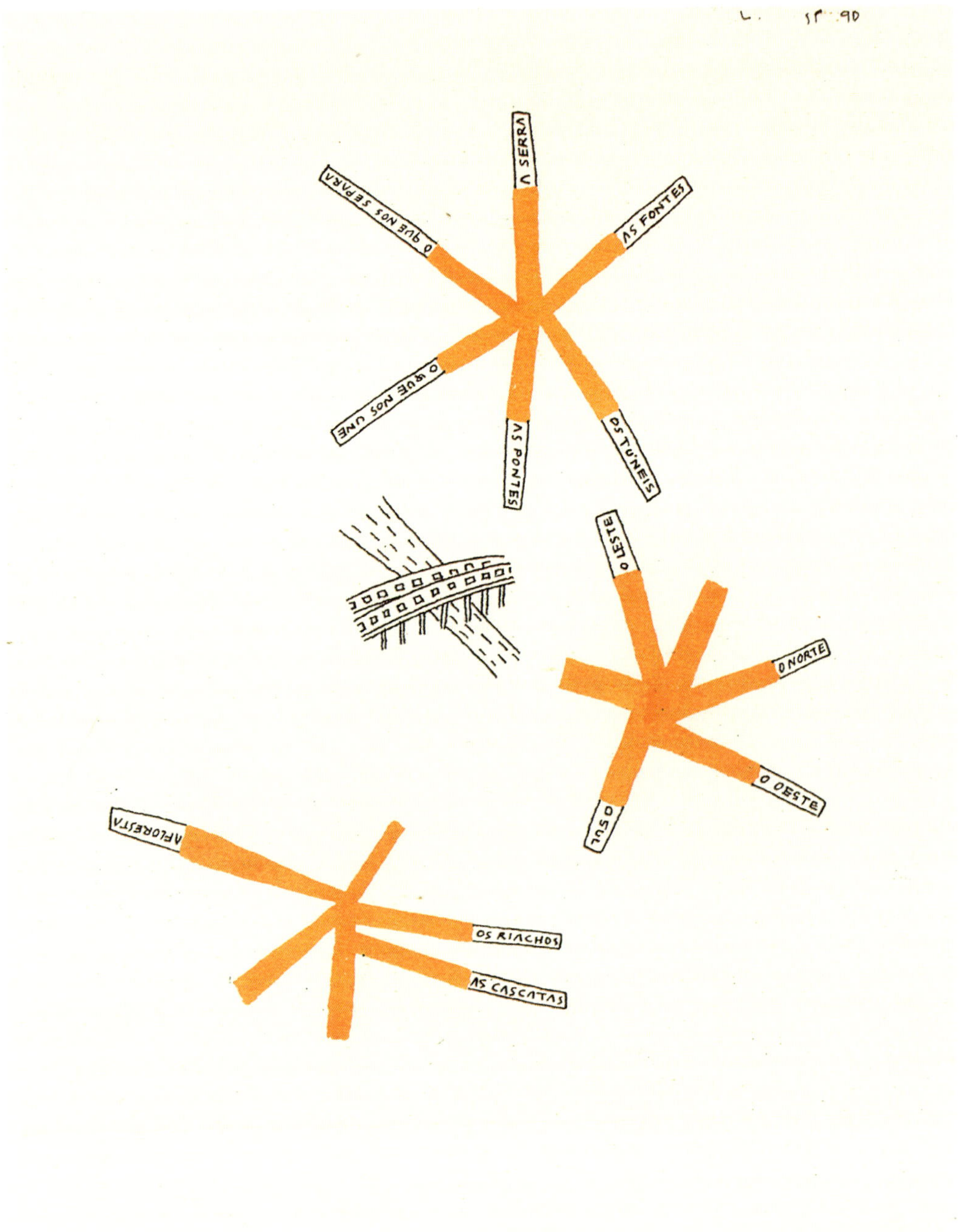

97. ***O que nos une, o que nos separa*** [What Unites Us, What Separates Us], 1990

China ink and watercolor on paper
31 × 23 cm
Museu de Arte Moderna do Rio de Janeiro, sponsor White Martins, Brazil
PL.1877.0/00

98. ***Os olhos atentos***
[The Wary Eyes], *circa* 1990

Watercolor and China ink on paper
31 × 23 cm
Museu de Arte Moderna
do Rio de Janeiro, sponsor
White Martins, Brazil
PL.1468.0/00

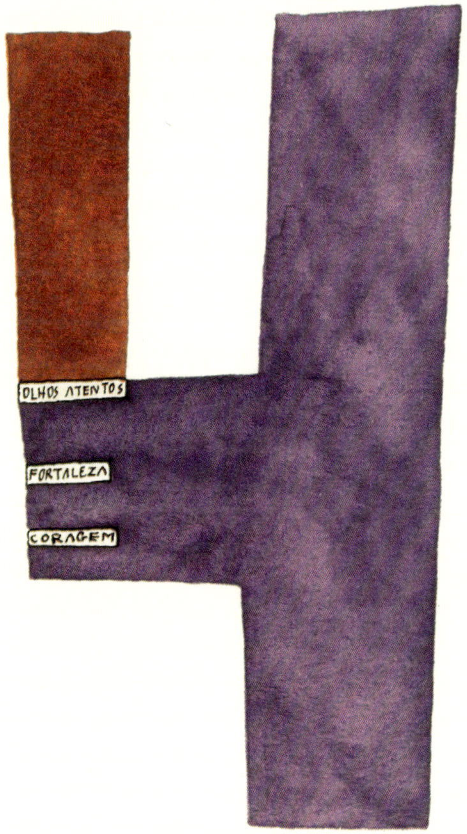

1990

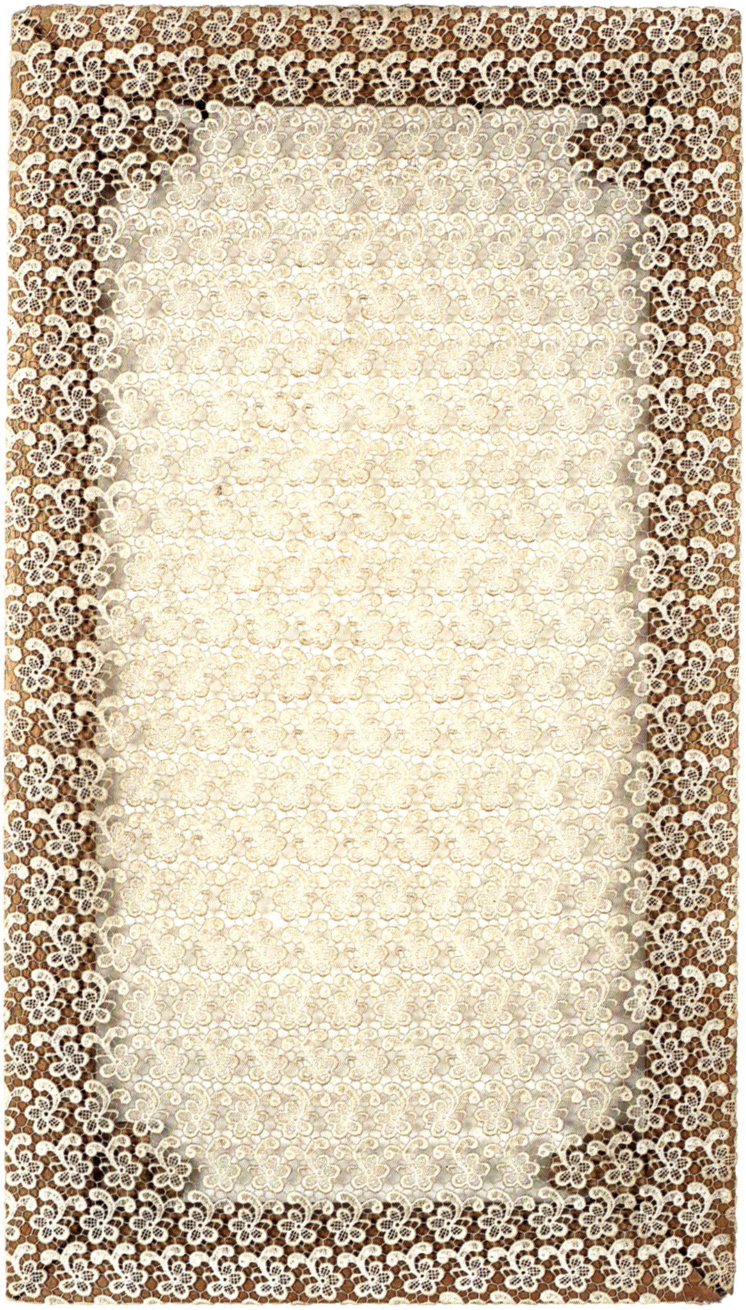

99. ***O singelo***
[The Plain One], *circa* 1990

Guipure lace canvas
70 × 40 cm
Private collection,
São Paulo, Brazil
PL.1132.0/00

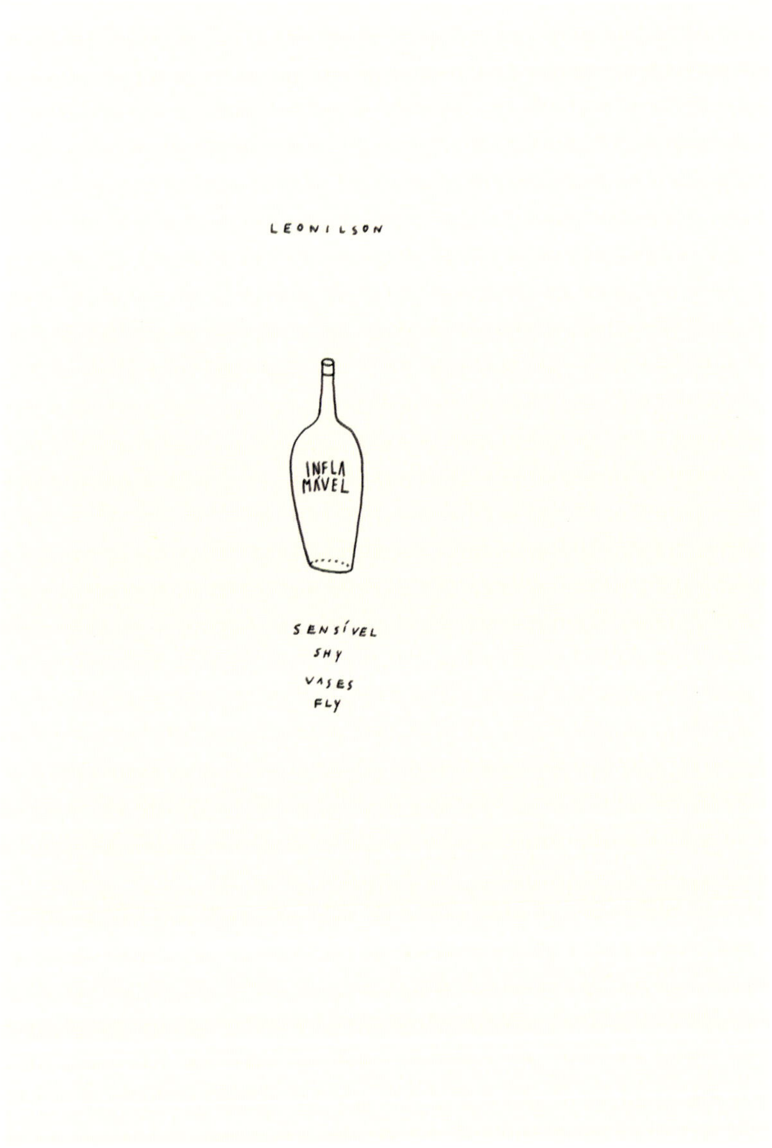

100. ***[Inflamável]***
[Inflammable], *circa* 1990

Permanent ink on paper
48 × 33 cm
Private collection,
São Paulo, Brazil
PL.0387.0/00

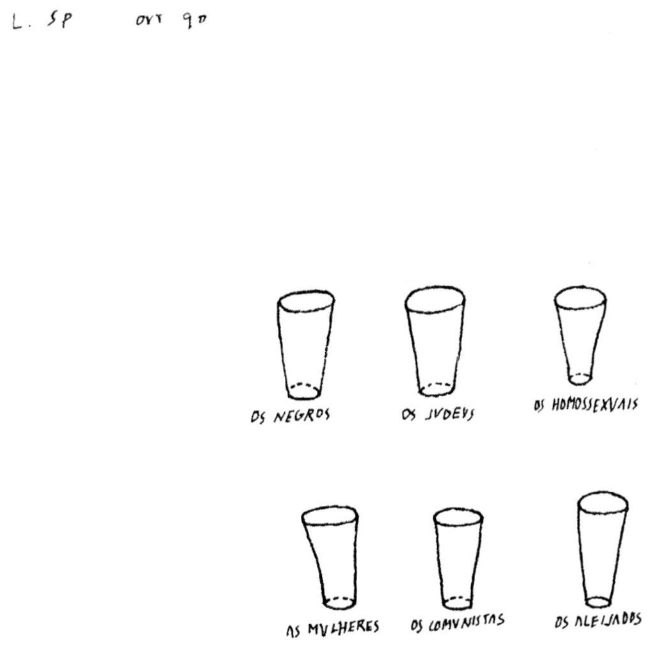

101. ***[Os negros; os judeus; os homossexuais; as mulheres; os comunistas; os aleijados]***
[The Blacks; The Jews; The Homosexuals; The Women; The Communists; The Crippled], 1990

Permanent ink on paper
30 × 22 cm
Collection of Luisa Malzoni Strina,
São Paulo, Brazil
PL.1139.0/00

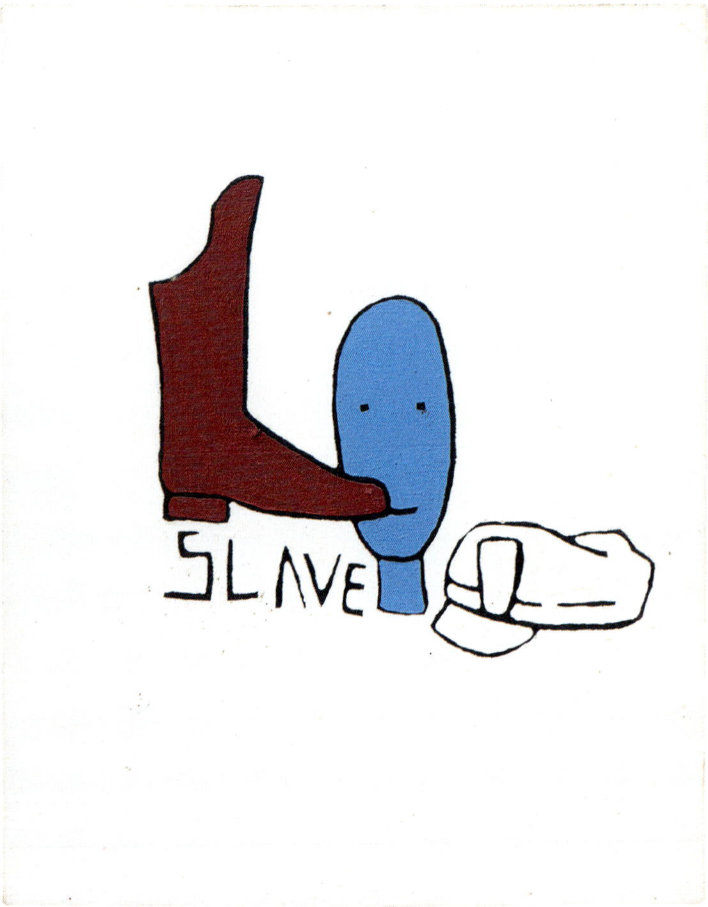

102. *[Slave]*, *circa* 1990

Acrylic paint on canvas
41 × 33 cm
Collection of Eduardo Brandão
and Jan Fjeld, São Paulo, Brazil
PL.0806.0/00

103. ***O q. você desejar, o q. você quiser, eu estou pronto para servi-lo*** [Whatever You Desire, Whatever You Want, I Am Ready to Serve You], 1990

Thread on voile and copper hanger
136 × 51 × 10 cm
Collection of Susana and Ricardo Steinbruch,
São Paulo, Brazil
PL.1000.0/00

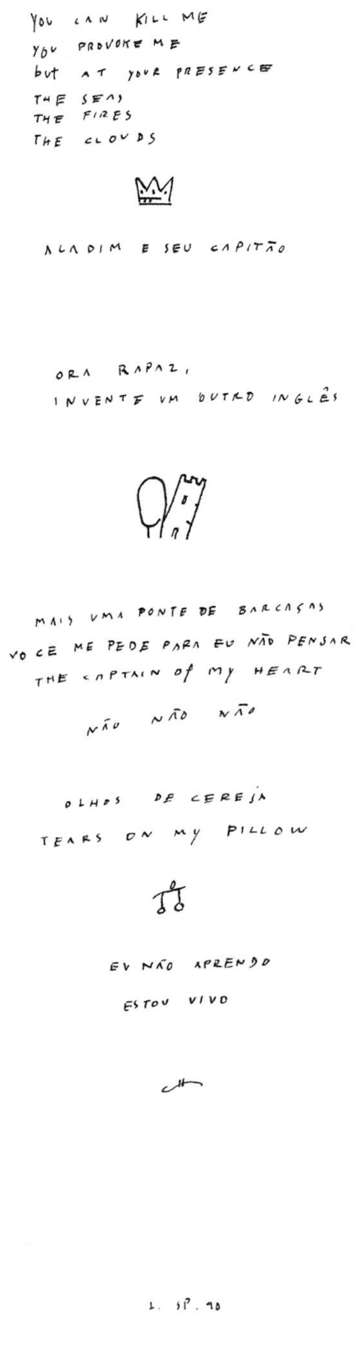

105. ***[Aladim e seu capitão]***
[Aladdin and His Captain], 1990

Permanent ink on paper
32 × 24 cm
Collection of Paulo A. W. Vieira,
Rio de Janeiro, Brazil
PL.1480.0/00

104. ***[Morro pela boca; vivo pelos olhos]***
[I Die Through My Mouth; I Live Through My Eyes], 1990

Permanent ink on paper
32 × 24 cm
Collection of Paulo A. W. Vieira,
Rio de Janeiro, Brazil
PL.1481.0/00

107. *[O ouro do artista]*
[The Artist's Gold], 1990

Permanent ink on paper
32 × 24 cm
Collection of Paulo A. W. Vieira,
Rio de Janeiro, Brazil
PL.1482.0/00

106. *[O músico]* [The Musician], 1990

Permanent ink on paper
32 × 24 cm
Collection of Paulo A. W. Vieira,
Rio de Janeiro, Brazil
PL.1479.0/00

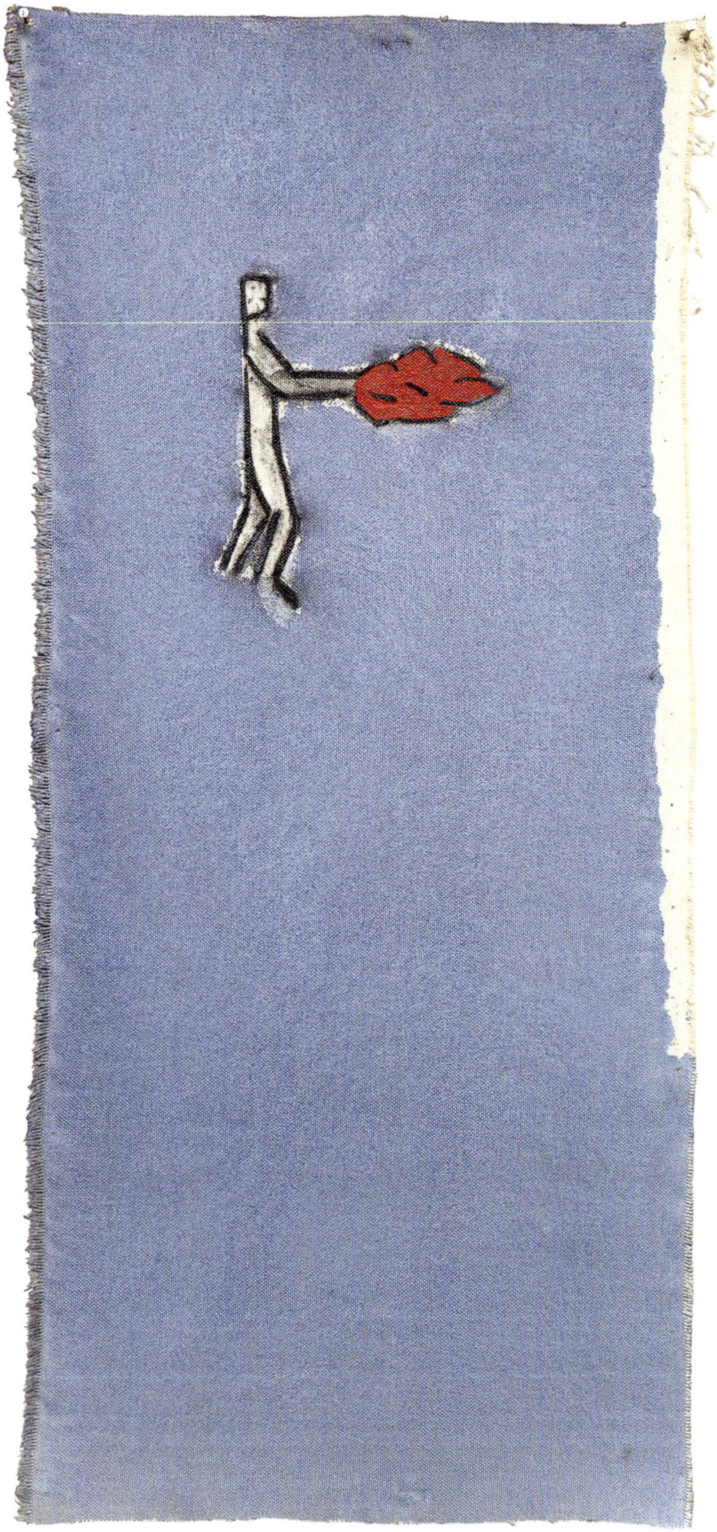

108. ***Homem c/ fogo nas mãos***
[Man With Fire on His Hand], *circa* 1990

Acrylic paint on unstretched canvas
61 × 29 cm
Collection of Eduardo Brandão
and Jan Fjeld, São Paulo, Brazil
PL.0813.0/00

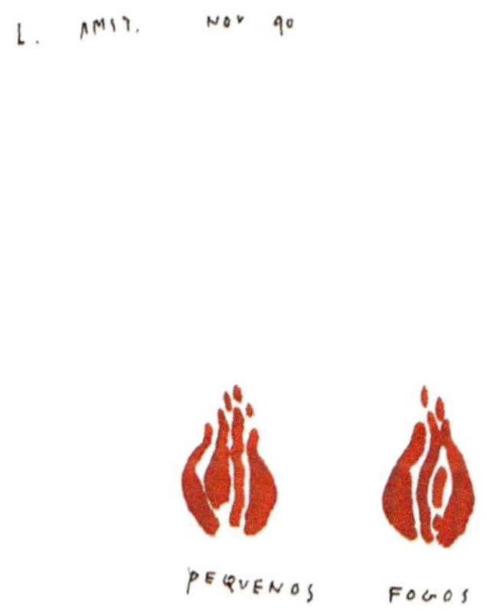

109. ***Pequenos fogos***
[Small Fires], 1990

Watercolor on paper
21 × 13.5 cm
Private collection,
Lisbon, Portugal
PL.1115.0/00

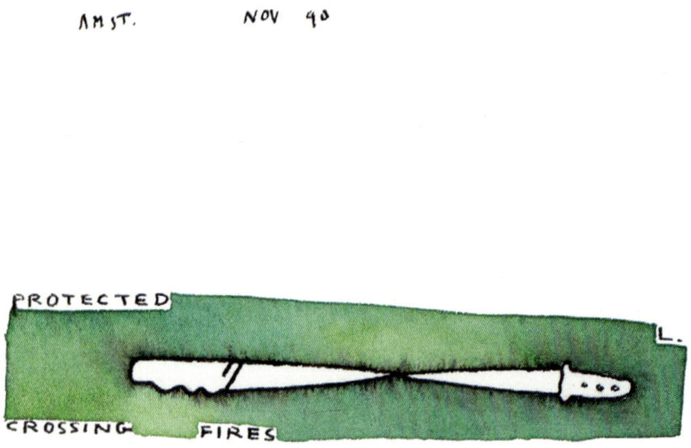

110. ***Protected, Crossing Fires*****,** 1990

Watercolor and
permanent ink on paper
22 × 14.5 cm
Museu de Arte Moderna de São Paulo,
gift Carmem Bezerra Dias and
Theodorino Torquato Dias, 1997,
Brazil
PL.1039.0/00

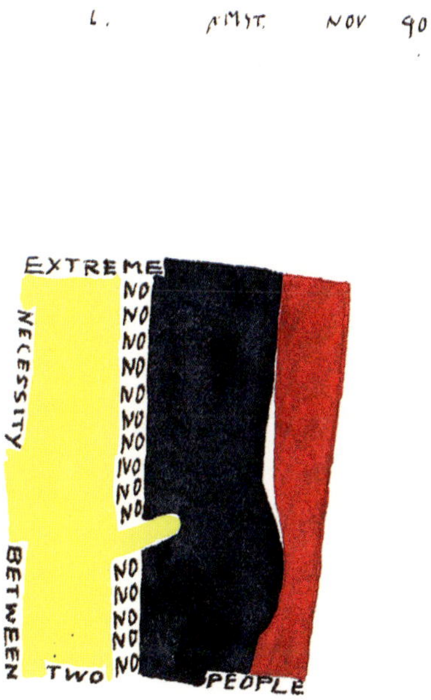

111. ***Extreme Necessity Between Two People*****,** 1990

Watercolor on paper
21 × 13.5 cm
Private collection,
Chicago, United States
PL.0038.0/00

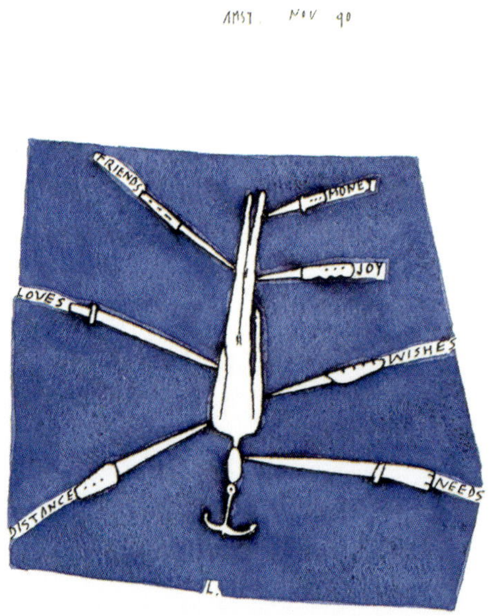

112. ***[Distance Needs]***, 1990

Ink and watercolor on paper
21 × 13.5 cm
Los Angeles County Museum of
Art, gift Gary and Tracy Mezzatesta,
2001, United States
PL.1525.0/00

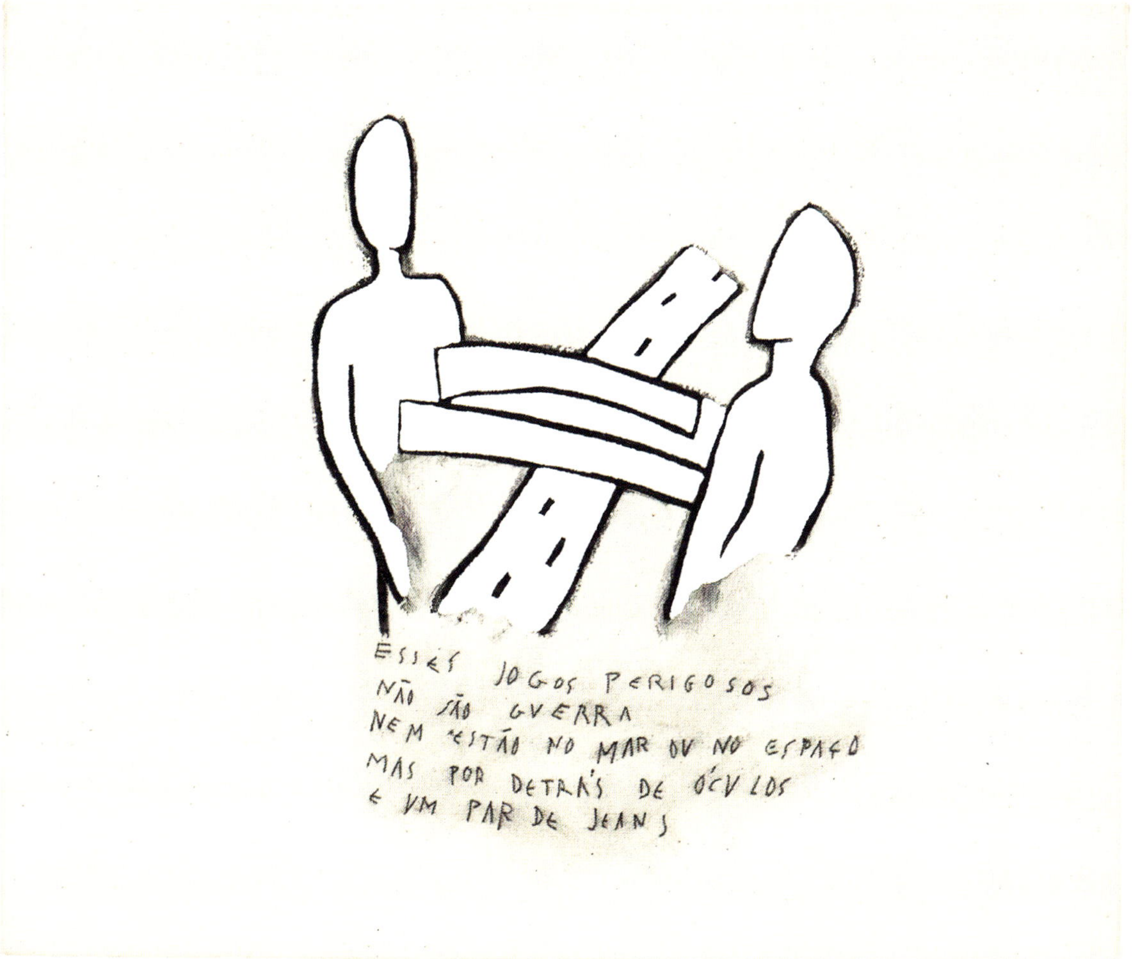

113. ***[Jogos perigosos]***
[Dangerous Games],
circa 1990

Acrylic paint on canvas
50 × 60 cm
Collection of Luisa Malzoni Strina,
São Paulo, Brazil
PL.1193.0/00

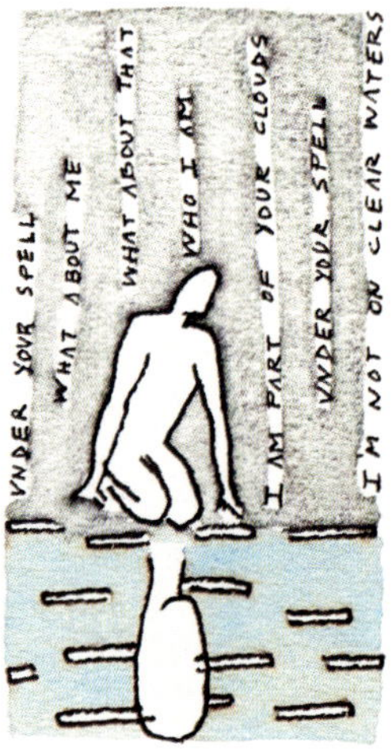

114. ***Under Your Spell I'm Not on Clear Waters*****,** 1990

Permanent ink and
watercolor on paper
30.5 × 23 cm
Collection of Cristina Secaf Rebello,
São Paulo, Brazil
PL.0784.0/00

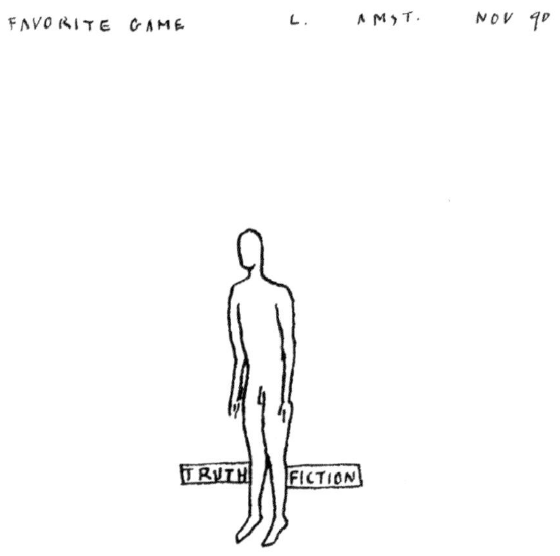

115. ***Favorite Game***, 1990

Permanent ink on paper
21 × 13.5 cm
Private collection,
São Paulo, Brazil
PL.0021.0/00

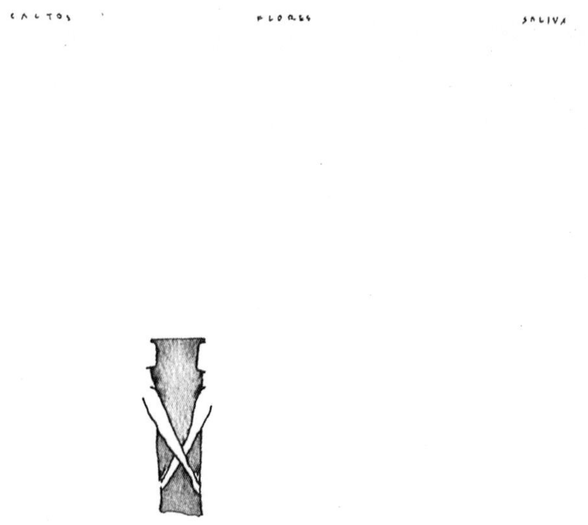

116. ***Masturbação mútua***
[Mutual Masturbation], 1990

Permanent ink and
watercolor on paper
30 × 23 cm
Museo de Arte Contemporáneo
de Castilla y León,
MUSAC collection, Spain
PL.1286.0/00

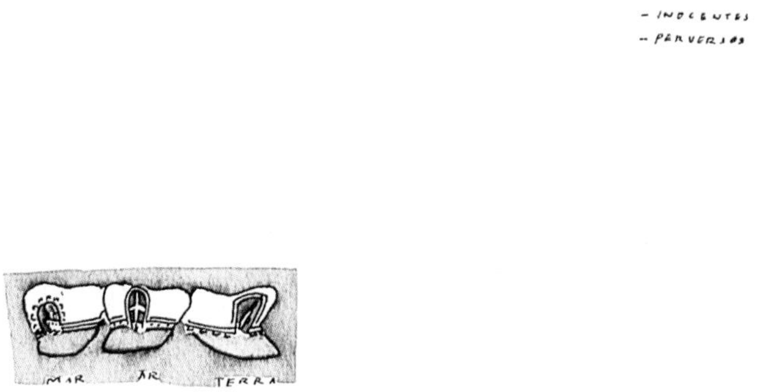

118. ***Fantasia — mar, ar, terra***
[Fantasy—Ocean, Air, Earth], 1990

Permanent ink and watercolor on paper
30 × 23 cm
Museo de Arte Contemporáneo
de Castilla y León,
MUSAC collection, Spain
PL.1288.0/00

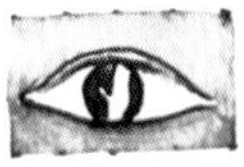

117. ***Voyerismo***
[Voyeurism], 1990

Permanent ink and
watercolor on paper
30 × 23 cm
Museo de Arte Contemporáneo
de Castilla y León,
MUSAC collection, Spain
PL.1287.0/00

119. ***Untitled***, 1990

Acrylic paint on canvas
70 × 65 cm
Banco Itaú collection,
São Paulo, Brazil
PL.0756.0/00

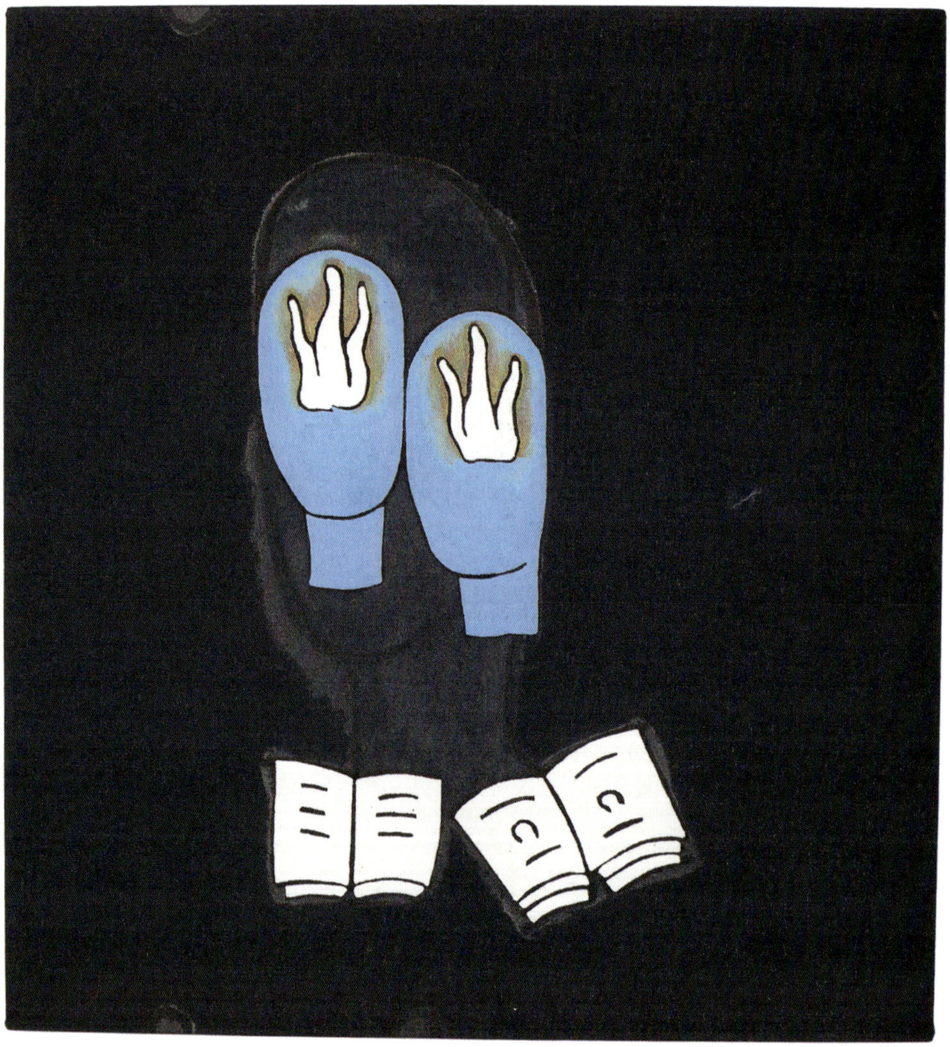

120. ***Untitled***, 1990

Acrylic paint on cotton fabric
140.5 × 75 cm
Collection of Rafael Moraes,
São Paulo, Brazil
PL.0716.0/00

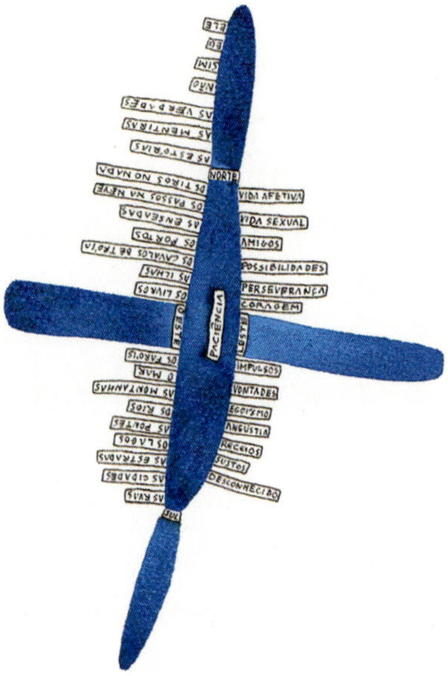

121. *[Paciência]*
[Patience], 1990

Watercolor and
permanent ink on paper
40.5 × 30.5 cm
Private collection,
São Paulo, Brazil
PL.1158.0/00

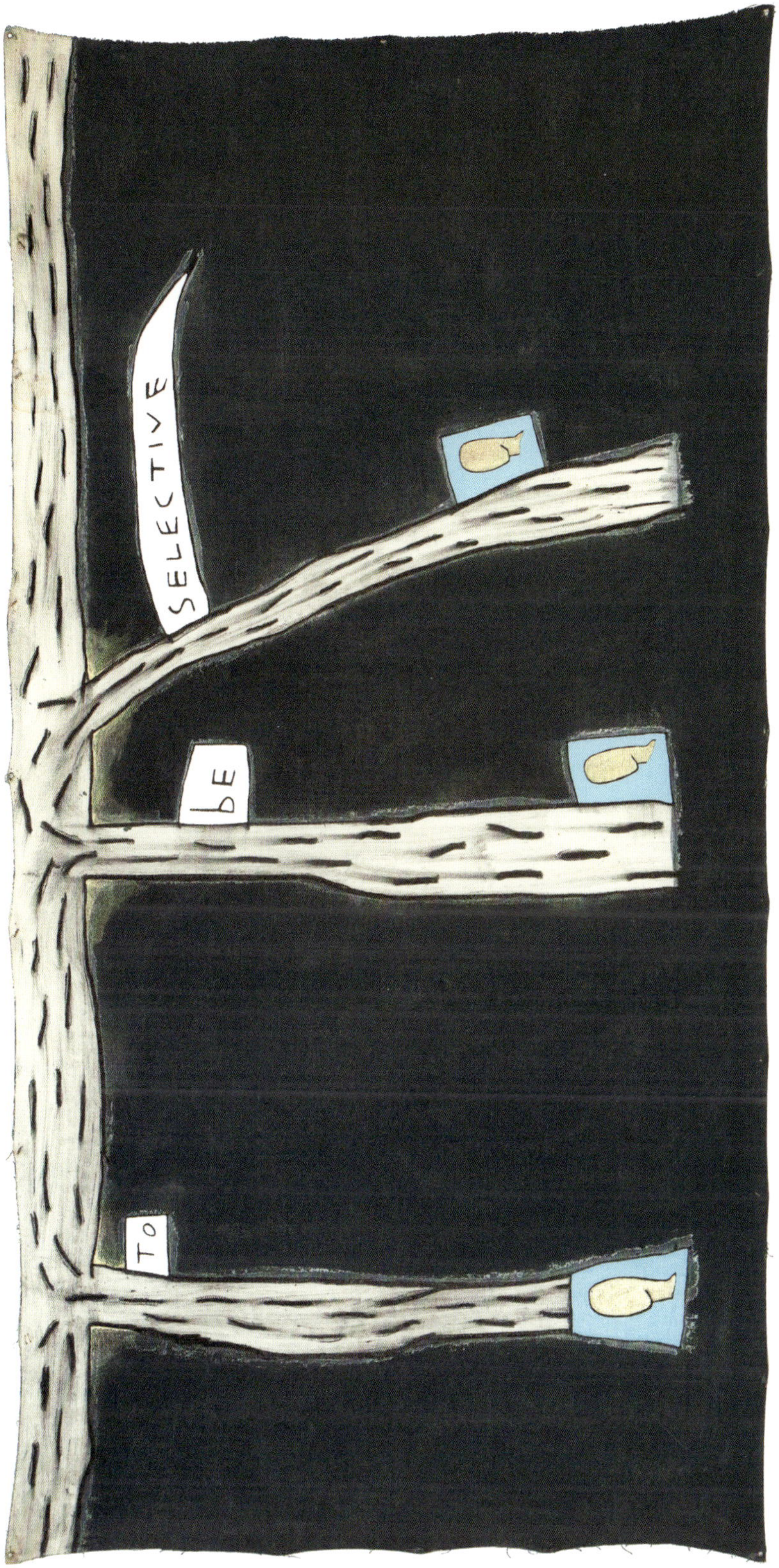

122. ***To Be Selective***, 1990

Acrylic paint, metallic paint and
colored pencil on unstretched canvas
203 × 105 cm
Collection of Luisa Malzoni Strina,
São Paulo, Brazil
PL.0647.0/00

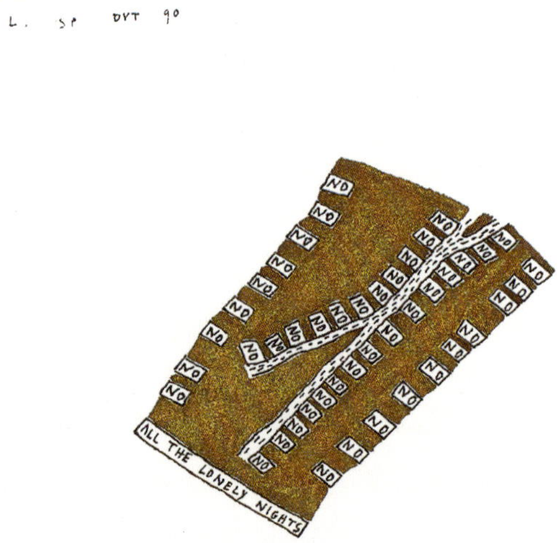

123. [*All the Lonely Nights*], 1990

Permanent ink and
metallic paint on paper
30.5 × 22.5 cm
Collection of Luisa Malzoni Strina,
São Paulo, Brazil
PL.1279.0/00

124. *[No Yes Please]*,
1990/91

Acrylic paint and
metallic paint on canvas
145 × 70 cm
Private collection,
São Paulo, Brazil
PL.0682.0/00

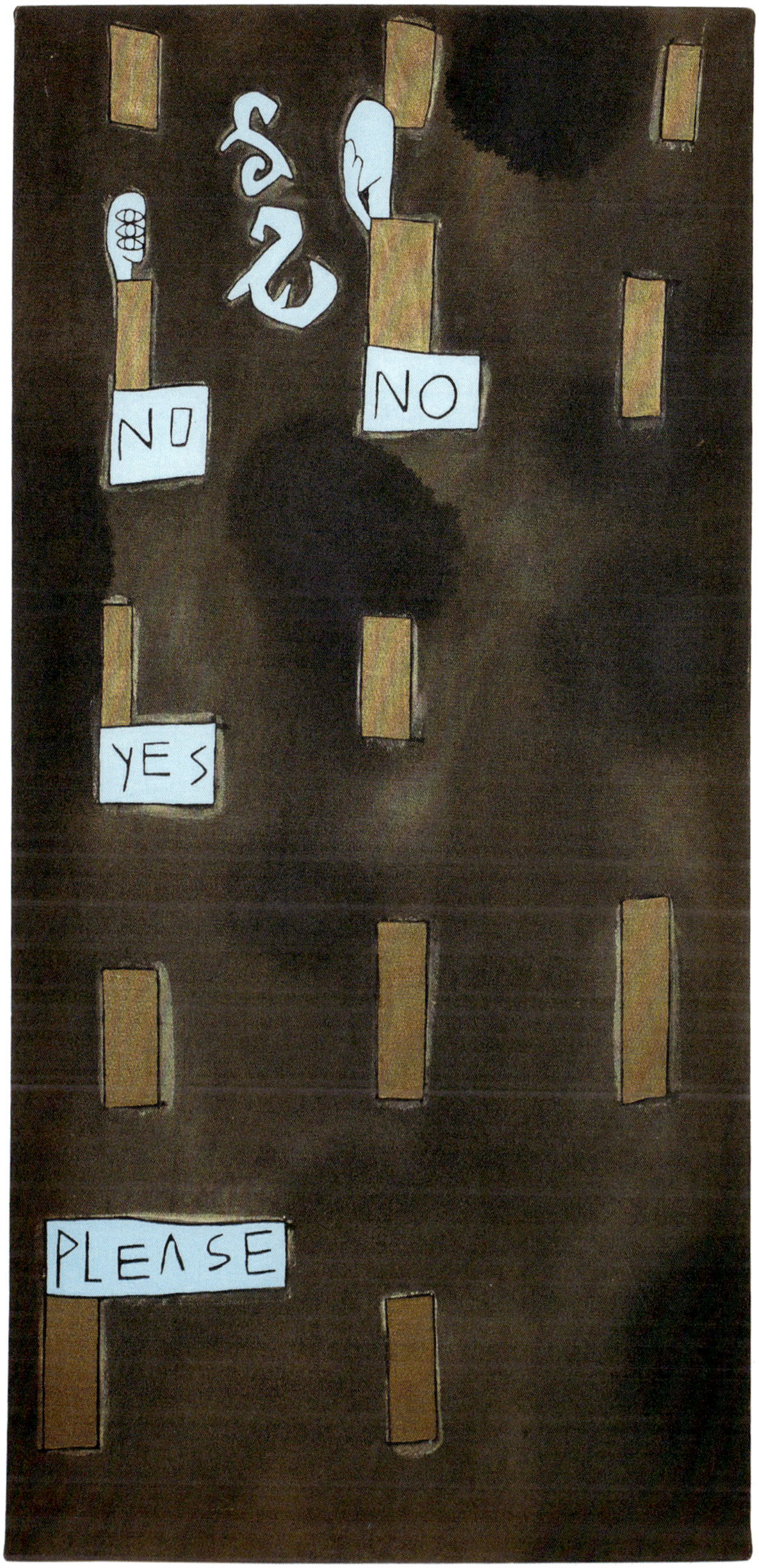

125. ***O dia do herói***
[The Day of the Hero], 1990

Thread on felt
104 × 156 cm
Collection of Susana
and Ricardo Steinbruch,
São Paulo, Brazil
PL.1189.0/00

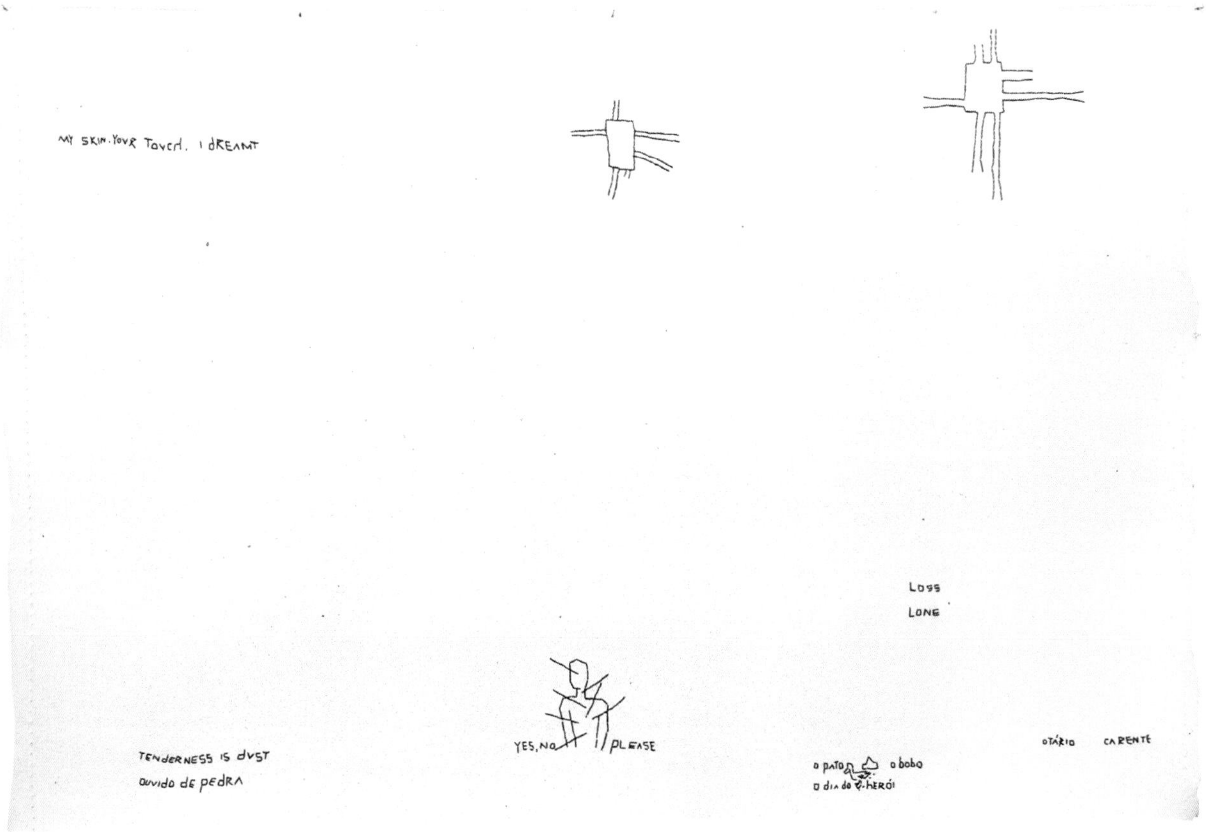
MY SKIN. YOUR TOUCH. I DREAMT
LOSS
LONE
TENDERNESS IS DUST
ouvido de PEDRA
YES, NO
PLEASE
o pato
o bobo
o dia do herói
OTÁRIO
CARENTE

171

126. ***[If You Dream With Clouds]***, **1990**

Permanent ink and gouache on papel
30 × 23.5 cm
Collection of Charlô Whately, São Paulo, Brazil
PL.1182.0/00

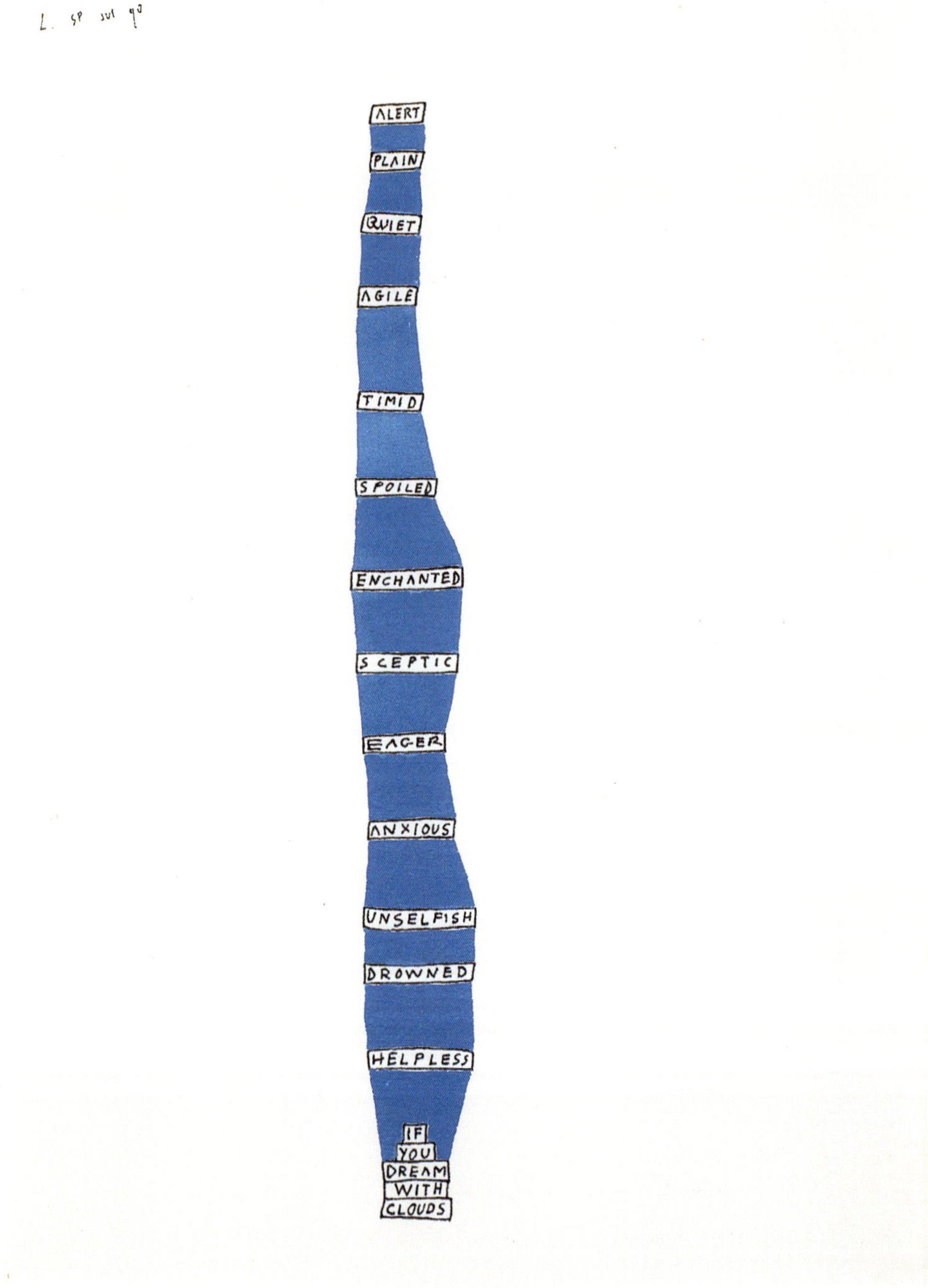

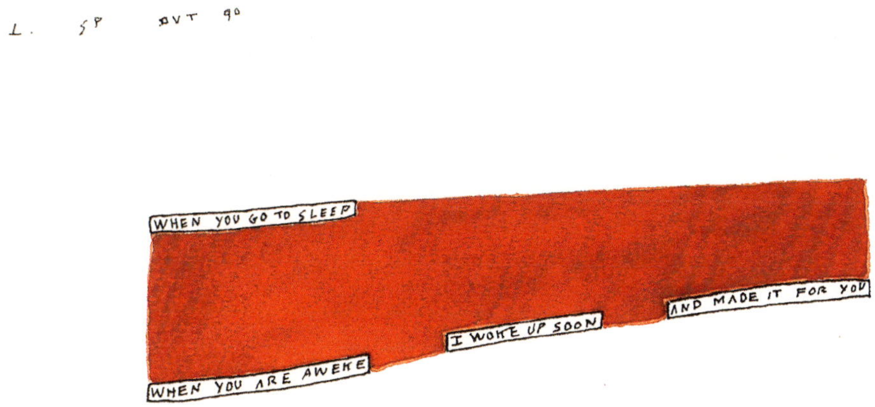

127. ***[When You Go to Sleep]***, 1990

Watercolor and permanent ink on paper
32 × 24 cm
Collection of Francisco Meirelles de Andrade,
São Paulo, Brazil
PL.1163.0/00

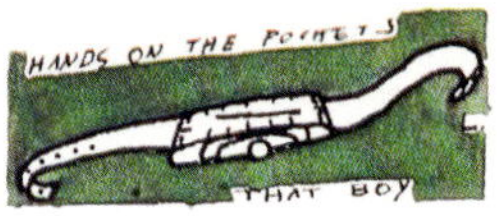

128. ***Hands on the Pockets, That Boy***, 1990

Permanent ink and
watercolor on paper
30 × 22.5 cm
Collection of Luisa Malzoni Strina,
São Paulo, Brazil
PL.0004.0/00

129. ***He Could Not Sleep Because of a Tel. Call***, 1990

Permanent ink and
watercolor on paper
32 × 24 cm
Collection of Paula Nazarian,
São Paulo, Brazil
PL.0330.0/00

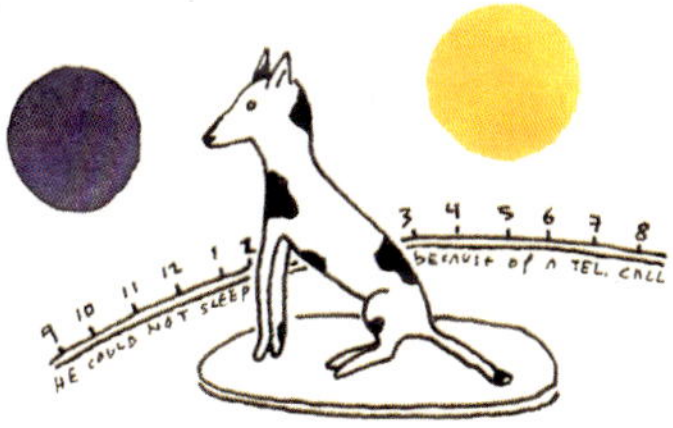

L. AMIT. 90

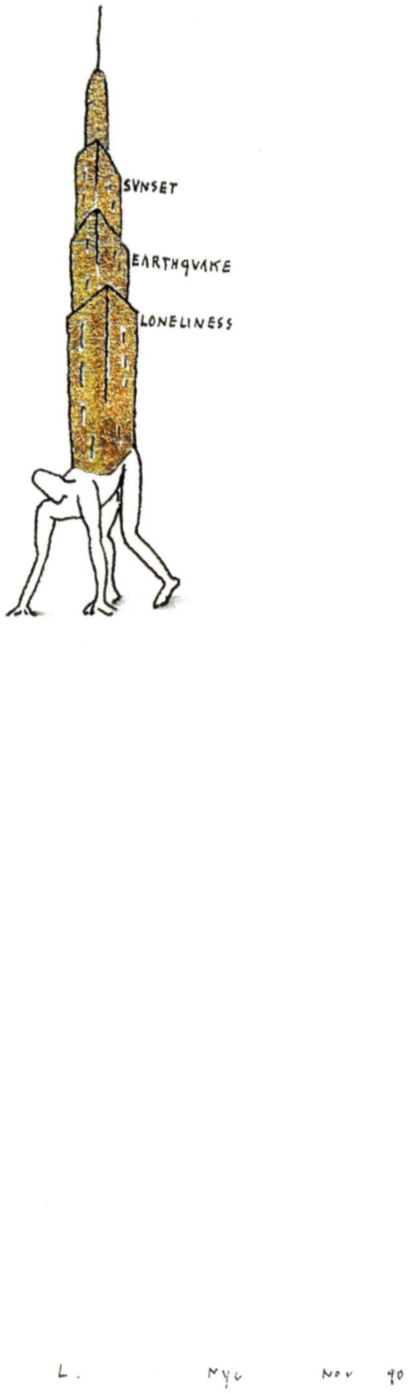

130. ***[Sunset; Earthquake; Loneliness]***, 1990

Permanent ink and
metallic paint on paper
30.5 × 23 cm
The Museum of Modern Art,
gift of família Bezerra Dias/
Projeto Leonilson, 1999,
New York, United States
PL.1532.0/00

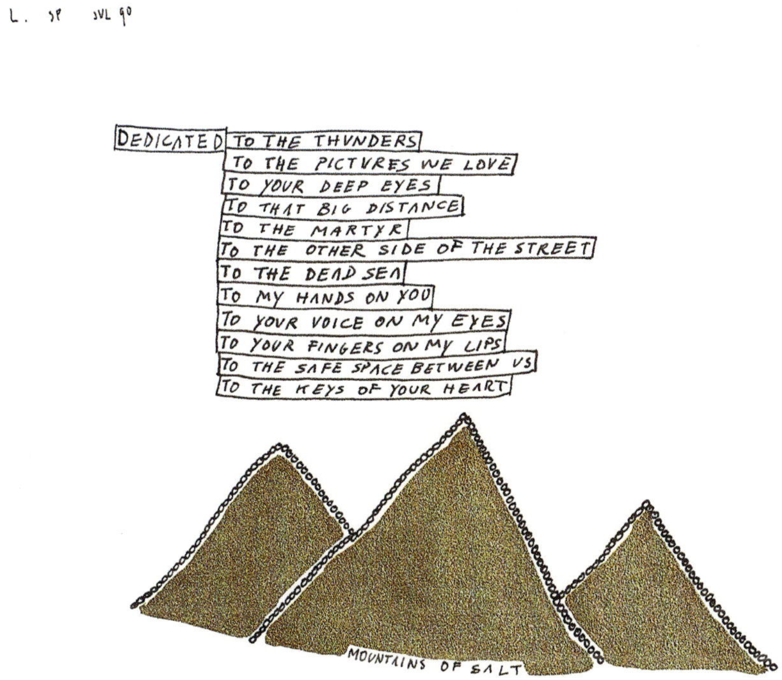

131. ***[Mountains of Salt]***, 1990

Permanent ink and
metallic paint on paper
25 × 20 cm
Private collection,
São Paulo, Brazil
PL.1245.0/00

132. ***[Mar do Japão]***
[Sea of Japan], 1990

Acrylic paint and
metallic paint on canvas
143 × 84 cm
Collection of Cristina Secaf Rebello,
São Paulo, Brazil
PL.0785.0/00

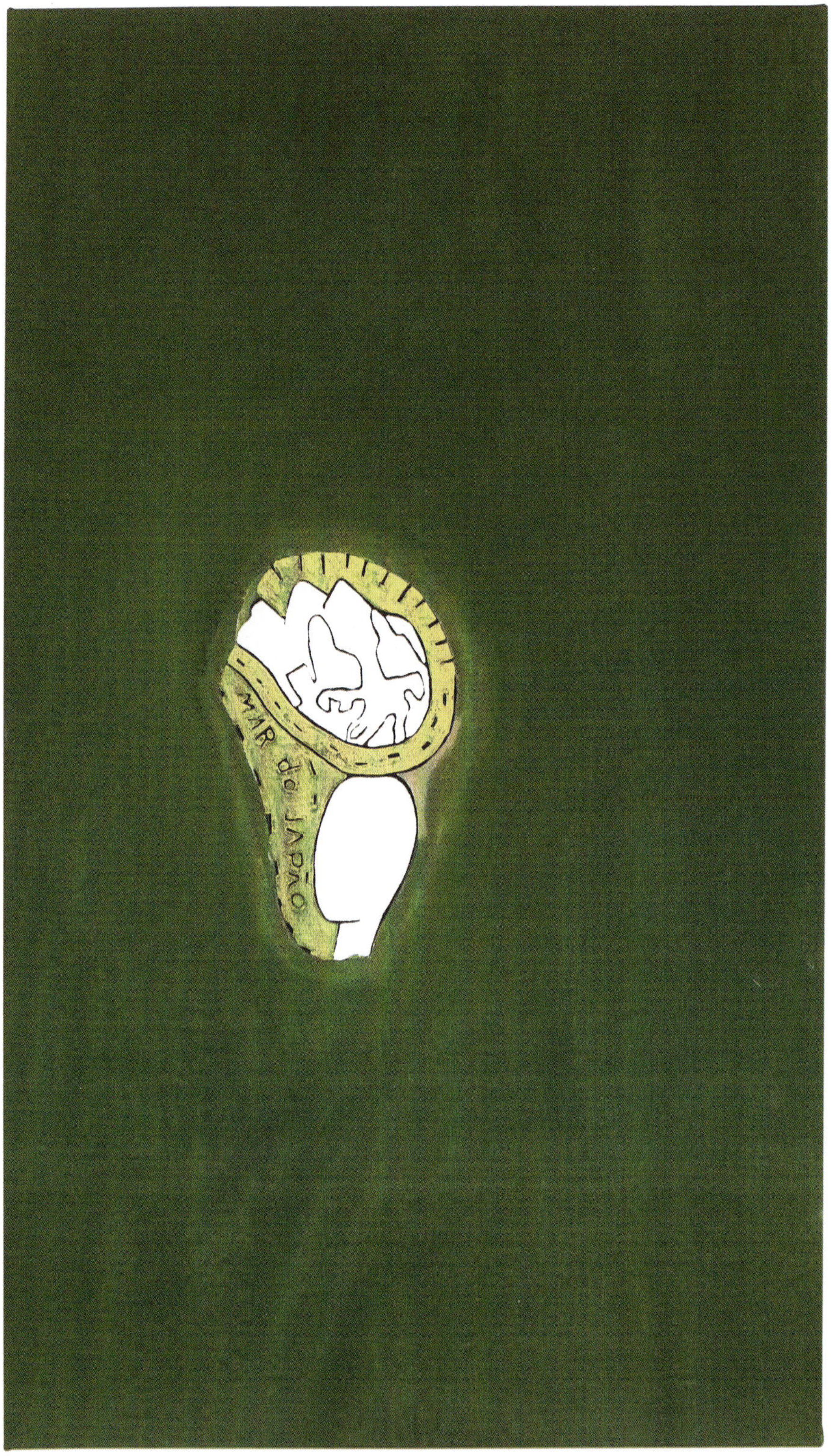

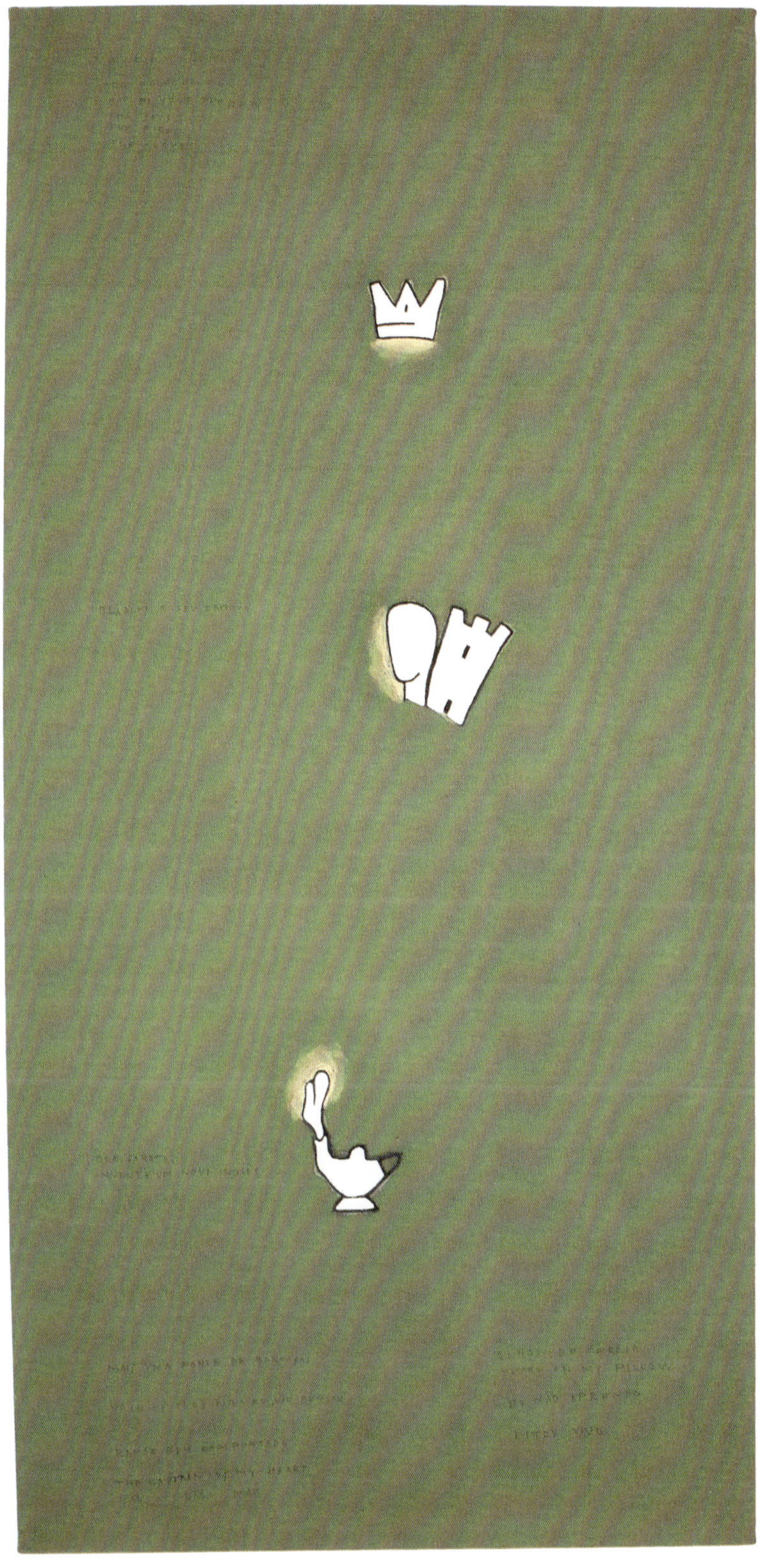

133. ***[Aladim e seu capitão]***
[Aladdin and His Captain],
circa 1990

Acrylic paint and
metallic paint on canvas
151 × 75 cm
Private collection,
São Paulo, Brazil
PL.0879.0/00

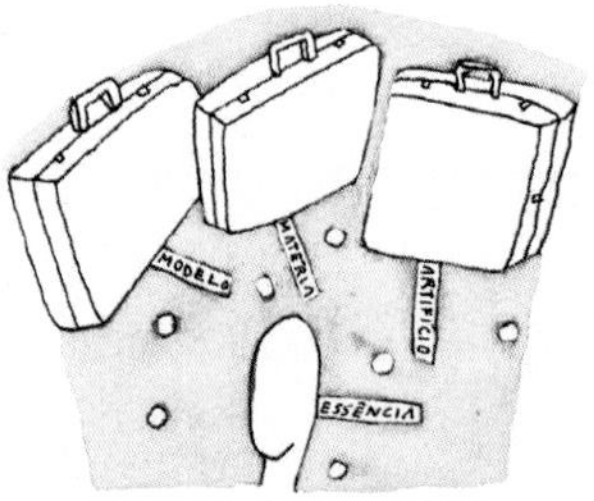

180

134. ***[Modelo; Matéria; Artifício; Essência]*** [Model; Matter; Artifice; Essence], 1990

Permanent ink on paper
31 × 41 cm
Collection of Luisa Malzoni Strina, São Paulo, Brazil
PL.1144.0/00

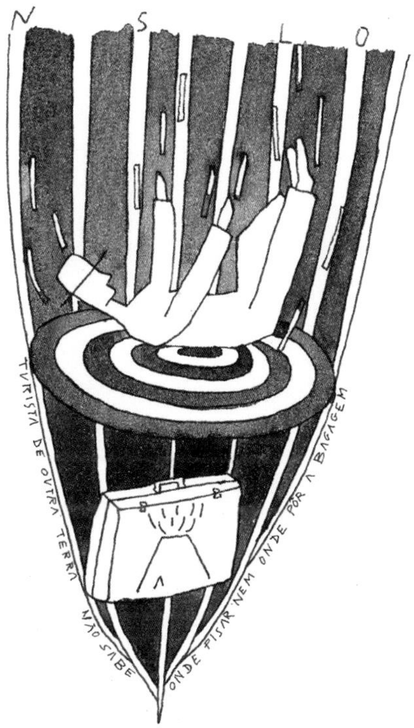

135. ***[Turista de outra terra]***
[Tourist From Another Land],
circa 1990

Permanent ink and
watercolor on paper
25.5 × 18 cm
Collection of Paulo A. W. Vieira,
Rio de Janeiro, Brazil
PL.1477.0/00

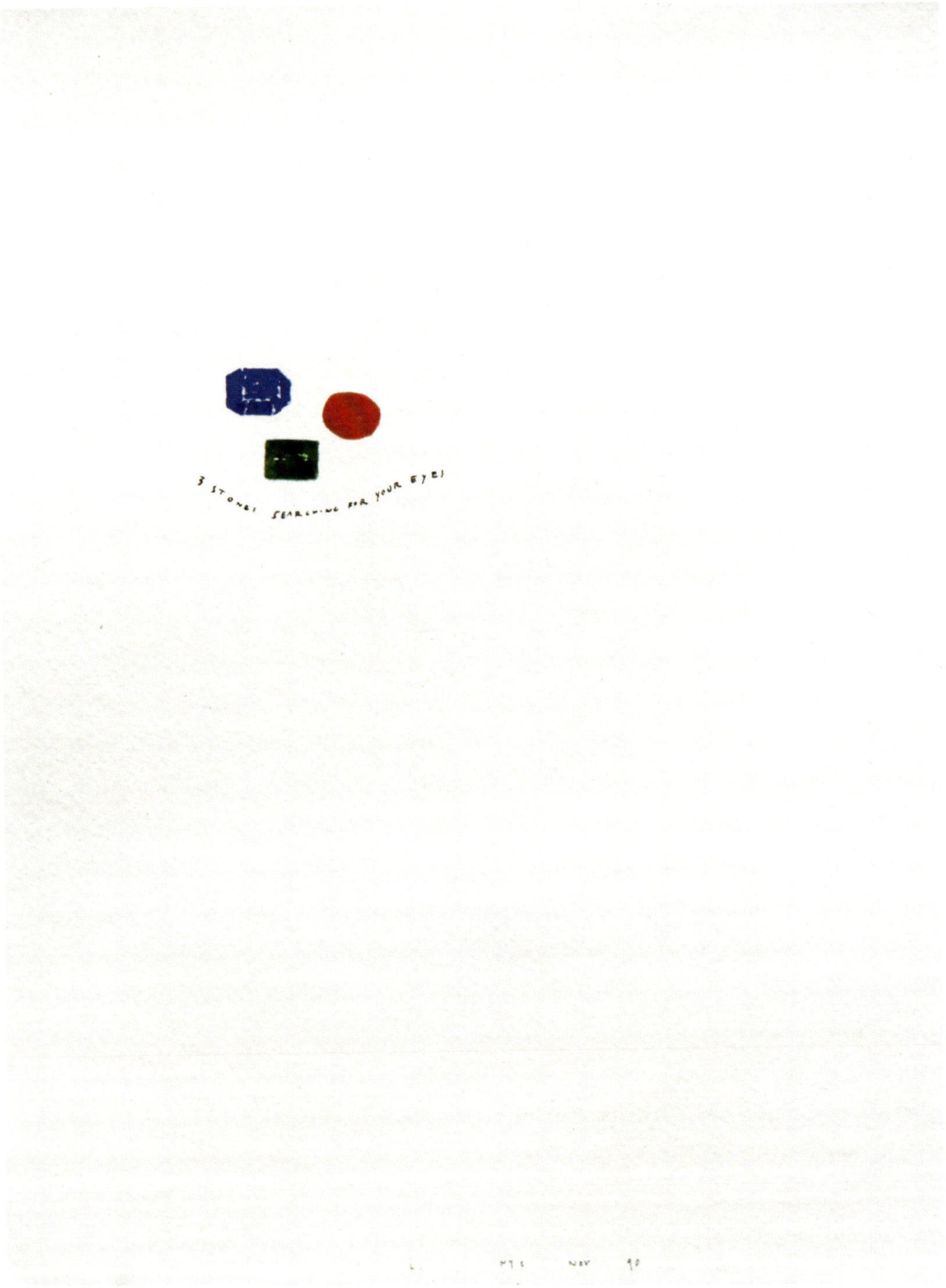

136. ***[3 Stones Searching for Your Eyes]***, 1990

Watercolor on paper
30.5 × 23 cm
Private collection,
Lisbon, Portugal
PL.0951.0/00

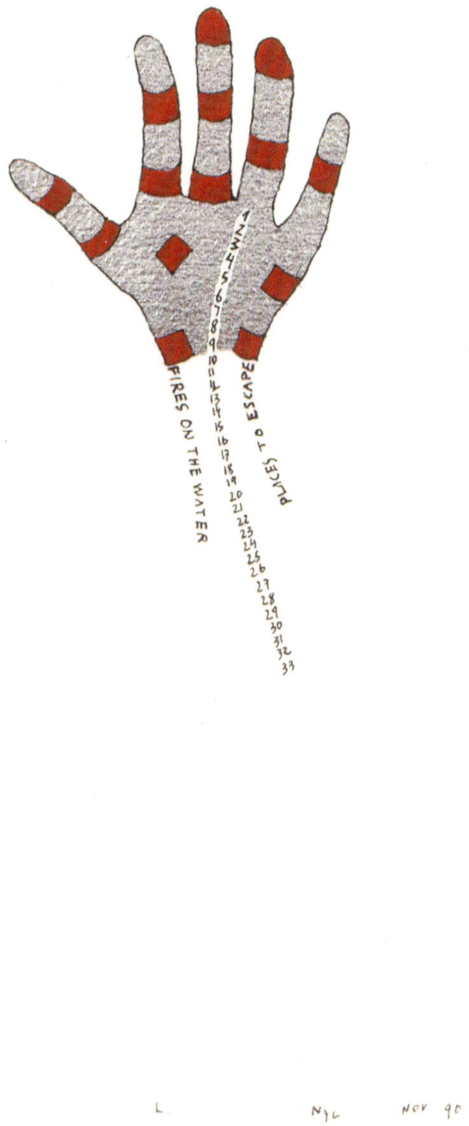

137. ***[Fire on the Water]***, 1990

Permanent ink, metallic paint,
and gouache on paper
30.5 × 23 cm
Private collection,
São Paulo, Brazil
PL.1565.0/00

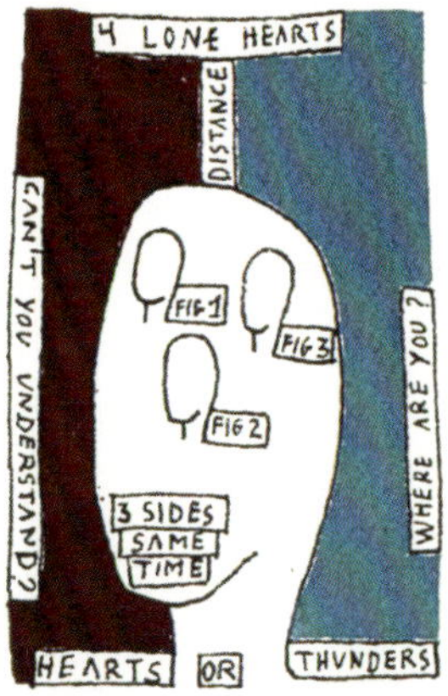

138. *[4 Lone Hearts]*, 1990

Permanent ink and
gouache on paper
32 × 24 cm
Private collection,
São Paulo, Brazil
PL.1188.0/00

139. ***[As oliveiras]***
[The Olive Trees], 1990

Watercolor, permanent ink,
and graphite on paper
27 × 21.5 × 3 cm
Museu de Arte Moderna de
São Paulo, gift Carmem Bezerra Dias
and Theodorino Torquato Dias, 1997,
Brazil
PL.1038.0/00

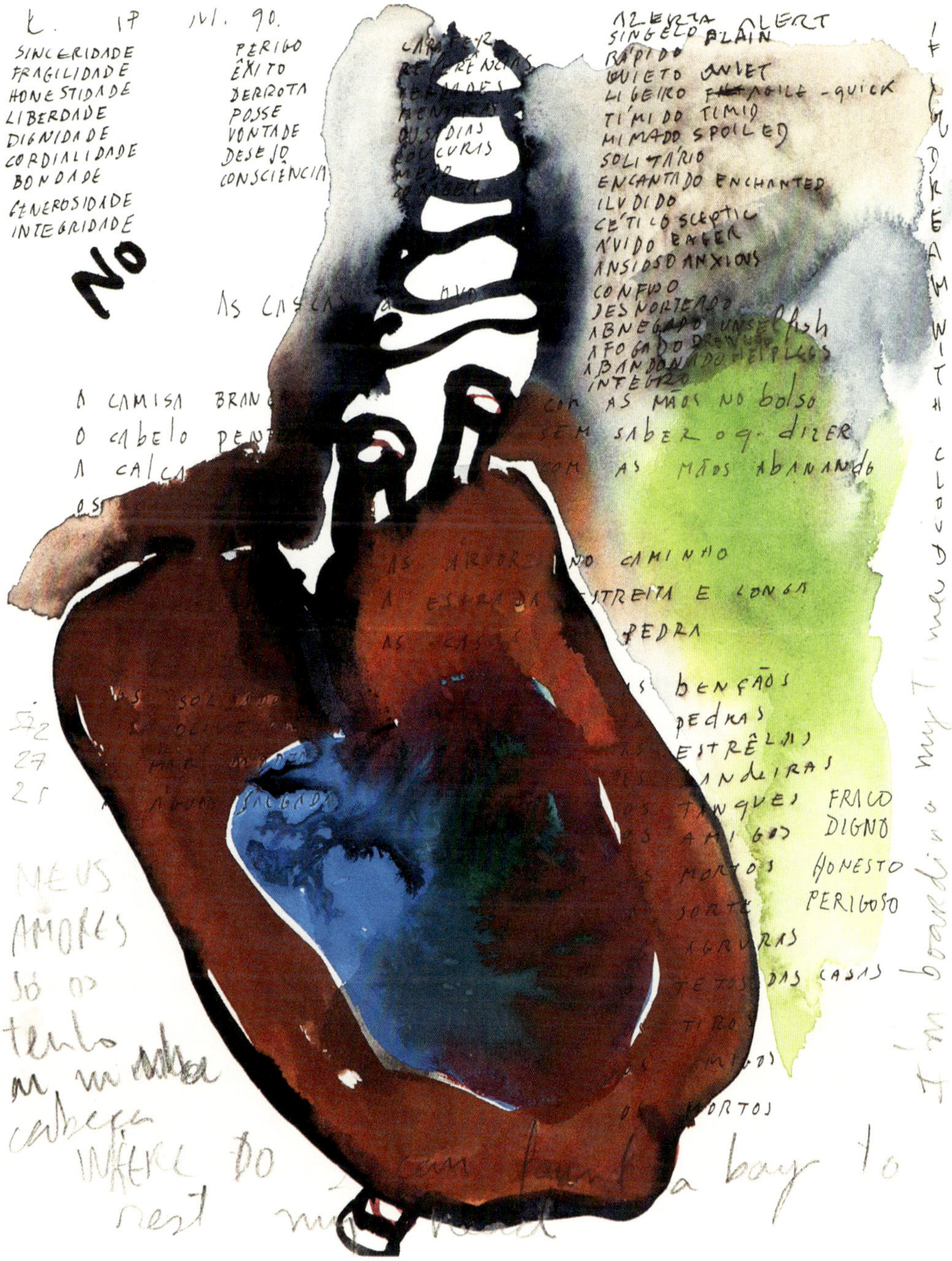

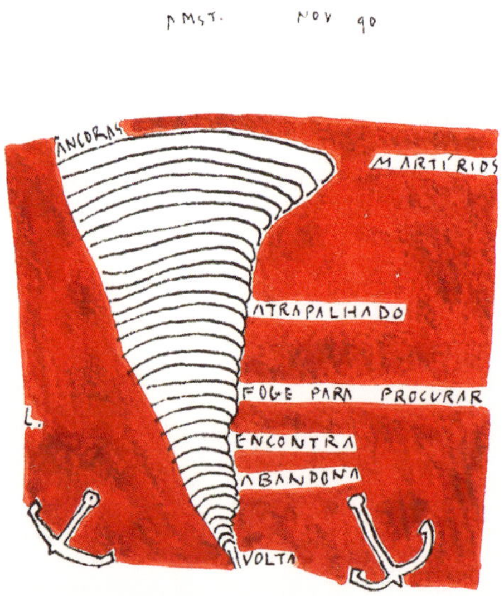

140. ***Foge para procurar***
[Runs Away to Find], 1990

Permanent ink and
watercolor on paper
21 × 13.5 cm
Collection of Ricardo Resende
and Jose Mauro Del Royo
Correa (*in memoriam*),
São Paulo, Brazil
PL.0882.0/00

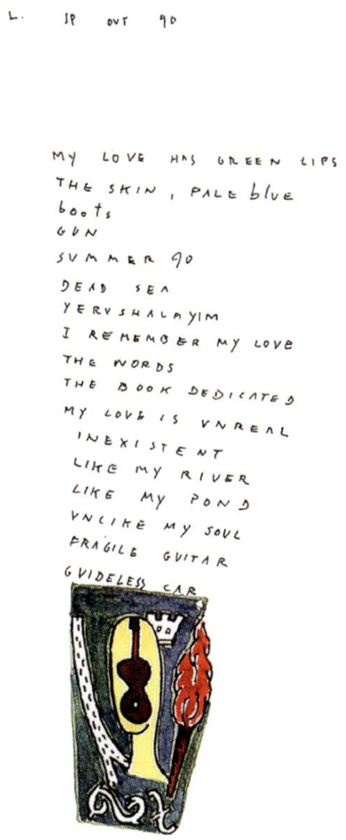

141. ***[My Love Has Green Lips]***, 1990

Permanent ink and
watercolor on paper
35 × 25 cm
Collection of Charlô Whately,
São Paulo, Brazil
PL.1168.0/00

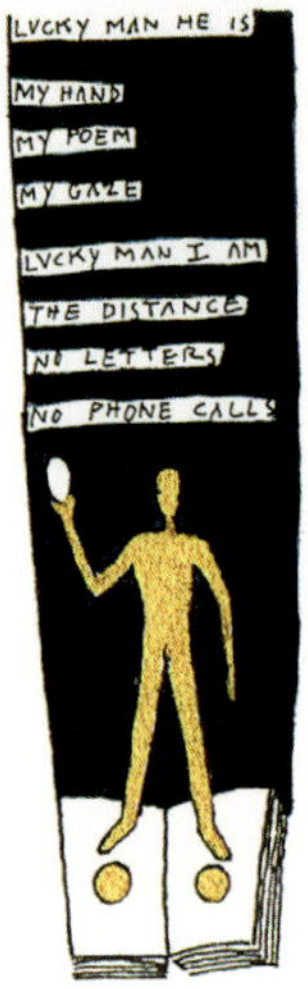

142. *[Lucky Man He Is]*, 1990

Permanent ink, China ink,
and metallic paint on paper
35 × 25 cm
Private collection,
São Paulo, Brazil
PL.1180.0/00

L. 28 jul. 90

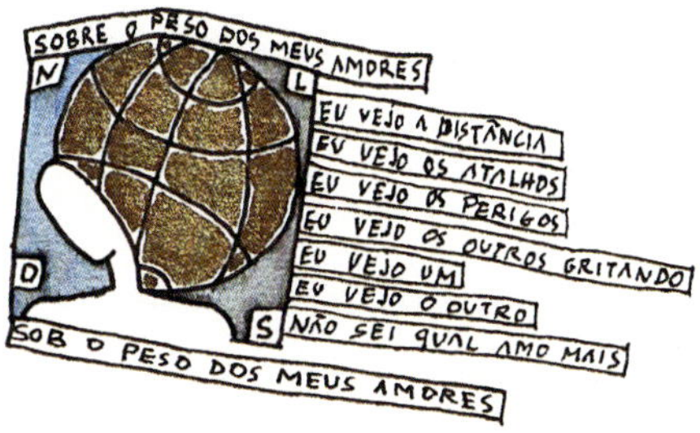

143. *[Sob o peso dos meus amores]* [Under the Weight of My Loves], 1990

Permanent ink, metallic paint, and watercolor on paper
29 × 21 cm
Private collection,
São Paulo, Brazil
PL.0982.0/00

144. ***Untitled (Zoo)***, 1990

Ink and watercolor on paper
30.5 × 23 cm
Los Angeles County Museum of Art,
gift Gary and Tracy Mezzatesta,
United States
PL.1524.0/00

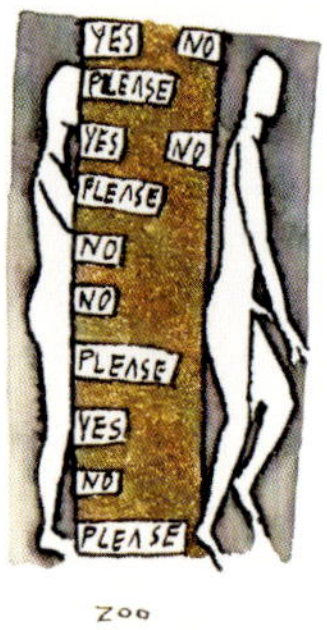

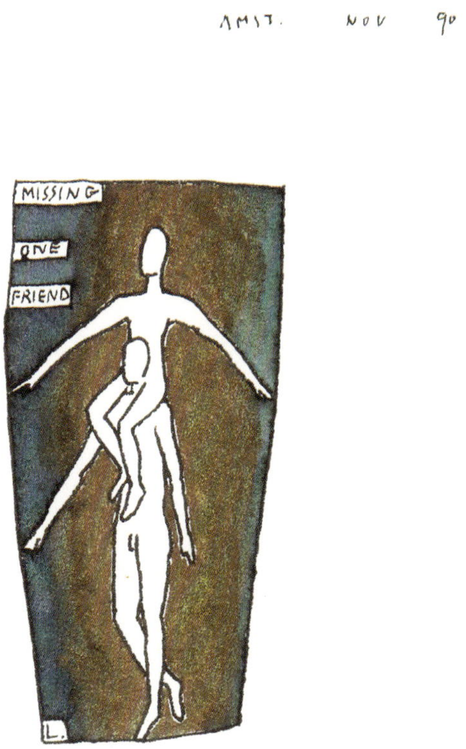

145. ***Missing One Friend***, 1990

Permanent ink, watercolor
and metallic paint on paper
21 × 13.5 cm
Private collection,
São Paulo, Brazil
PL.0848.0/00

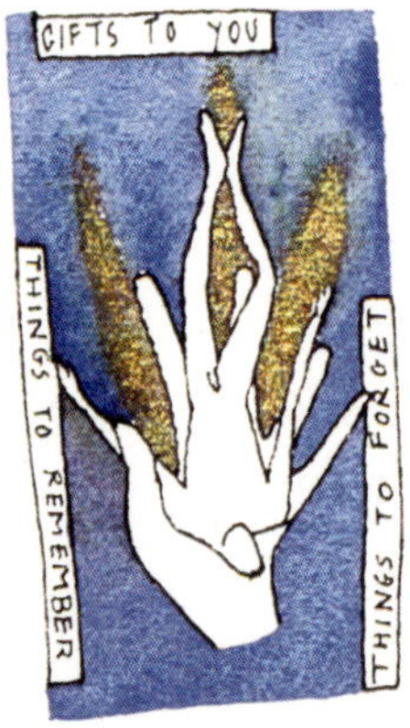

146. ***[Gifts to You]***, 1990

Permanent ink, watercolor
and metallic paint on paper
30.5 × 22.5 cm
Private collection,
São Paulo, Brazil
PL.1196.0/00

L. 5t jul 90

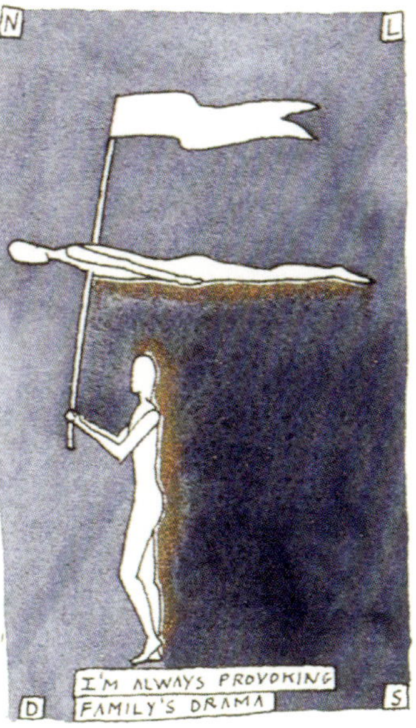

147. ***[I'm Always Provoking Family's Drama]***, 1990

Permanent ink, watercolor,
and metallic paint on paper
30 × 22 cm
Collection of Ricardo Resende and
Jose Mauro Del Royo Correa (*in memoriam*),
São Paulo, Brazil
PL.1512.0/00

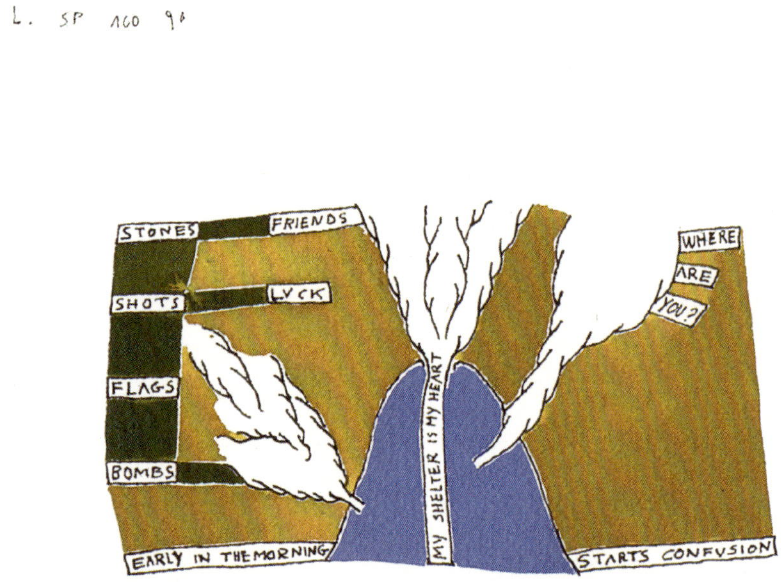

194

148. *[My Shelter Is My Heart]*, 1990

Permanent ink and
gouache on paper
32 × 22 cm
Private collection,
São Paulo, Brazil
PL.1156.0/00

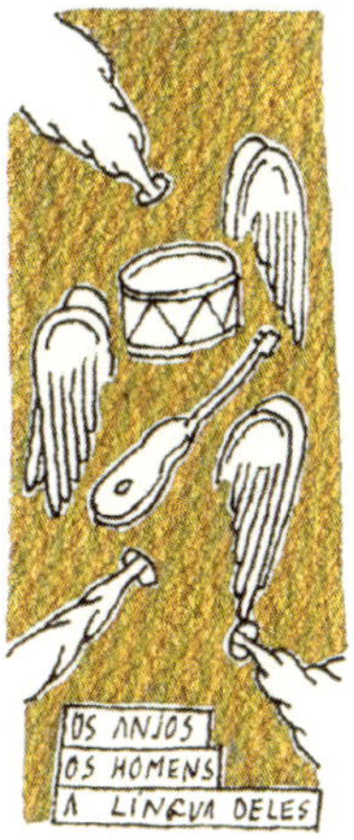

149. ***[Os anjos; os homens; a língua deles]*** [The Angels; The Men; Their Language, 1990

Permanent ink and
metallic paint on paper
30.5 × 22.5 cm
Private collection,
São Paulo, Brazil
PL.1154.0/00

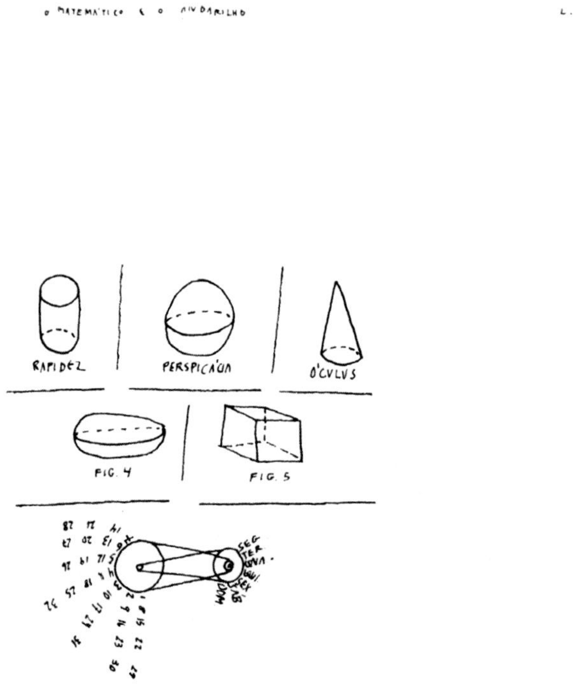

150. [*O matemático e o andarilho*]
[The Mathematician and the Wanderer],
circa 1990

Permanent ink on paper
24 × 32 cm
Centre Pompidou, Musée national d'art moderne, Centre de création industrielle, gift família Bezerra Dias/Sociedade Amigos do Projeto Leonilson, 2005,
Paris, France
PL.0036.0/00

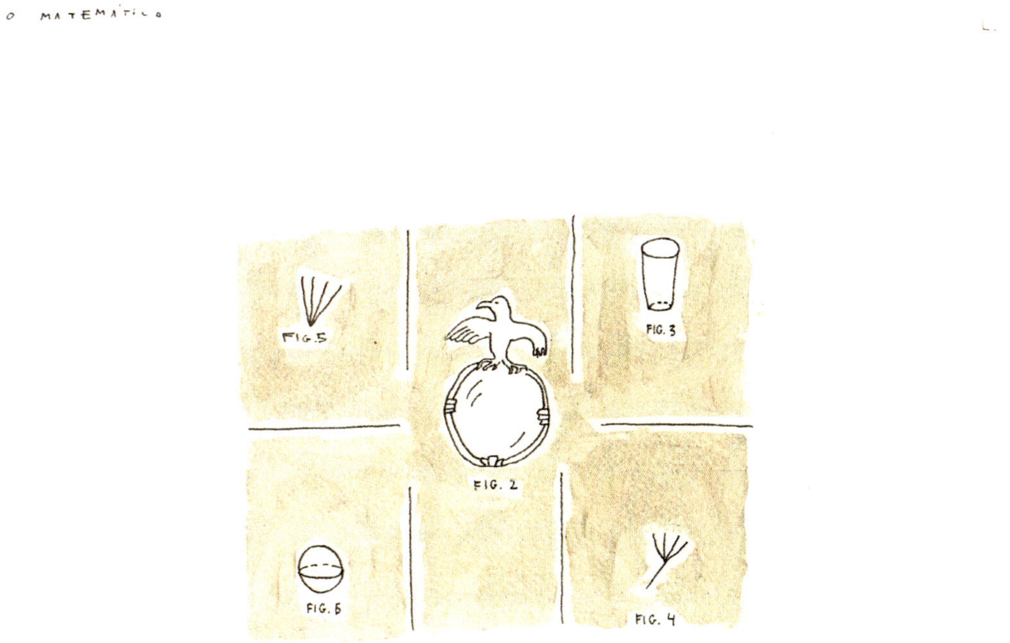

151. *[O matemático]*
[The Mathematician], 1990

Permanent ink and
watercolor on paper
24 × 32 cm
Collection of Luisa Malzoni Strina,
São Paulo, Brazil
PL.1294.0/00

1991

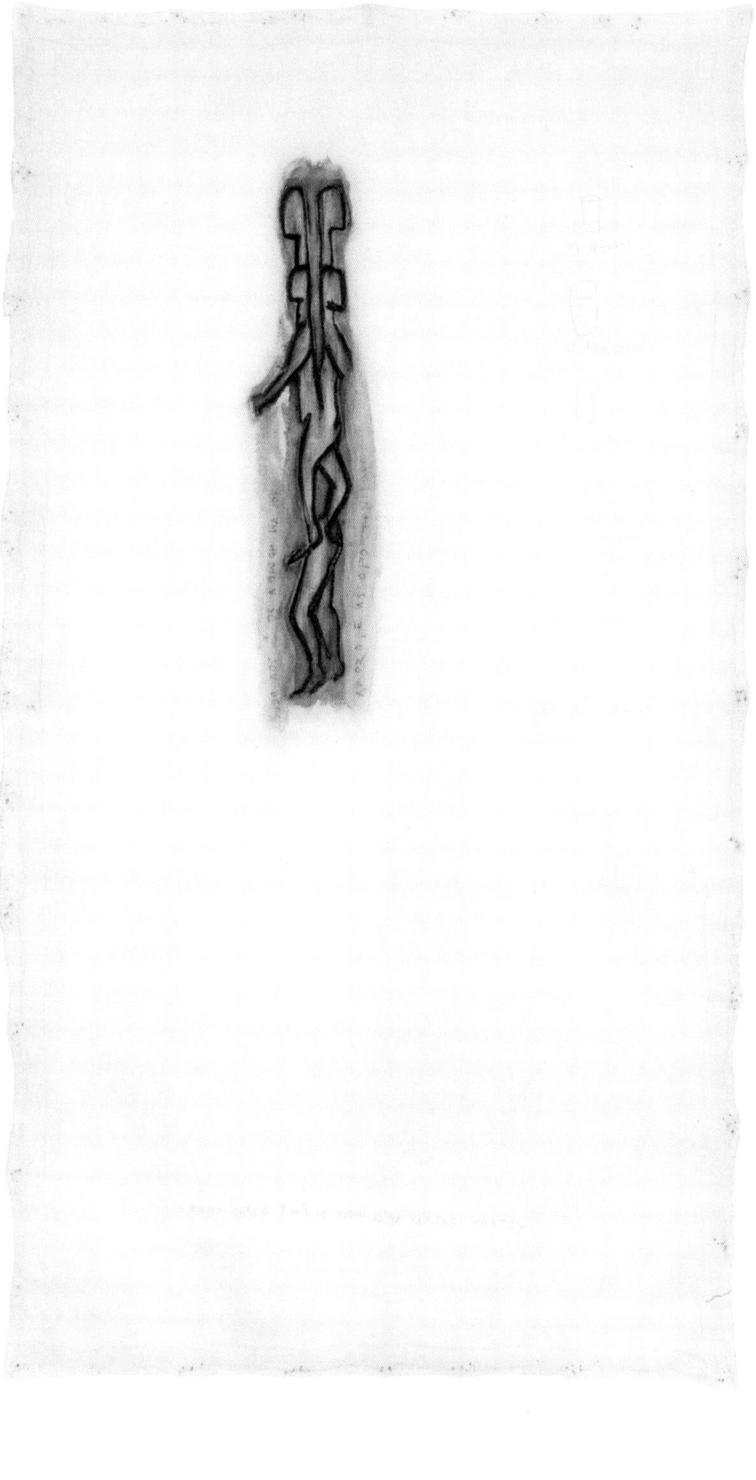

152. *Agora e as oportunidades*
[Now and Opportunities], 1991

Acrylic paint and colored pencil
on unstretched canvas
155 × 88 cm
Museu de Arte de São Paulo Assis
Chateaubriand, gift Fernanda Feitosa
and Heitor Martins, 2020, Brazil
MASP.11149
PL.0339.0/00

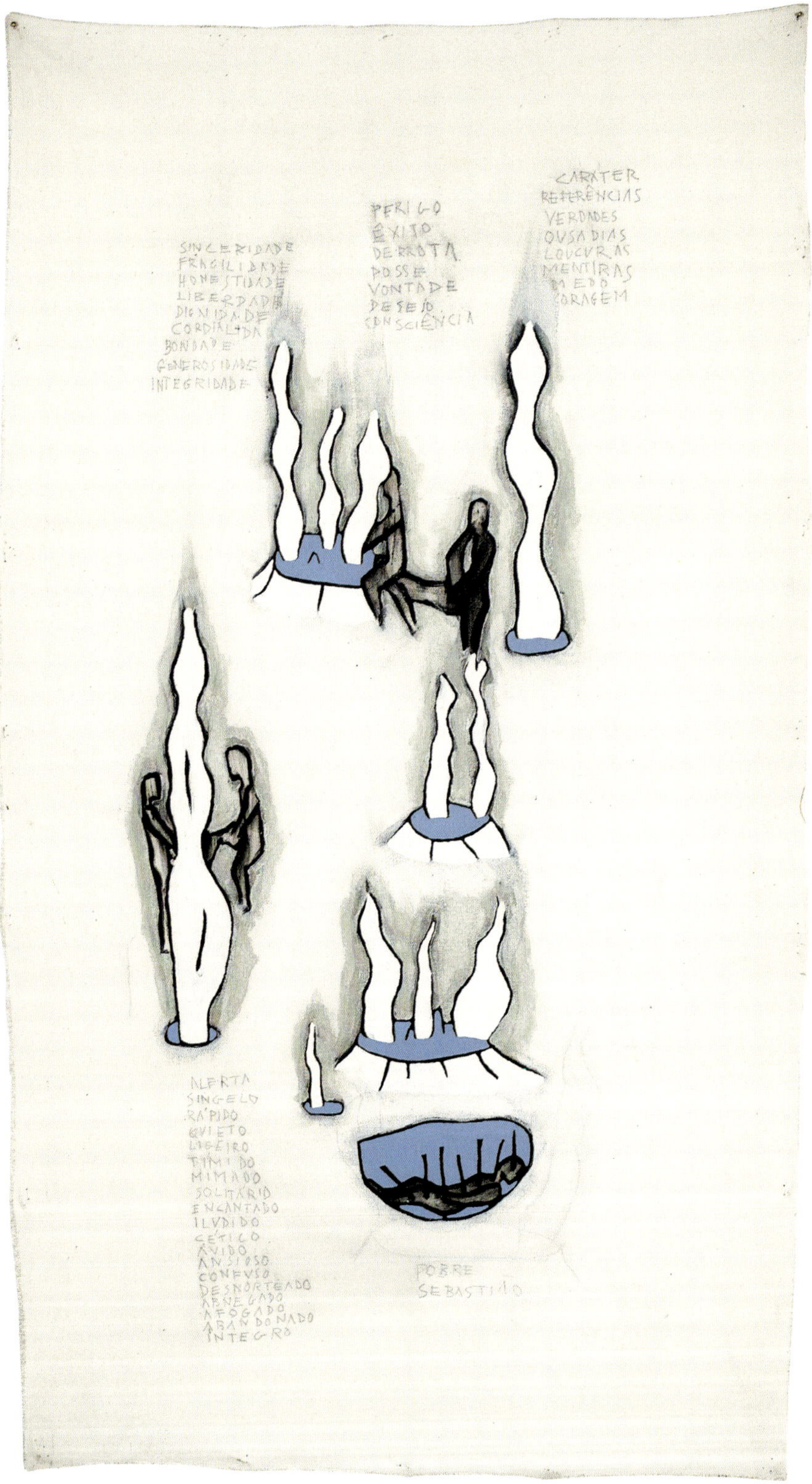

153. ***Pobre Sebastião***
[Poor Sebastião], 1991

Acrylic paint and colored pencil
on unstretched canvas
160 × 90 cm
Collection of Eduardo Brandão
and Jan Fjeld, São Paulo, Brazil
PL.0810.0/00

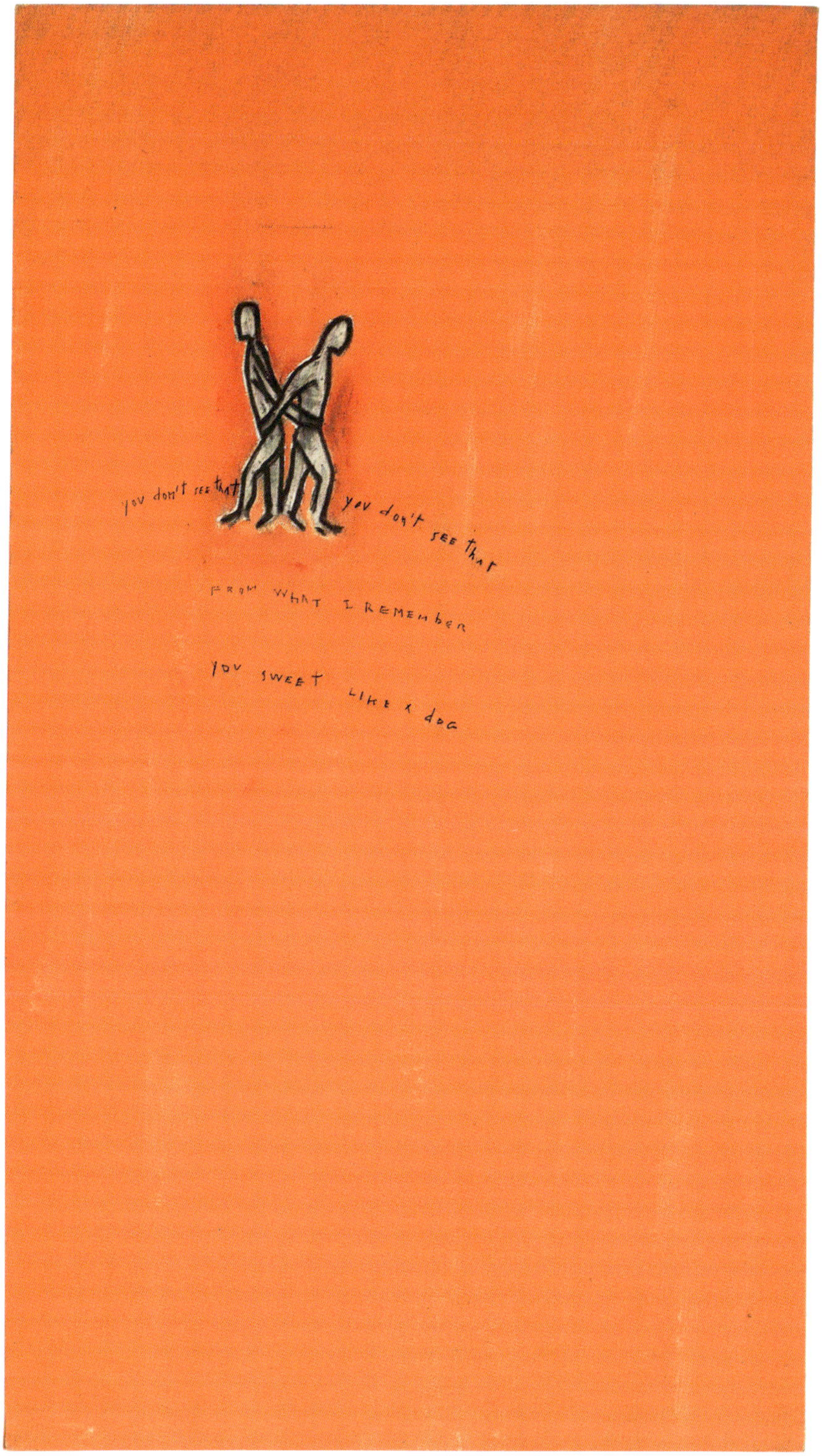

154. ***You Don't See That***, 1991

Acrylic paint and
colored pencil on canvas
149 × 85 cm
MEJME collection,
São Paulo, Brazil
PL.1084.0/00

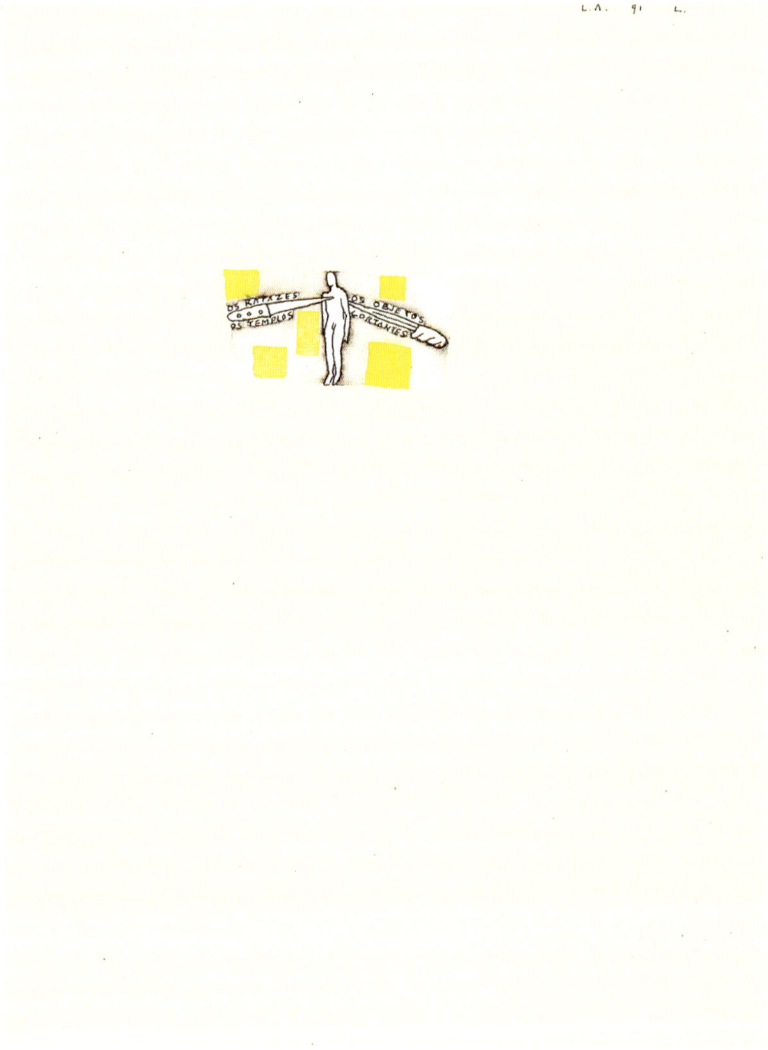

155. ***Os rapazes os templos***
[The Young Men the Temples], 1991

Permanent ink and
watercolor on paper
30 × 22.5 cm
Collection of Susana and
Ricardo Steinbruch,
São Paulo, Brazil
PL.1153.0/00

156. ***Leo não pode mudar o mundo*** [Leo Can't Change the World], 1991

Thread and unstretched canvas on voile
140.5 × 141 cm
Private collection, São Paulo, Brazil
PL.0340.0/00

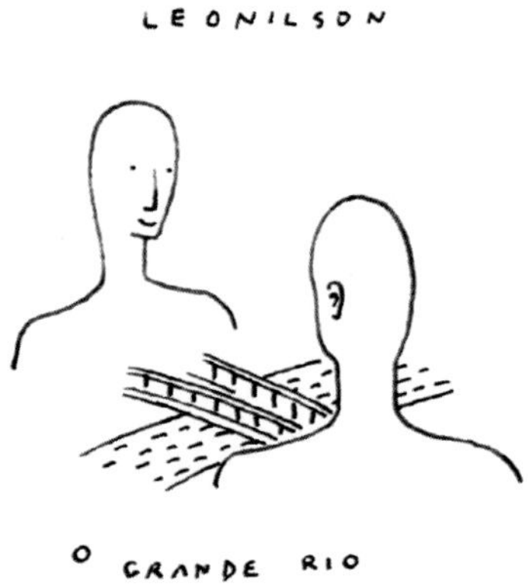

157. ***O grande rio***
[The Large River], *circa* 1991

Permanent ink on paper
15 × 22 cm
Collection of Marcelo Secaf,
São Paulo, Brazil
PL.1009.0/00

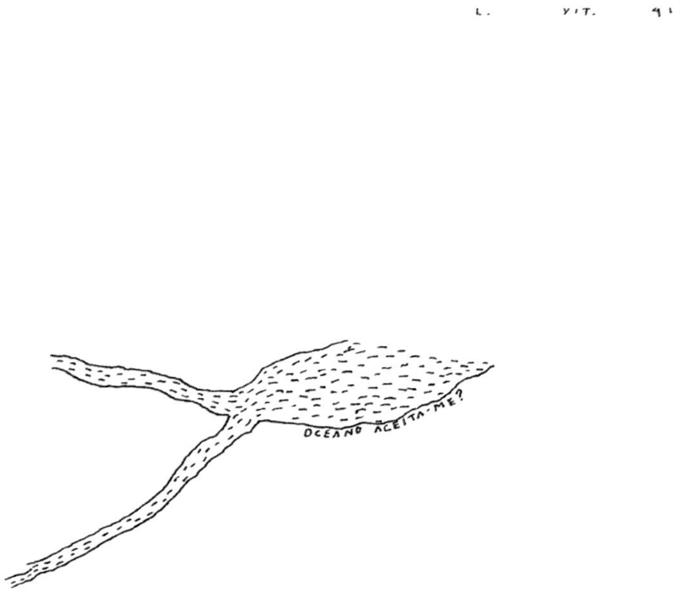

158. ***[Oceano, aceita-me?]***
[Ocean, Will You Accept Me?], 1991

Permanent ink on paper
30 × 23 cm
Private collection,
São Paulo, Brazil
PL.0658.0/00

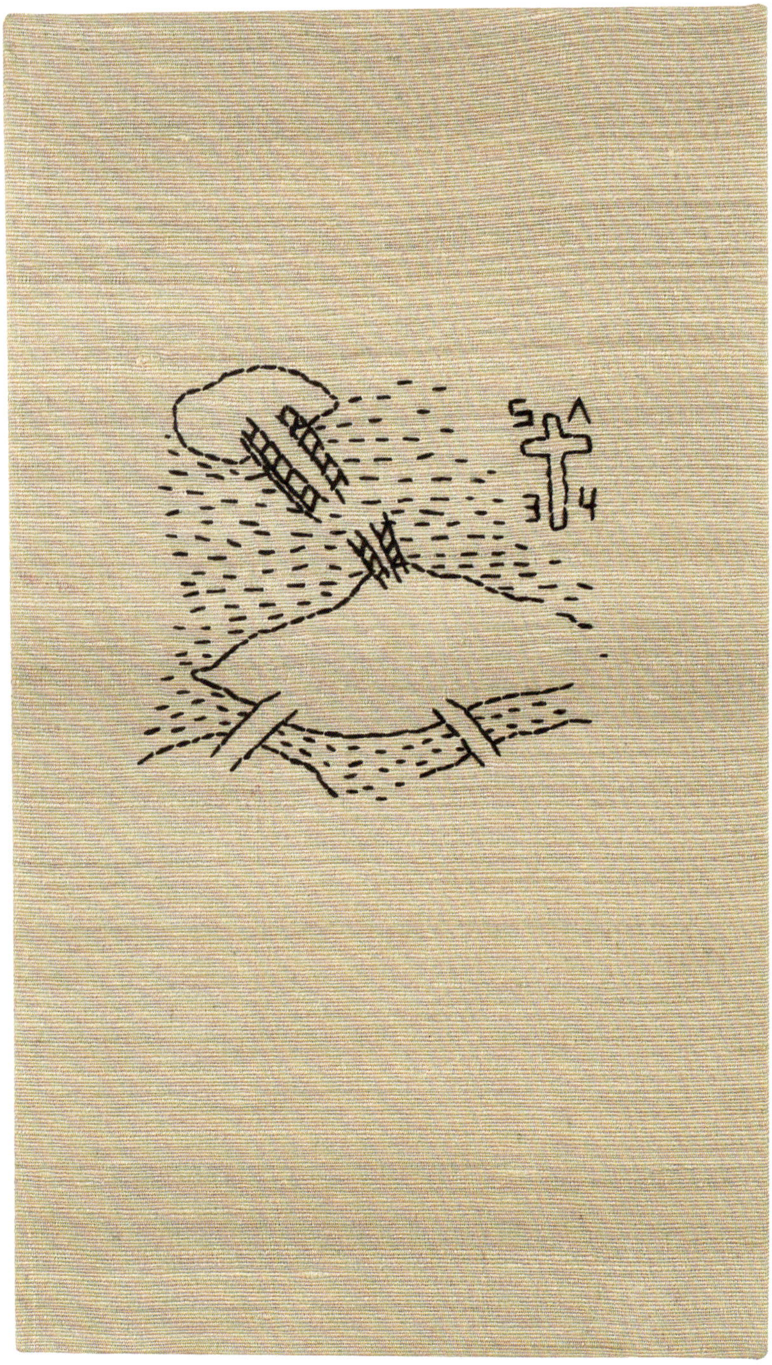

159. ***Síndrome de abandono***
[Abandonment Syndrome], 1991

Thread on rustic silk
41 × 23.5 cm
Collection of Valdirlei Dias Nunes,
São Paulo, Brazil
PL.1118.0/00

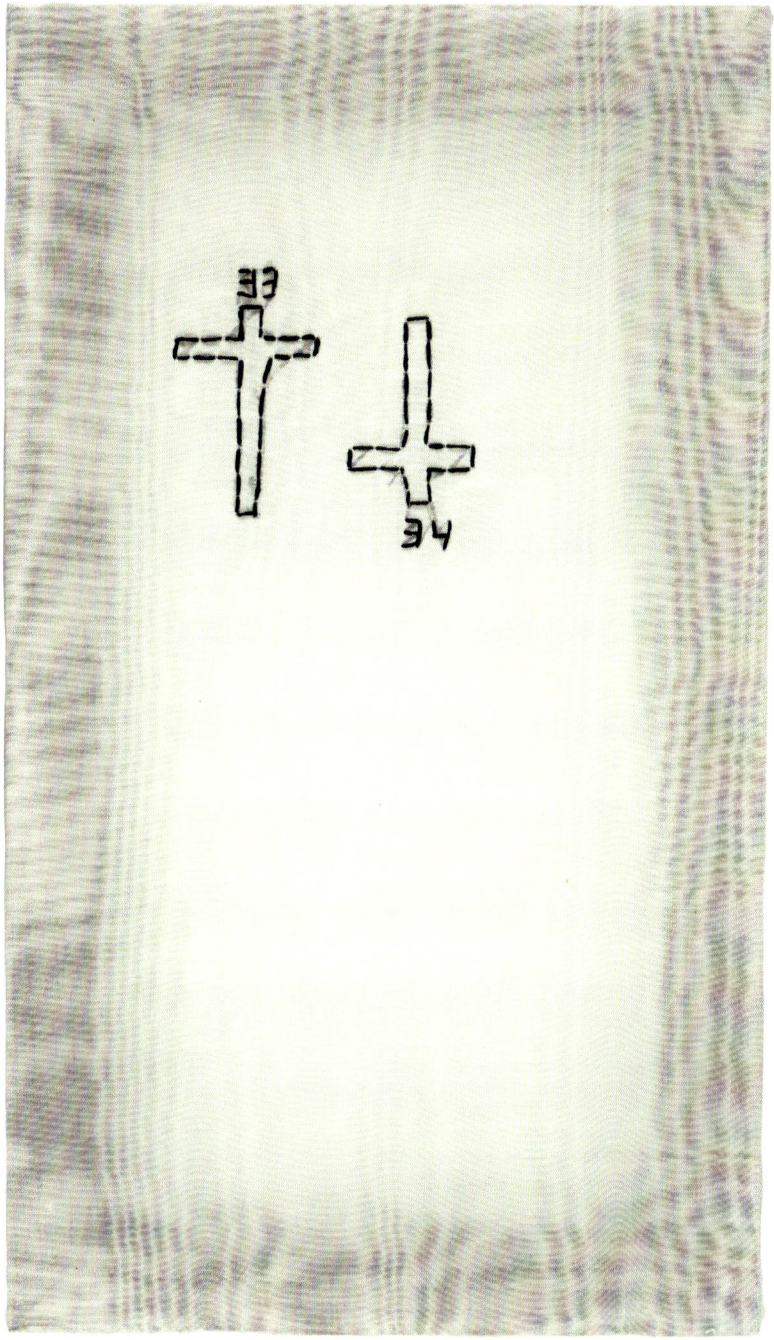

160. *33/34*, 1991

Black embroidery thread,
voile, wooden frame
41 × 24 cm
Centre Pompidou, Musée national
d'art moderne, Centre de création
industrielle, purchase,
2005, Paris, France
PL.0005.0/00

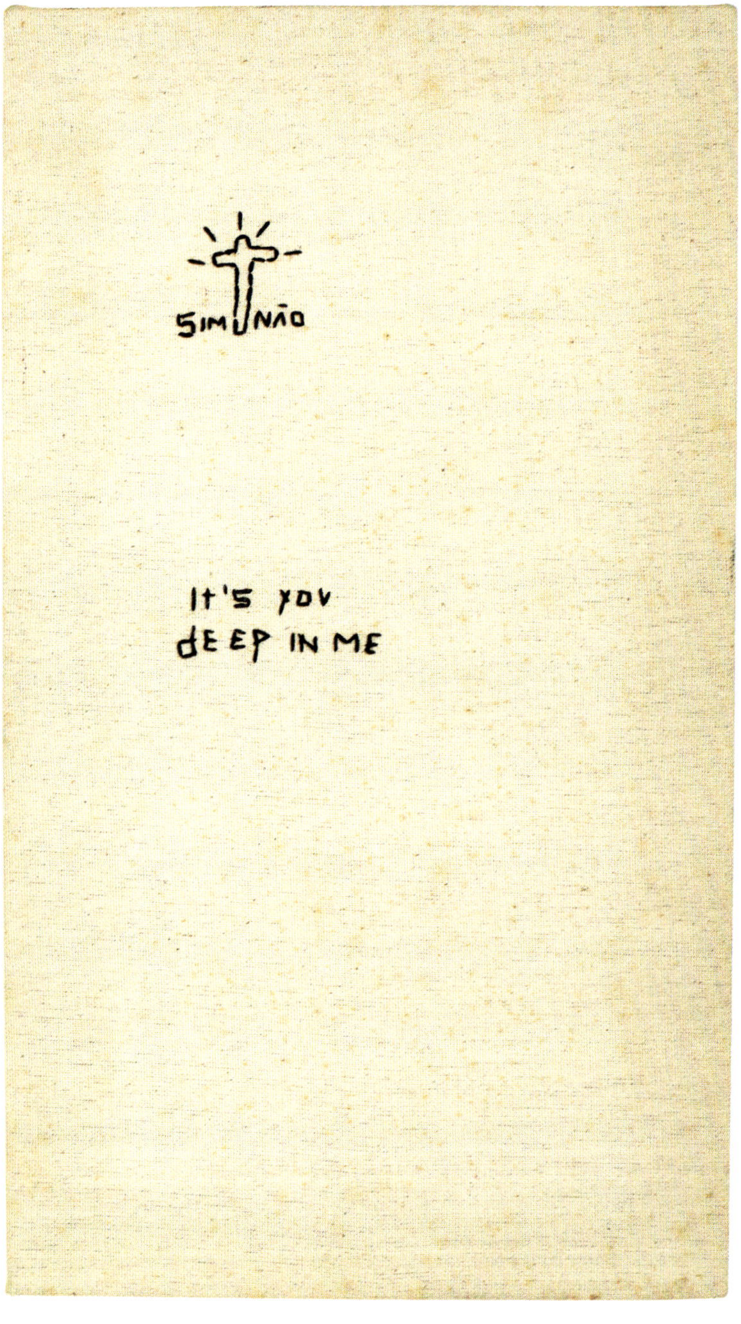

161. ***It's You Deep in Me****, circa* 1991

Thread on canvas
41 × 29 cm
Museu Nacional de Belas Artes/Ibram,
gift família Bezerra Dias/
Projeto Leonilson, 2004,
Rio de Janeiro, Brazil
PL.0015.0/00

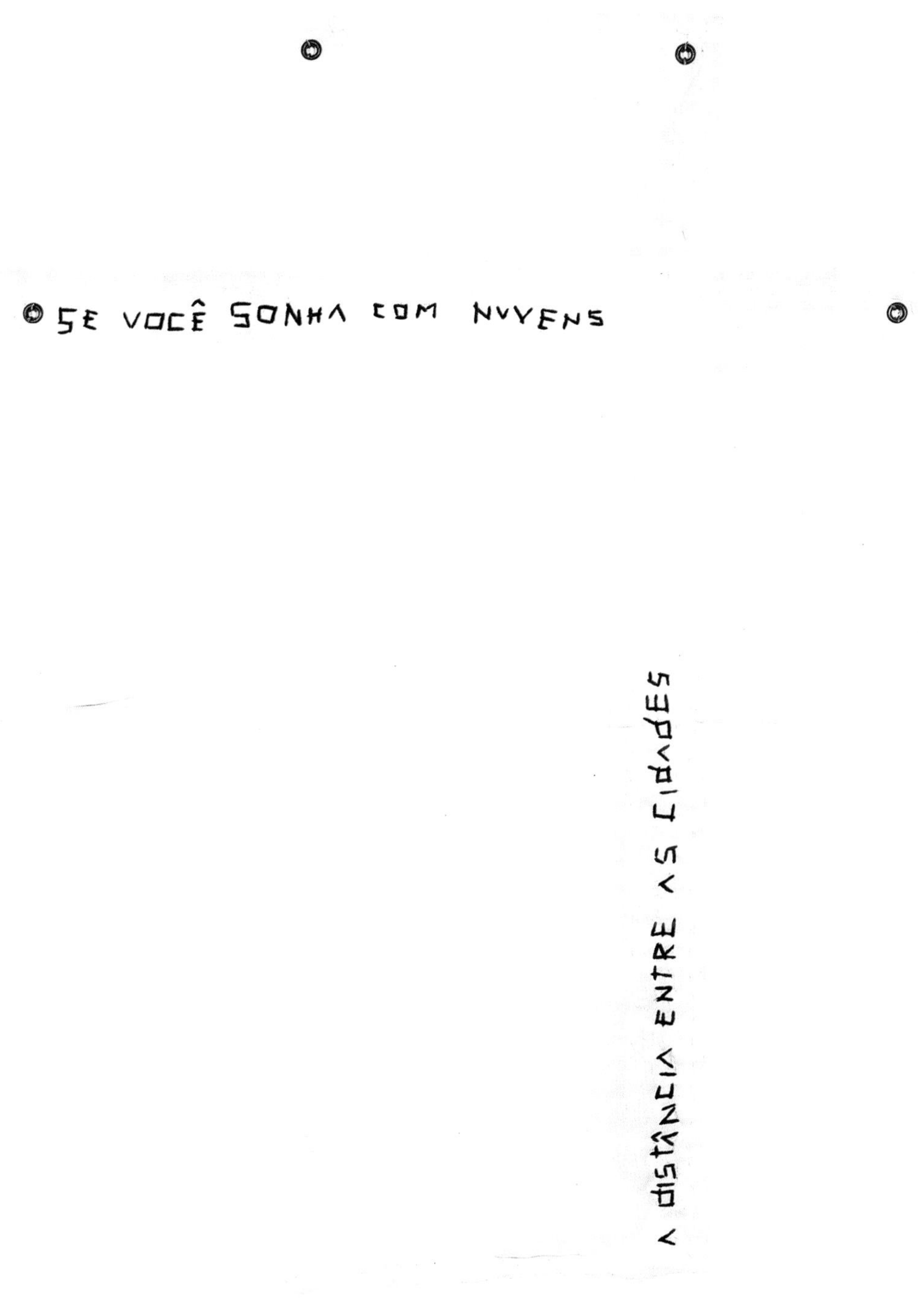

162. ***Se você sonha com nuvens***
[If You Dream of Clouds], *circa* 1991

Embroidery, sewing,
and metal eyelet on voile
57.5 × 47.5 × 4 cm
Museu de Arte Moderna de
São Paulo, gift Carmen Bezerra Dias
and Theodorino Torquato Dias, 1997,
Brazil
PL.1040.0/00

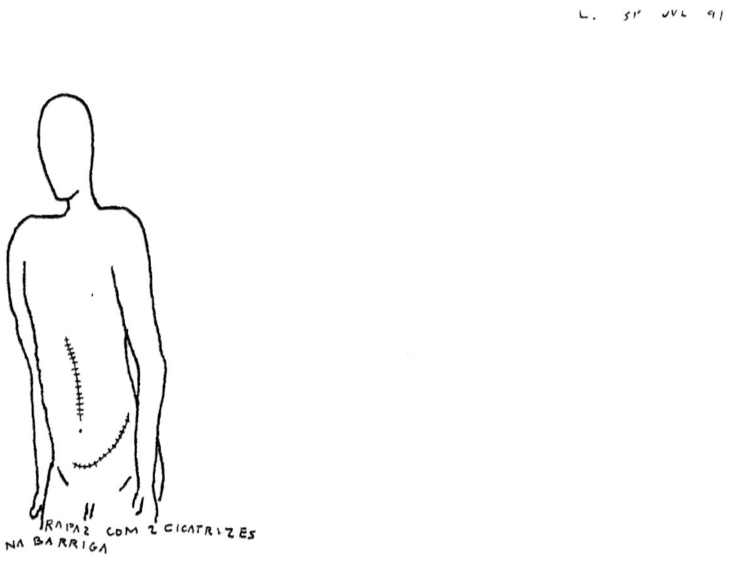

163. ***[Rapaz com 2 cicatrizes na barriga]*** [Young Man With 2 Scars in the Stomach], 1991

Permanent ink on paper
31 × 23 cm
Collection of Eduardo Brandão
and Jan Fjeld, São Paulo
PL.0818.0/00

164. ***[Jesus com rapaz acidentado]*** [Jesus With Accidented Young Man], 1991

Permanent ink and
gouache on paper
31 × 23 cm
Collection of Eduardo Brandão
and Jan Fjeld, São Paulo
PL.0823.0/00

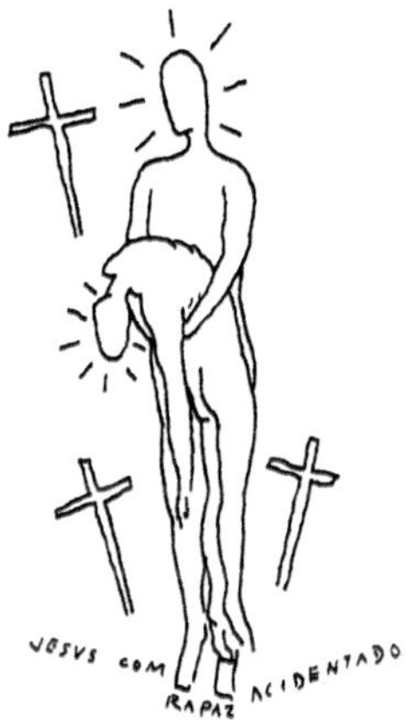

165. ***[Que estranho nome dão a isto?]*** [What Strange Name Do They Give to This?], 1991

Permanent ink and watercolor on paper
32 × 24 cm
Private collection, São Paulo, Brazil
PL.1166.0/00

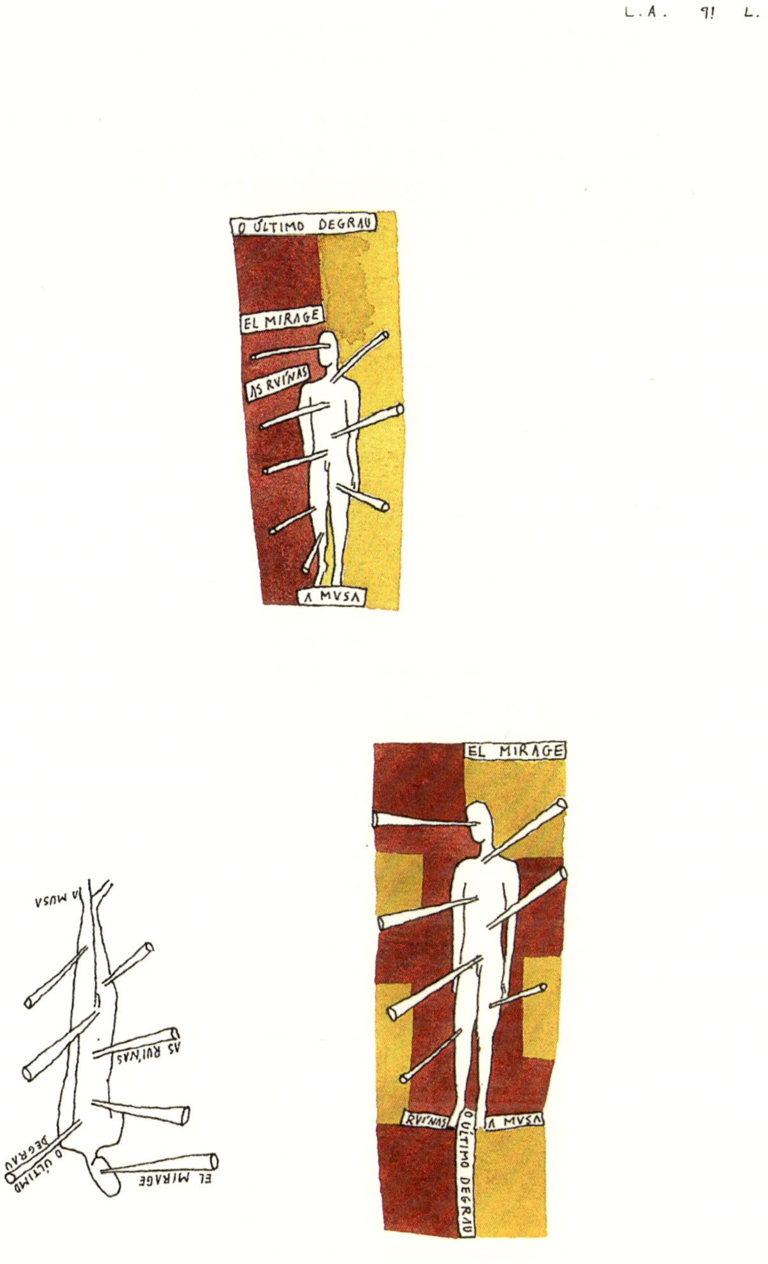

166. *El Mirage* [The Mirage], 1991

Permanent ink and
watercolor on paper
30.5 × 23 cm
Collection of Thiago Tannous,
São Paulo, Brazil
PL.2319.0/00

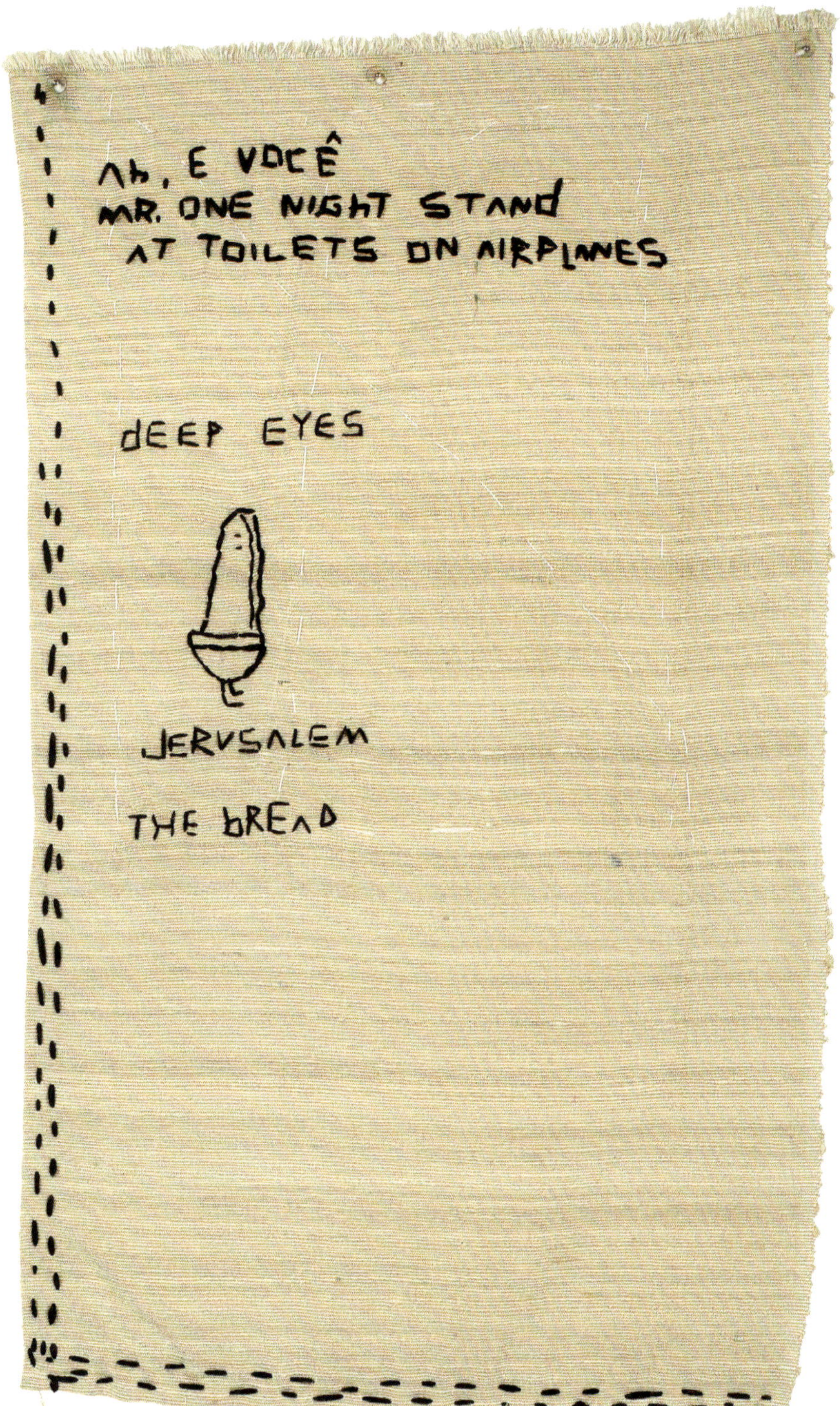

214

167. ***Mr. One Night Stand*** , 1991

Thread on rustic silk
47.5 × 28 cm
Private collection,
São Paulo, Brazil
PL.0014.0/00

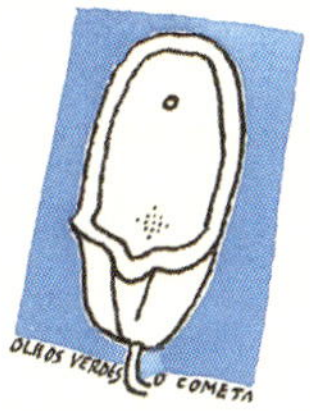

168. ***O cometa*** [The Comet],
from the series *Os dedicados*
[The Dedicated], 1991

Permanent ink and
watercolor on paper
30.5 × 23 cm
Collection of Francisco Meirelles de Andrade,
São Paulo, Brazil
PL.0019.0/00

169. *O vapor* [The Vapor], from the series *Os dedicados* [The Dedicated], 1991

Permanent ink and watercolor on paper
30.5 × 23 cm
Private collection, Chicago, United States
PL.0018.0/00

170. *Príncipe* [Prince], from the series *Os dedicados* [The Dedicated], 1991

Permanent ink and watercolor on paper
30.5 × 23 cm
Museu de Arte de São Paulo Assis Chateaubriand, gift Luisa Strina, 2024, Brazil
MASP.11532
PL.1194.0/00

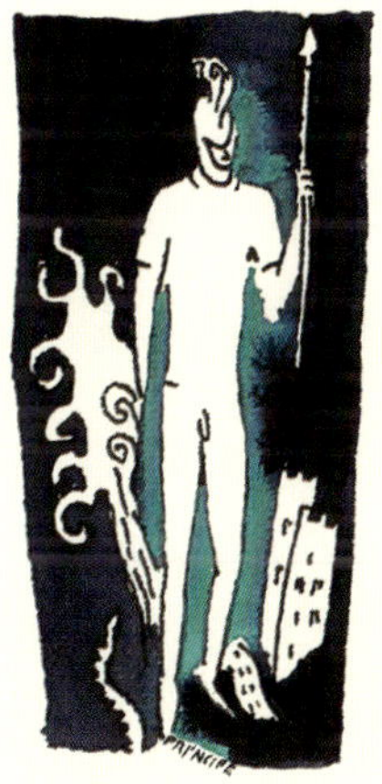

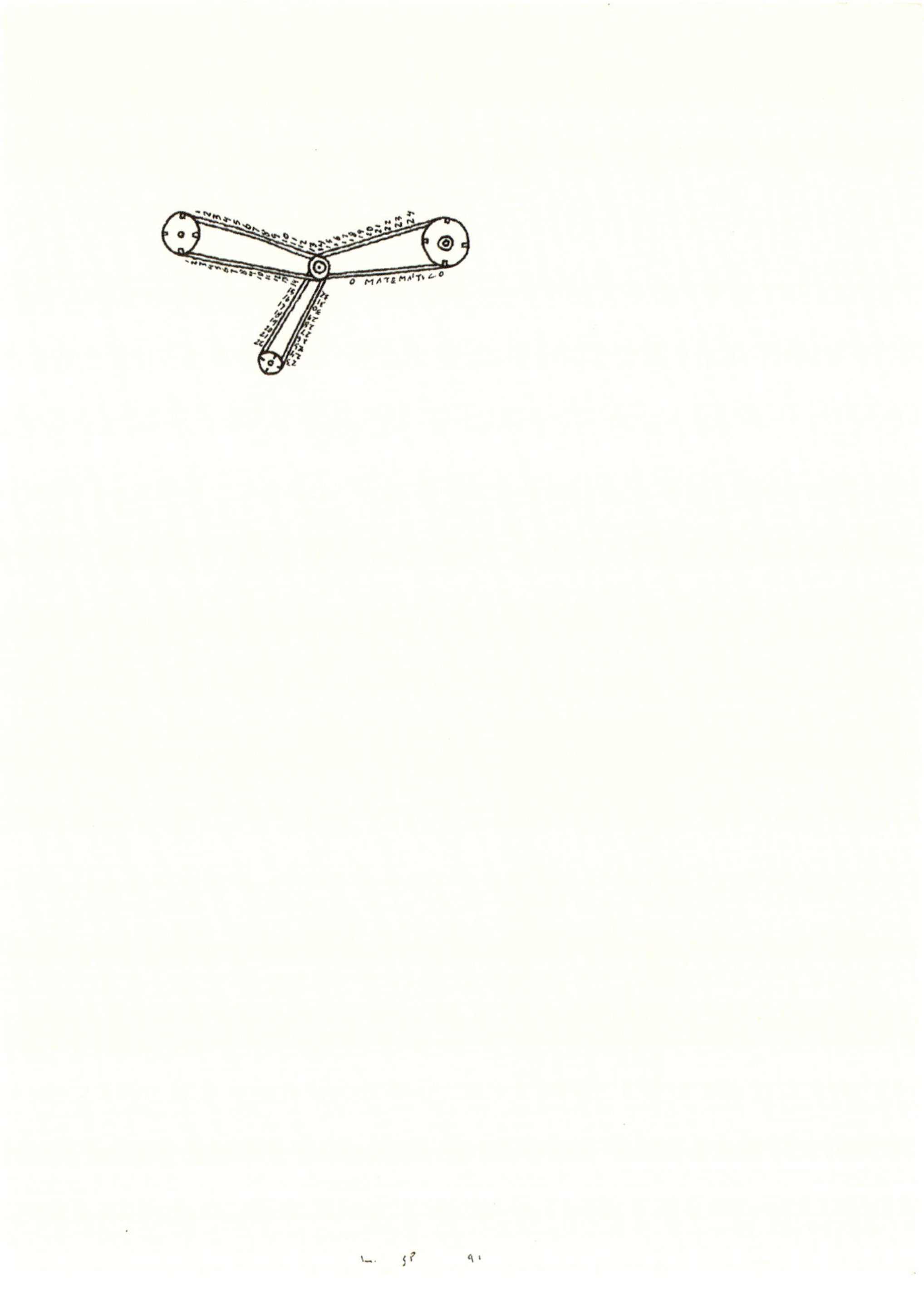

171. ***O matemático***
[The Mathematician],
from the series *Os dedicados*
[The Dedicated], 1991

Permanent ink on paper
30.5 × 23 cm
Private collection,
São Paulo, Brazil
PL.0020.0/00

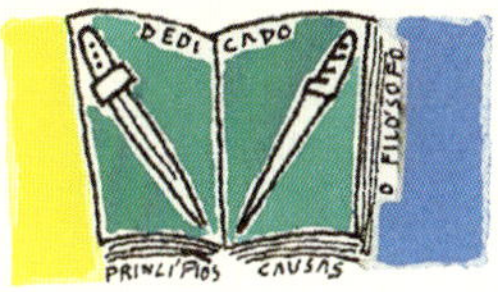

219

172. ***O filósofo***
[The Philosopher],
from the series *Os dedicados*
[The Dedicated], 1991

Permanent ink and
watercolor on paper
30.5 × 23 cm
Private collection,
São Paulo, Brazil
PL.0017.0/00

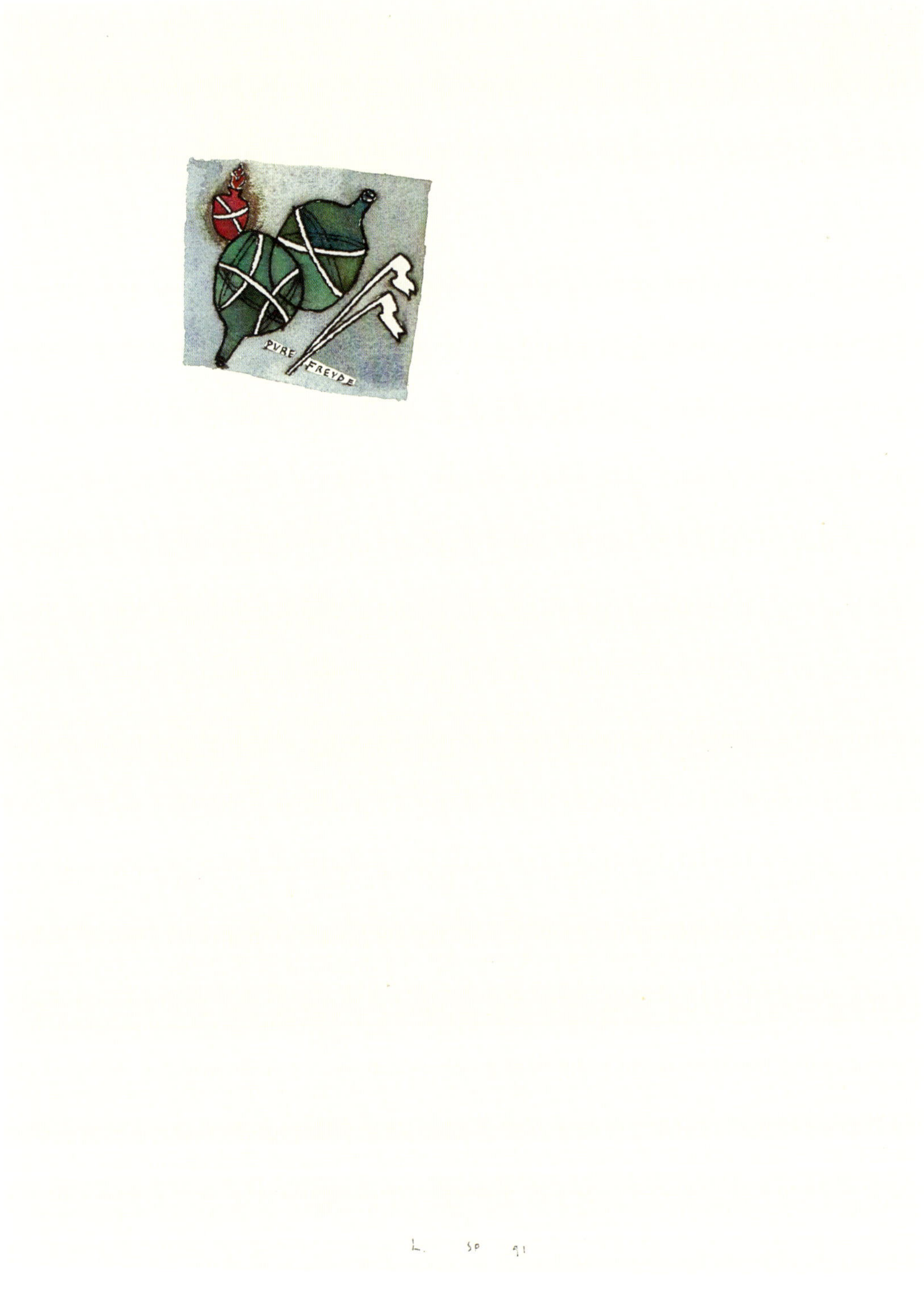

173. ***Pure freude*** [Pure Joy], from the series *Os dedicados* [The Dedicated], 1991

Permanent ink and watercolor on paper
30.5 × 23 cm
Collection of Luisa Malzoni Strina, São Paulo, Brazil
PL.1195.0/00

174. *O músico* [The Musician], from the series *Os dedicados* [The Dedicated], 1991

Watercolor and permanent ink on paper
30.5 × 23 cm
Collection of Rafael Moraes, São Paulo, Brazil
PL.2600.0/00

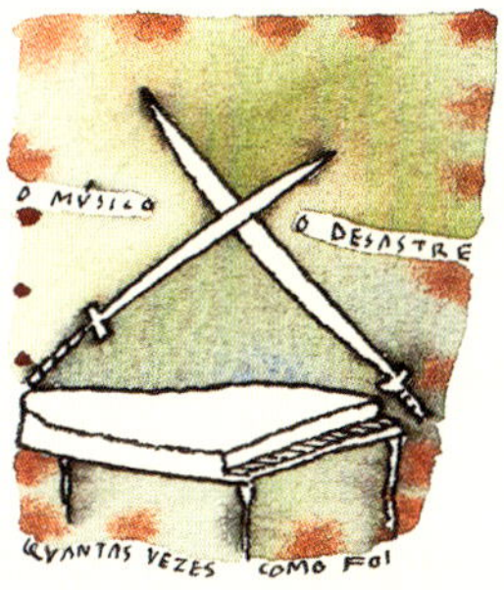

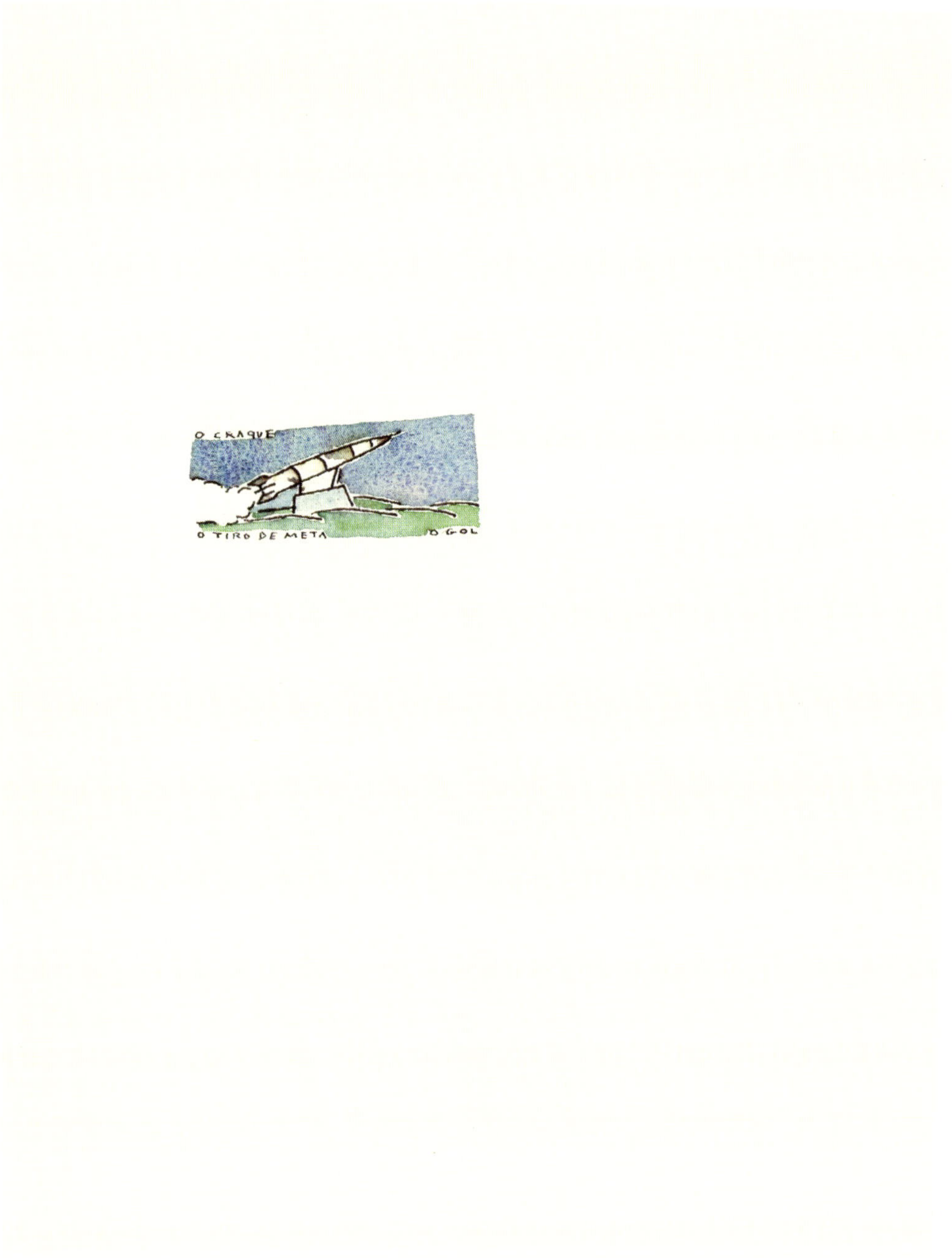

175. ***O craque*** [The Top Player], from the series *Os dedicados* [The Dedicated], 1991

Permanent ink and
watercolor on paper
30.5 × 23 cm
Private collection,
São Paulo, Brazil
PL.1101.0/00

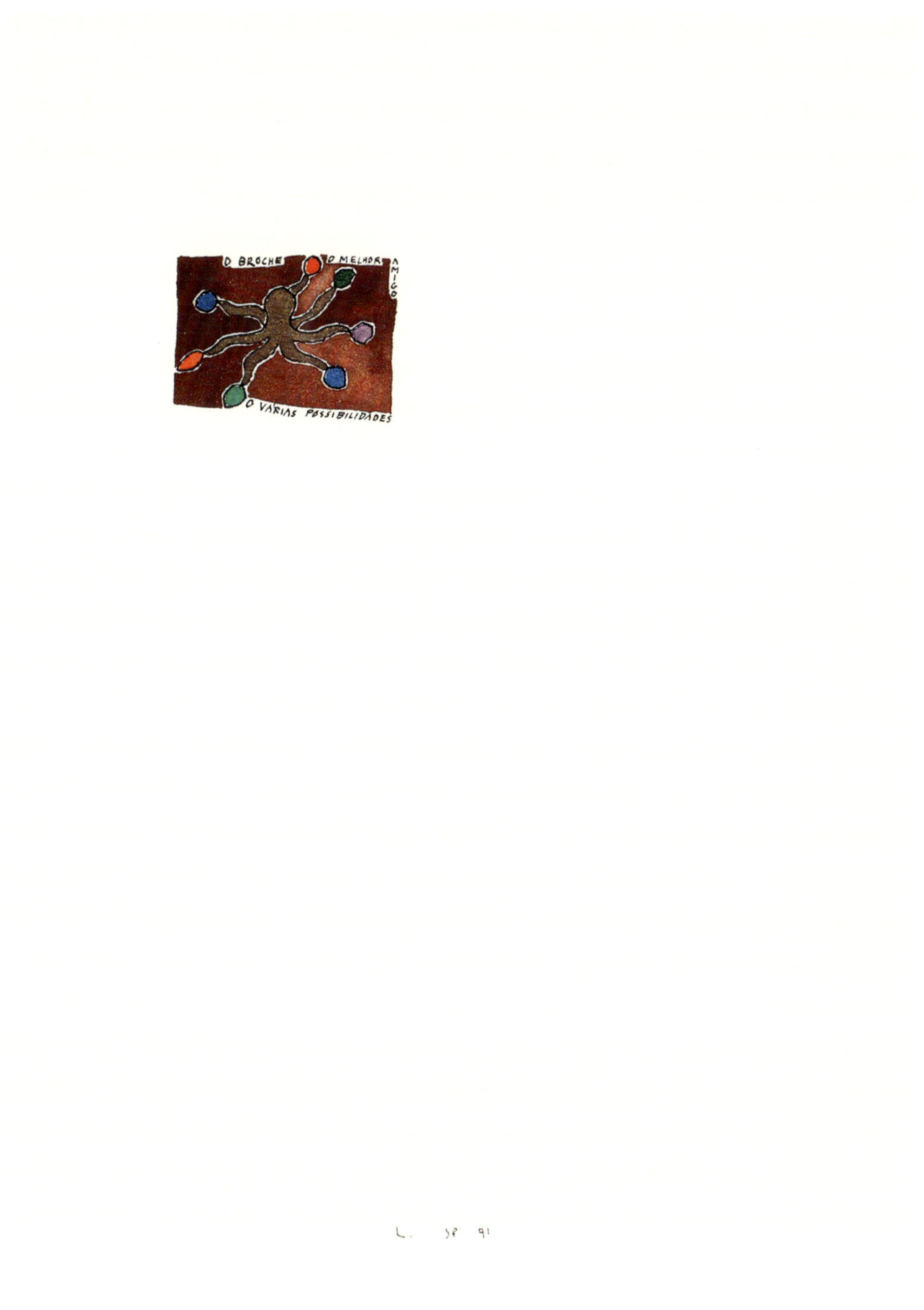

176. ***O broche*** [The Brooch], from the series *Os dedicados* [The Dedicated], 1991

Permanent ink and watercolor on paper
30.5 × 23 cm
Collection of Marcelo Secaf, São Paulo, Brazil
PL.2175.0/00

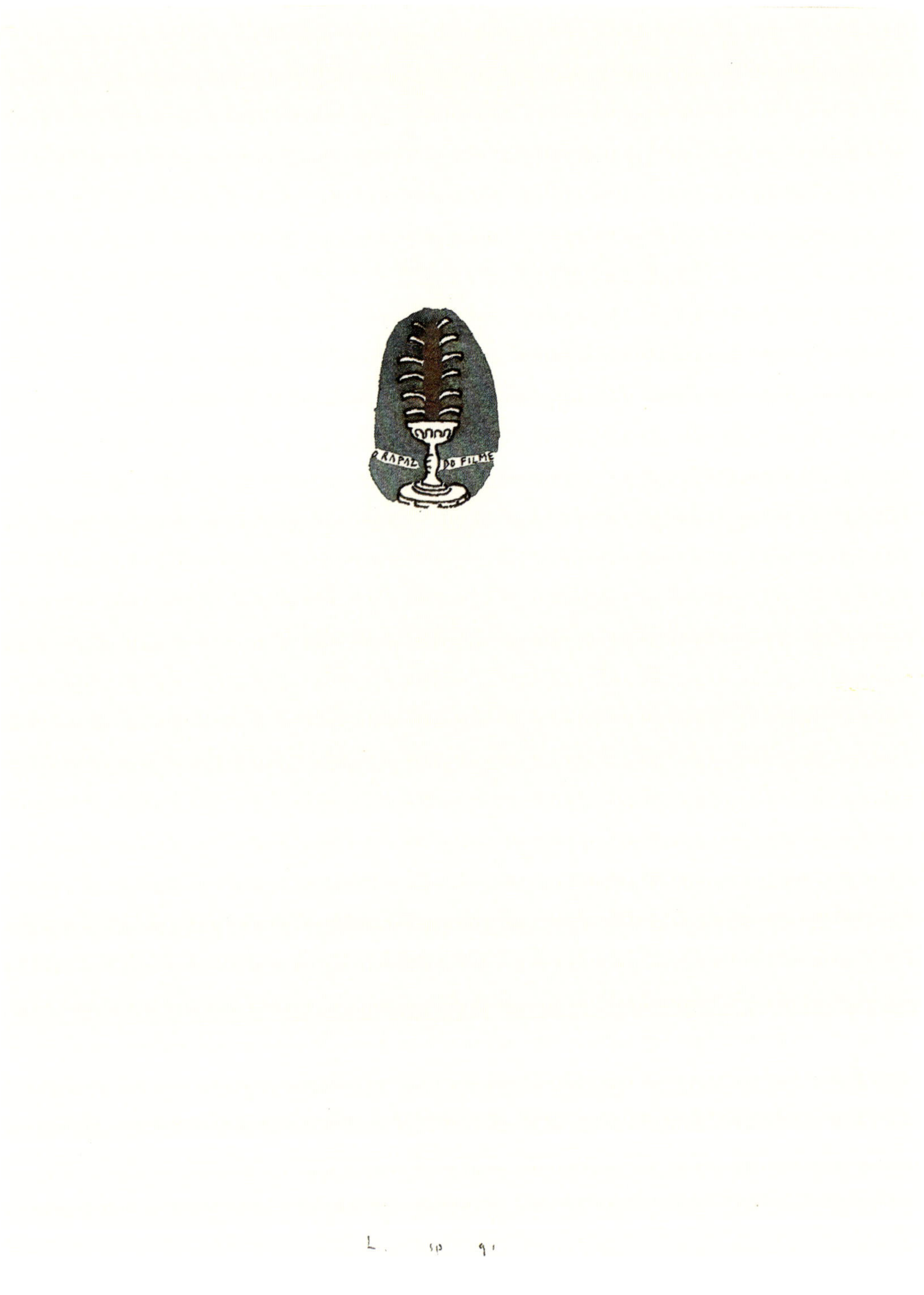

177. ***O rapaz do filme***
[The Young Man From
the Movies], from the series
Os dedicados [The Dedicated], 1991

Permanent ink and
watercolor on paper
30.5 × 23 cm
Collection of Luisa Malzoni Strina,
São Paulo, Brazil
PL.1078.0/00

178. ***Não me lembro*** [I Don't Remember], from the series *Os dedicados* [The Dedicated], 1991

Permanent ink and watercolor on paper
30.5 × 23 cm
Private collection,
São Paulo, Brazil
PL.0850.0/00

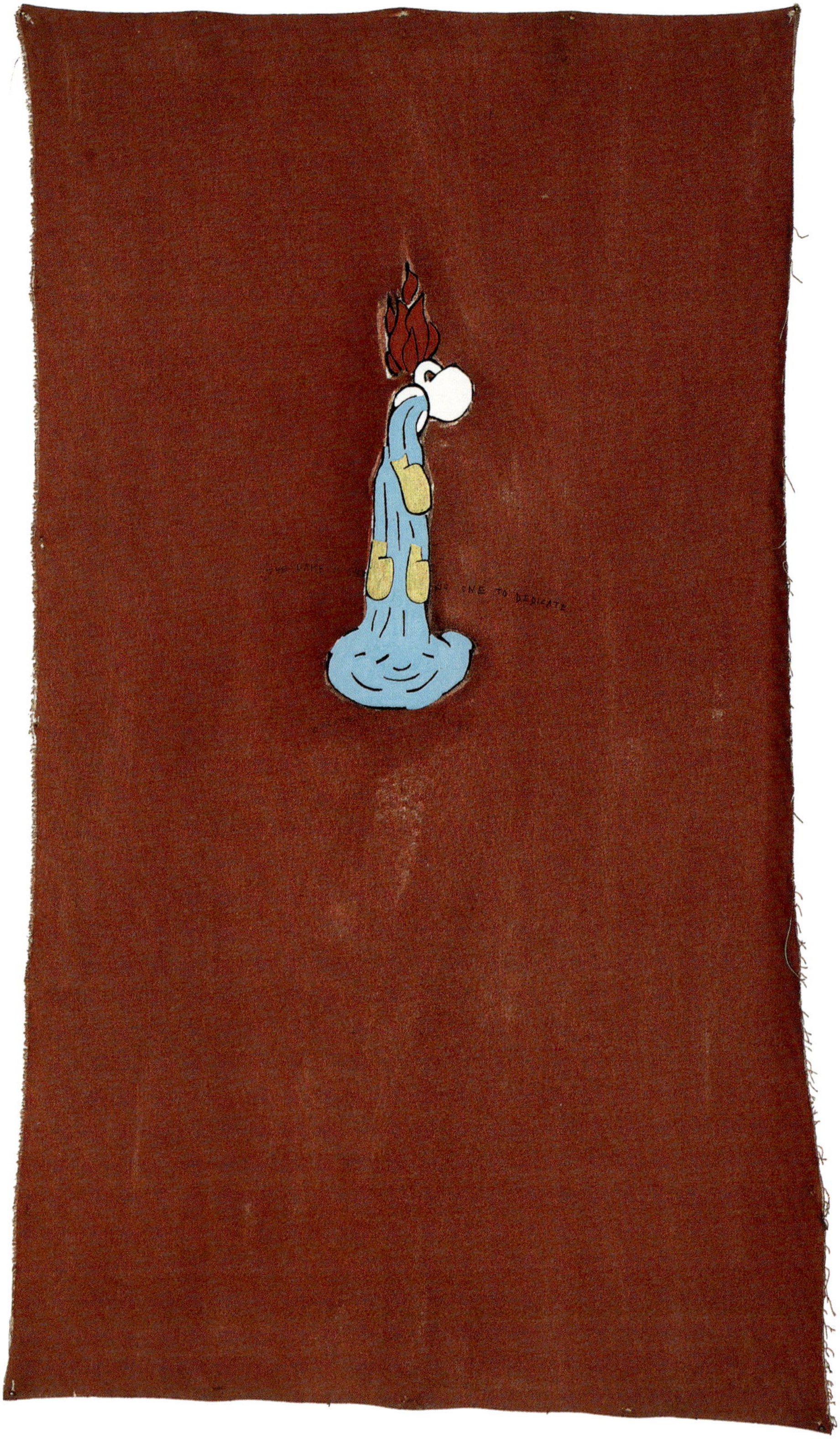

179. ***The Game Is Over***, *circa* 1991

Acrylic paint, metallic paint and
colored pencil on unstretched canvas
155 × 95 cm
Private collection,
São Paulo, Brazil
PL.1454.0/00

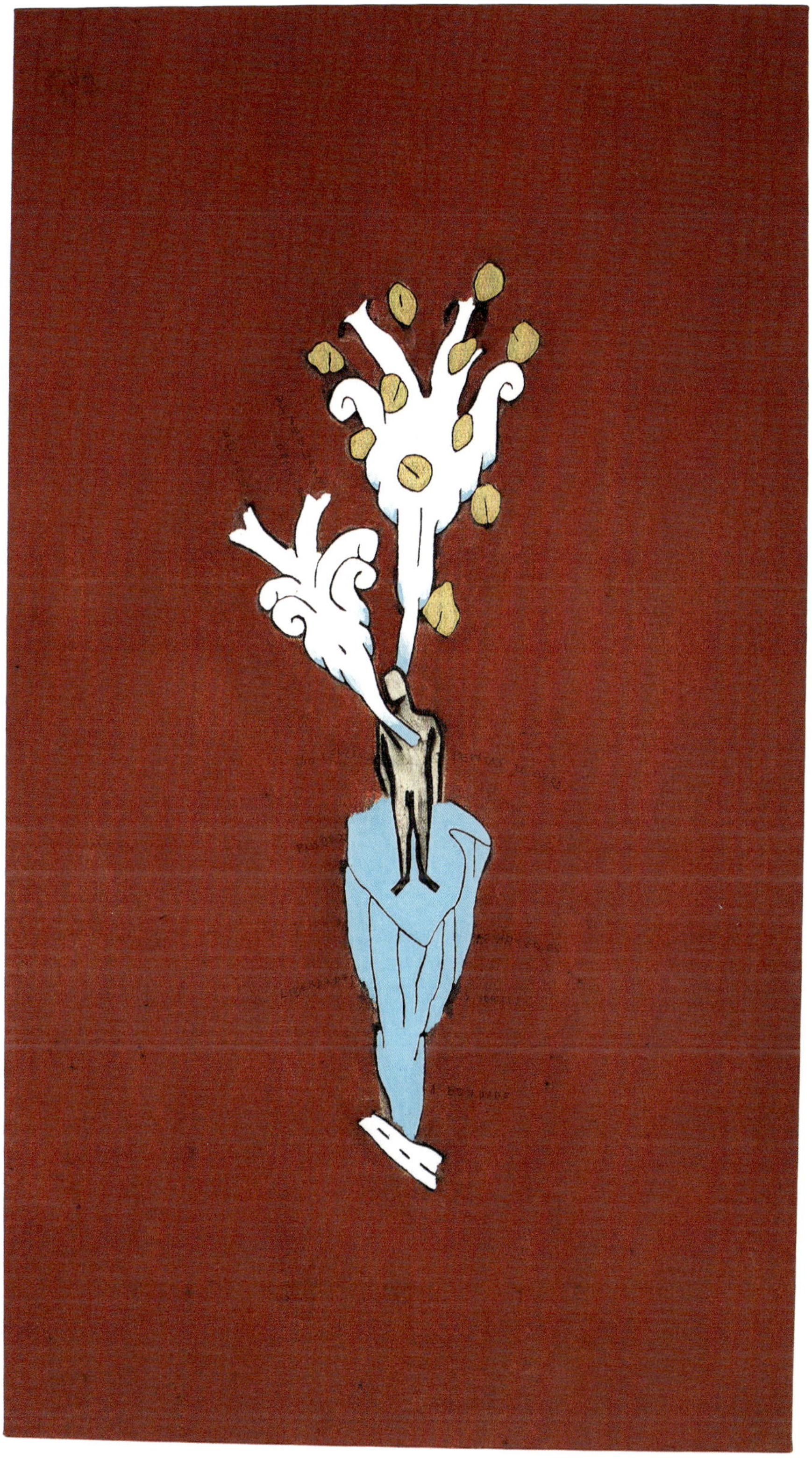

180. ***[Pepitas de ouro]***
[Gold Nuggets], 1991

Acrylic paint, metallic paint and
colored pencil on canvas
150 × 85 cm
Private collection,
São Paulo, Brazil
PL.1111.0/00

181. ***Rapaz dividido***
[Divided Young Man], [1991]

Acrylic paint and
colored pencil on canvas
149 × 92 cm
Private collection,
São Paulo, Brazil
PL.1205.0/00

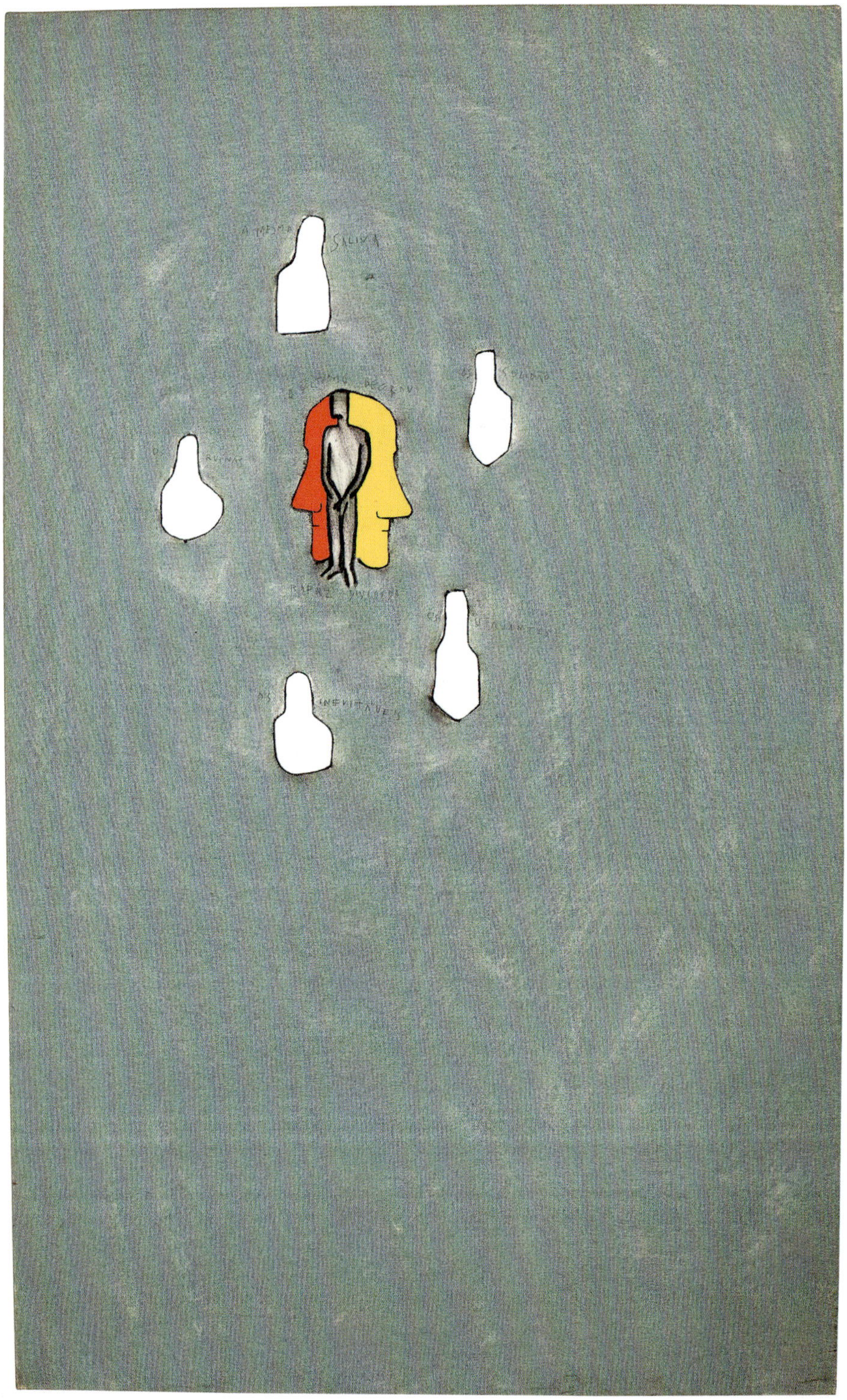

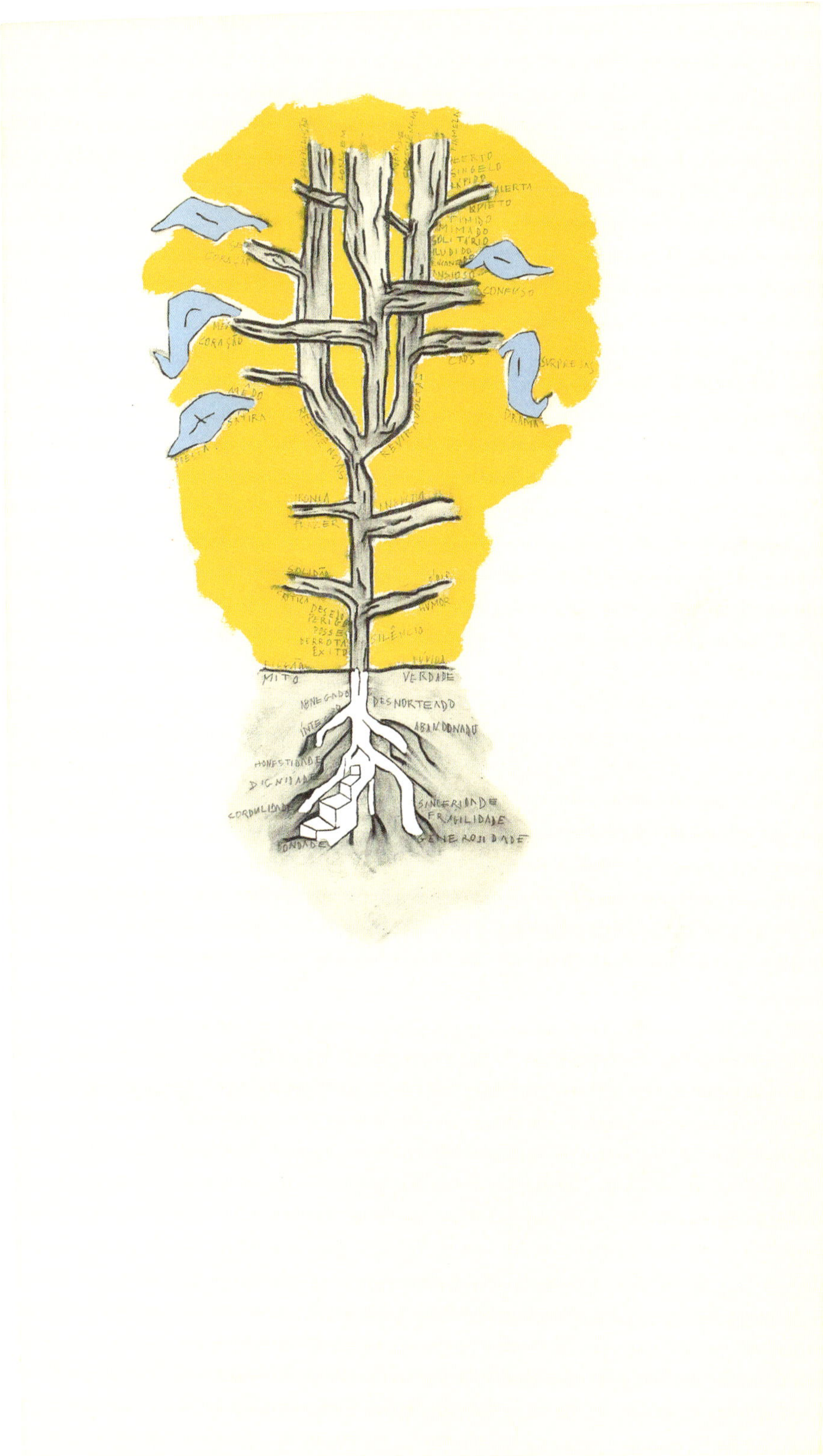

182. ***Meu coração, seu coração***
[My Heart, Your Heart], *circa* 1991

Acrylic paint and
colored pencil on canvas
155 × 90 cm
Collection of Andrea and
José Olympio Pereira,
São Paulo, Brazil
PL.1191.0/00

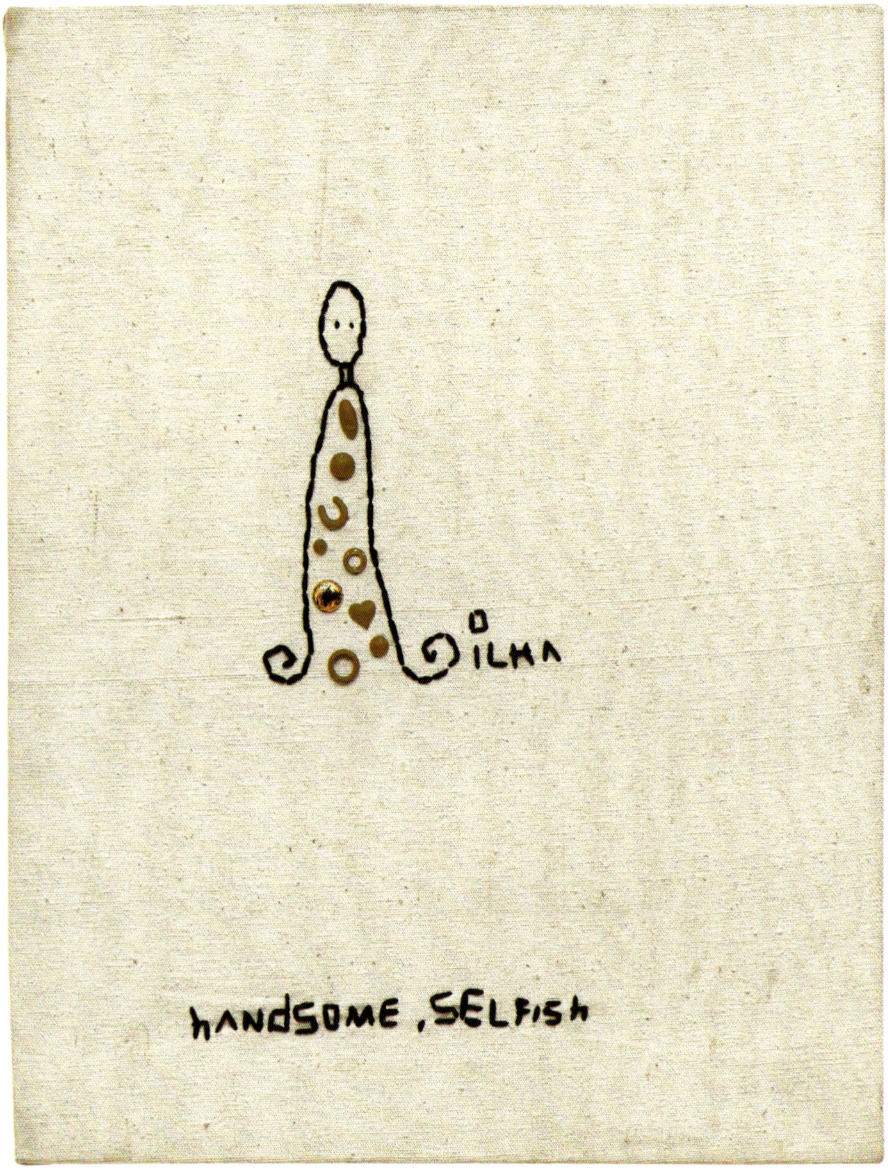

183. ***O ilha***
[The Island One], 1991

Thread and metal on canvas
35 × 27 cm
Private collection,
São Paulo, Brazil
PL.0905.0/00

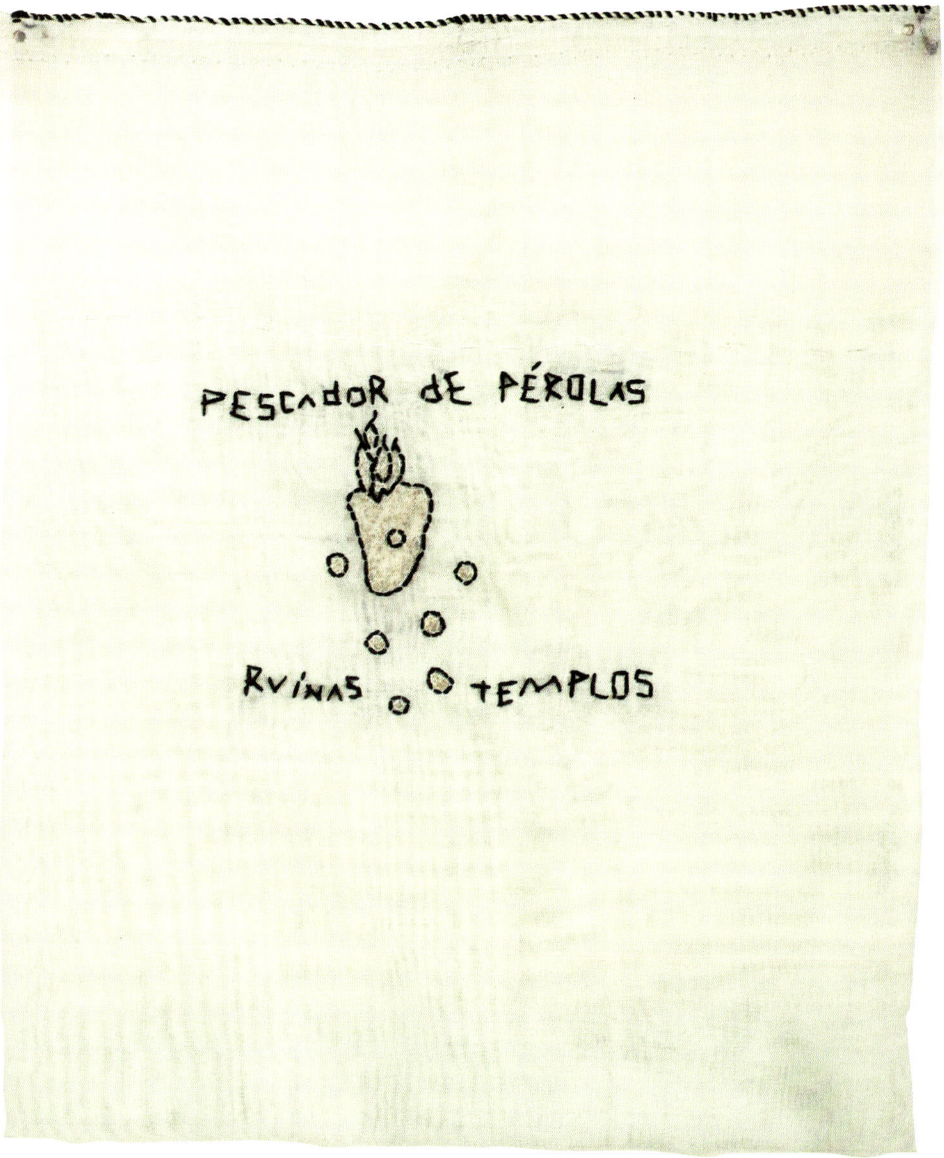

184. ***Pescador de pérolas***
[Pearl Fisher], 1991

Thread and metallic
paint on voile
36 × 31 cm
Private collection,
São Paulo, Brazil
PL.1063.0/00

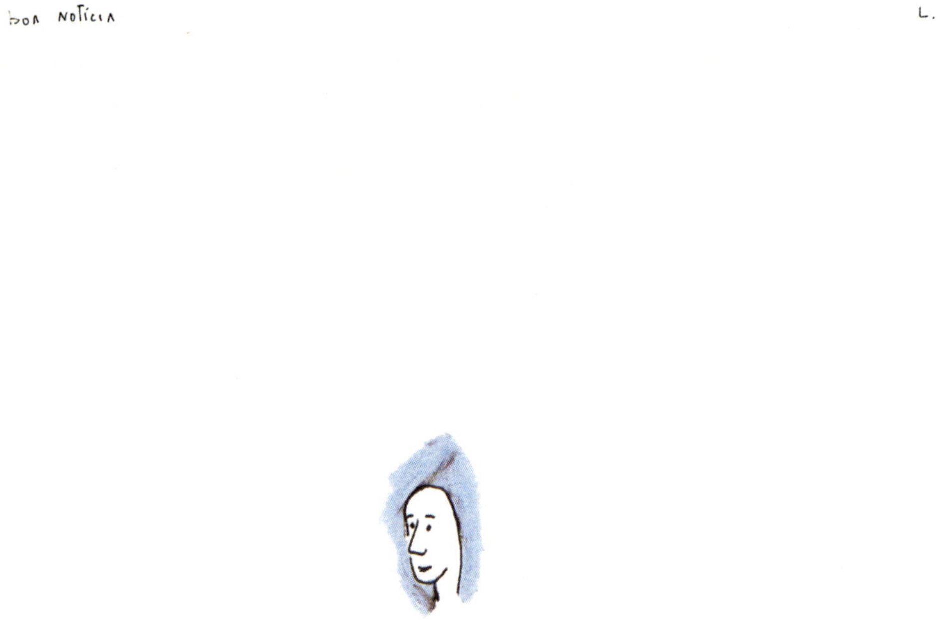

185. ***Boa notícia***
[Good News], *circa* 1991

Permanent ink and
colored pencil on paper
32 × 24 cm
Private collection,
São Paulo, Brazil
PL.0030.0/00

186. ***O apaixonado, o zig zag, 5 minutos*** [The Enamored One, the Zigzag, 5 Minutes], 1991

Guipure lace, thread and beads on unstretched canvas
33 × 20.5 cm
Private collection,
São Paulo, Brazil
PL.1455.0/00

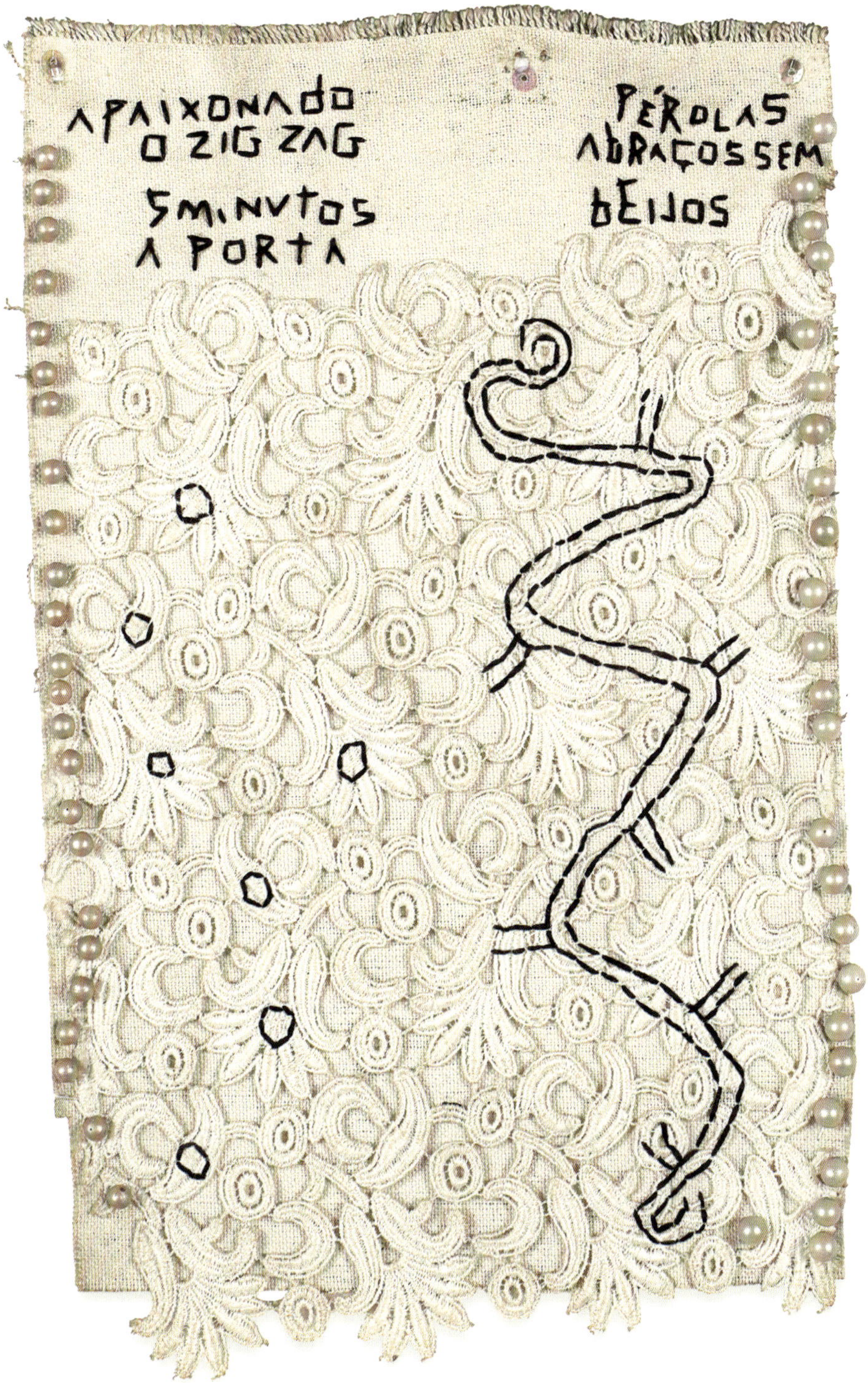

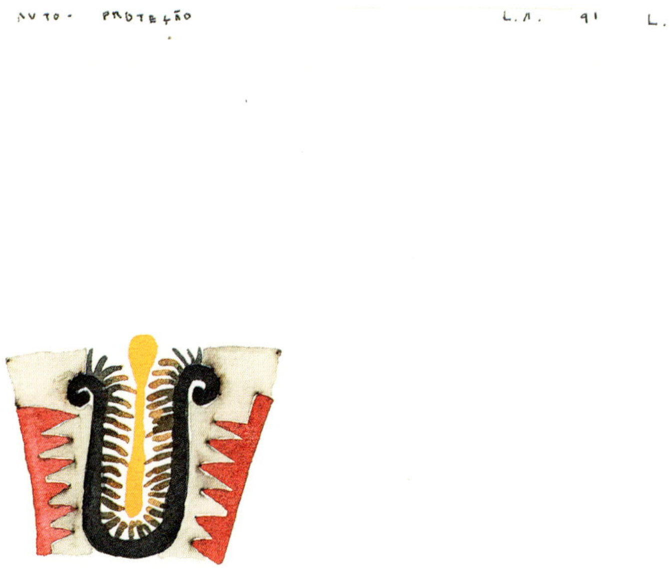

187. **[*Auto-proteção*]**
[Self-Protection], 1991

Watercolor on paper
30 × 22.5 cm
Collection of Luisa Malzoni Strina,
São Paulo, Brazil
PL.1164.0/00

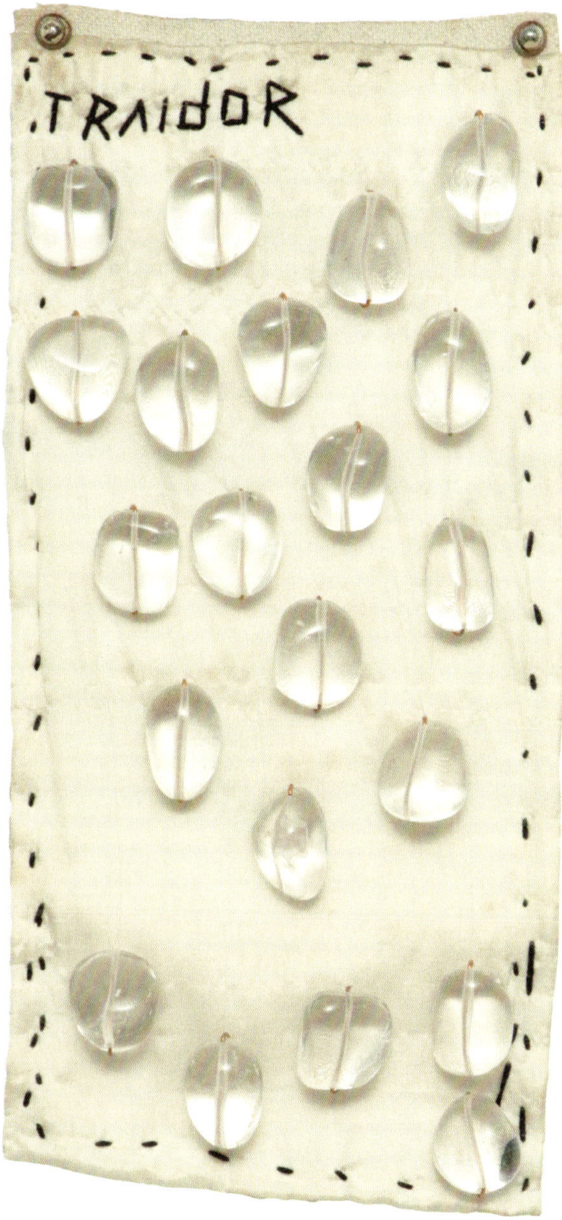

188. ***Traidor*** [Traitor], 1991

Thread, crystals, copper wire, and white wax on cotton fabric on unstretched canvas
24 × 12 × 2 cm
Collection of Luisa Malzoni Strina, São Paulo, Brazil
PL.1147.0/00

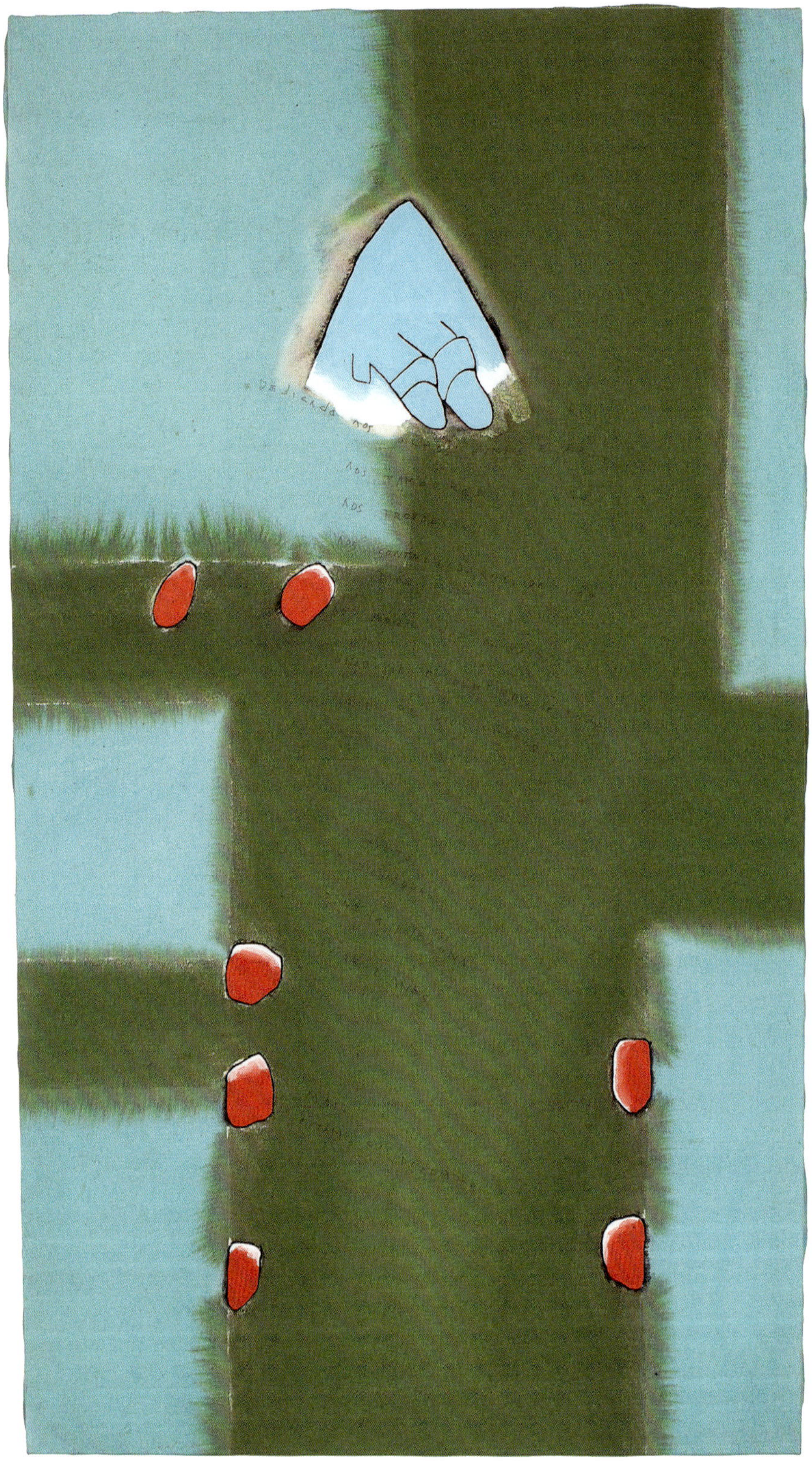

189. ***Dedicado aos olhos fundos e verdes***
[Dedicated to the Deep Green Eyes], [1991]

Acrylic paint and
colored pencil on canvas
163 × 95 cm
Collection of Evelyn and Ivoncy Ioschpe,
long term loan with
Pinacoteca de São Paulo, Brazil
PL.0878.0/00

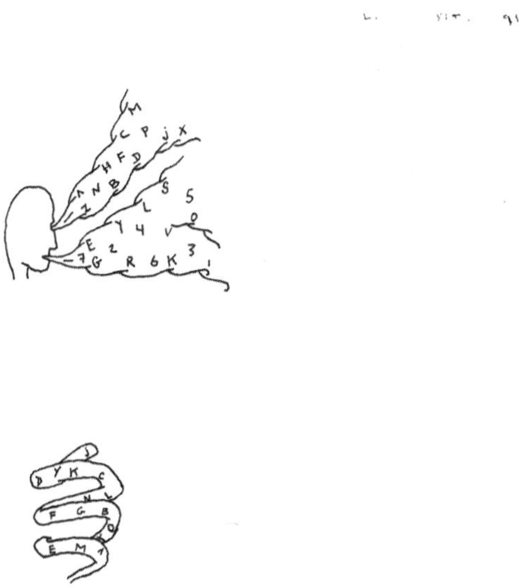

190. ***Untitled***, 1991

Permanent ink on paper
32 × 24 cm
Collection of Luisa Malzoni Strina,
São Paulo, Brazil
PL.1142.0/00

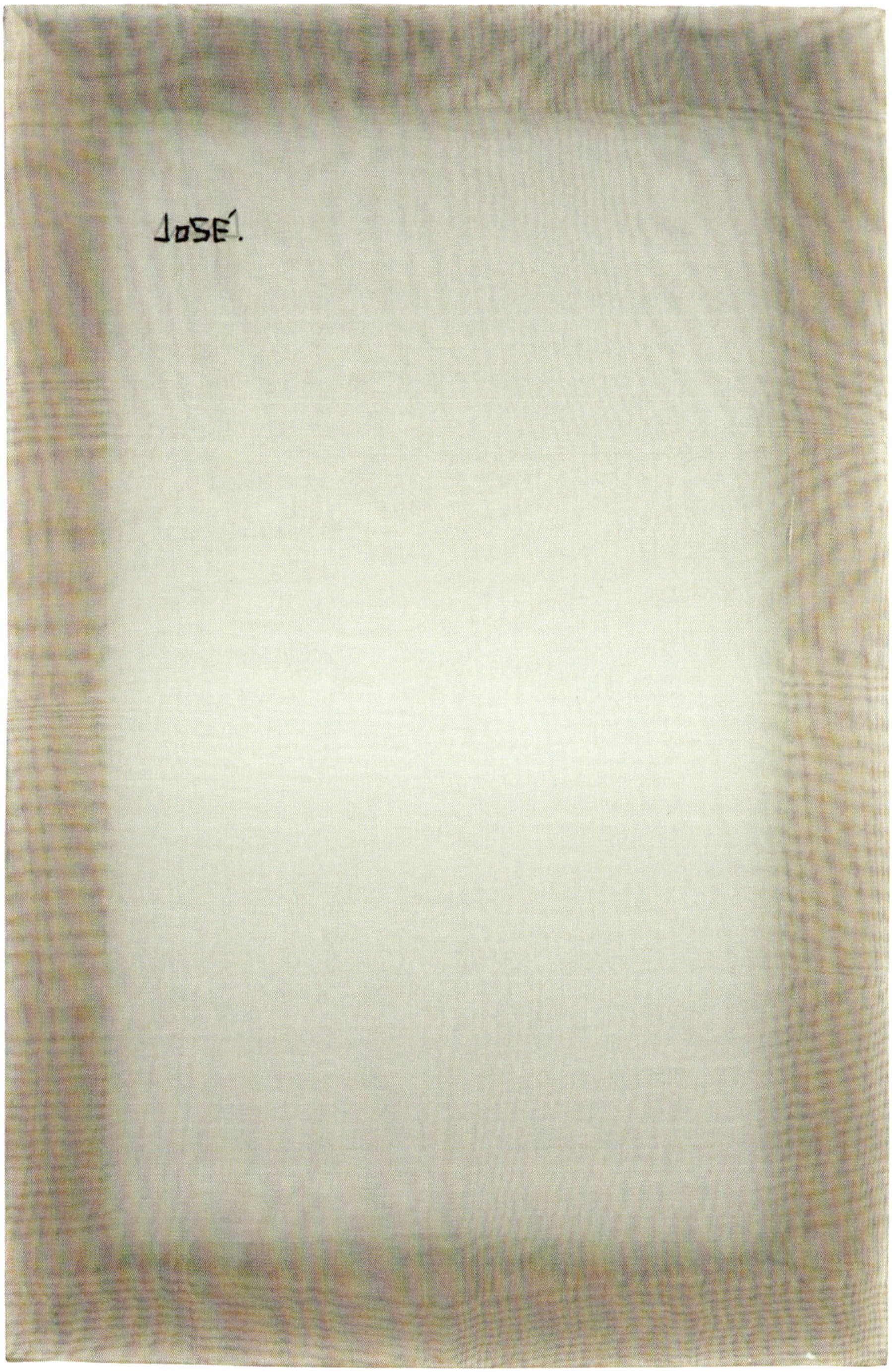

191. ***José***, 1991

Thread on voile
60 × 40 cm
Private collection,
São Paulo, Brazil
PL.0016.0/00

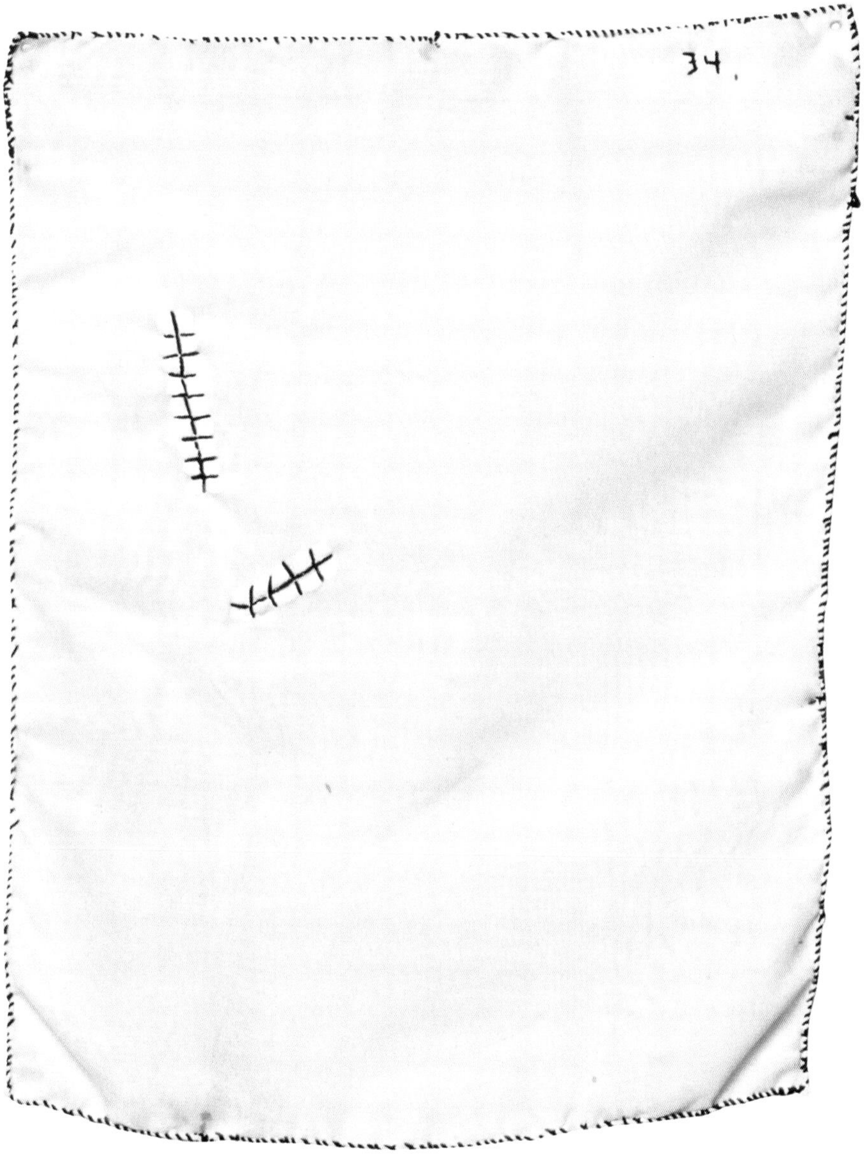

192. ***34 com Scars***
[34 With Scars], 1991

Thread and acrylic paint on voile
41 × 31 cm
The Museum of Modern Art,
gift Carmen Bezerra Dias in memory
of Theodorino Torquato Dias,
New York, United States
PL.0006.0/00

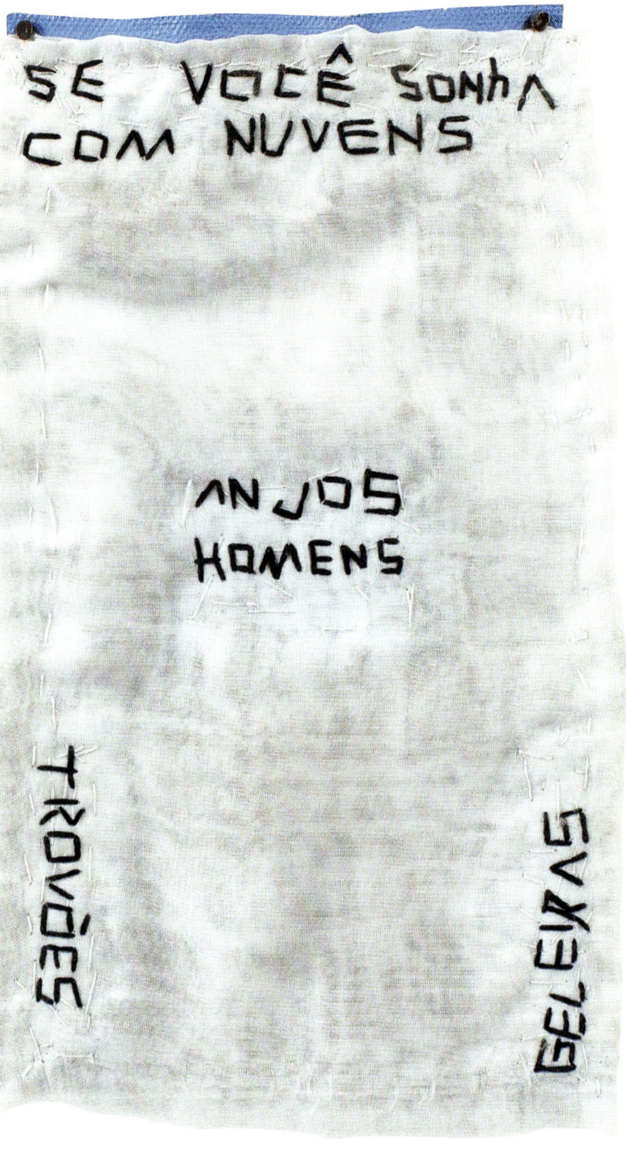

193. ***[Anjos; homens]***
[Angels; Men], 1991

Thread, acrylic paint and
unstretched canvas on voile
25.5 × 12.5 cm
Collection of Luisa Malzoni Strina,
São Paulo, Brazil
PL.1297.0/00

194. ***Provas de amor***
[Proofs of Love], 1991

Thread on unstretched
canvas and voile
50 × 37 cm
Collection of Susana
and Ricardo Steinbruch,
São Paulo, Brazil
PL.0013.0/00

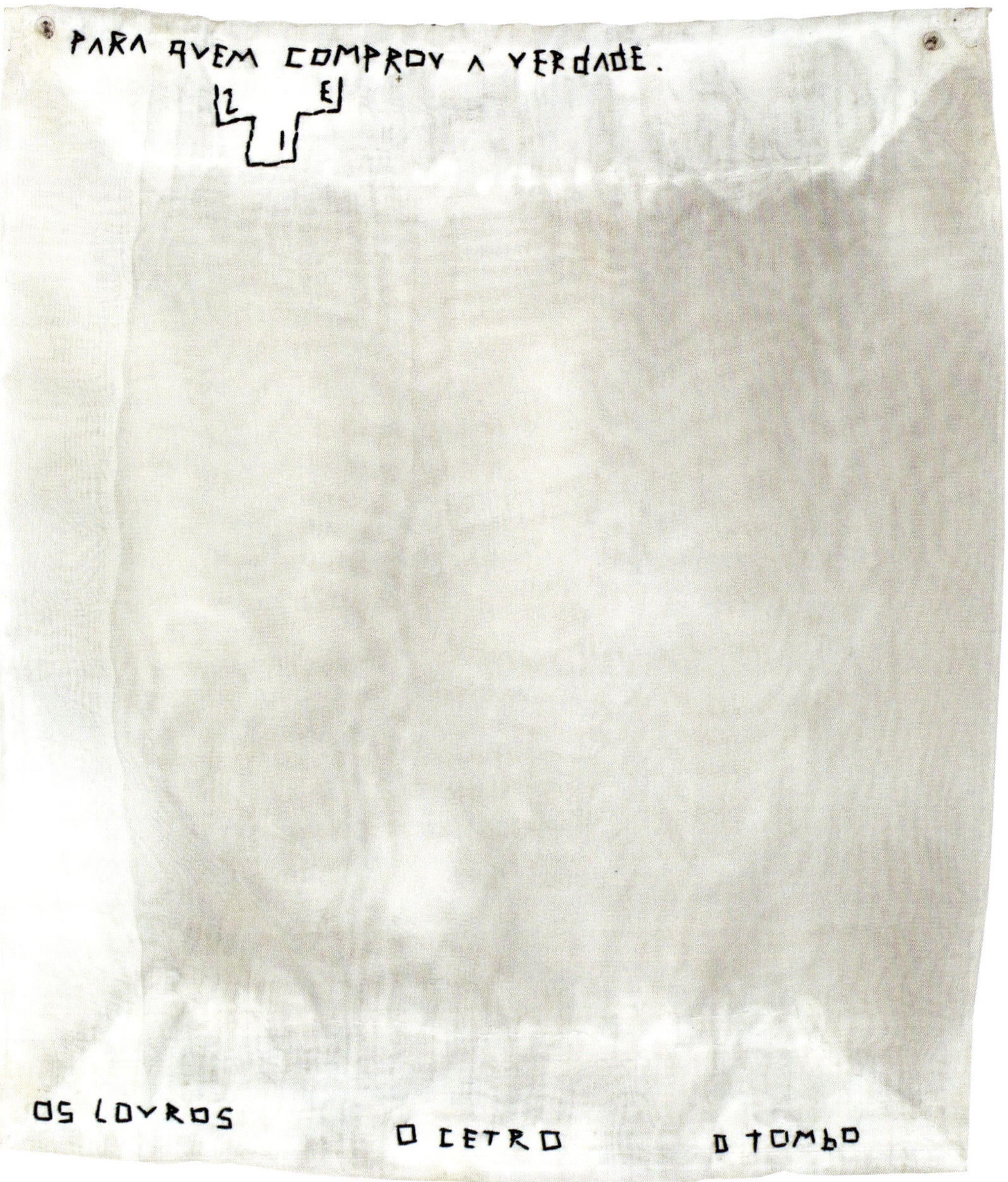

195. ***[Para quem comprou a verdade]*** [For Whoever Bought the Truth], *circa* 1991

Thread on voile
39 × 35 cm
Private collection,
São Paulo, Brazil
PL.0928.0/00

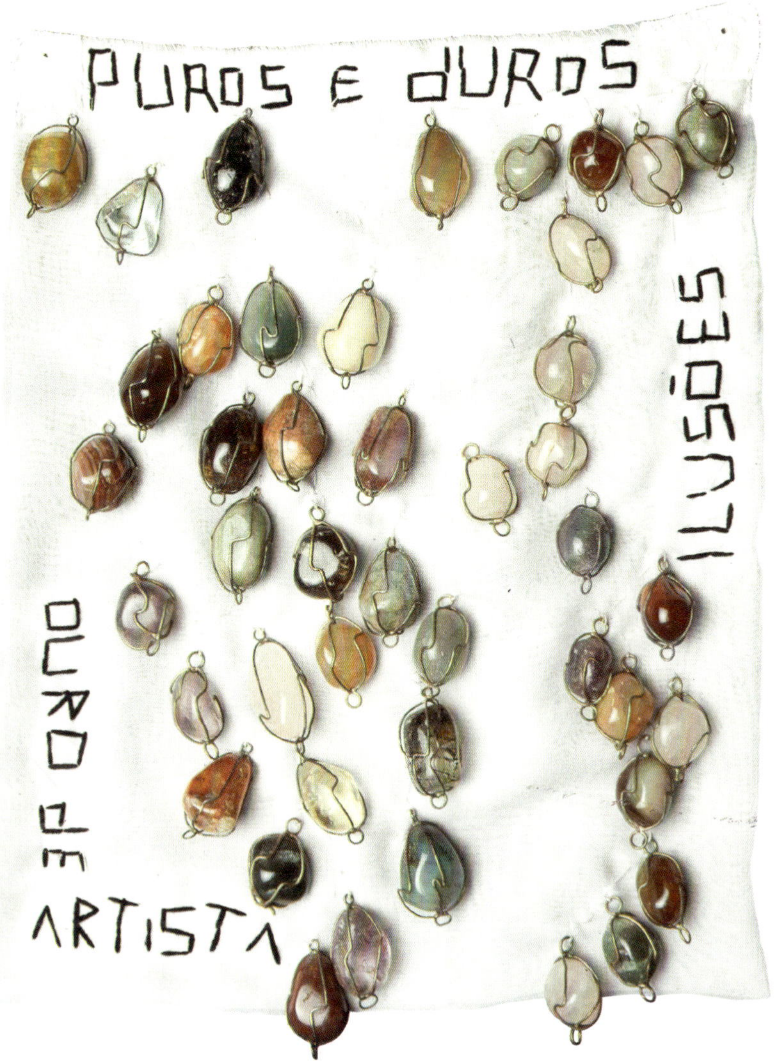

196. ***Puros e duros***
[The Pure and Hard], 1991

Embroidery and stones on cloth
26 × 21 × 1.5 cm
Los Angeles County Museum of Art,
gift família Bezerra Dias/Projeto Leonilson
and purchase with funds provided by
Gary and Tracy Mezzatesta, United States
PL.1523.0/00

244

197. ***Das tiranias***
[Of the Tyrannies], *circa* 1991

Acrylic paint on canvas
155 × 86 cm
Art Institute of Chicago, fund
Nancy Lauter McDougal and
Alfred L. McDougal, 2017,
United States
PL.0705.0/00

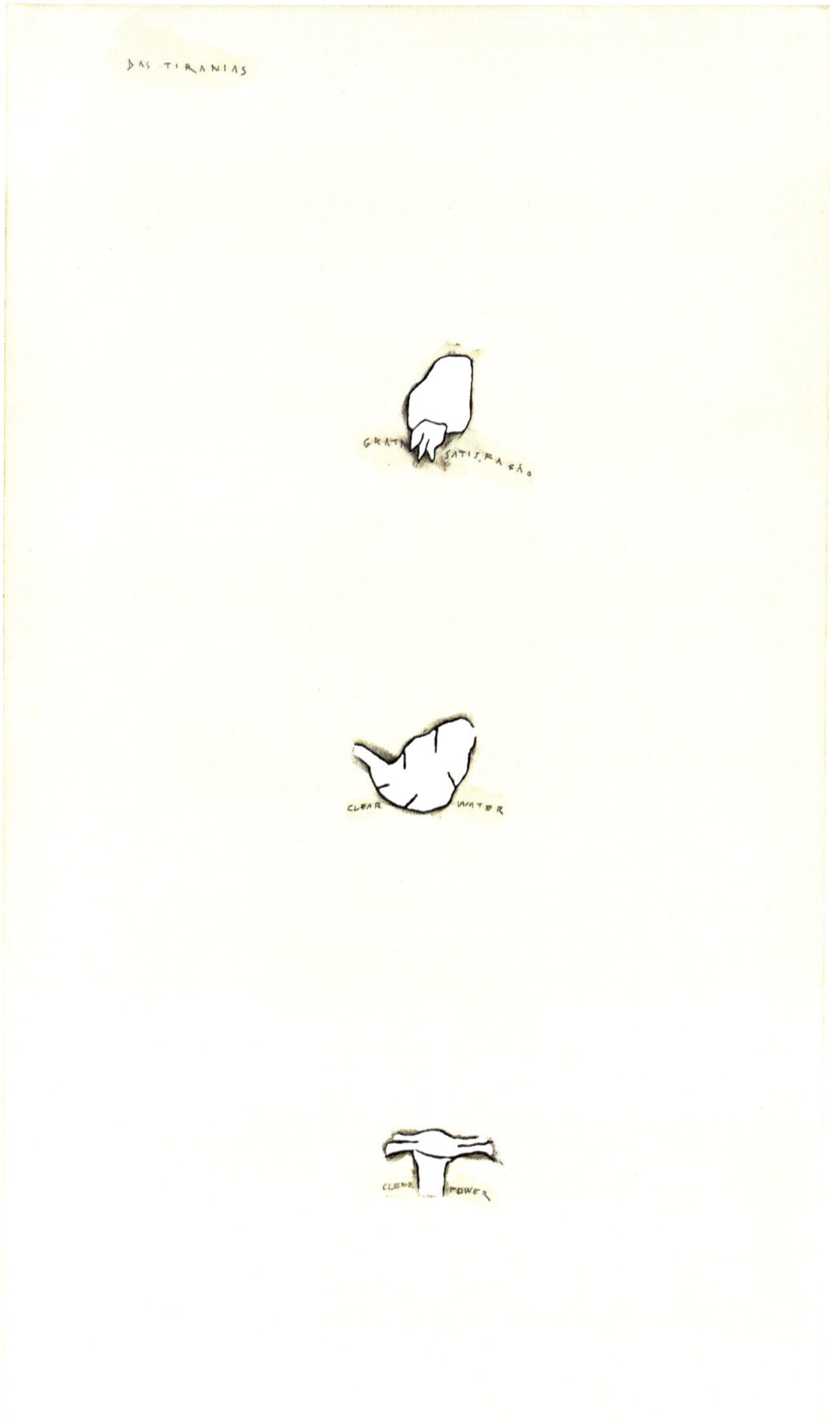
DAS TIRANIAS
SATISFAÇÃO
CLEAR
WATER
CLEAR
POWER

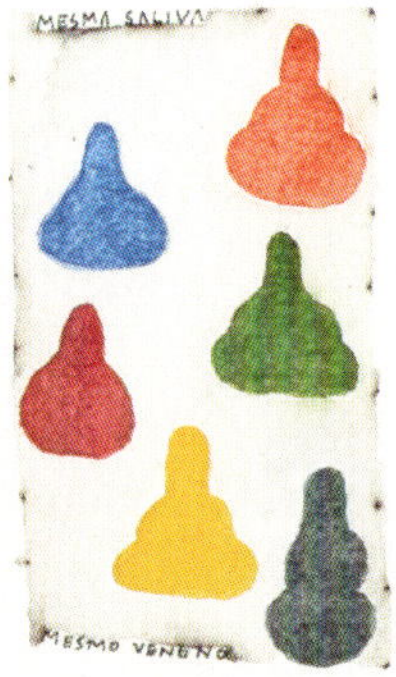

198. ***Mesma saliva mesmo veneno***
[Same Saliva Same Poison], 1991

Watercolor on white wove paper
30.5 × 23 cm
Art Institute of Chicago, fund
Nancy Lauter McDougal and
Alfred L. McDougal, 2017,
United States
PL.1169.0/00

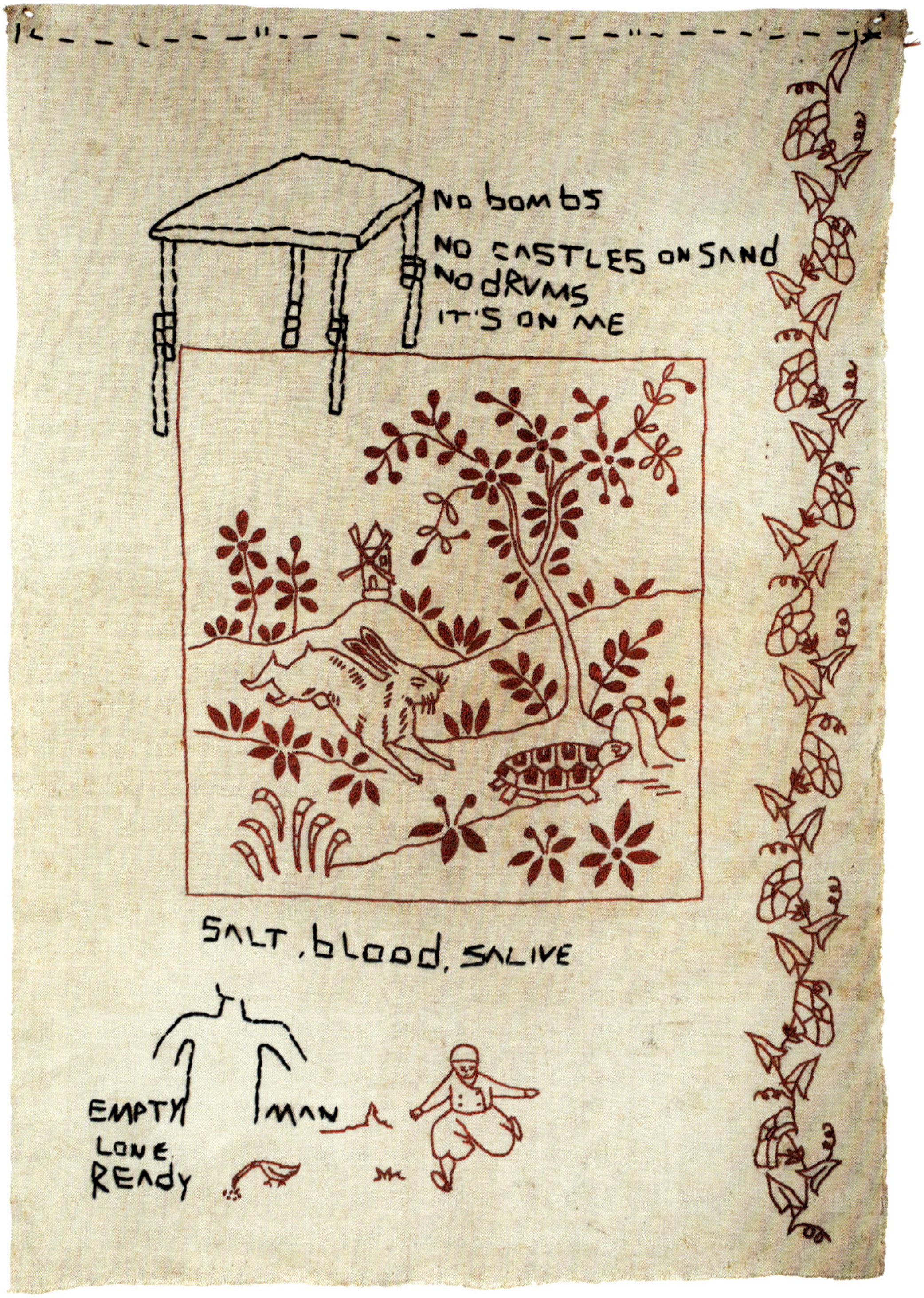

199. ***Empty Man*****, 1991**

Thread on embroidered linen
53 × 37 cm
Private collection,
São Paulo, Brazil
PL.0007.0/00

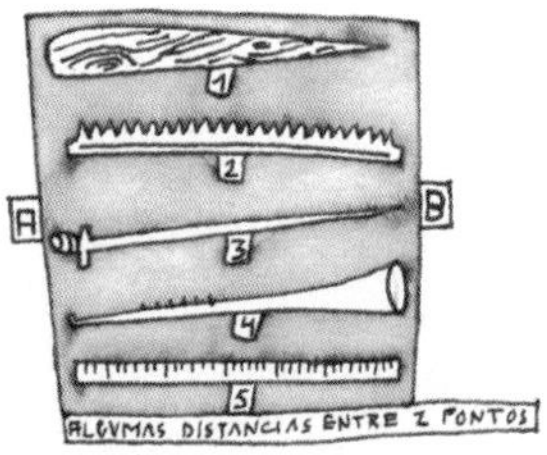

200. [***Algumas distâncias entre 2 pontos***] [Some Distances Between 2 Points], *circa* 1991

Permanent ink and
watercolor on paper
28 x 20 cm
Private collection,
São Paulo, Brazil
PL.0893.0/00

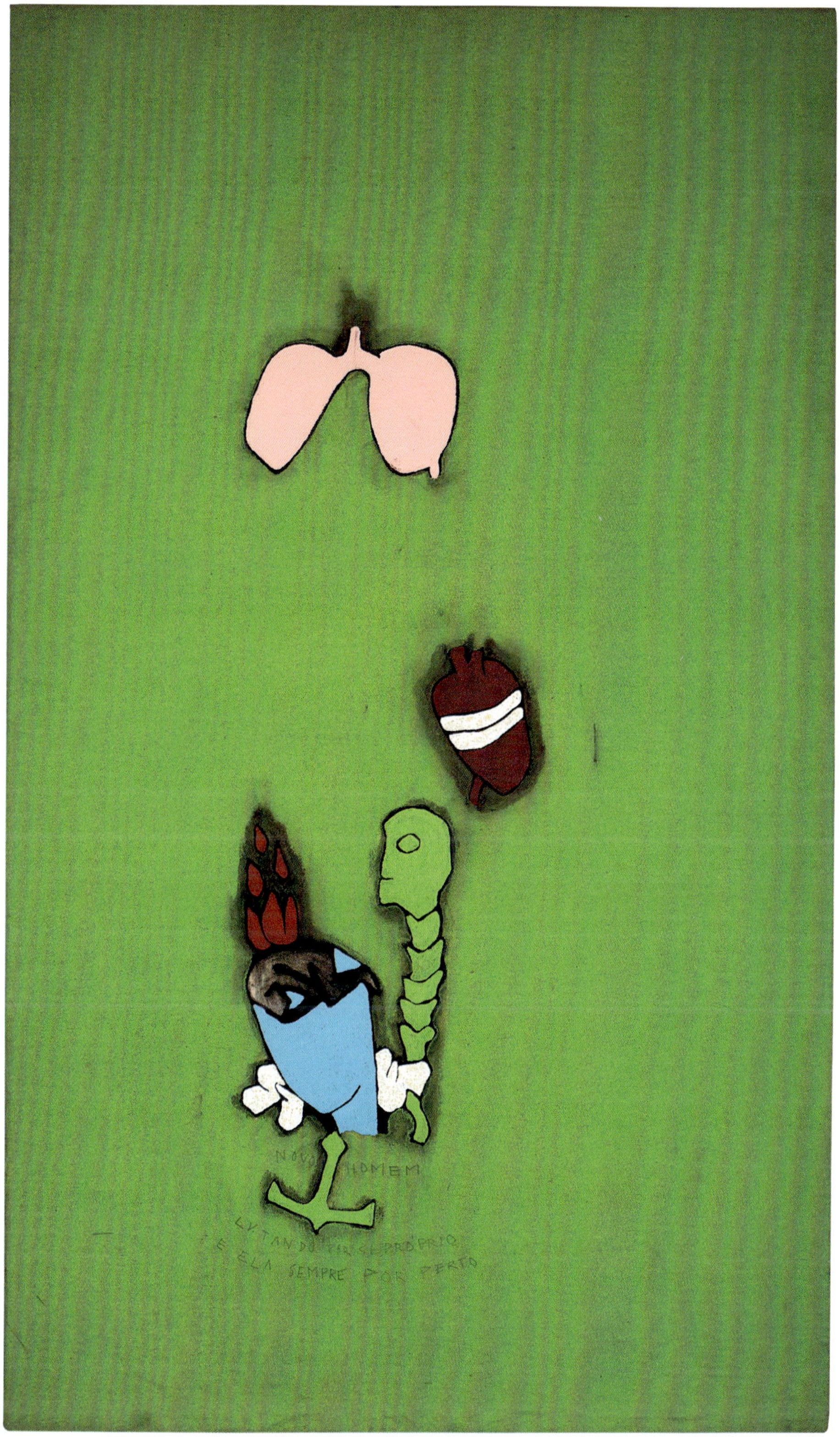

201. ***C/ ela sempre por perto***
[With Her Always Around], *circa* 1991

Acrylic paint and
colored pencil on canvas
143 x 85 cm
Collection of Jassanan Amoroso Dias Pastore,
São Paulo, Brazil
PL.0855.0/00

1992

202. ***O perigoso*** [The Dangerous One], from the series *O perigoso* [The Dangerous One], [1992]

Permanent ink and blood on paper
30.5 × 23 cm
Collection of Flávia and Guilherme Teixeira, Belo Horizonte, Brazil
PL.1070.0/00

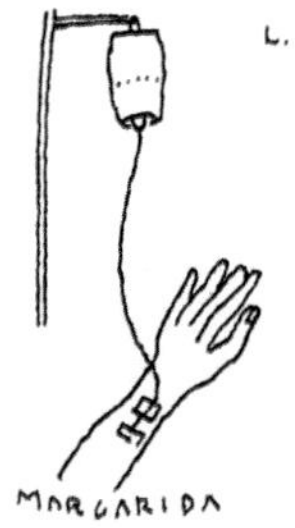

203. ***Margarida*** [Daisy],
from the series *O perigoso*
[The Dangerous One], [1992]

Permanent ink on paper
30.5 × 23 cm
Collection of Flávia and
Guilherme Teixeira,
Belo Horizonte, Brazil
PL.1071.0/00

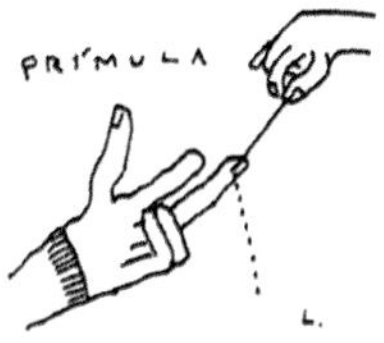

204. ***Prímula*** [Primrose], from the series *O perigoso* [The Dangerous One], [1992]

Permanent ink on paper
30.5 × 23 cm
Collection of Flávia and Guilherme Teixeira, Belo Horizonte, Brazil
PL.1072.0/00

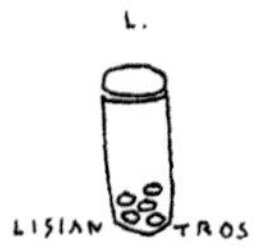

254

205. ***Lisiantros*** [Lisianthius], from the series O *perigoso* [The Dangerous One], [1992]

Permanent ink on paper
30.5 × 23 cm
Collection of Flávia and Guilherme Teixeira,
Belo Horizonte, Brazil
PL.1073.0/00

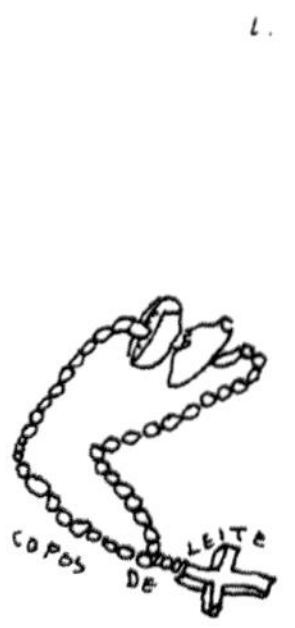

206. ***Copos-de-leite*** [Arum Lilies], from the series O *perigoso* [The Dangerous One], [1992]

Permanent ink on paper
30.5 × 23 cm
Collection of Flávia and Guilherme Teixeira, Belo Horizonte, Brazil
PL.1074.0/00

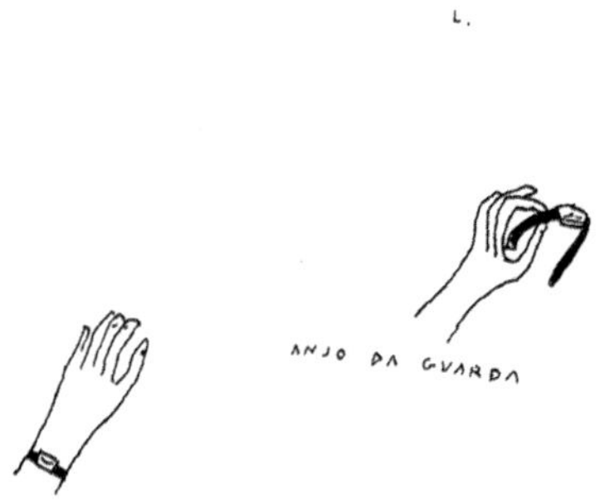

207. *Anjo da guarda* [Guardian Angel], from the series O *perigoso* [The Dangerous One], 1992

Permanent ink on paper
30.5 × 23 cm
Collection of Flávia and Guilherme Teixeira, Belo Horizonte, Brazil
PL.1075.0/00

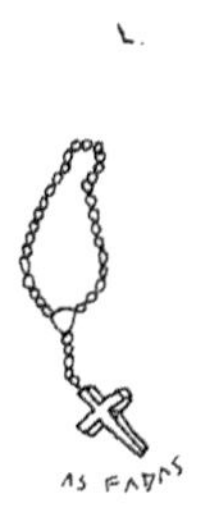

208. ***As fadas*** [The Fairies], from the series *O perigoso* [The Dangerous One], [1992]

Permanent ink on paper
30.5 × 23 cm
Collection of Flávia and Guilherme Teixeira, Belo Horizonte, Brazil
PL.1076.0/00

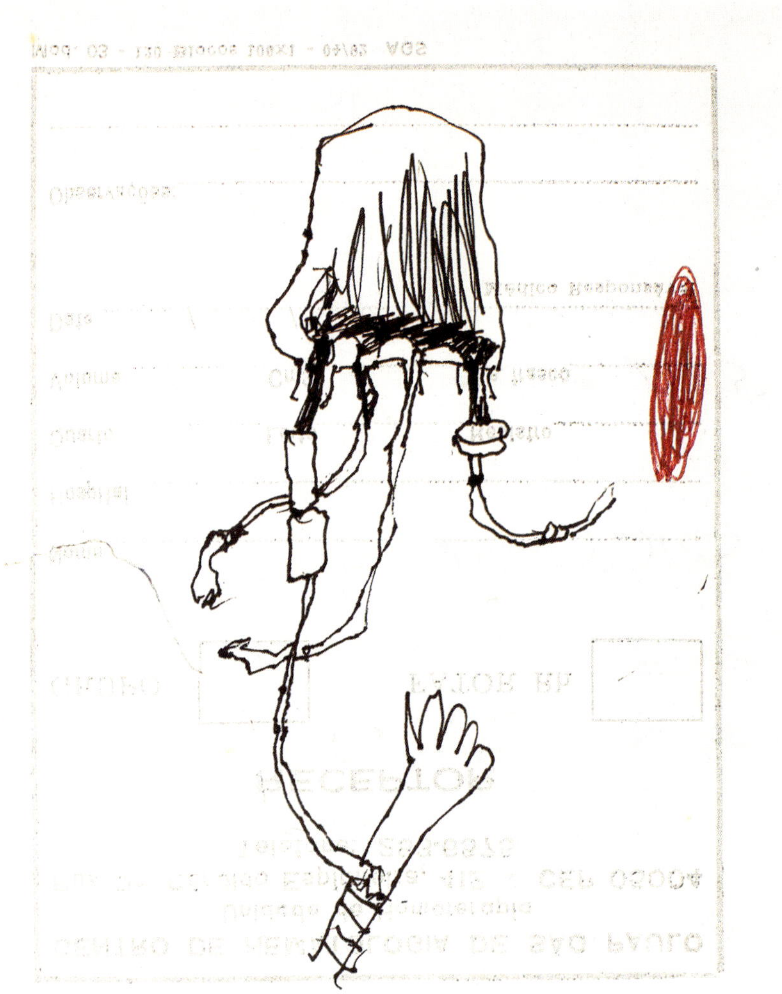

209. ***Untitled***, 1992

Marker on paper
12.5 × 9.5 cm
Private collection,
São Paulo, Brazil
PL.0448.0/00

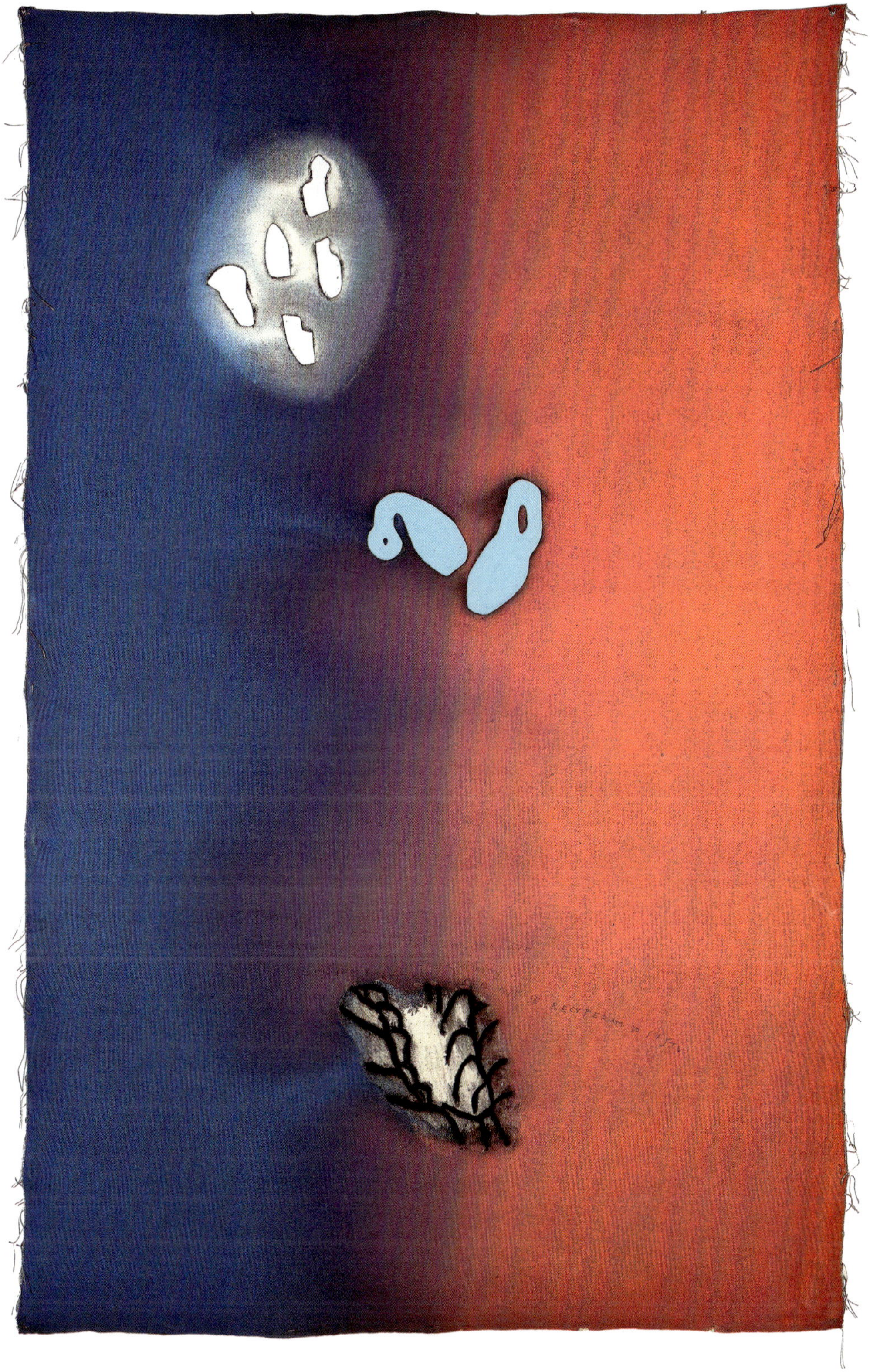

210. ***Quantos já se foram e pra que*** [How Many Are Already Gone and What For], 1992

Acrylic paint and colored pencil on unstretched canvas
160 × 102 cm
Collection of Rafael Moraes, São Paulo, Brazil
PL.2389.0/00

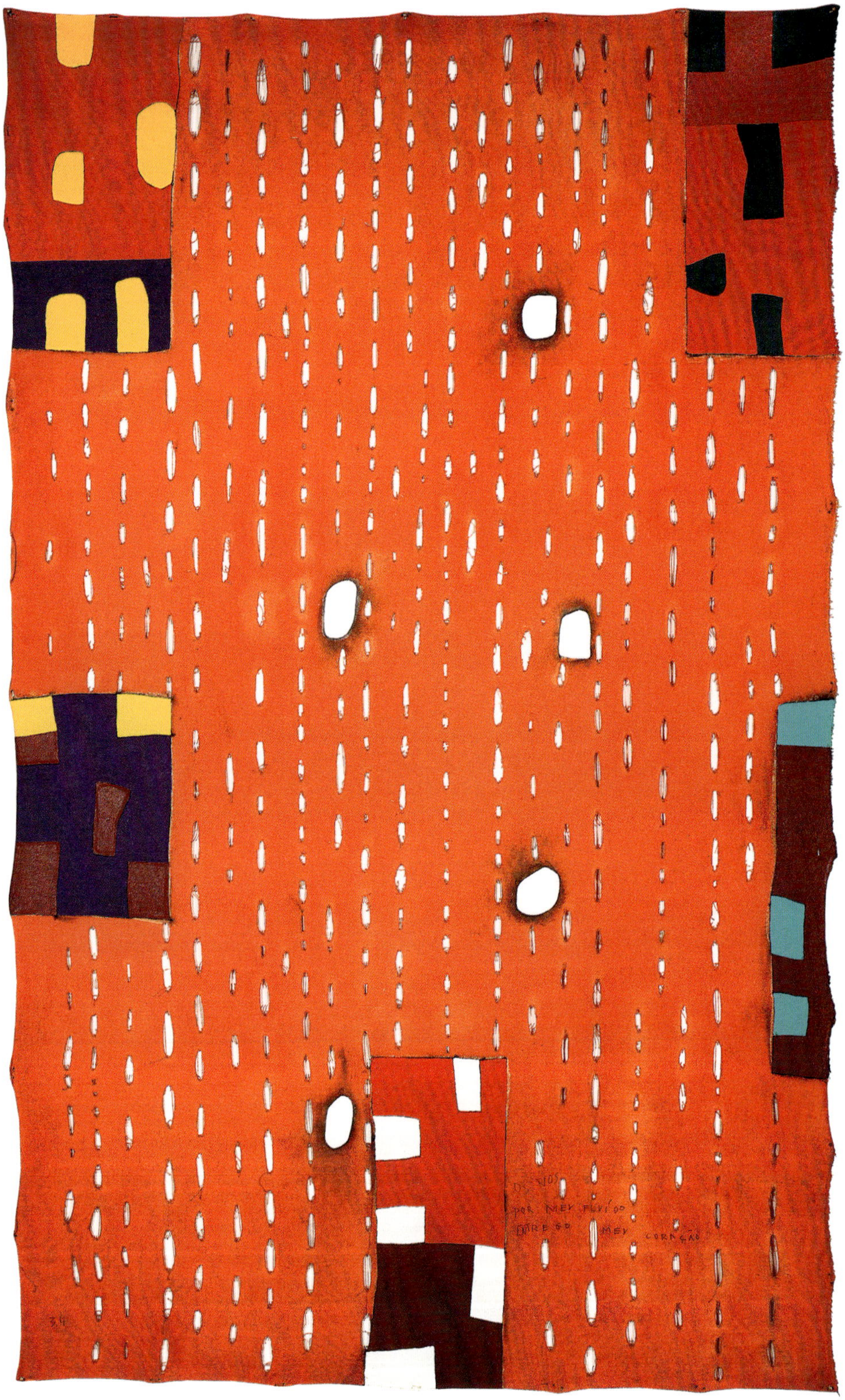

211. ***Os rios por meu fluído entrego meu coração***
[The Rivers Through My Fluid I Surrender My Heart], 1992

Acrylic paint and cutting on unstretched canvas
166.5 × 103 cm
Collection of Eduardo Brandão and Jan Fjeld,
São Paulo, Brazil
PL.0797.0/00

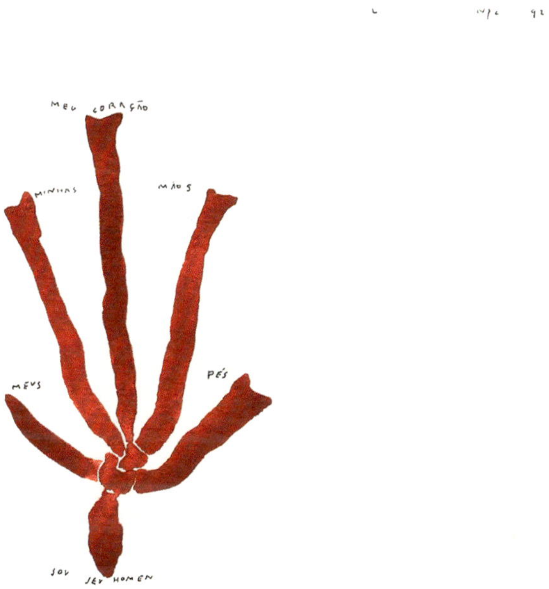

212. ***Sou seu homem*** [I'm Your Man], 1992

Watercolor and ink on paper
23 × 30.5 cm
The Museum of Modern Art,
gift Friends of Contemporary Drawing,
1999, New York, United States
PL.1533.0/00

213. ***Se você sonha com nuvens***
[If You Dream of Clouds], 1992

Embroidery on felt
and cotton fabric
100.5 × 18 cm
Museu de Arte Contemporânea
da Universidade de São Paulo,
gift família Bezerra Dias/
Projeto Leonilson, 1999, Brazil
PL.1050.0/00

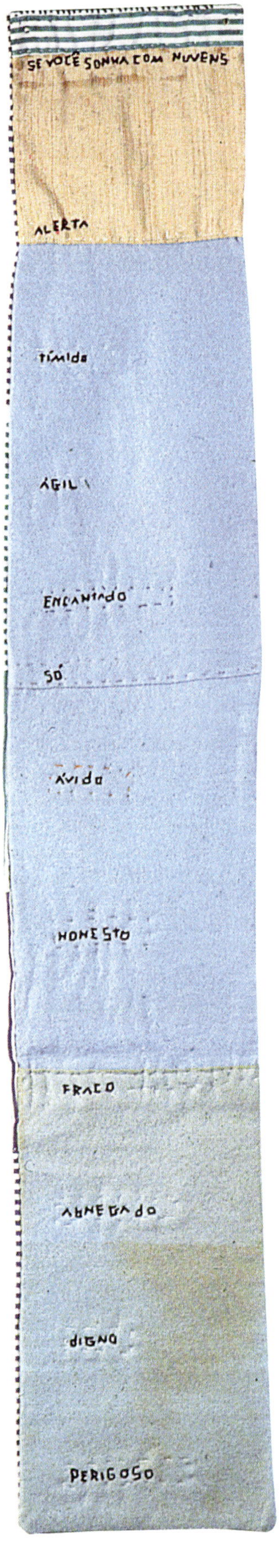

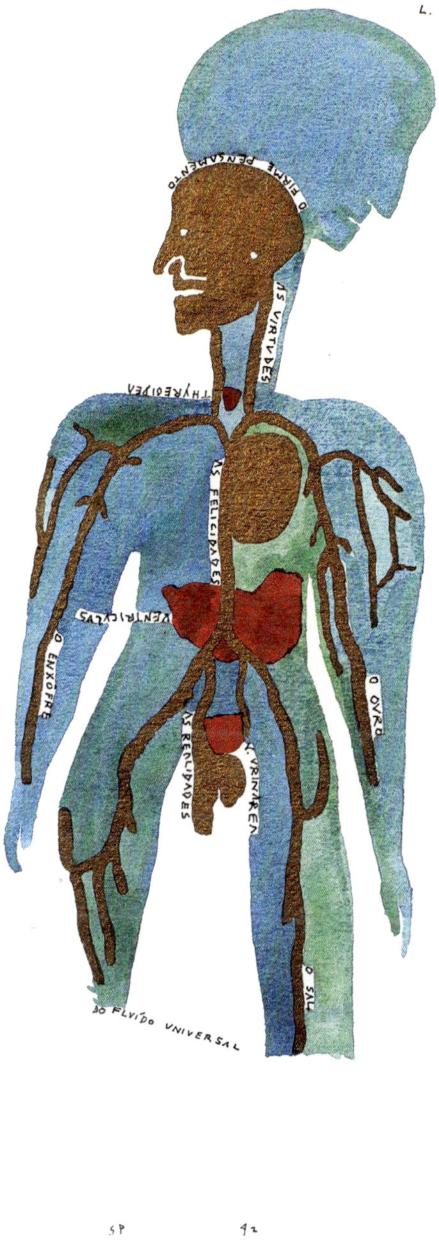

214. *[O firme pensamento]*
[The Firm Thought], 1992

Watercolor and
metallic paint on paper
30 × 23 cm
Collection of Luisa Malzoni Strina,
São Paulo, Brazil
PL.1155.0/00

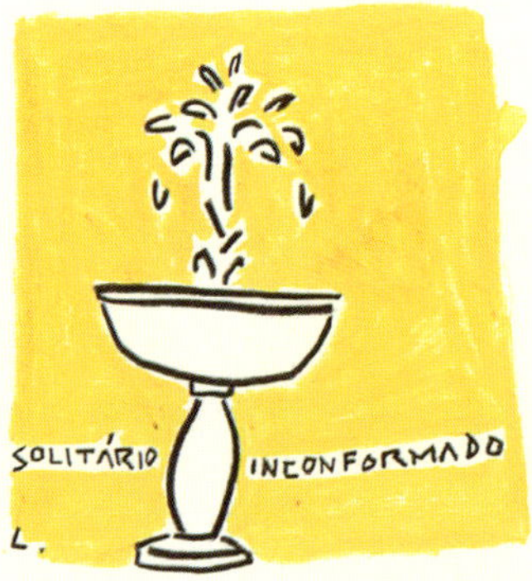

215. *[Solitário inconformado]*
[The Unreconciled Solitary],
circa 1992

Colored pencil on paper
32.5 × 23.5 cm
Private collection,
São Paulo, Brazil
PL.0398.0/00

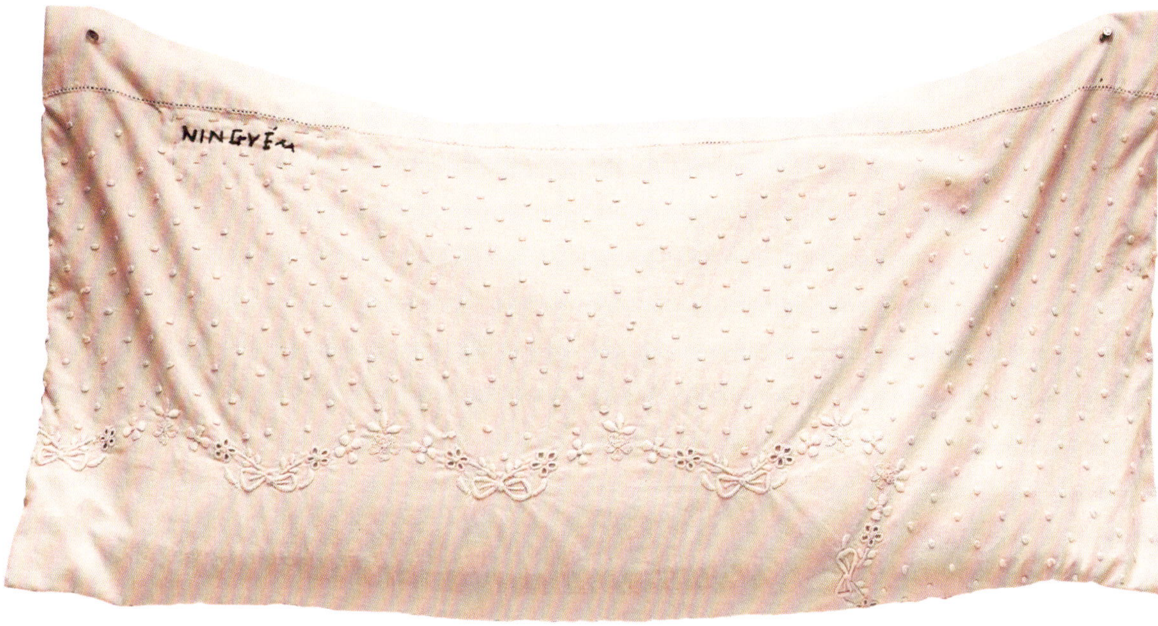

216. ***Ninguém*** [Nobody], [1992]

Thread on embroidered cotton pillowcase, chequered cotton fabric, and pillow
23.5 × 46 × 5 cm
Collection of Maria Pini Piva, São Paulo, Brazil
PL.0847.0/00

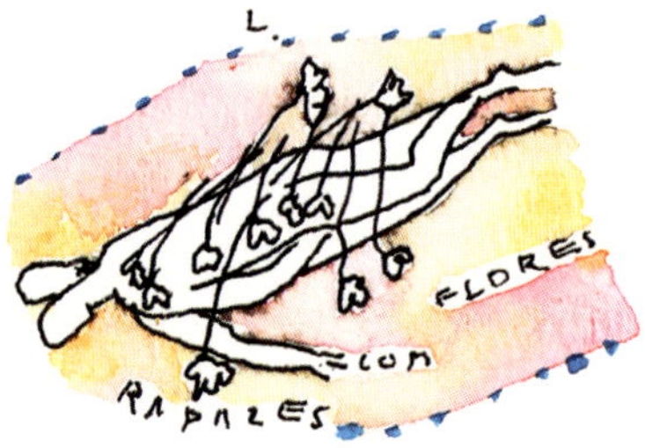

217. ***Rapazes com flores*** [Young Men With Flowers], 1992

Permanent ink and
watercolor on paper
26 × 16 cm
Collection of Leda Catunda,
São Paulo, Brazil
PL.0895.0/00

267

218. ***Les moments***
[The Moments], 1992

Thread on felt
31 × 20 cm
Collection of Janka Babenco,
São Paulo, Brazil
PL.0840.0/00

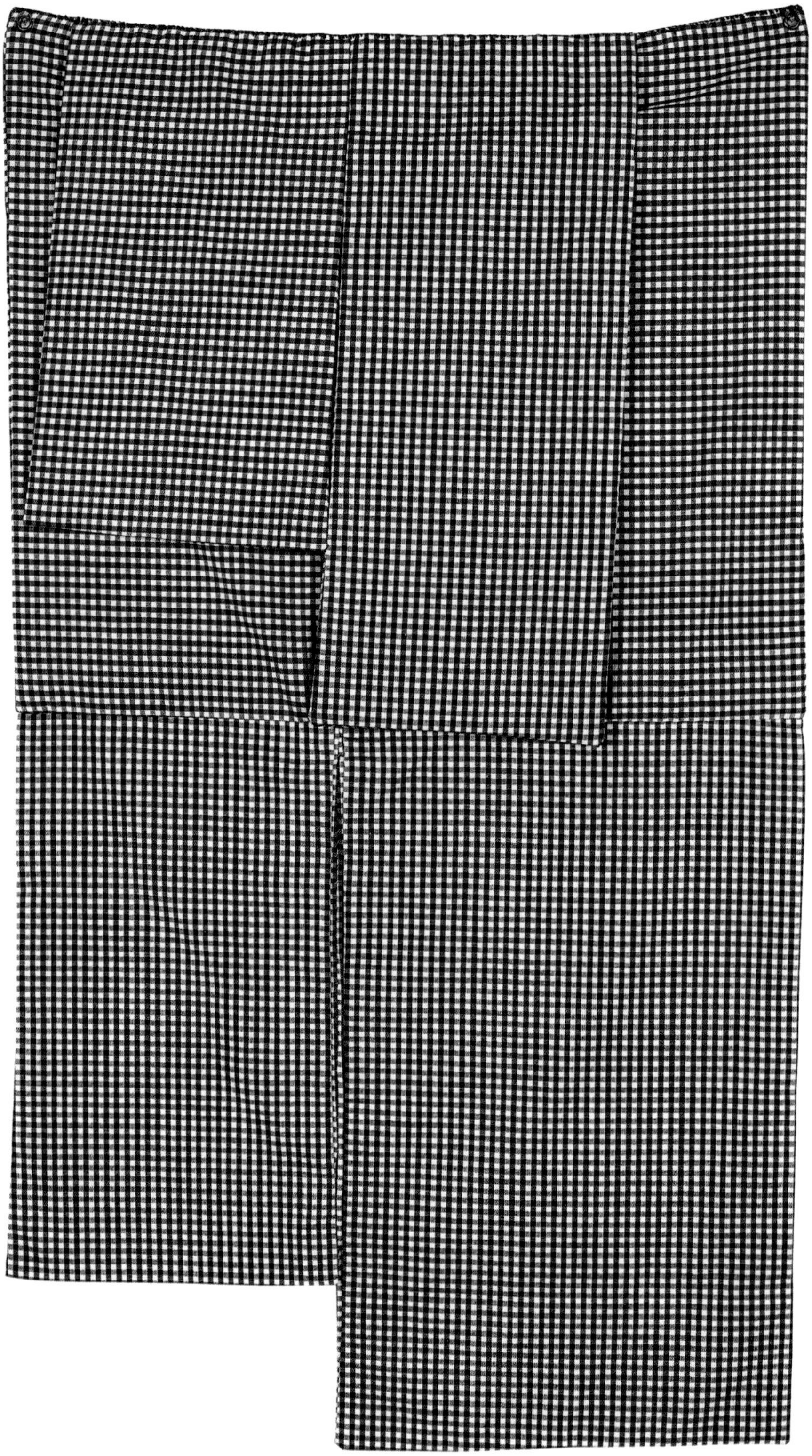

219. ***Roupa de homem***
[Men's Clothing], *circa* 1992

Thread on chequered
cotton fabric
64 × 36 cm
Private collection,
São Paulo, Brazil
PL.0022.0/00

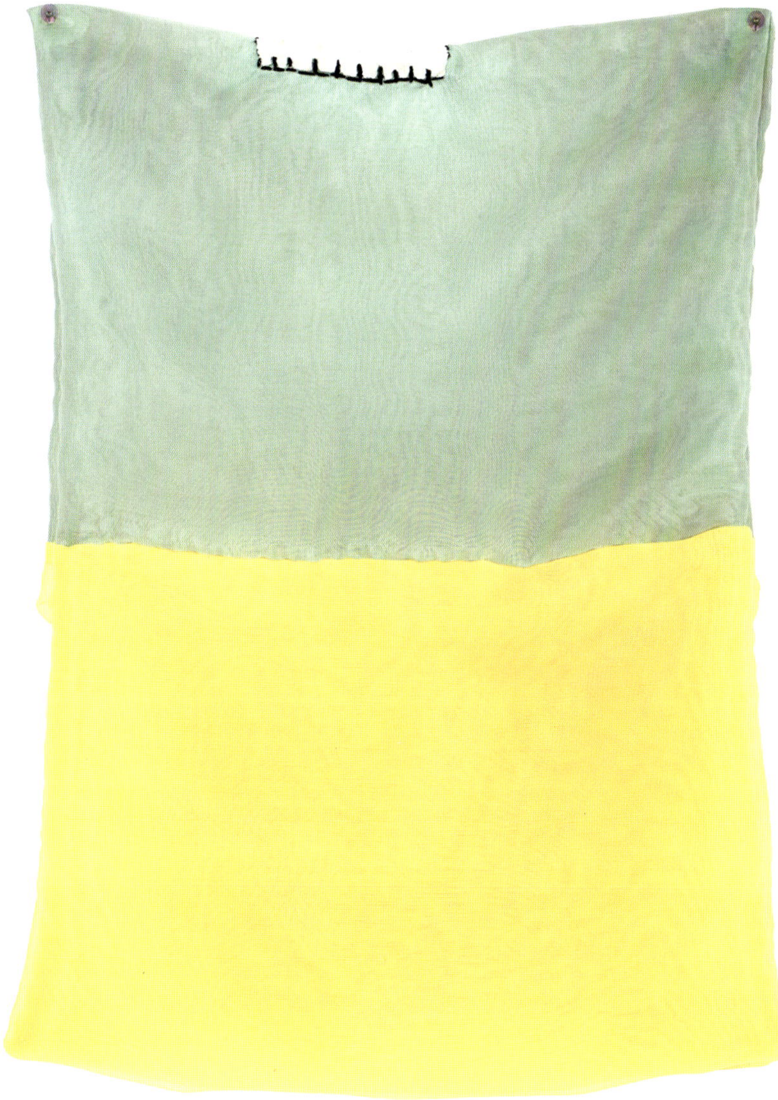

220. ***Verde e amarelo***
[Green and Yellow], 1992

Thread and acrylic
paint on voile
37 × 28.5 cm
Private collection,
São Paulo, Brazil
PL.0003.0/00

221. ***Águas divididas***
[Divided Waters], 1992

Thread on patterned silk
and striped cotton fabric
42 × 38 cm
Private collection,
São Paulo, Brazil
PL.0010.0/00

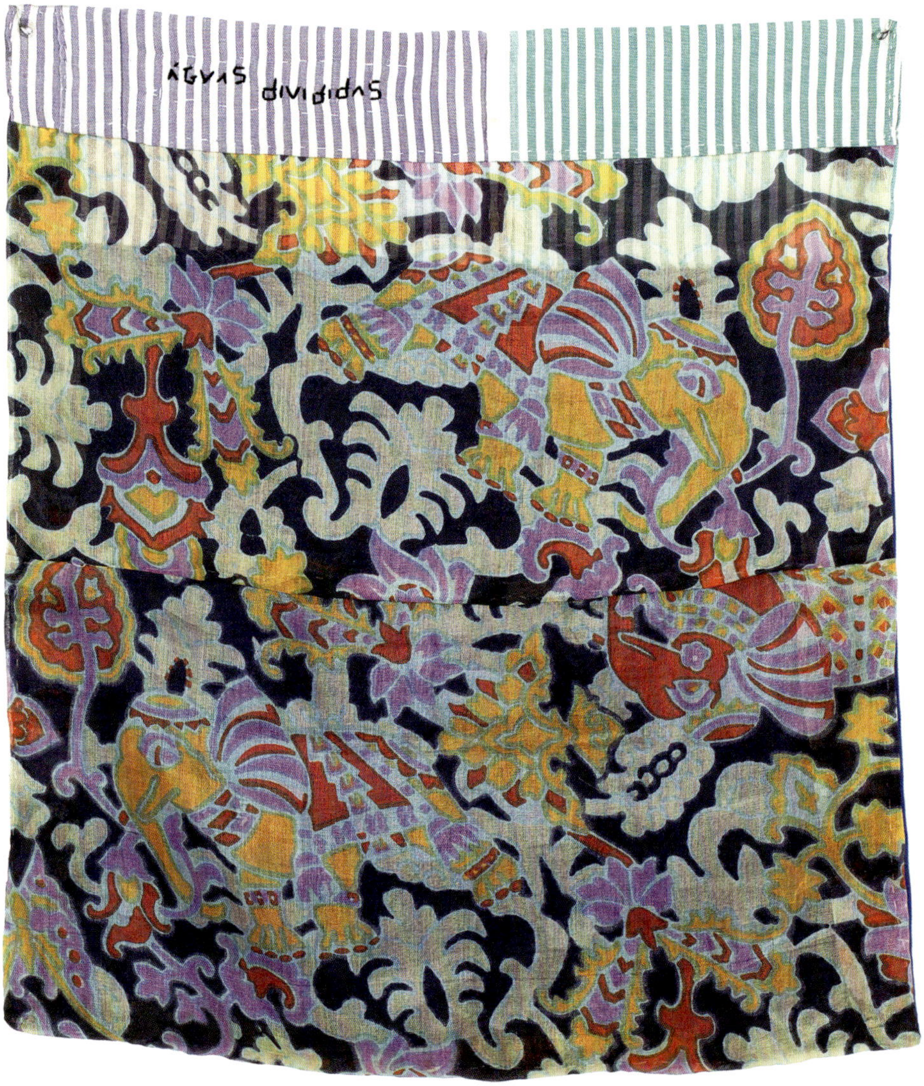

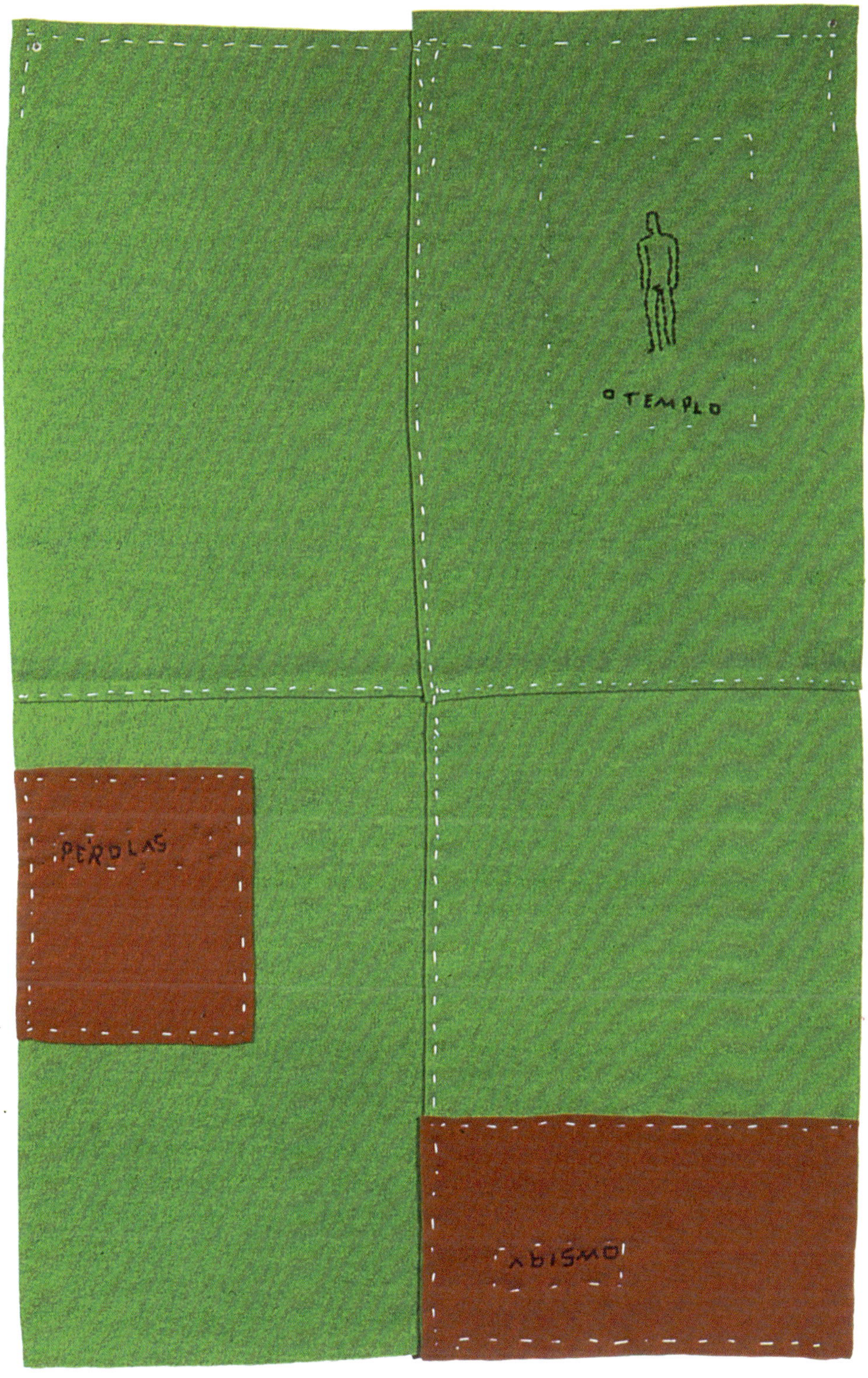

222. ***O templo***
[The Temple], 1992

Thread on felt
58 × 38 cm
Private collection,
São Paulo, Brazil
PL.1077.0/00

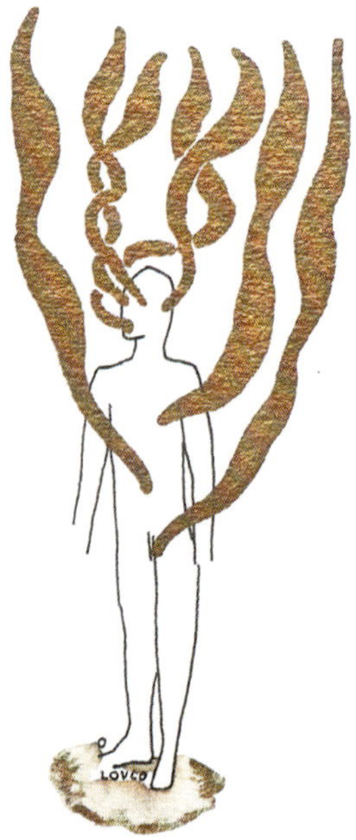

223

223. ***[O louco]***
[The Madman], 1992

Permanent ink and
metallic paint on paper
32 × 24 cm
Collection of Ricardo Resende
and Jose Mauro Del Royo Correa
(*in memoriam*),
São Paulo, Brazil
PL.1513.0/00

224. ***Barbara (com as mãos nos bolsos)*** [Barbara (With Her Hands in Her Pockets)], 1992

Thread on lace and fabric
152 × 92 cm
Brondesbury Art Collection
PL.1502.0/00

273

224

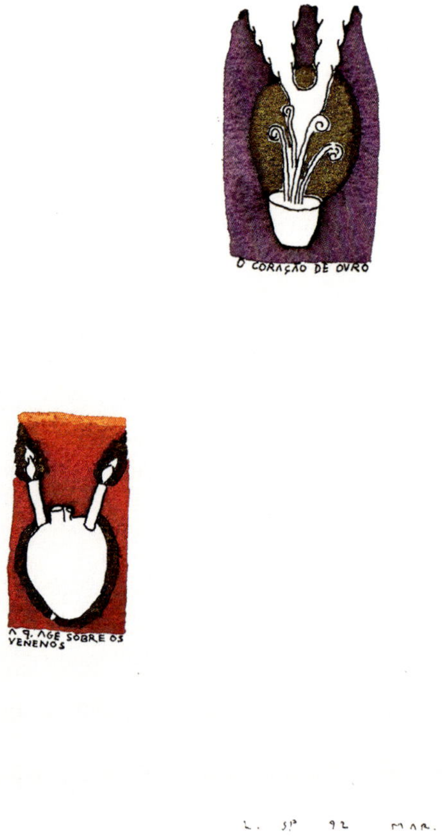

225. [***O coração de ouro***]
[The Heart of Gold], 1992

Permanent ink, watercolor,
and metallic paint on paper
30.5 × 22.5 cm
Collection of Luisa Malzoni Strina,
São Paulo, Brazil
PL.1173.0/00

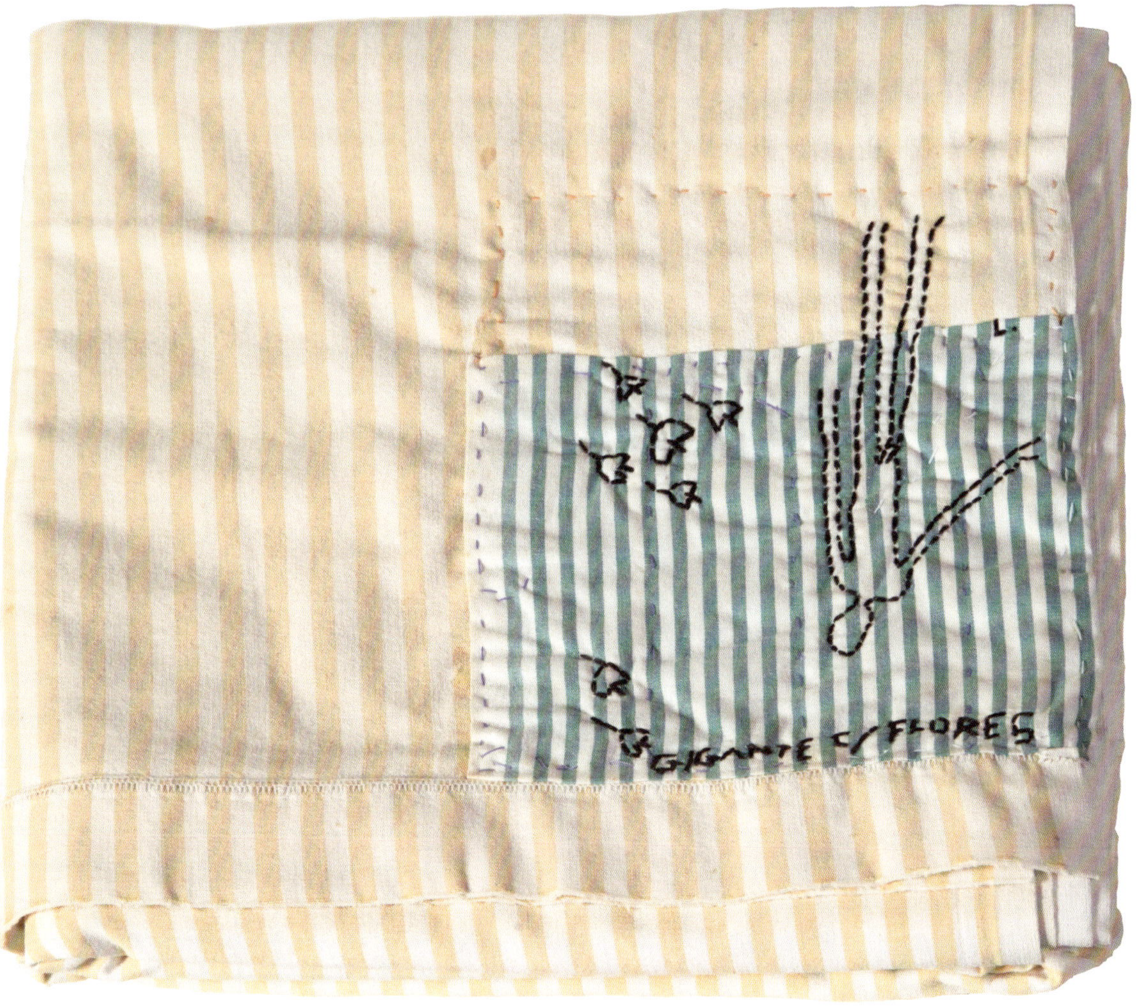

226. ***Gigante c/ flores***
[Giant with Flowers] (detail), [1992]

Thread on striped cotton bed
sheet and acrylic paint on iron base
105 × 35 × 35 cm
Private collection,
São Paulo, Brazil
PL.0341.0/00

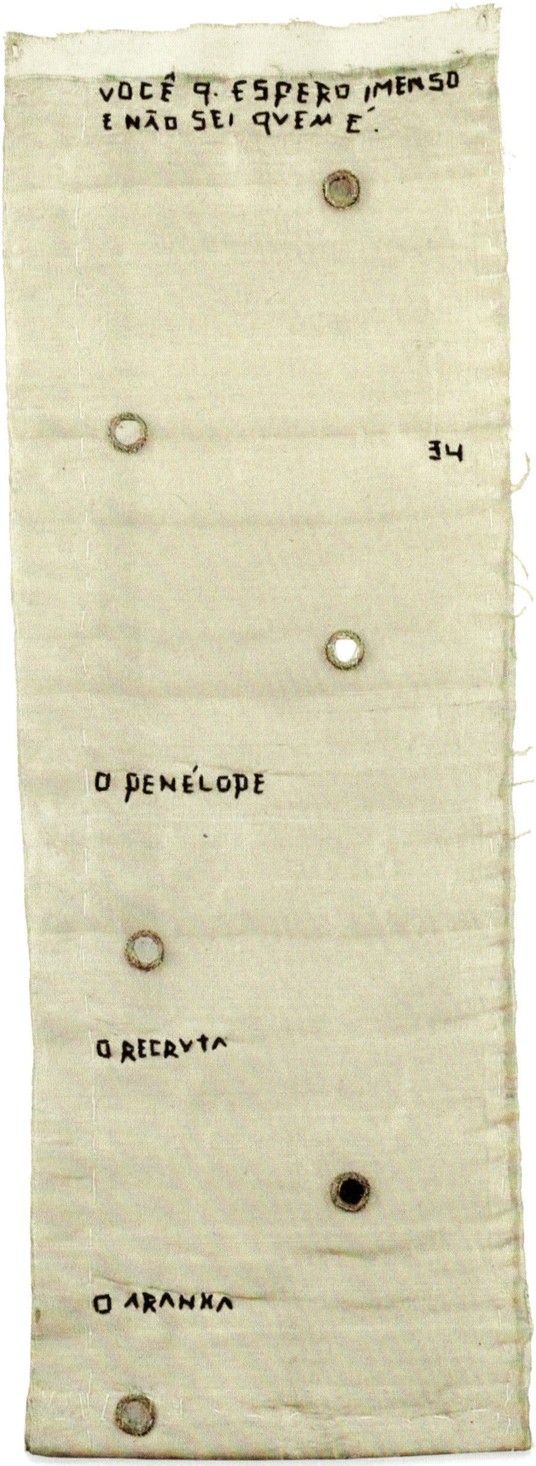

227. ***O Penélope, o Recruta, o Aranha***
[The Penelope, the Recruit, the Spider], *circa* 1992

Thread and sequins on voile
and unstretched canvas
50.5 × 18 cm
Private collection,
São Paulo, Brazil
PL.1355.0/00

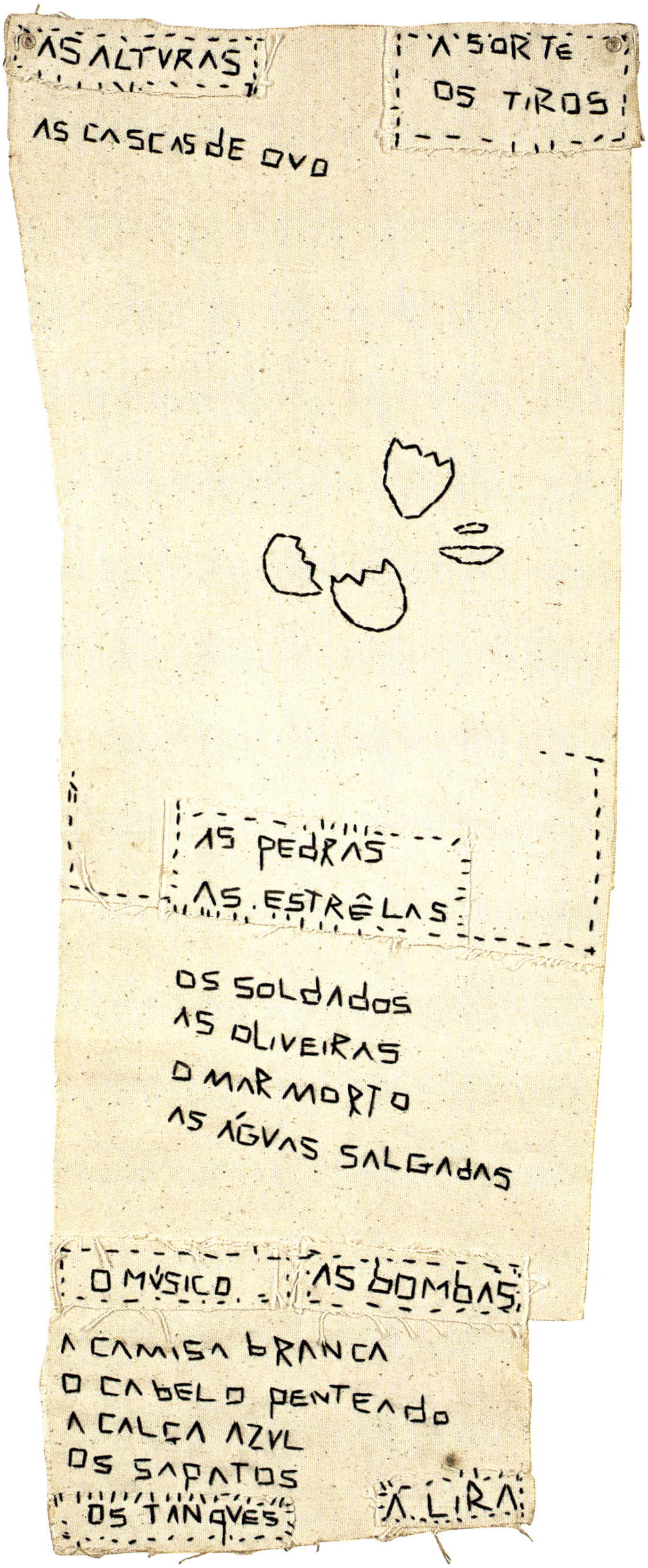

228. ***As cascas de ovo***
[The Egg Shells], 1992

Thread on unstretched canvas
65 × 24 cm
Private collection,
São Paulo, Brazil
PL.0676.0/00

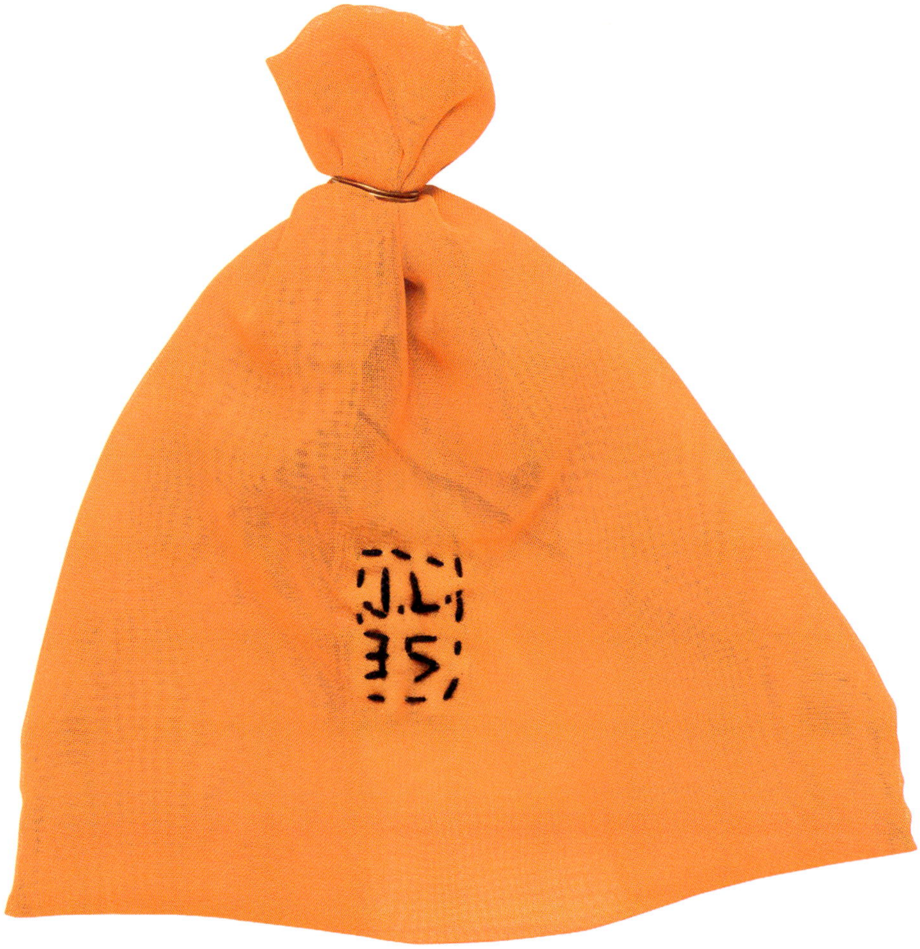

230. ***Saquinho***
[Small Bag], *circa* 1992

Thread and copper
wire on voile
15.5 × 15.5 cm
Private collection,
São Paulo, Brazil
PL.0002.0/00

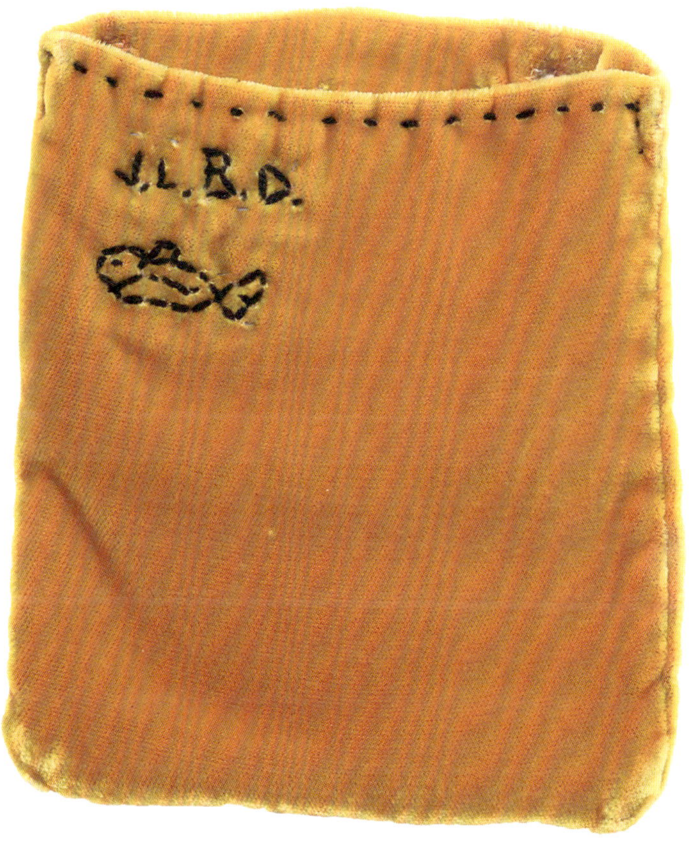

229. ***Bolsinho***
[Small Pocket], [1992]

Thread on velvet
14 × 12.5 cm
Private collection,
São Paulo, Brazil
PL.0001.0/00

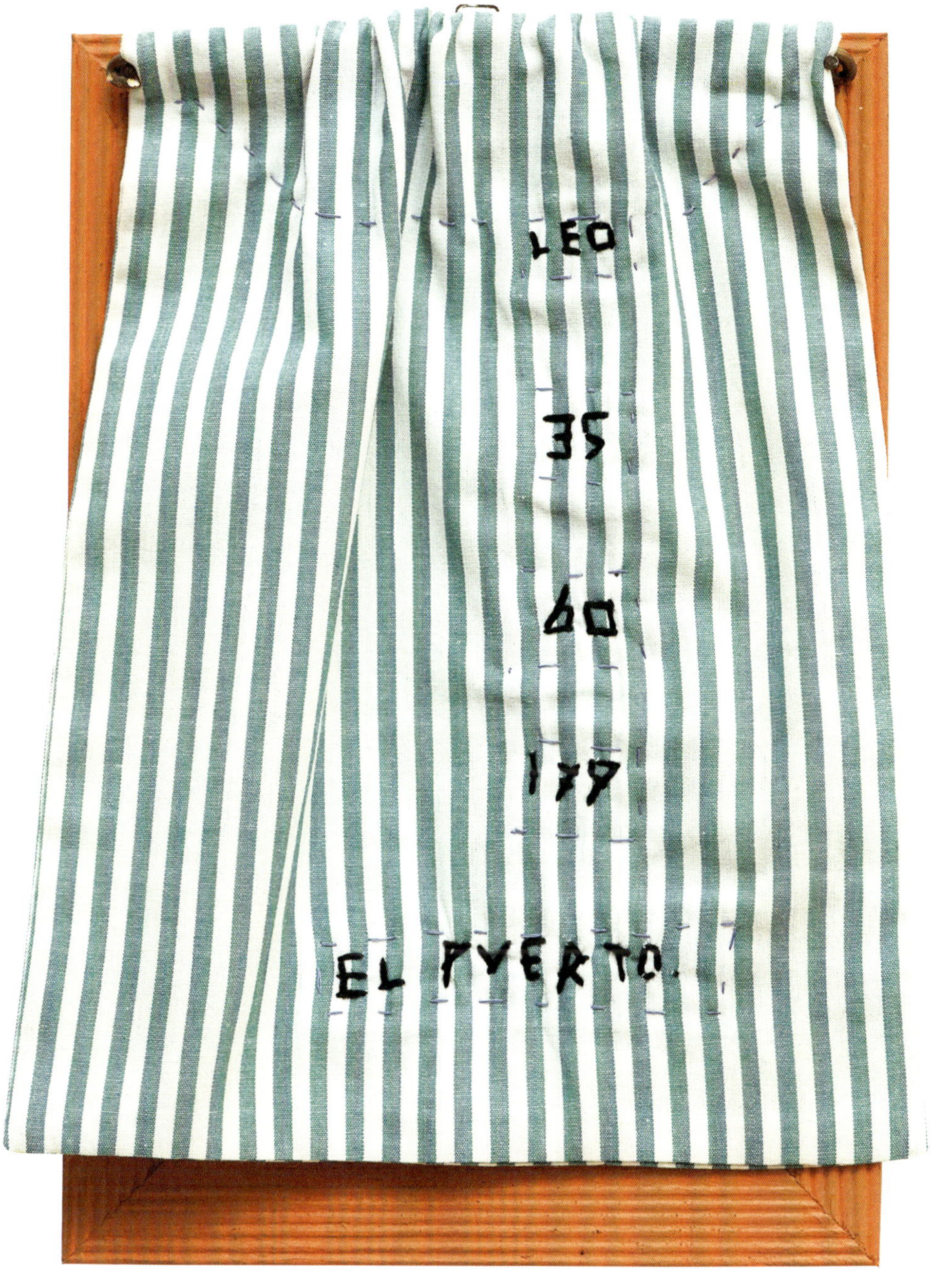

231. ***El puerto*** [The Harbor], [1992]

Thread on striped cotton fabric,
nail, copper wire, and acrylic paint
on mirror frame
23 × 16 × 2.5 cm
Private collection,
São Paulo, Brazil
PL.0009.0/00

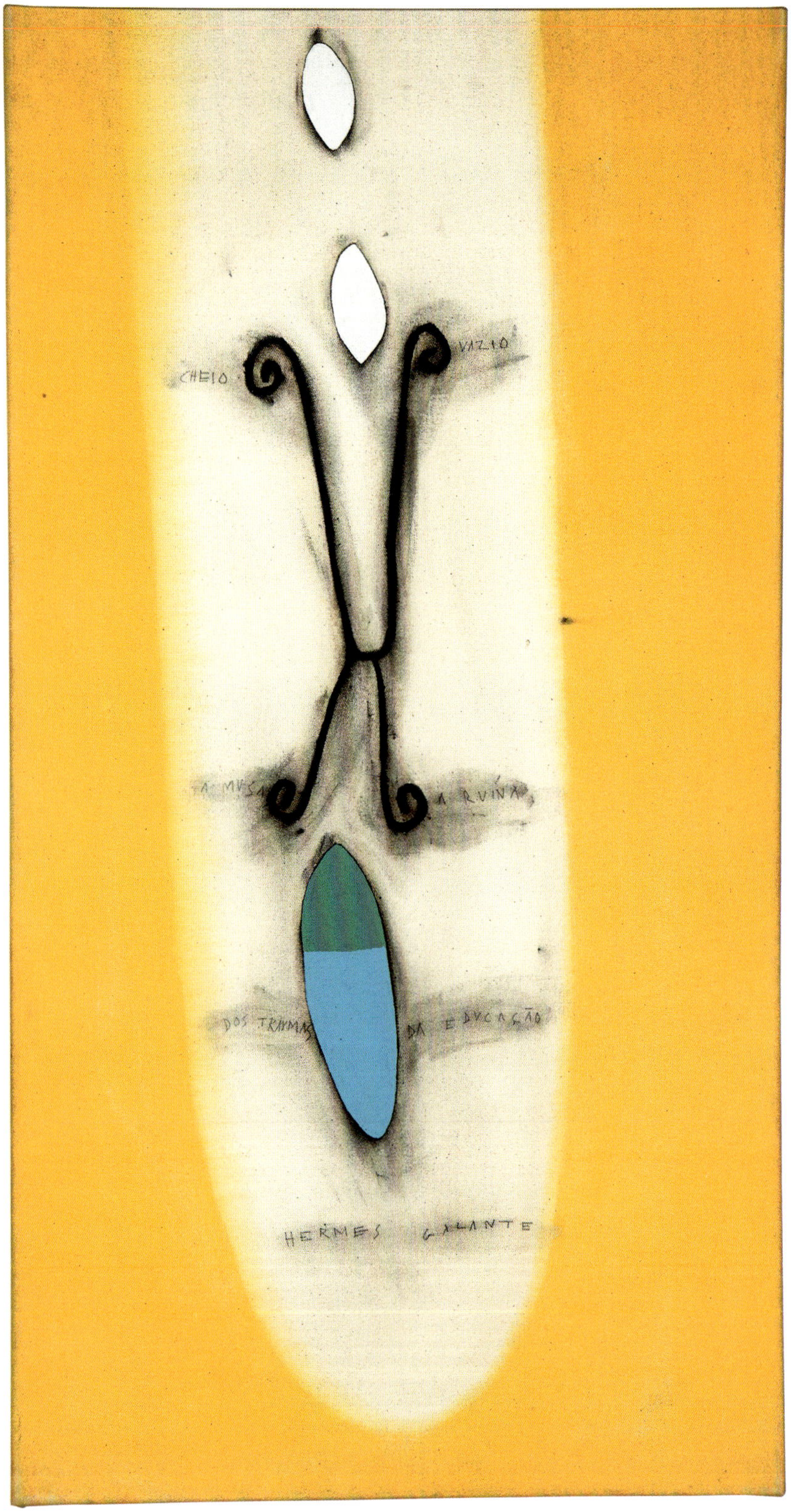

232. *[Cheio, vazio]*
[Full, Empty], 1992

Acrylic paint on canvas
115 × 62 cm
Collection of Marcelo Secaf,
São Paulo, Brazil
PL.1011.0/00

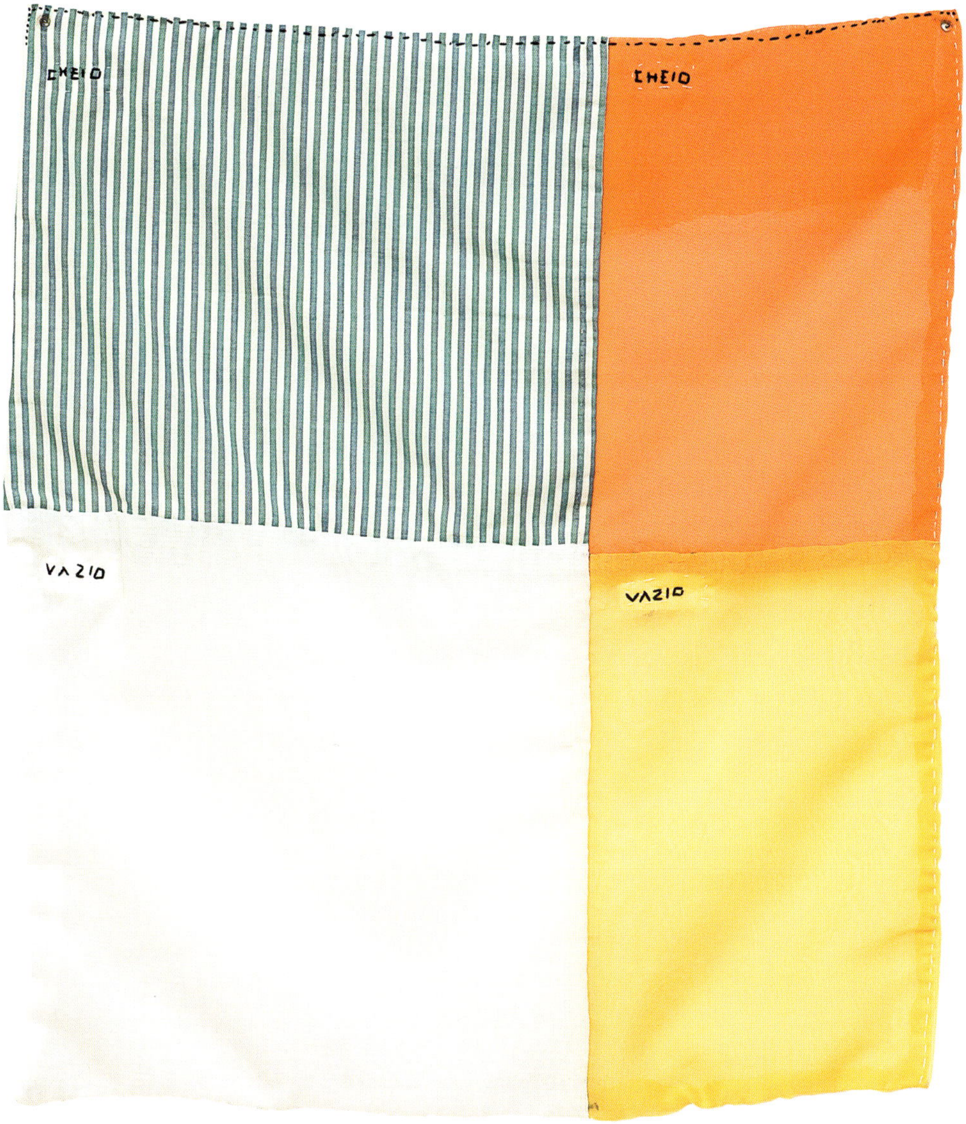

233. ***Cheio, vazio***
[Full, Empty], 1992

Embroidery and sewing
on voile and cotton fabric
66 × 61 cm
Museu de Arte Moderna
de São Paulo, gift Bayer S.A.,
1996, Brazil
PL.1043.0/00

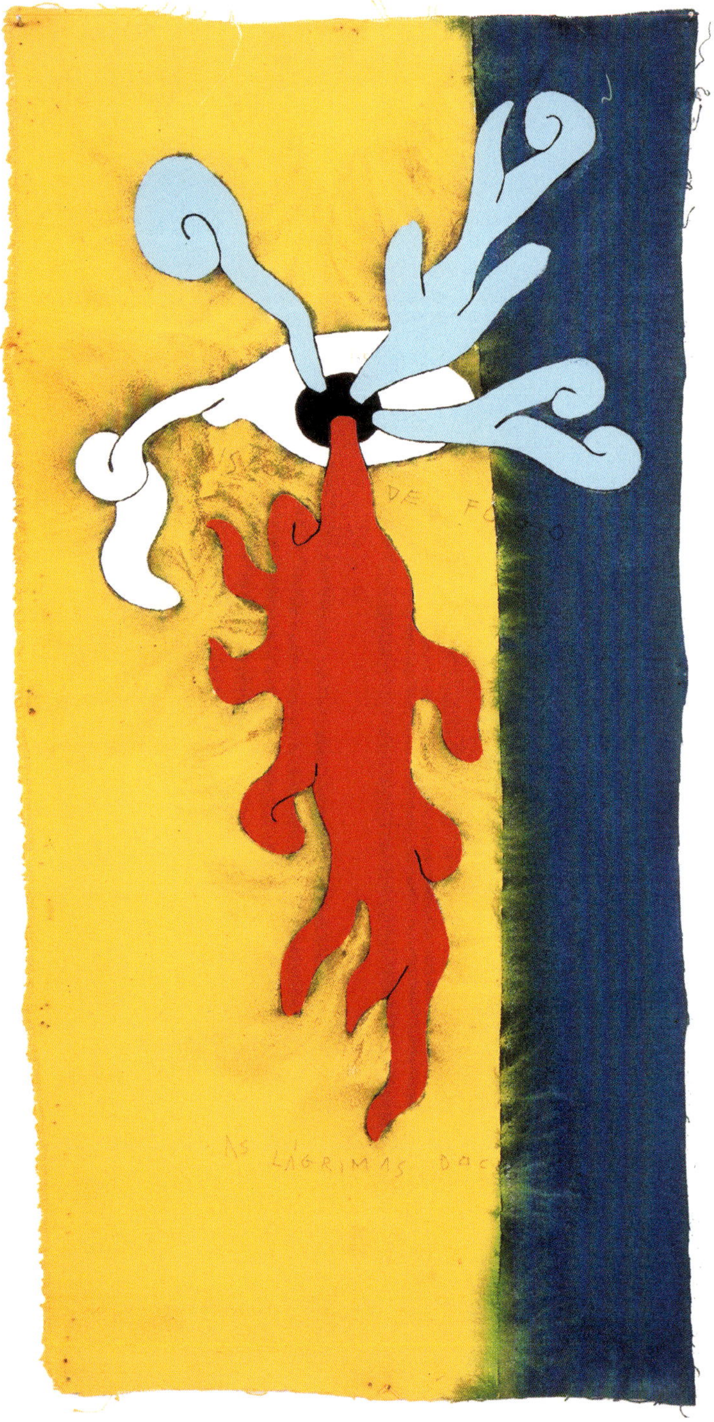

234. ***[A visão de fogo]***
[The Vision of Fire], *circa* 1992

Acrylic paint on unstretched canvas
80 × 40 cm
Collection of Guilherme Dias Salvatore,
São Paulo, Brazil
PL.0418.0/00

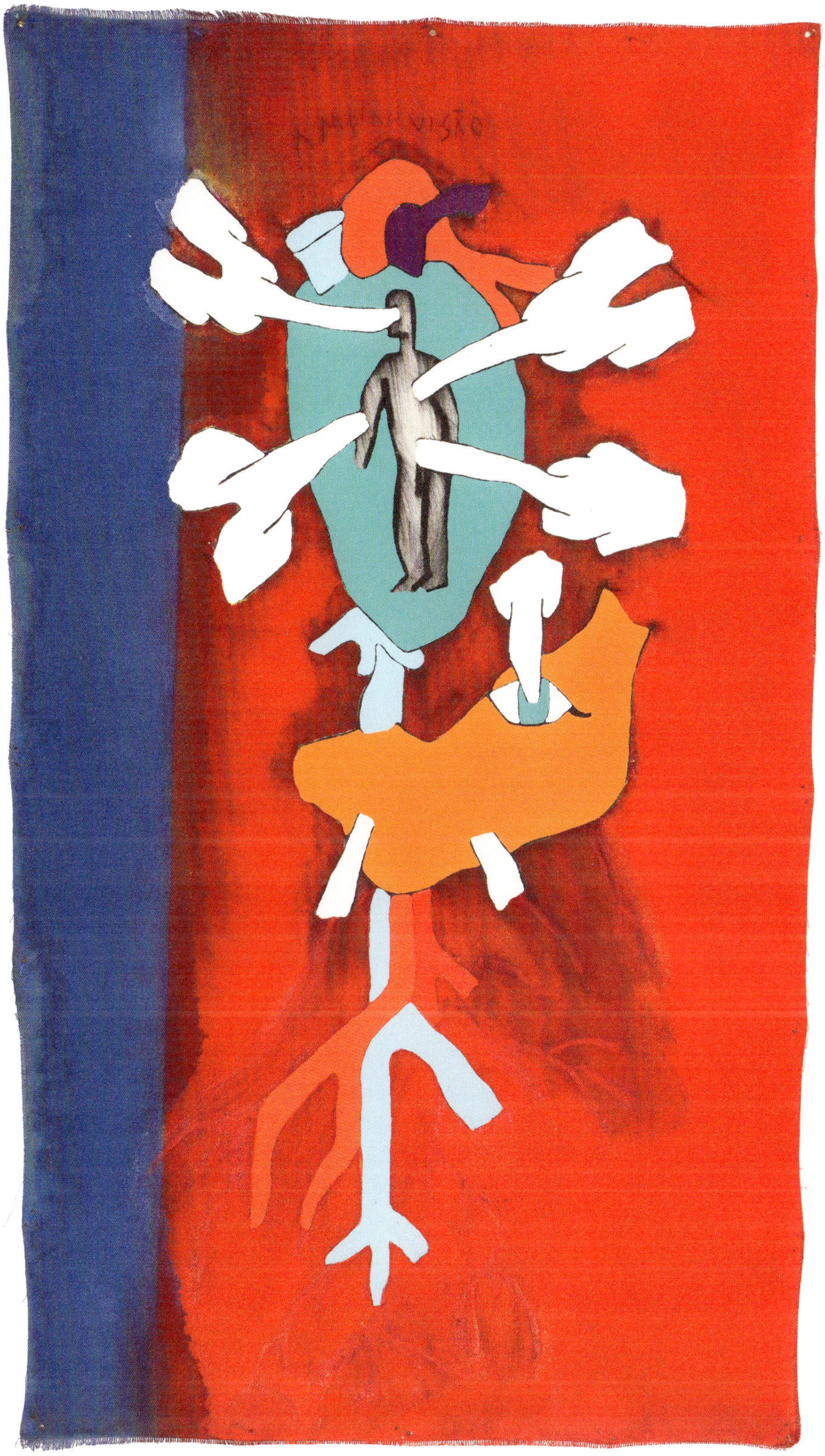

235. ***Ampla visão***
[Ample Vision], 1992

Acrylic paint on unstretched canvas
98 × 55.5 cm
Collection of Ricardo Bezerra
and Bete Dias, Fortaleza, Brazil
PL.1488.0/00

1993

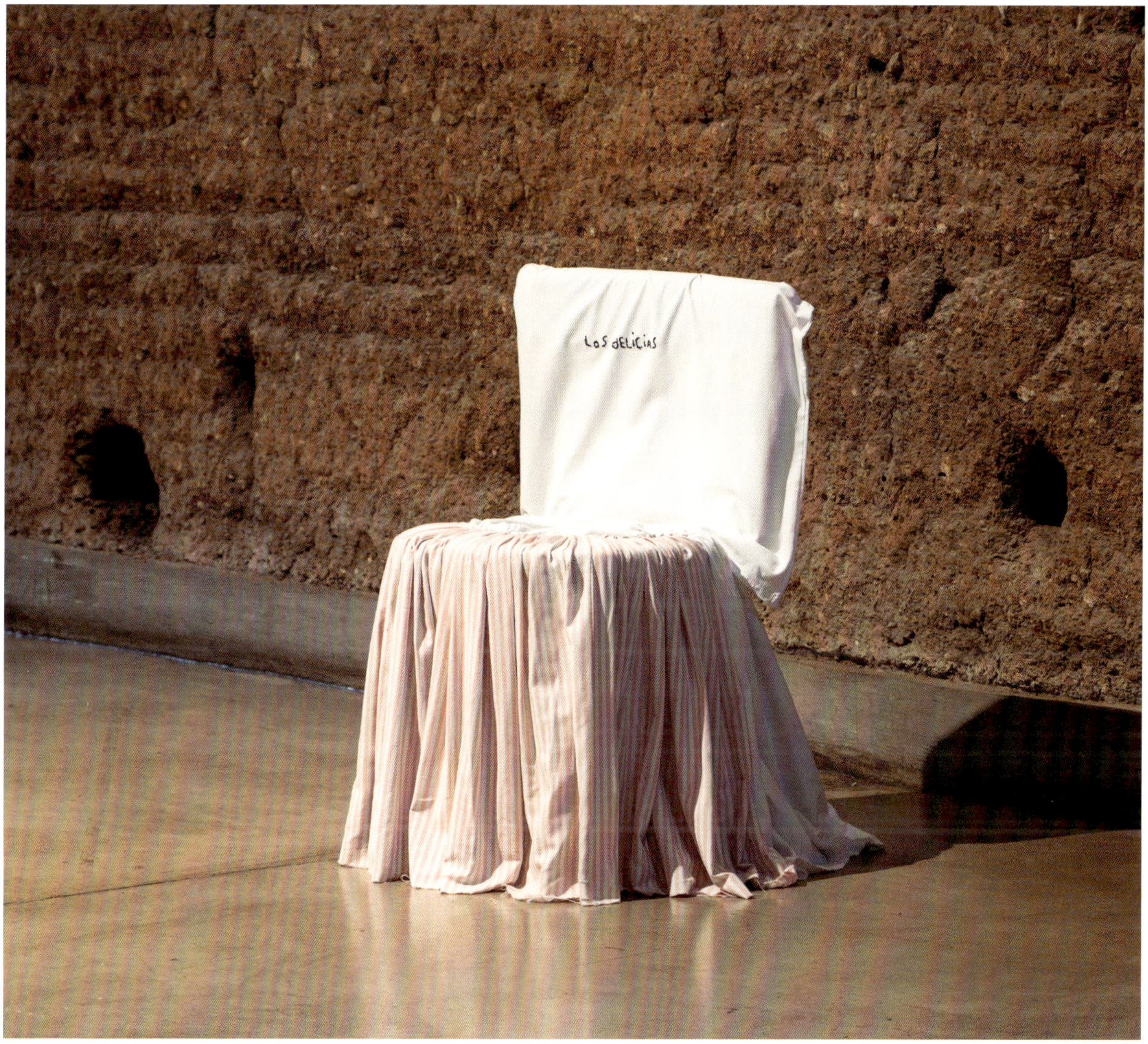

On the next page

236. ***Los delícias***, 1993

Thread on striped cotton fabric and cotton fabric, and iron chair
80 × 45 × 60 cm
Private collection,
São Paulo, Brazil
PL.0027.1/01

237. ***Instalação sobre duas figuras***
[Installation on Two Figures], 1993

Embroidery and needlework on cotton fabrics, striped cotton fabrics, cotton shirts, piqué shirts, voile, wire hanger, iron rack, wooden chairs, and metal chairs
179 × 600 × 1.200 cm
Private collection, São Paulo, Brazil
PL.0027.1/00

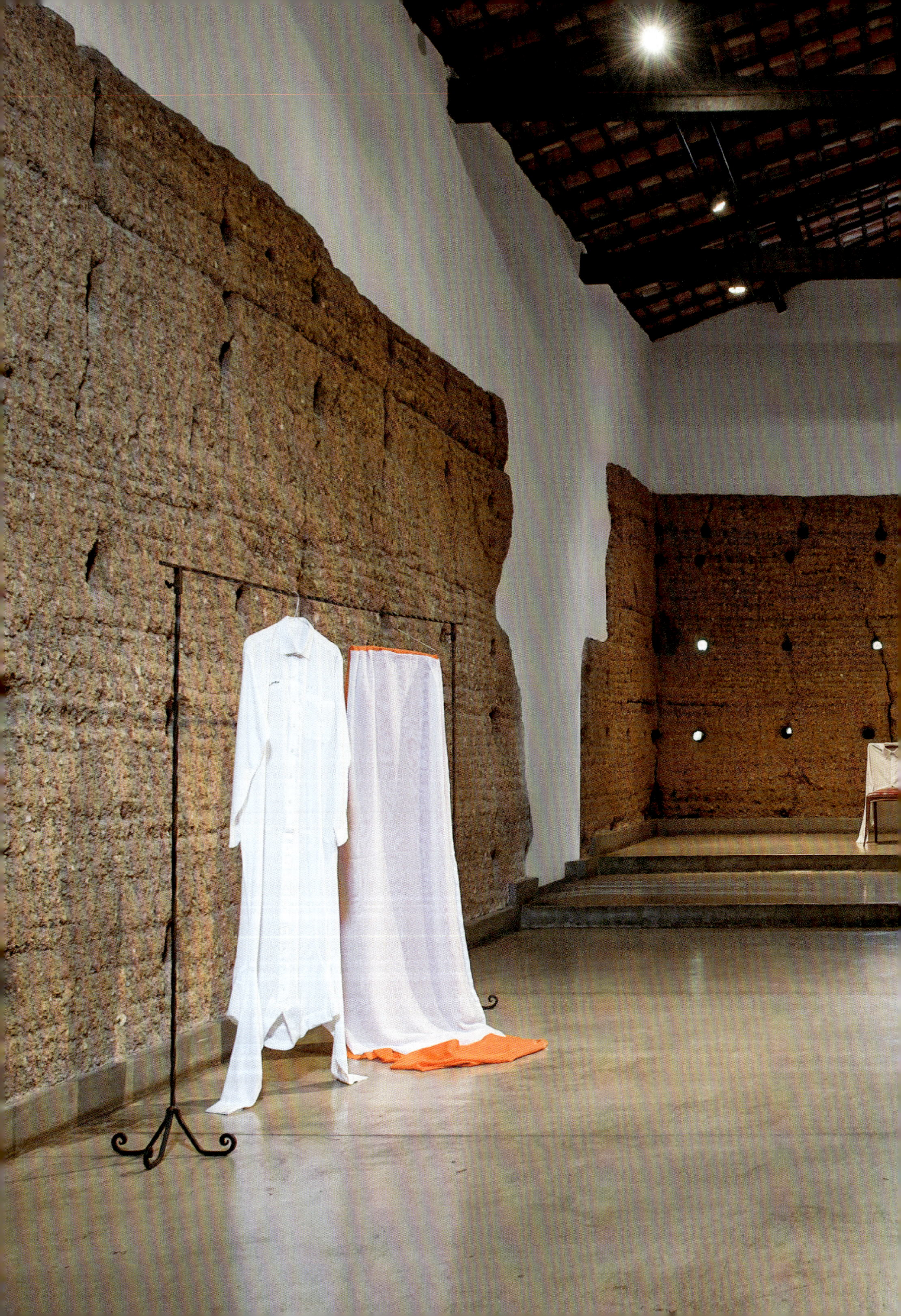

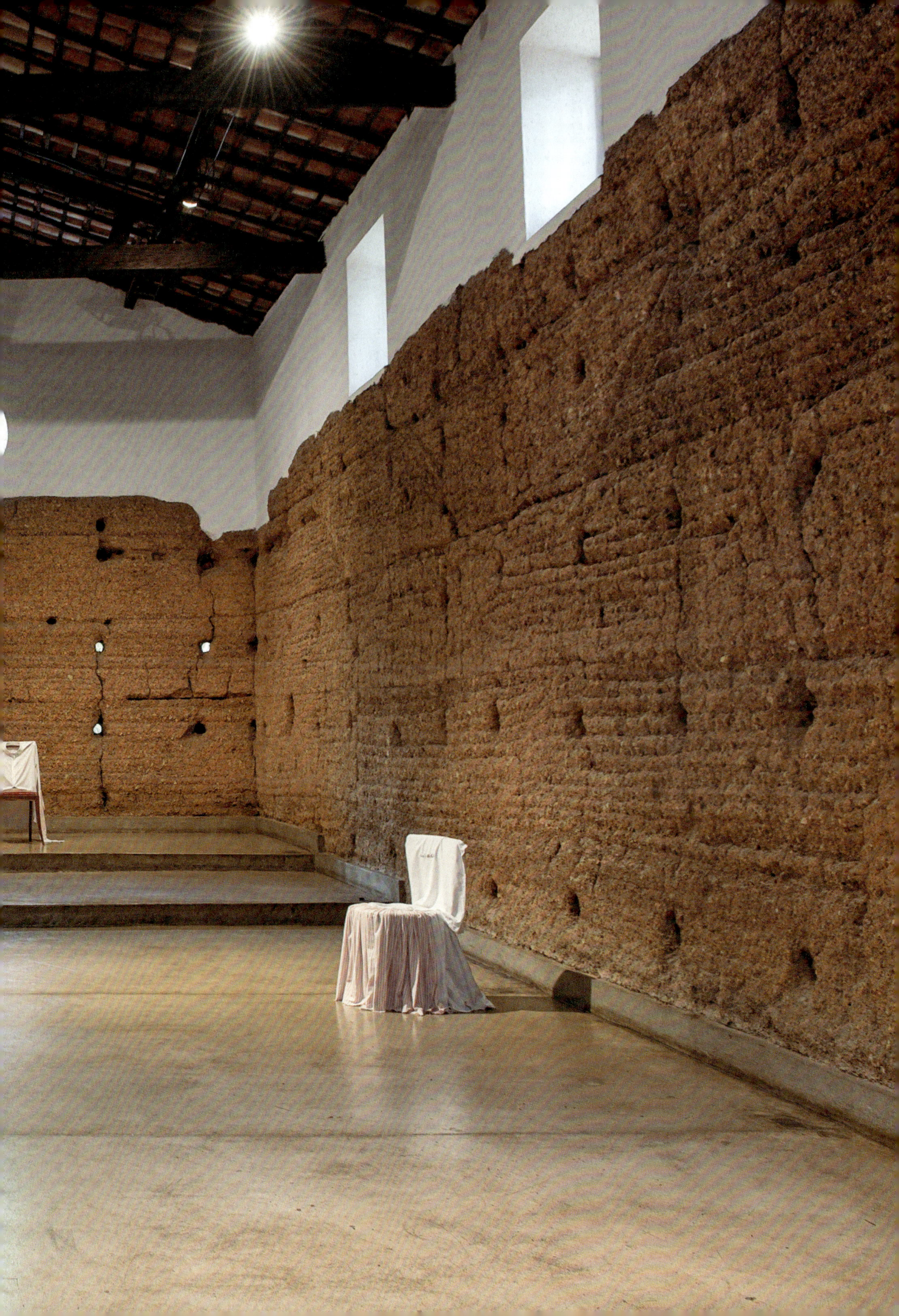

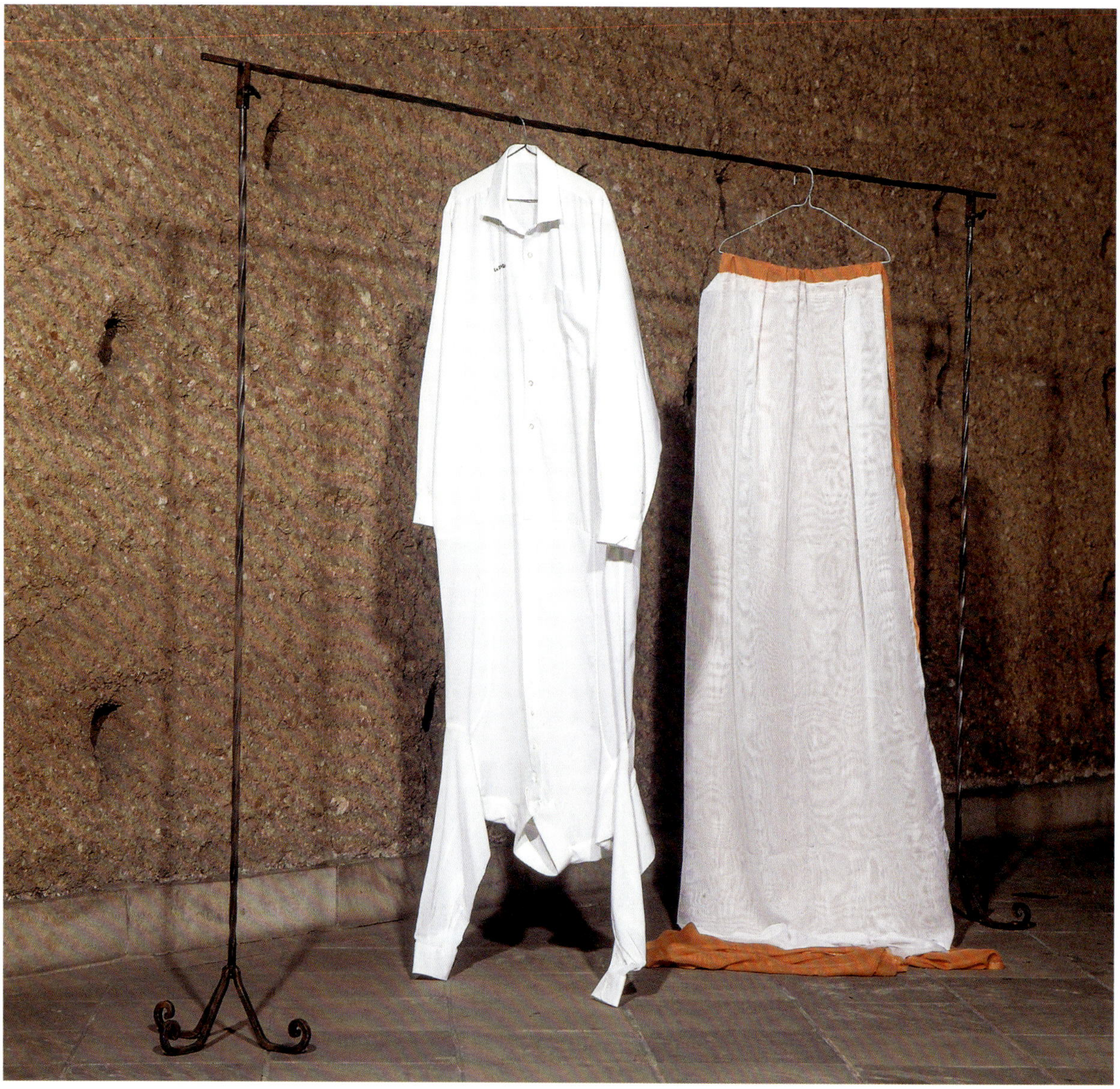

238. ***Lásaro***, 1993

Thread on cotton shirts, wire hanger, and iron hack
150 × 72 × 4 cm
Private collection,
São Paulo, Brazil
PL.0027.1/04

Untitled, 1993

Thread on voile,
wire hanger and iron rack
179 × 75 × 2 cm
Private collection,
São Paulo, Brazil
PL.0027.1/05

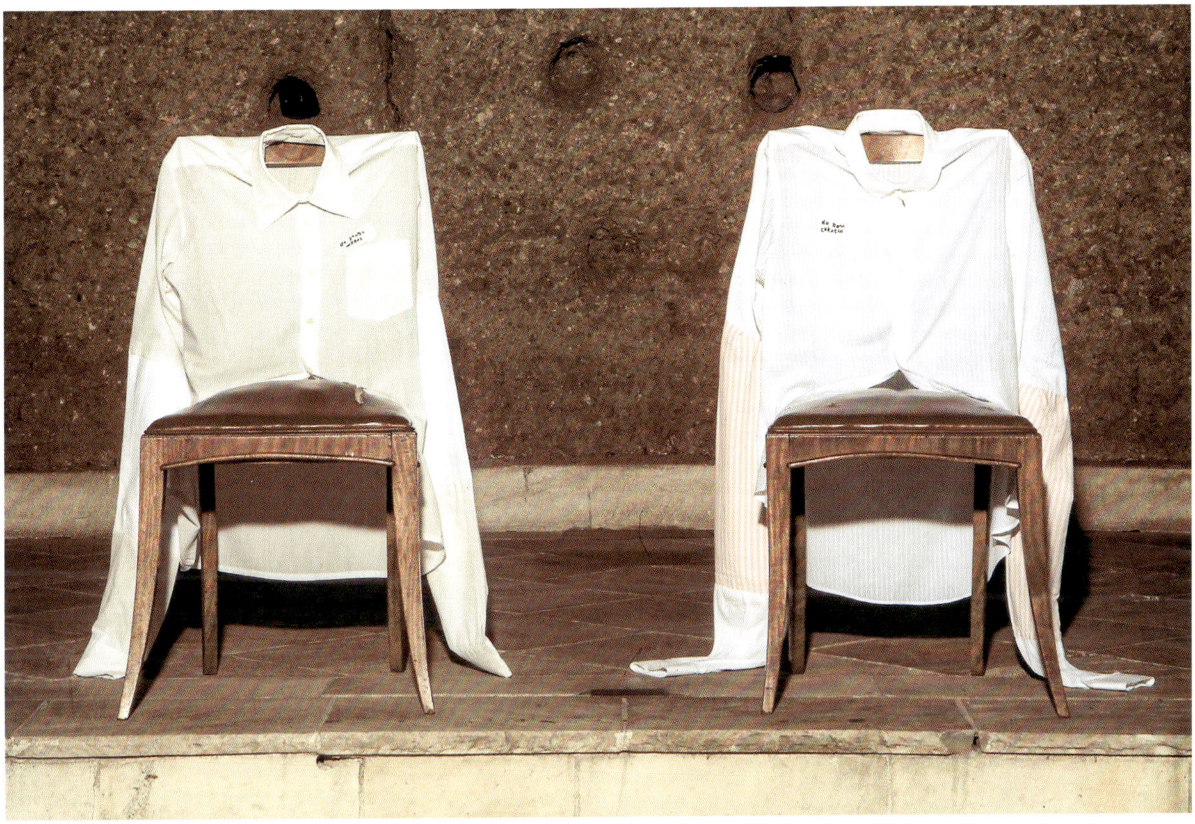

239. ***Da falsa moral***
[Of the False Morals], 1993

Thread on cotton fabric, piqué shirt, and wooden chair
92 × 55 × 50 cm
Private collection, São Paulo, Brazil
PL.0027.1/02

Do bom coração
[Of the Good Heart], 1993

Thread on cotton fabric, piqué shirt, and wooden chair
92 × 70 × 50 cm
Private collection, São Paulo, Brazil
PL.0027.1/03

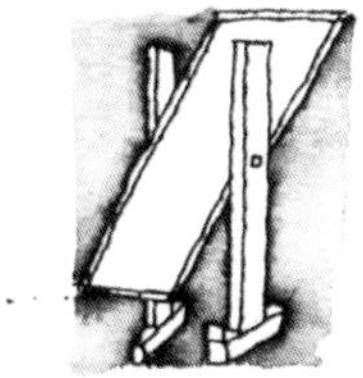

240. ***O espelho***
[The Mirror], 1993

Permanent ink and
watercolor on paper
30 × 23 cm
Private collection,
São Paulo, Brazil
PL.0670.0/00

241. ***O Penélope***
[The Penelope], 1993

Thread on voile
222 × 83 cm
Tate Gallery, gift Carmen Bezerra Dias
and Theodorino Torquato Dias/
Projeto Leonilson,
2001, London, England
PL.1531.0/00

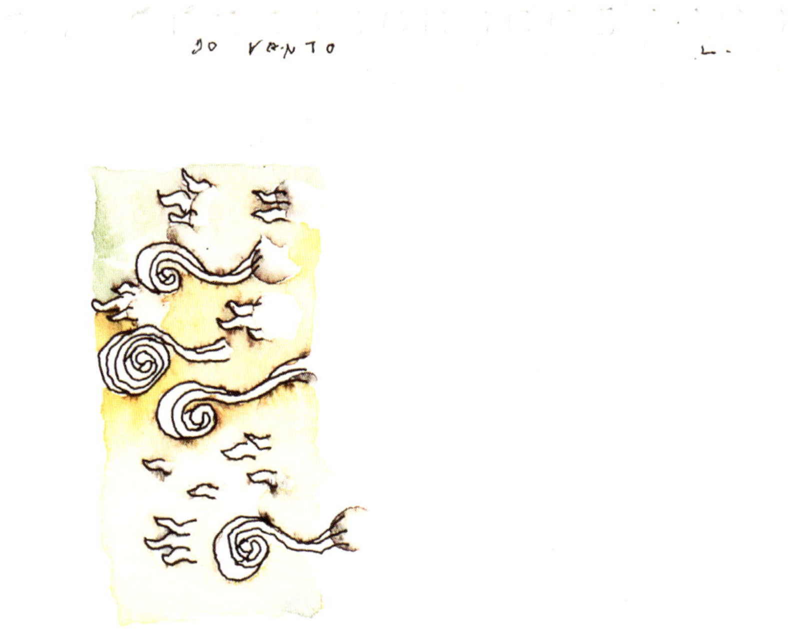

242. **[*Do vento*]**
[Of the Wind], *circa* 1993

Permanent ink and
watercolor on paper
25 × 18 cm
Private collection,
São Paulo, Brazil
PL.1206.0/00

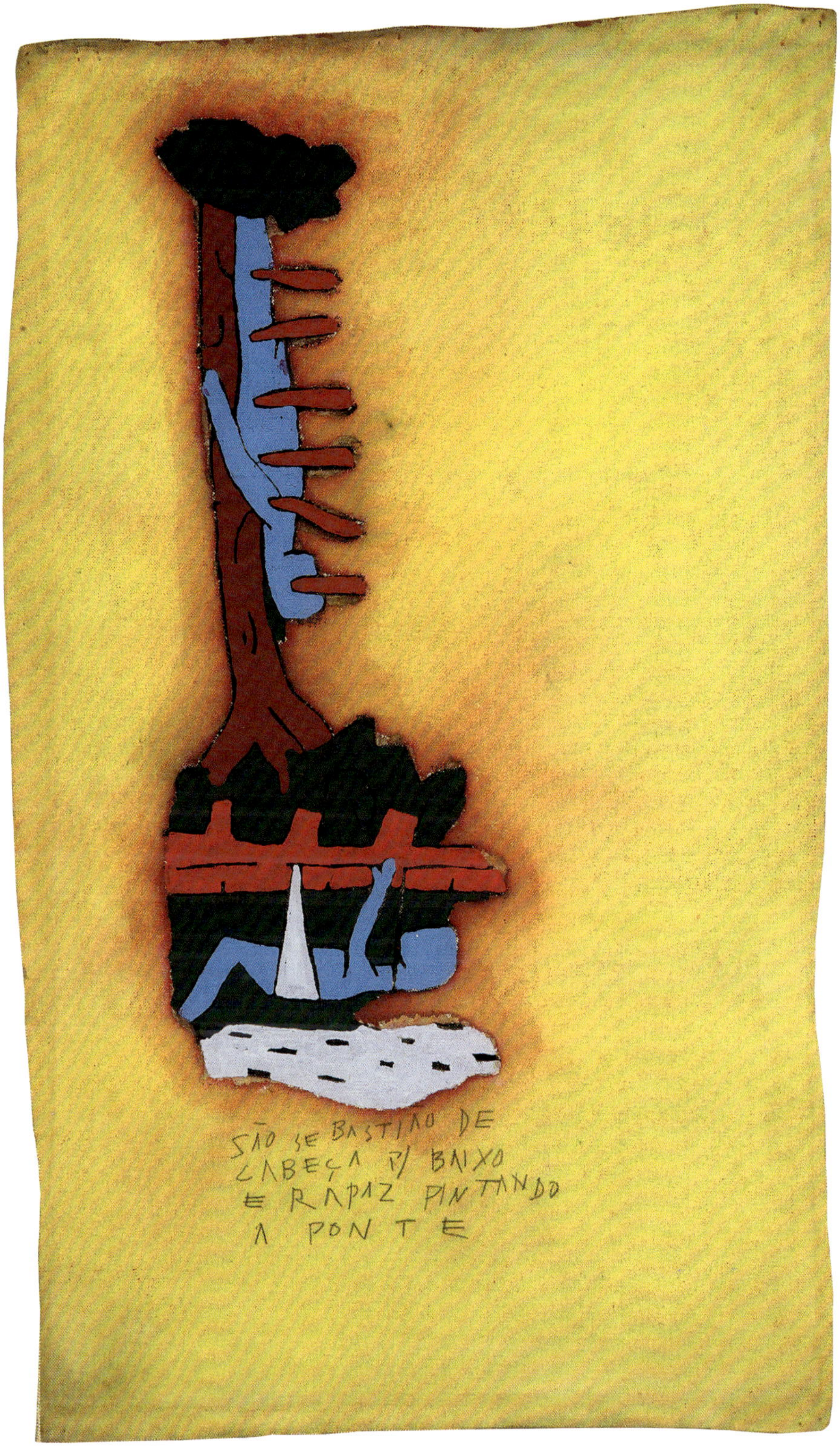

243. *São Sebastião de cabeça para baixo* [Saint Sebastian Upside Down], 1993

Acrylic paint on
unstretched canvas
70 × 41.5 cm
Private collection,
São Paulo, Brazil
PL.1100.0/00

ILLUS TRA TIONS FOR *FOLHA DE S. PAULO*

Illustrations created for Barbara Gancia's column in *Folha de S. Paulo*. All works are part of a private collection in São Paulo, and were made using permanent ink on paper, unless otherwise noted. The publication date is indicated by the acronym "FSP," except for the last two drawings, which were not published in the newspaper.

244. ***[Paulistanos ensopados dão com os burros n'água]*** [Soaked Paulistanos Go Down the Drain], 1991

17.5 × 13.5 cm
FSP 3.9.1991
PL.0135.0/00

245. ***[Quem é do bem não fica passado num alalaô]*** [Good People Don't Get Stunned by Carnival], 1991

Colored pencil on paper
19 × 12 cm
FSP 3.16.1991
PL.0061.0/00

246. ***[SP se arma para "tempestade em Interlagos"]*** [SP Arms Up for "Storm in Interlagos"], 1991

20 × 13 cm
FSP 3.23.1991
PL.0062.0/00

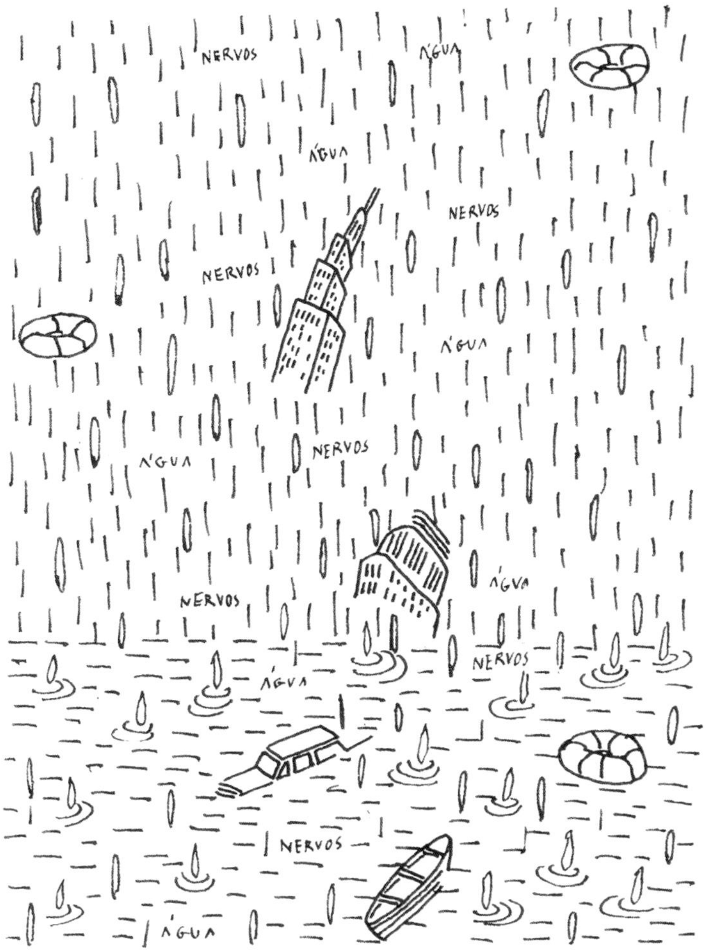

244

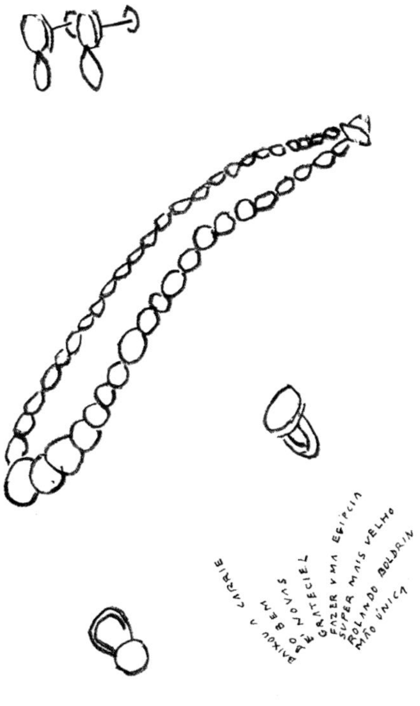

245

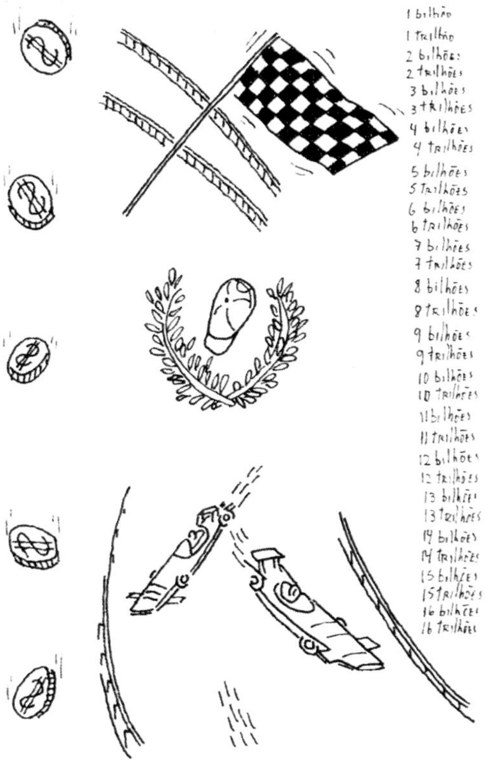

246

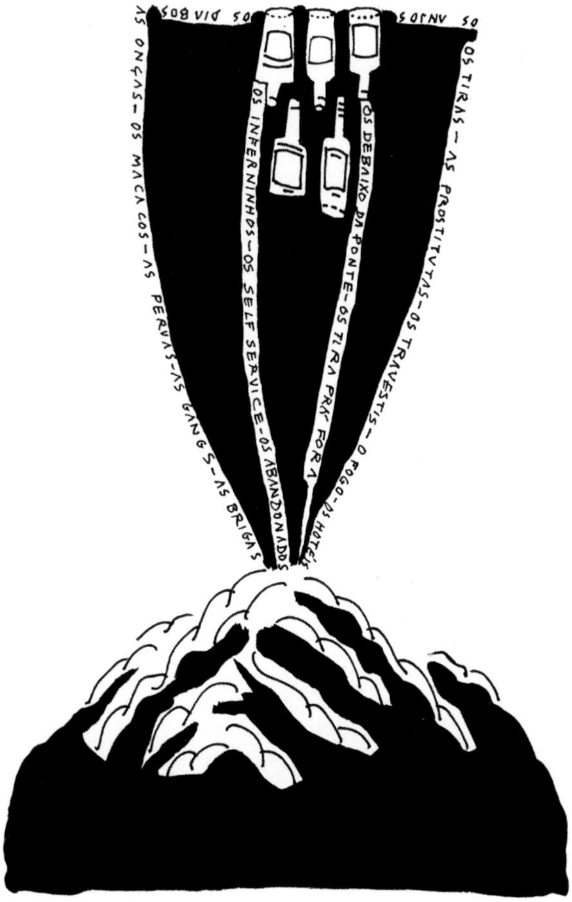

247

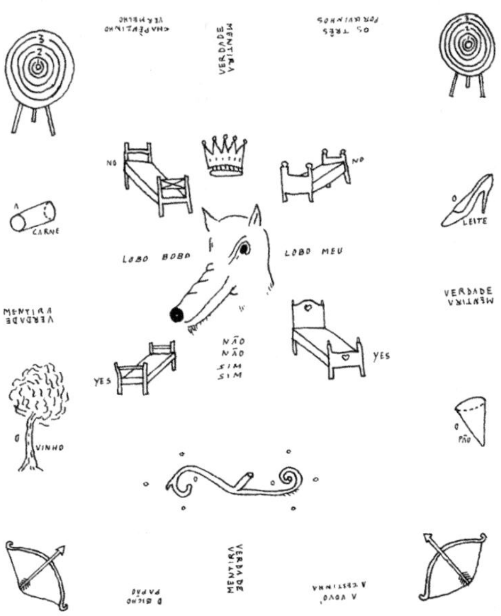

248

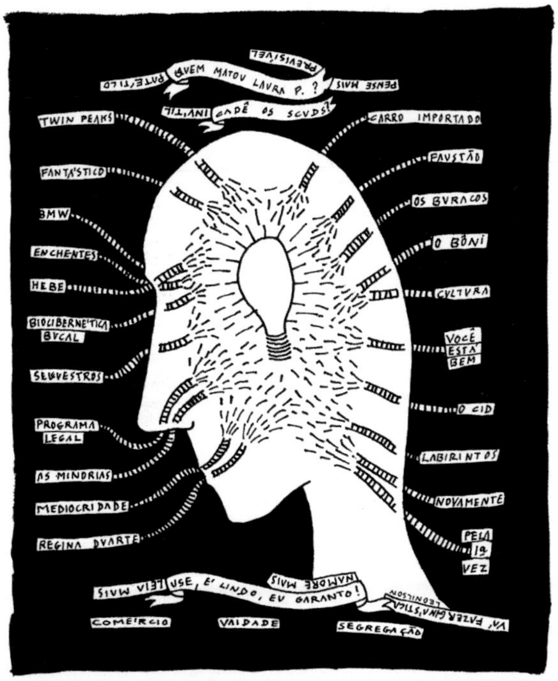

249

247. ***[Adivinhe quem vai estar na fila esta noite]*** [Guess Who's Gonna Be in Line Tonight], 1991

Permanent ink and
China ink on paper
25 × 16 cm
FSP 4.6.1991
PL.0064.0/00

248. ***[Paulistano está com síndrome de linha cruzada]*** [Paulistanos Suffer from Crossed Line Syndrome], 1991

22 × 19 cm
FSP 3.30.1991
PL.0063.0/00

249. ***[Moda bizarra aterrissa nas bocas e nas TVs]*** [Weird Fashion Lands in Mouths and TVs], 1991

Permanent ink and
China ink on paper
23 × 18 cm
FSP 4.13.1991
PL.0065.0/00

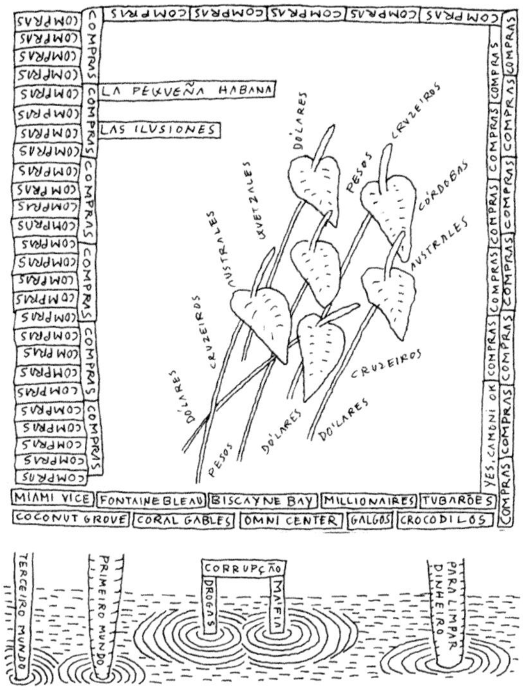

250

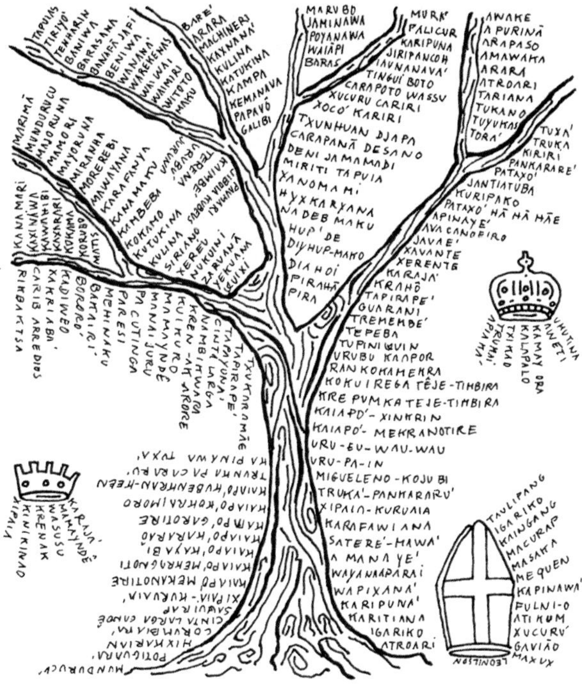

251

250. ***[Brasil vai a Miami em busca da "década perdida"]*** [Brazil Goes to Miami in Search of the "Lost Decade"], 1991

Permanent ink and
cut paper glued on paper
18 × 14.5 cm
FSP 4.20.1991
PL.0115.0/00

251. ***[Jamais toque em um membro da família real]*** [Never Touch a Member of the Royal Family], 1991

18 × 16 cm
FSP 4.27.1991
PL.0117.0/00

252. ***["Motoqueiros do chiclete" aceleram corações]*** ["Chewing-Gum Bikers" Speed Up Hearts], 1991

18.5 × 16.5 cm
FSP 5.4.1991
PL.0116.0/00

253. ***[Carro importado enfrenta asfalto thrash metal]*** [Imported Cars Face Thrash Metal Asphalt], 1991

17 × 14.5 cm
Unknown collection
FSP 5.18.1991
PL.2360.0/00

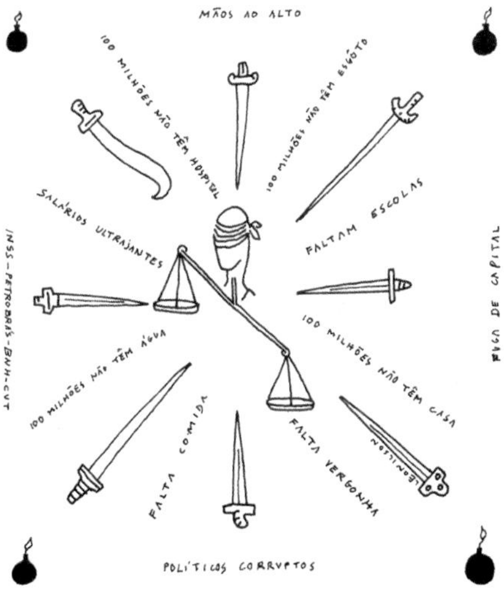

252

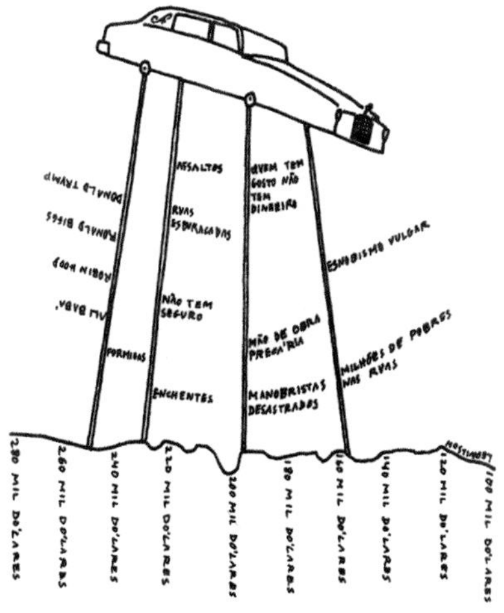

253

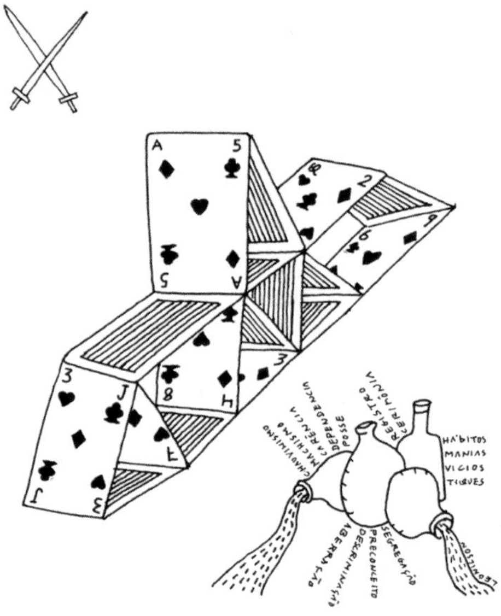

254

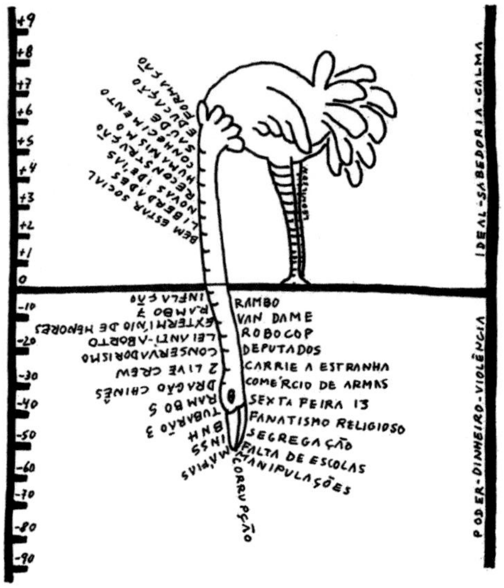

255

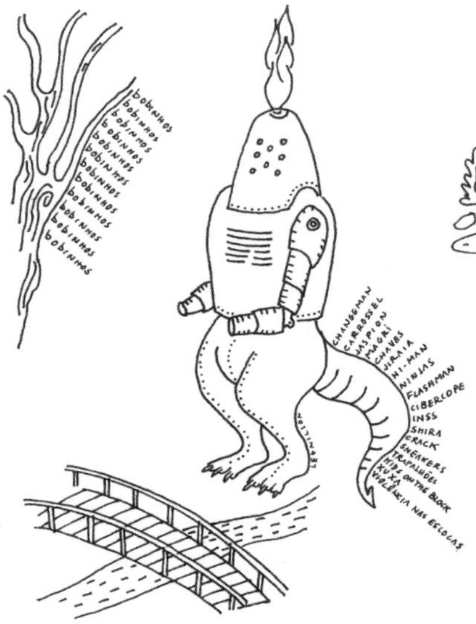

256

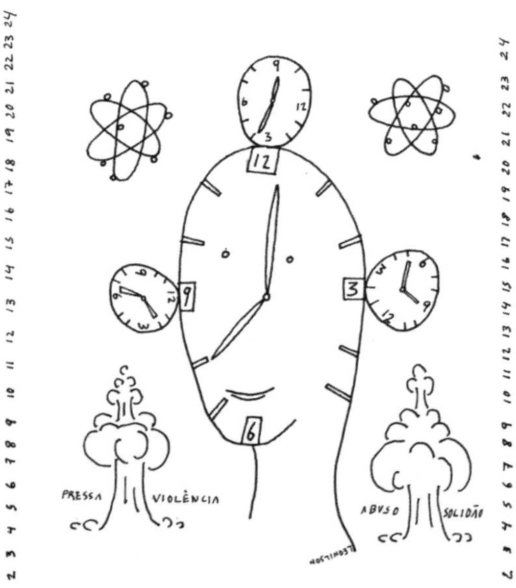

257

254. ***[Paulistanos estão com a cara do Meneguelli]*** [Paulistanos Are Looking Like Meneguelli], 1991

18 × 16 cm
FSP 5.25.1991
PL.0127.0/00

255. ***[Violência e terror agora divertem a juventude]*** [Violence and Terror Now Entertain the Youth], 1991

20 × 18 cm
Unknown collection
FSP 6.8.1991
PL.2361.0/00

256. ***[E se o advogado Murphy for assaltado no Rio?]*** [What if Lawyer Murphy Is Robbed in Rio?], 1991

18 × 17 cm
FSP 6.15.1991
PL.0100.0/00

257. ***[Vapt-vupt no Congresso causa perplexidade]*** [Top Speed in Congress Causes Perplexity], 1991

18 × 16 cm
FSP 6.1.1991
PL.0128.0/00

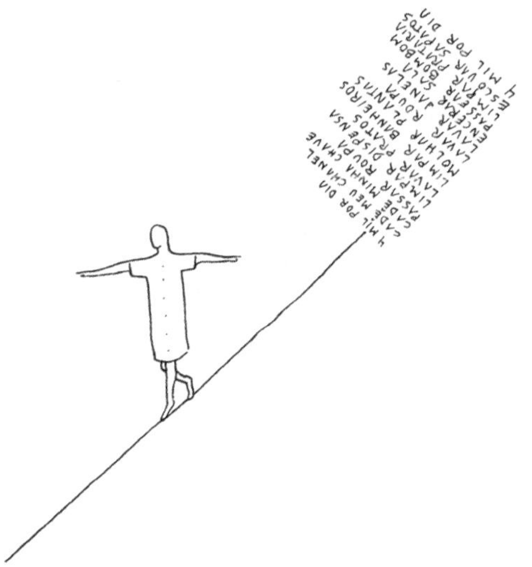

258

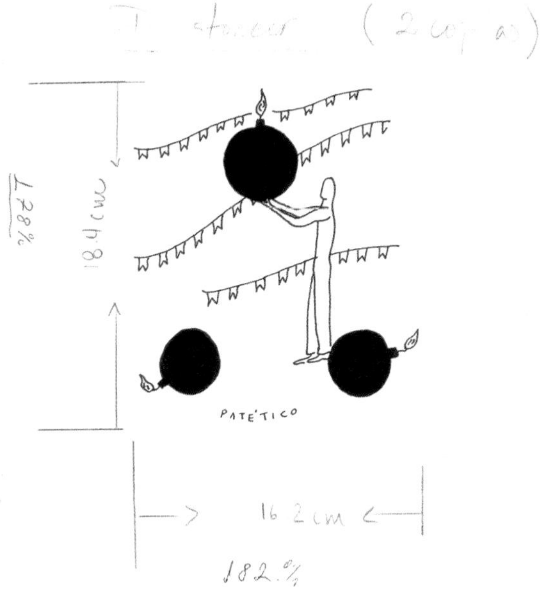

259

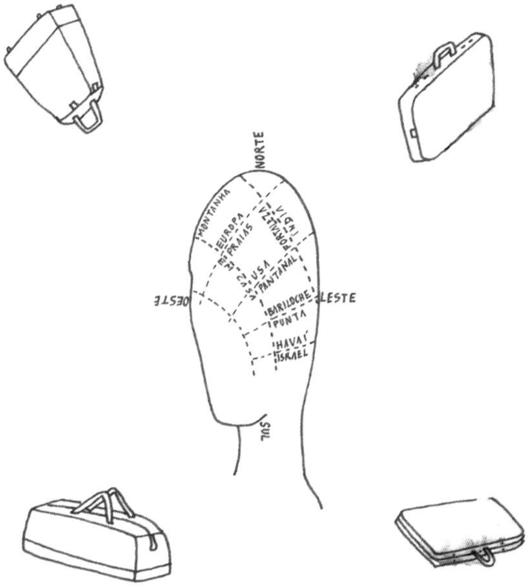

260

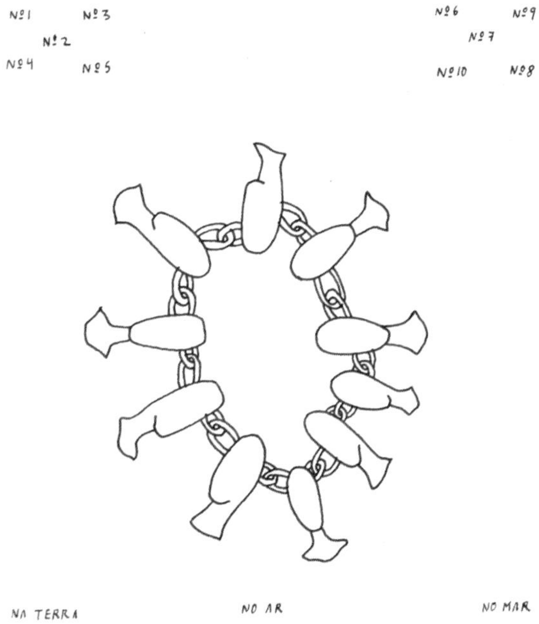

261

258. ***[Empregada de novela é mais chique que madame]*** [A Soap Opera Cleaning Woman Is Fancier Than a Lady], 1991

18 × 16 cm
FSP 6.22.1991
PL.0103.0/00

259. ***[Paulistano foge da cobra e da fumaça de ônibus]*** [Paulistano Runs Away From Snake and Bus Smoke], 1991

Permanent ink and
China ink on paper
18 × 17 cm
FSP 6.29.1991
PL.0091.0/00

260. ***[Brasileiro vira habitante do Planeta dos Macacos]*** [Brazilians Become Inhabitants of the Planet of the Apes], 1991

18.5 × 16.5 cm
FSP 7.6.1991
PL.0092.0/00

261. ***[Ricardona prefere jugulares comprometidas]*** [Ricardona Prefers Commited Jugulars], 1991

18 × 16 cm
FSP 7.13.1991
PL.0093.0/00

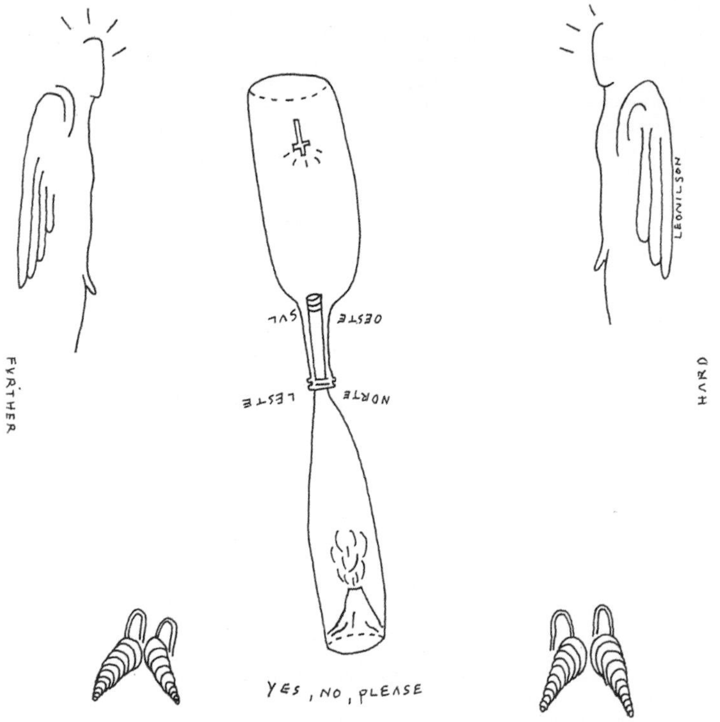

262

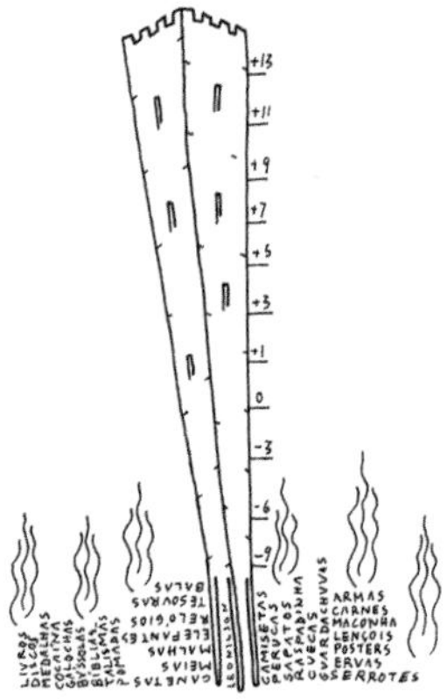

263

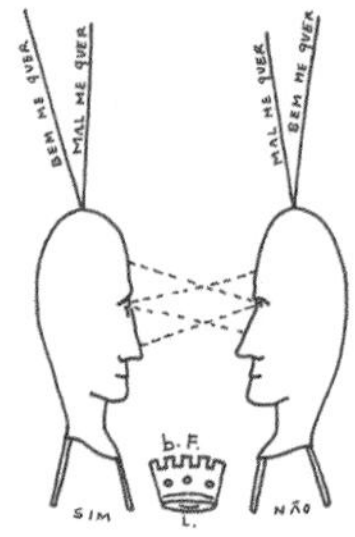

264

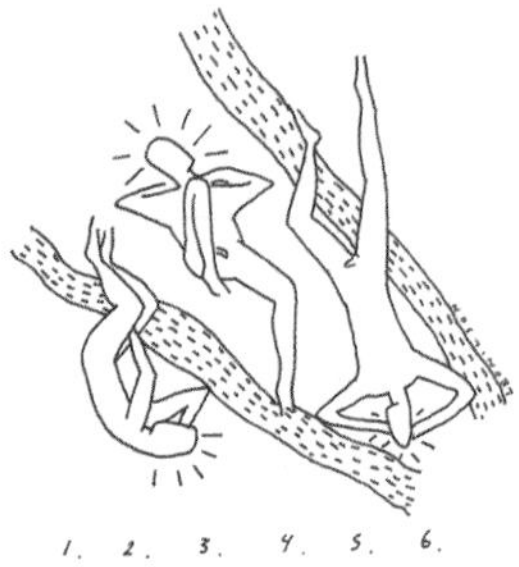

265

262. ***[Periquita de Madonna está solta por SP]*** [Madonna's Pussy Is Running Wild in SP], 1991

18 × 17 cm
FSP 7.27.1991
PL.0044.0/00

263. ***[Paulistano aterrissa na Istambul dos camelôs]*** [Paulistanos Land in the Istanbul of the Peddlers], 1991

18 × 16.5 cm
FSP 8.3.1991
PL.0066.0/00

264. ***[Melhor amigo do homem não abana o rabo]*** [Man's Best Friend Doesn't Wag His Tail], 1991

18 × 15 cm
FSP 8.7.1991
PL.0042.0/00

265. ***[Estrelas levam suas manias para a cama]*** [Stars Take Their Manias to Bed], 1991

18 × 13 cm
FSP 8.14.1991
PL.0101.0/00

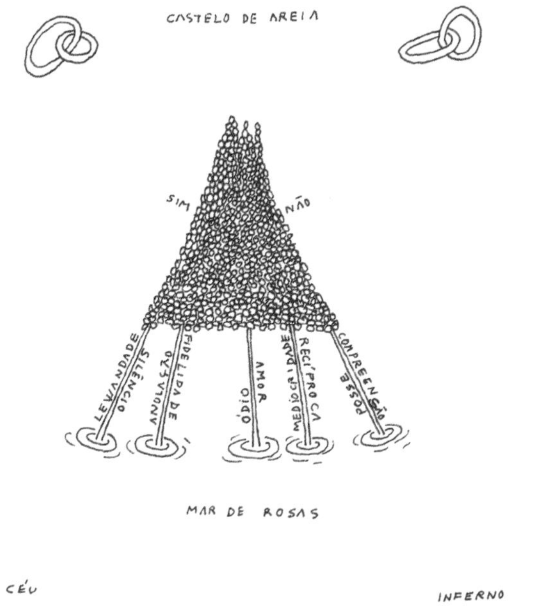

266

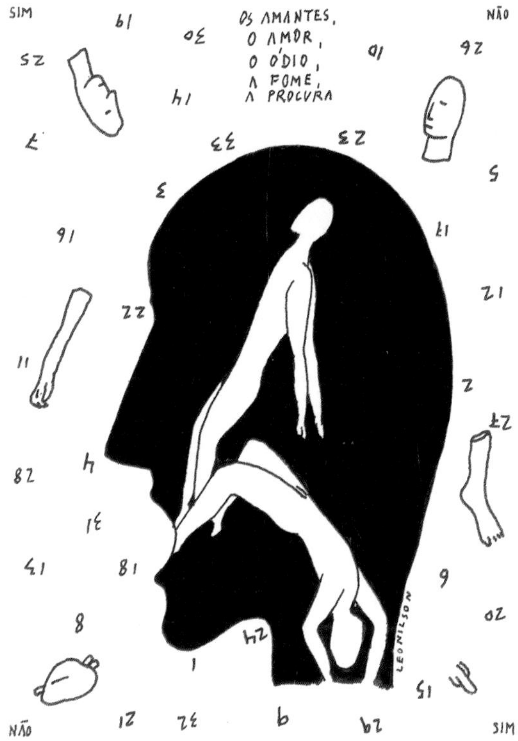

267

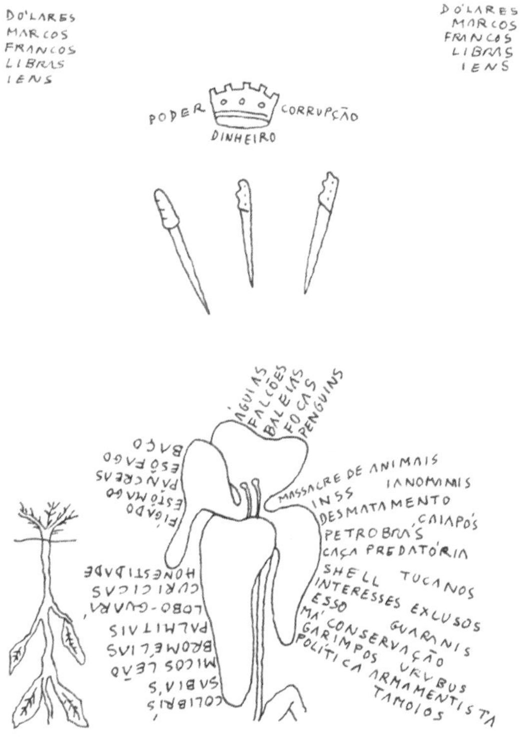

268

266. ***[Administração doméstica lava roupa suja]*** [Domestic Administration Airs Dirty Laudry], 1991

15 × 13 cm
FSP 8.28.1991
PL.0102.0/00

267. ***[Adivinhe quem vem para ser jantado?]*** [Guess Who's Coming to Be Dinner?], 1991

Permanent ink and
China ink on paper
18 × 13 cm
FSP 8.21.1991
PL.0043.0/00

268. ***[Defensores de pandas podem ser perigosos]*** [Panda Defenders Might Be Dangerous], 1991

18.5 × 13.5 cm
FSP 9.11.1991
PL.0130.0/00

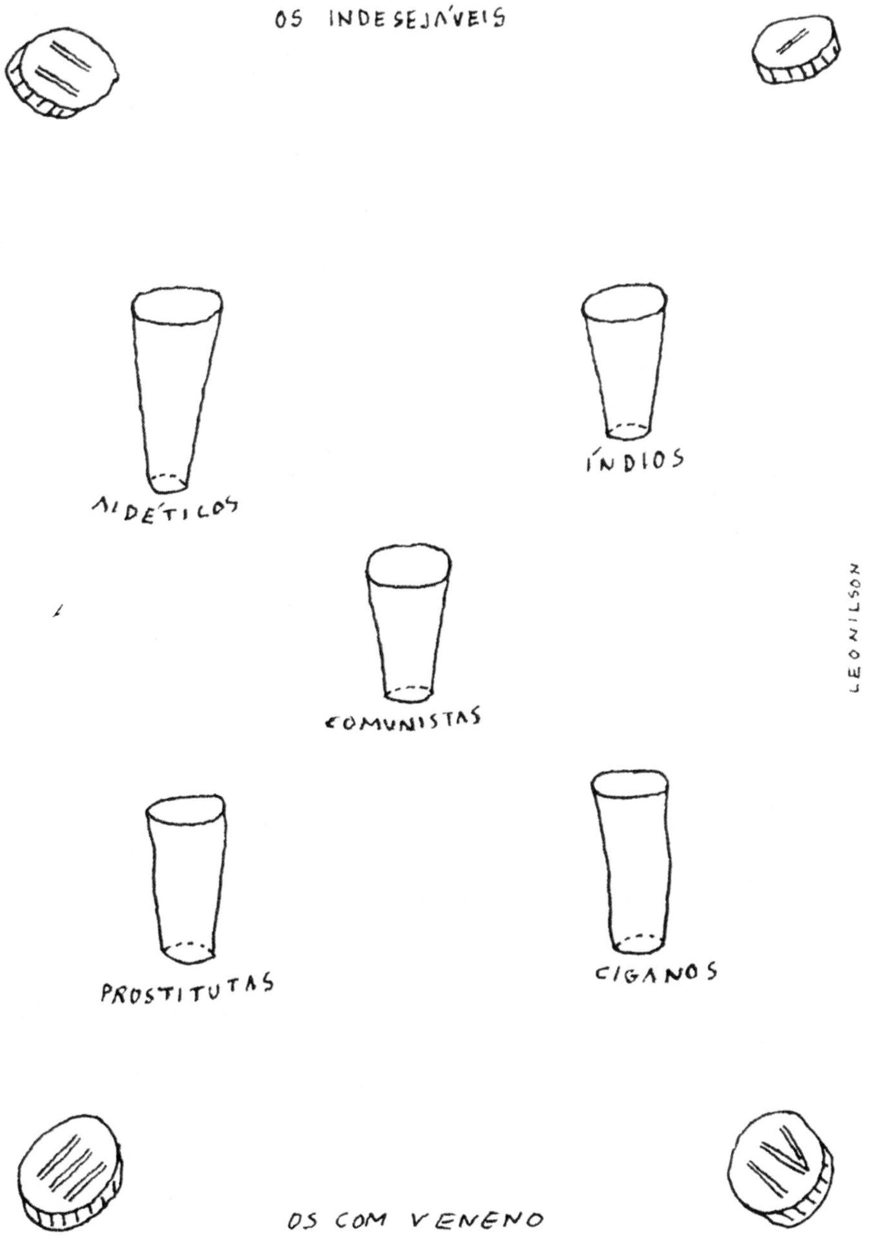

269

269. ***[Os chatos unidos foram enfim vencidos]*** [United Bores Were Finally Defeated], 1991

18 × 13 cm
FSP 9.4.1991
PL.0129.0/00

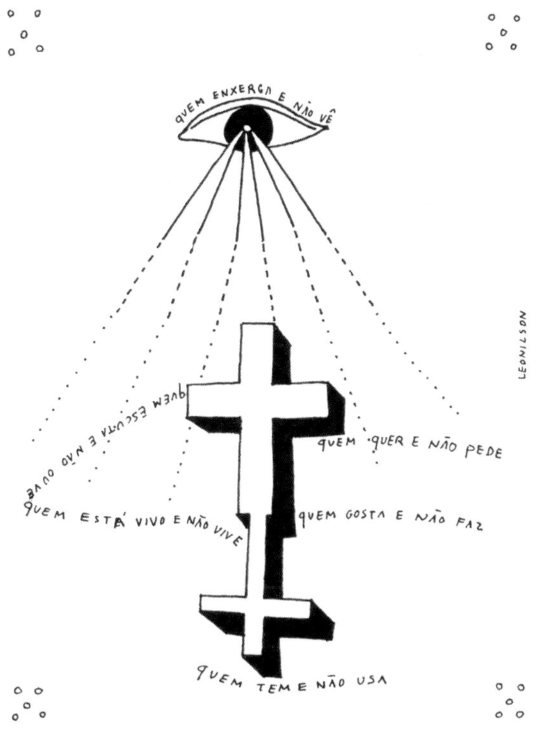

270

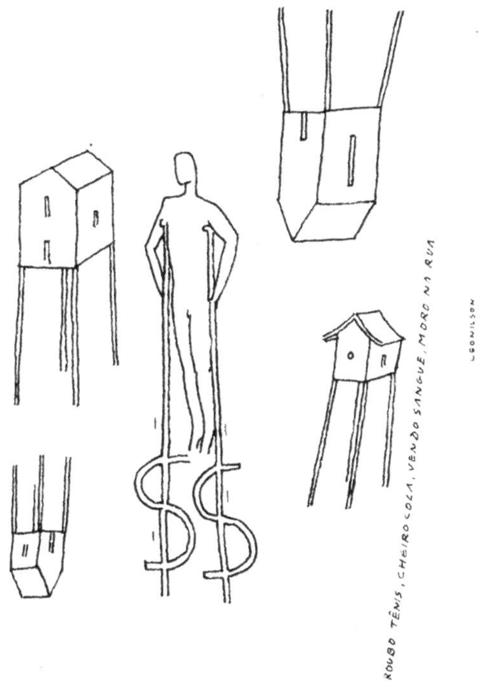

271

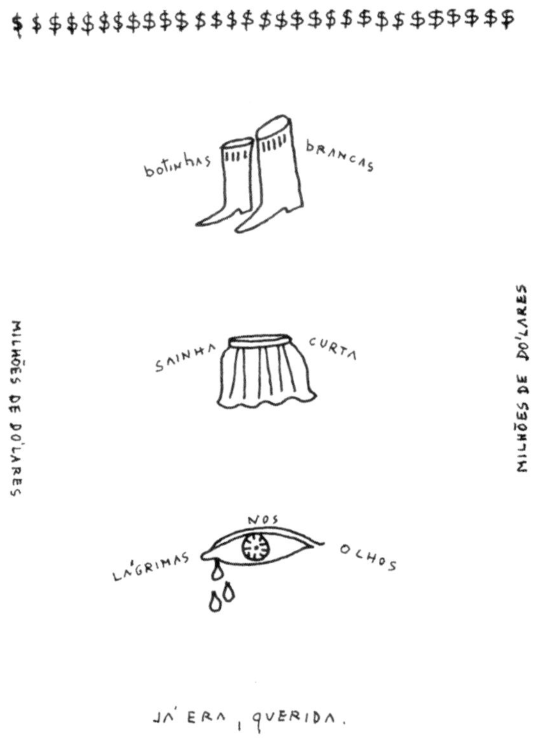

272

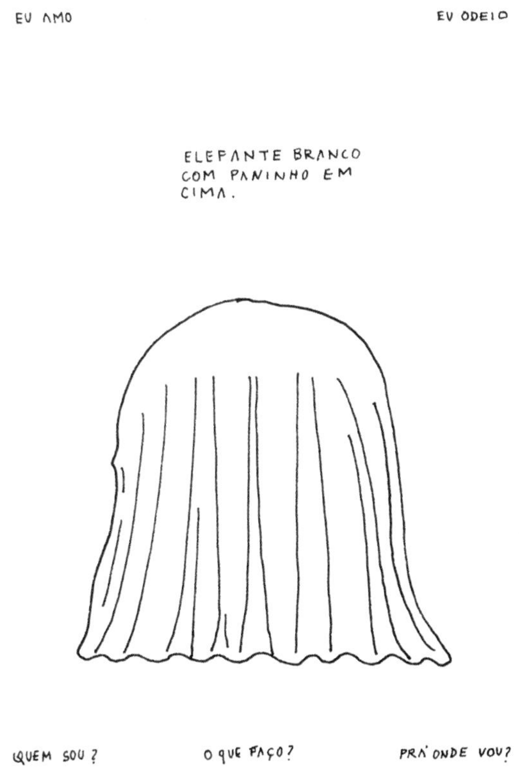

273

270. ***[Limpadores de ralo podem ser "pornô"]*** [Drain Cleaners May Be "Porn"], 1991

18 × 13.5 cm
FSP 9.18.1991
PL.0131.0/00

271. ***[Os jovens adoram ter pés de roquefort]*** [Youngsters Love Having Roquefort Feet], 1991

18 × 13.5 cm
FSP 9.25.1991
PL.0132.0/00

272. ***[Xuxa é um Lee Iacocca de botinha branca]*** [Xuxa Is a Lee Iacocca in White Booties], 1991

18 × 12.5 cm
FSP 10.2.1991
PL.0133.0/00

273. ***[A 21ª Bienal tem aroma de peixaria]*** [The 21ª Bienal Has the Scent of a Fishery], 1991

18 × 12.5 cm
FSP 10.9.1991
PL.0134.0/00

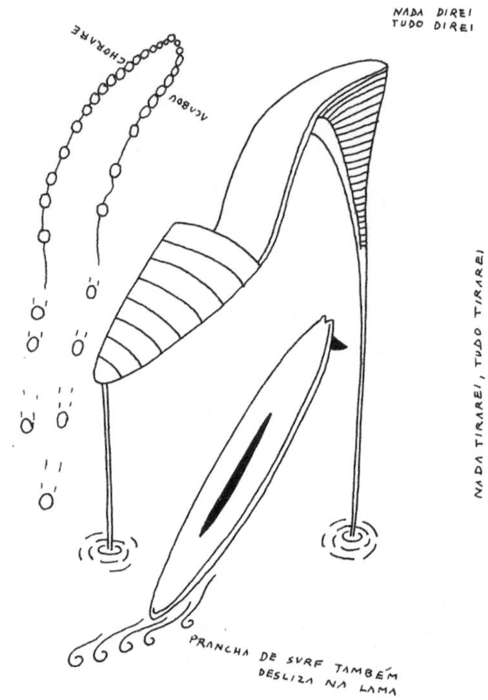

274

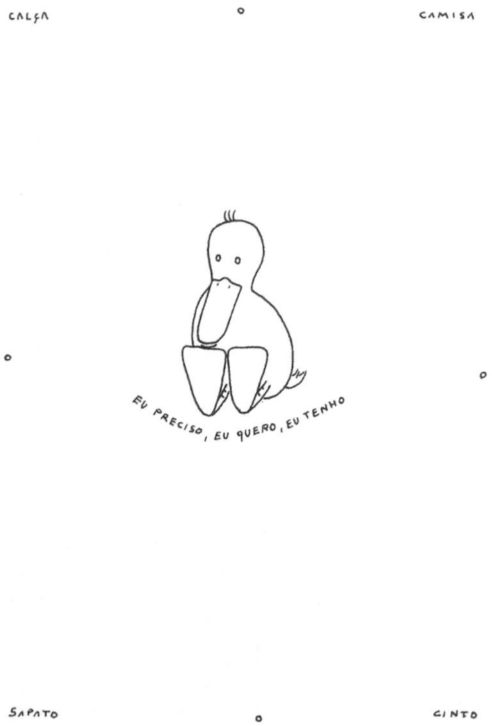

275

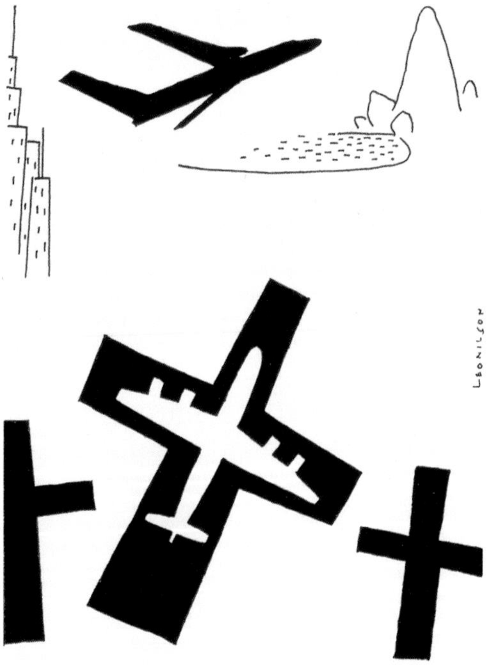

276

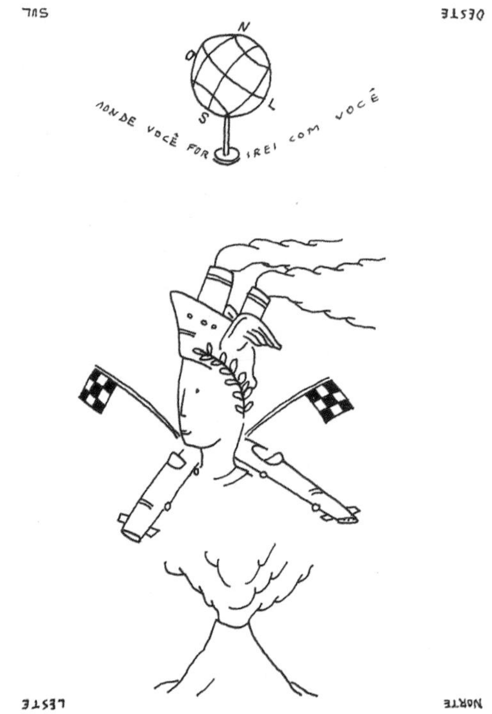

277

274. ***[Zélia entra para o "Vingativas F.C."]*** [Zélia Joins the "Vengeful Ladies F.C."], 1991

18 × 12.5 cm
FSP 10.23.1991
PL.0098.0/00

275. ***[Mauricinho é o troglodita arrumadinho]*** [Dandy Types Are Glummed-Up Troglodytes], 1991

18 × 12.5 cm
FSP 10.30.1991
PL.0046.0/00

276. ***[Na ponte aérea, voar não é um calvário]*** [In the Airlift, Flying Is Not a Calvary], 1991

Permanent ink and China ink on paper
18 × 12.5 cm
FSP 11.6.1991
PL.0099.0/00

277. ***[Senna imita Rosane e abre a torneira]*** [Senna Imitates Rosane and Opens the Faucet], 1991

18 × 12.5 cm
FSP 11.13.1991
PL.0088.0/00

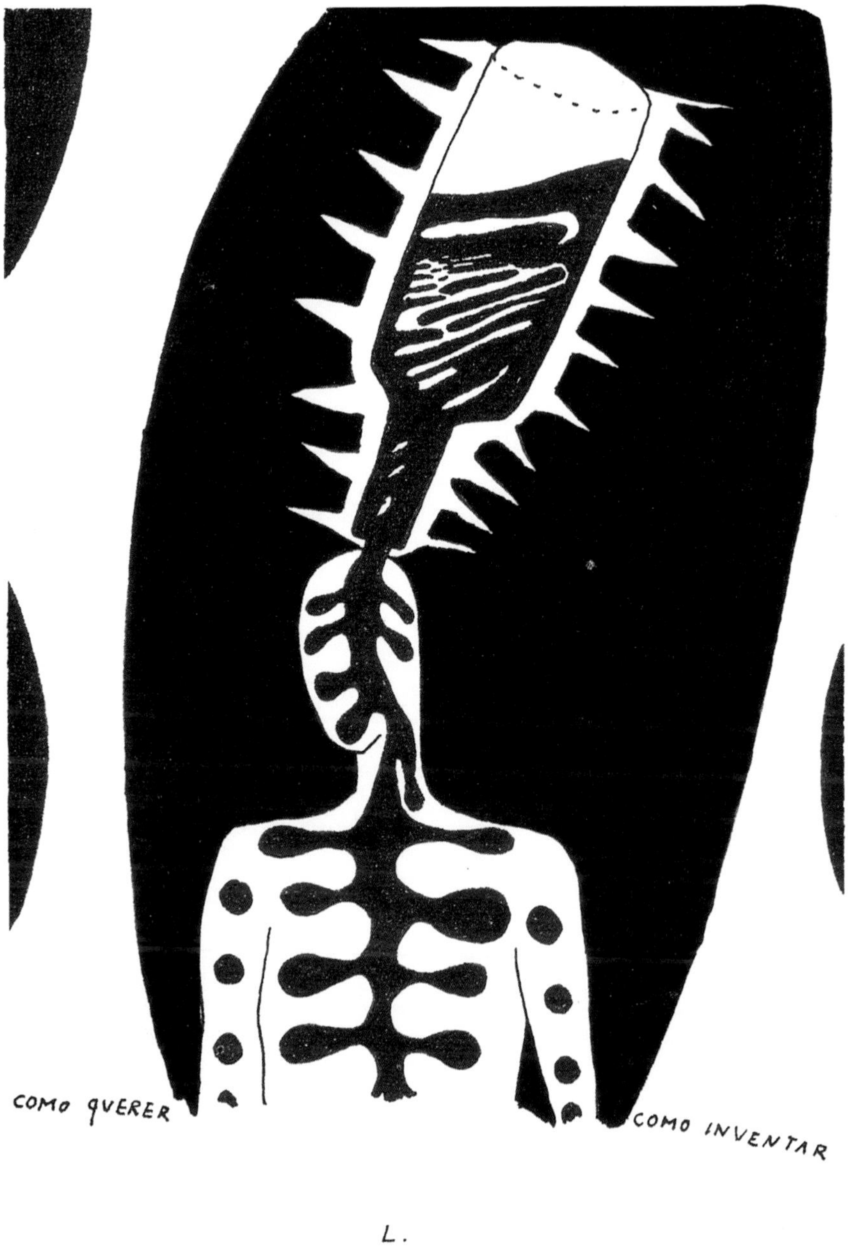

278

278. ***[Otimistas lutam contra natal macambúzio]***
[Optimists Fight Against Cloomy Christmas], 1991

Permanent ink and
China ink on paper
18 × 12.5 cm
FSP 12.4.1991
PL.0094.0/00

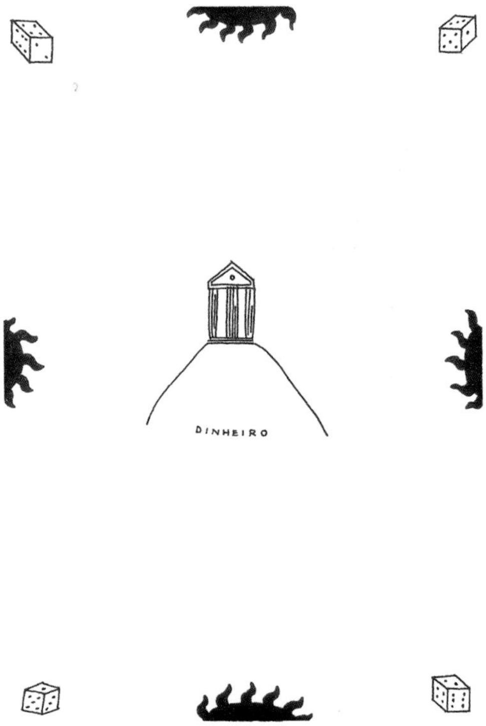

279

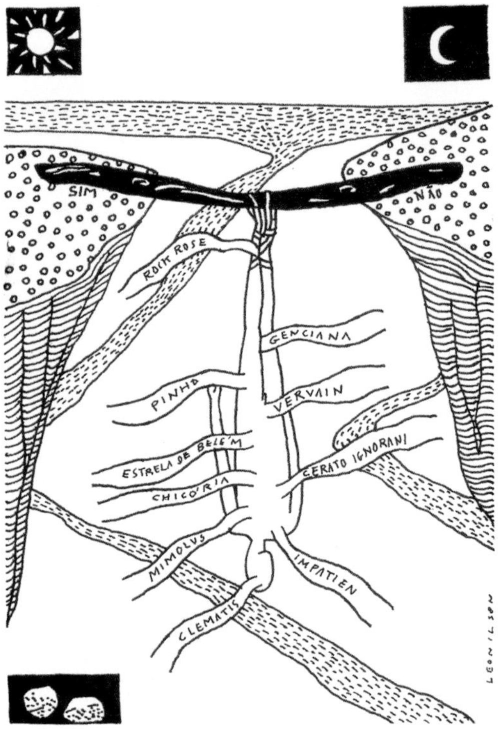

280

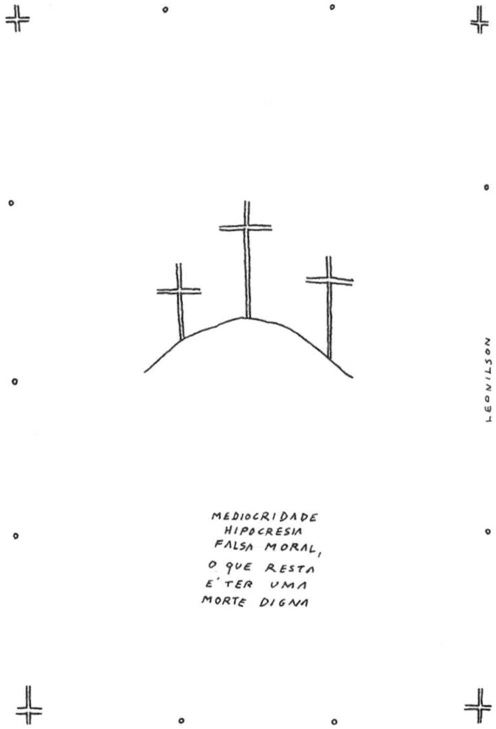

281

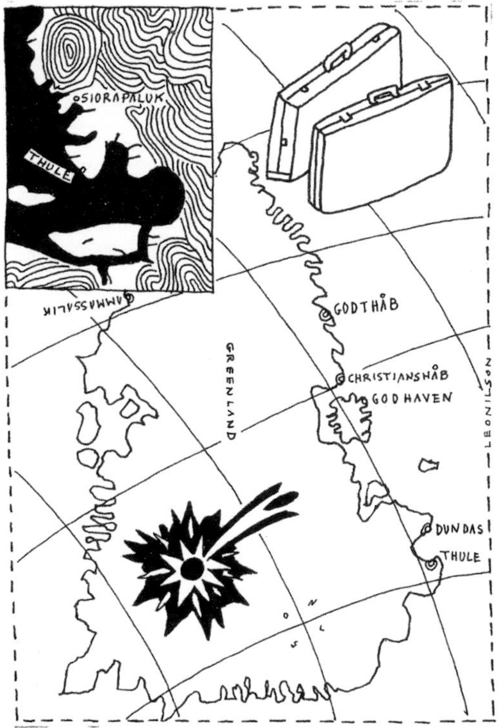

282

279. ***[Paulista se afoga em horrores kitschs]*** [Paulista Drowns in Kitsch Horrors], 1991

18 × 12.5 cm
FSP 11.20.1991
PL.0089.0/00

280. ***[Florais são moda entre desequilibrados]*** [Flower Remedies Are Fad Among the Unstable], 1991

18 × 12.5 cm
FSP 11.27.1991
PL.0090.0/00

281. ***[Neo-vitorianismo é o novo aliado da aids]*** [Neo-Victorianism Is AIDS' New Ally], 1991

18 × 12.5 cm
FSP 12.11.1991
PL.0095.0/00

282. ***[Trágico acidente aéreo mata Papai Noel]*** [Tragic Air Accident Kills Santa Klaus], 1991

18 × 12.5 cm
FSP 12.18.1991
PL.0096.0/00

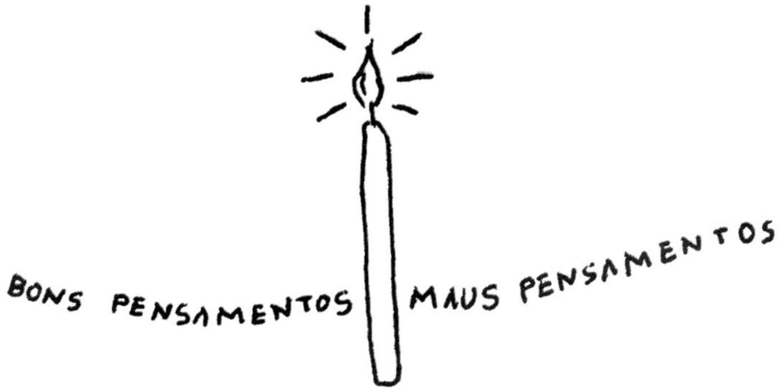

283

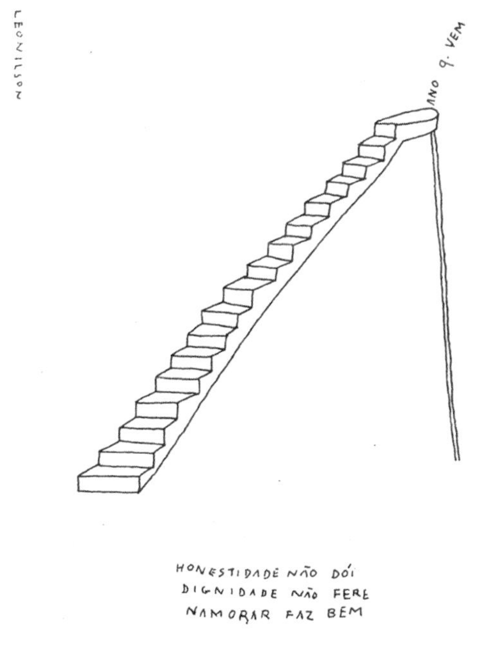

284

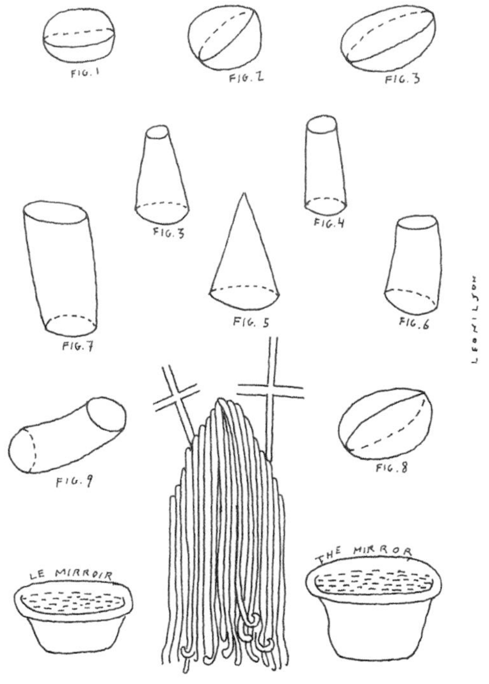

285

283. ***[Natal é época ideal para lavar roupa suja]*** [Christmas Is the Ideal Time to Air Dirty Laudry], 1991

6 × 10 cm
Unknown collection
FSP 12.25.1991
PL.2362.0/00

284. ***[Ano zero km sai por preço de banana]*** [Brand-New Year Sold for Peanuts], 1992

18 × 12.5 cm
FSP 1.8.1992
PL.0052.0/00

285. ***[Thomas deve ganhar eleição para Rei Sol]*** [Thomas Sounds to Win the Election for Sun King], 1992

18 × 12.5 cm
FSP 1.15.1992
PL.0053.0/00

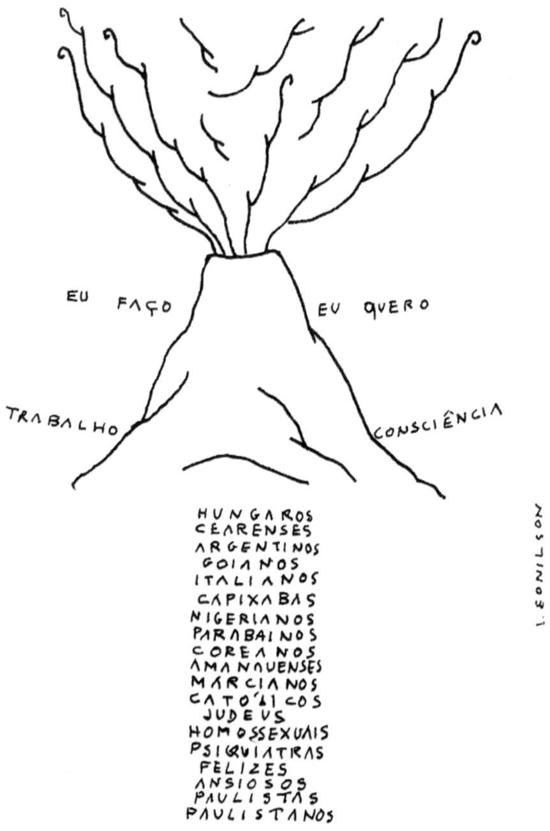

286

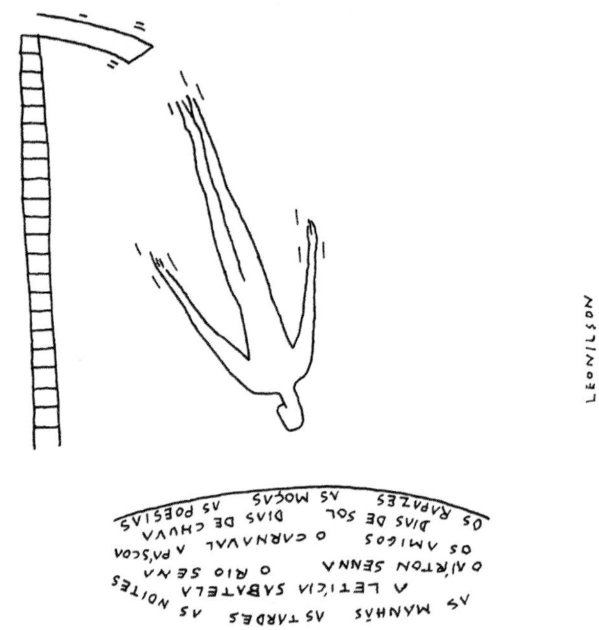

287

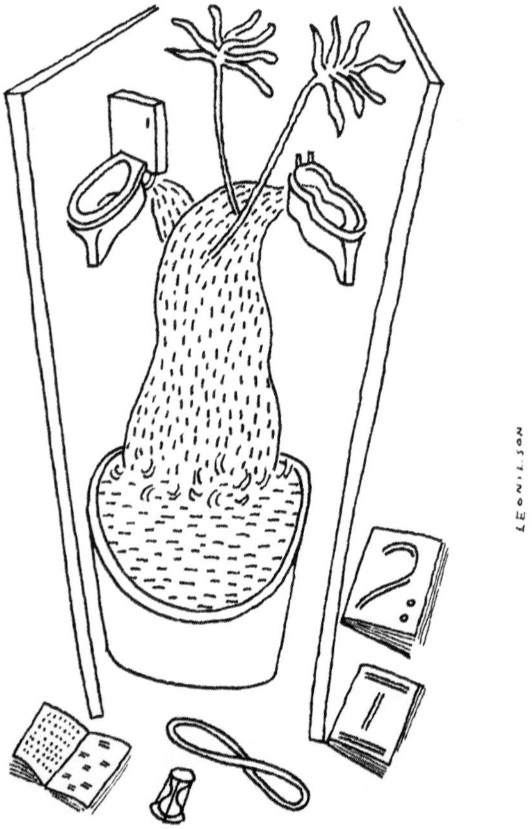

288

286. ***[São Paulo não é nenhuma Brastemp]*** [São Paulo Is No Brastemp], 1992

18 × 12.5 cm
FSP 1.22.1992
PL.0057.0/00

287. ***["N" razões para não se suicidar em 1992]*** ["N" Reasons Not to Commit Suicide in 1992], 1992

18 × 12.5 cm
FSP 1.29.1992
PL.0058.0/00

288. ***[O banheiro vai para o trono ou não vai?]*** [Does the Bathroom Go to the Throne or Not?], 1992

18 × 12.5 cm
FSP 2.5.1992
PL.0059.0/00

289. ***[Cariocas dão a volta por cima e se sacodem]*** [Cariocas Come Out on Top and Jiggle], 1992

12.5 × 18 cm
FSP 2.28.1992
PL.0120.0/00

290. ***[As melhores farpas, ups, frases do ano]*** [The Best Thorns, Ops, Thoughts of the Year], 1992

12.5 × 18 cm
FSP 3.6.1992
PL.0121.0/00

291. ***[Andorinhas abastadas procuram o photo]*** [Well-Off Swallows Patronize the Photo], 1992

Permanent ink and
China ink on paper
18 × 12.5 cm
FSP 2.12.1992
PL.0118.0/00

292. ***[Tyson serve chá com porrada para moças]*** [Tyson Serves Tea with Clobbering to Young Ladies], 1992

18 × 12.5 cm
FSP 2.21.1992
PL.0119.0/00

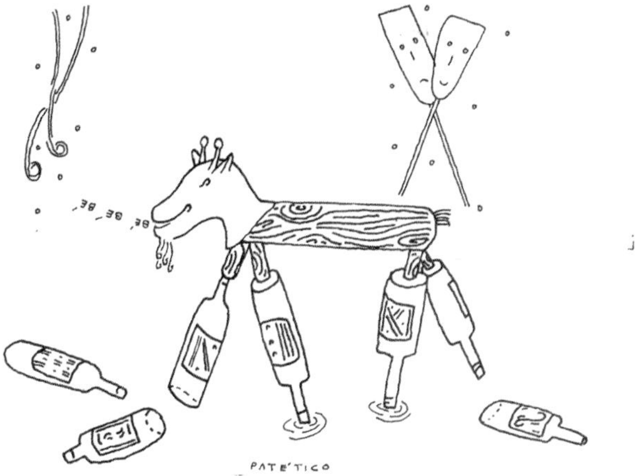

289

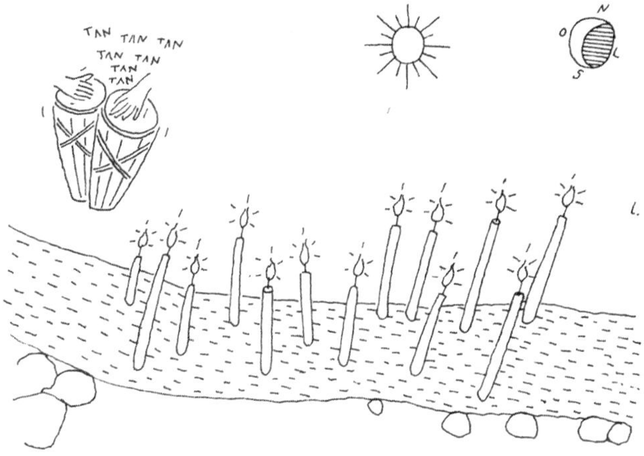

290

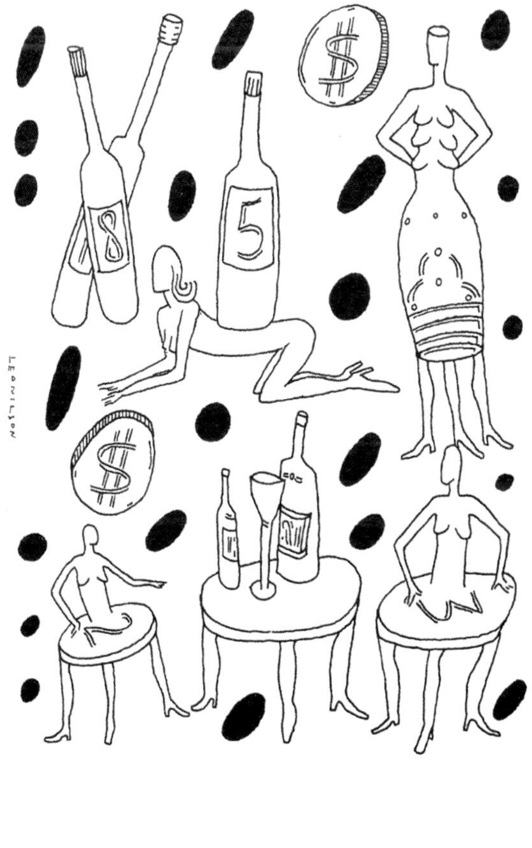

291

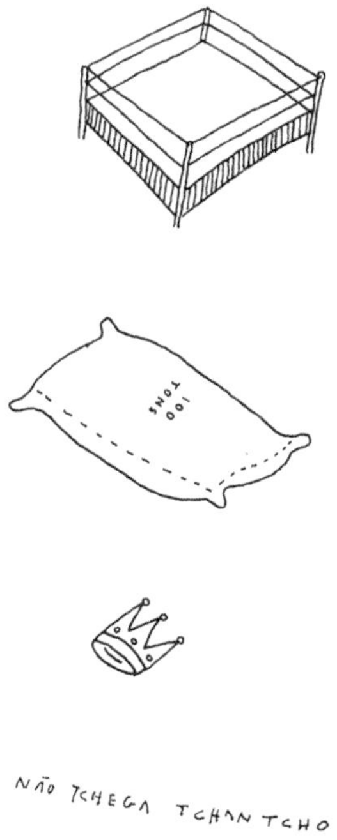

292

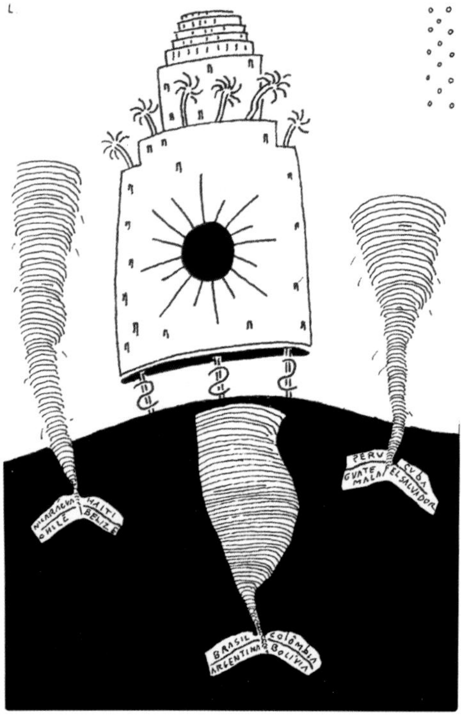

293

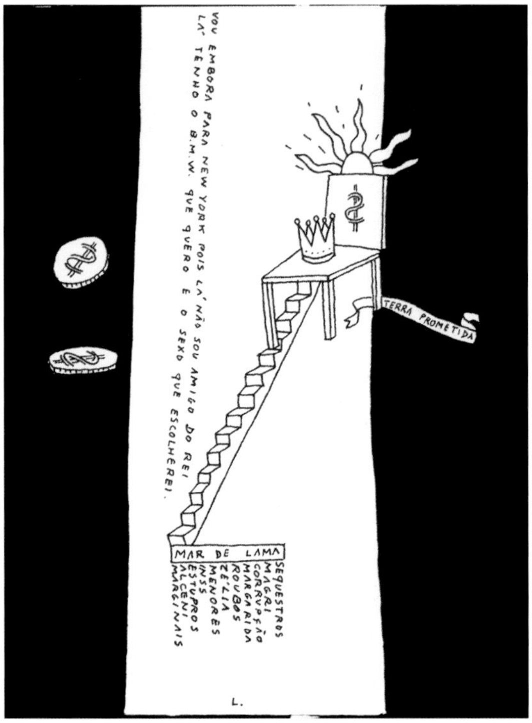

294

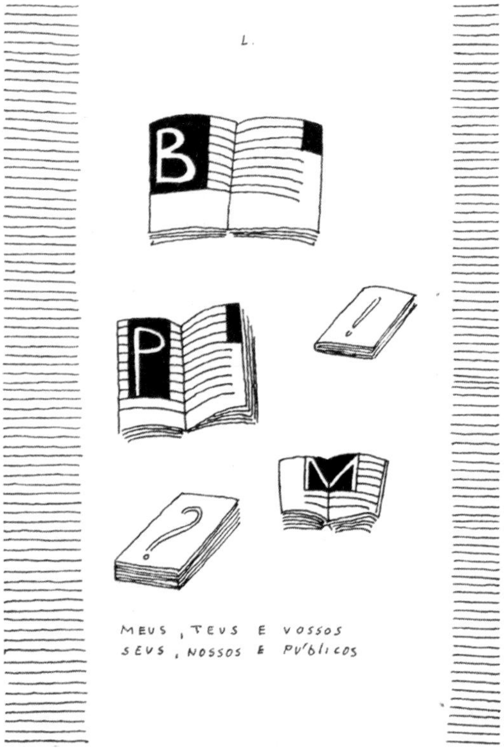

295

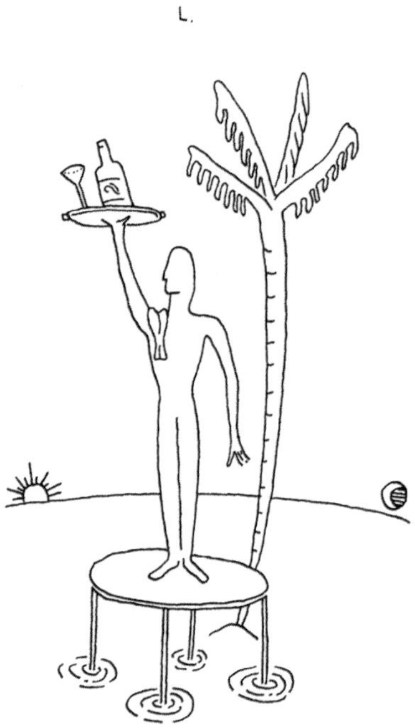

296

293. ***[Miami é o Rio de Janeiro que deu certo]*** [Miami Is a Successful Rio de Janeiro], 1992

Permanent ink and
China ink on paper
18 × 12.5 cm
FSP 3.13.1992
PL.0122.0/00

294. ***[Terra de Marlboro é a terra prometida]*** [Land of Marlboro Is the Promisse Land], 1992

Permanent ink and
China ink on paper
18 × 12.5 cm
FSP 3.20.1992
PL.0123.0/00

295. ***[Palavrão não é exclusividade de Magri]*** [Swear Word Is Not Magri's Prerogative], 1992

18 × 12.5 cm
FSP 3.27.1992
PL.0126.0/00

296. ***[Para lidar com garçons arrogantes, rosne]*** [To Deal With Arrogant Waiters, Snarl], 1992

18 × 12.5 cm
FSP 4.3.1992
PL.0124.0/00

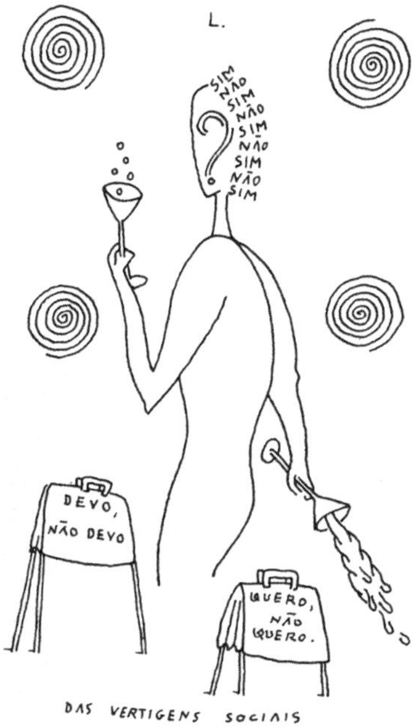

297

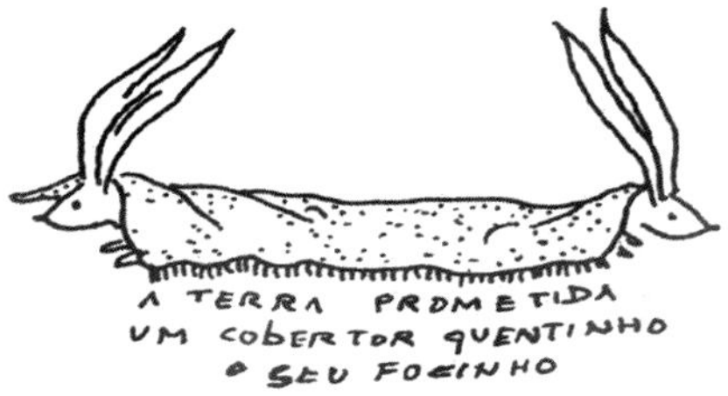

298

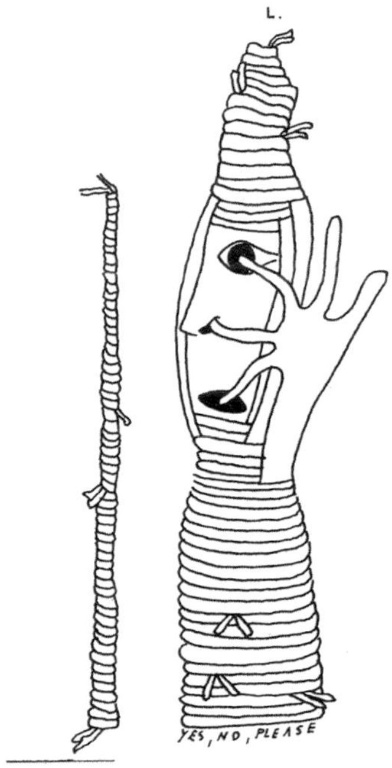

299

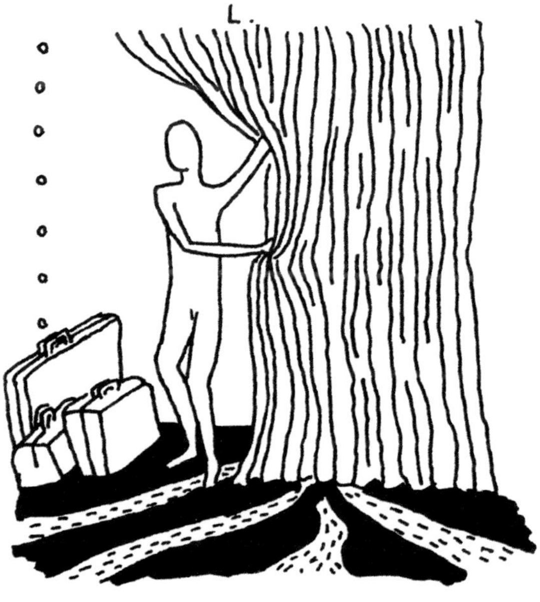

300

297. ***[Falta de educação virou mania nacional]*** [Bad Manners Became National Mania], 1992

18 × 12.5 cm
FSP 4.10.1992
PL.0125.0/00

298. ***[Páscoa é sinônimo de filmes chatos na TV]*** [Easter Is Synonymous With Boring Films on TV], 1992

14 × 13 cm
Unknown collection
FSP 4.17.1992
PL.2363.0/00

299. ***[Curso é coisa da época do avião a lenha]*** [Courses Are From the Time of the Timber Plane], 1992

18 × 12.5 cm
FSP 4.24.1992
PL.0097.0/00

300. ***[Para coçadores, feriado é prato cheio]*** [For Lazybones, Holiday Is a Feast], 1992

13.5 × 13.5 cm
Unknown collection
FSP 5.1.1992
PL.2364.0/00

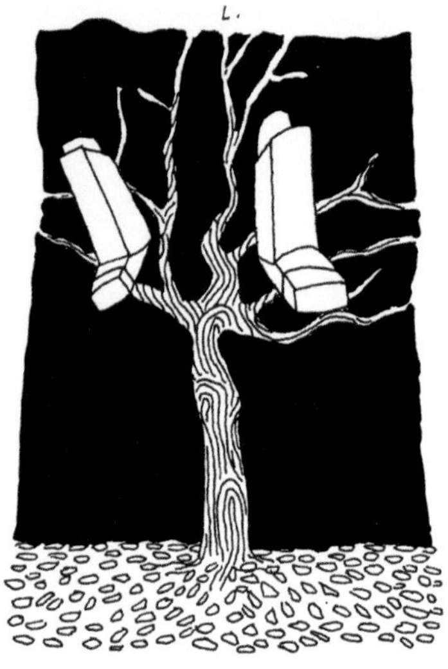

301

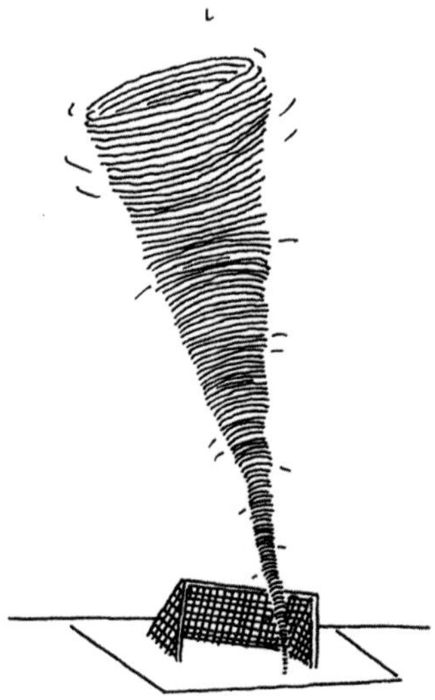

302

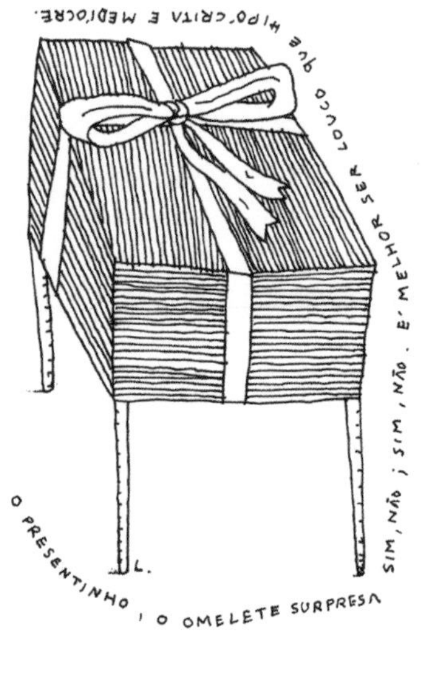

303

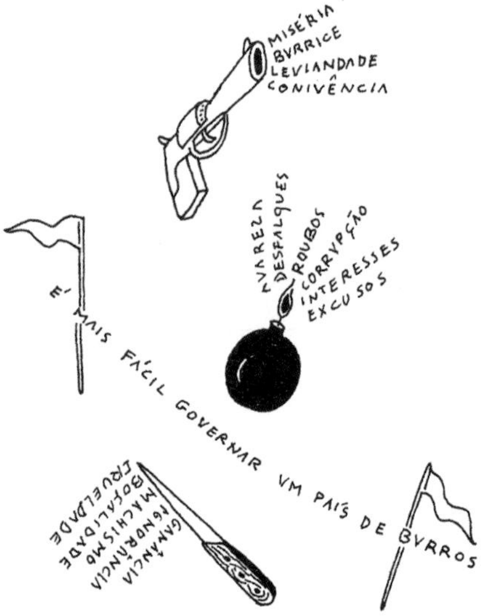

304

301. ***[Inverno em São Paulo pronuncia-se inferno]*** [Winter in São Paulo Is Pronounced Hell], 1992

Permanent ink and China ink on paper
18 × 12.5 cm
FSP 5.15.1992
PL.0067.0/00

302. ***[O Brasil, quem diria, acabou no Haiti]*** [Brazil Eventually Ended in Haiti], 1992

14 × 14 cm
Unknown collection
FSP 5.22.1992
PL.2365.0/00

303. ***[Traveca sai do armário para ser endeusada]*** [Drag Comes Out to Be Adored as a Goddess], 1992

Permanent ink and cut paper glued on paper
18 × 12.5 cm
FSP 6.5.1992
PL.0068.0/00

304. ***[Elite ou celite, eis a dilacerante questão]*** [Elite or Celite, That's the Dilacerating Question], 1992

Permanent ink and China ink on paper
16 × 12 cm
FSP 6.19.1992
PL.0069.0/00

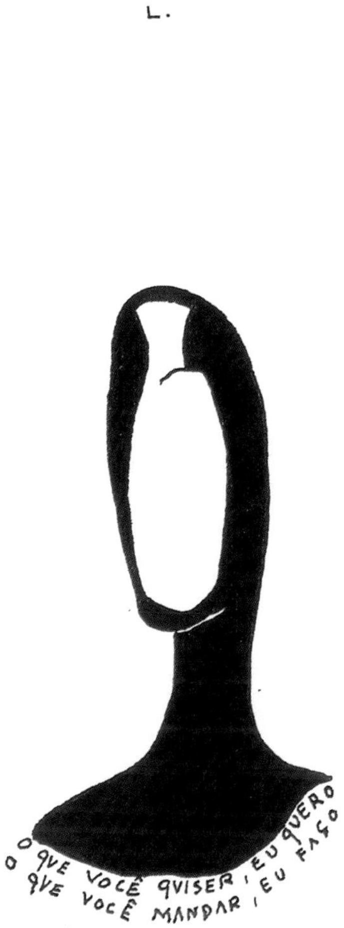

305

305. ***[Comemore sozinho o dia dos namorados]*** [Celebrate Valentine's Day Alone], 1992

Permanent ink and
China ink on paper
18 × 12.5 cm
FSP 6.12.1992
PL.0045.0/00

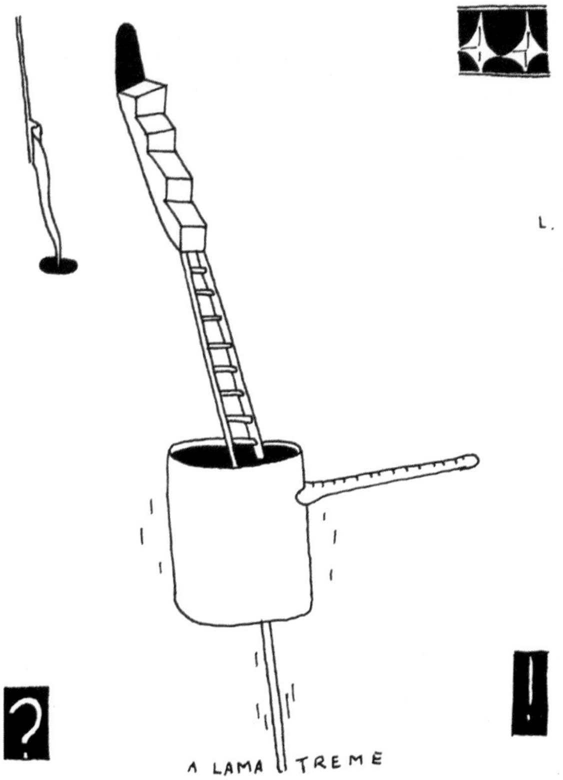

306

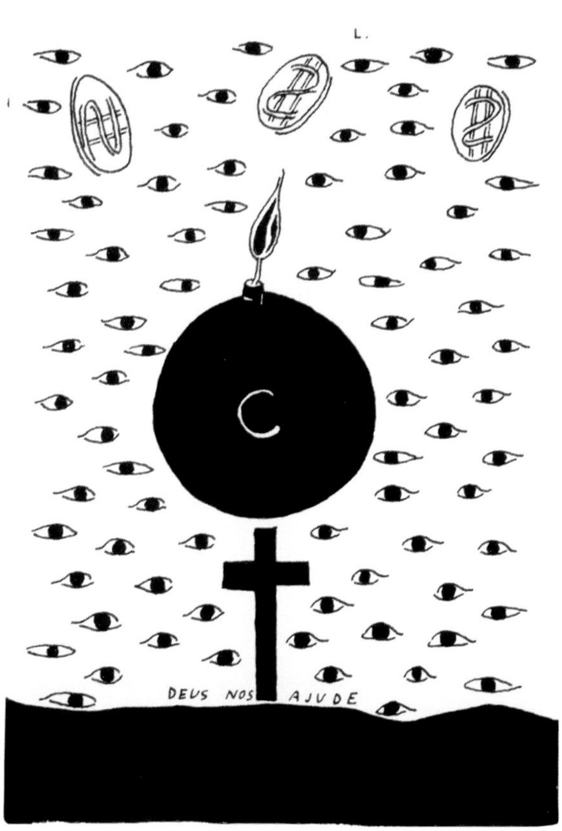

307

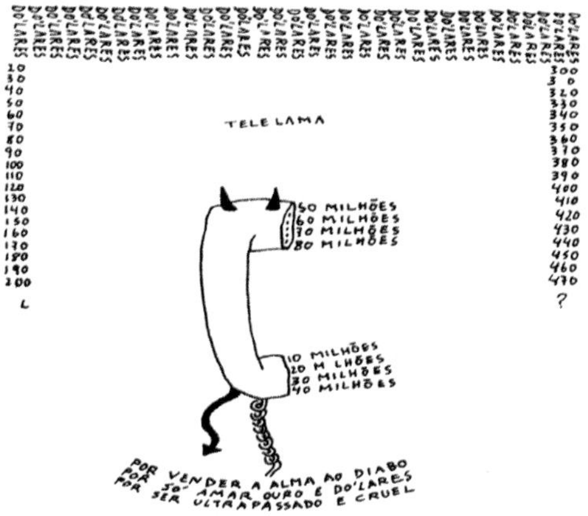

308

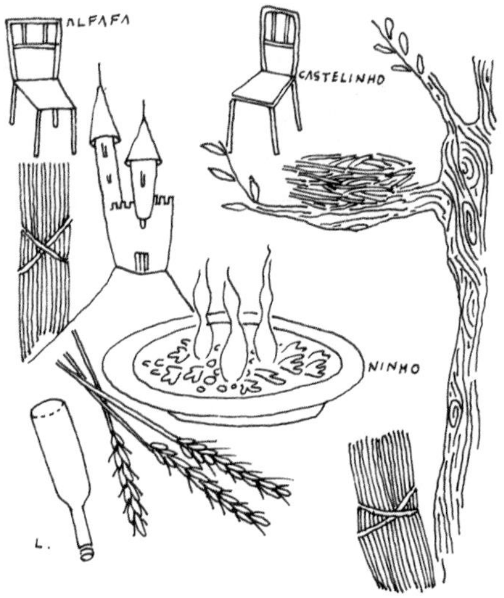

309

306. ***[Vice é vício desde os tempos de Sarney]*** [A Vice Is a Vicious Ever Since the Time of Sarney], 1992

Permanent ink and China ink on paper
18 × 12.5 cm
FSP 6.26.1992
PL.0070.0/00

307. ***[Você compraria um carro usado "delle"?]*** [Would You Buy an Used Car From "Him"?], 1992

Permanent ink and China ink on paper
18 × 12.5 cm
FSP 7.3.1992
PL.0071.0/00

308. ***[Descoberto novo furo no "affair" PC]*** [Another Blooper Found in PC "Affair"], 1992

10.5 × 14 cm
Unknow collection
FSP 7.10.1992
PL.2366.0/00

309. ***[Comida de hospital é a gororoba da moda]*** [Hospital Food Is the Grub in Vogue], 1992

16.5 × 14.5 cm
FSP 7.24.1992
PL.0072.0/00

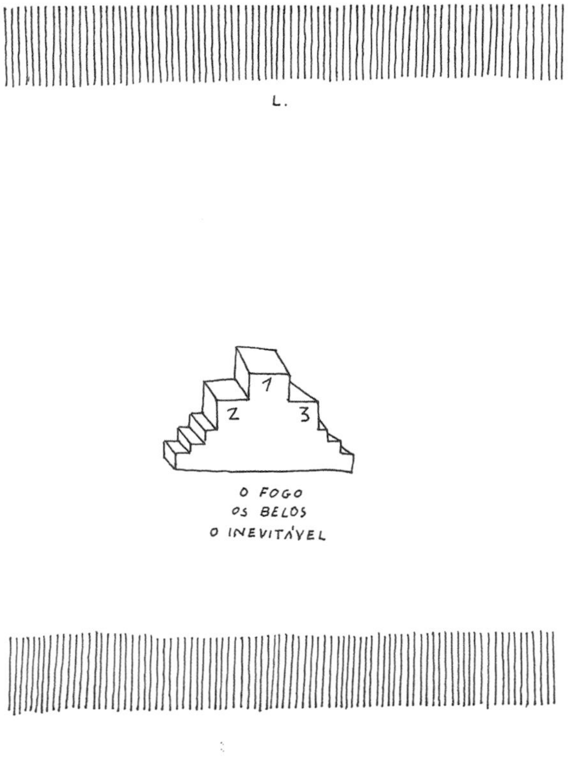

310

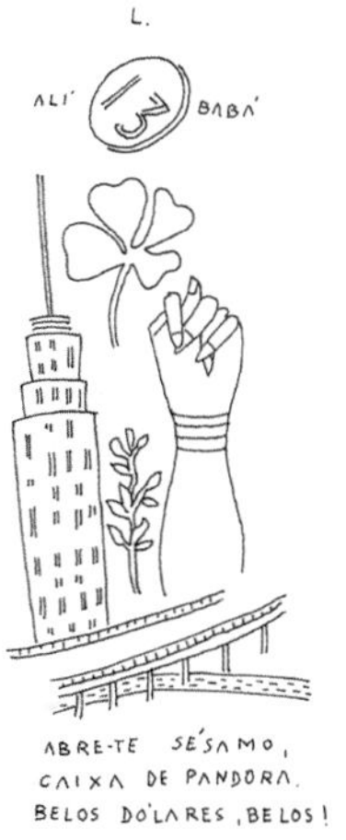

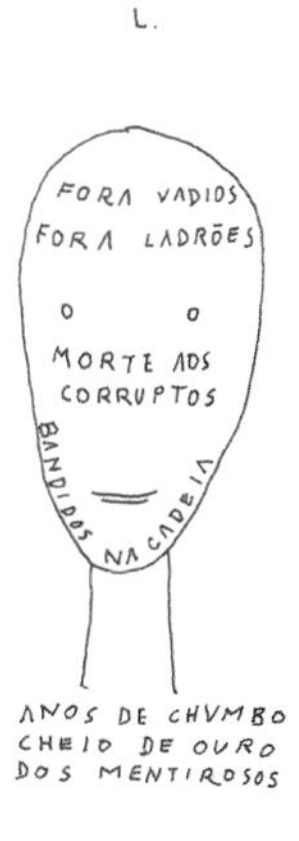

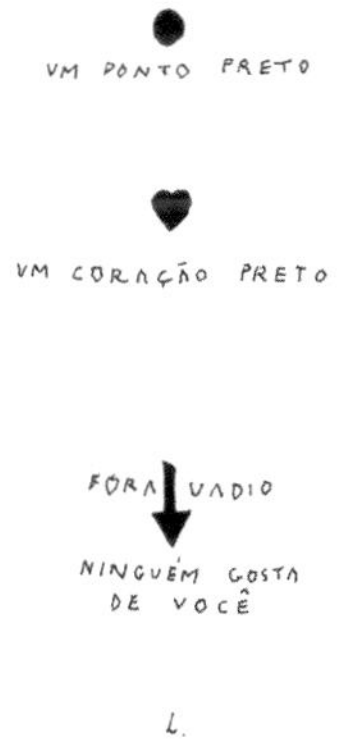

311

312

313

310. ***[Na Olimpíada, Brasil é ouro em jequice]*** [At Olympics, Brazil Takes Gold in Tawdriness], 1992

19.5 × 14 cm
FSP 7.31.1992
PL.0048.0/00

311. ***[Aberta a temporada de abobrinhas políticas]*** [Season of Political Baloney Opens], 1992

21 × 15 cm
FSP 8.7.1992
PL.0050.0/00

312. ***[Estudantes, enfim, saem do mundo da lua!]*** [Students Finally Get Their Heads Out of the Clouds!], 1992

19 × 11.5 cm
FSP 8.14.1992
PL.0049.0/00

313. ***[Com que roupa Rosane irá a Varennes?]*** [What Will Rosane Wear to Varennes?], 1992

19 × 11.5 cm
FSP 8.21.1992
PL.0078.0/00

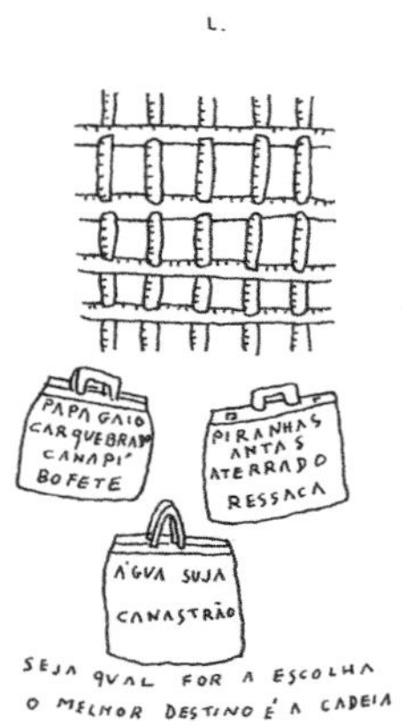

314

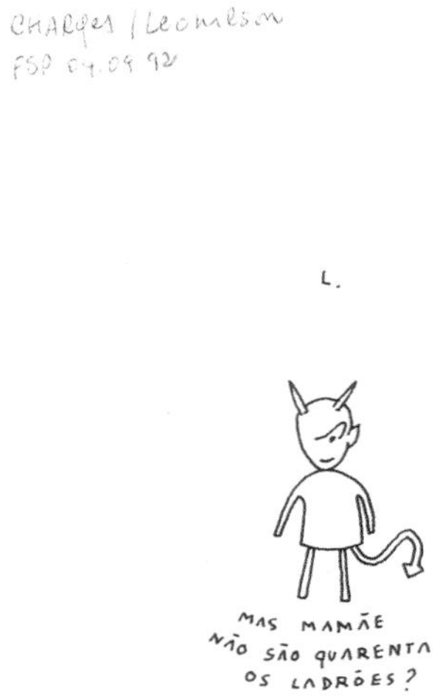

315

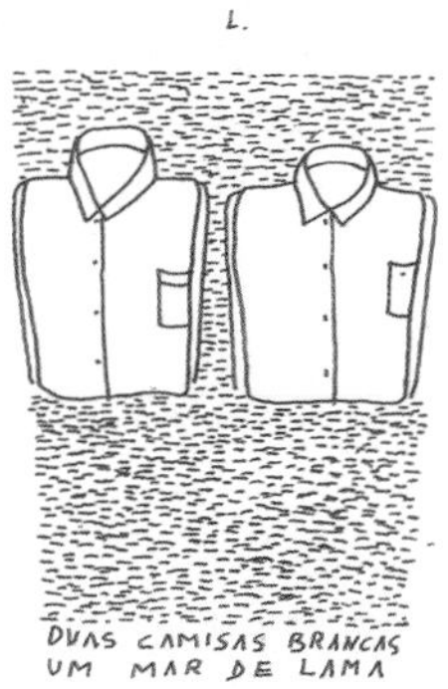

316

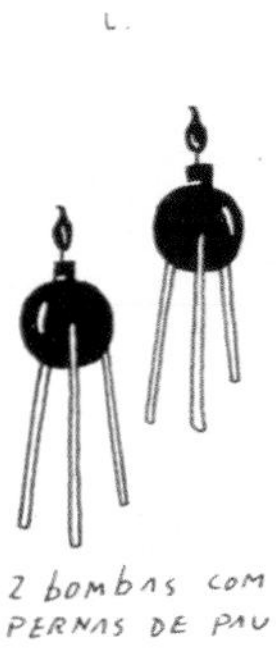

317

314. ***[Clima de despacho paira sobre caso PC]*** [Voodoo Atmosphere Looms Over PC Case], 1992

15.5 × 12.5 cm
FSP 8.28.1992
PL.0077.0/00

315. ***[O mundo gira, a lusitana roda e la nave va]*** [The World Spins, The Lusitana Goes Round and La Nave Va], 1992

19 × 11.5 cm
FSP 9.4.1992
PL.0076.0/00

316. ***[Quando Brasil e Itália têm algo em comum]*** [When Brazil and Italy Have Something in Common], 1992

19 × 11.5 cm
FSP 9.11.1992
PL.0041.0/00

317. ***[São Paulo é candidata a capital do Brasil]*** [São Paulo Is Running for Brazil's Capital], 1992

Permanent ink and
China ink on paper
19 × 11.5 cm
FSP 9.18.1992
PL.0105.0/00

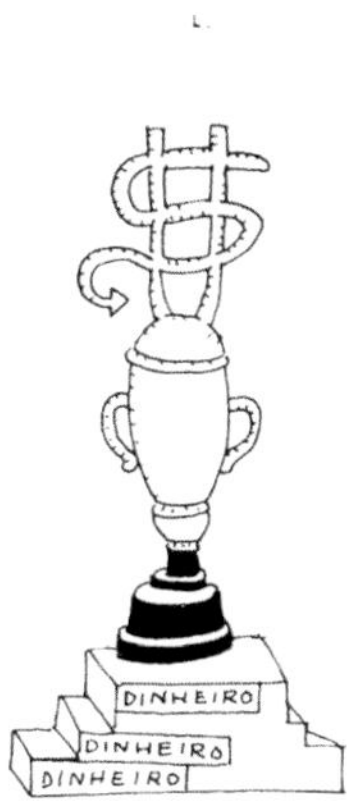

318

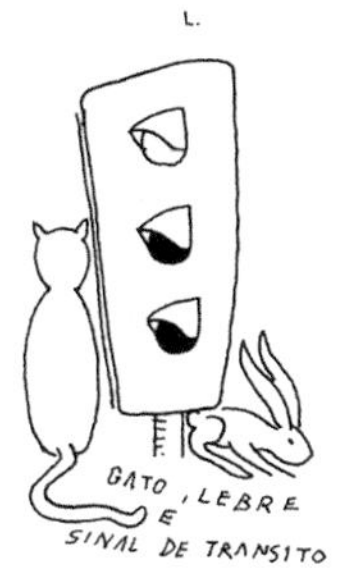

319

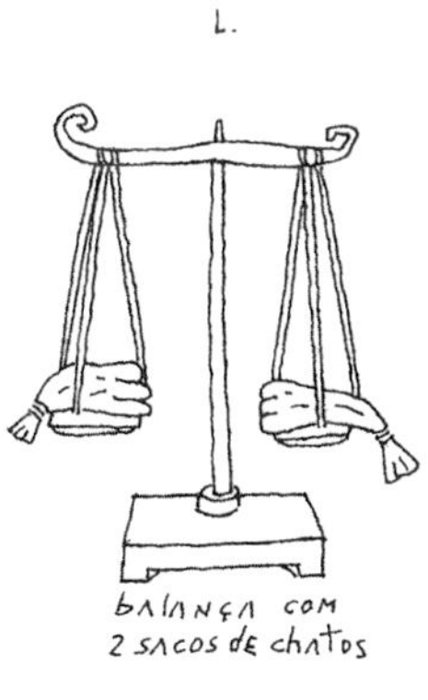

320

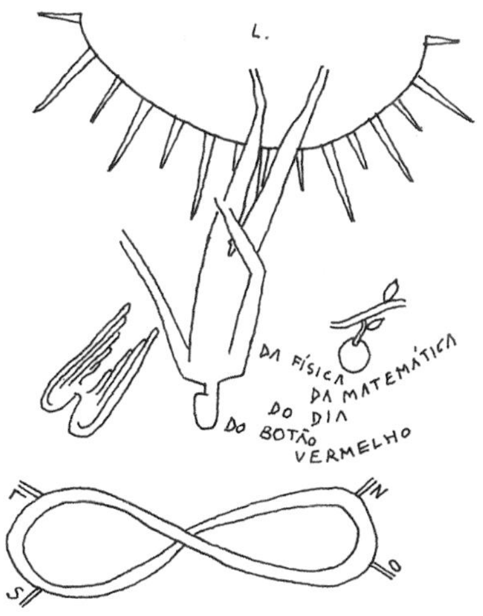

321

318. ***[Fórmula 1 mostra seu jeito PC de ser]*** [Formula 1 Shows Its PC Way of Being], 1992

19 × 11.5 cm
FSP 9.25.1992
PL.0104.0/00

319. ***[Odafas fisiologista amarga "day after"]*** [Odafas Fisiologista Suffers Day After], 1992

19 × 11.5 cm
FSP 10.2.1992
PL.0081.0/00

320. ***[O chato volta a atacar 30 anos depois]*** [The Bore Charges Again After 30 Years], 1992

18 × 10 cm
FSP 10.9.1992
PL.0082.0/00

321. ***[O último vôo do intrépido filho de Dédalo]*** [The Last Flight of Daedalus' Intrepid Son], 1992

14 × 11.5 cm
FSP 10.16.1992
PL.0084.0/00

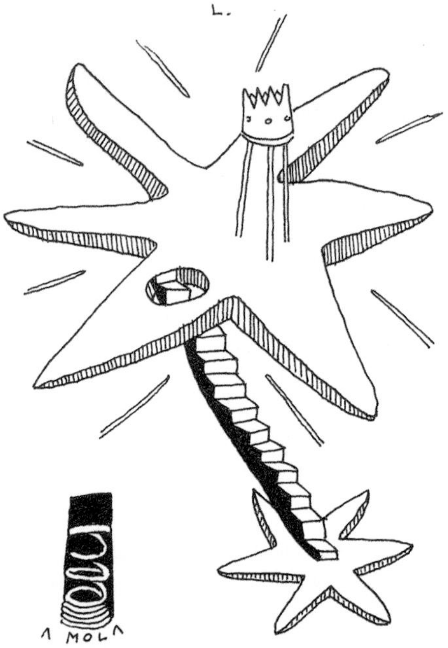

322

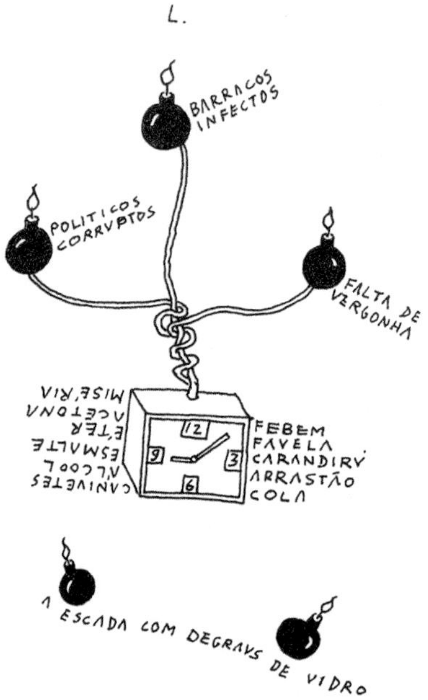

323

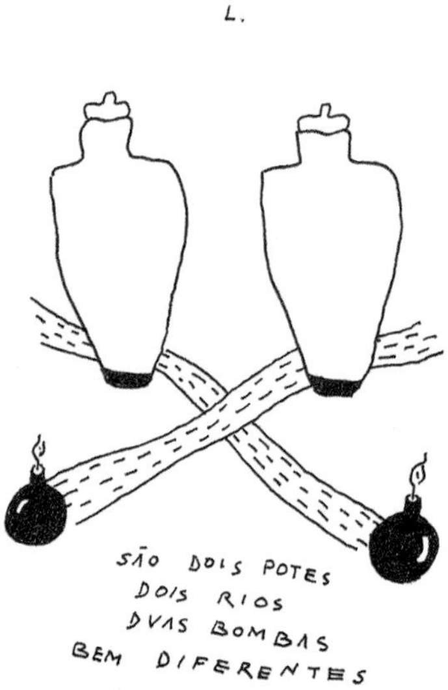

324

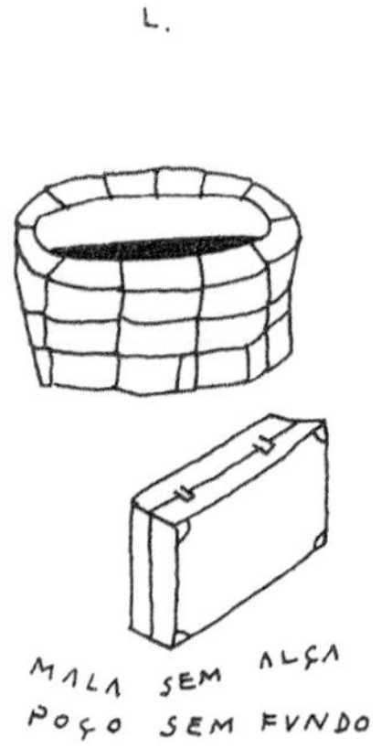

325

322. *[Bom mesmo é nascer virado para a lua]* [What's Really Good Is to Be Born Turned Toward the Moon], 1992

15 × 10.5 cm
FSP 10.23.1992
PL.0085.0/00

323. *[Não se faz mais baderna como antigamente]* [They Don't Make Messes Like in the Old Times Anymore], 1992

15.5 × 10.5 cm
FSP 10.30.1992
PL.0086.0/00

324. *[Saddam vai à luta e Bush veste pijama]* [Saddam Goes Fighting and Bush Wears Pijamas], 1992

15.5 × 10.5 cm
FSP 11.6.1992
PL.0087.0/00

325. *[Suplicy e Maluf formam par de vasos]* [Suplicy and Maluf Are Birds of a Feather], 1992

15.5 × 10.5 cm
FSP 11.13.1992
PL.0073.0/00

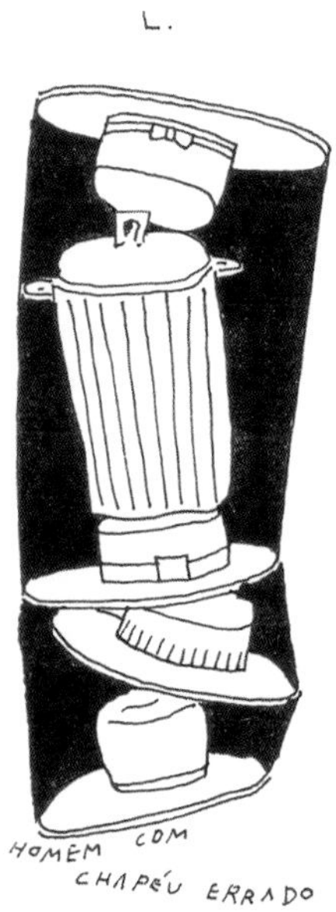

326

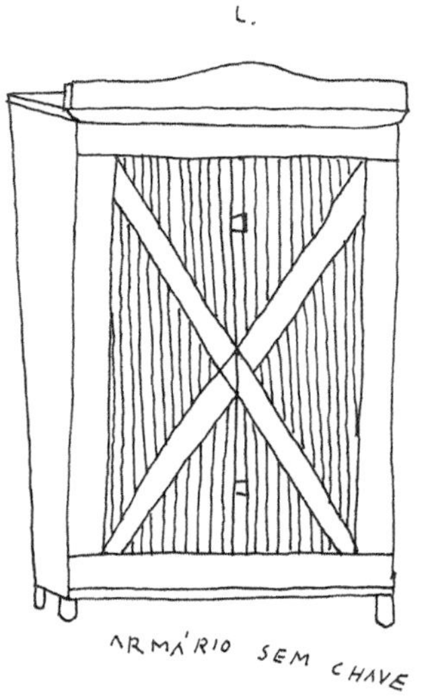

327

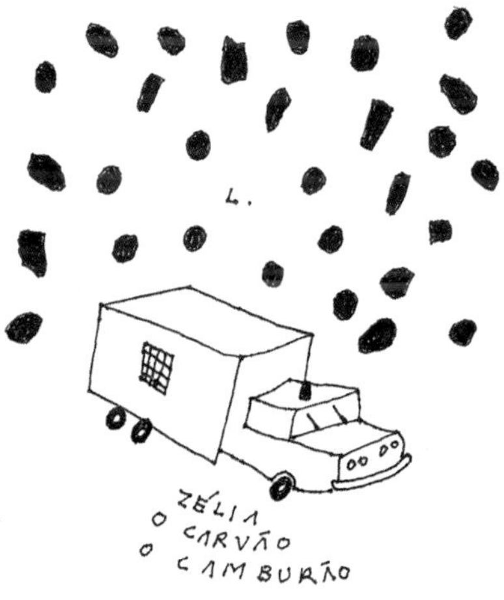

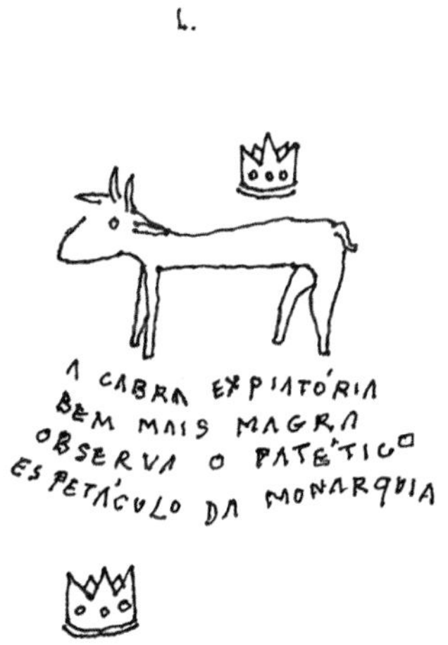

329

328

326. ***[Kissinger vence nobel na categoria vexame]*** [Kissinger Wins Nobel in Shame Category], 1992

Permanent ink and China ink on paper
15.5 × 10.5 cm
FSP 11.20.1992
PL.0074.0/00

327. ***[Tutu à mineira é inimigo do orgasmo]*** [Tutu à mineira Is an Enemy of Orgasm], 1992

15.5 × 10.5 cm
FSP 11.27.1992
PL.0075.0/00

328. ***[Papai Noel baixa na Dinda de saco cheio]*** [Santa Klauss Shows Up at Dinda with his Bag Full], 1992

Permanent ink on lined paper
17 × 10 cm
FSP 12.4.1992
PL.0079.0/00

329. ***[Diana roda baiana e azeda natal da rainha]*** [Diana Throws a Fit and Sours Queen's Christmas], 1992

14 × 13.5 cm
Unknown collection
FSP 12.11.1992
PL.2367.0/00

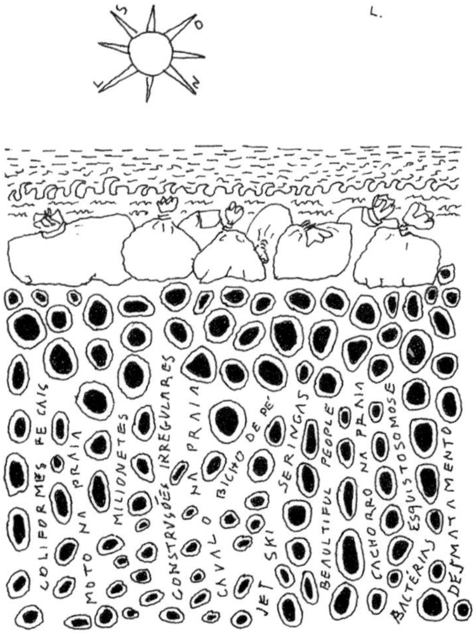

330

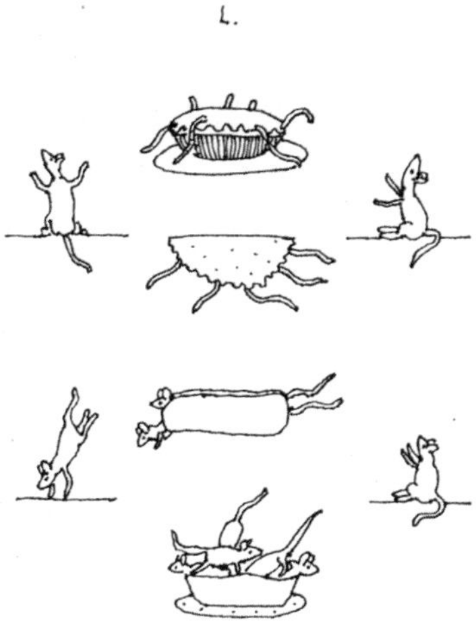

331

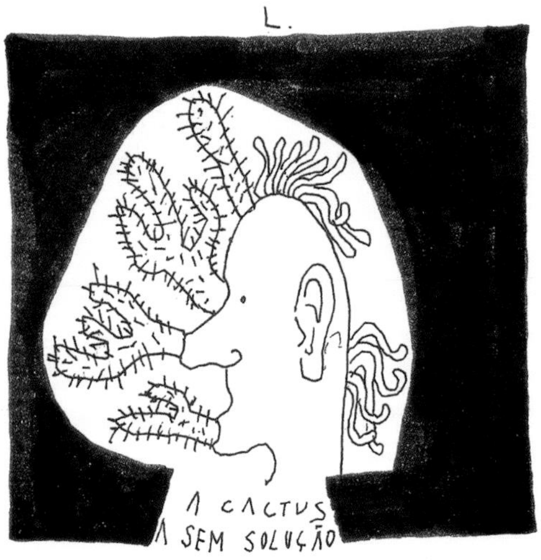

332

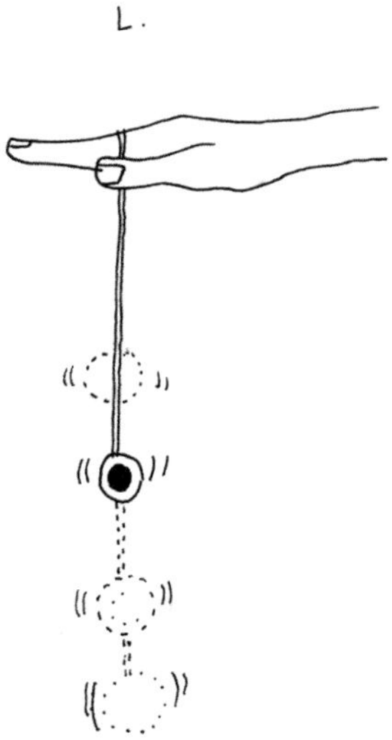

333

330. ***[Lugar de masoquista é na areia da praia]*** [A Masochist's Place Is on the Beach Sand], 1993

Permanent ink and China ink on paper
17 × 12.5 cm
FSP 1.8.1993
PL.0080.0/00

331. ***[Ratos são iguaria da culinária tradicional]*** [Rats Are Delicacy of Traditional Cooking], 1993

Permanent ink on lined paper
17 × 10.5 cm
FSP 1.15.1993
PL.0051.0/00

332. ***[Desculpe Vinicius, feiúra é fundamental]*** [Sorry Vinicius, Ugliness Is Fundamental], 1993

Permanent ink and marker on paper
14.5 × 10.5 cm
FSP 1.29.1993
PL.0047.0/00

333. ***[Português faz papagaio perder o lugar]*** [Portuguese Makes Parrot Lose its Place], 1993

14.5 × 10.5 cm
FSP 2.12.1993
PL.2368.0/00

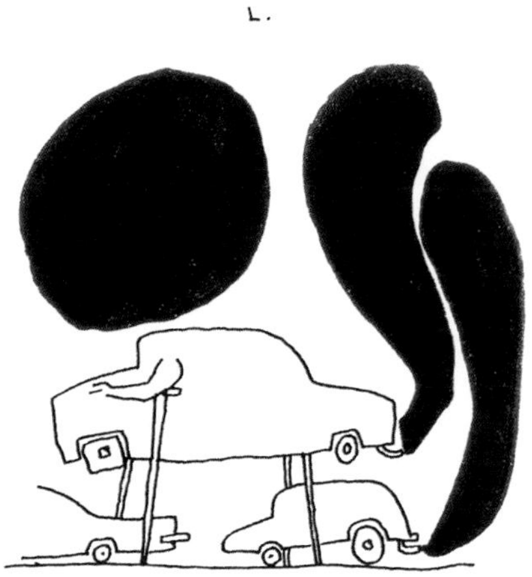

334

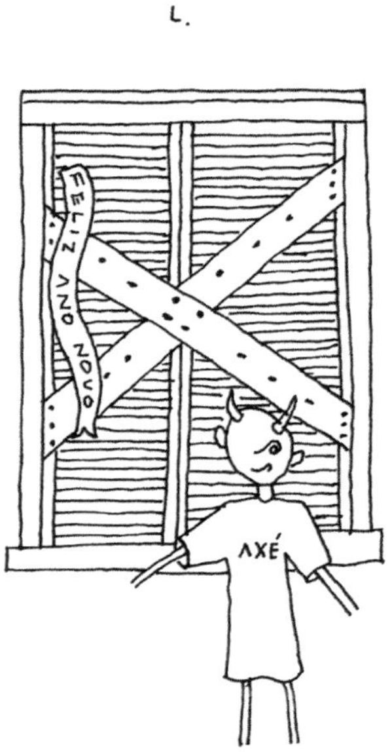

335

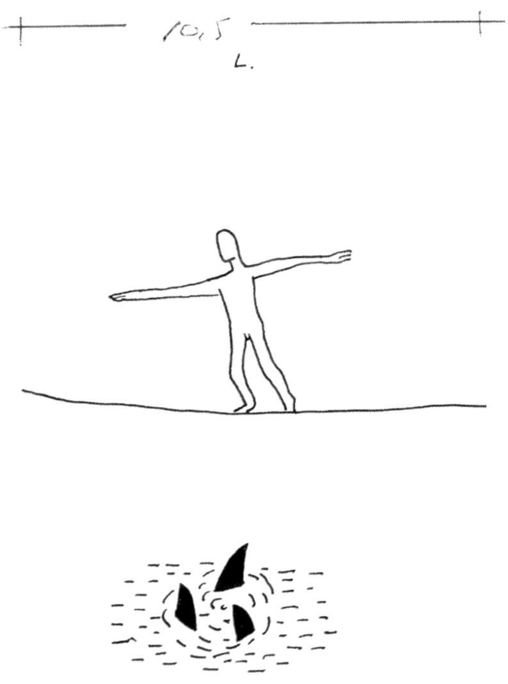

336

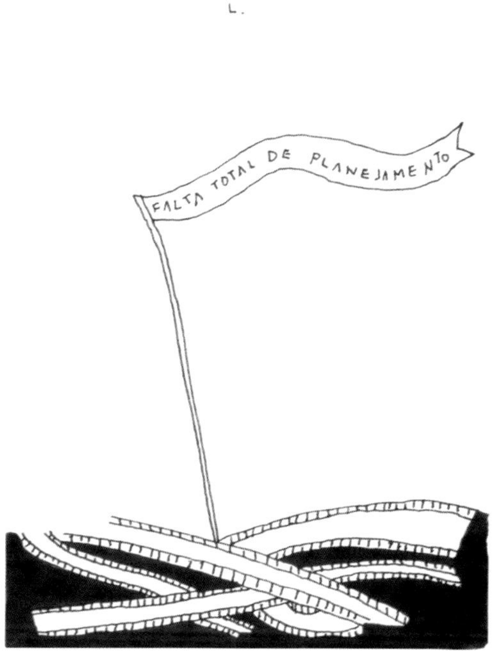

337

334. ***[Paulistano não consegue mais trocar o óleo]*** [Paulistano Can't Change Oil Anymore], 1993

Permanent ink and marker on paper
14.5 × 10.5 cm
FSP 2.19.1993
PL.0054.0/00

335. ***[Carnaval paulistano eleito o pior do mundo]*** [Paulistano Carnival Voted Worst in the World], 1993

14.5 × 10.5 cm
FSP 2.26.1993
PL.0055.0/00

336. ***[São Paulo, a cidade que é uma roubada]*** [São Paulo, the City That's a Rip-Off], 1993

14.5 × 10.5 cm
FSP 3.5.1993
PL.0056.0/00

337. ***[Paulo Maluf, um perfeito injustiçado]*** [Paulo Maluf, a Perfectly Wronged Person], 1993

Permanent ink and marker on paper
14.5 × 10.5 cm
FSP 3.12.1993
PL.0106.0/00

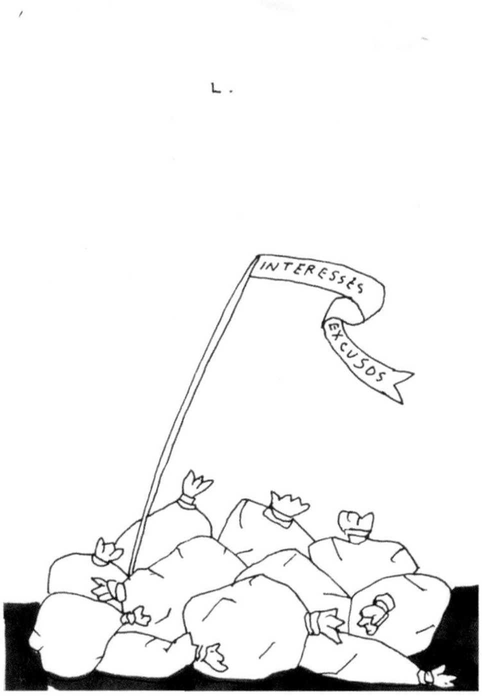

338

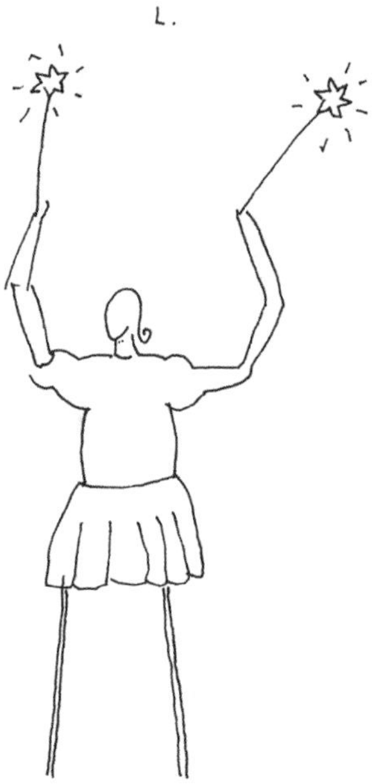

339

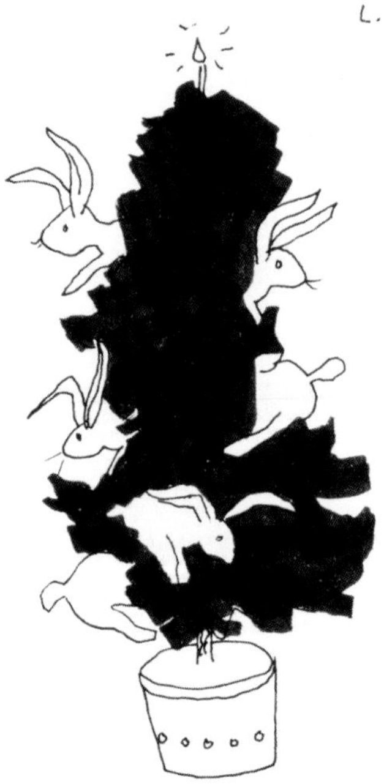

340

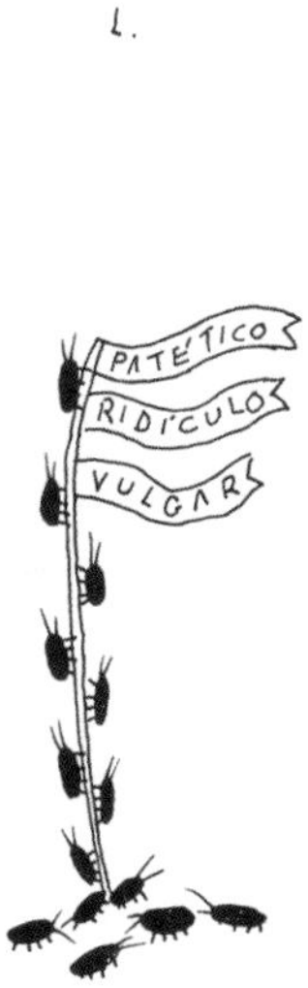

341

338. ***[Great Gatsby se esbalda nos Jardins]*** [Great Gatsby Has a Ball in Jardins], 1993

Permanent ink and marker on paper
14.5 × 10.5 cm
FSP 3.19.1993
PL.0107.0/00

339. ***[Drácula vem curtir o outono em Sampa]*** [Dracula Comes to Enjoy Autumn in Sampa], 1993

14.5 × 10.5 cm
FSP 4.16.1993
PL.0109.0/00

340. ***[Paixão é pior que andar em ônibus lotado]*** [A Passion Is Worse Than Riding a Crowded Bus], 1993

Permanent ink and marker on paper
14.5 × 10.5 cm
FSP 4.9.1993
PL.0111.0/00

341. ***[Comer barata é o novo barato da cidade]*** [Eating Roaches Is the New Craze in Town], 1993

15 × 8.5 cm
FSP 3.26.1993
PL.0108.0/00

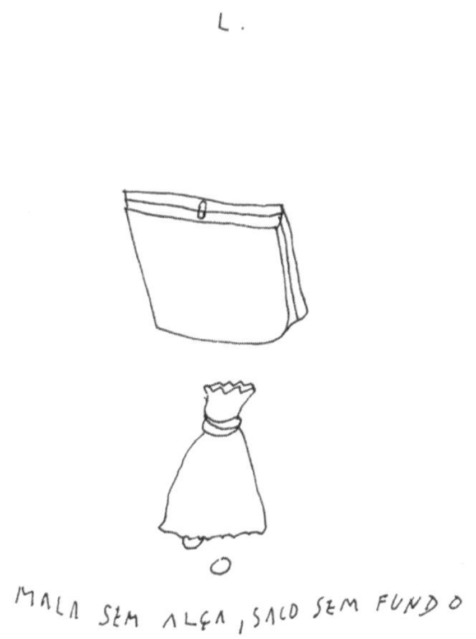

342

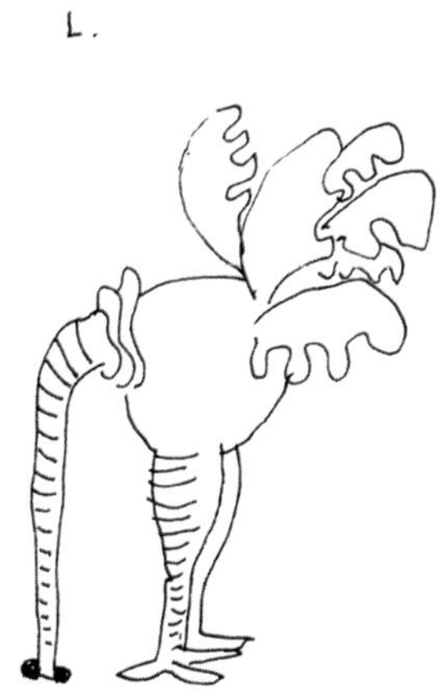

343

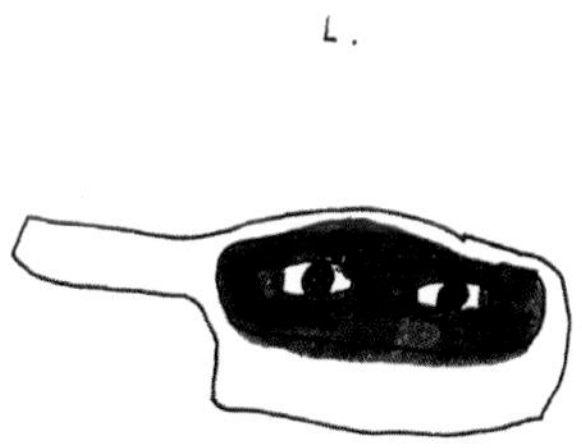

344

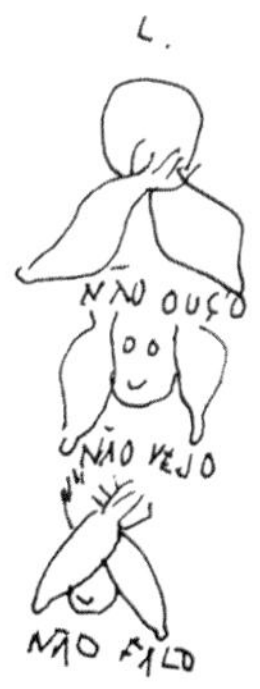

345

342. ***[Plebiscito revive quarta-feira de cinzas]*** [Plebiscite Reenacts Ash Wednesday], 1993

14.5 × 10.5 cm
FSP 4.23.1993
PL.0110.0/00

343. ***[Sexo moderno se pratica verbalmente]*** [Modern Sex Is Practiced Verbally], 1993

14.5 × 10.5 cm
FSP 4.30.1993
PL.0112.0/00

344. ***[Vida noturna de "mudernos" é uma Bósnia]*** [Nightlife of "Mudernos" People Is a Bosnia], 1993

Permanent ink and marker on paper
14.5 × 10.5 cm
FSP 5.7.1993
PL.0113.0/00

345. ***[E se Suzy Rego casasse com Gustavo Rosa?]*** [What if Suzy Rego Married Gustavo Rosa?], 1993

14.5 × 10.5 cm
FSP 5.14.1993
PL.0114.0/00

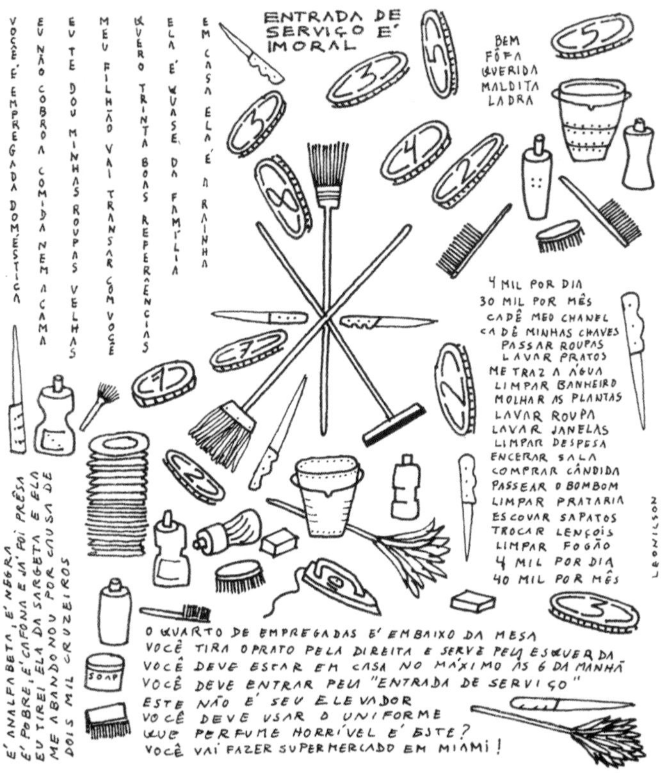

346

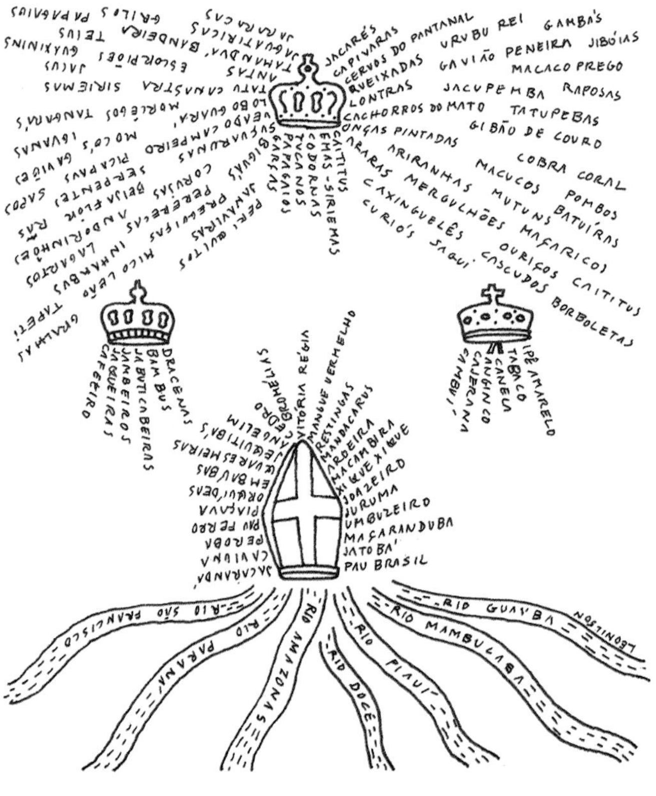

347

346. ***[Entrada de serviço é imoral 4]*** [Service Entrance Is Immoral 4], 1991

18.5 × 15 cm
PL.0136.0/00

347. ***[Família real]*** [Royal Family], 1991

18.5 × 15 cm
PL.0083.0/00

CONCEN TRATED CON VERSA TIONS

Leonilson
Adriano Pedrosa

SÃO PAULO, MARCH 4, 1991[1]

ADRIANO PEDROSA **When did you start at FAAP?**[2]
JOSÉ LEONILSON In the second half of 1978, to do visual arts. In early 1977, I enrolled at Belas Artes,[3] stayed a month and quit. In July [of the following year],[4] I passed the FAAP admission exam and enrolled.

AP **You were in class with Leda Catunda, Sérgio Romagnolo, Luiz Zerbini?**
JL No. I was in class with Zerbini, Ana Tavares, Jac Leirner, Margô Crescente, and Silvia Freitas. Leda and Sérgio were younger, they got in after me, in 1979.

AP **How long did you stay at FAAP?**
JL I left FAAP after a year, I don't remember very well, I think it was in 1980... Yes, in 1980 I went to study at Aster, which was Julio Plaza's [1937–2003] school.[5] I did work as a mentor there, which was great.

AP **You were already painting at the time you started at FAAP?**
JL No.

AP **Drawing?**
JL No, back then, I didn't do anything.

AP You entered without knowing what you wanted to do or whether you wanted to be an artist?

JL To be an artist? I wanted to work with art; I don't know whether I wanted to be an artist... Yes, I wanted to be an artist. I wanted to paint, to draw.

AP You didn't have any work previous to that?

JL No, not in the sense of a regular practice. Occasionally I did some paintings, some drawings.

AP Before entering FAAP?

JL Yes. During FAAP, I made works proposed by teachers at FAAP.

AP And nothing else?

JL And nothing else. But in the last year, in 1979, I already knew I wanted to do this, I wanted to paint, and thought I should have a studio. So, Zerbini and I set up our first studio and we stayed there for a year, working. We went there every morning and stayed until night, when I went to FAAP classes.

AP But you didn't complete the course?

JL No. In the first half of 1980, I paused my enrollment. We continued with this studio, and I, Zerbini, Jac, Ana Tavares, Eduardo Brandão—also some other artists, I think Rafael França [1957–1991]—we went to Aster.

AP Where was this school?

JL In Pacaembu [São Paulo]. It was a great school.

AP Was it a non-degree program?

JL We went there every Friday with all we had done during the week; we came together, showed our work [to each other], and discussed it.

AP You were born in 1957, so you were twenty-three years old?

JL Yes, exactly. That was in the first half of 1980. In the second [half of 1980], I enrolled at FAAP again, and finished the fifth semester. But then, I couldn't stay there any longer. I was already making my own work; I was drawing. I didn't want to go to school anymore, because I no longer wanted to do the stuff we had to do there. Teachers would propose certain tasks we should work on, and I didn't do any of them. Nelson Leirner [1932–2020], for example, kept saying that I had to leave FAAP, that it was no longer for me, that I needed to have a studio and work on my own. This was also encouraged by Julio Plaza. That year I made a series of about forty drawings.

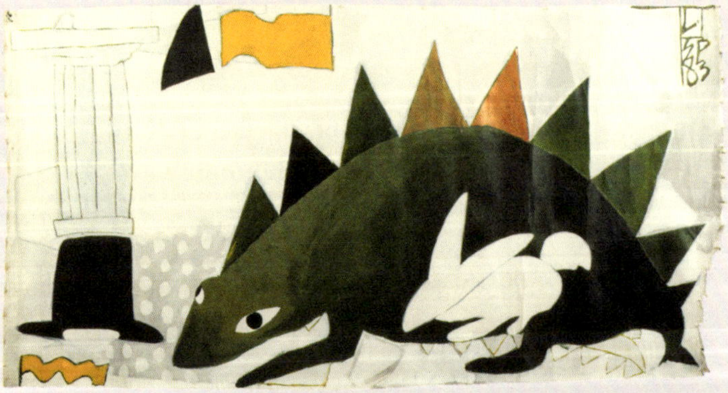

348

AP That same year you participated in *Panorama*?[6]

JL Yes.

AP And in *Desenho jovem*.[7] **So from 1978 onward, you began to develop a practice?**

JL From 1979 onward. Until 1978, I did nothing; I only made some works for FAAP. And they were bad. In 1979, I rented a studio and we made our first attempts. From the second half of the year, things started to work out much better.

AP It was a painting studio?

JL Yes, it was. There were two rooms. We painted, drew, made sculptures.

AP What did you show at *Panorama*?

JL Drawing.

AP But that famous work in the Gilberto Chateaubriand collection (*O coelho e o dinossauro*, 1983 [img. 348]) dates from this time?

JL No, that work is from 1983. But, what happened was this: I went to live in Madrid and I had these drawings.

AP You went alone?

JL Yes, I wanted to live in Europe and thought that Madrid would be the most familiar place in terms of language. And I had this kind of thing with... the painter I adored at the time was [Antoni] Tàpies [1923–2012] and I wanted to see his works.

348. Leonilson
O coelho e o dinossauro
[The Rabbit and the Dinosaur], 1983

Acrylic paint on unstretched canvas
89.5 × 175 cm
Museu de Arte Moderna do Rio de Janeiro, Gilberto Chateaubriand collection, Brazil
PL.1465.0/00

AP Had you been to Europe before?

JL Yes.

AP Did you used to go there as a child?

JL Not as a child; as a young man, when I was eighteen, nineteen, I think, and again when twenty-three. So I arrived in Madrid. I had my drawings and went to some galleries, and in one of them a woman said to me, "Look, I can't do anything for you, but where are you living?" "I live in a hotel," I replied. She said: "You don't have a studio, nothing?" and I told her, "No, I just arrived yesterday." She said: "I know the people from the Brazilian Embassy, maybe they can help you. I have a friend there who is married to an artist, she knows many people." So, they introduced me to Mazu Calvo from the Brazilian Embassy in Madrid, and Mazu introduced me to Claudio Telles.

AP She was a diplomat?

JL Yes.

AP And what was Claudio Telles doing in Madrid?

JL Not Claudio Telles, Claudio Leal. He was the director of Casa do Brasil, which was a Brazilian university residence in Madrid. Claudio saw the drawings, liked them, and said: "You must be broke, right?" "I have 2,000 dollars," I replied, and he said: "And how do you want to live here with 2,000 dollars?" I said: "I don't know, that's why I'm here to talk with you." He said: "You can live here in Casa do Brasil. You will have a nice room where you can also work.

Later on, we can arrange an exhibition with these drawings of yours." We arranged an exhibition for May and I kept working until the beginning of that month.

AP You weren't earning anything in Europe?

JL No. I just had these 2,000 dollars. Claudio bought my work, that very day, I think—he bought two works. He asked: "How much do want for a drawing?" I said: "Around fifty or one hundred dollars, something like that" I thought a drawing would cost one hundred dollars. Then he paid me. Next, I talked to my parents, who were also travelling when I left. I called and told them that I had found a place to live, and they sent me some money every month. In the meantime, I continued living in Madrid, getting to know the people there, going to openings. That's how I met a guy who had a very nice gallery called Ehrhardt, a German who has a gallery in Frankfurt now. He had an extraordinary library that I always used. It was him who showed me Eva Hesse [1936–1970], [Blinky] Palermo [1943–1977], Joseph Beuys [1921–1986]. He put on an exhibition of Beuys, Imi Knoebel, and [Jörg] Immendorff's [1945–2007] series *Café Deutschland* (Café Germany, 1977–84).[8]

AP You didn't get to know the work of Beuys at FAAP, for example?

JL Of course, I knew him, but not fully. There, I got to know the works.

AP You learned about him from books?

JL From books, from people talking about him, from Julio Plaza talking. I learned about him through my own research, too. At FAAP, they had all the magazines—*Artforum*, *Art in America*—and I saw his work there.

AP And Eva Hesse?

JL In 1979, I saw something by Eva Hesse for the first time, in a friend's house.

AP What impressed you in Eva Hesse's work?

JL [Silence] I found it different, I found it strange, and this was what I liked about it. With respect to the other [artist's] works, I thought I knew it all. But with respect to Eva Hesse's work, I found she had something. I don't know what impressed me. I think it was simply that it was different.

AP And who impressed you most at the time, Beuys, perhaps?

JL Beuys impressed me, but Palermo impressed me much more because of the poetry, the poetics of his work. I found it beautiful—there was a little blue triangle in the gallery, you know?

AP What was the exhibition like?

JL It was composed of small drawings only, like this, very small, five by seven [centimeters]. Like the ones I do now, on large paper: a little square of color in the corner of the paper or in the center, you know?

AP **Little geometric figures in the center of the paper?**
JL Yes, geometric figures. There were also painted panels on the wall. And this German had many books on German artists, I saw many more. I remember Palermo a lot, whom I liked most, whom I always liked most.

AP **Eva Hesse, Palermo, and who else?**
JL Eva Hesse and Blinky Palermo. And Paul Klee [1879-1940]. In May 1981, I saw this huge Paul Klee exhibition in Madrid. And I kept thinking a lot about Klee and Palermo, because their works were neither figurative nor abstract; they were none of that. They were feeling. I think they did what they wanted to do. I have this issue with doing what one likes, because I was always super stuck in my home. I always had to do what my parents wanted me to. This means that although I was quite free, there was a pattern of behavior; I was expected to do a series of things. And when I went to Europe, I started to do what I wanted. I wanted to conquer my liberty, I wanted to be free. What I appreciate about these people—Eva Hesse, Palermo, Klee—is their attitude of being free people. That's what I wanted, you know? I didn't want to be an artist like this or like that. I wanted to do everything. I didn't want to have rules. I didn't want to follow a behavior, to follow a law. I didn't want to say, "I'm a figurative artist. I'm an abstract artist." I wanted to do everything. Now, this is basically my attitude, you know? As long as I stayed in Brazil, I would have been stuck in my family, stuck in everything. I was completely suffocated. Everything feels very powerful around me, and sometimes I feel weak. I only feel strong when something responds to me, to my feelings. I think this is the strongest thing I have now: the will to do whatever I like. This initiation was the beginning of my spiritual education, of doing just what I really wanted. If it turns out to be wrong, I correct it afterward. And these people, like Eva Hesse—I understood that she had arrived at [her practice] without anybody teaching her... Maybe she had learnt it, but there was something different. She wanted to do that [thing], so she simply took it up and made it. She didn't chase history. She was straightforward. I remember that before leaving Brazil, I even made some works very influenced by Eva Hesse, in 1979.

AP **Sculptures?**
JL Yes, sculptures with cloth. I took some cloths, and sewed, folded, and aligned them.

AP **Organic?**
JL No. Not organic. It was kind of geometric, because I thought this was the simplest thing I could make. What impressed me most about Palermo and Klee was the simplicity of their works. It was then that I came up with the idea that sometimes when I'm making a work and I suddenly find it too complicated, I need to redo it, to start again. I prefer to throw something away when I can't work it out. It's not that I work hard, I work fast. You have to begin and finish a work. Without being finished, it is not

resolved. The point is not to complicate, you know? I think the work has to be as simple as possible.

AP **And you think that Klee, Palermo, and Hesse had this?**
JL Ah yes, they had this simplicity. Tàpies, for example.

AP **What was it about Tàpies that you liked so much when you went to Europe?**
JL I still like him a lot, but he's very complicated, very baroque. This was not what I wanted for myself. Although I do have some color planes, some elements that are very influenced by Tàpies. My artistic education really began when I left my parents' house and moved to Europe. FAAP served well for meeting people, to work out what I was doing together with others. Because [before that] I was completely isolated, I didn't have artist friends. I didn't know anybody who made work, who made anything. At FAAP, I knew a lot of people who discussed art, who discussed... ah, stuff like that [laughs].

AP **And what was being done in Spain at that time?**
JL Ah, it was bad. There was no Susana Solano, no Ferran García Sevilla, that explosion. I think they were there, but they didn't appear a lot. I went to see exhibitions... Ehrhardt, for example, did not show any Spanish artists. But he had some friends who were artists, young like me. There was Javier, who made drawings. What I really enjoyed was seeing the international exhibitions, and Madrid had many.

AP **Did you travel much at the time?**
JL No. I went once or twice to Paris. The first time I was very silly. I did the regular circuit. I went to the Beaubourg,[9] to the Musée [d'Art Moderne] de la Ville [de Paris]. I didn't go to the galleries. I think I went to Lelong, established places like that.

AP **It's hard, more so, if you don't know. But tell me one thing: when you went to Paris, was it the first time you saw the "modern classics?"**
JL Which "modern classics?"

AP **[Édouard] Manet [1832–1883], [Paul] Cézanne [1839–1906], [Jackson] Pollock [1912–1956], [Willem] de Kooning [1904–1997]...**
JL I didn't see any of them, but I remember one super important thing that happened to me in Paris: Robert Ryman's [1930–2019] [1981] exhibition at the Beaubourg. After seeing it, I started to make a lot of white works. I loved it. That's the Beaubourg catalog of Robert Ryman that I have, you know, the white one.

AP **Yes.**
JL I remember seeing that guy with all these white works. This was

something that impressed me so much. I remember that afterward, I began to make several white works. There was a figure, but I only left a black contour, you know?

AP **Yes.**
JL And it was all white. I painted, sometimes I worked with colored paper and sometimes I painted white on top. Or I tried different types of paper, but I would always paint white on top to have a white thing.

AP **How long did you stay in Madrid?**
JL I stayed for a year, from January to December.

AP **Did you ever have a studio there?**
JL I did, yes.

AP **And you formed a group?**
JL Not a group. But in the second half of the year I worked with Luiz Zerbini. He went to live there as well.

AP **Was it because you were living there?**
JL Yes, I kept telling him to come, and he also wanted to live in Europe for a while, and so he came. He had already lived in London. And then, I had a studio. The French government has a place called Casa de Velázquez, with studios for French artists living in Madrid. One day, I was riding my bike and visited this place. There I met an artist, a sculptor, who introduced me to the director. He asked me: "Don't you have a studio?" "No," I replied. He said: "Oh, so leave your name here, and if a studio becomes empty, I'll let you know." I think he saw my exhibition in May, and soon after he called me. He said, "Look, there's a vacant studio, if you want to use it."

AP **Your exhibition at Casa do Brasil?**
JL At Casa do Brasil. This exhibition was great.

AP **But was it a place people went to, was it on the circuit?**
JL No, not on the commercial exhibition circuit.

AP **Even if it was on the alternative circuit...**
JL Of the university. Because there was a theater where many things happened, a Brazilian film festival, jazz concerts...

AP **Isn't it a peripheral gallery, a kind of "Banco Bamerindus" gallery?**
JL No. It's a gallery of Casa do Brasil, the exhibition space of the university residence. Many students go there. It's in the middle of the University City of Madrid. Many people came to my exhibition. I sold all the works. It was the first time I spent plenty of money. I remember I made 5,000 dollars, at that time. It was supercool,

because I earned a lot of money, about 4,000 dollars, I think. It was fantastic. I met many people in Madrid. Ehrhardt's friends, for example, all of them came. Ehrhardt bought five works; his partner bought several.

AP **Are you still in touch with him?**
JL Occasionally. When I come across him at fairs, in places like Germany, I talk with him. He has all those works.

AP **And he still has a gallery?**
JL He does, in Frankfurt. Grässlin-Ehrhardt. Now it's just called Ehrhardt. He also dispensed with the woman.[10] I sold all the works, and then I went to Paris, I saw that Robert Ryman exhibition, which influenced me considerably. I was impressed. Because I had already gotten over Tàpies. I think Tàpies was a stage. Ryman I already liked much more than Tàpies. Although Tàpies wrote a very nice book of theory, *La práctica del arte* [The practice of art]. He's kind of a wizard.

AP **Where did you go in December 1981?**
JL I returned to Brazil.

AP **But you also lived in Italy?**
JL I was here [in Brazil] in December, then in January I went to Milan. At the end of 1981, I took a trip. First I went to Frankfurt to meet my brother-in-law. Then, I went to Paris again, where I met Arthur Luiz Piza [1928–2017], the graphic artist, through Dirce and Geraldo Holanda, who were the [Brazilian] ambassadors in Paris at the time. I stayed at their place. Piza said: "Will you meet Antonio Dias [1944–2018] in Milan?" I replied: "No." As I had told them, I was going to Milan to see exhibitions, galleries. Then he said: "When you go, you have to meet him. Antonio is very interested in young artists; he is a true supporter." So, I went to Milan in October 1981, and knocked on the door of Antonio Dias. I brought some recent drawings with me. He said: "I see, you're also an artist." "I am," I replied. I think I said "I am"—by that time I thought I was. He saw the drawings, liked them, and asked: "Where are you going now?" "Well, I don't know, I think I'll look for a hotel," I said, and he said: "No, come live here at my place." Back then he lived alone in a huge apartment.

AP **In October of...**
JL 1981. I had left Madrid in order to travel. And he said: "Come live here." So I went, and stayed with him for a fortnight. In the meantime, he introduced me to [Enzo] Cannaviello, who was my first gallerist.[11] I remember that Cannaviello bought fifteen works, and I made 1,500 dollars. One hundred dollars for each work, each drawing.

AP **But wasn't this very cheap for the time, a hundred dollars for a drawing?**
JL It was cheap, but it was still good money.

AP This wouldn't be the same today, of course. Shouldn't it be... some three hundred dollars today?
JL I think it would be one hundred dollars today.

AP Impossible, Leonilson, over ten years, there's inflation.
JL Well, I don't remember. Really, I don't remember. But, I do remember that once I sold him a drawing for a hundred dollars, and bought a wonderful cashmere pullover. Cannaviello bought the drawing, and said: "Let's make a contract in order to work together." I said: "Look, I'm going to Brazil, then we'll see."

AP And then you went to Brazil?
JL Oh, where's the light [on the recorder]?

AP The light is here. You went to Brazil, and then what followed?
JL I went to Brazil, and that's why Cannaviello got angry. I thought he didn't want to work with me anymore. When I came back in January... No... Before I went to Madrid, I stayed another month, and then went to Brazil.

AP What is the name of the gallery?
JL Cannaviello. When I returned to Milan in January, Cannaviello treated me kind of badly at first, but I was already determined to live there for six months. I stayed at Antonio Dias' place, then I stayed with [Antonio] Peticov. And sometimes Cannaviello bought a work. But I started to become really broke, and he introduced me to [Fernando] Pellegrino, a gallery in Bologna. So I lived in Milan between January and May, then moved to Bologna in June, and Pellegrino made an exhibition with me.[12] He had a huge gallery. He lived in a palace. There were some rooms where I could paint. He showed my works at the 1981 fair in Basel. Later, he showed them at the Düsseldorf art fair as well. I returned to Brazil in September 1981. In January 1982, I spent a week with Antonio Dias in Rio, and he introduced me to Thomas Cohn [1935–2018], who worked for a computer company, and wanted to open a gallery. I had some drawings, and Thomas said: "You make drawings, and I want to open a gallery next year, in 1983."
I said: "I'm going to Milan to get some work done." He bought some of my drawings. That's how I started. And I passed by at Luisa Strina before going to Milan in January 1982.

AP Whom you already knew?
JL I knew her by sight, from going to her exhibitions.

AP And you told her something...
JL Yes, that I would be represented by the gallery. I began to visit Luisa's gallery in 1978. I remember going to an exhibition of Wesley Duke Lee [1931–2010], and I think also of [Luiz Paulo] Baravelli. So, I stopped by at Luisa's and said: "Luisa, I have these works here..."

AP Without being introduced?
JL Without being introduced. I went

there and said: "Luisa, my name is Leonilson. I already know about you, from São Paulo, because I've visited your exhibitions. I went to Milan, and Antonio told me to come see you." I showed the drawings to her, she went through the pile and said, "I'll buy these." She asked: "Are you going to do an exhibition with anyone here in Brazil?" I said: "I met Thomas Cohn and he bought some drawings." She said: "I know Thomas, he's a collector, isn't he?" I said: "Yes, but he wants to open a gallery." "When you return to Brazil, come see me and we'll figure something out," she said. So, I went to Milan, and stayed there until May. Later, Luisa passed by there, and bought some more drawings. One time I was broke in Milan, and Antonio contacted her saying: "Luisa, Leo has no money, what can we do about that?" And she said: "Give him some money, and when he gets back to Brazil, he can give me some drawings." Antonio gave me about 400 dollars. I also went to Bologna. There I spent nothing, because Pellegrino paid for everything, he gave me money. They bought some works.

AP Was it a big gallery?
JL Yes. But they stole around twenty of my works. They ran away.

AP They conned you?
JL And various other people. They closed the gallery from one day to the next; they stopped at the door with a van, and disappeared. Nobody knows where they are.

AP When did you return to Brazil?
JL In August 1982. Thomas visited me, and asked: "Shall we arrange an exhibition?" He told me that he would open a gallery with [Carlos] Vergara, and wanted me to do the second show. I had returned from Bologna via Milan, first to São Paulo, spent about ten days there, and then went to stay in Rio, because I had started working with Asdrúbal Trouxe o Trombone.[13]

AP What did you do for them?
JL I did everything but act, because I couldn't act. I rehearsed with them, though, and began with set design. That was during the second half of 1982. In December, I had some personal problems, and returned to São Paulo. Both Luisa and Thomas had already planned an exhibition for May 1983. I worked with Asdrúbal until March 1983; I did the Marathon at Centro Cultural Vergueiro.[14]

AP Zerbini was there as well.
JL Yes.

AP Who else?
JL Regina Casé, Luiz Fernando [Guimarães], Lena Brito, Pedro Santos, from Porto Alegre. At that time, I began to paint some canvasses, because we made some big canvasses for Asdrúbal. I began to enjoy making big canvasses, as until then I had only made drawings.

AP In Spain and Italy...

JL I made some canvasses, but mostly I was drawing. First, I made some screens for Asdrúbal's sets, then I started making them for myself. I painted on the terrace; I didn't have a studio. I lived at my mother's place in São Paulo.

AP During your time in Rio, did you get to know the Cariocas of *Geração* 80?[15]

JL No.

AP Only Zerbini, but he is from São Paulo.

JL I only knew the people from the theater.

AP Daniel [Senise], Bia [Milhazes]?

JL I hadn't met either of them. I didn't even know they existed. I think Daniel wasn't around yet. He worked in a bank, if I remember well.

AP Back then he was already painting.

JL But I hadn't met him. I didn't even know Barrão, no one. I knew Milton Machado, Antonio Dias, and his friends: [Rubens] Gerchman [1942–2008], Sergio Camargo [1930–1990], Tunga [1952–2016], Waltercio [Caldas], Jorginho Guinle [1947–1987].

AP That was when your friendship with Jorge Guinle began?

JL Yes. In 1983, the following happened: Thomas eventually managed to open the gallery, and he would work with the artists whose work he collected: Waltercio, Tunga, Zé [José] Resende, Sergio Camargo. When he decided that I should be working for his gallery, there was this quarrel among the artists, which I never knew the truth of—what it was really about. Thomas told me they left the gallery because of me, because they didn't accept a figurative artist.

AP Who followed a different line?

JL Yes. There was even this famous lunch at Jorginho Guinle's place with Ronaldo Brito, Tunga, Ângelo de Aquino [1945–2017], and the other Aquino, who makes...

AP Adriano de Aquino. But Ângelo and Adriano also worked with Thomas?

JL No, they didn't. They started speaking badly about Leonilson at the table, and Jorginho didn't say that I was present.

AP But your exhibition had already taken place?

JL No, the exhibition was still to happen. It must have been March 1983.

AP And where did they know your work from?

JL Well, from Thomas Cohn. I had taken part in an exhibition entitled *À Flor da Pele* at Centro Empresarial Rio.[16] Thomas showed it to everyone. Also to Marcus Lontra, who liked the work. He actually put me in this exhibition.

Then there was this lunch, which was on the day of Vergara's exhibition. That evening, I was very sad, I met Thomas in the gallery and said, "Thomas, this and that happened... they kept speaking badly about me while I was there." [laughs] Thomas was angry, called the guys, and took care of them. I remember that Ângelo and Adriano went to the gallery that night, and Thomas had a fight with them, saying they were stupid, hypocritical. Thomas was very cool. I did the exhibition in May 1983.

AP **When you were already living in São Paulo.**
JL Yes. First, I did the one at Luisa's and then at Thomas Cohn's, in two consecutive weeks.[17]

AP **Were there any reviews?**
JL Reviews? No. Jorginho Guinle wrote a text for *Módulo* magazine,[18] a pretty good text. Casimiro [Xavier de Mendonça] [1947-1992] wrote something for *Veja*[19]—not a bad text, but not an essay, just an article. I think it was important, because then...

AP **You sold a lot of works?**
JL I did.

AP **And this work in the Gilberto Chateaubriand collection dates from when?**
JL It was part of the exhibition. He bought it on this occasion.

AP **So there was a painting in the exhibition?**
JL There was, there were both paintings and drawings.

AP **But at Luisa's there were only drawings?**
JL No. At Luisa's, both paintings and drawings were included. There were some cutouts made of black rubber, showing a lighthouse, a mountain, a shark's fin...

AP **What was this work like, Leonilson?**
JL At Luisa's, I hung the works up, close to the ceiling. Very few things hung close to the people, only some drawings. The frames were all made by Mário [Pinto]. At Thomas', too.

AP **Back then you even had some abstract works, didn't you? Some patterns?**
JL Yes, but they were not completely abstract. There was always some sort of figuration, without it being expressionist. It was abstract in the way my work is abstract today. The work is more of an object. I don't know what to call it.

AP **Alright. And the *Geração 80* show?**
JL That was also in 1983. I did an exhibition with Tina Presser [gallery] in Porto Alegre. [laughs] I didn't sell a single work. Still, it was nice because I met a lot of people. During this time, I met Angélica de Moraes, who came to write for the *Jornal da Tarde* in São Paulo.

She interviewed me for a Porto Alegre newspaper, or for television, something like that. In 1984, I made an exhibition in Fortaleza, at Arte Galeria. After that, I don't remember which month, there was the *Geração 80* show. Roberto Pontual [1939–1994], Paulo Roberto Leal [1946–1991], Sandra Magger [1956–2018], who was the editor of *Módulo* magazine, and Marcus Lontra, who at the time was the director of Parque Lage,[20] began to organize a big show with emerging artists of the moment. This was great because it brought everyone together; it was kind of a FENIT for artists.[21]

AP **This was when you met the people from Rio?**
JL Yes. Back then, I already knew [Hilton] Berredo [1954–2024], Jorge Duarte, Beatriz Milhazes, Barrão, [Ricardo] Basbaum, Marcus André, Paulinho Paes...

AP **[Daniel] Senise?**
JL Daniel I met the day of the opening of *Geração 80*. He put a Samson between the columns. It was the hit of the show, an enormous work.

AP **Where was your work located?**
JL In the library of Parque Lage. The library was reserved for Leda, Romagnolo, Ciro [Cozzolino], and me. We had done a really thorough study of the room. We put works that fit in that blank space up there. Then Ciro arrived with a six by six meter work, and destroyed our installation.

AP **But how did this group work?**
JL We worked as a group...

AP **Did you share a studio?**
JL I shared a studio with Romagnolo and Ciro. They lived at my place. Leda worked at her father's place.

AP **So you lived in this place at the time?**[22]
JL Yes. They stayed here for six months in 1984. But during this period I also spent a lot of time in Rio because of Humberto. I worked in Rio as well, at his place, and was going back and forth between Rio and São Paulo. Sergio and Leda got married in 1984. Ciro left, I sent him away, and stayed on my own.

AP **Where is Ciro from?**
JL He is from São Paulo. So then, the *Geração 80* show took place.

AP **What do you think *Geração 80* was about?**
JL "The pleasure of painting..."

AP **Some people elaborate a theoretical framework, however superficial or broad it may be, because after all, *Geração 80* included many people; the show had 123 artists. There are some texts that try to identify what this generation was, also by referring to "the pleasure of painting," hinting at a renewal of painting.**
JL I didn't read them. I only started reading texts after meeting you. When I

stayed at Antonio Dias' place, he would make me read things. I read Wittgenstein's *Tractatus*,[23] I read a lot of things, but I didn't read a single text about the *Geração* 80 show. Wait, I have to admit, there was one! A book written by Roberto Pontual,[24] I read some passages of that.

AP But after all, people spoke about...
JL "The pleasure of painting."

AP What do you think about that?
JL The pleasure of painting?

AP Did you take pleasure in painting? Because there was this group of people suddenly coming together. What do you think of this whole story?
JL This was what the critics said about us.

AP Do you think there was a movement?
JL A movement? Certainly not.

AP Do you think these people had something in common? Something other than just painting, and being young?
JL Something in common...

AP Besides making art and being young?
JL Well, these are two very important things to have in common. What else could you expect? It was a time when several artists of a similar age were painting, something that was not otherwise being done in Brazil.

AP But was there only painting in the exhibition?
JL No. But, painting was its strongest part, as something that had been generally rejected. Conceptual artists said that art had died. All those things they said—to tell the truth, I don't even know exactly what they said. I also think it was a natural consequence: after the generation of conceptual artists, of course a new generation came up, enrolled in art school, and then after dropping out of it wanted to enter the market. It just happened. I think that at that time everything just happened, and there were many things that came in handy. At that time, there were a lot of artists exhibiting... well not exhibiting, but working.

AP The spaces were emerging. And the market?
JL The market was greedy [laughs]. Because at that time you could sell so many works, you know? Everyone sold works: Berredo, [Luiz] Pizarro, Bia, Leda, me; we all sold a lot of works; we sold everything we'd painted. At the beginning of our career, when we started working, we made a lot of money, traveled, went to Europe, to Rio. Things were cheap, the cost of living was low. So I could rent this house, but I now have to argue with the landlord [over rent]. It cost eighty cruzeiros, which was about forty dollars.[25] We really made money

back then. But a group, a movement, this didn't exist anywhere in the world.

AP Nowhere?

JL Do you think in Germany there was such a group?

AP People come together in groups. You, Leda, Sergio, and Ciro formed a group.

JL Well, yes. We formed a group.

AP That's right. There are groups. For example, the CoBrA group.[26]

JL But I mean a group of *Geração 80*'s size! No. This exhibition brought together several different groups of artists. There were groups in Rio de Janeiro...

AP But the curators' intention was to try to show that these artists had something in common that was bigger or went beyond the simple facts of being young and making paintings.

JL I don't know what this was.

AP You mentioned one aspect yourself. Because [Eduardo] Sued also made paintings, didn't he? Your paintings wanted to go against...

JL I didn't want to go against anything!

AP Against the conceptual art of the 1970s.

JL I didn't want to go against it!

AP Calm down!

JL I didn't want to go against anything! The critics used this [idea] because they were sick and tired of the conceptual artists.

AP It's not that...

JL We made something different from what they did.

AP Was it a response to their work?

JL A response? Only if this response is something very subjective. It was not a response. I wasn't against anyone, I only made something different. I didn't want to do colored stripes like Sued again, what for? I wanted to make my own work. He had already done that. I wanted to do what I wanted. There was a bunch of people who did just what they wanted. That was great about the *Geração 80*. Whatever people said wasn't art, we did.

AP So, Sued wasn't doing what he wanted?

JL I think these people did what [they thought] should be done. Because they're committed to history, to aesthetics, to theory. Maybe this was what they wanted to do. We did what we wanted and it was different from them. And the gallerists thought the market was open for this, for us.

AP Because then, rightly or wrongly, we are in this conversation distinguishing between two groups, two very loose sets: the artists of the 1970s and those of the 1980s;

the artists who are committed to theory and the artists who are not, so to speak...

JL We couldn't have any theory, that was very new. There was no one talking about us. Could you name a critic of the 1980s? Who wrote essays like Ronaldo Brito wrote about the 1960s and 1970s? No one wrote essays about us. No one wrote anything about us, just gossip.

AP **Actually, [Ricardo] Basbaum wrote an essay on the texts about the *Geração 80*,[27] where he comments on the texts that were published. He analyzes, talks about Marcus Lontra, Jorge Guinle...**

JL He doesn't talk about me. How can you talk about the art of the 1980s without mentioning me?

AP **Who, Basbaum?**

JL Yes.

AP **But wait a moment, Leonilson, he's talking about the texts from the 1980s. That text is about the theory around the *Geração 80*. He doesn't mean to theorize the *Geração 80*, he means to identify the theory [of the time] based on texts that were produced in the 1980s.**

JL Not one of these texts was an essay. They were all exhibition texts.

AP **A catalog exhibition text can be an essay or not be an essay. But, these catalogs texts brought up certain theoretical issues—they did!**

JL Yes? And what did they say?

AP **They basically said...**

JL "The pleasure of painting."

AP **"The pleasure of painting." That is, to forget this very theoretical, very intellectual side of art, to return to pleasure itself.**

JL Now, this was a big marketing operation, wasn't it?

AP **I don't know.**

JL All of the published texts were marketing. All of the publications about us in the 1980s were marketing.

AP **Leonilson, did you read the texts?**

JL All I read is what had been written for magazines. Jorginho Guinle sometimes wrote [for them].

AP **Wait a moment, Leonilson, you just told me in this very conversation that you didn't read the texts.**

JL I didn't pay attention, but I read. I read like anyone who reads... I don't know, other things. But, nothing serious appeared about us, no one took the time to really study us... No one.

AP **Well, Basbaum wrote this early text as an attempt to understand all this. Even though he was also part of the *Geração 80*.**

JL Yes, but, you understand that the members of the *Opinião* group in 1964 and 1965,[28] and the people of the 1970s, had critics who worked closely with them. Ronaldo Brito worked with these people, wrote essays... We had none of that.

AP They debated... But this was kind of typical for artists who were more interested in theory. To—with a greater interest in theory—develop works that have a theoretical, let's say, conceptual background. Naturally, there is a closer rapport with the critic. And do you miss not having had that?

JL I do, because I'm not against it. I think that, even if I'm doing whatever I want, the works can be commented on. You can comment on what is there. Even if it's highly subjective, there should have already been a critic working on it, because this happened ten years ago... It's been six years since the *Geração* 80 show.

AP Seven years.

JL There could already be a critic working with us, writing essays. But the problem is that critics are committed to that conceptual issue. There is no critic trying to work on this [issue of the] artists' subjective [dimension]. A critic who doesn't follow such a hard line, but writes essays about us. It all comes down to gossip, talk, doesn't it? "So-and-so uses this, so-and-so uses that, so-and-so copies so-and-so..." No one talks about the works, no one talks about the spirit, about desire. That's what we have in us. We came out of a generation in which repression was extremely strong. Our generation came out of this, and we got up to new things. The communication with the world was much better.

AP Exactly, this is another reading of the *Geração* 80: that it came out of a dictatorial period. Do you think this really influenced your work?

JL Of course, imagine! We had access to the media in our early twenties. I don't know, I didn't want to think, I wanted to do a lot of things, I wanted to do everything I could think of. I didn't need an accompanying theory in order to do my work. I wanted to do what I was feeling. I fell in love with someone, and made many works for that person, and that was important to me. Now, I think that this, too, can be discussed in a critical or theoretical way.

AP And you lack someone who... well, a critic?

JL I lack someone who comes here to my house to see the works and to discuss them.

AP But you do this with some people.

JL I do this with you.

AP And who else? With Casimiro?

JL Even with Casimiro. But...

AP You think this is a problem for you. Sometimes I think this is a problem of the artist who reaches a point at which...

JL What?

AP Very few people have access to him and, let's say, even need some courage to go to his house and discuss his work.

JL But the critics… they have to do that. For example, I get up, and I have my daily work. The critic—isn't that what he is supposed to do? Doesn't he need to observe what's going on, isn't that his job? Doesn't he need to write? Ronaldo Brito, doesn't he do that? Doesn't he write? Isn't he a guy who thinks? Why didn't this happen to us? This is something I keep thinking about. Why didn't someone show up to write about us? Or is all criticism like this, some sort of gossip: "So-and-so copies so-and-so, so-and-so makes this, so-and-so makes that." People don't write about the work. Maybe… Do you think this is the critical approach of the 1980s, different from the approach of the 1970s?

AP I think it certainly has something to do with the fact that the work of the *Geração 80* is less intellectualized, less tied to theory. Don't you think?

JL I think so. But sometimes, I miss something more consistent.

AP Of course, that is also related to the feeble state of art criticism in Brazil.

JL And it keeps getting more feeble.

AP There are these magazines of criticism, like *Galeria* and *Guia das Artes*…

JL These are not "magazines of criticism."

AP Exactly. They are art magazines.

JL They gather a bunch of things. And yet, many texts are paid for, many are commissioned.[29] There is no criticism. There is no self-criticism of this criticism. Everything is very flawed, very precarious. The problem is that we are dealing with highly precarious issues. The market system in Brazil is precarious, criticism is precarious, and to tell the truth, the art system is also highly precarious. Because there are many people stalling, procrastinating, a lot of people making things and works just to be an artist. You see, if you are very mean, and if you are…

AP Extremely rigorous.

JL Then, you see the artists nowadays… few of them are doing good work. I think it's a general situation.

AP Out of your generation of the 1980s, who, in your opinion, has managed to acquire a certain quality, in the sense of developing their work beyond what it was back then?

JL This is a difficult question. [silence] I see an evolution in the work. I don't know who has already… [silence] Beatriz Milhazes has improved a lot, don't you think? If you want my opinion about who is making really good work at the moment…

AP Yes.

JL No one.

AP No one from the *Geração 80*?

JL Well, yes. Leda has developed her own style. Sergio Romagnolo has his personal style. I also have no idea how to discuss this. I don't even know how to discuss my own work.

AP **Alright, let's conclude this part. I thought it would be interesting... Do you want to go already?**
JL No.

AP **I thought we could also speak a little about the works that are here in the room. There are one, two, three, four, five, six, seven paintings, and some other works, right? These are paintings you made now, this year. This one, for example, is from last year, right?**
JL No. They are all from now, from January.

AP **Well, let's start with this one. What is the title of this one here?**
JL This one is called *The Game Is Over—No One to Dedicate.*[30] To begin with, all of these seven paintings have a colored background and sometimes the color is repeated in the figure. Because there is a figure that is more important, another that is less important, and other things that I want to feature, but that I don't want to be as important as the main figure. In *No One to Dedicate*, for example, there is a tipping jug, water pouring from it forms a pond; and in the middle of the water there are three falling heads, and flames that come out of the jug's handle. This basic thing about the work is that. I was in love three times, with three people, and none of these passions worked out. The three love relationships didn't work out. And so, the game was over. The game with those people was over, the game of passion. But, the little fire... I wanted to show that, despite the game being over, there was still some passion left, a strong relationship. I think I stayed strong, even after breaking up. Even without those people, my fire was still lit. That's why there's this fire. And the water falling into the pond represents the people leaving my life, passion itself.

AP **Do you think your work is a diary?**
JL Yes. The works are completely autobiographical.

AP **They are completely personal?**
JL They are completely personal. But if someone looks at this, don't you think it automatically establishes a relation with his issues? Because this is something present in everyone's life, right? We are always experiencing disappointments in love. I keep talking about myself, about my relationships. This is the diary.

AP **How do you think this can reach other people? It does reach, but...**
JL It reaches, but I don't know how.

AP **What do you think that is?**
JL The collective subconscious? [laughs]

AP **[Laughs] Something that speaks of feelings...**
JL It speaks of feelings. The things that I speak about are not mine. Everyone feels this, everyone goes through break ups...

AP And this reading, which is actually a writing on your work, do you think everyone does this, that it is important that people ought to know? Because that's what we're doing right now.
JL I think it's important that people know. I think it's important to reveal our feelings. Conceptual artists... they revealed their feelings in another way. When I see a work by Waltercio Caldas, I obviously see a load of strong feelings, only he reveals them differently. I think there was a turn in the way feelings are revealed. This has to do with behavior. We now take several things for granted that were more difficult to handle in the past. It's much easier for me to talk about one of my love relationships than it was for Zé Resende to put that in his work. Maybe it was not important for him. Perhaps he would rather keep his love relationship a secret, and reveal to people something else in his work. So he reveals an aesthetics, he reveals... I don't know what! But this here is what I can do; so, I do it. I could make a conceptual work. I could join two bricks, put a cork in the middle, and call it "inside and outside," "empty and full." But they've already taught us that. What worries me in life are my love relationships, my relationships with people. I think about different things—for example, I think a lot about fashion. These works here I made in summer time, and I wanted to use summer colors. It's a "summer collection." I wouldn't make a dark gray work at this time of year, like I would in winter. In winter, I remember certain things. In summer, I remember other things. In summer, I want a green work, a purple work, an orange work, a brown work, a work that mixes greens and yellows. This is extremely important for me: the conditions of where I am, being in a colder or a warmer place.

AP Your context?
JL Completely, my context. Because it is a diary.

AP So, if you wake up in a bad mood, you will make a work that somehow reflects this information.
JL Yes.

AP So there is a big narrative to the work? This work means this, that work means that. Obviously, people don't see this exactly, that there are three people [in the case of *No One to Dedicate*], and what they stand for.
JL Yes.

AP So the narrative is rather abstract.
JL And yet, people have come to my house, looked at this work and said: "Incredible, Leo, that's great! That fire means you are still alive. Despite all that is happening, you remain strong, right?" It was a businessman who told me that.

AP And the work over there, for example, how does it work in this sense? What's the title? It's a green work...
JL It's a green work with the title *Novo homem* [New Man] [img. 349].[31] The week I made it, I was sick, I had bad back pains. I couldn't move very well, and it was

difficult to work. I went to have acupuncture, and there were these figures of the human body showing the meridians. Then, I had to think about death. Which is…

AP **"O novo homem lutando" [The new man fighting]…**
JL "O novo homem lutando por si próprio e ela sempre por perto" [The new man fighting for himself with her always around]—where "her" is death.[32] Every time I'm sick, I always think: "Oh my, now I'm going to die. What shall I do? I'm finished."

AP **But there's a man burning in the head of another man…**
JL No. The fire always stands for the spirit, this strength that I have in me. Whenever you see fire in my work, it's this. It's a symbology.

AP **How interesting, because this is a vocabulary, right?**
JL Yes, I'm trying to establish a vocabulary. It may also change completely before it can work. For example, there is a man who is thinking inside a head, because there is also some selfishness. A doctor told me a story, an old tale from a book of Arab tales. There was a boy in a bar in Baghdad, in a café, and he saw death talking to someone. He knew that death had come to Baghdad to kill, to catch several people. It said: "I have to get so-and-so…" The boy thought to himself, "I think it wants to get me, too." So he fled to Samarkand. He was a disciple of a wise man. Death visited the wise man and asked him: "Did you see that disciple of yours, José?" The wise man replied, "No, I have not seen José, I think he disappeared, he must be running from something." And death said: "I am looking for him and have a meeting with him in Samarkand." I was very impressed with this story. We have a saying that no one dies the noon before. It's something I think about a lot. I keep thinking that death is prowling; every day I hear from a friend who is dying or rotting alive.

AP **And this work talks about that.**
JL Yes. While I was making it, I was thinking about that. I was sick. But there are these two flowers, which are

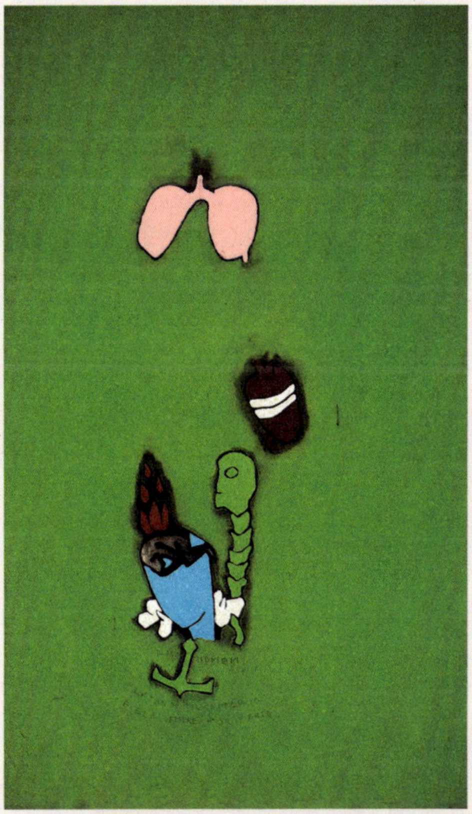

349

349

349. Leonilson
C/ ela sempre por perto
[With Her Always Around],
circa 1991 [img. 201]

something like rebirth to me. There is also the fire, which is this spirit that doesn't fade; so, I won't fade. There is an anchor...

AP **They are flowers?**
JL Yes. Two flowers. Two lilies.

AP **And this here?**
JL This is a heart and a lung.

AP **There is something around the heart.**
JL Yes. It's to secure the heart. The heart normally does not have this. There is the anchor, which is a symbol for my persistence in life, for still being alive; getting sick and becoming well again. Because death is around, though the time has not yet come. Before, I never thought about death: I was always very afraid of talking about death. And now it has become so apparent, so many people are dying, so it is much closer to me. I keep thinking about it, but I try not to worry. I have already become much less worried.

AP **And Leo, these little stones are another element that appear in some of your works, right?**
JL Yes. The stones... this is called... to tell you the truth, I don't know what it's called. I'll have to check... It's called *Tempestades no coração* [Storms in the Heart, 1991] [img. 350]. It has to do with the issue of people leaving my life, though they are always coming back. We don't forget, do we? I am talking about that issue of ex-lovers and friends. A former lover is a friend who stays with me. I don't have this normal relationship of breaking up with someone and not wanting to see them anymore. That is, you always think of that person, you think of what you had with that person, and that is a stone in your path. Now, this is a stone you don't want to break up with; it is a stone worth as much as gold, a precious stone, a stone you want to keep. You learn how to deal with it, because that's the great thing about relationships: you are learning how to deal with people, how to deal with this important thing you had. This purple work is called *Tempestades no coração, abismos, fendas e relâmpagos, que nome estranho dão a isso* [Storms in the Heart, Chasms, Fissures, and Lightning, What a Strange Name They Give to This]. What a strange name they give to this thing

350

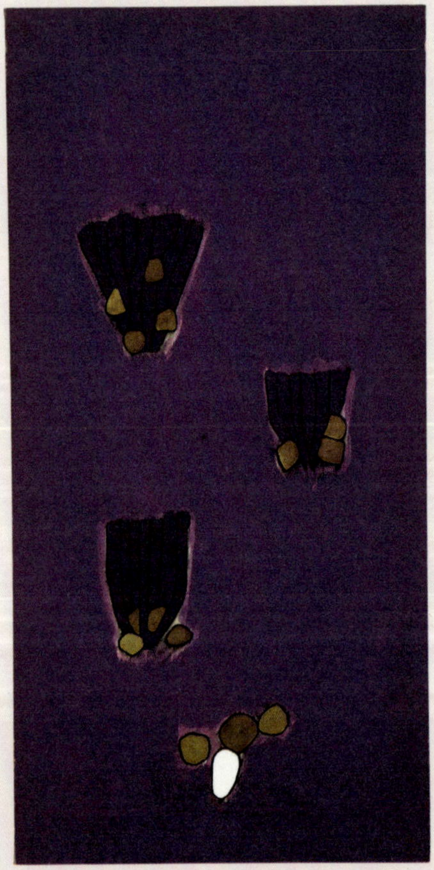

350

350. Leonilson
Tempestades no coração
[Storms in the Heart], 1991
[img. 35]

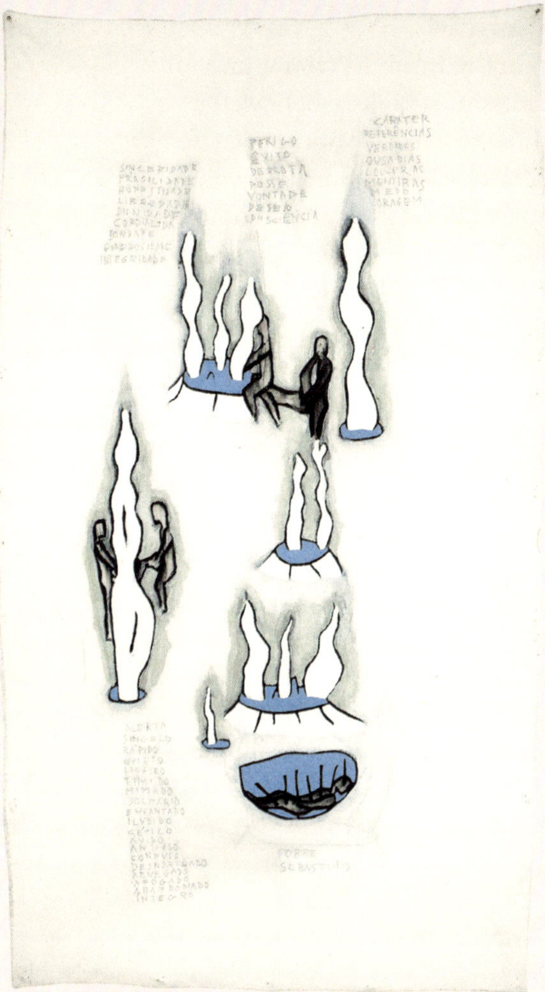

351

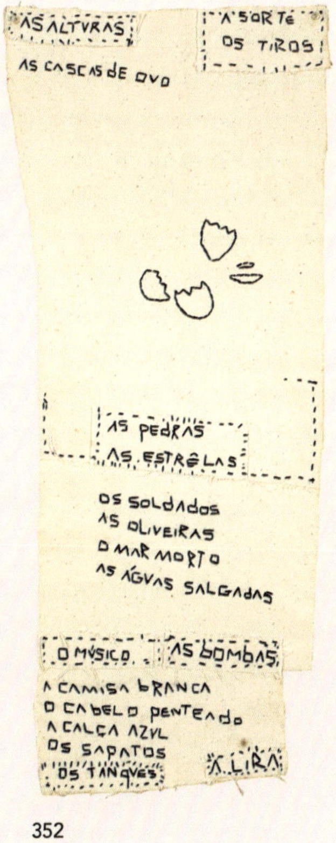

352

that… this way of acting that… ah, that's what I was hinting at, these people who come into our lives, and we don't want them to disappear, so we hold onto them even in difficult situations. That is what really matters in a relationship between people. You deal with difficulties, and see what you can do. It's this.

AP And this work here?
JL This here has to do with a work I wanted to make for a long time.

AP Its title is *Pobre Sebastião* [Poor Sebastião, 1991] [img. 351]?
JL Yes. *Pobre Sebastião*, as I wanted to make a work on Saint Sebastian. All these words that are written were already part of another work… in the work *Os cascas do ovo* [sic] [The Egg Shells, 1992] [img. 352] with the blue balls, the poem of that guy… he was a simple guy wearing a white shirt and blue pants. There's this poem in Marguerite Yourcenar's book *Fires*;[33] I don't remember if it's by Yourcenar or by [Marguerite] Duras… *Fires*, let me see who is it by… it's by Yourcenar. In the book, there's a poem that says: "A guy in Greece, a handsome, pure boy, every day he was wearing a starched white shirt." This is something that fascinates me—it's the simplest thing. Getting back to [Blinky] Palermo's work, you know? It's the simplest thing about a person: he has a white shirt, which his mother washed and ironed the day before and he is wearing today. He is a peasant, he works all day, but in the evening, there's the white house and the green light from the fields…

351. Leonilson
Pobre Sebastião
[Poor Sebastião], 1991
[img. 153]

352. Leonilson
As cascas de ovo
[The Egg Shells], 1992
[img. 228]

AP **A white house?**

JL Yes. A white house. At the end of the day he wears blue pants and a white shirt, puts his hands in his pockets with nothing inside, or he keeps his hands waving. All this constitutes a poetic universe. There is no boredom, no exuberant happiness, none of that. It is something simple. That's the greatest thing of all, just like this. I'm searching for the simplest thing possible. So, I had all these words related to a modest, simple boy. Yes—and there's the danger...

AP **Which is this other work you are talking about?**

JL It's this framed work here in the room, called *Os cascas do ovo*,[34] which depicts some broken eggs. A simple person is strong, but that person is like an egg, for if a bad person comes, it breaks.

AP **It's the felt piece?**

JL No, it's on canvas. There are some blue balls. It went to Brasília. It was stained. It has this poetry of the guy who is waving his hands. I had brought it together with something I did for Eitham, when he went to Israel. He seemed such a simple person to me.

AP **So, how did this one come together?**

JL I wanted to make a work about Saint Sebastian. But you told me that Saint Sebastian didn't die because of the arrows, right? That is, he was completely skewered...

AP **He survived.**

JL He survived and they threw him into a cauldron of boiling oil or water. So I wanted to make a work about Saint Sebastian in a cauldron of boiling oil. Because I think the story of Saint Sebastian has something super sexy about it... In Derek Jarman's movie *Sebastiane*...[35]

AP **Something sensual?**

JL Yes, sensual. In the movie *Sebastiane*, he had sex with almost everyone in the troop, but not with the captain, the sergeant; a guy more powerful than him. This guy had Sebastian killed, because he wanted to have sex with him. The guy who had him killed was martyred. He decided who he wanted to have sex with; herein lies his purity, in that he only did what he wanted. That, I feel extremely identified with, with what people want.

AP **"People"—who?**

JL With us, the boys we know. Because we're a kind of tribe, aren't we?

AP **Yes, we are.**

JL A group. And Saint Sebastian is a super strong symbol. Maybe now, São Paulo is starting to become a symbol. Now that things are being revealed. This is great, because of our Catholic education.

AP **And this other work here, with the minorities, that we already talked about...**

JL I had already made it on the wall of... I think it's very similar to this one.

AP What is the title?

JL *Tenho quase dois metros e estou só há várias noites* [I Am Almost Two Meters Tall and I Have Been Alone for Several Nights]. I don't think anything needs to be added. Its title runs as follows: *Não sou um homem só, sou dois — Agora e as oportunidades* [I'm not One Man, I'm Two — Now and Opportunities].[36] I keep thinking that we don't think *straight*;[37] we think in diverse ways. Our thoughts sometimes go this way, and sometimes come from that way.

AP You said *straight*.

JL Yes, that is, only following one line, just straight.

AP Heterosexual.

JL Heterosexual. We don't have a heterosexual mindset; it is much more diversified. And I keep thinking: we open up so many possibilities; we think about so many different things. Why are we always alone? Why are things...? What is it that can happen to me? Sometimes I get desperate thinking about things that have not yet happened. I am learning to be more patient, but still, sometimes I get very impatient, and I want to know where all the things they promised me are; all the things I see. So, I try to reach things, but they are abstract. Sometimes, this drives me crazy. Where is everything? What is this being constructed around me, what am I constructing?

AP These works now, of course, are still very personal, the two we just talked about, but they have one thing that hasn't been present before, which is the theme of sexuality.

JL And sociality, too.

AP Of the social aspect, you say...

JL Of sociality.

AP Of sociality?

JL Of the social aspect of the thing... Of the social aspect because...

AP Before you were talking about it in a personal way...

JL I can only be a social being when I prepare myself intimately, when I prepare myself as a person. Otherwise, how could I act socially if I am completely torn apart, without any relation to myself, without any connection to my inner self? You mentioned sexuality... yes, because now I'm a bit older. In the past, sexuality... you met someone and you had sex. Now there's a certain risk involved, a responsibility.

AP Almost ten years ago...

JL Ten years ago, it was different, completely different.

AP It's been known for seven years...

JL But now it is a proven fact and thrown in our faces more directly. Now, we have quite a clear idea of the risk involved. Things have changed, relationships have changed completely.

AP **This kind of, let's say, personal-political topic has only recently emerged in a more explicit way.**
JL Recently—I think my work was much emptier before.

AP **Much emptier or more abstract?**
JL More abstract. [silence] Or, not more abstract, but more immature. Well, I'm growing up. I think I have grown up a bit.

AP **Which year are the works you are talking about from?**
JL They are for example from 1983. These were completely personal, subjective. There was already the diary, but I had conversations that were not as concentrated as this one.

AP **More scattered?**
JL Yes, they were much more scattered. I think it was only after meeting you that I began to talk more about my works, I became much more responsible. You know, much more responsible with respect to my work, my stuff.

AP **But the 1989 Luisa Strina exhibition was a rigorous one.**
JL Yes. I was preparing myself for something. With each exhibition I'm preparing myself for something that will happen in my life.

AP **There was also that exhibition of yours in Munich at Kunstforum.[38] When was that [img. 353]?**
JL 1987. There were pieces, objects... I think by that point I had already started to deal with something stronger inside myself.

AP **With something that still has to do with your work today...**
JL It was about moving mountains; that is, about how to act in the situations we are confronted with. I think I had already been working on this. That exhibition was about moving a mountain: I had a room, a strange place, a pile of wood, and every day I had to think about what was happening to me. I kept constructing those things, working on what the work was giving me, you know? That, I think, is a great thing to practice. It is just like when sometimes I picture a person on a palm of hand [img. 354]. I remember an old song by Beto Guedes that goes like: "Dançar na mão do caçador, se entregar para o caçador" [Dance in the hunter's hand, surrender to the hunter]. There is something in that too, in how when I find myself in a dangerous situation, I completely lay down my arms and surrender to it, because sometimes I think that's the best thing you can do. You surrender and see what you can do. Sometimes it's only in my head, but sometimes it really works out. Life is all about trying. We try to see what happens. Until one day we die.

AP **But you...**
JL A funny thing I kept thinking about: the books. You made me read more. Now I'm reading theory, something I have not done before. I'm reading critical texts.

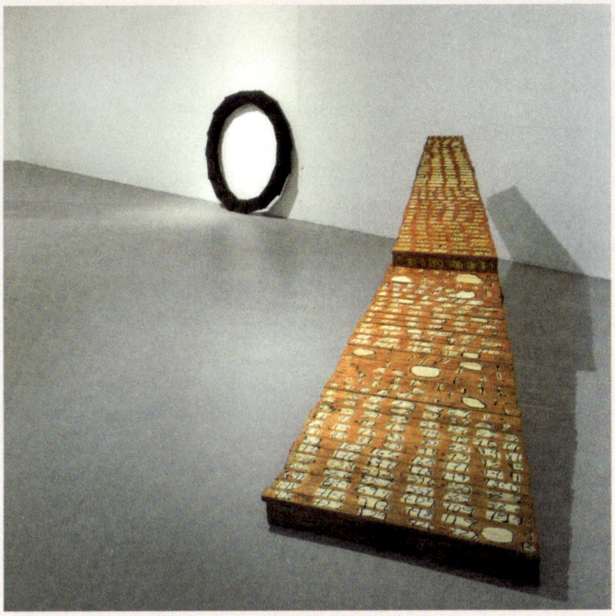

353

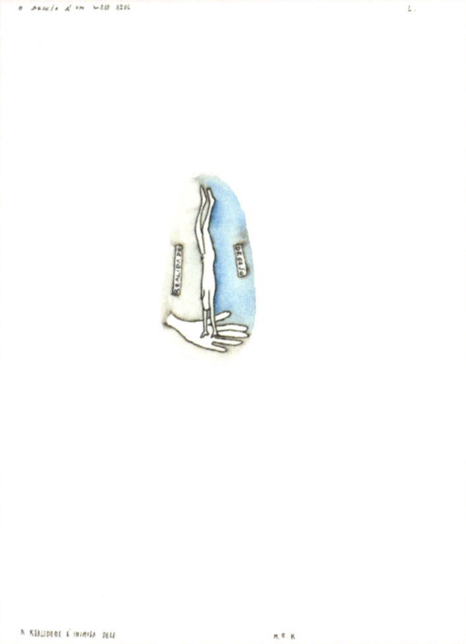

354

AP **That you were averse to?**

JL I was not averse, I just had no incentive to read them. I'm not averse like that... I'm stimulated by things. In the past I was stimulated by certain things; today I'm more stimulated by other things. One day, I was extremely depressed and I kept thinking... We read, we learn, we get more things for ourselves, and then one day we die. I kept thinking about that; thinking about what makes up our lives. We go through situations, through other people's lives; we set things up, read, become smarter, massage the brain, exercise... and then one day we die. Sometimes I think about this: Why am I doing all this? What do I keep painting and doing this whole diary for? I know that I do it because I think about what happened to me, and learn about what is happening to me. Do you remember I told you my learning really began when I went to Spain? This was nonsense. My learning began when I started establishing relationships with other people, when I was three or four years old, [learning] to relate myself and to detach what I wanted from what I didn't want. When I left my parents' house and decided to be an artist, [decided] that I wanted to do this, to develop this, to learn... I think that's why I'm doing a diary. It's the basis on which I began to nurture my life, on which I began to prepare my life. So I started to pay more attention to what I was doing, to what was happening to me, to my body, my sexuality, my desires, my wishes, my anxieties, to fear. I think that's why I specialized in talking about myself in my work. That's why I do this diary, because it's a study of what is happening to me. Today, I was reading a book by Paul Klee. I was excited about making new work; I wanted to make something, and I ended up making nothing.

353. View of Leonilson's exhibition *Moving Mountains*, Städtische Galerie im Lenbachhaus, Munich, Germany, 1987

354. Leonilson
[O desejo é um lago azul]
[Desire Is a Blue Lake], 1989
[img. 52]

But I think I'll make something soon. It stimulates things that are inside my head, you know? We have been talking here for three days and a lot of new things are popping up in my mind—relations. I already wanted to start working on it. But now I also feel more relaxed to wait a while and see how things develop. And later I can start to work. What were we talking about yesterday? That João Pedrosa was talking about a person who says everything he thinks... What did he say? This person is stupid or foolish, right?

AP **Yes.**
JL In the past, I felt much more like that. I had a thought, and I made the work. So, I made a lot of nonsense. I think nowadays I have a process of reflection on things. I have already established a practice of thinking. I told you I wanted to work today, but I'm not sure yet. Normally, I would take a sheet of paper and start drawing some things. But, I think it's enough to have it in my head, stored, until the moment I really start working. I also needed a long time before I could make this series of works here. Now it's finished. It's similar to the drawings dedicated to the boys I met; to the myths, the desired ones... I think this work is already much more mature. This here, too. That's why today I feel more secure talking about my sexuality.

SÃO PAULO, MARCH 6, 1991

AP **We ended the first part of the conversation talking about the fact that more recently, in the last two years, the question of sexuality has been more explicitly addressed in your work. That's how you manage to join together, let's say, a political and a personal issue.**
JL Yes.

AP **That's interesting because concurrently with the diary, you are addressing this issue. So, I would like to ask you: What is your opinion on "gay art"? The concept is super loose, but in the end it is used in theory: [Robert] Mapplethorpe [1946–1989] addresses the issue in some of his works; McDermott & McGough too, do you know them? They are also painting...**
JL Of course, yes, I saw one of their exhibitions.

AP **And our friend Duane Michals.**
JL Huh...

AP **Come on.**
JL It's true.

AP **Later I think we need to have a special conversation about Duane. And what about the guys from ACT UP, Gran Fury?**
JL I think the question of sexuality was always something that had been suppressed in my work. Because in the past, I

was much more repressed. But now, when it comes to this thing of "gay art"... I don't know if there is such a thing as "gay art."

AP **It's a super loose concept. But let us talk about art that speaks of the theme...**
JL Of homosexuality. But my work doesn't speak of the theme of homosexuality. The things that I'm making don't speak of that. Do you think they do? I think... well, maybe they do, they speak of something like that...

AP **Of homosexuality, definitely. Don't they? The speak of your...**
JL Of my...

AP **Sexual orientation.**
JL *Pobre Sebastião*... Who cannot even decide who to give it to. I'm not sure, Al, I don't think I want to reach a particular audience. But, as it turns out, this is already something very clear in my mind today. Before, I had many more doubts about my options, about what I wanted to do. Now this is already better defined, it has already become clearer. So, it forms a strong feature of the work. Isn't it a diary? Something of my daily life? I think about sex several times a day. And the sexual patterns I think of, my sexual fantasies, have a direct influence on the work. In as much as I think about it, I also work on it.

AP **Was there any influence of an artist or a book that helped you discover these things? For example, Duane Michals?**
JL Duane Michals. He's a great artist to me. He does photography. I've always liked photography more than any other form of artistic expression. In fact, I think it's the form I like most. More than painting, sculpture, printmaking, cinema, more than anything—it's photography. I was always super influenced by photography. Whether from magazines, books, or exhibitions. And when I first saw Duane Michals' book...

AP **Do you remember which year that was?**
JL I think that was in 1985, at Du's [Eduardo Brandão] house. A friend of his, Leda Vignette, had Duane Michals's book *Portraits*,[39] and Du showed it to me. I was immediately fascinated. It's one of the most beautiful books ever. There are several portraits and situations in it, and he put the titles below them. I don't have it, I never found out where to buy the book. Once I also saw a book by Duane and [Konstantinos] Kaváfis [1863–1933], with poems by Kaváfis, and photographs by Duane.[40] He impressed me—this man who wrote about sexuality without being "faggy," without being gay, well, without being...

AP **Effeminate.**
JL Yes, effeminate, or pretentious. They write about homosexuality in a beautiful, poetic way—both Kaváfis and Michals. You think Duane Michals' texts are weak...

AP **I never said that.**

JL You told me so. I think his texts are weak because he just wants to write that over there. It's very direct.

AP **I never said that.**

JL You said that when you read *Duane Duck.*[41]

AP **Well...**

JL For example, in my texts...

AP **So this was when you began to write?**

JL No, I was always writing in the works. Since 1979 my drawings were written all over, but the works also began to change; they changed a lot. Duane was the one who helped change my work. If there is somebody you come across at a certain moment—like Palermo and Eva Hesse, in the beginning, they influenced me very much. After those two, I'd say it was Duane Michals who influenced me the most. He influenced me not so much in terms of what concerns the image or what to make, but what to put inside the work.

AP **In terms of the concept.**

JL In terms of the concept, the courage, the attitude. He gave me strength. It's just like taking a shot of *Biotônico Fontoura.*[42] To me, he was the one telling me: "Do it." I think he was... well not he himself, but his books were the most important thing that has ever happened to me.

AP **In relationship to your work?**

JL Yes. Which means the support of an older artist who influences you, who guides you. I never talked to him, but I didn't have to. I just needed to see his books to get oriented.

AP **So since 1979, you have been writing on the actual works?**

JL Since 1979, 1980.

AP **But in the early paintings of, let's say, the *Geração 80*, there was sometimes something written, though only a little. Sometimes a title, sometimes nothing. Today, almost all of your paintings have written elements. And some paintings have nothing but writing on them...**

JL Yes, the drawings I made in the early 1980s did not have a lot of writing, but in the early 1980s, I didn't do much painting either. I had only just started to paint. I made some big canvasses like the ones for Asdrúbal.

AP **But in *Geração 80* you had...**

JL Wait a moment, I'll get there.

AP ***Sorry.***[43]

JL I started to make some paintings and wanted them to be different from the drawings. I didn't want to write. I had nothing to write; at least that was true at the beginning. There was nothing written on those big canvasses I made for Asdrúbal. Every once in a while, there appeared a word; nothing but nonsense.

The *Geração* 80 paintings only featured figures. They were almost abstract, weren't they? They had a lot of patterns, spots, some sparse things. That was what I was experiencing. To arrive at the paintings with drawings, with figures, and also with patterns, I had to go through that process. I was exercising— those paintings were exercises. For example, that painting in the Chateaubriand collection [img. 348], of the rabbit and the dinosaur, has no writing. I used to joke and say that this painting is the one that always appears in the books, so it seems that I'm a painter of only one painting. Anyway, this painting is very important, perhaps one of the most important from that time. Something that happened to me struck me a great deal, and left quite an impression on me. This was directly connected with my sexuality. I was living in Milan at Peticov's house. I practically lived in his library, which had a bed where I could sleep, books, and a place for me to work, on the top floor of the apartment. It was super nice. One day I was working there while they were having a little party. I wasn't with them, I was upstairs, and a guy who had come to the party came up; only—he was the bishop of Turin. And he came up and started talking about...

AP **That was in Turin?**
JL No, that was in Milan. But he was at the party. I didn't understand how the bishop of Turin could be at this wild party. And the guy started to make a move on me. Somehow, he wanted to have sex with me. But back then, I didn't have sex with guys. I had never had... No, I had, right, but I was not up to... I didn't use to flirt. And he kept chasing me, more and more, and more, and more, until I told him to leave my room. Then, he tried to be kind of violent.

AP **Was he dressed like a bishop?**
JL No, he was in regular clothes. He was wearing a black suit. And I was so struck by that guy coming up to me, giving this whole speech about being a bishop, starting to chase me, acting almost violently—you know, to get what he wanted. Then I don't remember if I pushed him away, [if] I threw him out of the room or called someone. Afterward, I made a drawing that is down there; a rabbit on a flowered sheet and a dragon approaching. That's when I made this work.

AP **What does that work in the Chateaubriand collection look like?**
JL There is a big dinosaur and...

AP **There is a rabbit...**
JL And there is a top hat with a rabbit inside. Except that the dinosaur in the Chateaubriand work has a nice face, because I couldn't make a bad one. At that point, some time had already passed since the Milan experience.

AP **Speaking of the relation between image and text, figure and pattern and text: for example, in this work, there is a figure, an abstract element, and text. How does the text contribute to the work? Is it a descriptive element? Are there several ways in which it works?**

JL The text is as important as the figure. It only works by telling something. Sometimes I feel like writing.

AP I want to know this: is the text here describing this, or does one thing substitute the other?
JL There is no substitution at all. It had to be a text. I thought about a text for this work. Instead of thinking about a figure or a form, I thought about a text. The text also works as a figure.

AP Would you say that the text is describing the figures in the work?
JL No. The text is as important as the figure. The text acts as a figure. The text is an element of the work. The green and yellow pattern in the background looks like a military curtain.

AP What is it called, Leo?
JL *Perversos inocentes* [Innocent Perverts, 1991]. It is green and yellow, there is an epaulette on it and the words "innocent perverts." These words are as strong as the epaulette, like the yellow spots on the green background. I don't differentiate a lot. In the work *Pobre Sebastião* [img. 351], there are various figures, situations, spots, and written elements, which are super strong. I could only make this in a written form. I wouldn't make a "Danger" drawing, a "Success" drawing, a "Defeat" drawing, a "Possession" drawing...

AP But at the same time, would you say the function of the text is to clarify something? Or does it also create an abstraction? Is the text abstract in a sense?
JL Also. I think it triggers an abstraction in so far as it is not a figure, but it clarifies...

AP No. I mean an abstraction in the sense of the text itself.
JL Ah no, that's not the case. Its function is more to clarify. It's an additional element.

AP Of course it's an additional element. But "innocent perverts" does not express something very clearly...
JL It reminds you of different things...

AP Well yes, but it's somehow abstract.
JL It's abstract. The work is abstract. We have already talked about that.

AP Would you make a work only with text? Proper text, like a book.
JL How?

AP Not in the form of a picture. Would you publish a book?
JL With pictures.

AP No, only text.
JL Maybe, at some point... I have already thought a lot about...

AP Only one thing: the text bears your handwriting, you see?

JL Yes. I've thought of this as much as I've thought about film. I've already thought of several films. But then I think film would be something much more explicit. For example, the other day I was watching [Pier Paolo] Pasolini's [1922–1975] *Teorema* [1968], and I realized that this was a film I would like to have made. It's something I think about a lot; this being that arrives and occupies a space and then goes away. Now, let's talk about something else.

AP So, may I ask you a question? You listen to a lot of music...

JL [Laughs] The interviewer is worthless!

AP [Laughs] And you are very attached to fashion and design. You pay a lot of attention to these things, don't you?

JL Yes.

AP How is it that all these things come together?

JL While I'm working, for example, I listen to music, to the radio or to records.

AP What kind of music?

JL I listen to dance music, rap, blues, and soul... never to classical music.

AP And to Brazilian music?

JL Of Brazilian music, only to Fellini and Kid Abelha, because those are the only records I have. Ah, sometimes also to bossa nova. But I never put on bossa nova to work. And not Fellini, because it makes me feel like crying, it touches me too much. His lyrics are the most beautiful I've ever heard. At the moment, I listen to a lot of rap, because I think it's the only thing we should listen to: it's today's culture, it's fast, throws things into your head. I put on a rap record and that energy, that wave hits me, so it keeps on working in my head. Sometimes I'm listening to a song and a phrase—I don't understand English very well, but sometimes I understand a few phrases— that is important to me, and I jot it down somewhere.

AP You made a work called *To Be Selective* [1990] [img. 355].

JL Yes. *To Be Selective* is this super cool Soul II Soul song.[44] It had so much to do with what I was thinking at that very time. It has a lot to do with this work here, with the waterfall, the pouring water and the heads. I think *to be selective* is something I need to learn.[45]

AP To be selective...

JL Yes... Not to be selective, but to really understand what I want, and to consciously select things. For me, this is growing up. So, this phrase was very important to me. It's the same with "you sweet like a dog." The work is called both *You Don't See That* [1991] [img. 356] and *You Sweet Like a Dog*. These are phrases from songs I heard. "You don't see that" is something Rickie Lee Jones sings on an Orb album, and "you sweet like a dog" is from LL Cool J.'s

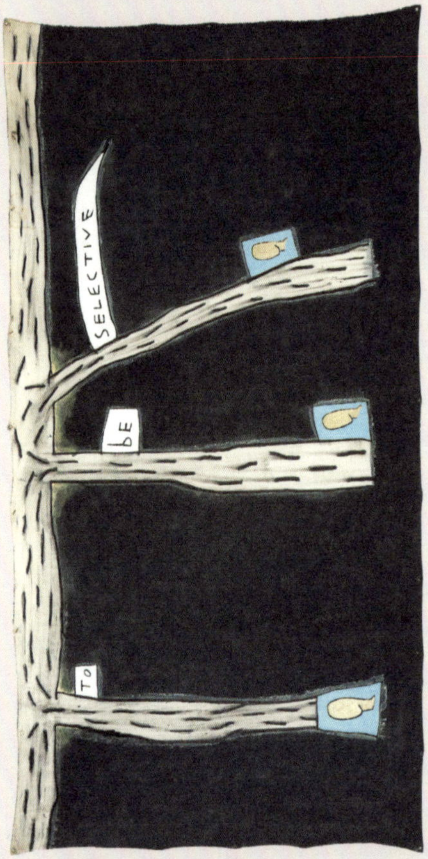

355

"I Need Love"—two things I would [like to] make, two things I think about. That's great. Sometimes, you see something you totally identify as yours. There are several songs I completely identify as mine. So many phrases that appear in my works are phrases I heard in songs. Sometimes I just understand one or two words to which I add other words to make my own phrase. Or sometimes, I listen to a phrase, copy it, and consider it completely mine, because removed from its original context, the context changes entirely when it enters my work.

AP And fashion?

JL Fashion influences me, because I look at fashion magazines, like *The Face* and *Vogue*. And some of my friends are working in fashion, like Marie Rucki in Paris. She's as important to me as my art teachers were. She's as important to me as Duane Michals. She once told me that fashion designers don't have time to get dressed. This is super important, and something that I apply to myself, to art. Anyone who makes art has no time to theorize it. Because you either make art or you do theory.

AP Or criticism.

JL Or criticism. And nowadays you can observe this process of criticism replacing art, of artists doing more as critics than as art-makers. Oh, that's what is happening.

AP I don't agree.

JL Ah, I agree, with myself.

AP [Laughs] Can you name an example of someone who is doing more criticism than art-making?

JL Nancy Dwyer.

AP Nancy Dwyer is doing more criticism than art-making?

JL Yes. I'm not talking about [Joseph] Kosuth, for example.

355. **Leonilson**
To Be Selective, 1990
[img. 122]

AP Are you referring to people doing criticism with their works or people that actually write art criticism?

JL I'm referring to people who talk and theorize about art a lot. Let's say you make a work. Then, you come to me, and talk, talk, talk about the work, but for me, by the time I see your work on the wall, it is much stronger than anything you want to tell me with your theory of it. I look at Kosuth's work… The other day I felt stupid at your house in Rio de Janeiro, because you said to me: "You don't know what this is, what he wants to say with it?" And I replied: "No." But for me that doesn't matter. The visual is much more important, because I'm seeing visual art. A book is different. Of course, theory is extremely important, what you tell me about the images is extremely important. Now…

AP Leonilson, the innovation of conceptual art is precisely about the aspect of the idea, you understand?

JL Sure. But what I see visually…

AP So, you still look at conceptual art with one pre-conceptual eye, prior to conceptual art.

JL No, because I read what is written, and I know what is meant. At least, I know for myself, although I cannot tell what it means to you.

AP If you apprehend something visually that is made to be apprehended conceptually…

JL This is what I call theory; this is something I call nonexistent.

AP Well it does exist… [laughs].

JL No, no, this is a preconception.

AP What is?

JL What you are saying.

AP Your attitude is quite romantic, in the sense that you are an artist who paints, or draws, or works with what you experience in life, what you are thinking. So, your work is a diary. Everything, all the issues that run through your work, also run through your life. Then, there is the other side of art, which would be conceptual art.

JL Do you think my work isn't conceptual?

AP Obviously, no. You've pointed out two artists who influenced you, who played an important role in your formation, and who somehow follow this conceptual line. Eva Hesse and who else?

JL Blinky Palermo.

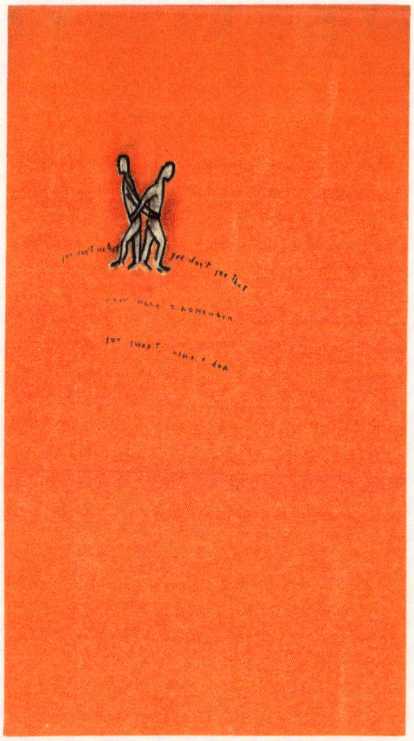

356

356. Leonilson
***You Don't See That*, 1991**
[img. 154]

AP Yes, Blinky Palermo. How do you view a conceptual work?

JL I already told you. When I see these works...

AP What is your interaction with them?

JL It's poetic. No matter if it's a Beuys or a Palermo, the same holds true for Walter De Maria [1935–2013], Robert Smithson [1938–1973], Eva Hesse, Imi Knoebel, I look at the works...

AP And Kosuth.

JL Kosuth... I look at his work and certainly realize many things. I don't strip off the theory of the work. Sometimes I even try to read about this theory, I try to understand it. For example, I look at Kosuth's work, I read, I establish the relations between what is written, photography, and the real chair [*One and Three Chairs*, 1965]. I completely interact with the poetic side of the work. And for me this is what matters most. I remember Walter De Maria's earth room [*The New York Earth Room*, 1977] and I remember that room full of earth. I think there must be a lot of really important things written about that, which I may even read, because I haven't read them yet. Actually, I read the Dia Art Foundation text. What I really remember is a room full of earth in the middle of New York, a gallery, a place, a space full of earth, one meter high. And this is something super important. I don't know what it is, or rather I should know inside myself. Now, a room full of earth is very strong. In the case of Eva Hesse, it's very strong to see all those braided things, that cobweb made of resin-soaked thread. Those texts by Kosuth, where he scratched a few words, put a stripe over some words, were very strong. Of course, I remember everything, I remember people's censorship, the censorship of feelings, the censorship of people's intimate thoughts. I'm pretty sure he must think a lot like me, except that he's a theoretical guy, he has a different background to me. For example, when I see Beuys's work [*Horns*, 1961] with two rhinoceros horns and two hanging tubes filled with rhinoceros blood—that is much, much stronger than anything ever written about him. The Robert Ryman exhibition, where he used different types of material—some canvases made of aluminum, that white paint on those canvases was very strong. I think it's as strong as an Expressionist painting by [Emil] Nolde or [Ernst Ludwig] Kirchner. I see Richard Serra, for example, you go into a place with two thick iron walls spanning across the room. Of course there must be a theory about it; Ronaldo Brito would talk for days about that...

AP [Laughs]

JL But for me... I go into that place and the feeling I get is very... and this feeling is way stronger than all those written things. Because the poetics of the work is very important, and people's poetics are very important. I may appreciate what people have to say, but what they represent is most important to me. Now this is my opinion, and this is not *naïf*.

NEW YORK, MAY 3, 1991

AP **Today is May 3, we are in New York and I would like to add some questions to complement the conversation we had in March in São Paulo. The first question has to do with what we were saying about your work being very personal and thus, a diary. But at the same time, you are making works like the one about minorities, which you had already made on the wall at the Escola de Artes Visuais do Parque Lage, and which you presented slightly differently in April, at Galeria Thomas Cohn [in Rio]. Is it a personal work?**

JL I'm not sure if it is a personal work, but it's something that interests me. It's an opinion I have about things that... [silence]

AP **In the conversation we had before, you understood your work as a diary; all the time you are recording things that happen in your life. But this work on minorities, what is it?[46] Do you think it is a personal work?**

JL I think it is a personal work. For example, this idea of the diary, the work being a diary, is something that speaks of my day; these are personal observations about my life, and I'm paying attention to them. For a long time, I wanted to do a public work that... I mentioned that my works have become more mature; at the same time I'm reflecting more on my sexuality, the way I relate to people, my way to face the world, to live day by day. I think the work is still personal, still a diary, even with those works on minorities. I only wanted to address these things I notice in the world. I do perceive the segregation that exists. And of course, I belong to one of these minorities, or to more than one. Several things that I speak of are subject of segregation. I reflect a lot more, and in particular, much more freely than an average citizen. I'm not a standard person, right? I'm part of a minority that thinks differently. So, I wanted to address that. This work is a general overview of what I call "minorities." There, I only included women, homosexuals, blacks, Indigenous people, people living with AIDS, communists, the disabled...

AP **How many glasses are there?**

JL Seven glasses.

AP **Did you say seven?**

JL No. Did I say seven? Maybe. Yes... Now, I wanted to bring this up because of the chance to make it public. I think what we can do with art is to give a heads up to society a little. We can't change the world, but we can show some some things. So, for example, rather than mounting that work inside the gallery, I preferred to put it in the window, a place many people passed by. The labels in the work are typewritten. You can't see them from a distance, but you notice that there is an art gallery with a window which usually showcases a painting or an artwork. Then, you see a glass shelf with glasses on top, which catches your eye, so you move closer to see what it is. You come in and see these written labels, these categories. I think there is always the chance that people will stop and think a little about what is written there, and I have the impression that, however subtle, it always makes the person think a little, always makes them reflect a little, because that is also a characteristic of art; it is a point of reflection. When I am walking in the street and see a hungry person, a person lying on the ground, I stop and think; as cold as I may be, I stop and think a little about life, about my existing social relationships. When I come across a person who says "that guy is a fag," I obviously stop and think, and I'm sure other people stop and think, too. So, I wanted to make a more public work, but this is still part of my diary. It's something I suffer and experience daily. It's something that influences me daily, too. All that I am making is building a character. I am not building a career. I am building my personality, I am maturing.

AP Do you think this also applies to your work about AIDS, the watercolors? *Beijo seco* [Dry kiss, *circa* 1990] [img. 357]...
JL I think so.

AP In the same way?
JL Yes. I think that work is great because of its subtlety. It is neither violent, nor ostentatious nor worthless, nor trying to instrumentalize AIDS, which is a very topical and much discussed issue. The work speaks subtly about it, and it's a beautiful, poetic work. I think we can explore the poetics of something without exploring the thing itself. It's the same with the exotic or the rare. I agreed to take part in that work, to make the corresponding drawing, because I think that, once exhibited and viewed by the public, it also gives them a heads up. What we can do is give a heads up to people from time to time.

AP I want to ask you this: is there any other work of yours that falls into this category? Because if you compare these two works to the voile works, they have a different aim or intention. Why give a heads up? Do those voile works give a heads up?
JL All my works want to give a heads up, don't they? Although it is personal, it is my attitude, and I think my attitude can give a heads up to people. I act differently today than I did some time ago, right? Nowadays, I feel more secure when I act. For example, with the works from the series with the boys who are "the dedicated," someone will see that and see the words "o craque" (the star), "o inatingível" (the unreachable). When someone views all that together, won't that provoke a feeling, a reaction?

AP But what I mean is, does your work generally provoke this or is this your attitude to it? To provoke a feeling, give a heads up as you say.
JL Yes. I don't know what the right word for it is.

AP Anyway, do these works about minorities put forward an educational proposal?
JL An educational proposal? I think they have a formative character...

AP Because it's not purely poetic. It has quite a different attitude.
JL It does. What about this one: *O q. você desejar, o q. você quiser eu estou pronto para servi-lo* [Whatever You Desire, Whatever You Want, I Am Here, Ready to Serve You, 1990] [img. 103], don't you think it has this same character?

AP No, I think it is quite different.
JL Really?

AP I think both are formally quite poetic. Obviously, the one about minorities is very poetic. But in it you are making a political statement.
JL Right. Perhaps this work goes more in that direction instead of being purely poetic, being passionate for someone like I am.

AP One is extremely personal...
JL They complement each other. For me, they form a body of work.

357

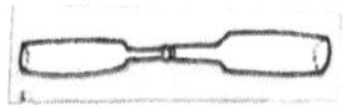

357. Leonilson
Beijo Seco [Dry Kiss], *circa* 1990

Permanent ink, watercolor
and gouache on paper
23 × 30 cm
Private collection,
Palma de Mallorca, Spain
PL.1255.0/00

AP Of course, together they form Leonilson's body of work. But I'm trying to identify the difference between them, which I think is there, but I would like to understand it together with you.
JL Whereas the other works speak more of myself, this work is more an observation of society. Perhaps other works may be a heads up to society, but they are also something particularly *mine*. This one, no. It's something I see in the street, something more public.

AP Do you think that they have a more specific aim?
JL Look, I don't think of an aim like that, you know.

AP No, I'm not talking... because it's very difficult.
JL But obviously, after finishing the work, you can establish this relationship, its aim as something broader, much broader than that.

AP And more specific.
JL More specific.

AP Let's say, more objective.
JL Yes.

AP It doesn't matter how much it...
JL No matter how subtle it is. It's not subtle at all!

AP **It's political work, isn't it?**
JL Yes. It can be political. It has a far more political attitude of social concern than other works, in which I keep talking about my loves, my most intimate relationships, my most private things, and which I, rudely speaking, make for myself. This work I also make for myself. In the moment I'm thinking of it, I think for myself. When I tell you that I decided to put it in the gallery window, so people could see it from outside, the attitude is political. Do you say a "political attitude"?

AP **Yes.**
JL That's what I would like to do. It's meant to make people think about it, isn't it? I don't know if it is a strong work.

AP **Would you say there is any other work with the same feature?**
JL In 1985, I participated in an exhibition in Rio. I don't remember the title...

AP **Where did it take place?**
JL I don't remember. It was a group show in Rio de Janeiro and I participated with a work about AIDS. I took a newspaper page that said "AIDS." Do you know this work? It features a pocket knife and is full of red and golden balls [img. 358].

AP **A drawing on newspaper?**
JL Yes. I took a page as soon as they started talking about AIDS in the Brazilian press. In the beginning they presented it as "the gay plague." That was actually an interesting situation, because on one side [of the page] they were talking about AIDS, and on the other about football. I found this interesting and drew a large pocket knife and some balls on it. I believe it was for a group exhibition curated by Casimiro. I really don't remember well, but I sent this work to the exhibition and it was also shown in Vitória. I believe my installation at Parque Lage had the same attitude.

AP **Which was more or less the work about minorities.**
JL It was more or less the work about the minorities. But it was the first time I made something so direct, so explicit.

AP **And what about the installation at Centro Cultural São Paulo?**[47]
JL Oh yes, there was also the Centro Cultural installation, though it was quite confusing. For example, the part of the installation that people paid no attention to but was very important to me, was the part with xerox copies [img. 359]. I came to realize that every exhibition I participated in at the Centro Cultural, and the things people were making, were very much like that... Of course, we are always copying, we always take up an artist we like a lot.

AP **What was the work like?**
JL I gathered the artists I thought people were copying the most.

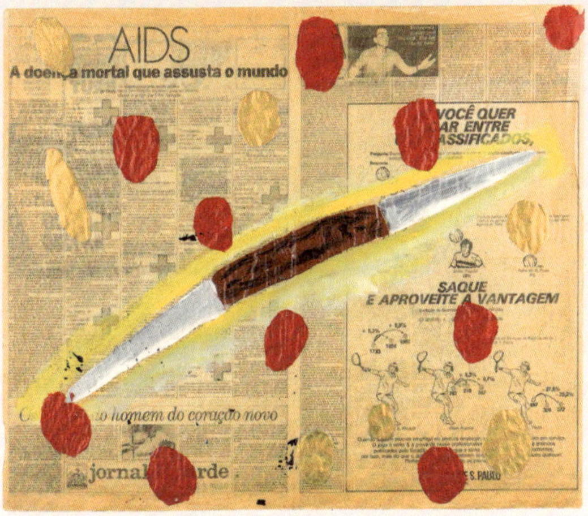

358

AP **Like who?**

JL Eva Hesse, [Richard] Sierra's stuff spilled on the floor, Alan Saret, Reiner Ruthenbeck, Beuys. For example, I noticed many people kept doing Eva Hesse, Arte Povera, without having any idea of what they were doing. Or they saw it in a book and did exactly the same. I mean, I'm saying this without knowing if these people... I *think* they did that. In my opinion, you can take a work from someone you like a lot and develop on that, and then you arrive at another result. I think that's just amazing! I made xerox copies from my books on Arte Povera, Eva Hesse, Donald Judd [1928–1994], Walter De Maria, Michelangelo Pistoletto. I xeroxed works that I thought people were emulating most; I simply copied them. I also tried to include people I liked most. There were photos of [works by] Palermo, photos of [works by] artists I liked most, and these were perhaps the artists this youngest generation of artists in São Paulo were working on. Once again, I think it's great they were doing this, but I would have liked to see another result. In some ways they are smart, not so in others. How is that possible? On one wall, I decided to make a kind of educational thing: to explicitly include what I thought was happening on the actual São Paulo contemporary art scene, as it had a deep connection to the Arte Povera and conceptual movements. I included things by Eva Hesse, her balls wrapped in fishermen's nets, and that Serra thing in which he threw molten lead on the floor, splattering it. For example, I made a work, a table with stilts, with fake legs, reaching up to the ceiling. Looking at the Arte Povera book, I think Reiner Ruthenbeck made a work like that in 1966. It was a little different, but I saw a very big connection. I said: "Gosh, it stays in our mind, I've seen this already." So if it's in our mind, it's up to you to change the idea a little. The funniest thing was that I did this, I showed all this here; people saw it, some were interested and wanted to know more about it. But the following month, there was an exhibition and this girl made the same Eva Hesse balls and said it was her work, which she had been developing for a long time. It was so obvious, you know? She didn't even want to assume the obvious, the copy, and just say: "I saw it and I wanted to make it." No. She had never seen Eva Hesse's work, and she insisted that it was her own work. It was so hypocritical to me that I wanted to slap her in the face when I saw it. I got mad at her. I was so angry on the day of the opening that I wanted to fight with the girl, because that was so outrageous.

AP **And your exhibition?**

JL The other part of the exhibition was more poetic. There was a table with a

358. Leonilson
Saque e aproveite a vantagem [Serve and Enjoy the Advantage], 1985

Acrylic paint, gouache, and varnish on newspaper
58 × 68.5 cm
Pinacoteca de São Paulo, gift Associação Pinacoteca Arte e Cultura (APAC) and Projeto Leonilson, acquisition made with resources from the Pinaball, in celebration of 110 years of Pinacoteca, 2015, Brazil
PL.0377.0/00

poem that I had made for a friend who went to Israel. There was something very nice, a little shelf with a piece of bread on which I wrote, "Na cor dos lábios do meu amor" [In the color of my love's lips]. More explicit than that, only if I had put in something pornographic. The bread was at the same height as my dick, like that, on the wall. It was piece like that, and it was also in the shape of a dick, and there were these words written.[48] I think it was a super strong work, but at the same time, it was super romantic. Some friends of mine were very moved. They said, "Wow, what a beautiful work this is," knowing what was behind it. I wanted to make a work that was almost... not pornographic, but erotic... I wanted to make something erotic. Then there was this work with stilts and a sandcastle. And another work, also, in which I assembled several of my books into a pile; it was a work that spoke of accumulating things. Both this work and the one with an island [and a sandcastle] had to do with accumulating things. You see, my place looks like a junkyard. I go to places, keep buying things, take them with me, find things on the street, take them home. These stones I made were books. There was my Latin dictionary, a folklore dictionary, the Brazilian literature I had as a boy. There was *Urupês* [by Monteiro Lobato]; there was *Grande Sertão: Veredas* [*The Devil to Pay in the Backlands*, by Guimarães Rosa], among others. I wrapped them in some old pants of mine and piled them up like the things I keep inside of me. I knew the stories from the Latin and folklore books, from *Urupês*, from *Grande Sertão*, so I made this work, which had to do with accumulation. Also, *O ilha* [The Island One, 1990] was about going far away and taking everything I wanted with me. All the things closest to me were supposed to be on the table: my tape recorder, my asthma inhaler, my pillow, my pillowcase, some clothes, books, tapes, drawings, paraphernalia. Eventually, I didn't put anything [on the table] because I wanted the work to be simpler. And there was a sandcastle, which for me is a primary artistic expression: we go to the beach and want to build something. It's very related to what I think I'm doing these days. I start making a work, I have an idea of what I want to do, but the work develops in the work process; that's the exercise of making it. The same happens with a sandcastle: you want to make

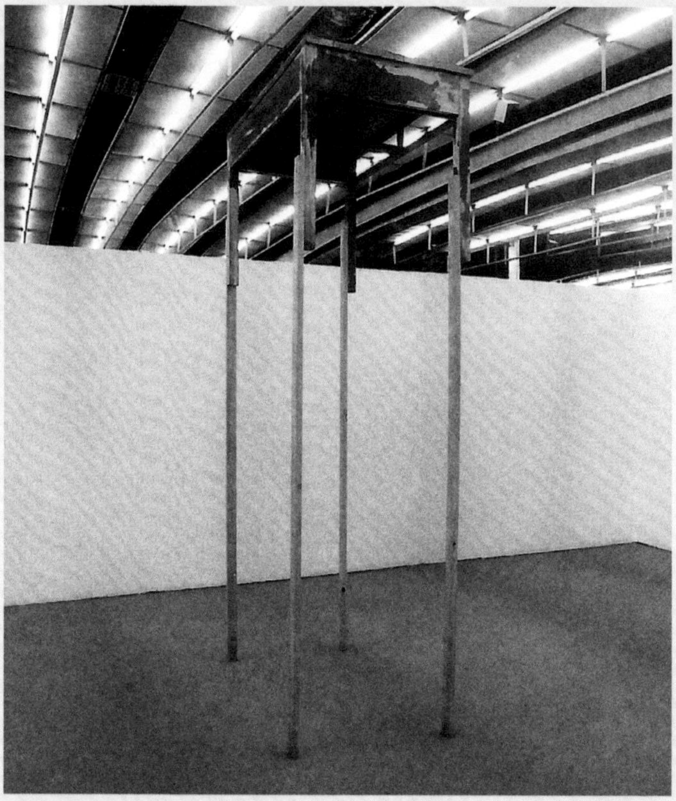

359

359. View of the work *O ilha* [The Island One] (1990) (PL.2534.0/00) at *Leonilson (Simultaneous Solo Exhibitions)* at the Centro Cultural São Paulo in 1990.

a sandcastle, and you start to pile up sand, but sometimes water comes and tears it down, and sometimes the sand falls down. You build until you arrive at something and that's the exercise: that's the work of art. While I'm working, I'm thinking about many things, some problems, in things I want to do, in things I don't want for myself. I keep thinking about people, about who I like, who I don't like; I keep arguing with myself. It's a labour of exercise.

AP Coming back to the two distinct objectives [personal and political, or subjective and objective], how do you think this will develop now? Are you going to continue in both approaches or has your attitude toward the work, the way you understand the work and its function, changed somehow? Because in fact, these two works could be said to have opposite functions: one very specific, objective, albeit with a great deal of poetry, and the other rather subjective.

JL I think this is opening doors. It's like expanding your universe. It's possible that from time to time I felt limited. It's good when these things come up because I know there is more than one area to work on; it's something normal.

AP Would you like to talk a little about your work process? What is this process like, from the moment you come up with an idea, how do you think of resolving it visually? An idea or a feeling...

JL Sometimes, I'm listening to a song and I write down some of the lyrics. In my notebook there are quite a few sentences from songs. Sometimes I'm in a place, something comes to my mind and I write it down. Or sometimes, I'm listening to a song and I remember a scene, or I meet someone who makes me remember something, and I store it. I used to produce a lot more work. I used to wake up and look for something to work on. Nowadays, I take it easy. I wait a little while to see if it appears too silly to me. In the past, my works were much sillier. Now, I get up every day and sometimes I work and sometimes I don't.

AP But then you decide to make a work—do you plan for it in advance?

JL No.

AP It's all in your head?

JL Yes. For example, I turn to my notebook and see the written sentences, some of which become titles of works.

AP When you begin to make a work, do you have a more or less clear idea of how it will be in the end?

JL I have an idea of how to start a work. How it will turn out in the end, I don't know.

AP So it's a working process in which you take a canvas and you have no idea what will emerge?

JL Well, no. I have a certain intention to make something. But I don't know how the work will turn out.

AP Not how it will turn out in the end, but are you clear about how the work should turn out more generally? I would like to know if you have a plan.
JL Yes. Sometimes I think a work is going to turn out in a certain way, I start working and it changes. It doesn't change completely, but some things happen that I connect to other things that arise during the work process.

AP This may even be a result, as you said the other day, of working quickly, of fast execution.
JL It has happened a few times that I placed the canvas on my table and had no idea what I was going to do. And it has happened that some of these works turned out well and some didn't; instead of turning out nicely, they turned out silly. Nowadays, I'm used to a certain amount of planning. I'm learning; I already have a practice, a practice of reflecting on work. That's how I can have an idea of how the work will turn out in the end. But sometimes it changes completely.

AP Why is that?
JL Well it may change considerably, though not completely. I already know how I want to make a work, that I want to do this or that.

AP In the previous conversation, you also mentioned that when the work starts to drag on, you might have trouble working it out, finding an interesting solution, and you think you have to throw the work away.
JL No. I might think that I have to stop.

AP Do you remember having said this?
JL I remember. I think it's necessary to pause when the work is getting too entangled, in order to understand what is happening. If I said something else, I change it now.

AP Do you throw many works away?
JL In the past... Yes. I was going to say that before I used to throw away more, but I remembered that before travelling, I threw away a lot of works, I cut them up and threw them away. But maybe I throw away fewer works now. Maybe I throw less because now I know when I should stop working. For example, sometimes I start going back to the process. I start making a work thinking it's going to become a certain thing, and in the middle of the process the work is already good, even though I didn't get to what I was planning. Sometimes, with only a few elements, the work is already great. And then I stop. That's why I've been throwing away less work. It may be that I'm working with more discretion, perhaps with a little maturity and better knowledge of the work.

AP Would you say that most of the time you carry out a plan that is in your head and the work is ready?
JL Most of the time, yes. But there are times that I stop in the middle because the work turns out better that way.

AP **The formal vocabulary of your paintings and drawings is quite large.**
JL Yes.

AP **There's the bridge, the river, the stones, the flames...**
JL The mountain, the volcano...

AP **The maps, the human body, the organs. Would you like to talk a little about that?**
JL Yes. You saw that the series of works on the boys, *Os dedicados* [The Dedicated, 1991] [imgs. 168-178], lack these things. I tried to make this series quite different. I kept remembering the guys I had met and what they reminded me of. I use very little of this symbology of mine. That's great, because it's becoming richer. From then on, this symbology will change a little. This is a basic symbology. These are the normal things, the things we have most contact with, the things I admire. Bridges are something I admire a lot; they are beautiful to me. I arrive in a city and see a river, which is something I like, with a bridge over it. There are people who like other things, but I like bridges. To me mountains and stones are beautiful. I love the seashore, the edge of the water.

AP **In our last conversation, you said that stones have quite a specific meaning to you. Do you remember that?**
JL I don't remember. But I think stones are...

AP **The things that stay...**
JL They are the things that stay. They are the things we want to break up with, or not, or we don't know how to get past them. They are something precious.

AP **Is this actually a vocabulary?**
JL I think you can answer that better than me.

AP **The bridge, for example, does it have a more or less specific meaning to you?**
JL I think it stands for a certain thing. On the Rio exhibition invitation [for Galeria Thomas Cohn, 1983] [img. 360], there are two guys with a river and a bridge in the middle. This bridge is the feeling.

AP **And the fire?**
JL The fire is our own fire. In the work with the three heads falling with the pouring water and the fire above [*The Game Is Over*], fire is this energy, something that we keep. Fire is like water, like wind; it's energy, it's what we have, it's the spirit, the persistence, this thing of wanting to continue.

AP **Perhaps we could make a division: on the one hand, there is a vocabulary of forms and figures, including stones, fire, water, and maybe even colors; on the other, there is a number of images that repeat themselves...**
JL The head...

AP **A group of images that is the human body, the maps...**

JL Which maps are you talking about?

AP **The rivers.**

JL Oh, right. Some people go into nature, get inspired and paint a landscape. I'm inspired by maps. I look at an atlas and that is everything for me. I look at an atlas as much as I look at the sea. They are the same to me, awakening several interests of mine. I wander the roads of the atlas, the rail tracks, and it's like looking at the sea or the sky, the clouds coming and going, or at a bunch of people. I include a lot of people because they interest me, but I don't draw people. I draw symbols that are people.

AP **Are you only drawing or also painting?**

JL I'm drawing more. I like to paint the background. Colors also have a huge symbology.

AP **I asked you this because we are talking about both drawing and painting. I even wanted to cut a little bit. But well, we'll come back to this issue of drawing and painting. Another question about vocabulary is how certain elements like gold always have a...**

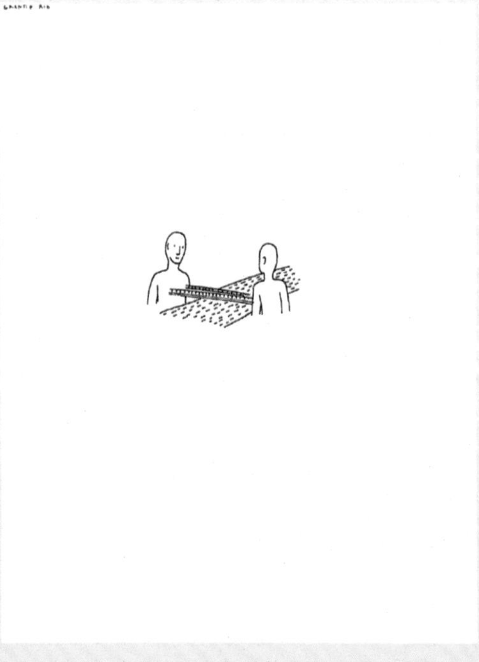

JL Yes. This is something I find beautiful, too, the gold. It is the power of gold. Especially after my doctor, Fernando, who I listen to and really adore, told me that I needed some gold in my body for balance, because of my allergies. He prescribed me gold. So every three months I take some liquid gold for balancing. It has to do with energy, with radiation.

AP **I don't know. But you have used it, that is, in the last...**

JL I always use what I can.

AP **In drawings.**

JL The gold?

AP **Yes.**

JL It's because I also like colors mixed with gold. It's more about having this energy, this radiation, this health thing, healthy balance. For the most important body parts, I like to use gold. I like to use it for the head, which is something like... there are people who talk about the aura that surrounds us. So, I like to use gold to make this emanation. It's like saying that it's a little bit sacred too, which interests me—I'm interested in the sacred, the holistic.

AP **The holistic?**

JL Yes. I don't even really know what that means.

AP **[Laughs] I'll explain it to you later. So, finally, are you painting or drawing?**
JL Me? I mix everything.

AP **Why?**
JL Because I make small and large scale watercolors, and they contain drawing. My canvasses from some time ago are like my small watercolors, only in larger scale. It's not that I make large watercolors, but they have a direct relationship, they are like large watercolors. And I think they have a lot of drawing [within them]. Drawing is as important as painting; they are the same, they merge.

AP **Yes, but distinguishing...**
JL It's like embroidery—there is no distinction.

AP **But making the technical distinction between drawing and painting: painting comes from the ground [the support] to the front, comes from the first [background] layers to the front; there are superimpositions of layers, whereas drawing is filling in...**
JL Yes, but I don't paint by filling layers.

AP **Not filling layers...**
JL I'm not painting with this...

AP **Filling forms.**
JL Yes. My painting is filling in from the outside, don't you think? I draw...

AP **This is a typical approach of drawing, but this is not a drawing. Do you see this distinction?**
JL Only that I paint on top of the drawing.

AP **Do you see the distinction I'm making?**
JL Ahem.

AP **Which is a distinction that is often made.**
JL Right.

AP **This here, for example, is a drawing, in which problems of drawing are at stake, even though it was filled in. Do you see what I mean?**
JL Yes.

AP **That over there and this here, too. You take any painting and you see its layers. Painting comes, it grows.**
JL The way you're talking, I think it's much more drawing than painting. Now, I consider it a mix.

AP **Of course, it's painting because you use paint.**
JL It's painting because I use paint.

AP **And a brush.**
JL So, it's painting and also drawing. I have the impression that the drawing is... No, the drawing is not stronger, because the color comes with the painting, because the drawing is always with black crayon.

360. Leonilson
Grande rio [Large River],
circa 1991

Permanent ink on paper
Unknown collection
PL.2959.0/00

AP Not necessarily. Black crayon?
JL Yes. I use black crayon. I use color with the paint.

AP Yes, but the drawing has another feature distinguishing it from painting which is the question of the ground. The ground is given by the color of the paper. That ground is visible. Otherwise, it is a painting on paper.
JL Right, in the drawings. But when it comes to the canvasses...

AP In some of your works, the color of the canvas is visible. Or even when the color of the canvas isn't visible, they often have a watercolor-type background.
JL Yes, the canvas has a color and there is a drawing on it, which is the work. Also, the white of the paper, when I leave it, is very important. That's why the drawing is small and not large. Sometimes I do want to make a large drawing, covering all of the white paper. It is still very important for me to use the white space. It is still very important for me to make it raw or else fill the canvas with a color or pattern and make a tiny drawing over it.

AP There is also the text, the writing. The other day we were talking about what you would do if you didn't paint, right? You said you wouldn't write.
JL I said that I wouldn't do anything.

AP And I said you could write, you could do poetry—couldn't you?
JL Could I make poetry only with the figure? I find it very difficult, because it's rather complementary. I'm not like Jenny Holzer, who comes and really only does writing. The figure for Jenny Holzer...

AP But don't think of Jenny Holzer...
JL No, I'm trying to establish...

AP Because Jenny Holzer is not doing poetry, Leonilson.
JL No, I know, but she writes.

AP She writes. But I'm referring to literature, do you see what I mean?
JL Ah, literature? I don't know if I could just do poetry anyway. Because I think of poetry together with the figure.

AP But some works only have written elements.
JL But the shape of the work, its size, the fabric, all of that is very important for me. It is like the painting.

AP I have been thinking about that and came to the conclusion...
JL I can't even say if I do painting, if I do drawing, if I do this or that. Because it's all very similar. Some works are on chiffon, so because of their transparency, the wall and the holes in the wall are visible, and so is the shine of the chiffon.

AP These are not paintings, right?
JL They're objects. I like to understand paintings as objects, too.

AP I was thinking about this the other day, whether you could be a poet, and thought maybe you could even give up drawing, the forms. Maybe your limit would be to write literature with your handwriting... It couldn't be printed letters, it would have to be at least your handwriting. Have you ever thought of such a project?
JL No.

AP And why do you sometimes write in English?
JL To train. [Silence] Then, I write incorrectly. I write in English, because there are some words... for example, handsome, that you can only say in English.[49] There are words that are beautiful in English, others that are beautiful in French; there are some things I find beautiful—*el desierto* [the desert] is a feeling that only exists in Spanish. That's great because now I even look them up in the dictionary. Now I only write [something] when I know it's correct. I still make a lot of mistakes in word matching.

AP Do you think that because of writing in another language, you are distanced from the word?
JL No. I sometimes write in English because I'm traveling. For example, the drawings I make when I'm traveling. When I'm in Amsterdam or here in New York and I speak English to people. Sometimes, I'm listening to a song in English and I take a sentence, and a whole sentence comes out that is not in the song, but is a new one that I create. For example, I have a work titled *O que é verdade para certos rapazes*.[50] I thought the song said "what is true for certain guys," which would be, "o que é verdade para certos rapazes," but the phrase in the song is actually: "What is true, what is true, when someone dies." And I think my sentence is much nicer. One thing leads to another.

AP Are you afraid someone will make a reading of your work like that, too?
JL What kind of reading?

AP Because you misread something, which has brought you something new.
JL Yes, some people sometimes do this and help me. It's nice. Some people correct, which I find even nicer.

AP And the volcano?
JL I think it strengthens what in theater is called "alienation."[51]

AP In theater?
JL Yes.

AP I really don't know.
JL [Laughs] Say "the volcano."

AP What is the volcano?

JL The volcano. That's what we have inside us, something that explodes, this load of feelings. The volcano is like when I feel full of things, ready to explode.

AP And the mountains?

JL Mountains are certain problems; they are something I don't know how to handle. I say: every pimple on my face is for a certain thing. At Thomas Cohn's, there was a work with several mountains and with writing: "a família" (the family), "o sexo" (the sex), "o amor" (the love), "o dinheiro" (the money), "os amigos" (the friends). Sometimes I get a pimply face, allergic reactions, and I think every time I have a problem a pimple appears. I compare them with the mountains.

AP And what about the "sheltering mountain"?

JL The "sheltering mountain"?

AP There's still this work, right?

JL There is still this sheltering mountain. But the sheltering mountain is the real mountain. The mountain that shelters, inside of it, a place of refuge, a kind of "sheltering dream". The dream is a powerful mountain that protects you.

AP And "moving mountains"?

JL I think "moving mountains" is more similar to this other explanation of mine for mountains. If you have quite a few problems, quite a few things to solve, you either go through them, inside a situation, or you go around them. Sometimes you stop, think, and solve the situation, or you simply push the problem aside. This is the moving mountain.

AP And the mathematician?

JL The mathematician, because I thought you were studying mathematics when I met you. You once told me you had studied mathematics... Oh, no, remember, you once told me about that place down in Rio, where people study mathematics?[52] I was so impressed to know that there is a place where some guys go to study mathematics. I was always pretty bad at math in school, but it always fascinated me the most, especially when I started to learn about the history of algebra, the philosophers... I remember when I met you, you told me this story of a place where these guys were studying. I asked: "Does the government pay them, are there scholarships?" And you said: "Yes, they stay there studying mathematics." It's something that I'm not at all close to, but that fascinates me completely. I would like very much to study it more, among the many things I would like to study more.

AP And the human body and organs?

JL The human body and organs is [about] this: I have a problem with blood; I cannot see it or smell it or I faint immediately. I could never look at pictures of surgery. I remember that once at school they showed a video of a child being born and I had a very bad time, I wanted to throw up, had to leave the classroom, and they gave me smelling salts. I had always this relationship of disgust to offal. One day I said, "I'm gonna end this." But I can't stop fainting as soon as I smell blood.

AP Smell?
JL Yes, blood, the smell of blood makes me pass out. And if I see someone get cut I get dizzy, dizzy. I sort of exorcised this thing. I started making works about it. I have an anatomy book and I keep looking...

AP Because you've been working on this for a long time.
JL Since 1988. Since that work called *As ruas da cidade* [The City Streets, *circa* 1988].

AP Whose work is that?
JL Mine.

AP Is it hanging somewhere?
JL It hangs in the back room. I thought it was like diagramming the human body with a map of a city, and the veins and the circling of things.

AP You talked about blood, what is *Blood Sucker* [1989] [img. 361] like?[53]
JL There's a work called *Blood Sucker*.

AP It's like a wooden man made from boards...
JL This culture of yours to read, read, read... It seemed you were sucking out something of yours. You were drawing blood. I can't explain it well, you know? This is a work I really can't explain.

AP You make many different types of works: you have drawings, works on paper, paintings, you make objects that are...
JL Made of cloth.

AP Cloth objects. And you also make three-dimensional objects.
JL I've also made objects out of wood and iron.

AP It would be nice if we chose one of each, more or less recent, to talk a little about them. For example, the voile works, or those with gold.
JL A. P. [1991] [img. 362].

AP There are three of them, right?[54]
JL Yes.

AP Would you like to talk a little about these works?
JL In these works, I wanted to see where my limit lies in how simply I can make a work. So, I wanted to work with voile.

AP Was this one of your first works with voile?
JL Yes.

AP **From last year?**
JL Exactly. I was trying to make the work as simple as possible, without figures, without anything. But I couldn't help it, I had to put something, so I decided to put the gold there. Just as protection. I used the gold also because the voile frays a lot. I could only use transparent resin, but I decided to use gold as well [on the edges of the work], which is beautiful; it is surrounded by this strength. While this is a very light work, easily swayed by the wind, the gold makes the textile work harder. Sometimes it curls, stretches, or wrinkles. In this way, the work appears more like an object.

AP **And those objects that are projects? The lamp.**
JL The lamp.

AP **The knives.**
JL The small knives. There is one I like a lot, a picture of Chantilly lace, which is a lace made of silk and cotton. A picture of green Chantilly lace on a wall and of a fakir's bed,[55] except that it is made of nails and with several points. It is called *Aos seus pés meus desejos* [At Your Feet, My Desires, *circa* 1991]. You can also call it *To My Captain*. It is about the contrast between the violence of the nail bed and the gentleness of the lace. When you want something from someone, when you are in love, or you've just met someone, and you have that fascination with them, you want to serve them, you want to give yourself to them, and at the same time you want

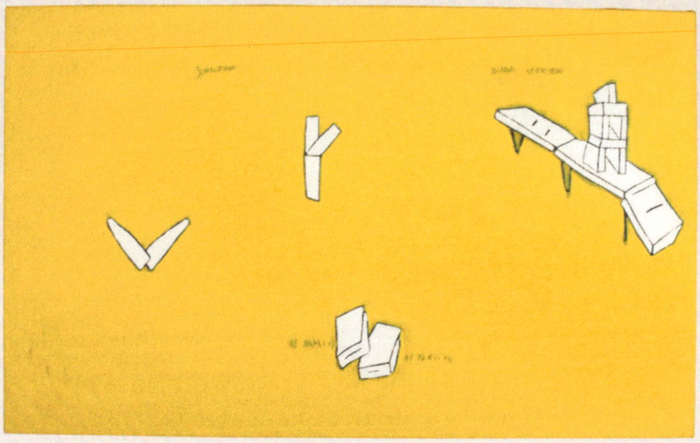

361

that person [all] for yourself. This is always a relationship of tenderness and violence. I had never paid much attention to this, then at one point I began to. I was really into someone, and I think I wanted, I didn't just want... I don't know, I paid attention to the fact that I wanted that person's tenderness, and I wanted to possess them too. I wanted to own that person. So the words, "at your feet, my desires," are me asking the person for something, and at the same time ordering them—I want something from them. I think this work is great; it's very representative of my works that speak of feelings. It is very similar to the work with the two knives that meet at the tip.

AP **What is it called?**
JL *Crossing fires*, or something like "cross fire" [*Protected, Crossing Fires*, 1990] [img. 363]. That is a very delicate relationship. Two people who are fascinated with each other, and they have this thing, the force of the knife, something that penetrates, but at the same time it is only the tip that penetrates,

361. Leonilson
***Blood Sucker*, 1989**

Acrylic paint on canvas
90 × 150 cm
Private collection,
São Paulo, Brazil
PL.2304.0/00

in a subtle, delicate, even fragile way. And it is a water line that can be broken at any time. You can break with feeling.

AP And it can hurt.
JL Yes, hurt. This does not mean that it is bad or not.

AP And *Pequenos fogos* [Small Fires, 1990], which is both a sculpture and a drawing?
JL This is a project involving both sculpture and drawing.

AP It's that story of the flame...
JL It is the purest, most beautiful feeling released by you. They are little fires that appear.

AP And the lamp?
JL The lamp is a very aesthetic work. The lamp is something that we want to have next to us, to leave beside the bed. When we are in the dark, we turn it on to illuminate. On the lamp's dome, a little truck is drawn with the] written [words], "inflamável, rapaz muito sensível" (inflammable, very sensitive boy). And behind the lampshade there is no bulb, but a candle. Every time I turned it on, I would see the drawing and remember someone very sensitive. It is also a work to keep remembering this person. That sensitive thing, which can explode at any moment because it is inflammable. People are inflammable. You see a very shy person, who is very restrained. Suddenly, the person explodes. Hence the relationship with the gasoline truck.

362

362. Leonilson
A.P., 1991

Metallic paint on voile
210 × 147 cm (210 × 49 cm;
134 × 94 cm)
Private collection,
São Paulo, Brazil
PL.0334.1/00

Translated from Portuguese by Sarah Poppel

Source: PEDROSA, Adriano. "Concentrated Conversations". In: GRUIJTHUIJSEN, Krist. *Leonilson: Drawn* (1975-1993). Berlin: Hatje Cantz Verlag, 2020.

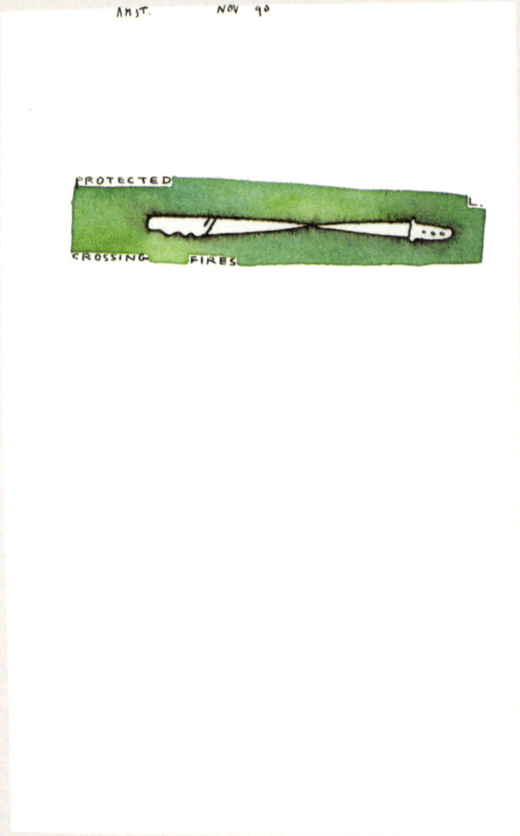

363

NOTES

1 This interview was first published in Portuguese in Adriano Pedrosa, *Leonilson: Truth, Fiction* (São Paulo /Rio de Janeiro: Pinacoteca/Cobogó, 2014).

2 Fundação Armando Alvares Penteado, a private college in São Paulo which has an undergraduate art program.

3 Today the Centro Universitário Belas Artes de São Paulo [Fine Arts University of São Paulo].

4 Text in [square brackets] has been inserted by either the translator or the editors.

5 Centro de Estudos Aster [Aster Study Center, 1978-81]. This school was co-founded by Julio Plaza, among other artists and art theorists.

6 12º Panorama de Arte Atual Brasileira (12th Panorama of Brazilian Art), Museu de Arte Moderna de São Paulo (MAM-SP), 1980.

7 *Desenho jovem* [Young drawing], Museu de Arte Contemporânea da Universidade de São Paulo (MAC-USP), 1980.

8 This series of paintings, drawings, and prints was actually created between 1977 and 1982, and appears with the additional title *Style Wars* in English language contexts.

9 Centre Georges Pompidou, informally called Beaubourg.

10 Despite Leonilson's remarks, the gallery continued to be called Grässlin-Ehrhardt, and announced its exhibitions in the March/April 1991 *FlashArt* issue under this name.

11 Studio d'Arte Cannaviello, Milan.

12 Leonilson's exhibition at Fernando Pellegrino actually took place in 1982.

13 The Asdrúbal Trouxe o Trombone [Asdrúbal Brought the Trombone] group, directed by Hamilton Vaz Pereira, were part of Rio de Janeiro's theater scene from the mid-1970s. Some of the group's best known plays are *Trate-me leão* [Treat me lion] (1977), *Aquela coisa toda* [That Whole Thing] (1980), and *A farra da Terra* [The Fun of the Earth] (1983).

14 The Marathon at the Centro Cultural Vergueiro in São Paulo took place in 1982. This was one of Asdrúbal's events, in which the artists revealed their process of creating the play *A farra da Terra*, which would premiere in 1983. Occupying all the rooms of the cultural center for two consecutive days, the public was invited to participate in various stages of the creative process: either by acting and dancing, or by assisting in the making of sets and costumes under the direction of Luiz Zerbini and Leonilson.

15 *Como vai você, Geração 80?* [How are you, 80s Generation?], Escola de Artes Visuais do Parque Lage, Rio de Janeiro, 1984. After the show, the participating artists became known as the *Geração 80*. *Carioca*, native or resident of Rio.

363. Leonilson
***[Protected, Crossing Fires]*,**
1990 [img. 110]

16 *Á flor da pele: pintura e prazer* [Skin Deep: Painting and Pleasure], Galeria do Centro Empresarial Rio, 1983.

17 These two exhibitions, showing in parallel at Thomas Cohn's in Rio de Janeiro and Luisa Strina's in São Paulo, were Leonilson's first solo shows in Brazil.

18 Jorge Guinle Filho, "A implosão da imagem," *Módulo*, no. 75, Mar. 1983.

19 Casimiro Xavier de Mendonça, "Arca modernista," *Veja*, Jun. 1, 1983.

20 Escola de Artes Visuais do Parque Lage (EAV, the School of Visual Arts of Lage Park), Rio de Janeiro.

21 Founded in 1958, Fenit, Feira Nacional da Industria Têxtil (National Textile Industry Fair), was the biggest fashion event in Brazil, a kind of forerunner of São Paulo Fashion Week.

22 Located on the Sud Mennucci Street, Vila Mariana, São Paulo.

23 Ludwig Wittgenstein, *Tractatus logico-philosophicus*, first published in Germany in 1921. Translated and published in Brazil by Edusp (University of São Paulo Press, 1968).

24 Roberto Pontual, *Explode geração* (Rio de Janeiro: Avenir Editora, 1987).

25 The cruzeiro was Brazil's currency from 1942 to 1986 and again between 1990 and 1993.

26 A group of artists formed in Europe in 1948 by Christian Dotremont, Asger Jorn, Joseph Noiret, and Karel Appel, among other artists, taking its name from the cities of Copenhagen, Brussels, and Amsterdam.

27 Ricardo Basbaum, "Pintura dos anos 80: algumas observações criticas," *Gávea*, no. 6, 1988.

28 Grupo Opinião [Group Opinion], Brazilian theater group.

29 What is meant here is not that the magazine commissions and pays for texts based on editorial interests, but that such texts are commissioned and paid for following commercial interests.

30 In the Project Leonilson catalog there are records of a work registered under the title *The Game Is Over* (1990) and another one under *No One To Dedicate* (*circa* 1991). The description in this answer matches *The Game Is Over*. [Editor's Note]

31 In the Projeto Leonilson catalog, this work is registered under the title *Com ela sempre por perto* [With Her Always Around] (1991).

32 In Portuguese, the word "death" is feminine gender (*a morte*).

33 Marguerite Yourcenar, *Feux* (Paris: Éditions Grasset, 1936). Translated as *Fogos* (Rio de Janeiro: Nova Fronteira, 1983).

34 Apparently the work was later modified by the artist, removed from its frame, and "blue balls" were painted on the cut out canvas, becoming *As cascas de ovo* (1992).

35 *Sebastiane* (1976), directed by Paul Humfress and Derek Jarman.

36 In the Projeto Leonilson catalog, this work is registered under the title *Agora e as oportunidades* (1991).

37 Leonilson uses the English word.

38 *Moving Mountains*, Kunstforum, Munich, Germany, 1987.

39 Duane Michals, *Album: The Portraits of Duane Michals, 1958–1988* (Santa Fe, NM: Twin Palms, 1988).

40 Duane Michals, *Homage to Cavafy. Ten Poems by Constantine Cavafy. Ten Photographs by Duane Michals* (Danbury, NH: Addison House, 1978).

41 Duane Michals, *Duane Duck: Photographs/Sequences/Texts* (1958–1984) (Oxford: Modern Art Oxford, 1984).

42 Brazilian medicinal tonic.

43 Adriano uses the English word. [Editor's Note]

44 The title of the Soul II Soul song is actually "Get A Life," and at one point the lyrics say "be selective."

45 Leonilson uses the English phrase.

46 In several of the artist's works, references to minorities become palpable.

47 This installation was part of the exhibition *Leonilson*, Centro Cultural São Paulo, 1990.

48 A colloquial expression for "dick" in Portuguese is "pau" (the word Leonilson uses in the original interview), homonymous with "pão," which translates to "bread" in English.

49 Leonilson uses the English word.

50 The work's actual title is *El desierto* [The desert] (1991) and includes the written phrase "O que é verdade para certos rapazes."

51 Leonilson seems to be referring to the alienation effect, also often referred to in dramatic theory as the estrangement effect or distancing effect (from the German "Verfremdungseffekt"), coined by Berthold Brecht.

52 Instituto de Matemática Pura e Aplicada (IMPA, National Institute for Pure and Applied Mathematics).

53 In the Projeto Leonilson catalog, this work is registered under the title *Blood Sucker* (1989).

54 In the Projeto Leonilson catalog, only a diptych is registered under this title.

55 Fakir, a Sufi Muslim ascetic.

BIO GRAPH ICAL NOTE

Teo Teotonio

José Leonilson Bezerra Dias[1] was born on March 1st, 1957, in Fortaleza, Ceará state, the fourth of five children. His parents, Carmem Bezerra Dias (1927-2017) and Theodorino Torquato Dias (1925-2000), born in Northern Brazil, met each other while traveling—the father, born in Guaporé,[2] was on a business trip, while the mother, who was from Manaus, was on her way to a convent to become a nun. After their wedding, they moved to Porto Velho, Rondônia state, due to Theodorino's trading activities, since he owned Casa Saudade, the main fabric store in that area. Due to the business' success, they decided to live in Fortaleza, where they stayed for ten years before settling in the Vila Mariana neighborhood in São Paulo, at the end of 1961.

Leonilson grew up in a moment of great economic, social, and cultural changes in the country, among them, the robust industrialization and internationalization of production means, the migration flow from Northeast to Southeast, and the civil-military dictatorship in Brazil (1964-1985). His family belonged to the upper middle class forming in São Paulo; it was traditional, loving, and deeply religious, which led Leonilson to study in private, Catholic schools for boys [img. 364]. He attended elementary school at the Colégio Sagrado Coração de Jesus and Colégio Arquidiocesano, where he deepened his studies on religion and Christian iconography. Considering the proper changes in perspective and meaning, this aspect accompanied him throughout his personal and artistic life—crosses, flaming hearts, crowns of thorns, and other elements of Christian vocabulary would emerge in his late visual production. Despite living in an exclusively male environment in school, while at home, Leonilson joined his mother and sisters in daily tasks, including embroidery and sewing, which were made easier considering his father's fabric store.

In 1975, he took his first international trip to Madrid, Spain. One year later, he enrolled in a technical course in tourism at the Colégio Ideal, in the Higienópolis neighborhood, São Paulo, where he concluded high school. During the brief period while he attended the course, he had classes with the art critic Casimiro Xavier de Mendonça (1947-1992), who would write texts about his work years later.[3]

These were the first signs of an interest in displacement, maps, and crossings which would become central to the development of his artistic research. His interest in traveling was familiar: his parents, migrants who met each other while traveling, visited their relatives often in Fortaleza and took advantage of their children's school breaks to find countryside and beach locations in São Paulo state. Moreover, the artist's father always told him stories about his wanderings during work, which would also fill his imagination with other cities and far distances.

***

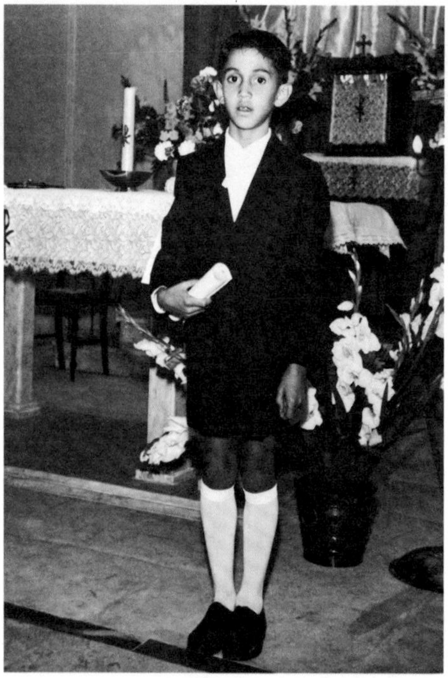

364

Leonilson showed his appreciation for artistic practice from early in life. Catalogs show that his first visual works date from 1971 when he was only 14. In his preadolescent age, the artist attended open drawing courses at the Escola Panamericana de Artes and in 1975, by the age of 18, he worked at the 13th Bienal de São Paulo as a Spanish interpreter. He then decided to devote himself to artistic study and practice, attending the Artistic Education undergraduate course at the Faculdade de Belas Artes (current Centro Universitário Belas Artes) in the first semester of 1977. However, he quit that program and entered the Fine Arts program at the Fundação Armando Álvares Penteado (FAAP) the next semester, with the artists Jac Leirner, Ana Maria Tavares, and Luiz Zerbini. That same year, he exhibited his works for the first time at the group show *Arte e pensamento ecológico* [Art and Ecological Thought] at the City Council Chamber in Santos, São Paulo.

At the beginning of college, Leonilson would produce according to the demands of his professors, among them Nelson Leirner (1932–2020), Julio Plaza (1937–2003), and Regina Silveira, especially from observation drawing exercises or those aimed at the depiction of human figures, landscapes and plants, and architectonic section drawings. After two years in the university, in 1979 the artist rented a studio in the Vila Previdência neighborhood with his friend Luiz Zerbini and started working actively to build a solid production and enter the artistic milieu. Leonilson spent his days immersed in the studio and attended classes at FAAP at night. However, as he devoted himself increasingly to his own practice, he would lose interest in the exercises proposed by the professors.

In the first semester of 1980, he interrupted the course and started attending Aster (1978–1981), a hybrid institution that merged the intents of a school, art studio, and research center created by Donato Ferrari, Julio Plaza, Regina Silveira, and Walter Zanini (1925–2013). There, he could discuss his and other students' productions in a horizontal organizational structure typical of a non-traditional school. He reenrolled at FAAP that same year, but abandoned the course for good with the support of his professors:

364. Leonilson at his first communion, 1964
Courtesy of Projeto Leonilson, São Paulo, Brazil

But then, I couldn't stay there any longer. I was already making my own work; I was drawing. I didn't want to go to school anymore, because I no longer wanted to do the stuff we had to do there. Teachers would propose certain tasks we should work on, and I didn't do any of them. Nelson Leirner, for example, kept saying that I had to leave FAAP, that it was no longer for me, that I needed to have a studio and work on my own. This was also encouraged by Julio Plaza. That year I made a series of about forty drawings.[4]

That same year, 1980, when he was 23, Leonilson had his first solo exhibition, *Cartas a um amigo* [Letters to a Friend], at the Museu de Arte Moderna da Bahia, in Salvador. Aiming to expand his contacts, participate in the international artistic scene, obtain independence from his family, and fulfill his insatiable desire to travel (even though he always returned home before planned),[5] Leonilson headed to Europe in January 1981, beginning his journey in Madrid. His great curiosity and sociability have helped him meet artists, curators, and gallerists with whom he would work in the future. On one of these occasions, he was told to go to the Brazilian Embassy in Madrid, where he met Cláudio Leal, director of the artistic residence for college students at Casa do Brasil. With financial support from his family, Leonilson lived there for a few months, using his studio to produce a series of drawings that were displayed in *Cartas al hombre* [Letters to the Man], his first international solo exhibition held at Casa do Brasil's gallery. After the exhibition opening in 1981, Leonilson invited Luiz Zerbini, with whom he had formerly shared a studio, to go to Spain. They shared a studio at Casa de Velázquez, a French artistic institution located in Madrid.[6] That same year, they opened the exhibition *José Leonilson/Luiz Zerbini*, also at Casa do Brasil.

At the end of 1981, Leonilson traveled to Germany, France, and Italy. Encouraged by the artist Arthur Luiz Piza (1928–2017), he went to Antonio Dias' (1944–2018) place in Milan. He recalls that he knocked on the door, introduced himself, and was promptly invited to live with Dias,[7] with whom he stayed for a few months, joining the artist in events and exhibition openings, as well as in trips through Germany and Portugal. It was in this context that Leonilson met his first gallerist, Enzo Cannaviello, from Studio d'Arte Cannaviello, located in Milan.

When Leonilson and Zerbini returned to Brazil in 1982, they were invited by his colleagues of the theater group Asdrúbal Trouxe o Trombone[8] to join the team in charge

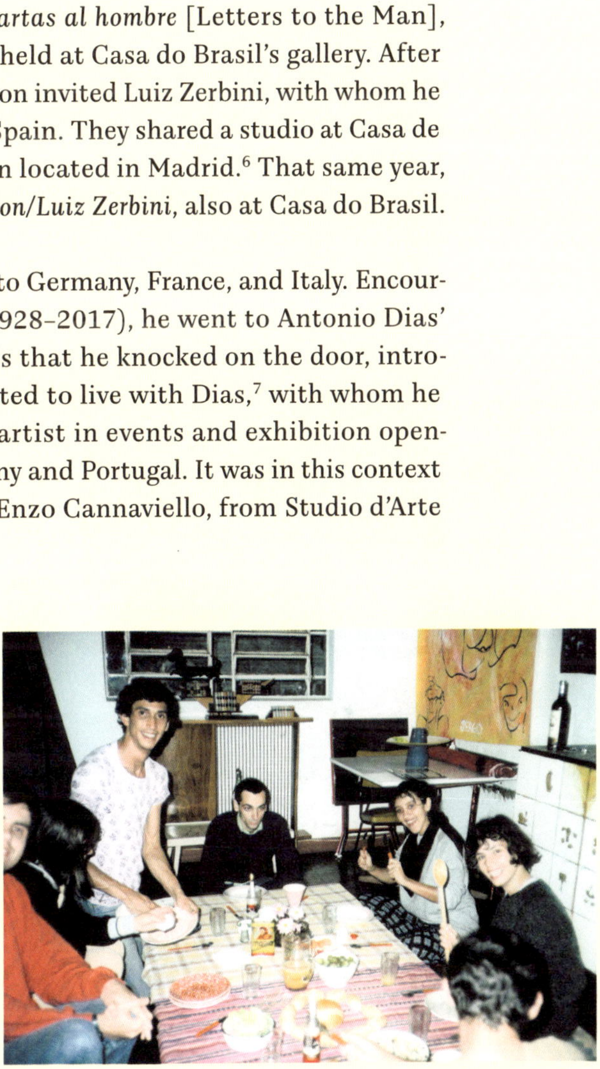

365. Dinner at Leonilson's house in São Paulo. From left to right: Sérgio Romagnolo, Patricia Casé, Leonilson, Luiz Zerbini, Regina Casé, Leda Catunda, and unidentified person, *circa* 1984

365

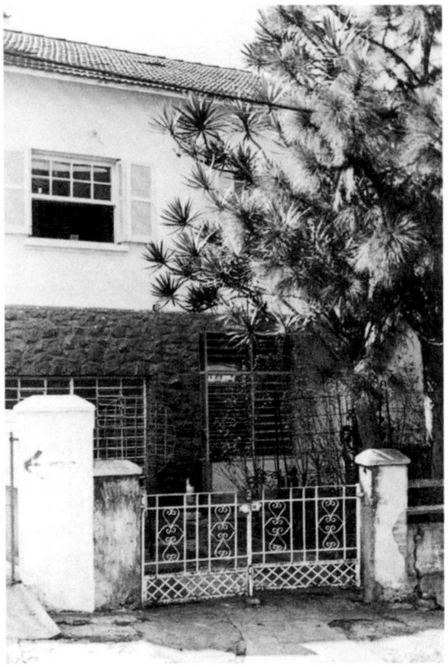
366

of the scenery and costumes of the play *A farra da Terra* [Earth's Spree] (1983) in Rio de Janeiro. The large dimensions of the paintings in the scenery and the group's experimental trait enabled a change in the tone and scale of Leonilson's production: his paintings became bigger and more explosive.

In 1983, the artist returned to São Paulo and rented a house with the financial support of his family in Sud Mennucci Street in Vila Mariana, where he lived for ten years. The place was a few blocks from his parents' house, which he visited frequently, especially during the meals. Leonilson lived by himself for a few months and soon his friends Sérgio Romagnolo and Ciro Cozzolino moved in there. The three artists shared the house and a studio in its garage for roughly one year [img. 366].

That same year, 1983, Leonilson had two simultaneous solo exhibitions at Galeria Luisa Strina in São Paulo, and Galeria Thomas Cohn, which had recently been founded in Rio de Janeiro. The exhibits were very successful and prompted him as the newest artist in the milieu. After that, in 1984, Leonilson took part in one of the most emblematic Brazilian exhibitions of the decade—*Como vai você, Geração 80?* [How Are You, 80s Generation?], held at the Escola de Artes Visuais Parque Lage in the Jardim Botânico neighborhood, Rio de Janeiro. The curators Marcus Lontra, Paulo Roberto Leal (1946-1991), and Sandra Magger (1956-2018) invited 123 artists—among them Beatriz Milhazes, Ana Maria Tavares, Cristina Canale, and Daniel Senise—to occupy different spaces in the historical building. Leonilson displayed large paintings and drawings in the library with his colleagues Leda Catunda, Ciro Cozzolino, and Sérgio Romagnolo [img. 367]. As a way of drawing a picture of the production of young artists from the Brazilian Southeast region of that time, the curatorial scope was restricted to painters between 20 and 30 years old living in Rio de Janeiro and São Paulo. The works bore an evident variety regarding their themes and both formal and technical approaches. However, the artists who stood out as the most emblematic of the 80s Generation shared similar subjective themes and eclectic references, expressed in a technically loose,

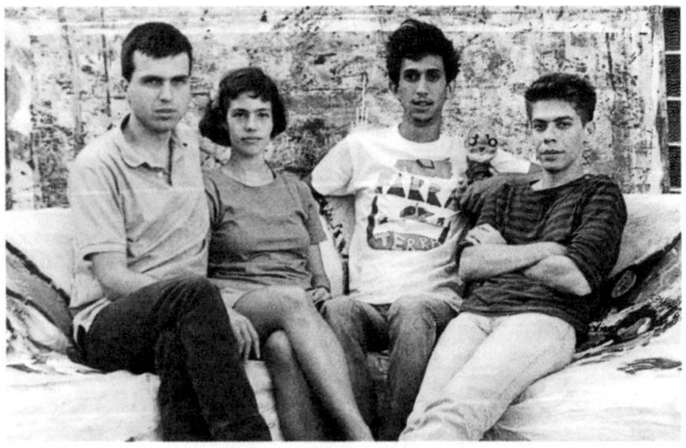
367

366. Façade of Leonilson's house/studio, São Paulo, undated
Courtesy of Projeto Leonilson, São Paulo, Brazil

367. Sérgio Romagnolo, Leda Catunda, Leonilson and Ciro Cozzolino at Leonilson's home/studio, São Paulo, 1983
Courtesy of Projeto Leonilson, São Paulo, Brazil

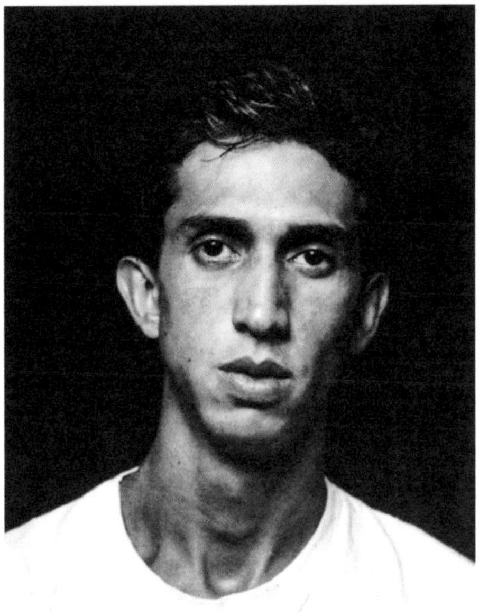

368

large-scaled, and bright-colored informal figurative painting. They also had an obvious correspondence with the German Neo-expressionism and the Italian Transavantgarde, theorized by Achille Bonito Oliva and highly in vogue in the international scene during that period—Leonilson had met Bonito Oliva years before in Milan thanks to Antonio Dias.

Even though one could not delimit an artistic movement, the necessity of determining new tendencies arose from a clear difference between the production of artists of the new generation and those from the previous decade, the 1970s, known for exploring political, social, and formal themes conceptually and using non-traditional media. Unlike the latter, who had experienced the *anos de chumbo* [Years of Lead][9] of the civil-military dictatorship, the 80s Generation had lived through the transition to democracy, with its political openness and decreasing repression. It was also a moment of international cultural influence, especially from the United States, with the advent of rock music, the so-called New Wave, of MTV, and the wide spread of fashion and lifestyle magazines. A feeling of relief and hope pointed out the overcoming of the past and focused on the experience of the present time. In the artistic production, the suppression of political themes, the theoretical and conceptual looseness, the resumption of traditional media, and a great dose of humor were evident, signaling a certain notion of pleasure in the act of doing and, mainly, of painting.

At the same time, with the growth of both income concentration and social inequity, the purchasing power of collectors increased and fostered the art market.[10] It was in this context that some of the artists from the 80s Generation entered the artistic milieu, legitimated by the exhibition at Parque Lage, by the media encouragement given by a press that still felt the traumas of political censorship, and by the selling and circulation of their artworks.

The market was greedy [laughs]. Because at that time you could sell so many works, you know? Everyone sold works: [Hilton] Berredo, [Luiz] Pizarro, Bia [Beatriz Milhazes], Leda [Catunda], me; we all sold a lot of works; we sold everything we'd painted. At the beginning of our career, when we started working, we made a lot of money, traveled, went to Europe, to Rio. Things were cheap, the cost of living was low.[11]

368. Portrait of Leonilson,
circa 1989
Courtesy of Projeto Leonilson,
São Paulo, Brazil

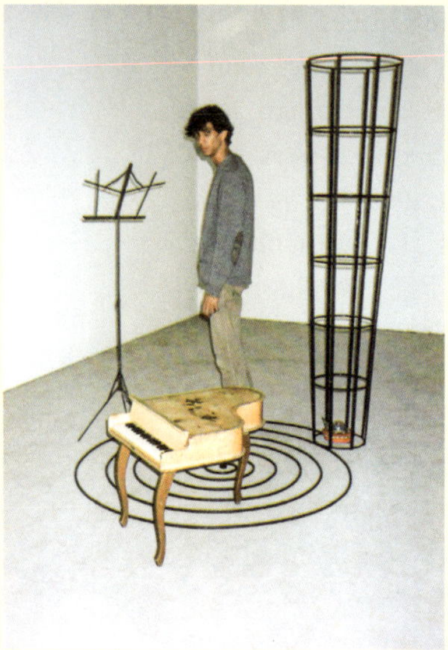

369

Leonilson not only exhibited his work in solo and group shows but also participated in two documentary films on the 80s Generation: *Tinta s/ tela* [Paint on Canvas] (1985) by Malu de Martino and *Spray Jet* (1985) by Ana Maria Magalhães. In 1985, he participated in two biennial exhibitions: the Nouvelle Biennale in Paris and the 18th Bienal de São Paulo, known for gathering artists from different nationalities and degrees of visibility that shared neo-expressionist and transavangardist features [img. 369]. Leonilson exhibited a group of sculptures, objects, paintings, and drawings, and that was the second time he showed tridimensional works—in the previous year, he produced the public sculpture *Torre na praia* [Tower on the Beach], commissioned by the City Hall of Fortaleza for the Projeto Arte Urbana [Urban Art Project].

During the 18th Bienal de São Paulo, Leonilson met the German artist Albert Hien. They traveled together through the historical cities of Minas Gerais state, becoming friends and work partners. The next year, they coproduced the installation *Vulcão de neve* [Snow Volcano] (1986) [img. 370], exhibited at Walter Storms Galerie in Munich. That same year, Leonilson presented a version of the work made of sand in the 1st Exposição Internacional de Esculturas Efêmeras [International Exhibition of Ephemeral Sculptures] in Fortaleza. Since then, the image of the volcano became part of his vocabulary of images and has been featured in many other works.

The volcano. That's what we have inside us, something that explodes, this load of feelings. The volcano is like when I feel full of things, ready to explode.[12]

The next year, after the Bienal, Leonilson began a new trip through France, Portugal, Germany, Spain, and Italy, where he participated in international exhibitions. In one of these excursions, he once more met Bonito de Oliva, who would include him in the exhibition *Transvanguarda e culturas nacionais* [Transavantgarde and National Cultures], curated by him and to be held at the Museu de Arte Moderna do Rio de Janeiro in 1986.

That same year, Eduardo Brandão (a gallerist, photographer, and, by that time, graphic designer) and Jan Fjeld (a collector, journalist, and, at that moment, English teacher), who were a couple, returned from Europe and started living in

369. Leonilson in one of the installations of *Por você não ter uma situação estável* [Because You Do Not Have a Stable Situation] (PL.2301.0/00), at the 18th Bienal de São Paulo, in 1985
Courtesy of Projeto Leonilson, São Paulo, Brazil

Leonilson's place in Vila Mariana. Eduardo had met Leonilson years before during Regina Silveira's and Julio Plaza's classes, but they hadn't become friends. However, they got close after a casual meeting and began a great friendship. The couple had moved to São Paulo from Los Angeles, United States, where the HIV and AIDS epidemic had killed many of their friends. At the end of the 1980s, the lack of medical knowledge associated with structural homophobia was responsible for quickly spreading the virus. Meanwhile, the governmental neglect regarding public health was justified by the illusion, disseminated by the most important media, that this was a "gay disease"—such an idea was widely embraced by the huge homophobic and conservative portion of the population. In Brazil, the process developed similarly, and the epidemic peaked in the following years.

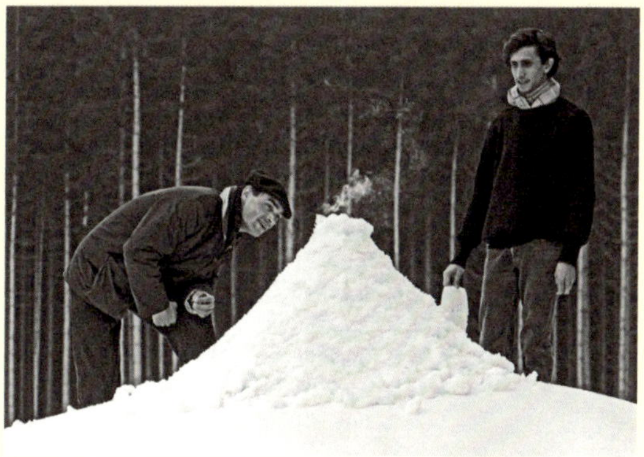

370

After some time in São Paulo, Brandão and Fjeld traveled to Norway. They returned to Brazil after Leonilson insisted they should live together, which they did until the last months of his life. They built a new family, even including some blood relatives—the couple established a friendship with Leonilson's parents, while the artist also became friends with Brandão's mother. They started doing a lot of things together, except for the household chores, which were handled by the couple, since Leonilson didn't take any responsibility for paying the bills or cleaning the house. Parties and visits from friends were common. Leonilson didn't drink too much and smoked weed. During the week, he usually went out for a coffee in the middle of the afternoon and always ordered a *pingado* (a cup of coffee with a drop of milk) and bread paired with butter. When they would go out to eat there was only one option: Oswaldo Aranha stake with fries rigorously prepared to avoid the artist's constant complaints

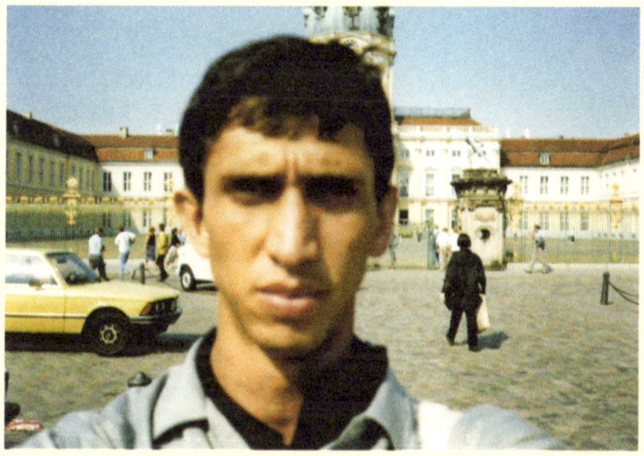

371

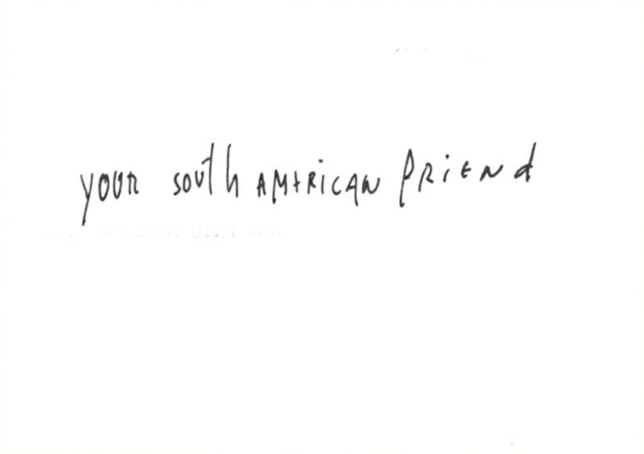

372

370. Leonilson and Albert Hien observing the ephemeral sculpture *Vulcão de neve* [Snow Volcano] (PL.2909.0/00), that they produced together, in Munich, Germany, 1986
Courtesy of Projeto Leonilson, São Paulo, Brazil

371, 372. Photo from Leonilson to Albert Hien, front and back, 1988
Courtesy of Projeto Leonilson, São Paulo, Brazil

to the waiters. He usually took flowers to the studio or to friends, to whom he also gave paintings and drawings, among other gifts [imgs. 371, 372].

By that time, Brandão worked as a photographer for fashion magazines, such as *Interview* and *Vogue*. Therefore, models and other people from that milieu attended the house frequently. Through this plethora of colleagues from the arts, Leonilson expanded even further his contact with literature, fashion, and music, with the last two already being great influences since his youth—in 1976, when he was 19, he manually produced a fictional magazine titled *Vogue Ideal* [Ideal Vogue] [imgs. 374, 375], which featured 30 pages divided into sections with details on fashion, the personality and both physical and behavioral traits of different characters, as well as interviews and testimonies from friends and family:

> **I dedicate this magazine to all those who can see ahead of some silly prejudices, to all enthusiasts of improvisation, happiness, and *joie de vivre*, and I apologize to those who haven't been pleased with me. To them, however, I say life is made to be lived, and not for saying such things as: Awful! Have you been there? Life to those who know how to live, and that's why I am alive. I have learned to like those who like me. A big kiss.**[13]

Since then, fashion has pervaded the artist's personal and professional lives, often influencing each other. The monochromatic layers of the Japanese designers Rei Kawakubo and Yohji Yamamoto were transferred to the paintings; beaded fabrics were also seen in the work by the Turkish Rifat Özbek [img. 373]; and the lightness of voile pieces that emerged at the end of his life resembled the transparencies by the Tunisian-born French designer Azzedine Alaïa (1935–2017) [img. 227].

Leonilson liked pop, rock, dance, blues, soul, and rap music. Just like fashion, the rhythms and lyrics also influenced his production. The title of the painting *You Don't See That* (1991) [img. 154], also inscribed on the canvas, was taken from the song "Little Fluffy Clouds," released in 1990 by the electronic music duo The Orb. The sentence "you sweet like a dog," also present in the

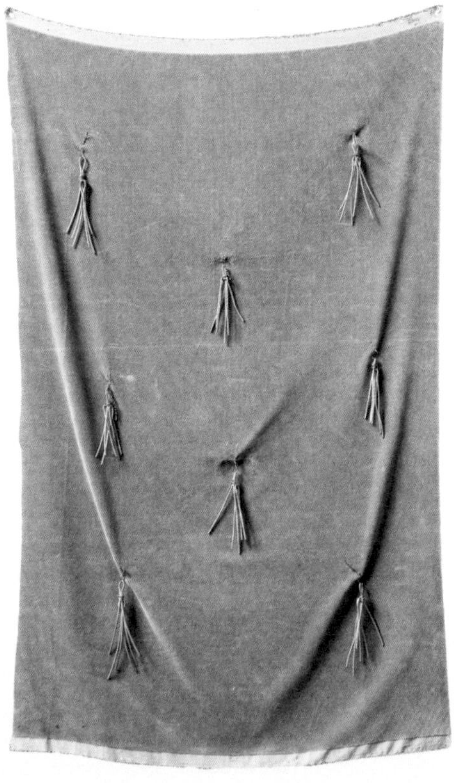

373

373. Leonilson
Rifat, *circa* 1988

Wire and copper
wire on velvet
93 × 58 × 3 cm
Private collection,
São Paulo, Brazil
PL.0411.0/00

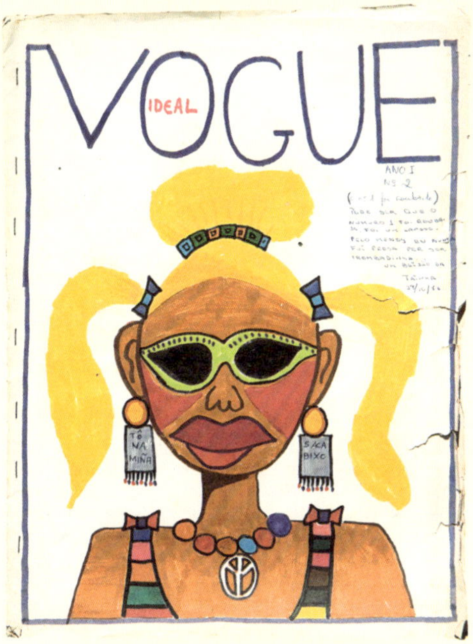

374

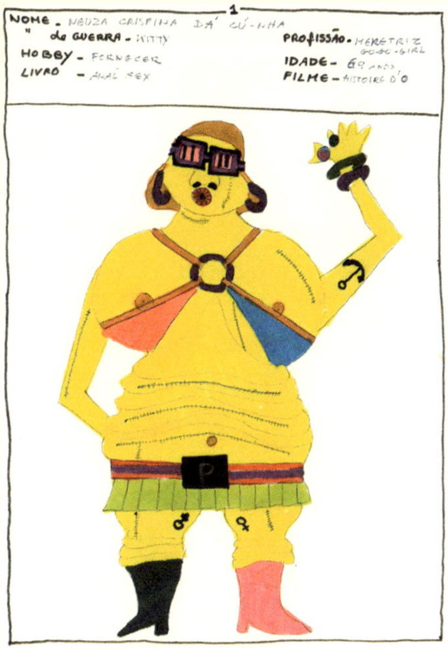

375

composition, is featured in the song "I Need Love," released in 1987 by the rapper and actor LL Cool J. There is a third one among these, "from what I remember," which testifies to the task of assigning a new meaning to references taken from their original contexts and its role in creating non-linear, subliminal narratives, a unique feature of his work. Plays on words were appropriated from literature, and Leonilson's interest in gay literature has led him to the books of Konstantinos Kaváfis (1863–1933), Joe Orton (1933–1967), Christopher Isherwood (1904–1986), and Gary Glickman, among others.

On the one hand, the context of the 1980s was marked by the achievement of rights by the queer community. Many bars attended by gays, lesbians, and *travestis*[14] were becoming famous in São Paulo, the circulation of the newspaper *O Lampião da Esquina* grew more and more, and the depathologization of homosexuality took its first steps. Leonilson felt increasingly freer to hang out with his friends and potential lovers at gay saunas and night parties in the city. On the other hand, some factors hindered his possibilities of sexual expression—homophobia, which was strengthened by HIV and AIDS epidemics from the second half of the 80s on, the fear of his profoundly Catholic family, to which he was close, and his internal repressions and traumas, common to most queer people who had been socialized in oppressive contexts.

It is no coincidence that his production gains a liminal tone between homosexual eroticism, abstraction, and poetry from the end of that decade on.

374. Leonilson
Vogue ideal (Fanzine)
[Ideal Vogue (Fanzine)], 1976

Marker, ballpoint pen,
and graphite on paper
34 × 25 cm
Private collection,
São Paulo, Brazil
PL.2550.1/01

375. Leonilson
Neuza, *circa* 1976

Marker, ballpoint pen,
and graphite on paper
29.5 × 21.5 cm
Private collection,
São Paulo, Brazil
PL.2289.0/00

Sexual iconography from the gay world, references to BDSM and phallic images start emerging in his work, while the boundaries between his public and private lives become increasingly indefinite.

***

After talking to his friend Ricardo Ferreira Henrique (a translator and literature teacher) about keeping a diary, Leonilson decided to begin his autobiography. The artist bought a portable recorder and on April 4, 1990, started his spoken diary, which would accompany him until a few months before his death in May 1993. In the recordings, Leonilson reports details of his personal and romantic lives, his sexual desires, episodes of Platonic love, professional relations, thoughts, dreams, and ideas for works.

The goal was to give the tapes to Ferreira, who would transcribe them into a book, as attested by the artist himself. After his passing, the tapes were kept in a dresser and recovered months later by Eduardo Brandão, becoming part of the archive of Projeto Leonilson, the institution in charge of the artist's estate. The first work made from the recordings was *Com o oceano inteiro para nadar* [With the Whole Ocean to Swim] (1997), a video about the life and work of the artist which was shot by Karen Harley. When listening to the recordings, the director came across the statement: "If one day I die, I will leave all these tapes as a gift for him [Ricardo]." She shared this excerpt with Brandão, who immediately sent the tapes to Ferreira. Between 1996 and 2000, Ferreira transcribed the tapes, which were proofread and edited by colleagues. To preserve the identity of those people Leonilson mentioned, he decided to change their names for the characters of Homer's *Odyssey*. The title, *Frescœ Ulisses*, had been suggested by Leonilson.

After the book was ready for release by the publishing house Siciliano, the artist's family prevented its publication, and the material never became public. Years later, Carlos Nader, with the support of Projeto Leonilson, retrieved the tapes and directed a second documentary, *A paixão de JL* [JL's Passion], released in 2014, which presented until then unrevealed excerpts from the recordings.

In both documentaries and in the tapes, one can track a series of romantic relationships and friendships. Leonilson depicted these men in several works without identifying them by their real names, using terms such as "Al," "A.P." and "the mathematician" or mentions to Rio de Janeiro, which refer to Adriano Pedrosa [imgs. 71, 151, 362]. The latter, then a young artist, and Leonilson met in 1989, at the Escola de Artes Visuais do Parque Lage in Rio de Janeiro, where Pedrosa studied. They had a romantic relationship and later became friends, establishing an intense intellectual exchange, as the interview published in this book attests. Around 1991, after visiting Valdirlei Dias Nunes' first solo exhibition at Casa Triângulo, in downtown São Paulo, Leonilson showed interest in meeting the artist and exchanging a painting with him. The first time they met, the artists found an intense aesthetic affinity, which evolved into a brief romantic relationship. They met only for a few weekends since Dias Nunes lived at that time in Maringá, Paraná state. A few weeks after they had met, Leonilson found out he was HIV-positive, a discovery that would change definitely the course of the relationship. Several works were produced in this context, such as *O apaixonado, o zig zag, 5 minutos* [The Enamored One, the Zigzag, 5 Minutes] (1991) [img. 186], *Das estrelas e de seus olhos* [Of the Stars and of Their Eyes] (1991), and *Se você sonha com nuvens* [If you Dream of Clouds] (*circa* 1991) [img. 162].

The autobiography in the artist's productions and oral accounts describes a romantic, passionate, and impulsive person. Nonetheless, his friends and ex-boyfriends say he was shy, reserved, methodic, and sometimes strict regarding his relationships, features that are not always present in the works.

[...] He wouldn't talk about his sexuality with other people, neither with Jan nor me. He didn't go to meet guys—or, he didn't seem to be very romantic. He was very theoretical: "This guy is super nice. He's a doctor and I think I like him very much." But in the end, he wouldn't even talk to the guy, which I found a very funny way of being gay. It was more in his dreams and in his mind than it was actually about meeting people, talking to them, getting interested, and kissing. There was none of that. [15]

On the other side, the consolidation and wide circulation of his production, especially after his death, proved that investigating the truthfulness of the facts can be a hard task since such stories have become each time more concrete in the audience's imagination as they have been repeatedly told through his works.

In the public sphere, the moment during which his sexuality was externalized through work changed his image, turning it into that of an artist belonging to a minority and, at the same time, bringing it closer to a political dimension. In 1990, he

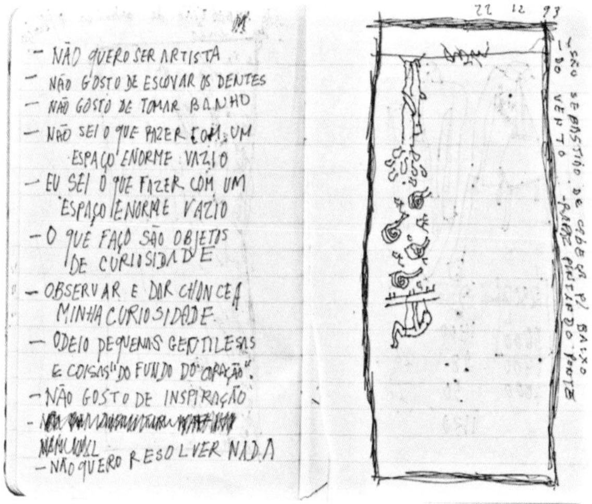

376

376. Leonilson

Artist's Notebook 26, pages 22-23, 1992-93
Courtesy of Projeto Leonilson, São Paulo, Brazil

opened his solo exhibition at the Centro Cultural São Paulo (CCSP), maybe his most openly political show, featuring works with sexual content, romantic and erotic dedications, as well as critical references to other artists and their productions. The next year, he started illustrating the lifestyle column "Talk of the town—o ti-ti-ti da cidade," written by journalist Barbara Gancia for *Folha de S. Paulo*. The column appeared in several sections of the newspaper, such as "Acontece São Paulo," "Ilustrada," "Cotidiano," and "Fim de Semana." The 106 drawings, published weekly from March 1991 to May 1993, were caustic, ironic, critical, and strictly aligned with the subjects in question, which would always address social, cultural, and political issues.

***

On August 22, 1991, Leonilson took an HIV test, and the result was positive. By that time, the number of people contaminated was rising exponentially, and the artist had already expressed his fear of getting infected and how this influenced the way he related to other people. The artist told his diagnosis to Brandão and kept it a secret from other friends and family for months until it was virtually impossible to hide his condition. Leonilson, who at that time was gaining great recognition and visibility, kept producing, going out with friends, and traveling for both work and leisure purposes.

In 1992, the artist traveled to Fortaleza, and his health condition, which up until then wasn't severe, worsened. He was debilitated when he returned to São Paulo and moved in with Brandão and Fjeld so he could receive medical care and help from both the couple and nurses. He transferred his studio to the Pinheiros neighborhood and didn't stop working. That was when the artist started producing exclusively drawings and embroideries, since the paints were toxic and caused allergies in his skin.

Leonilson had always been asthmatic. During his childhood, he would often go to medical appointments, and as an adult, he couldn't run out of his medication. His condition, associated with the effects of the virus, was responsible for drastically aggravating his condition after he got pneumonia, which required blood transfusions. From 1992 on, he lost weight, and his appearance made his sickness evident even before he could talk about it. People around him were worried and feared his death. Therefore, friends and colleagues who loved and admired him visited him frequently, with people "queueing up"[16] to see him. His relatives became even closer to him, supplicating and collectively praying in the hope of curing him. At the beginning of 1993, Leonilson got worse and moved to the Alphaville neighborhood with his sister Ana Lenilda Dias to live in a broad space, far from the city, where he would have more privacy and quietness.

Despite being debilitated, Leonilson began his last work, one of the most significant of his career. *Instalação sobre duas figuras* [Installation on Two Figures] (1993) [imgs. 236-39], exhibited at the Capela do Morumbi, currently a museum in São Paulo, became famous for turning the absence, ethereality and ephemerality related to a decaying body into something physical. In a symbolic circle, the religiosity that accompanied him since his birth emerged as a closure for his artistic journey, even though assuming subverted values and traditions.

Leonilson passed away on May 28, 1993, at his parents' house, while sleeping. A few months after that, friends, family, and colleagues from work gathered to find ways of preserving his work. In a collaborative initiative, they started developing what would become Projeto Leonilson, a non-profit institution founded officially in 1995. The project, led by Leonilson's sister, Ana Lenice Dias, has over four thousand cataloged works, and new entries are still being processed.

More than three decades after his death, the artist's production stands out for its autobiographical and subjective traits, marked by existential reflections, moments of affection, expressions of sexuality, and gender performativity. Circulating both nationally and internationally, his legacy remains alive, powerful, and fresh.

Translated from Portuguese by Lara Rivetti

Teo Teotonio, Assistant Curator, MASP

NOTES

1 This biographical note was written based on texts and interviews published in Lisette Lagnado, *Leonilson: são tantas as verdades [So Many Are the Truths]* (São Paulo: Projeto Leonilson, 2019); Adriano Pedrosa, *Leonilson: Truth, Fiction* (São Paulo/Rio de Janeiro: Pinacoteca do Estado/Cobogó, 2014); Ana Lenice Dias and Gabriela Dias Clemente (eds.), *Leonilson: catálogo raisonné* (São Paulo: Projeto Leonilson, 2017); and Krist Gruijthuijsen, *Leonilson: Drawn* (1975-1993) (Berlin: Hatje Cantz Verlag, 2020). Interviews were also made with Dora Longo Bahia, Eduardo Brandão, and Gabriela Dias, whom I thank.

2 This region was incorporated into the Amazonas state until 1943 when the Federal Territory of Guaporé was made official. Currently, the area corresponds to the Rondônia state.

3 The text that had the greatest repercussion was "Cartilha secreta" [Secret Guidebook], published in the exhibition catalog *Leonilson* (São Paulo: Galeria de Arte São Paulo, 1991).

4 Leonilson and Adriano Pedrosa, "Concentrated Conversations." In: Krist Gruijthuijsen, *Leonilson: Drawn* (1975-1993) (Berlin: Hatje Cantz Verlag, 2020), 259.

5 See Jan Fjeld, "Um Leo Possível." In: Ana Lenice Dias and Gabriela Dias Clemente (eds.), 2017, op. cit.

6 The Casa de Velázquez holds open art courses, artistic residencies, and research and investigation centers in arts and human sciences. The institution comprises five French schools based in Madrid, Spain: The French School of Athens, the French School of Rome, the French Institute for Oriental Archaeology of Cairo, and the French School of the Middle East.

7 Leonilson and Adriano Pedrosa, 2015, op. cit., 264.

8 The group, founded in 1974, became famous after enlivening the theatrical scene in Rio de Janeiro during the dictatorship, especially due to the informal, experimental, and critical features of its plays. Its leading members were Regina Casé, Luiz Fernando Guimarães, Perfeito Fortuna, Patrícia Travassos, Evandro Mesquita, and Hamilton Vaz Pereira. *A farra da Terra*, presented in 1983, was the group's last performance.

9 The period between 1968 and 1978 is usually called the "Years of Lead," marked by the violent set of repressive measures enforced by the civil-military dictatorship at the time. [Editor's Note]

10 Pedro H. G. Ferreira de Souza, *Uma história da desigualdade: a concentração de renda entre os ricos no Brasil* (1926-2013) (São Paulo: Hucitec, 2018).

11 Leonilson and Adriano Pedrosa, 2020, op. cit., 269.

12 Ibid., 303.

13 Inscription by Leonilson on the magazine's first page. In: Ana Lenice Dias and Gabriela Dias Clemente, 2017, op. cit., 85.

14 *Travesti* is a Latin-American gender identity. The term was coined during the years of military dictatorships in Latin America (*circa* 1960s–80s) to pejoratively refer to feminine-presenting transgender people identities, marginalized, persecuted, and killed by the regime. The term was later adopted by the LGBTQIA+ community as a way to honor the particular experience and identity of *travestis* in Latin America.

15 Eduardo Brandão in the interview "Conversation with Eduardo Brandão and Jan Fjeld," by Krist Gruijthuijsen. In: Krist Gruijthuijsen, 2020, op. cit., 117.

16 Eduardo Brandão, in a private conversation with the author in April 2024.

EXHI BITION HISTO RY

SOLO EXHIBITIONS

1980
Cartas a um amigo. Museu de Arte Moderna da Bahia, Salvador

1981
Cartas al hombre. Casa do Brasil, Madrid, Spain

1982
José Leonilson. Galleria Fernando Pellegrino, Bologna, Italy

1983
Leonilson. Galeria Tina Presser, Porto Alegre, Brazil
Leonilson — desenhos pinturas. Galeria Luisa Strina, São Paulo, Brazil
Leonilson — pinturas e desenhos. Thomas Cohn Arte Contemporânea, Rio de Janeiro, Brazil

1984
Leonilson. Arte Galeria, Fortaleza, Brazil

1985
Leonilson. Espaço Capital Arte Contemporânea, Brasília, Brazil
Leonilson. Galeria Luisa Strina, São Paulo, Brazil
Leonilson. Thomas Cohn Arte Contemporânea, Rio de Janeiro, Brazil

1986
Leonilson — Dibujos. Casa do Brasil, Madrid, Spain

1987
Leonilson. Usina Arte Contemporânea, Vitória, Brazil
Leonilson — Trabalhos recentes. Galeria Luisa Strina, São Paulo, Brazil
Moving Mountains. Städtische Galerie im Lenbachhaus, Munich, Germany

1988
Leonilson — O inconformado. Thomas Cohn Arte Contemporânea, Rio de Janeiro, Brazil

1989
Leonilson. Galeria Luisa Strina, São Paulo, Brazil

1990
Leonilson. Pulitzer Art Gallery, Amsterdam, Netherlands
Leonilson (Exposições individuais simultâneas). Centro Cultural São Paulo (CCSP), Brazil

1991
Leonilson. Galeria São Paulo, Brazil
Leonilson. Thomas Cohn Arte Contemporânea, Rio de Janeiro, Brazil

1993
Leonilson. Capela do Morumbi, São Paulo, Brazil
Leonilson. Galeria São Paulo, Brazil
Leonilson 1993. Thomas Cohn Arte Contemporânea, Rio de Janeiro, Brazil
Lembrando Leonilson. Thomas Cohn Arte Contemporânea, Rio de Janeiro, Brazil

1994
Projeto Leonilson. Galeria Luisa Strina, São Paulo, Brazil

1995
Leonilson: são tantas as verdades. Centro Cultural Fiesp/Galeria de Arte do Sesi, São Paulo, Brazil
Zé. Paço Imperial, Rio de Janeiro, Brazil

1996
Leonilson: são tantas as verdades. Centro Cultural Banco do Brasil, Rio de Janeiro, Brazil
Leonilson: Selected Works. Randolph Street Gallery, Chicago, United States

1997
Leonilson. Centro Cultural Light, Rio de Janeiro, Brazil
Leonilson: o solitário inconformado. Museu de Arte Contemporânea de Americana, São Paulo, Brazil
Leonilson: são tantas as verdades. Museu de Arte da Pampulha, Belo Horizonte, Brazil

1998
Leonilson. Galeria Thomas Cohn, Rio de Janeiro, Brazil

2003
A moda e Leonilson. Galeria do Hotel Lycra, São Paulo, Brazil
Leonilson "Fique firme, seja forte." Galeria Luisa Strina, São Paulo, Brazil
Leonilson na 18ª Bienal de São Paulo, Brazil — 1985. Pinacoteca do Estado de São Paulo, Brazil

2005
Leonilson — desenhos. Galeria Luisa Strina, São Paulo, Brazil

2006
Leonilson. Centro Cultural Banco do Nordeste — Cariri, Juazeiro do Norte, Ceará, Brazil
Leonilson em Fortaleza. Centro Cultural Banco do Nordeste, Fortaleza, Brazil

2007
Diário de bordo: uma viagem com Leonilson. Caixa Cultural São Paulo, Brazil

2008
Diário de bordo: uma viagem com Leonilson. Caixa Cultural Brasília, Brazil
Diário de bordo: uma viagem com Leonilson. Caixa Cultural Salvador, Brazil
Leonilson — desenhos. Centro Universitário Maria Antonia da Universidade de São Paulo, Brazil

2009
O jovem Leonilson: desenhos 1974-1982. Galeria Luisa Strina, São Paulo, Brazil
Diário de bordo: uma viagem com Leonilson. Espaço Cultural Unifor, Fortaleza, Brazil

2011
Solitário inconformado e outras gravuras de Leonilson. Galeria Logo, São Paulo, Brazil

2012
Leonilson — sob o peso dos meus amores. Fundação Iberê Camargo, Porto Alegre, Brazil

2013
Leonilson: inflamável. Museu de Arte Contemporânea do Ceará, Fortaleza, Brazil

2014
Leonilson: verdades e mentiras. Galeria Superfície, São Paulo, Brazil
Leonilson: Truth, Fiction. Estação Pinacoteca, São Paulo, Brazil

2015
Leonilson: Truth, Fiction. Centro Cultural Banco do Brasil, Rio de Janeiro, Brazil

2017
Do silêncio: vers Leonilson. Galeria Marilia Razuk, São Paulo, Brazil
Leonilson: arquivo e memória vivos. Espaço Cultural Unifor, Fortaleza, Brazil
José Leonilson: Empty Man. Americas Society, New York, United States

2019
Leonilson: arquivo e memória vivos. Galeria de Arte do Centro Cultural Fiesp, São Paulo, Brazil
Leonilson por Antonio Dias. Galeria Multiarte, Fortaleza, Brazil
Leonilson por Antonio Dias. Pinakotheke Cultural, Rio de Janeiro, Brazil
Leonilson por Antonio Dias. Pinakotheke, São Paulo, Brazil

2020
Leonilson: Drawn (1975-1993). KW Institute for Contemporary Art, Berlin, Germany

2021
Leonilson: Drawn (1975-1993). Malmö Konsthall, Sweden

2022
Leonilson: Drawn (1975-1993). Fundação de Serralves, Museu de Arte Contemporânea, Porto, Portugal

2023
Leonilson. Corpo político. Almeida & Dale, São Paulo, Brazil
Leonilson: das montanhas protetoras e ao longe, vulcões, rios, furacões, mares, abismos e das amizades. Pinacoteca do Ceará, Fortaleza, Brazil
Leonilson e o artista do nosso tempo. Verve Galeria, São Paulo, Brazil
Leonilson: territórios em travessias. Espaço Cultural Unifor, Fortaleza, Brazil
O menino Leonilson. Galeria Desconexo, Fortaleza, Brazil

2024

Leonilson em cartaz. Galeria Mapa, São Paulo, Brazil

Leonilson: Now and Opportunities. Museu de Arte de São Paulo Assis Chateaubriand, Brazil

GROUP EXHIBITIONS

1977

Arte e pensamento ecológico. Faculdade de Arquitetura e Urbanismo de Santos, São Paulo, Brazil

1979

IV Salão de Arte Contemporânea da Associação dos Artistas Plásticos de Jundiaí. Centro Cultural Bandeirantes, São Paulo, Brazil

1980

II Mostra Nova — Grupo Três. Centro de Artes Shopping News, São Paulo, Brazil

III Salão Jovem de Arte Contemporânea. Centro Cívico de Santo André, São Paulo, Brazil

V SARP — Salão de Arte Contemporânea de Ribeirão Preto. Casa da Cultura de Ribeirão Preto, São Paulo, Brazil

Desenho jovem. Museu de Arte Contemporânea da Universidade de São Paulo, Brazil

José Leonilson/Luiz Zerbini. Teatro Lira Paulistana, São Paulo, Brazil

Panorama de arte atual brasileira 80: desenho e gravura. Museu de Arte Moderna de São Paulo, Brazil

1981

Giovane Arte Internazionale. Galleria Giuli, Lecce, Italy

José Leonilson/Luiz Zerbini. Casa do Brasil, Madrid, Spain

Viva arte brasileña. Casa do Brasil, Madrid, Spain

1982

Galleria Fernando Pellegrino, Bologna, Italy

1983

6° Salão Nacional de Artes Plásticas. Museu de Arte Moderna do Rio de Janeiro, Brazil

13 Artistas — 13 Obras. Thomas Cohn Arte Contemporânea, Rio de Janeiro, Brazil

À flor da pele: pintura e prazer. Centro Empresarial Rio, Rio de Janeiro, Brazil

Arte Galeria: exposição de inauguração. Arte Galeria, Fortaleza, Brazil

Brasil pintura. Palácio das Artes, Belo Horizonte, Brazil

1984

Arte Brasileira Atual: 1984. Galeria de Artes UFF, Rio de Janeiro, Brazil

Coleção Gilberto Chateaubriand: retrato e auto-retrato da arte brasileira. Museu de Arte Moderna de São Paulo, Brazil

Como vai você, Geração 80?. Escola de Artes Visuais do Parque Lage, Rio de Janeiro, Brazil

Leda Catunda/Sergio/Leonilson/Cozzolino. Galeria Luisa Strina, São Paulo, Brazil

Stand 320: jovem pintura brasileira. Thomas Cohn Arte Contemporânea, Rio de Janeiro, Brazil

1985

18ª Bienal Internacional de São Paulo. Fundação Bienal de São Paulo, Brazil

Arte em São Paulo. Galeria São Paulo, Brazil

Brasilidade e independência. Foyer do Teatro Nacional de Brasília, Brazil

Brasilidade e independência. Museu da Casa Brasileira, São Paulo, Brazil

Fall-out—Aspetti della pittura Internazionale senza centro né margini. Convitto Nazionale Pasquale Galluppi, Catanzaro, Italy

Nouvelle Biennale de Paris. Grande Halle du Parc de la Villette, France

Nueva Pintura Brasileña. Centro de Arte y Comunicación, Buenos Aires, Argentina

Velha mania: desenho brasileiro. Escola de Artes Visuais do Parque Lage, Rio de Janeiro, Brazil

1986

I Exposição Internacional de Esculturas Efêmeras. Parque Ecológico do Cocó, Fortaleza, Brazil

A conquista do espaço. Rio Design Center, Rio de Janeiro, Brazil

A nova dimensão do objeto. Museu de Arte Contemporânea da Universidade de São Paulo, Brazil

Albert Hien: transatlantik, transatlantique, transatlantico. Josef-Haubrich-Kunsthalle, Cologne, Germany

Arte contemporânea brasileira. Petite Galerie, Rio de Janeiro, Brazil

Bienal Latinoamericana de Arte sobre Papel. Salas Nacionales de Exposición, Buenos Aires, Argentina

Caminhos do desenho brasileiro. Museu de Arte do Rio Grande do Sul Ado Malagoli, Porto Alegre, Brazil

Coletiva do acervo. Galeria Luisa Strina, São Paulo, Brazil

Coleção Rubem Knijnik — arte brasileira anos 60/70/80. Museu de Arte do Rio Grande do Sul Ado Malagoli, Porto Alegre, Brazil

Doze anos de trabalho conjunto. Galeria Luisa Strina, São Paulo, Brazil

Hien/Leonilson. Walter Storms Galerie, Munich, Germany

Imagine — o planeta saúda o cometa. Arte Galeria, Fortaleza, Brazil

Transvanguarda e culturas nacionais. Museu de Arte Moderna do Rio de Janeiro, Brazil

1987

Ao colecionador. Museu de Arte Moderna do Rio de Janeiro, Brazil

Coletiva. Galeria Paulo Figueiredo, São Paulo, Brazil

Coletiva de pinturas. Thomas Cohn Arte Contemporânea, Rio de Janeiro, Brazil

Modernidade: art brésilien du 20e. siècle. Musée d'Art Moderne de la Ville de Paris, France

Ouverture Brésilienne. Centre d'Art Contemporain — Galerie Fernand Léger, Paris, France

1988

34 artistas contemporâneos brasileiros. Subdistrito Comercial de Arte, São Paulo, Brazil

1981-1987. Galeria Arco Arte Contemporânea, Madrid, Spain

Albert Hien/Leonilson. Pulitzer Art Gallery, Amsterdam, Netherlands

Arte Hoje — 88/XIII Salão de Arte de Ribeirão Preto Nacional — Contemporâneo. Casa da Cultura, Ribeirão Preto, São Paulo, Brazil

Brasil Já: Beispiele zeitgenössischer brasilianischer Malerei. Galerie Landesgirokasse, Stuttgart, Germany

Brasil Já: Beispiele zeitgenössischer brasilianischer Malerei. Museum Morsbroich, Leverkusen, Germany

Coletiva — Arco arte contemporânea. Arco Arte Contemporânea, Madrid, Spain

Geração 80 pensando 68. Espaço Cultural Sérgio Porto, Rio de Janeiro, Brazil

Modernidade arte brasileira século XX. Museu de Arte Moderna de São Paulo, Brazil

Seven Artists on Invitation. Pulitzer Art Gallery, Amsterdam, Netherlands.

1989

8 artistas pintam a revolução francesa. Casa de Cultura Laura Alvim, Rio de Janeiro, Brazil

Arte contemporânea São Paulo — perspectivas recentes. Centro Cultural São Paulo (CCSP), Brazil

Brasil Já: Beispiele zeitgenössischer brasilianischer Malerei. Sprengel Museum, Hanover, Germany

Cada cabeça uma sentença. Centro Cultural da Universidade Federal de Minas Gerais, Belo Horizonte, Brazil

Cada cabeça uma sentença. Museu de Arte Moderna de São Paulo, Brazil

Cada cabeça uma sentença. Museu Mariano Procópio, Juiz de Fora, Minas Gerais, Brazil

Cada cabeça uma sentença. Museu Nacional de Belas Artes, Rio de Janeiro, Brazil

Coleção particular de Eduardo Brandão. Casa Triângulo, São Paulo, Brazil

Estampes et Révolution, 200 Ans Après. Fondation Nationale des Arts Graphiques et Plastiques, Paris, France

Fabio Cardoso, Leonilson, Daniel Senise, Luiz Zerbini. Museu de Arte de São Paulo Assis Chateaubriand, Brazil

Nada hás de temer. Galeria Gesto Gráfico, Belo Horizonte, Brazil

Os bombeiros não são corruptos. Espaço Capital Arte Contemporânea, São Paulo, Brazil

Panorama da arte atual brasileira. Museu de Arte Moderna de São Paulo, Brazil

1990

[EAV 15 anos]. Escola de Artes Visuais do Parque Lage, Rio de Janeiro, Brazil

Estampes et Révolution, 200 ans aprés. Chapelle de L'Oratoire, Clermont-Ferrand, France

Galeria Gesto Gráfico 10 Anos. Galeria Gesto Gráfico, Belo Horizonte, Brazil

Prêmio Brasília de Artes Plásticas. Museu de Arte de Brasília, Brazil

1991

Arte contemporânea no centro histórico. Sede da Indústria Santa Matilde, Rio de Janeiro, Brazil

Artistas contemporâneos no Engenho Central. Engenho Central, São Paulo, Brazil

BR 80 — Pintura Brasil década 80. Itaú Cultural, São Paulo, Brazil

Brasil — La Nueva Generación. Museo de Bellas Artes, Caracas, Venezuela

Calendário da anistia internacional — Seção Brasileira. Museu de Arte Moderna do Rio de Janeiro, Brazil

Coleção João Pedrosa — Arte dos anos 80. Galeria Millan, São Paulo, Brazil

Instalação Porto 91. Porto de Vitória, Brazil

Viva Brasil Viva. Liljevalchs Konsthall, Stockholm, Sweden

1992

X Mostra da gravura cidade de Curitiba. Museu da Gravura Cidade de Curitiba, Brazil

10ª Exposição Brasil-Japão de arte contemporânea. Gobankan Seibu Akarenga Hall, Sapporo, Japan

10ª Exposição Brasil-Japão de Arte Contemporânea. MOA Museum of Art, Atami, Japan
10ª Exposição Brasil-Japão de Arte Contemporânea. Nagoya Shimin Gallery, Japan
10ª Exposição Brasil-Japão de Arte Contemporânea. Tokyo Central Museum of Art, Japan
A caminho de Niterói. Paço Imperial, Rio de Janeiro, Brazil
Abertura temporada 1992. Subdistrito Comercial de Arte, São Paulo, Brazil
Branco dominante. Galeria São Paulo, Brazil
Visões de Vitória. Capela Santa Luzia, Vitória, Brazil
Moritz Ebinger, Albert Hien, Leonilson. Pulitzer Art Gallery, Amsterdam, Netherlands

1993

A caminho de Niterói II. Paço Imperial, Rio de Janeiro, Brazil
Aids — consciência e arte. Museu de Arte Contemporânea do Paraná, Curitiba, Brazil
Arte erótica. Museu de Arte Moderna do Rio de Janeiro, Brazil
Arte moderna brasileira na Coleção Gilberto Chateaubriand. Museu de Arte Moderna do Rio de Janeiro, Brazil
Brasil: segni d'Arte — Libri e video — 1950-1993. Biblioteca Nazionale Braidense, Milan, Italy
Brasil: segni d'Arte — Libri e video — 1950-1993. Fondazione Scientifica Querini Stampalia, Venice, Italy
Brasil: segni d'Arte — Libri e video — 1950-1993. Galeria Candido Portinari, Rio de Janeiro, Brazil
Brazil: Images Of The 80's & 90's. Art Museum of the Americas, Washington, D.C., United States
Brazilian Contemporary Art. Museu de Arte Contemporânea da Universidade de São Paulo, Brazil
Cartografías. Museo de Artes Visuales Alejandro Otero, Caracas, Venezuela
Cartografías: 14 artistas latinoamericanos. Biblioteca Luis-Angel Arango, Casa Luis Lópes de Mesa, Bogotá, Colombia
Cartographies: 14 Artists from Latin America. The Winnipeg Art Gallery, Canada
Encontros e tendências. Museu de Arte Contemporânea da Universidade de São Paulo, Brazil
Projetos figurativos na arte brasileira. Museu de Arte do Rio Grande do Sul Ado Malagoli, Porto Alegre, Brazil
Representação, presenças decisivas. Paço das Artes, São Paulo, Brazil

1994

Bastidores da criação. Oficina Cultural Oswald de Andrade, São Paulo, Brazil
Bienal Brasil Século XX. Pavilhão Ciccillo Matarazzo, São Paulo, Brazil
Brasil — Imagens dos anos 80 e 90. Casa das Rosas, São Paulo, Brazil
Brasil — Imagens dos anos 80 e 90. Museu de Arte Moderna do Rio de Janeiro, Brazil
Cartographies: 14 Artists from Latin America. National Gallery of Canada, Ottawa
Cartographies: 14 Artists from Latin America. The Bronx Museum of the Arts, New York, United States
Luisa Strina — 20 anos de arte brasileira. Museu de Arte de São Paulo Assis Chateaubriand, Brazil
Outros territórios: travessia pela sexualidade. Museu da Imagem e do Som, São Paulo, Brazil
Paisagens. Galeria São Paulo, Brazil
Presença White Martins no MAM. Museu de Arte Moderna do Rio de Janeiro, Brazil

1995

Anos 80: o palco da diversidade. Centro Cultural Fiesp/Galeria de Arte do Sesi, São Paulo, Brazil
Artistas colecionistas. Valu Oria Galeria de Arte, São Paulo, Brazil
Cartografías. Fundación La Caixa, Madrid, Spain
Infância perversa — fábulas sobre a memória e o tempo. Museu de Arte Moderna da Bahia, Salvador, Brazil
Infância perversa — fábulas sobre a memória e o tempo. Museu de Arte Moderna do Rio de Janeiro, Brazil
O desenho em São Paulo, Brazil 1956-1995. Galeria Nara Roesler, São Paulo, Brazil
Pinturas de Laura. Casa de Cultura Laura Alvim, Rio de Janeiro, Brazil
Resumo Hoje. Museu Mineiro, Belo Horizonte, Brazil
Selections Brazil. The Drawing Center, New York, United States
Thomas Cohn Arte Contemporânea visita Galeria Millan. Galeria Millan, São Paulo, Brazil

1996

15 artistas brasileiros. Museu de Arte Moderna de São Paulo, Brazil
Acervo. Galeria São Paulo, Brazil
Arte brasileira contemporânea. Museu de Arte Moderna de São Paulo, Brazil
Arte brasileira contemporânea. Bayer AG – Feierabendlhaus, Germany
Arte contemporânea brasileira na Coleção João Sattamini. Museu de Arte Contemporânea de Niterói, Rio de Janeiro, Brazil
Coleção Carioca. Espaço Cultural dos Correios, Rio de Janeiro, Brazil
Ouro de artista. Galeria Casa Triângulo, São Paulo, Brazil
Pequenas mãos. Centro Cultural Alumni, São Paulo, Brazil
Pequenas mãos. Paço Imperial, Rio de Janeiro, Brazil
Projects 53: Oliver Herring/Leonilson. The Museum of Modern Art, New York, United States

1997

XXV Salão de Arte Contemporânea de Santo André. Paço Municipal de Santo André, São Paulo, Brazil
5th International Istanbul Biennial: on life, beauty, translations and other difficulties. Türkiye
15 artistas brasileiros. Museu de Arte Moderna da Bahia, Salvador, Brazil
15 artistas brasileiros. Museu de Arte Moderna do Rio de Janeiro, Brazil
200 anos de Litografia Brasil-Estados Unidos. Museu da Gravura Cidade de Curitiba, Brazil
Acervo 1997. Galeria São Paulo, Brazil
Ar. Paço Imperial, Rio de Janeiro, Brazil
Así está la cosa: instalación y arte objeto en América Latina. Centro Cultural Arte Contemporáneo, Mexico City
Brasil — Reflexão 97 — A arte contemporânea da gravura. Museu Metropolitano de Arte de Curitiba, Brazil
Brito Cimino: arte contemporânea e moderna. Brito Cimino Arte Contemporânea e Moderna, São Paulo, Brazil
Doações recentes — Coleção Theodorino Torquato Dias e Carmen Bezerra Dias. Museu de Arte Moderna de São Paulo, Brazil
Heranças contemporâneas. Museu de Arte Contemporânea da Universidade de São Paulo, Brazil
MAC 1 ano. Museu de Arte Contemporânea de Niterói, Rio de Janeiro, Brazil
Magnetic: drawings in dialogue. Sean Kelly Gallery, New York, United States
Visões e (sub)versões: cada olhar uma história. Museu de Arte Contemporânea de Niterói, Rio de Janeiro, Brazil

1998

Afinidades eletivas I — O olhar do colecionador: Coleção Kim Esteve. Casa das Rosas, São Paulo, Brazil
Arte contemporânea brasileira: um e outro, 24ª Bienal Internacional de São Paulo. Brazil
COHNtemporânea. Galeria Thomas Cohn, Rio de Janeiro, Brazil
Doações Recentes 1997-1998. Museu de Arte Moderna de São Paulo, Brazil
Espelho da Bienal. Museu de Arte Contemporânea de Niterói, Rio de Janeiro, Brazil
Leonilson e Rochelle Costi. Brito Cimino Arte Contemporânea e Moderna, São Paulo, Brazil
Loose threads. Serpentine Gallery, London, England
Medidas de si. Itaú Cultural, Campinas, São Paulo, Brazil
Medidas de si. Museu de Arte Moderna de São Paulo, Brazil
Múltiplos. Valu Oria Galeria de Arte, São Paulo, Brazil
Os anos 80. Marina Potrich Galeria de Arte, Goiânia, Brazil
O moderno e o contemporâneo na arte brasileira: Coleção Gilberto Chateaubriand — MAM-RJ. Museu de Arte de São Paulo Assis Chateaubriand, Brazil
O suporte da palavra. Itaú Cultural, Belo Horizonte, Brazil
O suporte da palavra. Museu de Arte Moderna de São Paulo, Brazil
Preview 98. Galeria Cohn Edelstein, São Paulo, Brazil
Seleção. Brito Cimino Arte Contemporânea e Moderna, São Paulo, Brazil

1999

80 anos de arte no Brasil. Museu de Arte Moderna de São Paulo, Brazil
Devoção. Museu de Arte Moderna de São Paulo, Brazil
Figuras, quase figuras. Museu de Arte Moderna de São Paulo, Brazil
Paisagem sublime. Museu de Arte Moderna de São Paulo, Brazil

2000

XII Mostra da Gravura de Curitiba — Marcas do corpo, dobras da alma. Museu da Gravura Cidade de Curitiba, Brazil
A figura humana na Coleção Itaú. Itaú Cultural, São Paulo, Brazil
Acervo da Galeria São Paulo. Galeria São Paulo, Brazil
Arte e erotismo. Galeria Nara Roesler, São Paulo, Brazil
Brasil: psicanálise e modernismo. Museu de Arte de São Paulo Assis Chateaubriand, Brazil
F[r]icciones — Versiones del Sur: cinco propuestas en torno al arte en América. Museo Nacional Centro de Arte Reina Sofia, Madrid, Spain

Galeria São Paulo — Acervo 2000. Galeria São Paulo, Brazil
Mostra do Redescobrimento — Brasil 500 anos. Fundação Bienal de São Paulo, Brazil
O papel da arte. Centro Cultural Fiesp/ Galeria de Arte do Sesi, São Paulo, Brazil
Palavra/imagem. Museu de Arte Moderna do Rio de Janeiro, Brazil
Século 20: arte do Brasil. Fundação Calouste Gulbenkian, Rio de Janeiro, Brazil
Um oceano inteiro para nadar. Edifício Sede da Caixa Geral de Depósitos, Lisboa, Portugal

2001

Aquarela brasileira. Centro Cultural Light, Rio de Janeiro, Brazil
ARS 01 — Unfolding Perspectives. Kiasma Museum of Contemporary Art, Helsinki, Finland
Coleção Liba e Rubem Knijnik — Arte brasileira contemporânea. Museu de Arte do Rio Grande do Sul Ado Malagoli, Porto Alegre, Brazil
Coleção MAC. Museu de Arte Contemporânea da Universidade de São Paulo, Brazil
Espelho cego — Seleções de uma coleção contemporânea. Museu de Arte Moderna de São Paulo, Brazil
Espelho cego — Seleções de uma coleção contemporânea. Paço Imperial, Rio de Janeiro, Brazil
Gesto, matéria, cor, imagem. Museu de Arte Moderna do Rio de Janeiro, Brazil
Gilberto Chateaubriand: aspectos de uma coleção. Museu de Arte Moderna do Rio de Janeiro, Brazil
O espírito da nossa época — Coleção Dulce e João de Figueiredo Ferraz. Museu de Arte Moderna de São Paulo, Brazil
O espírito da nossa época — Coleção Dulce e João de Figueiredo Ferraz. Museu de Arte Moderna do Rio de Janeiro, Brazil
O Fio da Trama/The Thread Unraveled – Contemporary Brazilian Art. El Museo del Barrio, New York, United States
Palavra/imagem. Museu de Arte Moderna Aloisio Magalhães, Recife, Brazil
Trajetória da luz na arte brasileira. Itaú Cultural, São Paulo, Brazil

2002

28 (+) pintura. Espaço Virgilio Arte Contemporânea, São Paulo, Brazil
Amor no MAM. Museu de Arte Moderna de São Paulo, Brazil
Archivo Pons. Koldo Mitxelena Kulturunea, San Sebastián, Spain
Arte contemporânea: Colecção Caixa Geral de Depósitos – Novas Aquisições. Fundação Caixa Geral de Depósitos — Culturgest, Lisbon, Portugal
Caminhos do contemporâneo. Paço Imperial, Rio de Janeiro, Brazil
Ceará Redescobre o Brasil. Museu de Arte Contemporânea do Ceará, Fortaleza, Brazil
Diálogo, antagonismo e replicação na Coleção João Sattamini. Museu de Arte Contemporânea de Niterói, Rio de Janeiro, Brazil
El hilo de la trama/O fio da trama — Arte contemporáneo brasileño. Museo de Arte Latinoamericano de Buenos Aires
Espelho cego — Seleções de uma coleção contemporânea. Museu de Arte Moderna Aloisio Magalhães, Recife, Brazil
Fragmentos a seu imã — obras primas do MAB. Espaço Cultural Contemporâneo Venâncio (ECCO), Brasília, Brazil
Mapa do agora. Instituto Tomie Ohtake, São Paulo, Brazil
Matéria prima. Museu Oscar Niemeyer, Curitiba, Brazil
Nefelibatas. Museu de Arte Moderna de São Paulo, Brazil
O plano como estrutura/o plano como figura. Museu de Arte Moderna de São Paulo, Brazil
Pintura dos anos 80. Shopping Città America, Rio de Janeiro, Brazil
Recorrências — Coleção Gilberto Chateaubriand. Museu de Arte Moderna do Rio de Janeiro, Brazil

2003

1ª Exposição de arte brasileira — pinturas e desenhos. Centro Cultural Oboé, Fortaleza, Brazil
2080. Museu de Arte Moderna de São Paulo, Brazil
A arte atrás da arte — onde ficam e como viajam as obras de arte. Museu de Arte Moderna de São Paulo, Brazil
Arte em movimento. Galeria de Arte do BNDES, Rio de Janeiro, Brazil
Arteconhecimento — 70 anos USP. Museu de Arte Contemporânea da Universidade de São Paulo, Brazil
Compressores e condensadores. Museu de Arte Moderna de São Paulo, Brazil
Imagetica. Memorial de Curitiba, Brazil
MAC USP 40 anos: interfaces contemporâneas. Museu de Arte Contemporânea da Universidade de São Paulo, Brazil
Meus amigos. Museu de Arte Moderna de São Paulo, Brazil
Mostra coletiva de arte contemporânea. Espaço Cultural Marcantonio Vilaça, Brasília, Brazil
Ordenação e vertigem. Centro Cultural Banco do Brasil, São Paulo, Brazil
Panorama da arte brasileira 2003 (desarrumado) 19 desarranjos. Museu de Arte Moderna de São Paulo, Brazil
Panorama da arte brasileira 2003 (desarrumado) 19 desarranjos. Paço Imperial, Rio de Janeiro, Brazil
Projeto em preto e branco. Silvia Cintra Galeria de Arte, Rio de Janeiro, Brazil
Pulse: Art, Healing and Transformation. The Institute of Contemporary Art, Massachusetts, United States
Tomie Ohtake na trama espiritual da arte brasileira. Instituto Tomie Ohtake, São Paulo, Brazil

2004

A face icônica da arte brasileira. Museu de Arte Moderna do Rio de Janeiro, Brazil
A nova geometria. Galeria Fortes Vilaça, São Paulo, Brazil
Arte contemporânea brasileira nas coleções do Rio. Museu de Arte Moderna do Rio de Janeiro, Brazil
Entre outros... uma coleção. Arte 57, São Paulo, Brazil
Encontros com o Modernismo — destaques do Stedelijk Museum Amsterdam. Estação Pinacoteca, São Paulo, Brazil
Encontros com o Modernismo — destaques do Stedelijk Museum Amsterdam. Museu de Arte Moderna do Rio de Janeiro, Brazil
Espaço lúdico: um olhar sobre a infância na arte brasileira. Galeria de Arte do BNDES, Rio de Janeiro, Brazil
HIV/Aids in the Age of Globalization. Världskulturmuseerna, Stockholm, Sweden
Invenção de mundos — Coleção Marcantonio Vilaça. Museu Vale do Rio Doce, Vila Velha, Brazil
MoMA at el MUSEO — Latin American & Caribbean Art from The Collection of The Museum of Modern Art. El Museo del Barrio, New York, United States
Onde está você, Geração 80?. Centro Cultural Banco do Brasil, Rio de Janeiro, Brazil
Onde está você, Geração 80?. Museu do Estado de Pernambuco, Recife, Brazil
Panorama da arte brasileira 2003 (desarrumado) 19 desarranjos. Museu de Arte Moderna Aloísio Magalhães, Recife, Pernambuco
Tomie Ohtake na trama espiritual da arte brasileira. Museu Nacional de Belas Artes, Rio de Janeiro, Brazil
Tomie Ohtake na trama espiritual da arte brasileira. Museu Oscar Niemeyer, Curitiba, Brazil

2005

20 desarranjos — Panorama da arte brasileira. Museo de Arte Contemporánea de Vigo, Spain
25 Years of The Deutsche Bank Collection. Deutsche Guggenheim, Berlin, Germany
[NE] fronteiras, fluxos e personas. Centro Cultural Banco do Nordeste, Fortaleza, Brazil
Arte brasileira nas coleções públicas e privadas do Ceará. Espaço Cultural Unifor, Fortaleza, Brazil
Desenhos: A-Z. Porta 33, Funchal, Portugal
Doações Recentes 2005 — 3ª edição. Museu de Arte Contemporânea do Ceará, Fortaleza, Brazil
Dor, forma, beleza. Estação Pinacoteca, São Paulo, Brazil
Entre a palavra e a imagem: Coleção Gilberto Chateaubriand. Espaço Cultural Contemporâneo, Brasília, Brazil
Farsites: Urban Crisis and Domestic Symptoms in Recent Contemporary Art. San Diego Museum of Art, Centro Cultural Tijuana, Mexico
Festival Vida & Arte. Centro de Convenções do Ceará, Fortaleza, Brazil
Inverting the Map: Latin American Art from the Tate Collection. Tate, Liverpool, England
Jogo da memória. Museu de Arte Moderna do Rio de Janeiro, Brazil
Longo caminho de um rapaz apaixonado. Fundación Centro de Estudos Brasileiros, Buenos Aires, Argentina
Nmúltiplos. Arte 21 Galeria, Rio de Janeiro, Brazil
Romance *[a novel].* Cristina Guerra Contemporary Art, Lisboa, Portugal

2006

Arte Brasileira no Acervo da Pinacoteca do Estado de São Paulo. Museu de Arte de Ribeirão Preto Pedro Manuel-Gismondi, São Paulo, Brazil
Arte no Brasil no século 20. Museu de Arte do Rio Grande do Sul Ado Malagoli, Porto Alegre, Brazil
Blind Date. Prelacy of the Benedictine Monastery, Galerie Kunstforum Altes Haus, Germany
Deserto. Museu Victor Meirelles, Florianópolis, Santa Catarina
Designu — desdobramentos. Museu de Arte Contemporânea do Ceará, Fortaleza, Brazil
Entre la Palabra y la Imagen. Fundación Luis Seoane, Corunha, Spain
Entrelinhas. Museu de Arte Contemporânea do Ceará, Fortaleza, Brazil

Galeria de Arte Brasileira Moderna e Contemporânea. Museu Nacional de Belas Artes, Rio de Janeiro, Brazil
Longo caminho de um rapaz apaixonado. Museo de Arte Contemporáneo de Rosario, Santa Fé, Argentina
MAM na Oca: arte brasileira do acervo do Museu de Arte Moderna de São Paulo. Brazil
Obras em destaque. Museu de Arte Contemporânea do Ceará, Fortaleza, Brazil
Transforming Chronologies: an Atlas of Drawings — Part Two. The Museum of Modern Art, New York, United States
Um século de arte brasileira — Coleção Gilberto Chateaubriand. Museu de Arte Moderna do Rio de Janeiro, Brazil
Um século de arte brasileira — Coleção Gilberto Chateaubriand. Museu Oscar Niemeyer, Curitiba, Brazil
Um século de arte brasileira — Coleção Gilberto Chateaubriand. Pinacoteca do Estado de São Paulo, Brazil

2007

52ª Biennale di Venezia — pensa com i sensi/senti con la mente — l'arte al presente. Venice, Italy
80/90 — Modernos pós-modernos etc. Instituto Tomie Ohtake, São Paulo, Brazil
A linha do tempo. Galeria Gesto Gráfico, Belo Horizonte, Brazil
Acervo do MARGS — Expressividade na arte brasileira. Galeria Municipal de Arte Gerd Bornheim, Caxias do Sul, Brazil
Acervo do MARGS — Expressividade na arte brasileira. Memorial das Artes de Santa Cruz do Sul, Brazil
Constructing a Poetic Universe: The Diane and Bruce Halle Collection of Latin American Art. The Museum of Fine Arts, Texas, United States
Entre a palavra e a imagem. Palácio Vila Flor, Guimarães, Portugal

Gabinete de desenhos. Museu de Arte Moderna de São Paulo, Brazil
II Edital Caixa de adoção de entidades culturais. Museu de Arte Contemporânea do Ceará, Fortaleza, Brazil
Intimidades — Jogos perigosos. Galeria Marilia Razuk, São Paulo, Brazil
Itaú Contemporâneo – Arte no Brasil 1981-2006. Itaú Cultural, São Paulo, Brazil
L. 50. Museu de Arte Contemporânea do Ceará, Fortaleza, Brazil
Leo, 50. Estação Pinacoteca, São Paulo, Brazil
Mirada: Latino-americanos do MAC USP no Memorial. Galeria Marta Traba, Memorial da América Latina, São Paulo, Brazil
New Perspectives in Latin American Art, 1930-2006: Selections from a Decade of Acquisitions. The Museum of Modern Art, New York, United States
Pintura brasileira no acervo do Museu de Arte Moderna de São Paulo. Museu de Arte do Espírito Santo Dionísio Del Santo, Vitória, Brazil
Um século de arte brasileira — Coleção Gilberto Chateaubriand. Museu de Arte Moderna da Bahia, Salvador, Brazil

2008

20 desarreglos. Museo de Arte Miguel Urrutia, Bogotá, Colombia
41 Salón Nacional de Artistas. Museo de Arte Moderno La Tertulia, Valle del Cauca, Colombia
Acervo do MARGS — Expressividade na Arte Brasileira. Museu de Arte Leopoldo Gotuzzo, Pelotas, Rio Grande do Sul, Brazil
Acervo do MARGS — Expressividade na Arte Brasileira. Museu de Artes Visuais Ruth Schneider, Passo Fundo, Rio Grande do Sul, Brazil
Brasil Brasileiro. Centro Cultural Banco do Brasil, Rio de Janeiro, Brazil
Cover = Reencenação + Repetição. Museu de Arte Moderna de São Paulo, Brazil
Desenhos Estranhos: Colecção Madeira Corporate Services. Porta 33, Funchal, Portugal
Figurações, sonhos e desejos. Museu de Arte Contemporânea de Niterói, Rio de Janeiro, Brazil
Gravuras contemporâneas — Diálogos. Museu da Gravura Cidade de Curitiba, Brazil
Here is Every. Four Decades of Contemporary Art. The Museum of Modern Art, New York, United States
Make Art/Stop AIDS. Fowler Museum at UCLA, California, United States
MAM 60 anos. Museu de Arte Moderna do Rio de Janeiro, Brazil
MAM 60 anos. Pavilhão Lucas Nogueira Garcez (Oca), São Paulo, Brazil
Mercado de arte nº 13. Ricardo Camargo Galeria, São Paulo, Brazil
Moderno ou contemporâneo?. Museu de Arte Moderna de São Paulo, Brazil
Order. Desire. Light. An exhibition of contemporary drawings. Irish Museum of Modern Art, Dublin, Ireland
Par avion — exercícios de epistolografia. Memorial da América Latina, São Paulo, Brazil
Pequenos formatos. Sesc Avenida Paulista, São Paulo, Brazil
Quando vidas se tornam forma: diálogo com o futuro — Brasil/Japão. Museu de Arte Moderna de São Paulo, Brazil
Sintomas, os ateliês de gravura em 25 anos (e um pouco mais). Museu da Gravura Cidade de Curitiba, Brazil
Traçados modernos e contemporâneos. Galeria de Arte Marcelo Guarnieri, São Paulo, Brazil
Um século de arte brasileira — Coleção Gilberto Chateaubriand. Museu de Arte de Santa Catarina, Florianópolis, Brazil
Vou-te contar uma história: Colecção Madeira Corporate Services. Porta 33, Funchal, Portugal
When Lives Become Form. Museum of Contemporary Art Tokyo, Japan

2009

Atenção: estratégias para perceber a arte. Museu de Arte Moderna de São Paulo, Brazil
Arte Contemporânea Brasileira nas Coleções João Sattamini e MAC Niterói. Museu de Arte Contemporânea de Niterói, Rio de Janeiro, Brazil
Contemporâneo x Moderno. Galeria Daslu, São Paulo, Brazil
Coletiva 09. Mercedes Viegas Arte Contemporânea, Rio de Janeiro, Brazil
Desenhos: A-Z. Museu da Cidade, Lisboa, Portugal
En todas as partes — políticas da diversidade sexual na arte. Centro Galego de Arte Contemporânea, Santiago de Compostela, Spain
ENTRE/SÉCULOS — Acervos Públicos do Distrito Federal. Museu Nacional, Brasília, Brazil
Expressividade na Arte Brasileira — Acervo MON e MARGS. Museu Oscar Niemeyer, Curitiba, Brazil
Gabinete de desenhos — obras do acervo do MAM-SP. Caixa Cultural Salvador, Brazil
Memorial revisitado — 20 anos. Memorial da América Latina, São Paulo, Brazil
Pianíssimo. Museu de Arte Contemporânea do Ceará, Fortaleza
Um brinde à arte brasileira. Ricardo Camargo Galeria, São Paulo, Brazil
Um mundo sem molduras. Museu de Arte Contemporânea da Universidade de São Paulo, Brazil
Viagem a Campos: o MAM-SP visita o Palácio Boa Vista. Palácio Boa Vista, São Paulo, Brazil
When Lives Become Form. The Hiroshima City Museum of Contemporary Art, Japan
When Lives Become Form: Contemporary Brazilian Art, 1960s to the Present. Yerba Buena Center for the Arts, California, United States

2010

29ª Bienal Internacional de São Paulo — Há sempre um copo de mar para um homem navegar. São Paulo, Brazil
Arte brasileira nos acervos de Curitiba — um percurso junto aos museus da FCC. Museu da Gravura Cidade de Curitiba, Brazil
Arte e política: outros olhares. Museu de Arte de Ribeirão Preto Pedro Manuel Gismondi, São Paulo, Brazil
Colección MACBA. Museu d'Art Contemporani de Barcelona, Spain
Contemporary Art from the Collection. The Museum of Modern Art, New York, United States
Gravuras contemporâneas. Centro Cultural Martha Watts, São Paulo, Brazil
Gravuras contemporâneas. Museu de Arte Contemporânea de Sorocaba, São Paulo, Brazil
Modelos para armar. Pensar Latinoamérica desde la Colección MUSAC. Museo de Arte Contemporáneo de Castilla y León, Spain
Estampes et Révolution, 200 ans aprés — une comande du bicentenaire. Musée de la Révolution française, Vizille, France
Parede — II Festival Internacional de Pôster Arte do Rio de Janeiro. Centro Cultural Justiça Federal, Rio de Janeiro, Brazil
Preto no branco — do concreto ao contemporâneo. Galeria Berenice Arvani, São Paulo, Brazil
Recortes de uma coleção. Ricardo Camargo Galeria, São Paulo, Brazil

2011

12th Istanbul Biennial: Untitled. Antrepo 3 & 5 (Meclis-i Mebusan Caddesi), Türkiye
1911-2011 — Arte brasileira e depois, na Coleção Itaú. Palácio das Artes, Centro de Arte Contemporânea e Fotografia, Belo Horizonte, Brazil
1911-2011 — Arte brasileira e depois, na Coleção Itaú. Paço Imperial, Rio de Janeiro, Brazil
29ª Bienal de São Paulo — Obras selecionadas. Museu de Arte Moderna Aloisio Magalhães, Recife, Brazil
29ª Bienal de São Paulo — Obras selecionadas. Palácio das Artes, Centro de Arte Contemporânea e Fotografia, Belo Horizonte, Brazil

Campelo Costa e o desenho cearense. Sobrado Dr. José Lourenço, Fortaleza, Brazil
Doações Recentes. Museu de Arte Contemporânea da Universidade de São Paulo, Brazil
I Am Still Alive: Politics and Everyday Life in Contemporary Drawing. The Museum of Modern Art, New York, United States
Labirintos da Iconografia. Museu de Arte do Rio Grande do Sul Ado Malagoli, Porto Alegre, Brazil
Mostra Acervo MACC. Museu de Arte Contemporânea de Campinas José Pancetti, São Paulo, Brazil
O colecionador de sonhos. Instituto Figueiredo Ferraz, Ribeirão Preto, São Paulo, Brazil
Panorâmica 1: breve histórico das artes visuais do Ceará. Palácio da Abolição, Fortaleza, Brazil
Présentation des collections permanentes (collections contemporaines). Musée national d'art moderne, Centre de création industrielle, Centre Pompidou, Paris, France
Recortes de uma coleção. Ricardo Camargo Galeria, São Paulo, Brazil
Sob o peso dos meus amores. Itaú Cultural e Capela do Morumbi, São Paulo, Brazil
Sobrevitória — Usina de Arte Contemporânea, 25 anos depois. Museu de Arte do Espírito Santo Dionísio Del Santo, Vitória, Brazil
Wishing and Praying. CRG Gallery, New York, United States

2012

3ra Trienal Poli/gráfica de San Juan: América Latina y El Caribe – El Panal/The Hive. Galeria Nacional, Museu Casa Blanca e Casa de los Contrafuertes, Puerto Rico
1911-2011 — Arte brasileira e depois, na coleção Itaú. Museu Oscar Niemeyer, Curitiba, Brazil
A cada peça um universo — a construção de uma coleção de arte. Museu Victor Meirelles, Florianópolis, Brazil
Arte à primeira vista. Sesc São Carlos, São Paulo, Brazil
Contraproposta (Coletiva de encerramento da galeria). Galeria Thomas Cohn, Rio de Janeiro, Brazil
Viagem em torno do museu: 60 anos de Museu Victor Meirelles. Museu Victor Meirelles, Florianópolis, Brazil

2013

XVII Unifor Plástica. Espaço Cultural Unifor, Fortaleza, Brazil
93. Centro Galego de Arte Contemporánea, Santiago de Compostela, Spain
Acervos em movimento. Museu Nacional, Rio de Janeiro, Brazil
Arte à primeira vista. Sesc Sorocaba, São Paulo, Brazil
As tramas do tempo na arte contemporânea: estética ou poética?. Instituto Figueiredo Ferraz, Ribeirão Preto, São Paulo, Brazil
Geração 80. Galeria Berenice Arvani, São Paulo, Brazil
La conclusión nunca llega — Colección de dibujos de Madeira — Coleção de desenhos da Madeira. Sala de Arte El Broncense, Cáceres, Spain
Objects For Mending: Chen Zhen and Leonilson. Tate Modern, London, England
O Artista como Autor/o artista como editor. Museu de Arte Contemporânea da Universidade de São Paulo, Brazil
Order, Chaos, and the Space Between. Phoenix Art Museum, United States
30 × Bienal — Transformações na arte brasileira da 1ª à 30ª edição. Fundação Bienal de São Paulo, Brazil
Trajetórias — Arte brasileira na Coleção Fundação Edson Queiroz. Espaço Cultural Unifor, Fortaleza, Brazil

2014

A Galeria Luisa Strina na Coleção Figueiredo Ferraz. Instituto Figueiredo Ferraz, Ribeirão Preto, São Paulo, Brazil
A tara por livros ou a tara de papel. Galeria Bergamin, São Paulo, Brazil
Abstrações — Coleção Fundação Edson Queiroz e Coleção Roberto Marinho. Espaço Cultural Unifor, Fortaleza, Brazil
Afetividades eletivas: Coleção Luiz Sérgio Arantes. Galeria de Arte do Centro Cultural Minas Tênis Clube, Belo Horizonte, Brazil
Arte à primeira vista. Palácio das Artes, Belo Horizonte, Brazil
Carneiro. Museu de Arte Contemporânea do Ceará, Fortaleza, Brazil
Das viagens, dos desejos, dos caminhos. Museu Vale, Vitória, Brazil
Diálogos com Palatnik. Museu de Arte Moderna de São Paulo, Brazil
Distrações da memória — O museu como modo de rever o mundo. Museu de Arte do Rio Grande do Sul Ado Malagoli, Porto Alegre, Brazil
Edições e múltiplos: do concretismo ao contemporâneo. Galeria Superfície, São Paulo, Brazil
Entrecopas — Arte brasileira 1950 2014. Museu Nacional, Rio de Janeiro, Brazil
Eu represento os artistas, Revisited. Galeria Luisa Strina, São Paulo, Brazil
Inventário da paixão. Museu Histórico Nacional, Rio de Janeiro, Brazil
Luminares da arte cearense. Sobrado Dr. José Lourenço, Fortaleza, Brazil
Manifesto: poder, desejo, intervenção. Museu de Arte do Rio Grande do Sul Ado Malagoli, Porto Alegre, Brazil
140 caracteres. Museu de Arte Moderna de São Paulo, Brazil
Roesler Hotel # 25 — Dispositivos para um mundo (im)possível. Galeria Nara Roesler, São Paulo, Brazil
Tupi or not Tupi. Museu Oscar Niemeyer, Curitiba, Brazil
The Marvelous Real. Contemporary Spanish and Latin American Art from the MUSAC Collection. Museum of Contemporary Art Tokyo, Japan
10 años después: Post Emergencias en la Colección MUSAC. Museo de Arte Contemporáneo de Castilla y León, Spain
Unbound: Contemporary Art after Frida Kahlo. Museum of Contemporary Art Chicago, United States

2015

10ª Bienal do Mercosul — Mensagem de uma Nova América. Museu de Arte do Rio Grande do Sul Ado Malagoli, Porto Alegre, Brazil
A queda do céu. Paço das Artes, São Paulo, Brazil
Arthur Bispo do Rosário e Leonilson: Os Penélope. Sesc Jundiaí, São Paulo, Brazil
Arthur Bispo do Rosário e Leonilson: Os Penélope. Sesc Sorocaba, São Paulo, Brazil
Bidimensionais e tridimensionais. Museu de Arte Contemporânea de Campinas José Pancetti, São Paulo, Brazil
Concrete Matter. Warm São Paulo, Brazil
Corpo da obra. Museu de Arte Contemporânea do Ceará, Fortaleza, Brazil
Geometries On and Off the Grid: At from 1950 to the present. The Warehouse, Texas, United States
Geração 80: Ousadia & Afirmação. Simões de Assis Galeria de Arte, São Paulo, Brazil
O dia se renova todo dia. Galeria dotART, Belo Horizonte, Brazil
O espírito de cada época. Instituto Figueiredo Ferraz, Ribeirão Preto, São Paulo, Brazil
Paisagem opaca. Museu de Arte Moderna de São Paulo, Brazil
Recortes do Acervo — Pintura. Museu de Arte do Rio Grande do Sul Ado Malagoli, Porto Alegre, Brazil
Retratos: The Last Headline. Galeria Bergamin, São Paulo, Brazil

2016

A queda do céu. Sesc São José do Rio Preto, São Paulo, Brazil
Aquilo que nos une. Caixa Cultural Rio de Janeiro, Brazil
Arte à primeira vista. Sesc Bauru, São Paulo, Brazil
Coleção Airton Queiroz. Espaço Cultural Airton Queiroz, Fortaleza, Brazil
Distantes mundos/próximos lugares. Museu de Arte Contemporânea do Ceará, Fortaleza, Brazil
Hiato. SIM Galeria, São Paulo, Brazil
Homo Ludens. Galeria Luisa Strina, São Paulo, Brazil
In Between. Galeria Bergamin & Gomide, São Paulo, Brazil
Natureza franciscana. Museu de Arte Moderna de São Paulo, Brazil
O estado da arte. Instituto Figueiredo Ferraz, Ribeirão Preto, São Paulo, Brazil
O útero do mundo. Museu de Arte Moderna de São Paulo, Brazil
Os muitos e o um: arte contemporânea brasileira. Instituto Tomie Ohtake, São Paulo, Brazil
Por aqui tudo é novo. Instituto Inhotim, Brumadinho, Minas Gerais, Brazil
Vontade de mundo. Museu de Arte Contemporânea de Niterói, Rio de Janeiro, Brazil

2017

Acervo MVM em perspectiva. Museu Victor Meirelles, Florianópolis, Brazil
Al Margen del Amor. Museo Provincial de Teruel, Spain
Aquilo que nos une. Caixa Cultural São Paulo, Brazil
Arte à primeira vista. Sesc Jundiaí, São Paulo, Brazil
Arte à primeira vista. Sesc Piracicaba, São Paulo, Brazil
Dja Guata Porã: Rio de Janeiro, Brazil indígena. Museu de Arte do Rio, Rio de Janeiro, Brazil
Histórias da sexualidade. Museu de Arte de São Paulo Assis Chateaubriand, Brazil
Lugares do delírio. Museu de Arte do Rio, Rio de Janeiro, Brazil
Metrópole: experiência paulistana. Pina Estação, São Paulo, Brazil
Modos de ver o Brasil: Itaú Cultural 30 anos. Pavilhão Lucas Nogueira Garcez (Oca), São Paulo, Brazil
Past/Future/Present. Phoenix Art Museum, United States
Queermuseu — Cartografias da diferença na arte brasileira. Santander Cultural, São Paulo, Brazil
Todas as direções. Galeria Casa D'Alva, Fortaleza, Brazil

2018

A poesia e as artes visuais. Galeria Superfície, São Paulo, Brazil
Acervo. Ricardo Camargo Galeria, São Paulo, Brazil
Arte-veículo. Sesc Pompeia, São Paulo, Brazil
Brasile. Il coltello nella carne. PAC—Padiglione d'Arte Contemporanea, Milan, Italy
Com o ar pesado demais pra respirar. Galeria Athena, Rio de Janeiro, Brazil
Grandes obras, pequenos formatos. Galeria Mapa, São Paulo, Brazil
Lugares do delírio. Sesc Pompeia, São Paulo, Brazil
Matriz do tempo real. Museu de Arte Contemporânea da Universidade de São Paulo, Brazil
Passe a mão. Mercedes Viegas Arte Contemporânea, Rio de Janeiro, Brazil
Queermuseu — Cartografias da diferença na arte brasileira. Escola de Artes Visuais do Parque Lage, Rio de Janeiro, Brazil
Visiones de la tierra — El mundo planeado. Santander Cultural, Madrid, Spain

2019

A parte maldita: um esboço. SIM Galeria, São Paulo, Brazil
À Nordeste. Sesc 24 de maio, São Paulo, Brazil
A queda do céu. Caixa Cultural Brasília, Distrito Federal
Abertura 1980. Instituto Figueiredo Ferraz, Ribeirão Preto, São Paulo, Brazil
Amar em tempos de cólera. Galeria Verve, São Paulo, Brazil
Arte-veículo. Sesc Santos, São Paulo, Brazil
Chão de giz. Galeria Luisa Strina, São Paulo, Brazil
Da Terra Brasilis à aldeia global — Coleção Fundação Edson Queiroz. Espaço Cultural Unifor, Fortaleza, Brazil
Exposição permanente. Fama Museu, Itu, São Paulo, Brazil
I-D. Galeria Luisa Strina, São Paulo, Brazil
Memorial do desenho. Museu de Arte Contemporânea da Universidade de São Paulo, Brazil
No habrá nunca una puerta. Estás adentro. Santander Cultural, São Paulo, Brazil
Passado/futuro/presente: arte contemporânea brasileira no acervo do MAM. Museu de Arte Moderna de São Paulo, Brazil

2020

DECATEGORIZED. Artists From Brazil. Instituto Distrital de las Artes de Bogotá, Colombia
Leonilson + max wíllà morais. Auroras, São Paulo, Brazil
Pinacoteca: acervo. Pinacoteca do Estado de São Paulo, Brazil
Transbordar — Transgressões do bordado na arte. Sesc Pinheiros, São Paulo, Brazil

2021

4x5. Galeria Marilia Razuk, São Paulo, Brazil
Acervo em exposição. Fama Museu, Itu, São Paulo, Brazil
Acervo em transformação. Museu de Arte de São Paulo Assis Chateaubriand, Brazil
1981/2021: arte contemporânea brasileira na coleção Andrea e José Olympio Pereira. Centro Cultural Banco do Brasil, São Paulo, Brazil
Coreografia da atenção. Museu da Almada Casa da Cidade, Portugal
El sentido de la escultura. Fundación Joan Miró, Barcelona, Spain

Língua solta. Museu da Língua Portuguesa, São Paulo, Brazil
Máscaras: fetiches e fantasmagorias. Paço das Artes, São Paulo, Brazil
Zipper Open. Zipper Galeria, São Paulo, Brazil

2022

Acervo em exposição. Fama Museu, Itu, São Paulo, Brazil
Acervo em transformação: doações recentes. Museu de Arte de São Paulo Assis Chateaubriand, Brazil
Alegria aqui é mato. Instituto Casa Roberto Marinho, Rio de Janeiro, Brazil
Afinidades eletivas. Casa Zalszupin, São Paulo, Brazil
Bispo do Rosário — Eu vim: aparição, impregnação e impacto. Itaú Cultural, São Paulo, Brazil
Centelhas em movimento. Instituto Tomie Ohtake, São Paulo, Brazil
Condenado ao Moderno?. Instituto Figueiredo Ferraz, Ribeirão Preto, São Paulo, Brazil
Desvairar 22. Sesc Pinheiros, São Paulo, Brazil
Entrepanos — modernismo|contemporâneo. Casa Fiat de Cultura, Belo Horizonte, Brazil
Obscura luz. Galeria Luisa Strina, São Paulo, Brazil
Pequenos fogos. Galeria da Brotéria, Lisbon, Portugal
Que sejam muitas as manhãs de verão. Galeria Superfície, São Paulo, Brazil
Rafael Rg e Leonilson. Edifício Eifell, São Paulo, Brazil
Se arar. Pinacoteca do Ceará, Fortaleza, Brazil
Tempo e transparência. Casa Gabriel, São Paulo, Brazil
Un acto de ver que se despliega. Colección Susana y Ricardo Steinbruch. Museo Nacional Centro de Arte Reina Sofía, Madrid, Spain

2023

A coleção imaginária de Paulo Kuczynski. Instituto Tomie Ohtake, São Paulo, Brazil
Apaixonados. Galpão da Lapa, São Paulo, Brazil
Conversas entre coleções. Instituto Casa Roberto Marinho, Rio de Janeiro, Brazil
Elementar: fazer junto. Museu de Arte Moderna de São Paulo, Brazil
Hors de la nuit des nomes — hors de l'énorme ennui. Palais de Tokyo, Paris, France
Instalação sobre duas figuras. Capela do Morumbi, São Paulo, Brazil
Leonilson e a Geração 80. Galeria Multiarte, Fortaleza, Brazil
Leonilson e a Geração 80. Pinakotheke Cultural, Rio de Janeiro, Brazil
Linhas tortas. Mendes Wood DM, São Paulo, Brazil
Pedra Viva — Serra da Capivara, o legado de Niède Guidon. Museu Brasileiro da Escultura e da Ecologia, São Paulo, Brazil
Rosas Brasileiras. Farol Santander, São Paulo, Brazil
Tempos Fraturados. Museu de Arte Contemporânea da Universidade de São Paulo, Brazil
Tridimensional: entre o sagrado e o estético — Um recorte da coleção Vera e Miguel Chaia. Arte 132 Galeria, São Paulo, Brazil

2024

Centelhas em movimento. Espaço Cultural Unifor, Fortaleza, Brazil
De onde surgem os sonhos — Coleção Andrea e José Olympio Pereira. Palácio Anchieta, Vitória, Brazil
Gestos de amor, práticas de sedução. Almeida & Dale, São Paulo, Brazil
Unravel—The Power and Politics of Textiles in Art. Barbican Centre, London, England

EXHI BITION CHECK LIST

[Domingo é na pele] [Sunday Is on the Skin], 1989
Permanent ink and gouache
on paper, 32 × 24 cm
Private collection, São Paulo, Brazil
PL.1175.0/00 Image 84

[Eu; ele] [Me; Him], 1989
Permanent ink and watercolor
on paper, 32 × 24 cm
Collection of Marcia and Luiz Chrysostomo,
Rio de Janeiro, Brazil
PL.1289.0/00 Image 56

[He Thinks About Many Things, All at the Same Time], 1989
Permanent ink on paper, 23.5 × 16.5 cm
Collection of Luisa Malzoni Strina,
São Paulo, Brazil
PL.1146.0/00 Image 54

[Homem com chapéu] [Man With Hat], 1989
Permanent ink and watercolor
on paper, 40.5 × 30.5 cm
Collection of Luisa Malzoni Strina,
São Paulo, Brazil
PL.1157.0/00 Image 50

Isto é a lua, Not the Last Chance [This Is the Moon, Not the Last Chance], 1989
Acrylic paint on unstretched canvas,
83 × 50 cm
Collection of Jardis Volpe,
São Paulo, Brazil
PL.0746.0/00 Image 55

Leo Can't Change the World, 1989
Permanent ink and watercolor
on paper, 30 × 21 cm
Private collection, São Paulo, Brazil
PL.0910.0/00 Image 72

Leo não consegue mudar o mundo [Leo Can't Change the World], 1989
Acrylic paint and metallic paint on
unstretched canvas, 156 × 95 cm
Private collection, São Paulo, Brazil
PL.0615.0/00 Image 73

[Liberec], 1989
Permanent ink and watercolor
on paper, 40.5 × 30.5 cm
Collection of Ana Eliza and Paulo Setubal,
São Paulo, Brazil
PL.1160.0/00 Image 89

Luta de espadas sobre veludo roxo [Sword Fight on Purple Velvet], 1989
Miniature swords and metal heart,
staple, and thread on velvet on
unstretched canvas, 12 × 15 × 1 cm
Collection of Luisa Malzoni Strina,
São Paulo, Brazil
PL.1284.0/00 Image 68

[Man With No Shelter], 1989
Permanent ink and watercolor
on paper, 24 × 16.5 cm
Collection of Adriano Sammarone,
São Paulo, Brazil
PL.1275.0/00 Image 70

O litoral [The Shore], 1989
Watercolor and China ink
on paper, 41 × 31 cm
Museu de Arte Moderna do Rio de
Janeiro, sponsor White Martins, Brazil
PL.1470.0/00 Image 88

O porta fortuna [The Fortune Bearer], 1989
Acrylic paint on canvas, 150 × 100 cm
Collection of Susana and Ricardo Steinbruch,
São Paulo, Brazil
PL.2207.0/00 Image 48

[O q. ñ abdica] [He Who Does Not Resign], 1989
Permanent ink and watercolor
on paper, 41 × 31 cm
Collection of Luisa Malzoni Strina,
São Paulo, Brazil
PL.1187.0/00 Image 83

[Olhos pretos; cabelos pretos] [Black Eyes; Black Hair], 1989
Permanent ink and watercolor
on paper, 30 × 21 cm
Collection of Luisa Malzoni Strina,
São Paulo, Brazil
PL.1159.0/00 Image 66

[Os anéis do rapaz] [The Young Man's Rings], 1989
Permanent ink and watercolor
on paper, 25.5 × 17.5 cm
Collection of Luisa Malzoni Strina,
São Paulo, Brazil
PL.1281.0/00 Image 53

[Rapaz lembrando-se da Baía de Guanabara] [Young Man Recalling the Guanabara Bay], 1989
Permanent ink and watercolor
on paper, 32 × 24 cm
Collection of Francisco Meirelles de Andrade,
São Paulo, Brazil
PL.1202.0/00 Image 81

Rios afluentes e rio principal [Affluent Rivers and Main River], 1989
Watercolor and China ink
on paper, 41 × 31 cm
Museu de Arte Moderna do Rio de
Janeiro, sponsor White Martins, Brazil
PL.1469.0/00 Image 92

So Many Days, 1989
Permanent ink on paper, 29 × 21 cm
Private collection, São Paulo, Brazil
PL.0035.0/00 Image 64

[Very Sensitive Boy], 1989
Permanent ink on paper, 30 × 21 cm
Private collection, São Paulo, Brazil
PL.0984.0/00 Image 51

[O coração do homem] [Man's Heart], *circa* 1989
Watercolor and permanent ink
on paper, 32 × 24 cm
Collection of Patricia Levy, Rio de Janeiro, Brazil
PL.1323.0/00 Image 86

[Homem certo com molde certo] [Right Man With Right Mold], *circa* 1989
Permanent ink and watercolor
on paper, 32 × 24 cm
Collection of Thiago Tannous,
São Paulo, Brazil
PL.1199.0/00 Image 65

[O que não abdica] [He Who Does Not Resign], *circa* 1989
Permanent ink and watercolor
on paper, 24 × 16.5 cm
Collection of Mary Miranda,
São Paulo, Brazil
PL.0299.0/00 Image 82

[Quando não há bombas, óculos ou lábios] [When There Are No Bombs, Eyeglasses, or Lips], *circa* 1989
Permanent ink on paper, 26.5 × 33.5 cm
Private collection, São Paulo, Brazil
PL.0999.0/00 Image 62

Untitled, 1989
Acrylic paint on unstretched
canvas, 160 × 95 cm
Collection of Luisa Malzoni Strina,
São Paulo, Brazil
PL.0814.0/00 Image 60

Untitled, 1989
Permanent ink and watercolor
on paper, 30 × 21 cm
Collection of Graham Steele and
Ulysses de Santi, United States
PL.1165.0/00 Image 59

Untitled, 1989
Permanent ink and watercolor
on paper, 32 × 24 cm
Collection of Guilherme Salvatore,
São Paulo, Brazil
PL.0660.0/00 Image 58

Untitled, 1989
Silk thread fringe on chassis, 47 × 22 × 3 cm
Private collection, São Paulo, Brazil
PL.1240.0/00 Image 67

Untitled, from the series *Onde está o oceano* [Where Is the Ocean], 1989
Permanent ink on paper, 41 × 31 cm
Collection of Daniel Senise,
Rio de Janeiro, Brazil
PL.3056.0/00 Image 80

Untitled, from the series *Onde está o oceano* [Where Is the Ocean], 1989
Permanent ink on paper, 41 × 31 cm
Private collection, São Paulo, Brazil
PL.3053.0/00 Image 77

Untitled, *circa* 1989
Marker and metallic paint on paper, 32 × 20 cm
Private collection, São Paulo, Brazil
PL.0446.0/00 Image 87

Voilà mon coeur [Here Is My Heart], *circa* 1989
Crystals, thread, felt, and metallic paint
on unstretched canvas, 22 × 30 × 2 cm
Collection of Susana and Ricardo Steinbruch,
São Paulo, Brazil
PL.1296.0/00 Image 69

[4 Lone Hearts], 1990
Permanent ink and gouache
on paper, 32 × 24 cm
Private collection, São Paulo, Brazil
PL.1188.0/00 Image 138

[Aladim e seu capitão] [Aladdin and His Captain], 1990
Permanent ink on paper, 32 × 24 cm
Collection of Paulo A. W. Vieira, Rio de Janeiro, Brazil
PL.1480.0/00 Image 105

[All the Lonely Nights], 1990
Permanent ink and metallic paint on paper, 30.5 × 22.5 cm
Collection of Luisa Malzoni Strina, São Paulo, Brazil
PL.1279.0/00 Image 123

Aos próximos anos [To the Coming Years], 1990
Watercolor on paper, 31 × 23 cm
Museu de Arte Moderna do Rio de Janeiro, sponsor White Martins, Brazil
PL.1471.0/00 Image 93

[As oliveiras] [The Olive Trees], 1990
Watercolor, permanent ink, and graphite on paper, 27 × 21.5 × 3 cm
Museu de Arte Moderna de São Paulo, gift Carmem Bezerra Dias and Theodorino Torquato Dias, 1997, Brazil
PL.1038.0/00 Image 139

Favorite Game, 1990
Permanent ink on paper, 21 × 13.5 cm
Private collection, São Paulo, Brazil
PL.0021.0/00 Image 115

Foge para procurar [Runs Away to Find], 1990
Permanent ink and watercolor on paper, 21 × 13.5 cm
Collection of Ricardo Resende and Jose Mauro Del Royo Correa (*in memoriam*), São Paulo, Brazil
PL.0882.0/00 Image 140

[Gifts to You], 1990
Permanent ink, watercolor and metallic paint on paper, 30.5 × 22.5 cm
Private collection, São Paulo, Brazil
PL.1196.0/00 Image 146

Hands on the Pockets, That Boy, 1990
Permanent ink and watercolor on paper, 30 × 22.5 cm
Collection of Luisa Malzoni Strina, São Paulo, Brazil
PL.0004.0/00 Image 128

He Could Not Sleep Because of a Tel. Call, 1990
Permanent ink and watercolor on paper, 32 × 24 cm
Collection of Paula Nazarian, São Paulo, Brazil
PL.0330.0/00 Image 129

[If You Dream With Clouds], 1990
Permanent ink and gouache on papel, 30 × 23.5 cm
Collection of Charlô Whately, São Paulo, Brazil
PL.1182.0/00 Image 126

[I'm Always Provoking Family's Drama], 1990
Permanent ink, watercolor, and metallic paint on paper, 30 × 22 cm
Collection of Ricardo Resende and Jose Mauro Del Royo Correa (*in memoriam*), São Paulo, Brazil
PL.1512.0/00 Image 147

Mantiqueira Bocaina Tijuca, 1990
Watercolor and China ink on paper, 41 × 31 cm
Museu de Arte Moderna do Rio de Janeiro, sponsor White Martins, Brazil
PL.1466.0/00 Image 91

[Mar do Japão] [Sea of Japan], 1990
Acrylic paint and metallic paint on canvas, 143 × 84 cm
Collection of Cristina Secaf Rebello, São Paulo, Brazil
PL.0785.0/00 Image 132

Missing One Friend, 1990
Permanent ink, watercolor and metallic paint on paper, 21 × 13.5 cm
Private collection, São Paulo, Brazil
PL.0848/00 Image 145

[Modelo; Matéria; Artifício; Essência] [Model; Matter; Artifice; Essence], 1990
Permanent ink on paper, 31 × 41 cm
Collection of Luisa Malzoni Strina, São Paulo, Brazil
PL.1144.0/00 Image 134

[Morro pela boca; vivo pelos olhos] [I Die Through My Mouth; I Live Through My Eyes], 1990
Permanent ink on paper, 32 × 24 cm
Collection of Paulo A. W. Vieira, Rio de Janeiro, Brazil
PL.1481.0/00 Image 104

[My Love Has Green Lips], 1990
Permanent ink and watercolor on paper, 35 × 25 cm
Collection of Charlô Whately, São Paulo, Brazil
PL.1168.0/00 Image 141

[My Shelter Is My Heart], 1990
Permanent ink and gouache on paper, 32 × 22 cm
Private collection, São Paulo, Brazil
PL.1156.0/00 Image 148

O dia do herói [The Day of the Hero], 1990
Thread on felt, 104 × 156 cm
Collection of Susana and Ricardo Steinbruch, São Paulo, Brazil
PL.1189.0/00 Image 125

[O matemático] [The Mathematician], 1990
Permanent ink and watercolor on paper, 24 × 32 cm
Collection of Luisa Malzoni Strina, São Paulo, Brazil
PL.1294.0/00 Image 151

[O músico] [The Musician], 1990
Permanent ink on paper, 32 × 24 cm
Collection of Paulo A. W. Vieira, Rio de Janeiro, Brazil
PL.1479.0/00 Image 106

O oceano, o deserto [The Ocean, the Desert], 1990
Watercolor and China ink on paper, 31 × 23 cm
Museu de Arte Moderna do Rio de Janeiro, sponsor White Martins, Brazil
PL.1879.0/00 Image 96

[O ouro do artista] [The Artist's Gold], 1990
Permanent ink on paper, 32 × 24 cm
Collection of Paulo A. W. Vieira, Rio de Janeiro, Brazil
PL.1482.0/00 Image 107

O q. você desejar, o q. você quiser, eu estou pronto para servi-lo [Whatever You Desire, Whatever You Want, I Am Ready to Serve You], 1990
Thread on voile and copper hanger, 136 × 51 × 10 cm
Collection of Susana and Ricardo Steinbruch, São Paulo, Brazil
PL.1000.0/00 Image 103

O que nos une, o que nos separa [What Unites Us, What Separates Us], 1990
China ink and watercolor on paper, 31 × 23 cm
Museu de Arte Moderna do Rio de Janeiro, sponsor White Martins, Brazil
PL.1877.0/00 Image 97

[Os negros; os judeus; os homossexuais; as mulheres; os comunistas; os aleijados] [The Blacks; The Jews; The Homosexuals; The Women; The Communists; The Crippled], 1990
Permanent ink on paper, 30 × 22 cm
Collection of Luisa Malzoni Strina, São Paulo, Brazil
PL.1139.0/00 Image 101

[Paciência] [Patience], 1990
Watercolor and permanent ink on paper, 40.5 × 30.5 cm
Private collection, São Paulo, Brazil
PL.1158.0/00 Image 121

Protected, Crossing Fires, 1990
Watercolor and permanent ink on paper, 22 × 14.5 cm
Museu de Arte Moderna de São Paulo, gift Carmem Bezerra Dias and Theodorino Torquato Dias, 1997, Brazil
PL.1039.0/00 Image 110

Sem título n° 1 [Untitled #1], 1990
Watercolor and China ink on paper, 31 × 23 cm
Museu de Arte Moderna do Rio de Janeiro, sponsor White Martins, Brazil
PL.1467.0/00 Image 90

[Sob o peso dos meus amores] [Under the Weight of My Loves], 1990
Permanent ink, metallic paint, and watercolor on paper, 29 × 21 cm
Private collection, São Paulo, Brazil
PL.0982.0/00 Image 143

To Be Selective, 1990
Acrylic paint, metallic paint and colored pencil on unstretched canvas, 203 × 105 cm
Collection of Luisa Malzoni Strina, São Paulo, Brazil
PL.0647.0/00 Image 122

Under Your Spell I'm Not on Clear Waters, 1990
Permanent ink and watercolor on paper, 30.5 × 23 cm
Collection of Cristina Secaf Rebello, São Paulo, Brazil
PL.0784.0/00 Image 114

[When You Go to Sleep], 1990
Watercolor and permanent ink on paper, 32 × 24 cm
Collection of Francisco Meirelles de Andrade, São Paulo, Brazil
PL.1163.0/00 Image 127

[Aladim e seu capitão] [Aladdin and His Captain], *circa* 1990
Acrylic paint and metallic paint on canvas, 151 × 75 cm
Private collection, São Paulo, Brazil
PL.0879.0/00 Image 133

Homem c/ fogo nas mãos [Man With Fire on His Hand], *circa* 1990
Acrylic paint on unstretched canvas, 61 × 29 cm
Collection of Eduardo Brandão and Jan Fjeld, São Paulo, Brazil
PL.0813.0/00 Image 108

[Inflamável] [Inflammable], *circa* 1990
Permanent ink on paper, 48 × 33 cm
Private collection, São Paulo, Brazil
PL.0387.0/00 Image 100

[Jogos perigosos] [Dangerous Games], *circa* 1990
Acrylic paint on canvas, 50 × 60 cm
Collection of Luisa Malzoni Strina, São Paulo, Brazil
PL.1193.0/00 Image 113

Os olhos atentos [The Wary Eyes], *circa* 1990
Watercolor and China ink on paper, 31 × 23 cm
Museu de Arte Moderna do Rio de Janeiro, sponsor White Martins, Brazil
PL.1468.0/00 Image 98

Próximo futuro desejado [Coming Desired Future], *circa* 1990
Watercolor and China ink on paper, 31 × 23 cm
Museu de Arte Moderna do Rio de Janeiro, sponsor White Martins, Brazil
PL.1878.0/00 Image 94

[Slave], *circa* 1990
Acrylic paint on canvas, 41 × 33 cm
Collection of Eduardo Brandão and Jan Fjeld, São Paulo, Brazil
PL.0806.0/00 Image 102

[Turista de outra terra] [Tourist From Another Land], *circa* 1990
Permanent ink and watercolor on paper, 25.5 × 18 cm
Collection of Paulo A. W. Vieira, Rio de Janeiro, Brazil
PL.1477.0/00 Image 135

Untitled, 1990
Acrylic paint on canvas, 70 × 65 cm
Banco Itaú collection, São Paulo, Brazil
PL.0756.0/00 Image 119

Untitled, 1990
Acrylic paint on cotton fabric, 140.5 × 75 cm
Collection of Rafael Moraes, São Paulo, Brazil
PL.0716.0/00 Image 120

Untitled, from the series *Onde está o oceano* [Where Is the Ocean], 1990
Permanent ink and gouache on paper, 41 × 31 cm
Collection of Daniel Senise, Rio de Janeiro, Brazil
PL.3055.0/00 Image 76

[No Yes Please], 1990/91
Acrylic paint and metallic paint on canvas, 145 × 70 cm
Private collection, São Paulo, Brazil
PL.0682.0/00 Image 124

[A 21ª Bienal tem aroma de peixaria] [The 21st Bienal Has the Scent of a Fishery], 1991
Permanent ink on paper, 18 × 12.5 cm
Private collection, São Paulo, Brazil
PL.0134.0/00 Image 273

[Adivinhe quem vai estar na fila esta noite] [Guess Who's Gonna Be in Line Tonight], 1991
Permanent ink and China ink on paper, 25 × 16 cm
Private collection, São Paulo, Brazil
PL.0064.0/00 Image 247

[Adivinhe quem vem para ser jantado?] [Guess Who's Coming to Be Dinner?], 1991
Permanent ink and China ink on paper, 18 × 13 cm
Private collection, São Paulo, Brazil
PL.0043.0/00 Image 267

[Administração doméstica lava roupa suja] [Domestic Administration Airs Dirty Laudry], 1991
Permanent ink on paper, 15 × 13 cm
Private collection, São Paulo, Brazil
PL.0102.0/00 Image 266

Agora e as oportunidades [Now and Opportunities], 1991
Acrylic paint and colored pencil on unstretched canvas, 155 × 88 cm
Museu de Arte de São Paulo Assis Chateaubriand, gift Fernanda Feitosa and Heitor Martins, 2020, Brazil, MASP.11149
PL.0339.0/00 Image 152

[Anjos; homens] [Angels; Men], 1991
Thread, acrylic paint and unstretched canvas on voile, 25.5 × 12.5 cm
Collection of Luisa Malzoni Strina, São Paulo, Brazil
PL.1297.0/00 Image 193

As minorias [The Minorities], [1991/2024]
Glasses, water, and typing on paper, on glass shelves
45 × 45 × 10 cm
Private collection, São Paulo, Brazil
PL.3042.0/00 Image 7

[Auto-proteção] [Self-Protection] , 1991
Watercolor on paper, 30 × 22.5 cm
Collection of Luisa Malzoni Strina, São Paulo, Brazil
PL.1164.0/00 Image 187

[Brasil vai a Miami em busca da "década perdida"] [Brazil Goes to Miami in Search of the "Lost Decade"], 1991
Permanent ink and cut paper glued on paper, 18 × 14.5 cm
Private collection, São Paulo, Brazil
PL.0115.0/00 Image 250

[Brasileiro vira habitante do Planeta dos Macacos] [Brazilians Become Inhabitants of the Planet of the Apes], 1991
Permanent ink on paper, 18.5 × 16.5 cm
Private collection, São Paulo, Brazil
PL.0092.0/00 Image 260

Dedicado aos olhos fundos e verdes [Dedicated to the Deep Green Eyes], [1991]
Acrylic paint and colored pencil on canvas, 163 × 95 cm
Collection of Evelyn and Ivoncy Ioschpe, long term loan with Pinacoteca de São Paulo, Brazil
PL.0878.0/00 Image 189

[Defensores de pandas podem ser perigosos] [Panda Defenders Might Be Dangerous], 1991
Permanent ink on paper, 18.5 × 13.5 cm
Private collection, São Paulo, Brazil
PL.0130.0/00 Image 268

[E se o advogado Murphy for assaltado no Rio?] [What if Lawyer Murphy Is Robbed in Rio?], 1991
Permanent ink on paper, 18 × 17 cm
Private collection, São Paulo, Brazil
PL.0100.0/00 Image 256

El Mirage [The Mirage], 1991
Permanent ink and watercolor on paper, 30.5 × 23 cm
Collection of Thiago Tannous, São Paulo, Brazil
PL.2319.0/00 Image 166

[Empregada de novela é mais chique que madame] [A Soap Opera Cleaning Woman Is Fancier Than a Lady], 1991
Permanent ink on paper, 18 × 16 cm
Private collection, São Paulo, Brazil
PL.0103.0/00 Image 258

Empty Man, 1991
Thread on embroidered linen, 53 × 37 cm
Private collection, São Paulo, Brazil
PL.0007.0/00 Image 199

[Entrada de serviço é imoral 4] [Service Entrance Is Immoral 4], 1991
Permanent ink on paper, 18.5 × 15 cm
Private collection, São Paulo, Brazil
PL.0136.0/00 Image 346

[Estrelas levam suas manias para a cama] [Stars Take Their Manias to Bed], 1991
Permanent ink on paper, 18 × 13 cm
Private collection, São Paulo, Brazil
PL.0101.0.0/00 Image 265

[Família real] [Royal Family], 1991
Permanent ink on paper, 18.5 × 15 cm
Private collection, São Paulo, Brazil
PL.0083.0/00 Image 347

[Florais são moda entre desequilibrados] [Flower Remedies Are Fad Among the Unstable], 1991
Permanent ink on paper, 18 × 12.5 cm
Private collection, São Paulo, Brazil
PL.0090.0/00 Image 280

[Jamais toque em um membro da família real] [Never Touch a Member of the Royal Family], 1991
Permanent ink on paper, 18 × 16 cm
Private collection, São Paulo, Brazil
PL.0117.0/00 Image 251

[Jesus com rapaz acidentado] [Jesus With Accidented Young Man], 1991
Permanent ink and gouache on paper, 31 × 23 cm
Collection of Eduardo Brandão and Jan Fjeld, São Paulo, Brazil
PL.0823.0/00 Image 164

José, 1991
Thread on voile, 60 × 40 cm
Private collection, São Paulo, Brazil
PL.0016.0/00 Image 191

Leo não pode mudar o mundo [Leo Can't Change the World], 1991
Thread and unstretched canvas on voile, 140.5 × 141 cm
Private collection, São Paulo, Brazil
PL.0340.0/00 Image 156

[Limpadores de ralo podem ser "pornô"] [Drain Cleaners May Be "Porn"], 1991
Permanent ink on paper, 18 × 13.5 cm
Private collection, São Paulo, Brazil
PL.0131.0/00 Image 270

[Mauricinho é o troglodita arrumadinho] [Dandy Types Are Glummed-Up Troglodytes], 1991
Permanent ink on paper, 18 × 12.5 cm
Private collection, São Paulo, Brazil
PL.0046.0/00 Image 275

[Melhor amigo do homem não abana o rabo] [Man's Best Friend Doesn't Wag His Tail], 1991
Permanent ink on paper, 18 × 15 cm
Private collection, São Paulo, Brazil
PL.0042.0/00 Image 264

[Moda bizarra aterrissa nas bocas e nas TVs] [Weird Fashion Lands in Mouths and TVs], 1991
Permanent ink and China ink on paper, 23 × 18 cm
Private collection, São Paulo, Brazil
PL.0065.0/00 Image 249

["Motoqueiros do chiclete" aceleram corações] ["Chewing-Gum Bikers" Speed Up Hearts], 1991
Permanent ink on paper, 18.5 × 16.5 cm
Private collection, São Paulo, Brazil
PL.0116.0/00 Image 252

Mr. One Night Stand, 1991
Thread on rustic silk, 47.5 × 28 cm
Private collection, São Paulo, Brazil
PL.0014.0/00 Image 167

[Na ponte aérea, voar não é um calvário] [In the Airlift, Flying Is Not a Calvary], 1991
Permanent ink and China ink on paper, 18 × 12.5 cm
Private collection, São Paulo, Brazil
PL.0099.0/00 Image 276

[Neo-vitorianismo é o novo aliado da aids] [Neo-Victorianism Is AIDS' New Ally], 1991
Permanent ink on paper, 18 × 12.5 cm
Private collection, São Paulo, Brazil
PL.0095.0/00 Image 281

O apaixonado, o zig zag, 5 minutos [The Enamored One, the Zigzag, 5 Minutes], 1991
Guipure lace, thread and beads on unstretched canvas, 33 × 20.5 cm
Private collection, São Paulo, Brazil
PL.1455.0/00 Image 186

O broche [The Brooch], from the series *Os dedicados* [The Dedicated], 1991
Permanent ink and watercolor on paper, 30.5 × 23 cm
Collection of Marcelo Secaf, São Paulo, Brazil
PL.2175.0/00 Image 176

O cometa [The Comet], from the series *Os dedicados* [The Dedicated], 1991
Permanent ink and watercolor on paper, 30.5 × 23 cm
Collection of Francisco Meirelles de Andrade, São Paulo, Brazil
PL.0019.0/00 Image 168

O filósofo [The Philosopher], from the series *Os dedicados* [The Dedicated], 1991
Permanent ink and watercolor on paper, 30.5 × 23 cm
Private collection, São Paulo, Brazil
PL.0017.0/00 Image 172

O ilha [The Island One], 1991
Thread and metal on canvas, 35 × 27 cm
Private collection, São Paulo, Brazil
PL.0905.0/00 Image 183

O matemático [The Mathematician], from the series *Os dedicados* [The Dedicated], 1991
Permanent ink on paper, 30.5 × 23 cm
Private collection, São Paulo, Brazil
PL.0020.0/00 Image 171

O músico [The Musician], from the series *Os dedicados* [The Dedicated], 1991
Watercolor and permanent ink on paper, 30.5 × 23 cm
Collection of Rafael Moraes, São Paulo, Brazil
PL.2600.0/00 Image 174

O rapaz do filme [The Young Man From the Movies], from the series *Os dedicados* [The Dedicated], 1991
Permanent ink and watercolor on paper, 30.5 × 23 cm
Collection of Luisa Malzoni Strina, São Paulo, Brazil
PL.1078.0/00 Image 177

[Oceano, aceita-me?] [Ocean, Will You Accept Me?], 1991
Permanent ink on paper, 30 × 23 cm
Private collection, São Paulo, Brazil
PL.0658.0/00 Image 158

[Os chatos unidos foram enfim vencidos] [United Bores Were Finally Defeated], 1991
Permanent ink on paper, 18 × 13 cm
Private collection, São Paulo, Brazil
PL.0129.0/00 Image 269

[Os jovens adoram ter pés de roquefort] [Youngsters Love Having Roquefort Feet], 1991
Permanent ink on paper, 18 × 13.5 cm
Private collection, São Paulo, Brazil
PL.0132.0/00 Image 271

Os rapazes os templos [The Young Men the Temples], 1991
Permanent ink and watercolor on paper, 30 × 22.5 cm
Collection of Susana and Ricardo Steinbruch, São Paulo, Brazil
PL.1153.0/00 Image 155

[Otimistas lutam contra natal macambúzio] [Optimists Fight Against Cloomy Christmas], 1991
Permanent ink and China ink on paper, 18 × 12.5 cm
Private collection, São Paulo, Brazil
PL.0094.0/00 Image 278

[Paulista se afoga em horrores kitschs] [Paulista Drowns in Kitsch Horrors], 1991
Permanent ink on paper, 18 × 12.5 cm
Private collection, São Paulo, Brazil
PL.0089.0/00 Image 279

[Paulistano aterrissa na Istambul dos camelôs] [Paulistanos Land in the Istanbul of the Peddlers], 1991
Permanent ink on paper, 18 × 16.5 cm
Private collection, São Paulo, Brazil
PL.0066.0/00 Image 263

[Paulistano está com síndrome de linha cruzada] [Paulistanos Suffer From Crossed Line Syndrome], 1991
Permanent ink on paper, 22 × 19 cm
Private collection, São Paulo, Brazil
PL.0063.0/00 Image 248

[Paulistano foge da cobra e da fumaça de ônibus] [Paulistano Runs Away From Snake and Bus Smoke], 1991
Permanent ink and China ink on paper, 18 × 17 cm
Private collection, São Paulo, Brazil
PL.0091.0/00 Image 259

[Paulistanos ensopados dão com os burros n'água] [Soaked Paulistanos Go Down the Drain], 1991
Permanent ink on paper, 17.5 × 13.5 cm
Private collection, São Paulo, Brazil
PL.0135.0/00 Image 244

[Paulistanos estão com a cara do Meneguelli] [Paulistanos Are Looking Like Meneguelli], 1991
Permanent ink on paper, 18 × 16 cm
Private collection, São Paulo, Brazil
PL.0127.0/00 Image 254

[Pepitas de ouro] [Gold Nuggets], 1991
Acrylic paint, metallic paint and colored pencil on canvas, 150 × 85 cm
Private collection, São Paulo, Brazil
PL.1111.0/00 Image 180

[Periquita de Madonna está solta por SP] [Madonna's Pussy Is Running Wild in SP], 1991
Permanent ink on paper, 18 × 17 cm
Private collection, São Paulo, Brazil
PL.0044.0/00 Image 262

Pescador de pérolas [Pearl Fisher], 1991
Thread and metallic paint on voile, 36 × 31 cm
Private collection, São Paulo, Brazil
PL.1063.0/00 Image 184

Pobre Sebastião [Poor Sebastião], 1991
Acrylic paint and colored pencil on unstretched canvas, 160 × 90 cm
Collection of Eduardo Brandão and Jan Fjeld, São Paulo, Brazil
PL.0810.0/00 Image 153

Príncipe [Prince], from the series *Os dedicados* [The Dedicated], 1991
Permanent ink and watercolor on paper, 30.5 × 23 cm
Museu de Arte de São Paulo Assis Chateaubriand, gift Luisa Strina, 2024, Brazil, MASP.11532
PL.1194.0/00 Image 170

Provas de amor [Proofs of Love], 1991
Thread on unstretched canvas and voile, 50 × 37 cm
Collection of Susana and Ricardo Steinbruch, São Paulo, Brazil
PL.0013.0/00 Image 194

Pure Freude [Pure Joy], from the series *Os dedicados* [The Dedicated], 1991
Permanent ink and watercolor on paper, 30.5 × 23 cm
Collection of Luisa Malzoni Strina, São Paulo, Brazil
PL.1195.0/00 Image 173

[Que estranho nome dão a isto?] [What Strange Name Do They Give to This?], 1991
Permanent ink and watercolor on paper, 32 × 24 cm
Private collection, São Paulo, Brazil
PL.1166.0/00 Image 165

[Quem é do bem não fica passado num alalaô] [Good People Don't Get Stunned by Carnival], 1991
Colored pencil on paper, 19 × 12 cm
Private collection, São Paulo, Brazil
PL.0061.0/00 Image 245

[Rapaz com 2 cicatrizes na barriga] [Young Man With 2 Scars in the Stomach], 1991
Permanent ink on paper, 31 × 23 cm
Collection of Eduardo Brandão and Jan Fjeld, São Paulo, Brazil
PL.0818.0/00 Image 163

[Ricardona prefere jugulares comprometidas] [Ricardona Prefers Commited Jugulars], 1991
Permanent ink on paper, 18 × 16 cm
Private collection, São Paulo, Brazil
PL.0093.0/00 Image 261

[Senna imita Rosane e abre a torneira] [Senna Imitates Rosane and Opens the Faucet], 1991
Permanent ink on paper, 18 × 12.5 cm
Private collection, São Paulo, Brazil
PL.0088.0/00 Image 277

Síndrome de abandono [Abandonment Syndrome], 1991
Thread on rustic silk, 41 × 23.5 cm
Collection of Valdirlei Dias Nunes, São Paulo, Brazil
PL.1118.0/00 Image 159

[SP se arma para "tempestade em Interlagos"] [SP Arms Up for "Storm in Interlagos"], 1991
Permanent ink on paper, 20 × 13 cm
Private collection, São Paulo, Brazil
PL.0062.0/00 Image 246

[Trágico acidente aéreo mata Papai Noel] [Tragic Air Accident Kills Santa Klaus], 1991
Permanent ink on paper, 18 × 12.5 cm
Private collection, São Paulo, Brazil
PL.0096.0/00 Image 282

Traidor [Traitor], 1991
Thread, crystals, copper wire, and white wax on cotton fabric on unstretched canvas, 24 × 12 × 2 cm
Collection of Luisa Malzoni Strina, São Paulo, Brazil
PL.1147.0/00 Image 188

[Vapt-vupt no Congresso causa perplexidade] [Top Speed in Congress Causes Perplexity], 1991
Permanent ink on paper, 18 × 16 cm
Private collection, São Paulo, Brazil
PL.0128.0/00 Image 257

[Xuxa é um Lee Iacocca de botinha branca] [Xuxa Is a Lee Iacocca in White Booties], 1991
Permanent ink on paper, 18 × 12.5 cm
Private collection, São Paulo, Brazil
PL.0133.0/00 Image 272

You Don't See That, 1991
Acrylic paint and colored pencil on canvas, 149 × 85 cm
MEJME collection, São Paulo, Brazil
PL.1084.0/00 Image 154

[Zélia entra para o "Vingativas F.C."] [Zélia Joins the "Vengeful Ladies F.C."], 1991
Permanent ink on paper, 18 × 12.5 cm
Private collection, São Paulo, Brazil
PL.0098.0/00 Image 274

[Algumas distâncias entre 2 pontos] [Some Distances Between 2 Points], *circa* 1991
Permanent ink and watercolor on paper, 28 × 20 cm
Private collection, São Paulo, Brazil
PL.0893.0/00 Image 200

Boa notícia [Good News], *circa* 1991
Permanent ink and colored pencil on paper, 32 × 24 cm
Private collection, São Paulo, Brazil
PL.0030.0/00 Image 185

C/ ela sempre por perto [With Her Always Around], *circa* 1991
Acrylic paint and colored pencil on canvas, 143 × 85 cm
Collection of Jassanan Amoroso Dias Pastore, São Paulo, Brazil
PL.0855.0/00 Image 201

[Dedicate], *circa* 1991
Permanent ink on paper, 22 × 8 cm
Collection of Francisco Meirelles de Andrade, São Paulo, Brazil
PL.1200.0/00 Image 1

It's You Deep in Me, *circa* 1991
Thread on canvas, 41 × 29 cm
Museu Nacional de Belas Artes/ Ibram, gift família Bezerra Dias/Projeto Leonilson, 2004, Rio de Janeiro
PL.0015.0/00 Image 161

Meu coração, seu coração [My Heart, Your Heart], *circa* 1991
Acrylic paint and colored pencil on canvas, 155 × 90 cm
Collection of Andrea and José Olympio Pereira, São Paulo, Brazil
PL.1191.0/00 Image 182

O grande rio [The Large River], *circa* 1991
Permanent ink on paper, 15 × 22 cm
Collection of Marcelo Secaf, São Paulo, Brazil
PL.1009.0/00 Image 157

[Para quem comprou a verdade] [For Whoever Bought the Truth], *circa* 1991
Thread on voile, 39 × 35 cm
Private collection, São Paulo, Brazil
PL.0928.0/00 Image 195

Se você sonha com nuvens [If You Dream of Clouds], *circa* 1991
Embroidery, sewing, and metal eyelet on voile, 57.5 × 47.5 × 4 cm
Museu de Arte Moderna de São Paulo, gift Carmen Bezerra Dias and Theodorino Torquato Dias, 1997, Brazil
PL.1040.0/00 Image 162

The Game Is Over, *circa* 1991
Acrylic paint, metallic paint and colored pencil on unstretched canvas, 155 × 95 cm
Private collection, São Paulo, Brazil
PL.1454.0/00 Image 179

Untitled, 1991
Permanent ink on paper, 32 × 24 cm
Collection of Luisa Malzoni Strina, São Paulo, Brazil
PL.1142.0/00 Image 190

[Aberta a temporada de abobrinhas políticas] [Season of Political Baloney Opens], 1992
Permanent ink on paper, 21 × 15 cm
Private collection, São Paulo, Brazil
PL.0050.0/00 Image 311

Águas divididas [Divided Waters], 1992
Thread on patterned silk and striped cotton fabric, 42 × 38 cm
Private collection, São Paulo, Brazil
PL.0010.0/00 Image 221

Ampla visão [Ample Vision], 1992
Acrylic paint on unstretched canvas, 98 × 55.5 cm
Collection of Ricardo Bezerra and Bete Dias, Fortaleza, Brazil
PL.1488.0/00 Image 235

[Andorinhas abastadas procuram o photo] [Well-Off Swallows Patronize the Photo], 1992
Permanent ink and China ink on paper, 18 × 12.5 cm
Private collection, São Paulo, Brazil
PL.0118.0/00 Image 291

Anjo da guarda [Guardian Angel], from the series *O perigoso* [The Dangerous One], 1992
Permanent ink on paper, 30.5 × 23 cm
Collection of Flávia and Guilherme Teixeira, Belo Horizonte, Brazil
PL.1075.0/00 Image 207

[Ano zero km sai por preço de banana] [Brand-New Year Sold for Peanuts], 1992
Permanent ink on paper, 18 × 12.5 cm
Private collection, São Paulo, Brazil
PL.0052.0/00 Image 284

As cascas de ovo [The Egg Shells], 1992
Thread on unstretched canvas, 65 × 24 cm
Private collection, São Paulo, Brazil
PL.0676.0/00 Image 228

As fadas [The Fairies], from the series *O perigoso* [The Dangerous One], [1992]
Permanent ink on paper, 30.5 × 23 cm
Collection of Flávia and Guilherme Teixeira, Belo Horizonte, Brazil
PL.1076.0/00 Image 208

[As melhores farpas, ups, frases do ano] [The Best Thorns, Ops, Thoughts of the Year], 1992
Permanent ink on paper, 12.5 × 18 cm
Private collection, São Paulo, Brazil
PL.0121.0/00 Image 290

Bolsinho [Small Pocket], [1992]
Thread on velvet, 14 × 12.5 cm
Private collection, São Paulo, Brazil
PL.0001.0/00 Image 229

[Bom mesmo é nascer virado para a lua] [What's Really Good Is to Be Born Turned Toward the Moon], 1992
Permanent ink on paper, 15 × 10.5 cm
Private collection, São Paulo, Brazil
PL.0085.0/00 Image 322

[Cariocas dão a volta por cima e se sacodem] [Cariocas Come Out on Top and Jiggle], 1992
Permanent ink on paper, 12.5 × 18 cm
Private collection, São Paulo, Brazil
PL.0120.0/00 Image 289

[Cheio, vazio] [Full, Empty], 1992
Acrylic paint on canvas, 115 × 62 cm
Collection of Marcelo Secaf, São Paulo, Brazil
PL.1011.0/00 Image 232

Cheio, vazio [Full, Empty], 1992
Embroidery and sewing on voile and cotton fabric, 66 × 61 cm
Museu de Arte Moderna de São Paulo, gift Bayer S.A., 1996, Brazil
PL.1043.0/00 Image 233

[Clima de despacho paira sobre caso PC] [Voodoo Atmosphere Looms Over PC Case], 1992
Permanent ink on paper, 15.5 × 12.5 cm
Private collection, São Paulo, Brazil
PL.0077.0/00 Image 314

[Com que roupa Rosane irá a Varennes? [What Will Rosane Wear to Varennes?], 1992
Permanent ink on paper, 19 × 11.5 cm
Private collection, São Paulo, Brazil
PL.0078.0/00 Image 313

[Comemore sozinho o dia dos namorados] [Celebrate Valentine's Day Alone], 1992
Permanent ink and China ink on paper, 18 × 12.5 cm
Private collection, São Paulo, Brazil
PL.0045.0/00 Image 305

[Comida de hospital é a gororoba da moda] [Hospital Food Is the Grub in Vogue], 1992
Permanent ink on paper, 16.5 × 14.5 cm
Private collection, São Paulo, Brazil
PL.0072.0/00 Image 309

Copos-de-leite [Arum Lilies], from the series *O perigoso* [The Dangerous One], [1992]
Permanent ink on paper, 30.5 × 23 cm
Collection of Flávia and Guilherme Teixeira, Belo Horizonte, Brazil
PL.1074.0/00 Image 206

[Curso é coisa da época do avião a lenha] [Courses Are From the Time of the Timber Plane], 1992
Permanent ink on paper, 18 × 12.5 cm
Private collection, São Paulo, Brazil
PL.0097.0/00 Image 299

El puerto [The Harbor], [1992]
Thread on striped cotton fabric, nail, copper wire, and acrylic paint on mirror frame, 23 × 16 × 2.5 cm
Private collection, São Paulo, Brazil
PL.0009.0/00 Image 231

[Elite ou celite, eis a dilacerante questão] [Elite or Celite, That's the Dilacerating Question], 1992
Permanent ink and China ink on paper, 16 × 12 cm
Private collection, São Paulo, Brazil
PL.0069.0/00 Image 304

[Estudantes, enfim, saem do mundo da lua!] [Students Finally Get Their Heads Out of the Clouds!], 1992
Permanent ink on paper, 19 × 11.5 cm
Private collection, São Paulo, Brazil
PL.0049.0/00 Image 312

[Falta de educação virou mania nacional] [Bad Manners Became National Mania], 1992
Permanent ink on paper, 18 × 12.5 cm
Private collection, São Paulo, Brazil
PL.0125.0/00 Image 297

[Fórmula 1 mostra seu jeito PC de ser] [Formula 1 Shows Its PC Way of Being], 1992
Permanent ink on paper, 19 × 11.5 cm
Private collection, São Paulo, Brazil
PL.0104.0/00 Image 318

Gigante c/ flores [Giant With Flowers], [1992]
Thread on striped cotton bed sheet and acrylic paint on iron base, 105 × 35 × 35 cm
Private collection, São Paulo, Brazil
PL.0341.0/00 Image 226

[Inverno em São Paulo pronuncia-se inferno] [Winter in São Paulo Is Pronounced Hell], 1992
Permanent ink and China ink on paper, 18 × 12.5 cm
Private collection, São Paulo, Brazil
PL.0067.0/00 Image 301

[Kissinger vence Nobel na categoria vexame] [Kissinger Wins Nobel in Shame Category], 1992
Permanent ink and China ink on paper, 15.5 × 10.5 cm
Private collection, São Paulo, Brazil
PL.0074.0/00 Image 326

Les moments [The Moments], 1992
Thread on felt, 31 × 20 cm
Collection of Janka Babenco, São Paulo, Brazil
PL.0840.0/00 Image 218

Lisiantros [Lisianthius], from the series *O perigoso* [The Dangerous One], [1992]
Permanent ink on paper, 30.5 × 23 cm
Collection of Flávia and Guilherme Teixeira, Belo Horizonte, Brazil
PL.1073.0/00 Image 205

Margarida [Daisy], from the series *O perigoso* [The Dangerous One], [1992]
Permanent ink on paper, 30.5 × 23 cm
Collection of Flávia and Guilherme Teixeira, Belo Horizonte, Brazil
PL.1071.0/00 Image 203

[Miami é o Rio de Janeiro que deu certo] [Miami Is a Successful Rio de Janeiro], 1992
Permanent ink and China ink on paper, 18 × 12.5 cm
Private collection, São Paulo, Brazil
PL.0122.0/00 Image 293

["N" razões para não se suicidar em 1992] ["N" Reasons Not to Commit Suicide in 1992], 1992
Permanent ink on paper, 18 × 12.5 cm
Private collection, São Paulo, Brazil
PL.0058.0/00 Image 287

[Na Olimpíada, Brasil é ouro em jequice] [At Olympics, Brazil Takes Gold in Tawdriness], 1992
Permanent ink on paper, 19.5 × 14 cm
Private collection, São Paulo, Brazil
PL.0048.0/00 Image 310

[Não se faz mais baderna como antigamente] [They Don't Make Messes Like in the Old Times Anymore], 1992
Permanent ink on paper, 15.5 × 10.5 cm
Private collection, São Paulo, Brazil
PL.0086.0/00 Image 323

Ninguém [Nobody], [1992]
Thread on embroidered cotton pillowcase, chequered cotton fabric, and pillow, 23.5 × 46 × 5 cm
Collection of Maria Pini Piva, São Paulo, Brazil
PL.0847.0/00 Image 216

[O banheiro vai para o trono ou não vai?] [Does the Bathroom Go to the Throne or Not?], 1992
Permanent ink on paper, 18 × 12.5 cm
Private collection, São Paulo, Brazil
PL.0059.0/00 Image 288

[O chato volta a atacar 30 anos depois] [The Bore Charges Again After 30 Years], 1992
Permanent ink on paper, 18 × 10 cm
Private collection, São Paulo, Brazil
PL.0082.0/00 Image 320

[O coração de ouro] [The Heart of Gold], 1992
Permanent ink, watercolor, and metallic paint on paper, 30.5 × 22.5
Collection of Luisa Malzoni Strina, São Paulo
PL.1173.0/00 Image 225

[O firme pensamento] [The Firm Thought], 1992
Watercolor and metallic paint on paper, 30 × 23 cm
Collection of Luisa Malzoni Strina, São Paulo, Brazil
PL.1155.0/00 Image 214

[O louco] [The Madman], 1992
Permanent ink and metallic paint on paper, 32 × 24 cm
Collection of Ricardo Resende and Jose Mauro Del Royo Correa (*in memoriam*), São Paulo, Brazil
PL.1513.0/00 Image 223

[O mundo gira, a lusitana roda e La Nave Va] [The World Spins, The Lusitana Goes Round and La Nave Va], 1992
Permanent ink on paper, 19 × 11.5 cm
Private collection, São Paulo, Brazil
PL.0076.0/00 Image 315

O perigoso [The Dangerous One], from the series *O perigoso* [The Dangerous One], [1992]
Permanent ink and blood on paper, 30.5 × 23 cm
Collection of Flávia and Guilherme Teixeira, Belo Horizonte, Brazil
PL.1070.0/00 Image 202

O templo [The Temple], 1992
Thread on felt, 58 × 38 cm
Private collection, São Paulo, Brazil
PL.1077.0/00 Image 222

[O último vôo do intrépido filho de Dédalo] [The Last Flight of Daedalus's Intrepid Son], 1992
Permanent ink on paper, 14 × 11.5 cm
Private collection, São Paulo, Brazil
PL.0084.0/00 Image 321

[Odafas fisiologista amarga "day after"] [Odafas Fisiologista Suffers Day After], 1992
Permanent ink on paper, 19 × 11.5 cm
Private collection, São Paulo, Brazil
PL.0081.0/00 Image 319

Os rios por meu fluído entrego meu coração [The Rivers Through My Fluid I Surrender My Heart], 1992
Acrylic paint and cutting on unstretched canvas, 166.5 × 103 cm
Collection of Eduardo Brandão and Jan Fjeld, São Paulo, Brazil
PL.0797.0/00 Image 211

[Palavrão não é exclusividade de Magri] [Swear Word Is Not Magri's Prerogative], 1992
Permanent ink on paper, 18 × 12.5 cm
Private collection, São Paulo, Brazil
PL.0126.0/00 Image 295

[Papai Noel baixa na Dinda de saco cheio] [Santa Klaus Shows Up at Dinda With his Bag Full], 1992
Permanent ink on lined paper, 17 × 10 cm
Private collection, São Paulo, Brazil
PL.0079.0/00 Image 328

[Para lidar com garçons arrogantes, rosne] [To Deal With Arrogant Waiters, Snarl], 1992
Permanent ink on paper, 18 × 12.5 cm
Private collection, São Paulo, Brazil
PL.0124.0/00 Image 296

Prímula [Primrose], from the series *O perigoso* [The Dangerous One], [1992]
Permanent ink on paper, 30.5 × 23 cm
Collection of Flávia and Guilherme Teixeira, Belo Horizonte, Brazil
PL.1072.0/00 Image 204

[Quando Brasil e Itália têm algo em comum] [When Brazil and Italy Have Something in Common], 1992
Permanent ink on paper, 19 × 11.5 cm
Private collection, São Paulo, Brazil
PL.0041.0/00 Image 316

Quantos já se foram e pra que [How Many Are Already Gone and What For], 1992
Acrylic paint and colored pencil on unstretched canvas, 160 × 102 cm
Collection of Rafael Moraes, São Paulo, Brazil
PL.2389.0/00 Image 210

Rapazes com flores [Young Men With Flowers], 1992
Permanent ink and watercolor on paper, 26 × 16 cm
Collection of Leda Catunda, São Paulo, Brazil
PL.0895.0/00 Image 217

[Saddam vai à luta e Bush veste pijama] [Saddam Goes Fighting and Bush Wears Pijamas], 1992
Permanent ink on paper, 15.5 × 10.5 cm
Private collection, São Paulo, Brazil
PL.0087.0/00 Image 324

[São Paulo é candidata a capital do Brasil] [São Paulo Is Running for Brazil's Capital], 1992
Permanent ink and China ink on paper, 19 × 11.5 cm
Private collection, São Paulo, Brazil
PL.0105.0/00 Image 317

[São Paulo não é nenhuma Brastemp] [São Paulo Is No Brastemp], 1992
Permanent ink on paper, 18 × 12.5 cm
Private collection, São Paulo, Brazil
PL.0057.0/00 Image 286

[Suplicy e Maluf formam par de vasos] [Suplicy and Maluf Are Birds of a Feather], 1992
Permanent ink on paper, 15.5 × 10.5 cm
Private collection, São Paulo, Brazil
PL.0073.0/00 Image 325

[Terra de Marlboro é a terra prometida] [Land of Marlboro Is the Promisse Land], 1992
Permanent ink and China ink on paper, 18 × 12.5 cm
Private collection, São Paulo, Brazil
PL.0123.0/00 Image 294

[Thomas deve ganhar eleição para Rei Sol] [Thomas Sounds to Win the Election for Sun King], 1992
Permanent ink on paper, 18 × 12.5 cm
Private collection, São Paulo, Brazil
PL.0053.0/00 Image 285

[Traveca sai do armário para ser endeusada] [Drag Comes Out to Be Adored as a Goddess], 1992
Permanent ink and cut paper glued on paper, 18 × 12.5 cm
Private collection, São Paulo, Brazil
PL.0068.0/00 Image 303

[Tutu à mineira é inimigo do orgasmo] [Tutu à Mineira Is an Enemy of Orgasm], 1992
Permanent ink on paper, 15.5 × 10.5 cm
Private collection, São Paulo, Brazil
PL.0075.0/00 Image 327

[Tyson serve chá com porrada para moças] [Tyson Serves Tea With Clobbering to Young Ladies], 1992
Permanent ink on paper, 18 × 12.5 cm
Private collection, São Paulo, Brazil
PL.0119.0/00 Image 292

[Vice é vício desde os tempos de Sarney] [A Vice Is a Vicious Ever Since the Time of Sarney], 1992
Permanent ink and China ink on paper, 18 × 12.5 cm
Private collection, São Paulo, Brazil
PL.0070.0/00 Image 306

[Você compraria um carro usado "delle"?] [Would You Buy a Used Car From "Him"?], 1992
Permanent ink and China ink on paper, 18 × 12.5 cm
Private collection, São Paulo, Brazil
PL.0071.0/00 Image 307

[A visão de fogo] [The Vision of Fire], *circa* 1992
Acrylic paint on unstretched canvas, 80 × 40 cm
Collection of Guilherme Dias Salvatore, São Paulo, Brazil
PL.0418.0/00 Image 234

O Penélope, o Recruta, o Aranha [The Penelope, the Recruit, the Spider], *circa* 1992
Thread and sequins on voile and unstretched canvas, 50.5 × 18 cm
Private collection, São Paulo, Brazil
PL.1355.0/00 Image 227

Roupa de homem [Men's Clothing], *circa* 1992
Thread on chequered cotton fabric, 64 × 36 cm
Private collection, São Paulo, Brazil
PL.0022.0/00 Image 219

Saquinho [Small Bag], *circa* 1992
Thread and copper wire on voile, 15.5 × 15.5 cm
Private collection, São Paulo, Brazil
PL.0002.0/00 Image 230

[Solitário inconformado] [The Unreconciled Solitary], *circa* 1992
Colored pencil on paper, 32.5 × 23.5 cm
Private collection, São Paulo, Brazil
PL.0398.0/00 Image 215

Untitled, 1992
Marker on paper, 12.5 × 9.5 cm
Private collection, São Paulo, Brazil
PL.0448.0/00 Image 209

[Carnaval paulistano eleito o pior do mundo] [Paulistano Carnival Voted Worst in the World], 1993
Permanent ink on paper, 14.5 × 10.5 cm
Private collection, São Paulo, Brazil
PL.0055.0/00 Image 335

[Comer barata é o novo barato da cidade] [Eating Roaches Is the New Craze in Town], 1993
Permanent ink on paper, 15 × 8.5 cm
Private collection, São Paulo, Brazil
PL.0108.0/00 Image 341

Da falsa moral [Of the False Morals], 1993
Thread on cotton fabric, piqué shirt, and wooden chair, 92 × 55 × 50 cm
Private collection, São Paulo, Brazil
PL.0027.1/02 Image 239 (left)

[Desculpe Vinicius, feiúra é fundamental] [Sorry Vinicius, Ugliness Is Fundamental], 1993
Permanent ink and marker on paper, 14.5 × 10.5 cm
Private collection, São Paulo, Brazil
PL.0047.0/00 Image 332

Do bom coração [Of the Good Heart], 1993
Thread on cotton fabric, piqué shirt, and wooden chair, 92 × 70 × 50 cm
Private collection, São Paulo, Brazil
PL.0027.1/03 Image 239 (right)

[Drácula vem curtir o outono em Sampa] [Dracula Comes to Enjoy Autumn in Sampa], 1993
Permanent ink on paper, 14.5 × 10.5 cm
Private collection, São Paulo, Brazil
PL.0109.0/00 Image 339

[E se Suzy Rego casasse com Gustavo Rosa?] [What if Suzy Rego Married Gustavo Rosa?], 1993
Permanent ink on paper, 14.5 × 10.5 cm
Private collection, São Paulo, Brazil
PL.0114.0/00 Image 345

[Great Gatsby se esbalda nos Jardins] [Great Gatsby Has a Ball in Jardins], 1993
Permanent ink and marker on paper, 14.5 × 10.5 cm
Private collection, São Paulo, Brazil
PL.0107.0/00 Image 338

Instalação sobre duas figuras [Installation on Two Figures], 1993
Embroidery and needlework on cotton fabrics, striped cotton fabrics, cotton shirts, piqué shirts, voile, wire hanger, iron rack, wooden chairs, and metal chairs, 179 × 600 × 1,200 cm
Private collection, São Paulo, Brazil
PL.0027.1/00 Images 236–39

Lásaro, 1993
Thread on cotton shirts, wire hanger, and iron hack, 150 × 72 × 4 cm
Private collection, São Paulo, Brazil
PL.0027.1/04 Image 238 (left)

Los delícias, 1993
Thread on striped cotton fabric and cotton fabric, and iron chair, 80 × 45 × 60 cm
Private collection, São Paulo, Brazil
PL.0027.1/01 Image 236

[Lugar de masoquista é na areia da praia] [A Masochist's Place Is on the Beach Sand], 1993
Permanent ink and China ink on paper, 17 × 12.5 cm
Private collection, São Paulo, Brazil
PL.0080.0/00 Image 330

O espelho [The Mirror], 1993
Permanent ink and watercolor on paper, 30 × 23 cm
Private collection, São Paulo, Brazil
PL.0670.0/00 Image 240

[Paixão é pior que andar em ônibus lotado] [A Passion Is Worse Than Riding a Crowded Bus], 1993
Permanent ink and marker on paper, 14.5 × 10.5 cm
Private collection, São Paulo, Brazil
PL.0111.0/00 Image 340

[Paulistano não consegue mais trocar o óleo] [Paulistano Can't Change Oil Anymore], 1993
Permanent ink and marker on paper, 14.5 × 10.5 cm
Private collection, São Paulo, Brazil
PL.0054.0/00 Image 334

[Paulo Maluf, um perfeito injustiçado] [Paulo Maluf, a Perfectly Wronged Person], 1993
Permanent ink and marker on paper, 14.5 × 10.5 cm
Private collection, São Paulo, Brazil
PL.0106.0/00 Image 337

[Plebiscito revive quarta-feira de cinzas] [Plebiscite Reenacts Ash Wednesday], 1993
Permanent ink on paper, 14.5 × 10.5 cm
Private collection, São Paulo, Brazil
PL.0110.0/00 Image 342

[Português faz papagaio perder o lugar] [Portuguese Makes Parrot Lose Its Place], 1993
Permanent ink on paper, 14.5 × 10.5 cm
Private collection, São Paulo, Brazil
PL.2368.0/00 Image 333

[Ratos são iguaria da culinária tradicional] [Rats Are Delicacy of Traditional Cooking], 1993
Permanent ink on lined paper, 17 × 10.5 cm
Private collection, São Paulo, Brazil
PL.0051.0/00 Image 331

[São Paulo, a cidade que é uma roubada] [São Paulo, the City That's a Rip-Off], 1993
Permanent ink on paper, 14.5 × 10.5 cm
Private collection, São Paulo, Brazil
PL.0056.0/00 Image 336

São Sebastião de cabeça para baixo [Saint Sebastian Upside Down], 1993
Acrylic paint on unstretched canvas, 70 × 41.5 cm
Private collection, São Paulo, Brazil
PL.1100.0/00 Image 243

[Sexo moderno se pratica verbalmente] [Modern Sex Is Practiced Verbally], 1993
Permanent ink on paper, 14.5 × 10.5 cm
Private collection, São Paulo, Brazil
PL.0112.0/00 Image 343

[Vida noturna de "mudernos" é uma Bósnia] [Nightlife of "Mudernos" People Is a Bosnia], 1993
Permanent ink and marker on paper, 14.5 × 10.5 cm
Private collection, São Paulo, Brazil
PL.0113.0/00 Image 344

Untitled, 1993
Thread on voile, wire hanger and iron rack, 179 × 75 × 2 cm
Private collection, São Paulo, Brazil
PL.0027.1/05 Image 238

[Do vento] [Of the Wind], *circa* 1993
Permanent ink and watercolor on paper, 25 × 18 cm
Private collection, São Paulo, Brazil
PL.1206.0/00 Image 242

Carlos Nader
A paixão de JL [JL's Passion], 2014
Digital video, sound, 82'
Collection Banco Itaú, São Paulo, Brazil

Karen Harley
Com o oceano inteiro para nadar [With the Whole Ocean to Swim], 1997
Digital video, sound, 19'35"
Collection of Karen Harley, Rio de Janeiro, Brazil

The exhibition also included publications, artist notebooks, and documents not listed here.

SELECT ED BIBLI OGRA PHY

EXHIBITION CATALOGS

[NE] Fronteiras, fluxos e personas. Fortaleza: Centro Cultural Banco do Nordeste, 2005.

5º Festival Mix Brasil da diversidade sexual 97. São Paulo: Mix Brasil, 1997.

5th International Istanbul Biennial. Istanbul: Istanbul Foundantion for Culture and Arts, 1997.

6º Salão Nacional de Artes Plásticas: premiados. Rio de Janeiro: Funarte, 1983.

6º Salão Nacional de Artes Plásticas. Rio de Janeiro: Funarte, 1983.

9º Cinema Mostra Aids. São Paulo: Grupo Pela Vidda/SP, 2013.

18ª Bienal Internacional de São Paulo: catálogo geral. São Paulo: Fundação Bienal de São Paulo, 1985.

25 Visuell. Frankfurt: Deutsche Bank Kunst, 2005.

29ª Bienal de São Paulo: documentação: há sempre um copo de mar para um homem navegar. São Paulo: Fundação Bienal de São Paulo, 2011.

1981/2021 Arte Contemporânea Brasileira na Coleção Andrea e José Olympio Pereira. Rio de Janeiro: Tisara, 2021.

A figura humana na coleção Itaú. São Paulo: Itaú Cultural, 2000.

À flor da pele: pintura e prazer. Rio de Janeiro: Centro Empresarial Rio, 1983.

À Nordeste. São Paulo: Sesc 24 de maio, 2019.

A presença da White Martins no MAM/RJ. Rio de Janeiro: Museu de Arte Moderna, 1994.

Acervo–Guia de Visitação. São Paulo: Pinacoteca do Estado, 2020.

Albert Hien: transatlantik, transatlantique, transatlantico. Cologne: Josef-Haubrich-Kunsthalle, 1986.

ARCO'05: Feria Internacional de Arte Contemporáneo. Madrid: Arco/ Ifema, Feria de Madrid, 2005.

ARCO8: Brasil. Madrid: Arco/Ifema, Feria de Madrid, 2008.

Ars 01: artists. Helsinki: Museum of Contemporary Art Kiasma, 2001.

Arte brasileira atual: 1984. Niterói: Galeria de Arte UFF, 1984.

Arte brasileira contemporânea: doações recentes 96 [CONTEMPORARY Brazilian art: recent donations/96]. São Paulo: Museu de Arte Moderna, 1996.

Arte Galeria: exposição de inauguração. Fortaleza: Arte Galeria, 1983.

Arte no ônibus. Belo Horizonte: Genial Projetos de Arte/BHTrans, 2002.

Arte-Veículo. Santos: Sesc Santos, 2019.

Arte-Veículo. São Paulo: Sesc, 2018.

Arthur Bispo do Rosário e Leonilson: os Penélope. Jundiaí: Sesc Jundiaí, 2015.

Bispo do Rosário eu vim – aparição impregnação e impacto. São Paulo: Itaú Cultural, 2022.

Bob Wolfenson: Retratos. Porto Seguro: Espaço Cultural Porto Seguro, 2018.

Brasil 500 anos artes visuais. São Paulo: Associação Brasil 500 Anos Artes Visuais: Fundação Bienal de São Paulo, 2000.

Centelhas em movimento. São Paulo: Instituto Tomie Ohtake, 2023.

Coleção Airton Queiroz. Fortaleza: Espaço Cultural Unifor, 2016.

Cotidiano contemporâneo. Fortaleza: Centro Cultural Banco do Nordeste, 2005.

Cotidiano contemporâneo. Fortaleza: Centro Cultural Banco do Nordeste, 2008.

É Tudo Verdade [It's All True]: 20º Festival Internacional de Documentários. São Paulo: É Tudo Verdade/Imprensa Oficial, 2015.

Elementar: fazer junto. São Paulo: Ipsis, 2023.

Encontros com o modernismo. Rio de Janeiro: Museu de Arte Moderna, 2004.

Espaço lúdico: um olhar sobre a infância na arte brasileira. Rio de Janeiro: Galeria do BNDES, 2004.

Exposição Brasil-Japão de Arte Contemporânea. São Paulo: Fundação Brasil-Japão, 1992.

Histórias da sexualidade. São Paulo: Museu de Arte de São Paulo Assis Chateaubriand, 2017.

Leonilson – arquivo e memória vivos. Fortaleza: Unifor, 2024.

Leonilson [Art Basel]. São Paulo: Galeria Marilia Razuk, 2024.

Leonilson 1993. Rio de Janeiro: Thomas Cohn Arte Contemporânea, 1993.

Leonilson. Corpo político. São Paulo: Almeida & Dale, 2023.

Leonilson e a geração 80 (CE). Fortaleza: Multiarte, 2023.

Leonilson e a geração 80 (RJ). Rio de Janeiro: Edições Pinakotheke, 2023.

Leonilson inflamável. Fortaleza: Museu de Arte Contemporânea do Ceará, 2013.

Leonilson. São Paulo: Galeria Marilia Razuk, 2016.

Loose threads. Londres: Serpentine Gallery, 1988.

Mercado de arte nº 13. São Paulo: Ricardo Camargo Galeria, 2008.

Mostra Sesc de Artes 08. São Paulo: Sesc, 2008.

Museu de Arte Moderna 60 anos: arte brasileira 1963-1978, cinemateca, formação das coleções, pré bienal de Paris 1969, construção. Rio de Janeiro: Museu de Arte Moderna, 2009.

Neo Tropicália: when lives become form: contemporary Brazilian art 1960s to the present. Tokyo/Hiroshima: Museum of Contemporary Art/ Museum of Contemporary Art, 2008.

No habrá nunca una puerta. Estás adentro. Obras de la coleção Teixeira de Freitas. Madrid: Fundación Banco Santander, colección Teixeira de Freitas, 2019.

Nouvelle Biennale de Paris. Paris: Electa Moniteur, 1985.

Onde está você, Geração 80? Rio de Janeiro: Centro Cultural Banco do Brasil, 2004.

Os muitos e o um. São Paulo: Instituto Tomie Ohtake, 2017.

Past/Future/Present - Contemporary Brazilian Art. Phoenix/São Paulo: Phoenix Art Museum/Museu de Arte Moderna de São Paulo, 2017.

Pequenos Fogos. Brotéria: Associação Cultural e Científica, 2023.

Pinturas de Laura. Rio de Janeiro: Casa de Cultura Laura Alvim, 1995.

Prêmio Brasília de Artes Plásticas 1990. Brasília: Museu de Arte de Brasília, 1990.

Que sejam muitas as manhãs de verão. São Paulo: Galeria Superfície, 2022.

Rosas Brasileiras. São Paulo: Farol Santander, 2023.

Salão Nacional de Artes Plásticas. Rio de Janeiro: Funarte, 1983.

Salão Sobral 2000 Artes Plásticas. Sobral: Prefeitura Municipal de Sobral/ Secretaria da Cultura, Desporto e Mobilização Social, 2000.

Sandra Cinto: das ideias na cabeça aos olhos no céu. São Paulo: Itaú Cultural, 2021.

Sem título, 2006: comodato Eduardo Brandão e Jan Fjeld. São Paulo: Museu de Arte Moderna, 2006.

SP-ARTE/2005: Feira Internacional de Arte de São Paulo. São Paulo: Fundação Bienal de São Paulo, 2005.

SP-ARTE/2006: Feira Internacional de Arte Moderna e Contemporânea de São Paulo. São Paulo: Fundação Bienal de São Paulo, 2006.

Tempo e Transparência. São Paulo: Casa Gabriel, 2023.

Think with the senses, fell with the mind: art in the present tense: short guide. Venice: Fondazione La Biennale di Venezia/Marsilio, 2007.

Todos somos um. Brasília/São Paulo: Escola Superior do Ministério Público da União/FAAP, 2008.

Transbordar – transgressões do bordado na arte. São Paulo: Sesc, 2020.

Tridimensional: entre o sagrado e o estético – Um recorte da coleção Vera e Miguel Chaia. São Paulo: Arte 132, 2023.

Urgente! 41 Salón Nacional de Artistas. Cali: Asociacion para la Promocion de las Artes, 2010.

Visuell: blind date. Frankfurt: Deutsche Bank, 2006.

Viva arte brasileña. Madrid: Casa do Brasil, 1981.

Viva Brasil viva: konst från Brasilien. Stockholm: Kulturhuset, 1991.

Zona tórrida: certa pintura do Nordeste. Recife: Santander Cultural, 2012.

ABRAMO, Radha; LISBOA, Noris (eds.). *34 Artistas contemporâneos brasileiros*. São Paulo: Subdistrito Comercial de Arte, 1988.

ADAMS, Beverly. *Constructing a poetic universe: the Diane and Bruce Halle collection of Latin American art*. Houston: The Museum of Fine Arts, 2007.

______; DAVIDSON, Vanessa K. *Order, chaos, and the space between: contemporary Latin American art from the Diane and Bruce Halle collection*. Phoenix: Phoenix Art Museum, 2013.

AGUILAR, Nelson (ed.). *Bienal Brasil século XX*. São Paulo: Fundação Bienal de São Paulo, 1994.

______. *Ceará redescobre o Brasil*. São Paulo/Fortaleza: BrasilConnects/Centro Dragão do Mar de Arte e Cultura, 2002.

______; BRETT, Guy; DAVID, Catherine. *Mostra do Redescobrimento: arte contemporânea [contemporary art]*. São Paulo: Associação Brasil 500 Anos Artes Visuais/Fundação Bienal de São Paulo, 2000.

______; ANDRADE, Mário; PEDROSA, Mário; GULLAR, Ferreira. *Século 20: arte do Brasil*. São Paulo: Fundação Calouste Gulbenkian-Centro de Arte Moderna/Associação Brasil 500 Anos Artes Visuais, 2000.

AJZENBERG, Elza. *MAC USP 40 anos: interfaces contemporâneas*. São Paulo: Museu de Arte Contemporânea da Universidade de São Paulo, 2003.

ALIAGA, Juan Vicente; LEBOVICI, Elisabeth; OLIVEIRA, Manuel; LORD, Catherine; MELLAD, Justo Pastor. *Em todas partes: politicas de la diversidad sexual en el arte*. Santiago de Compostela: Centro Galego de Arte Contemporánea/Xunta de Galicia, 2009.

AMARAL, Aracy. *A nova dimensão do objeto*. São Paulo: Museu de Arte Contemporânea da Universidade de São Paulo, 1986.

______. *Brasil: la nueva generación*. Caracas: Fundación Museo de Bellas Artes, 1991.

______; BRIOT, Marie Odile Briot (eds.). *Modernidade: art brésilien du 20e. siècle*. Paris: Musée d'Art Moderne de la Ville de Paris, 1987.

AMOR, Mónica; BASUALDO, Carlos; KATZENSTEIN, Inés; MEREWETHER, Charles. *Archivo Pons - Artxiboa*. San Sebastián: Koldo Mitxelena Kulturunea, 2002.

ANJOS, Moacir dos. *A queda do céu*. São Paulo/São José do Rio Preto: Paço das Artes/Sesc Rio Preto, 2016.

ANTUNES, Cláudia Rejane Dornelles (ed.); MEDEIROS, Maria Tereza Silveira de. *MARGS: Catálogo de exposições 2015-2018*. Porto Alegre: AMARGS, 2018.

ÁQUILA, Luiz; CAVALCANTI, Lauro. *Ar: exposição de artes plásticas, brinquedos, objetos e maquetes*. Rio de Janeiro: Paço Imperial, 1997.

ARAÚJO, Olívio Tavares de. *BRASILIDADE e independência*. São Paulo: Pancrom Indústria Gráfica Ltda, 1985.

______; NOSEK, Leopold; ARAÚJO, Olívio Tavares de. *Dor, forma, beleza: a representação criadora de experiência traumática*. São Paulo: Estação Pinacoteca, 2005.

BARJA, Wagner (ed.). *Entrecopas: arte brasileira 1950-2014*. Brasília: Museu Nacional do Conjunto Cultural da República, 2014.

______; CHAVES, Xico. *Entre séculos: acervos públicos do Distrito Federal*. Brasília: Museu Nacional do Conjunto Cultural da República, 2009.

______; TAVEIRA, Ana. *Acervos em movimento: Museu de Arte de Brasília MAB, Museu Nacional MUN*. Brasília: Museu Nacional do Conjunto Cultural da República, 2013.

BARROS, Regina Teixeira de. *Arte e política: outros olhares*. Ribeirão Preto/São Paulo: Museu de Arte de Ribeirão Preto Pedro Manuel-Gismondi/Pinacoteca do Estado, 2010.

BARROS, Stella Teixeira de (ed.). *CCSP: 20 artistas, 20 anos*. São Paulo: Centro Cultural São Paulo, 2002.

______; MESQUITA, Ivo. *Artistas colecionistas*. São Paulo: Valu Oria Galeria de Arte, 1995.

BARTIRA, Uiara; MILLIET, Maria Alice. *Brasil reflexão 97: a arte contemporânea da gravura*. Curitiba: Fundação Cultural de Curitiba, 1997.

BASILIO, Miriam; BERCHT, Fatima; CULLEN, Deborah; GARRELS, Gary; PÉREZ-ORAMAS, Luis Enrique. *Latin American & Caribbean art: MoMA at El Museo*. New York: The Museum of Modern Art/El Museo del Barrio, 2004.

BERCHT, Fátima; CHIARELLI, Tadeu. *O fio da trama [The Thread Unraveled: Contemporary Brazilian Art]*. New York: El Museo del Barrio, 2001.

BESTUÉ, David. *El sentido de la escultura / The Point of Sculpture*. Barcelona: Fundació Joan Miró, 2021.

BOUSSO, Vitoria Daniela. *Representação, presenças decisivas*. São Paulo: Paço das Artes, 1993.

BRITO, Luciana; CIMINO, Fabio. *1: Galeria Brito Cimino*. São Paulo: Galeria Brito Cimino, 1998.

______; CIMINO, Fábio. *Brito Cimino: Arte Contemporânea e Moderna*. São Paulo: Galeria Brito Cimino, 1997.

BRITO, Ronaldo; BUENO, Guilherme; SALCEDO, Sonia. *Art in Brazil: 1950-2011*. Brussels/Antwerp: Europalia International/Ludion, 2011.

BUENO, Guilherme. *Arte contemporânea brasileira: coleções João Sattamini e MAC de Niterói: guia do visitante*. Niterói: Museu de Arte Contemporânea de Niterói, 2009.

CAMARGO, Ricardo; COSTA, Oswaldo Corrêa. *Recortes de uma coleção*. São Paulo: Ricardo Camargo Galeria, 2011.

______; MUSATTI, Bruno. *Recortes de uma coleção*. São Paulo: Ricardo Camargo Galeria, 2010.

CAMPOFIORITO, Italo; REIS, Paulo; PEDROSA, Mário. *Espelho da Bienal*. Niterói: Museu de Arte Contemporânea de Niterói, 1998.

CANTON, Katia; GONÇALVES, Lisbeth Rebollo (eds.). *Um mundo sem molduras*. São Paulo: Museu de Arte Contemporânea da Universidade de São Paulo, 2010.

______. *Heranças contemporâneas*. São Paulo: Museu de Arte Contemporânea da Universidade de São Paulo, 1997.

CASSUNDÉ, Bitú (ed.). *Das viagens, dos desejos, dos caminhos [Of Journeys, of Desires, of Paths]*. Vila Velha: Museu Vale, 2014.

CAVALCANTI, Lauro. *Caminhos do contemporâneo: 1952/2002*. Rio de Janeiro: Paço Imperial, 2002.

______; RODRIGUES, Maria Clara. *Abstrações: coleção Fundação Edson Queiroz e coleção Roberto Marinho*. Fortaleza: Espaço Cultural Unifor, 2014.

CATUNDA, Leda. *Leonilson: verdades e mentiras*. São Paulo: Galeria Superfície, 2014.

CHAIMOVICH, Felipe. *Leonilson*. São Paulo: Galeria Thomas Cohn, 1998.

______. *Quando vidas se tornam forma: diálogo com o futuro Brasil/Japão*. São Paulo: Museu de Arte Moderna, 2008.

______. *140 Caracteres*. São Paulo: Museu de Arte Moderna, 2014.

______; FABRIS, Annateresa; COSTA, Cacilda Teixeira da; OSORIO, Luiz Camillo. *MAM 60*. São Paulo: Museu de Arte Moderna, 2008.

CHIARELLI, Tadeu. *15 Artistas brasileiros*. São Paulo: Museu de Arte Moderna, 1996.

______.*Metrópole: Experiência Paulistana*. São Paulo: Pinacoteca do Estado, 2017.

______; CHAIMOVICH, Felipe; ALVES, Cauê. *MAM[na]Oca: arte brasileira no acervo do Museu de Arte Moderna de São Paulo*. São Paulo: Museu de Arte Moderna, 2006.

______; CINTRÃO, Rejane. *Arte brasileira no acervo do Museu de Arte Moderna de São Paulo: doações recentes 1996-1998*. Rio de Janeiro: Centro Cultural Banco do Brasil, 1998.

______; SANT'ANNA, Margarida. *Arte brasileira: século XX*. São Paulo: Museu de Arte Moderna: Imprensa Oficial, 2006.

CINTRÃO, Rejane. *XXV Salão de Arte Contemporânea de Santo André: sala especial*. Santo André: Paço Municipal, 1997.

______; BARROS, Stella Teixeira de. *O espírito da nossa época: coleção Dulce e João Carlos de Figueiredo Ferraz.* São Paulo: Museu de Arte Moderna, 2001.

COCCHIARALE, Fernando; MANATA, Franz; ROELS JR., Reynaldo. *Um século de arte brasileira: coleção Gilberto Chateaubriand.* Florianópolis: Museu de Arte de Santa Catarina, 2007.

______; MANATA, Franz. *Um século de arte brasileira: coleção Gilberto Chateaubriand.* São Paulo: Tekné Projetos Culturais, 2006.

COELHO, Teixeira (ed.). *1911-2011 arte brasileira e depois, na coleção Itaú [1922-2011 Brazilian art and after, the Itaú collection].* São Paulo: Itaú Cultural, 2012.

COELHO, Aguinaldo. *Os anos 80.* Goiânia: Marina Potrich Galeria de Arte, 1998.

COSTA, Cacilda Teixeira da. *Branco dominante.* São Paulo: Galeria de Arte São Paulo, 1992.

COSTA, Magnólia. *Gabinete de desenhos: obras do acervo do MAM-SP.* São Paulo/Salvador: Museu de Arte Moderna/Caixa Cultural, 2009.

______; OLIVA, Fernando; KIHN, Christophe; REZENDE, Marcelo. *Cover = reencenação + repetição.* São Paulo: Museu de Arte Moderna, 2008.

COSTA, Marcus de Lontra. *Infância perversa: fábulas sobre a memória e o tempo.* Rio de Janeiro/Salvador: Museu de Arte Moderna/Museu de Arte Moderna da Bahia, 1995.

______; RODRÍGUEZ, Bélgica. *Brazil: images of the 80's & 90's [Brasil: imagens dos anos 80 e 90].* Washington, D.C./Rio de Janeiro: Art Museum of the Americas/Museu de Arte Moderna do Rio de Janeiro, 1993.

COUTINHO, Fábio Luiz Borgatti; CARVALHO, Ana Albani de; COHN, Thomas. *Coleção Liba e Rubem Knijnik: arte brasileira contemporânea.* Porto Alegre: Museu de Arte do Rio Grande do Sul Ado Malagoli, 2001.

DUARTE, Luisa; BOGOSSIAN, Gabriel. *Dispositivos para um mundo (im)possível: Roesler Hotel # 25.* São Paulo: Galeria Nara Roesler, 2014.

FARIAS, Agnaldo. *Galeria Luisa Strina: 20 anos de arte brasileira.* São Paulo: Museu de Arte de São Paulo Assis Chateaubriand, 1994.

______. *80/90: Modernos, pós-modernos etc.* São Paulo: Instituto Tomie Ohtake, 2009.

FARIAS, Agnaldo et al. *Ordenação e vertigem: artes plásticas, cinema, fotografia, dança, música.* São Paulo: Centro Cultural Banco do Brasil, 2003.

______; ANJOS, Moacir dos. *Catálogo da 29ª Bienal de São Paulo: há sempre um copo de mar para um homem navegar.* São Paulo: Fundação Bienal de São Paulo, 2010.

______; ANJOS, Moacir dos. *Catalogue of 29ª Bienal de São Paulo: há sempre um copo de mar para um homem navegar.* São Paulo: Fundação Bienal de São Paulo, 2010.

FIDELIS, Gaudêncio. *Queermuseu: Cartografias da diferença na arte brasileira.* Porto Alegra: Santander Cultural, 2017.

______. *Queermuseu: Cartografias da Diferença na Arte Brasileira.* Rio de Janeiro: AMEAV, 2018.

______; ALVES, José Francisco. *Labirintos da iconografia.* Porto Alegre: Museu de Arte do Rio Grande do Sul/Gráf. Palloti, 2014.

FISCHER, André; CAPÓ, Suzy. *MIX Brasil: II Festival de Manifestações das Sexualidades.* São Paulo: Museu da Imagem e do Som, 1994.

FJELD, Jan. *Leonilson.* São Paulo: Galeria Luisa Strina, 1987.

______. *Leonilson: o inconformado.* Rio de Janeiro: Thomas Cohn Arte Contemporânea, 1988.

FORTES, Márcia; (ed.) *Espelho cego: seleções de uma coleção contemporânea.* São Paulo: Museu de Arte Moderna, 2001.

FRIEDEL, Helmut. *Moving mountains.* Munich: Städtische Galerie im Lenbachhaus, 1987.

GALVÃO, João Cândido. *Paisagens.* São Paulo: Galeria São Paulo, 1994.

______. *Leonilson.* São Paulo: Galeria São Paulo, 1993.

GENOCCHIO, Benjamin; LAGNADO, Lisette; BOND, Anthony. *Material immaterial.* Sydney: The Art Gallery of New South Wales, 1997.

GENSCHER, Hans-Dietrich; SODRÉ, Roberto Costa de Abreu; HERKENHOFF, Paulo. *Brasil já: Beispiele zeitgenössischer brasilianischer Malerei.* Leverkusen: Der Oberstadtdirektor, 1988.

GONÇALVES, Lisbeth Rebolo; SILVA, Aparício Basílio da. *Panorama da Arte Atual Brasileira/89: pintura.* São Paulo: Museu de Arte Moderna, 1989.

GRUIJTHUIJSEN, Krist. *Leonilson: Drawn (1975–1993).* Berlin: Hatje Cantz Verlag, 2020.

______ *Leonilson: Drawn (1975–1993).* Hatje Cantz Verlag/Fundação Serralves, 2022.

HERKENHOFF, Paulo. *Tomie Ohtake na trama espiritual da arte brasileira: exposição comemorativa dos 90 anos da artista.* São Paulo/Curitiba: Instituto Tomie Ohtake/Museu Oscar Niemeyer, 2004.

______; CAMPOS, Marcelo; QUEIROZ, Airton. *Trajetórias: arte brasileira na coleção Fundação Edson Queiroz: Unifor 40 anos.* Fortaleza: Espaço Cultural Unifor, 2013.

______; PEDROSA, Adriano (eds.). *Marcas do corpo, dobras da alma [Marks of the Body, Folds of the Soul].* Curitiba: Museu da Gravura de Curitiba, 2000.

HOFFMANN, Jens; PEDROSA, Adriano. *Isimsiz (12.Istanbul Bienali), 2011 [Untitled (12th Istanbul Biennial), 2011].* Istambul: Foundantion for Culture and Arts, 2011.

JAUKKURI, Maaretta; PAPASTERGIADIS, Nikos; ROGOFF, Irit. *ARS 01: unfolding perspectives.* Helsinki: Museum of Contemporary Art Kiasma, 2001.

JESUS, Eduardo de. *O que é verdade para certos rapazes: sobre A paixão de JL, de Carlos Nader.* In: FORUMDOC.BH.2015: 19° festival do Filme Documentário e Etnográfico/Fórum de Antropologia e Cinema. Belo Horizonte: Associação Filmes de Quintal, 2015.

JUNCOSA, Enrique; COLOMBO, Paolo; LAMPERT, Catherine. *Order. Desire. Light.* Dublin: Irish Museum of Modern Art, 2008.

KAITAVUORI, Kaija. *ARS 01: perspectives.* Helsinki: Museum of Contemporary Art Kiasma, 2001.

KALMAN, Regina Dragiça (ed.). *IV Salão de Arte Contemporânea da A.A.P.J.* Jundiaí: Associação dos Artistas Plásticos de Jundiaí (AAPJ), 1979.

KAPLAN, Alberto; Xaxéo, Pedro Martins Caldas. *Aquarela brasileira.* Rio de Janeiro: Centro Cultural Light, 2001.

KLEIN, Paulo. *VOA Leo.* Campinas: AT | AL | 609, 2013.

______. *69° Salão de Abril.* Prefeitura Municipal de Fortaleza, 2018.

KUCZYNSKI, Paulo. *A Coleção Imaginária de Paulo Kuczynski.* São Paulo: Ipsis, 2023.

LAGNADO, Lisette; VOGT, Rafael ; ROSA, Maia; GUIMARÃES, Cao. *Leonilson, Flávia Ribeiro, Rivane Neuenschwander: 5th International Istanbul Biennial.* São Paulo: Fundação Bienal de São Paulo, 1997.

______. "For those who did not buy the truth". In: *International Istanbul Biennial, 5.* Istambul: Istanbul Foundantion for Culture and Arts, 1997.

LANG, Jack; NARDIN, Anne Nardin; PONTUAL, Roberto. *Estampes et Révolution, 200 ans après.* Paris: Ministère de la Culture, de la Communication, des Grands Travaux et du Bicentenaire, 1989.

LAURO, Cavalcanti. *Conversas entre coleções.* Rio de Janeiro: Casa Roberto Marinho, 2024.

LEDIS, Lori; FLAM, Robert; SABBATINO, Mary (eds.). *Art from Brazil in New York.* New York: LedsFlam/Galerie Lelong, 1995.

LITTMAN, Robert R.; HOLLANDER, Kurt et al. *Así está la cosa, instalación y arte objeto en América Latina.* Mexico City: Centro Cultural Arte Contemporáneo, 1997.

MACEDO, Carlos. *PANORÂMICA 1: breve histórico das artes visuais do Ceará.* Fortaleza: Palácio da Abolição, 2011.

MACNAIR, Jennifer; FRICK, Thomas; BUTLER, Nola. *The Broad Contemporary Art Museum at the Los Angeles County Museum of Art, 2008.* Los Angeles: Los Angeles County Museum of Art, 2008.

MAGALHÃES, Fábio. *Brasil brasileiro: nossa terra, nossa gente.* São Paulo/Rio de Janeiro: Centro Cultural Banco do Brasil, 2008.

MARTA, Karen; RANGEL, Gabriela. *José Leonilson Empty Man.* New York: Koening Books/Americas Society, 2017.

MARTINS, Miriam Celeste. *Catálogo do aprendiz de arte: Brasil + 500 Mostra do Redescobrimento.* São Paulo: Carta Editorial/Associação Brasil 500 Anos Artes Visuais, 2000.

MASTROBUONO, Pedro. *Projeto felicidade – Grandes Coleções.* São Paulo: Salão Marc Chagall Clube Hebraica São Paulo, 2019.

MATTOS, Armando; COSTA, Marcus de Lontra. *Anos 80: o palco da diversidade: coleção Gilberto Chateaubriand MAM-RJ.* São Paulo: Galeria de Arte do Sesi, 1995.

MENDONÇA, Casimiro Xavier de. *Leonilson.* São Paulo: Galeria São Paulo, 1991.

MESQUITA, Ivo; HERKENHOFF, Paulo; MELLADO, Justo Pastor. *Cartographies.* Winnipeg: Winnipeg Art Gallery, 1993.

______; PEDROSA, Adriano; ANTELO, Raul; HERKENHOFF, Paulo. *Versiones del Sur: F[r]icciones.* Madrid: Museo Nacional Centro de Arte Reina Sofía, 2000.

MILLIET, Maria Alice. *Cada cabeça uma sentença: 1789-1989.* Juiz de Fora: Universidade Federal de Juiz de Fora, 1989.

MIRANDA, Danilo Santos de; RESENDE, Ricardo. *Arthur Bispo do Rosário e Leonilson: os Penélope.* Sorocaba: Sesc Sorocaba, 2015.

MONTENEGRO, Luís Paulo. *Visiones de la tierra – El mundo planeado.* Madrid: Lerner & TF Editores, 2018.

MORAIS, Frederico. *Coleção Gilberto Chateaubriand: retrato e auto-retrato da arte brasileira.* São Paulo: Museu de Arte Moderna, 1984.

MORAIS, Frederico et al. *BR 80: pintura Brasil década 80.* São Paulo: Itaú Cultural, 1991.

MORGAN, Jessica. *Pulse: art, healing, and transformation.* Boston: The Institute of Contemporary Art, 2003.

MOSQUERA, Gerardo; SAMOS, Adrienne Samos. *20 Desarranxos: Panorama da Arte Brasileira.* Vigo: Museo de Arte Contemporánea de Vigo, 2005.

NAVAS, Adolfo Montejo. *Obras primas do MAB: fragmentos a seu imã.* Brasília: Arte 21, 2003.

NAVES, Rodrigo. *Arte hoje 88.* Ribeirão Preto: Prefeitura Municipal – Casa da Cultura, 1988.

NETTO, José Teixeira Coelho. *O papel da arte.* São Paulo: Museu de Arte Contemporânea da Universidade de São Paulo/Sesi/Centro Cultural Fiesp, 2000.

NETTO, Karla Osório; COCCHIARALE, Fernando. *Entre a palavra e a imagem: coleção Gilberto Chateaubriand Museu de Arte Moderna do Rio de Janeiro.* Brasília: Espaço Cultural Contemporâneo Venâncio (ECCO), 2005.

NEVES, Julio; ARAÚJO, Olívio Tavares de. *Brasil: psicanálise e modernismo.* São Paulo: Museu de Arte de São Paulo Assis Chateaubriand, 2000.

NÓBREGA, Gustavo. *A poesia e as artes visuais.* São Paulo: Galeria Superfície, 2018.

ODAKA, Hikari; HASEGAWA, Yuko; GUZMÁN, Kristine. *The Marvelous Real: Contemporary Spanish and Latin American art from the MUSAC Collection.* Tokyo: Museum of Contemporary Art, 2014.

OHTAKE, Ricardo; FARIAS, Agnaldo; BUENO, Guilherme. *Mapa do agora: arte brasileira recente na coleção João Sattamini do Museu de Arte Contemporânea de Niterói.* São Paulo: Instituto Tomie Ohtake, 2002.

ORDÁS, Carlos. *Variantes discursivas: colección Musac III [Discursive variants: Musac collection III].* León/Barcelona: Museo de Arte Contemporáneo de Castilla y León/Actar, 2010.

PADILLA, Roberto; KORNIS, George. *Arte em movimento.* Rio de Janeiro: Galeria de Arte do BNDES, 2003.

PEDROSA, Adriano; HERKENHOFF, Paulo (eds.). *XXIV Bienal de São Paulo: arte contemporânea brasileira: um e/entre outro/s.* São Paulo: Fundação Bienal de São Paulo, 1998.

______; DUNN, Julie. *Farsites: urban crisis and domestic symptoms in recent contemporary art [Sitios distantes: crisis urbanas y síntomas domésticos en el arte contemporáneo reciente].* San Diego/Tijuana: San Diego Museum of Art /Centro Cultural Tijuana, 2005.

PEDROSA, Adriano. *Romance [a novel].* Lisbon: Cristina Guerra Contemporary Art, 2006.

______. *Leonilson: Truth, Fiction.* São Paulo/ Rio de Janeiro: Pinacoteca do Estado/ Cobogó, 2014.

______. *Leonilson: Truth, Fiction.* Belo Horizonte: Centro Cultural Banco do Brasil, 2015.

______. *Leonilson: Now and Opportunities.* São Paulo: Museu de Arte de São Paulo Assis Chateaubriand, 2024.

______; MELO, Alexandre; ZACCAGNINI, Carla. *Desenhos [drawings]: A-Z: Colecção Madeira Corporate Services.* Funchal: Colecção Madeira Corporate Services, 2006.

PEDROSA, João. *Fabio Cardoso, Leonilson, Daniel Senise, Luiz Zerbini.* São Paulo: Museu de Arte de São Paulo Assis Chateaubriand, 1989.

PEDROSO, Franklin Espath; TJABBES, Pieter; VASQUEZ, Pedro Karp. *Jogo da memória.* Rio de Janeiro: Museu de Arte Moderna, 2005.

PEREJAUME; GULLAR, Ferreira; PEREIRA, Cecilia; HERVÉS, Rubén Blanco; LAMBERT, Fátima; REIS, Paulo. *Entre a palavra e a imagem [Entre la palabra y la imagen].* A Coruña: Fundación Luis Seoane, 2007.

PÉREZ-ORAMAS, Luis. *An Atlas of Drawings: Transforming Chronologies.* New York: Museum of Modern Art, 2006.

PERLINGEIRO, Max (ed.); CHIEREGATO, Paola. *Leonilson por Antonio Dias Perfil de uma Coleção.* Edições Pinakotheke, 2019.

PETRUS, Nicholas. *Par Avion: exercícios de epistemografia.* São Paulo: Memorial da América Latina, 2008.

PFLEGER, Manfred; REIMELT, Helge Karsten; SOARES, Marcelo Lacerda. *Brasilianische Kunst der Gegenwart [Arte brasileira contemporânea] [Contemporary Brazilian art].* Leverkusen: Bayer AG/ Museu de Arte Moderna, 1996.

PONTUAL, Roberto. *Velha mania: desenho brasileiro.* Rio de Janeiro: Escola de Artes Visuais do Parque Lage, 1985.

______; CYROULNIK, Philippe (eds.). *Ouverture brésilienne.* Ivry-sur-Seine: Crédac-Centre d'Art Contemporain - Galerie Fernand Léger, 1987.

PORTELLA, Isabel Sanson. *Aquilo que nos une.* Rio de Janeiro: Caixa Cultural, 2016.

PRESTES, Cézar; LEAL, Mônica; CRUSIUS, Yeda Crusius; AMARAL, José Luiz do. *Acervo do MARGS: expressividade na arte brasileira.* Porto Alegre: Museu de Arte do Rio Grande do Sul Ado Malagoli, 2009.

Projeto Leonilson (ed.). *Diário de bordo: uma viagem com Leonilson.* São Paulo: Caixa Cultural, 2007.

______. *Diário de bordo: uma viagem com Leonilson.* Brasília/Salvador: Caixa Cultural, 2008.

______. *Diário de bordo: uma viagem com Leonilson.* Fortaleza: Espaço Cultural Unifor, 2009.

QUEIROZ, Airton; PERLINGEIRO, Max. *Arte brasileira nas coleções públicas e privadas do Ceará.* Fortaleza: Espaço Cultural Unifor, 2005.

RAMALHO, Claudia. *Inventário da paixão: homenagem a Marcantonio Vilaça.* Rio de Janeiro: Museu Histórico Nacional, 2014.

RAMOS, Fátima; RIBEIRO, António Pinto. *Arte contemporânea: colecção Caixa Geral de Depósitos: novas aquisições.* Lisbon: Caixa Geral de Depósitos - Culturgest, 2002.

REIS, Paulo; ROSENGARTEN, Ruth. *Um oceano inteiro para nadar.* Lisbon: Culturgest, 2000.

RESENDE, Ricardo. *Longo caminho de um rapaz apaixonado.* Buenos Aires: Funceb, 2005.

RESENDE, Ricardo et al. *Leonilson.* Fortaleza: Prefeitura, 2006.

______; CASSUNDÉ, Bitu; MACIEL, Maria Esther. *Leonilson: sob o peso dos meus amores.* Porto Alegre: Fundação Iberê Camargo, 2012.

RIBENBOIM, Ricardo; BORGES, Adélia; NERO, Cyro del; MORAIS, Frederico. *Cotidiano/Arte: consumo.* São Paulo: Itaú Cultural, 1999.

RITO, Lucia; COUTINHO, Wilson. *Coca-Cola 50 anos com arte [Coca-Cola 50 years of art].* São Paulo: Coca-Cola - Divisão de Atividades Públicas, 1992.

RIVERA, Tania. *Lugares do Delírio: arte e expressão, loucura e política.* São Paulo: N-1 Edições. 2018.

ROCHA, Lauro Santos; BARCELOS, Paulo; MENDONÇA, Casimiro Xavier de; MORAIS, Frederico. *Caminhos do desenho brasileiro.* Porto Alegre: Museu de Arte do Rio Grande do Sul Ado Malagoli, 1986.

ROELS JR., Reynaldo. *Arte erótica.* Rio de Janeiro: Museu de Arte Moderna, 1993.

______. *Arte contemporânea brasileira na coleção João Sattamini.* Niterói: Museu de Arte Contemporânea de Niterói, 1996.

SACCÀ, Lucilla. *Brasil, segni d'arte: libri e video 1950-1993.* Mariano Comense: Grafiche Mariano, 1993.

SACRAMENTO, Enock. *III Salão Jovem de Arte Contemporânea.* Santo André: Prefeitura Municipal, 1980.

SALZSTEIN, Sônia; ROELS JR., Reynaldo. *O moderno e o contemporâneo na arte brasileira: coleção Gilberto Chateaubriand do Museu de Arte Moderna do Rio de Janeiro.* São Paulo: Museu de Arte de São Paulo Assis Chateaubriand, 1998.

SAMOS, Adrienne; MOSQUERA, Gerardo; SANT'ANNA, Margarida. *Panorama da Arte Brasileira 2003: (Desarrumado) 19 desarranjos.* São Paulo: Museu de Arte Moderna, 2003.

SANT'ANNA, Margarida. *Afetividades eletivas: coleção Luiz Sérgio Arantes.* Belo Horizonte: Galeria de Arte do Centro Cultural Minas Tênis Clube, 2015.

______; CINTRÃO, Rejane. *2080.* São Paulo: Museu de Arte Moderna, 2003.

SANT'ANNA, Renata, PRATES, Valquíria. *Arte à primeira vista.* Bauru: Sesc Bauru, 2016.

______*Arte à primeira vista.* São Carlos: Sesc São Carlos, 2012.

______*Arte à primeira vista.* Sorocaba: Sesc Sorocaba, 2013.

______*Arte à primeira vista: páginas de uma história.* Belo Horizonte: Fundação Clóvis Salgado, 2014.

SARDENBERG, Ricardo. *A tara por livros ou a tara de papel.* São Paulo: Galeria Bergamin, 2014.

SCHWARTZMAN, Allan. *Geometries on and of the grid: Art from 1950 to the present.* Dallas: The Warehouse, 2016.

SCOVINO, Felipe; SALEM, Renato Schreiner. *Diálogos com Palatnik.* São Paulo: Museu de Arte Moderna, 2014.

SEILER, Evangelina; TEOBALDO, Marco Antonio; HOLLANDA, Heloisa Buarque de. *A céu aberto.* Rio de Janeiro: Casa França-Brasil, 2010.

SERÁPHICO, Luiz. *Panorama de Arte Atual Brasileira 80: desenho e gravura.* São Paulo: Museu de Arte Moderna, 1980.

SICOLI, Tonino. *Fall-Out: aspetti della pittura internazionale senza centro né margini.* Catanzaro: Convitto Nazionale Pasquale Galluppi, 1985.

SILVEIRA, Dôra; ROELS JR., Reynaldo; OSORIO, Luiz Camillo; VERGARA, Luiz Guilherme. *MAC: 1 ano: Jorge Guinle. Entre esculturas e objetos. Visões & (sub) versões: cada olhar uma história.* Niterói: Museu de Arte Contemporânea de Niterói, 1997.

SUZUKI, Katsuo; MIWA, Kenjin. *Brazil: body nostalgia.* Tokyo: National Museum of Modern Art, 2004.

CASTRO, Francisco de; CHAIMOVICH, Felipe; LAGNADO, Lisette; SORIN, Pierrick. *Galeria Brito Cimino: dois.* São Paulo: Galeria Brito Cimino, 1999.

VENANCIO FILHO, Paulo. *30 x Bienal: transformações na arte brasileira da 1ª a 30ª edição.* São Paulo: Fundação Bienal de São Paulo, 2013.

VIÇOSI, José Paulo; HORTA, Leila; VASCONCELLOS, Luiz Eduardo Meira de. *Sobrevitória: Usina Arte Contemporânea: 25 anos depois.* Vitória: Museu de Arte do Espírito Santo Dionísio Del Santo, 2011.

VILLELA, Milú; STIGGER, Veronica. *O útero do mundo.* São Paulo: Museu de Arte Moderna, 2016.

VISCONTI, Jacopo Crivelli; SILEO, Diego. *Brasile. Il coltello nella carne/Brazil. [Knife in the skin].* Silvana Ed./PAC, 2018.

______. *Matriz do tempo real.* São Paulo: Base7 Projetos Culturais, 2018.

BOOKS

ABREU, Caio Fernando. *Morangos Mofados.* São Paulo: Companhia das Letras, 2019.

______. *Limite Branco.* São Paulo: Companhia das Letras, 2022.

______. *Triângulo das tristezas.* São Paulo: Companhia das Letras, 2023.

ABREU, Laura Maria Neves; DIAS, Mariza Guimarães; XEXÉO, Pedro Martins Caldas. *Galeria de arte brasileira moderna e contemporânea.* Rio de Janeiro: Museu Nacional de Belas Artes, 2009.

AIDAR, Flávia; ALVES, Januária Cristina. *Para ler e ver com olhos livres.* Rio de Janeiro: Nova Fronteira, 2013.

AJZENBERG, Elza (ed.). *MAC USP: acervo virtual.* São Paulo: Museu de Arte Contemporânea da Universidade de São Paulo, 2006.

ALIAGA, Juan Vicente; CORTÉS, José Miguel G. *Desobediencias: cuerpos disidentes y espacios subvertidos en el arte en América Latina y España: 1960-2010.* Barcelona: Egales, 2015.

ALMEIDA, Caetano de; HERKENHOFF, Paulo. *O delicioso jardim do vizinho.* Rio de Janeiro: Cobogó, 2016.

ALZUGARAY, Paula (ed.). *Subjetiva vizinhos.* São Paulo: Akrobatika, 2003.

AMARAL, Aracy; BARROS, Regina Teixeira de (eds.). *Coleção Fundação Edson Queiroz.* Rio de Janeiro: Pinakotheke, 2018.

______. *Textos do Trópico de Capricórnio: artigos e ensaios (1980-2005) – vol. 3: bienais e artistas contemporâneos no Brasil.* São Paulo: Editora 34, 2006.

______. *Textos do Trópico de Capricórnio: artigos e ensaios (1980-2005) – vol. 2: circuitos de arte na América Latina e no Brasil.* São Paulo: Editora 34, 2006.

Antarctica artes com a Folha. São Paulo: Cosac Naify, 1998.

ARANHA, Maria Lúcia de Arruda; MARTINS, Maria Helena Pires. *Filosofando: introdução à Filosofia.* 3 ed. São Paulo: Moderna, 2004.

ARAÚJO, Olívio Tavares de. *Silva: Pinturas, 1947-1995.* São Paulo: Pinacoteca do Estado de São Paulo, 1998.

______. *Brazilianart VII: livro de arte brasileira.* São Paulo: JC Ed., 2007.

______. *Um Novo Olhar Amoroso.* São Paulo: Cult Arte e Comunicação, 2021.

ARÊAS, Vilma. *Trouxa frouxa.* São Paulo: Companhia das Letras, 2000.

ASBURY, Michael. *Today Is Always Yesterday: Contemporary Brazilian Art.* London: Reaktion Books, 2023.

AZEVEDO, Elizabeth. *O papel na arte brasileira no século XX.* São Paulo: DBA, 2010.

BACH, Cristina. *Jorge Guinle.* São Paulo: Cosac Naify, 2001.

BALDACCI, Cristina; GIACON, Danka (eds.). *La Donazione Bianca e Mario Bertolini: Museo del Novecento.* Milan: Silvana Ed., 2015.

BALTAZAR, Marina. *Textos e Têxteis: questões de intermidialidade.* Belo Horizonte: Tradição Planalto, 2021.

______. *Escrever Leonilson: expansão da poesia.* Belo Horizonte: Relicário, 2022.

BARREIROS, Edmundo; SÓ, Pedro. *1985: o ano em que o Brasil recomeçou.* Rio de Janeiro: Ediouro, 2005.

BARROS, Stella Teixeira (ed.). *Perfil da coleção Itaú.* São Paulo: Itaú Cultural, 1998.

BAYÓN, Damián; PONTUAL, Roberto. *La peinture de l'Amérique latine au XX siècle: identité et modernité.* Paris: Mengès, 1990.

BESSA, Marcelo Secron. *Os perigosos: autobiografias & Aids.* Rio de Janeiro: Aeroplano, 2002.

BLEYS, Rudi C. *Images of Ambiente: Homotextuality and Latin American Art 1810-today.* London: Continuum, 2000.

BORGATTO, Ana; BERTIN, Terezinha; MARCHEZI, Vera. *Tudo é linguagem: 9º ano.* São Paulo: Ática, 2009.

BOTELHO, André; SCHWARCZ, Lilia Moritz (eds.). *Agenda brasileira: temas de uma sociedade em mudança.* São Paulo: Companhia das Letras, 2011.

BUORO, Anamelia Bueno; KOK, Beth; ATIHÉ, Eliana Aloia. *O outro lado da moeda.* São Paulo: Companhia Editora Nacional, 2007.

CAMINHA, Adolfo. *Bom-Crioulo.* São Paulo: Ática, 2012.

CAMPOS, Marcelo. *Escultura contemporânea no Brasil: reflexões em dez percursos.* Salvador: Editora Carumarê, 2016.

CANONGIA, Ligia. *Anos 80: embates de uma geração.* Rio de Janeiro: Francisco Alves/Barléu, 2010.

CANONGIA, Ligia. *Anos 60 a 80 na coleção Gilberto Chateaubriand.* Rio de Janeiro: Barléu, 2012.

CANTON, Katia. *Novíssima arte brasileira: um guia de tendências.* São Paulo: Iluminuras, 2000.

______. *O trem da história: uma viagem pelo mundo da arte.* São Paulo: Companhia das Letrinhas, 2003.

CARMONA, Lissa; TEIXEIRA, Ruy. *Entre(tempos): casa zalszupin.* São Paulo: Act. Editora, 2022.

CHAIMOVICH, Felipe (ed.). *Inventário: catálogo geral do acervo do Museu de Arte Moderna de São Paulo – 2001 a 2007.* São Paulo: Museu de Arte Moderna, 2008.

______. *Grupo de estudos de curadoria do Museu de Arte Moderna de São Paulo: exposições organizadas em 1998 e 1999.* São Paulo: Museu de Arte Moderna, 2008.

CHIARELLI, Tadeu (ed.). *O Museu de Arte Moderna de São Paulo.* São Paulo: Banco Safra, 1998.

______. *Grupo de estudos em curadoria: exposições organizadas em 1998.* São Paulo: Museu de Arte Moderna, 1999.

______. *Grupo de estudos sobre curadoria: exposições organizadas em 1999.* São Paulo: Museu de Arte Moderna, 2000.

______. *Alegoria: arte brasileira – século XX/Museu de Arte Moderna de São Paulo.* São Paulo: Lemos, 2002.

______. *Acervo: outras abordagens.* São Paulo: Museu de Arte Contemporânea da Universidade de São Paulo, 2015.

______. *Arte internacional brasileira.* São Paulo: Lemos, 1999.

______. *Inventário: catálogo geral do acervo do Museu de Arte Moderna de São Paulo.* São Paulo: Museu de Arte Moderna de São Paulo/Lemos, 2002.

CHORPENING, Kelly; FORNUM, Rebecca (eds.). *A Companion to Contemporary Drawing.* Hoboken: Wiley-Blackwell, 2021.

CINTRÃO, Rejane; FERRAZ, João Carlos de Figueiredo (eds.). *A Arte nos anos 80: textos imperdíveis para entender a década.* Ribeirão Preto: Instituto Figueiredo Ferraz, 2020.

CIORNAI, Selma (ed.). *Percursos em arteterapia: ateliê terapêutico, arteterapia no trabalho comunitário, trabalho plástico e linguagem expressiva, arteterapia e história da arte.* São Paulo: Summus, 2004.

COELHO, Teixeira (ed.). *Coleção Itaú contemporâneo: arte no Brasil 1981-2006.* São Paulo: Itaú Cultural, 2006.

______; GROSSMAN, Martin (eds.). *Coleção MAC Collection.* São Paulo: Comunique/ Museu de Arte Contemporânea da Universidade de São Paulo, 2003.

COSTA, Cacilda Teixeira da. *Arte no Brasil 1950-2000: movimentos e meios.* São Paulo: Alameda, 2006.

______. *Roupa de artista: o vestuário na obra de arte.* São Paulo: Edusp/ Imprensa Oficial, 2009.

COUTINHO, Fábio Luiz Borgatti (ed). *Aquisições: 1999-2002.* Porto Alegre: Museu de Arte do Rio Grande do Sul Ado Malagoli, 2002.

CUNHA, Amanda S. Torres. *Ateliê de artes visuais: pintura.* Curitiba: Editora Intersaberes, 2016.

______. *Caminhos em poéticas visuais bidimensionais.* Curitiba: Editora Intersaberes, 2017.

DEMIRDJIAN, Tiqui. *For Art's Sake: Inside the Homes of Art Dealers.* New York: Rizzoli International Publications, 2020.

DIAS, Ana Lenice; CLEMENTE, Gabriela Dias (eds.). *Leonilson: catálogo raisonné.* São Paulo: Projeto Leonilson, 2017.

DIEGUES, Isabel; FORTES, Márcia; KERTI, Mini; LOPES, Priscila. *Arte brasileira para crianças: 100 artistas e atividades para você brincar.* Rio de Janeiro: Cobogó, 2016.

DIMENSTEIN, Gilberto; STRECKER, Heidi; GIANSANTI, Alvaro Cesar. *Dez lições de filosofia para um Brasil cidadão.* São Paulo: FTD, 2008.

Do conceitual à arte contemporânea: marcos históricos. São Paulo: Instituto Cultural Itaú, 1994.

DOMENECK, Ricardo. *Cabeça de galinha no chão de cimento.* São Paulo: Editora 34, 2023.

DOMINGUES, Joelza Ester; FIUSA, Layla Paranhos Leite. *História: o Brasil em foco.* São Paulo: FTD, 1996.

EID, Vilma; MONTE-MÓR, Germana (eds.). *Arte popular brasileira: olhares contemporâneos.* São Paulo: WMF Martins Fontes/Instituto do Imaginário do Povo Brasileiro, 2018.

FARIAS, Agnaldo (ed.). *50 anos da Bienal de São Paulo [50 years of the São Paulo Biennial: 1951-2001]: homenagem a Francisco Matarazzo Sobrinho [in honor of Francisco Matarazzo Sobrinho].* São Paulo: Fundação Bienal de São Paulo: Unisys, 2001.

______. *Luiz Zerbini.* Rio de Janeiro: Aeroplano, 2010.

FERRAZ, João Carlos de Figueiredo (ed.). *Instituto Figueiredo Ferraz.* São Paulo: Ed. Bamboo, 2014.

FERREIRA, Glória (ed.). *Arte contemporáneo brasileño: documentos y críticas [Contemporary Brazilian art: documents and critical texts].* Santiago de Compostela: Artedardo, 2009.

FLORES, Livia; SOMMER, Michekke (eds.). *Cadernos Desilha.* Rio de Janeiro: PPGAV ABA UFRJ/ Editora Circuito, 2017.

FOUCALT, Michel. *Dizer a verdade sobre si.* FRUCHAUD, Henri-Paul; LORENZIN, Daniele (eds.). São Paulo: Ubu Editora, 2022.

FREITAS, Newton. *Dicionário Oboé de artes.* 3ed. rev e ampl. Fortaleza: Oboé Financeira, 2004.

GALVÃO, Roberto. *Uma visão da arte no Ceará.* Fortaleza: Grafisa, 1987.

GARCIA, Wilton. **"Corpo e poética em jogos perigosos de José Leonilson".** In: LYRA, Bernadette; GARCIA, Wilton (eds.). *Corpo & imagem.* São Paulo: Arte & Ciência, 2002.

GONÇALVES FILHO, Antonio. *Primeira individual: 25 anos de crítica de arte.* São Paulo: Cosac Naify, 2009.

GRINSPUM, Denise; JAFFE, Noemi. *Ver palavras, ler imagens: literatura e arte.* São Paulo: Global/Ação Educativa, 2003.

GUIMARÃES, Andréa Camargo (ed.). *Cronologia de artes plásticas: referências 1975-1995.* São Paulo: Centro Cultural São Paulo-IDART, 2010.

GUNZI, Elisa Kiyoko. *A relação do desenho com o ensino da arte.* Curitiba: Editora Intersaberes, 2016.

HERNÁNDEZ, Andrés I. Martín; SOARES, Carolina (eds.). *Obras comentadas da coleção do Museu de Arte Moderna de São Paulo.* São Paulo: Museu de Arte Moderna, 2007.

HIEN, Albert; STORMS, Walter (eds.). *Albert Hien Scultura Poetica 1982-1990.* Berlin: Kerber Verlag, 2018.

HOLLANDA, Heloisa Buarque de. *Asdrúbal Trouxe o Trombone: memórias de uma trupe solitária de comediantes que abalou os anos 70.* Rio de Janeiro: Aeroplano, 2004.

HOLTZ, Raul (ed.). *Museu de Arte do Rio Grande do Sul: catálogo geral.* Porto Alegre: Museu de Arte do Rio Grande do Sul, 2013.

IOSCHPE, Evelyn Berg (ed.). *25: 25 artistas: 25 obras: 25 arte-educadores: 25 leituras: 25 anos Instituto Arte na Escola.* Porto Alegre/São Paulo: Penso Editora/ Instituto Arte na Escola, 2014.

IZIDIO, William. "Uma topografia de si na errância e na precariedade", In: FILHOS, Osvaldo Fontes; FERREIRA. Carolin Overhoff (eds.). *Arte e Política: algumas narrativas e poéticas.* Brasília: G3 Comunicação, 2023.

KAZ, Leonel; LODDI, Nigge (eds.). *Arte e ousadia: o Brasil na coleção Sattamini.* Rio de Janeiro: Aprazível, 2009.

LAGNADO, Lisette. *Leonilson: são tantas as verdades.* São Paulo: Projeto Leonilson/Sesi, 1995.

______. *Leonilson: são tantas as verdades.* 2ed. São Paulo: DBA Melhoramentos, 1998.

______. *Cultural Anthropophagy: The 24th Bienal de São Paulo 1998.* London: Afterall Books, 2015.

______. *Leonilson: são tantas as verdades [So Many Are the Truths].* São Paulo: Projeto Leonilson, 2019.

LE JUEZ, Brigitte; SHIEL, Nina; WALLACE, Mark (eds.). *(Re)Writing Without Borders.* Champaign: Common Ground Research Networks, 2018.

LEFFINGWELL, Edward. *A memória do guardião: a coleção Kim Esteve e uma história da Chácara Flora.* São Paulo: Terceiro Nome, 2003.

LEITE, Edson; ARANHA, Carmen S. G.; IAVELBERG, Rosa; NICOLAU, Evandro (eds.). *IV Simpósio Internacional Digital: Espaços da Mediação - Desenho como prática da memória.* São Paulo: Museu de Arte Contemporânea da Universidade de São Paulo, 2021.

LEONZINI, Nessia. *Coleções de artistas.* São Paulo: Ed. Bei, 2017.

LIMA, Manoel Ricardo de. *Quando todos os acidentes acontecem.* Rio de Janeiro: 7 Letras, 2009.

LORD, Catherine; MEYER, Richard. *Art & Queer Culture.* London: Phaidon, 2013.

LUZ, Afonso; FERRON, Fabio Maleronka; HERENCIA, José Luiz; ZAVAZONI, Rodrigo; COHN, Sergio (eds.). *Produção cultural no Brasil.* Rio de Janeiro: Beco do Azougue, 2010.

MACHADO, Hilda. *Nuvens.* São Paulo: Editora 34, 2018.

MANGE, Marilyn Diggs. *Arte brasileira para crianças.* São Paulo: Martins Fontes, 1988.

MATTAR, Gilda. *Gilda Mattar.* São Paulo: DBA, 2010.

MCBRINN, Joseph. *Queering the Subversive Stitch: Men and the Culture of Needlework.* London: Bloomsbury Visual Arts, 2021.

MEDINA, Cuauhtémoc et al. *Arte global, arte latinoamericano: nuevas estrategias.* Buenos Aires: ArteBA Fundación, 2009.

MEIRA, Beá et al. *Projeto Mosaico: Arte: 6º ano - Ensino Fundamental - anos finais: manual do professor.* São Paulo: Scipione, 2015.

______; PRESTO, Rafael; SOTER, Silvia. *Percursos da arte.* São Paulo: Scipione, 2016.

______. *Arte: 7. série: 8. ano do Ensino Fundamental.* São Paulo: Scipione, 2009.

MELENDI, Maria Angélica. *O corpo vulnerado.* Rio de Janeiro: Cobogó, 2024.

MELIM, Regina (ed.). *AMOR: leve com você [LOVE: take with you].* Florianópolis: Nauemblu/Parentesis, 2007.

MELLER, André e CAMPOS, Eduardo. *Projeto de Vida Ensino médio Volume único – Caminhar e construir.* Saraiva, 2020.

MELLO, Luiza (ed.). *Marcos Chaves.* Rio de Janeiro: Casa da Palavra, 2007.

MELLO, Ramon Nunes (ed.). *Tente entender o que tento dizer: poesia + HIV/AIDS.* Rio de Janeiro: Editora Bazar do Tempo, 2018.

MELO, Chico Homem de; COIMBRA, Elaine Ramos (eds.). *Linha do tempo do design gráfico no Brasil.* São Paulo: Cosac Naify, 2011.

MENDES, Ricardo (ed.). *Retratos do imaginário de São Paulo: fotógrafos e personagens.* São Paulo: FormArte, 2001.

Mensagem à assembleia 2023. Fortaleza: Governo do Ceará, 2023.

MESQUITA, Ivo. *Leonilson: use, é lindo, eu garanto.* São Paulo: Cosac Naify, 1997.

______. *Leonilson: use, é lindo, eu garanto.* São Paulo: Cosac Naify, 2006.

MESSIAS, Rudiran. *Tabus, perversões e outras catarses.* Porto Alegre: Nova Prova, 2005.

MÍCOLI, Roberto. *Roberto Mícoli.* São Paulo: Bei, 2010.

MORAIS, Frederico. *Cronologia das artes plásticas no Rio de Janeiro: da missão artística francesa à geração 90: 1816-1994.* Rio de Janeiro: Topbooks, 1995.

______. *Arte é o que eu e você chamamos arte: 801 definições sobre arte e o sistema da arte.* 4ed. Rio de Janeiro: Record, 2002.

______. *O Brasil na visão do artista: o país e sua cultura [Brazil in the eyes of the artist: a country and its culture].* São Paulo: Prêmio, 2003.

MOUTINHO, Marcelo (ed.). *Contos sobre tela.* Rio de Janeiro: Pinakotheke:, 2005.

MURILO, Claudio. *As quatro estações.* Madrid: Leopardi, 1987.

NEWBERY, Elizabeth. *Como e por que se faz arte.* São Paulo: Ática, 2003.

NOSEK, Leopold. *A disposição para o assombro.* São Paulo: Editora Perspectiva, 2017.

O Museu de Arte Moderna do Rio de Janeiro. São Paulo: Banco Safra, 1999.

OLIVA, Achille Bonito. *A arte até o ano 2000 [Art Towards the Year 2000].* São Paulo/Milão: Museu Brasileiro da Escultura/Torcular, 1998.

ORMUNDO, Wilton; SINISCALCHI, Cristiane; C D'AGOSTINI, Ana Carolina. *Projeto de vida – Se liga na vida.* Moderna, 2020.

PACQUEMENT, Alfred; BEAUMELLE, Agnès de la. *Collection art graphique: la collection du Centre Pompidou: Musée National d'Art Moderne.* Paris: Éditions du Centre Pompidou, 2008.

Papéis e panos: oficina de artesanato. Rio de Janeiro: Editora Senac Nacional, 2002.

PATRIOTA, Erika; NOGUEIRA, Ana Beatriz; PICCHETTI, Vanessa (eds.). *Brazilian Art in the Museums of New York city [Arte brasileira nos museus de Nova York].* Brasília: Coordenação de Divulgação/Ministério das Relações Exteriores, 2011.

PECCININI, Daisy. *Pintura no Brasil: um olhar no século XX.* São Paulo: Empresa das Artes, 2000.

PEDRO, Alexandre. *Flores do ócio: poesia brasileira.* São Paulo: Giostri, 2013.

PEDROSA, Adriano (ed.). *ArtNexus Brasil en Colombia: antología de textos.* Bogotá/ São Paulo: ArtNexus/Associação Brasileira de Arte Contemporânea (ABACT)/Apex Brasil, 2011.

PEDROSA, Sebastião; ZACCARA, Madalena (eds.). *Artes visuais: conversando sobre.* Recife: Ed. Universitária da UFPE, 2008.

PEREIRA, Helena Bonito; PELACHIN, Marcia Maisa. *Português na trama do texto: Ensino Médio – volume único.* São Paulo: FTD, 2004.

______. *Toda a literatura portuguesa e brasileira: Ensino Médio: volume único.* São Paulo: FTD, 2000.

PEREIRA, Maria de Fátima Rodrigues. *Concepções de História na proposta curricular do Estado de Santa Catarina.* Chapecó: Grifos, 2000.

PERLINGEIRO, Camila (ed.). *Coleção Airton Queiroz.* Rio de Janeiro: Pinakotheke, 2016.

PIMENTA, Angélica (ed.). *O Museu de Arte Contemporânea de Niterói: as coleções [The Museum of Contemporary Art of Niterói: the collections].* Niterói: Fundação de Arte de Niterói/Museu de Arte Contemporânea de Niterói, 2010.

PONTUAL, Roberto. *Explode geração!* Rio de Janeiro: Avenir, 1984.

______. *Entre dois séculos: arte brasileira do século XX na coleção Gilberto Chateaubriand.* Rio de Janeiro: Edições JB, 1987.

PORTO, Graça (ed.). *MAC de Niterói 10 anos.* Niterói: Niterói Livros, 2006.

REMESEIRA, Claudio Iván (ed.). *Hispanic New York: a sourcebook.* New York: Columbia University Press, 2010.

RESENDE, Ricardo. *Posição amorosa: Hudinilson Jr.* São Paulo: WMF Martins Fontes, 2016.

RUBIANO CABALLERO, Germán. *Art of Latin America: 1981-2000.* Washington: Inter-American Development Bank, 2001.

SALGADO, Renata. *Imagem escrita.* Rio de Janeiro: Graal, 1999.

SALLES, Claudia Moreira. *Claudia Moreira Salles.* São Pauio: Bei, 2013.

SANT'ANNA, Renata; PRATES, Valquíria. *Leonilson: gigante com flores.* São Paulo: Paulinas, 2007.

______. *Histórias da arte.* São Paulo: Globo, 2007.

______. *Saber e ensinar arte contemporânea.* São Paulo: Panda Books, 2009.

SANTA ROSA, Nereide Schilaro. *Cores e formas: a segunda metade do século XX.* Rio de Janeiro: Pinakotheke, 2002.

SARDO, Delfim; BRANDÃO, Mariano Viterbo. *Abrir a caixa: obras da colecção da Caixa Geral de Depósitos.* Lisbon: Caixa Geral de Depósitos/Culturgest, 2009.

SILVA, Fernando Pedro da; RIBEIRO, Marília Andrés (eds.). *Regina e Delcir da Costa.* Belo Horizonte: C/Arte, 2009.

SILVA, Márcia. *Artes: Ensino Fundamental.* São Paulo: Anglo, 2005.

SOUSA, Ivan Vale de (ed.). *A produção do conhecimento nas Letras, Linguísticas e Artes 2.* Ponta Grossa: Atena Editora, 2019.

TEIXEIRA, Virna. *Visita.* Rio de Janeiro: 7 Letras, 2000.

______. *Distância.* Rio de Janeiro: 7 Letras, 2005.

THOMAS, Catherine (ed.). *The Edge of Everything: Reflections on Curatorial Practice.* Toronto: Banff Centre Press, 2002.

TORRES CUNHA, Amanda Siqueira. *Ateliê de artes visuais: pintura.* Curitiba: Intersaberes, 2023.

TRENCH, Belkis (ed.). *Almanaque Zero.* São Paulo/Brasília: Nepaids Ministério da Saúde, 1997.

TREVISAN, João Silvério. *Devassos no paraíso: a homossexualidade no Brasil, da colônia à atualidade.* Rio de Janeiro: Record, 2004.

VAINER, André; FERRAZ, Marcelo (eds.). *Cidadela da liberdade: Lina Bo Bardi e o Sesc Pompeia.* São Paulo: Editora Sesc SP, 2013.

VARGAS, Jayme; TEIXEIRA, Ruy (eds.). *Horizonte ampliado: design moderno brasileiro.* São Paulo: Olhares, 2023.

Various authors. *8° Ano – Arte Fundamento: Material do Professor.* São Paulo: Ético Sistema de Ensino, 2014.

Various authors. *Alter – Revista de Estudos Psicanalíticos.* Brasília: Positiva - gráfica e editora, 2016.

Various authors. *Linguagens, códigos e suas tecnologias, ciências humanas e suas tecnologias: 3° ano - Ensino Médio - Caderno 2.* São Paulo: Editora Educacional, 2018.

VARNEDOE, Kirk; ANTONELLI, Paola; SIEGEL, Joshua (eds.). *Modern contemporary: art since 1980 at MoMA.* New York: Museum of Modern Art, 2000.

VASCONCELLOS, Eduardo Meira de. *Sobrevitória: coleção Marcio Espindula.* Vitória: Museu de Arte do Espírito Santo Dionísio Del Santo, 2011.

VASCONCELOS, Tania. *A arte pública de Fortaleza [Public art in Fortaleza].* São Paulo: Creativemidia/Governo do Estado do Ceará, 2003.

VELLO, Valdemar; COLUCCI, Mônica; ARIANE, Paula. *Artes: pranchas de linguagem visual: viver feliz com muita arte!* São Paulo: Scipione, 2008.

VENEROSO, Maria do Carmo de Freitas. *Caligrafias e escrituras: diálogo e intertexto no processo escritural nas artes no século XX.* Belo Horizonte: C/Arte, 2012.

VICENTINI, Daniela; BURJATO, Fernando. *Arte brasileira nos acervos de Curitiba.* Curitiba: Segesta, 2010.

VILAÇA, Maria do Carmo, et.al. *Marcantonio Vilaça.* São Paulo: Cosac Naify, 2001.

VILELA, Andréa de Paula Xavier. *Ensino Fundamental Anos Iniciais: Arte: 4° ano: caderno 4.* São Paulo: Somos, 2020.

WANNER, Maria Celeste de Almeida. *Paisagens sígnicas: uma reflexão sobre as artes contemporâneas.* Salvador: EDUFBA, 2010.

WOLFENSON, Bob. *Jardim da Luz.* São Paulo: Dórea Books and Art/ Companhia das Letras, 1996.

ACADEMIC PRODUCTION

ABREU, Carla Luzia de. ***Sexualidades desobedientes.*** Master's Thesis. Universitat de Barcelona, 2009.

ANDRADE, Karlene; CHAGAS, Juliana. ***Tramas narrativas, um mergulho com o artista Leonilson.*** Undergraduate Thesis. Universidade Federal do Ceará, 2017.

BAHIA, Ana Beatriz; DERDYK, Edith; BARRETO, Lia Menna. ***Bordaduras na arte contemporânea brasileira.*** Undergraduate Thesis. Universidade do Estado de Santa Catarina, 2002.

BAKKER, Claudia. ***A poética de Leonilson.*** Undergraduate Thesis. Pontifícia Universidade Católica do Rio de Janeiro, 1993.

BECK, Ana Lúcia. ***Palavras fora de lugar: Leonilson e a inserção de palavras nas artes visuais.*** Master's Thesis. Universidade Federal do Rio Grande do Sul, 2004.

______. ***Entre eu e o outro: realidade e desejo no processo de criação de José Leonilson e Louise Bourgeois.*** PhD Dissertation. Universidade Federal do Rio Grande do Sul, 2016.

______. "O gesto poético – uma reflexão a partir da produção de Louise Bourgeois, José Leonilson e William Yeats". In: ***Encontro Nacional da Associação Nacional de Pesquisadores em Artes Plásticas, 28, Origens, 2019, Cidade de Goiás. Anais.*** Universidade Federal de Goiás, 2019.

BECKER, Sandra Bancovsky. ***O corpo representado, apresentado e metaforizado na obra de arte: reflexão sobre o processo artístico e a utilização do corpo neste processo.*** Master's Thesis. Faculdade Santa Marcelina, 2006.

BITTENCOURT, Rita Lenira de Freitas. ***Poéticas do presente: limiares.*** PhD Dissertation. Universidade Federal de Santa Catarina, 2005.

CARVALHO, Clarissa Andrade. ***Tessitura de segredos e silêncios: o viver com aids.*** Master's Thesis. Universidade Federal de Pernambuco, 2000.

CASSUNDÉ, Carlos Eduardo Bitu. ***Leonilson: a natureza do sentir.*** Master's Thesis. Universidade Federal de Minas Gerais, 2011.

COUTINHO, Roberta Saraiva. ***José Leonilson: sistemática e poética.*** Undergraduate Thesis. Universidade de São Paulo, 2002.

CRUZ, Gleyce. ***Atratores de desenho.*** Master's Thesis. Universidade do Estado de Santa Catarina, 2012.

D'ÁVILA, Caroline Maria Gurgel. ***Presente ausência: escrevendo o corpo com Leonilson.*** Master's Thesis. Universidade Federal Fluminense, 2014.

DIAS, Camila et al. ***Leonilson.*** Fundação Armando Álvares Penteado, 2012.

DINIZ, Auana; LOPES, Levi Fernando; OLIVEIRA, Lucas; BREDARIOLLI, Rita Luciana Berti; LOPES, Rodrigo; LIMA, Sidiney Peterson F. de (eds.). ***Partilhas sensíveis: diálogos sobre imagem, história e memória, mediação, arte e educação.*** Universidade Estadual Paulista Julio de Mesquita Plaza, 2021.

DUARTE, Rodrigo A. de Paiva (ed.). ***Colóquio nacional morte da arte hoje, 1993, Belo Horizonte.*** Anais. Universidade Federal de Minas Gerais, 1993.

DULTRA, Maruzia. ***O silêncio da imagem: perspectiva micropolítica na vídeo-carta Letter to Jane: an investigation about a still (1972), de Jean-Luc Godard e Jean-Pierre Gorin.*** Universidade de Fortaleza, 2018.

FARIAS, Fábio. ***Avaliação e diagnóstico do Projeto Leonilson.*** Universidade de São Paulo, 2005.

FREITAS, Carlos Eduardo Riccioppo. ***Leonilson, 1980-1990.*** Master's Thesis. Universidade de São Paulo, 2010.

FRÓES, Maria Cristina. ***A dança das agulhas – o bordado como expressão plástica.*** Universidade Estadual de Minas Gerais, 2008.

GOIS, Wilma Farias. ***Afetos da obra de Leonilson: arte e vida, mapas e escrita.*** Master's Thesis. Universidade Federal do Ceará, 2015.

IZIDIO, William. ***Costuras do eu – poética visual e objetualidades em Leonilson.*** Master's Thesis. Universidade Federal de São Paulo, 2023.

KAWASIMA, Igor Yuji. ***Una distancia entre A y B: Leonilson, São Paulo-Madrid, 1981.*** Master's Thesis. Universidad Complutense de Madrid, 2013.

______. "Biografiar un viaje: Leonilson, São Paulo-Madrid, 1981". In: ***Seminario Autobiografía: Narración y construcción de la subjetividad en la creación artística contemporánea.*** Universidad Internacional Menéndez Pelayo, 2015.

LAMPERT, Jociele. ***Arte contemporânea, cultura visual e formação docente.*** PhD Dissertation. Universidade de São Paulo, 2009.

LUIZ, Eliana Patrícia. ***Arte como integradora da cultura na escola e na comunidade.*** Relatório de produção didático-pedagógica. Universidade Estadual de Londrina, 2012.

MATTOS, Marina Baltazar; SILVA, Lúcio Flávio Gondim. "Lugar do corpo: individuação e alteridade a partir de Leonilson". In: ***Anais do I Diálogos Convergentes do IX Curta O Gênero,*** 2021.

OLIVEIRA, Kris Herk de. ***De encontros, verdades e afetos: cartografias da sexualidade.*** Master's Thesis. Universidade Estadual de Campinas, 2019.

PAIVA, Ana Carolina Campos. ***Leonilson: o testamento da agonia na ilustração da mídia.*** Undergraduate Thesis. Universidade de Fortaleza, 2003.

PARENTE, Tiago Coutinho. ***Iracema, horizonte de memórias do mito incessante.*** PhD Dissertation. Universidade Federal do Rio de Janeiro, 2019.

PEGORARO, Cássia de Abreu. A relação entre arte e morte na obra de Leonilson. In: ***Encontro anual de iniciação científica.*** Universidade Estadual do Centro-Oeste, 2010.

PEGORARO, Cássia de Abreu. ***O desejo é um lago azul: o erotismo sagrado em Leonilson.*** Undergraduate Thesis. Universidade Estadual de Londrina, 2012.

RAMOS, Rafael. ***Cartas ao Leo: a literatura expandida na produção visual de José Leonilson.*** Master's Thesis. Universidade Federal de São Paulo, ***2022.***

REIS, Paulo Roberto de Oliveira. ***A construção do desenho: sujeito, temporalidade e cartografias em Leonilson.*** PhD Dissertation. Pontifícia Universidade Católica do Rio de Janeiro, 1998.

SILVA, Francisco Thiago Camêlo. ***Cartografias da Infância.*** Master's Thesis. Pontifícia Universidade Católica do Rio de Janeiro, 2017.

SILVA, Lúcio Flávio Gondim. ***Leonilson expandido.*** PhD Dissertation. Universidade Federal do Ceará, ***2022.***

SILVA, Priscilla Ramos da. ***Corpo e artes visuais nos anos 1990: Panorama de 97 e Bienal de 98.*** Master's Thesis. Universidade Estadual de Campinas, 2007.

SIQUEIRA, Aline. ***Espelhos de uma condição: reflexos da soropositividade nas obras de Félix González-Torres e Leonilson.*** Master's Thesis. Universidade do Estado do Rio de Janeiro, ***2021.***

TREVISAN, Paulo Sérgio. ***A figuração na arte brasileira dos anos 1980: análise de obra de Adir Sodré, José Leonilson, Alex Vallauri e Victor Arruda.*** Master's Thesis. Universidade de São Paulo, 2004.

TRINDADE, Denise Jorge. "Inscrições efêmeras, instantes singulares: uso e consumo dos 'panos encarnados' de Leonilson". In: ***Congresso brasileiro de ciências da comunicação. Anais.*** Universidade de Brasília, 2006.

TUTTOILMONDO, Joana. ***Presente nos museus: processo de formação de acervos de arte contemporânea brasileira.*** PhD Dissertation. Universidade de São Paulo, 2010.

VIEIRA, Camila. ***Do cheio ao vazio: uma análise do silêncio na obra de Leonilson.*** Undergraduate Thesis. Universidade Federal do Ceará, 2005.

Compiled by Projeto Leonilson.

Regina Pinho de Almeida
Ronaldo Cezar Coelho
Sonia and Hamilton Dias de Souza
Susana and Ricardo Steinbruch
Susie and Guido Padovano
Tania Haddad Nobre and Alexandre Nobre
Vania and José Roberto Marinho
Vera Lucia dos Santos Diniz

SILVER PATRONS
Alessandra (*in memoriam*) and Rodrigo Bresser-Pereira
Ana Karina Bortoni Dias and Marcos Fernandes Navarro
Ana Lucia and Sergio Comolatti
Ana Maria Igel and Mario Higino Leonel
Ana Paula Capricho de Azevedo Motta and Daniel Augusto Motta
Ana Paula and Sergio Spinelli
Ana Paula Martinez and Daniel K. Goldberg
Andrea and José Olympio da Veiga Pereira
Andrea Pinheiro and Newton Simões Filho
Carolina and Patrice Etlin
Cecília and Abram Szajman
Eduardo Salomão Neto
Fabiana and Marcelo Marangon
Janaina Dobbeck Fiorini and Reinaldo Carlos Fiorini
Juliana Freitas Calheiros and Grenfel Schwartz Calheiros
Julio Roberto Magnus Landmann
Karin Baumgart Srougi and Thomaz Srougi
Larissa Fortes de Almeida and Denis Caldeira de Almeida
Lavínia and Ricardo Setubal
Luciana de Oliveira Cezar Coelho
Luiza and Marcelo Hallack
Marcela and Alfredo Nugent Setubal
Marcia Bossa Graça Scripilliti and Clóvis Ermirio de Moraes Scripilliti
Marguerite and Jean Etlin
Maria Alice Setubal
Maria Eduarda and Ricardo Brito Pereira
Maria Flavia Barbosa Carvalho and Guilherme Moreira Teixeira
Maria Luiza and Tito da Silva Neto
Marta and Hecilda Fadel
Paula and Bruno Rizzo Setubal
Paula Pires Paoliello de Medeiros and Marcelo Medeiros
Paula Proushan
Sandra and José Luiz Setubal
Sonia and Luis Terepins
Stefania Pelusi Cestero and Francisco Cestero
Thiago Saddi Tannous
Vera Alves de Lima Parreiras and Luiz Paulo Parreiras
Vera Novis
Vera Sarnes Negrão
Vicente Furletti Assis
Vivian Jessica Blair Bigoni and Marcio Verri Bigoni

PATRONS
Alexandra Mollof
Ana Paula Vilela Vianna and Jose Luiz Vianna
Andrea and Guilherme Johannpeter
Andréa and Tom Waslander
Angela and Ricard Akagawa
Antonia Bergamin and Mateus Ferreira
Antonio Almeida and Carlos Dale
Augusto Livio Malzoni
Bruno Baptistella
Camila and Walter Appel
Claudete Brochmann and Silvano Gersztel
Daniela and Helio Seibel
Daniela Johannpeter
Danielle Silbergleid and Antônio Pitombo
Eduardo Saron
Fabio Magalhães
Fernanda and Alberto Fernandes
Fernanda Feitosa and Heitor Martins
Flávia Buarque de Almeida and Rodrigo Ferreira Leite
Flávia and Jean Sigrist
Gabriela and Adriano Borges
Heloisa and Amos Genish
Jackson Schneider
James Acacio Lisboa
Jane Hayre de Sousa Antunes and Fábio Lima Mourão
Karla Meneghel
Liane and Roberto Bielawski
Luisa Strina
Luiz Carlos Schmidt Ritter and Clelio da Costa Alves
Márcia Fortes, Alessandra D'aloia and Alex Gabriel
Maria Eugênia Abàtayguara-Örneberg and John Harald Örneberg
Maria Monteiro
Mariana Guarini Berenguer
Marilia Razuk and Marcela Razuk
Marina and Marcos Gouvêa
Marjorie and Geraldo Carbone
Marta and Paulo Kuczynski
Max Perlingeiro
Monize Neves and Ricardo Vasques
Myra Arnaud Babenco
Nara, Alexandre and Daniel Roesler
Neide Helena de Moraes
Paula Depieri
Paulo Donizete Martinez
Pedro Mendes Siruffo
Priscilla and Marcelo Parodi
Rafael Moraes
Rafael Reali Esposito and Fernanda Yumi Kuninari
Raquel and Marcio Kogan
Raul Juste Lores
Renata Bittencourt
Renata de Paula David
Renata Tubini
Ricardo Ohtake
Roberta Mendes Pereira Whately and Wagner Dias Coelho
Sabina and Abrão Lowenthal
Salo Seibel
Sandra and William Ling
Sílvia Teixeira Penteado
Silvio Tini de Araújo
Sonia and Paulo de Barros Carvalho
Thaissa and Alexandre Bertoldi
Thalita Cefali Zaher
Thiago Gomide Nunes
Titiza Nogueira and Renata Nogueira Beyruti
Ulisses Eliezer Simonetti Cohn and Flavio Isaias Simonetti Cohn

YOUNG PATRONS

SILVER YOUNG PATRONS
André Montanholi Mileski
Eliza Correa de Almeida Nobre
Francisco Fernando Correa de Almeida Nobre
Luiz and Ludwig Danielian

YOUNG PATRONS
Alessandra and Guilherme Simões de Assis
Ana Clara Medeiros de Almeida
Ana Luiza Tesser Arguello and Ary Cera Zanetta Neto
Ana Varella and Samuel Varella Pedrosa
Ananda and Leonardo Lopes
Anne Carolline Wilians
Arthur Jafet
Arthur Masi Uzum and Maria Helena Loureiro Masi Uzum
Beatriz Viabone and Thomaz Henrique Pacheco
Camila Yunes and Conrado Mesquita
Candido de Azeredo Gomes and Deyllison Cintra de Melo
Carolina da Costa Carvalho and Luiz Carlos da Costa Carvalho Jr.
Carolina Junqueira Bull and Edmar Mendoza Bull
Caroline Ficker
Clara Roorda
Daiane Santos and Joana Barros
Dhafyni Mendes
Edmar Pinto Costa
Fabio Pinheiro Molina and Lucas de Carvalho Tironi
Felipe Calil de Melo and Julia Suslick
Felipe Hegg and William Heuseler
Fernanda and Suzana Resstom
Gabriela Azevedo Forlin
Guilherme Nagel and Eduardo Cherez Pavia
Guilherme Pesenti
Ian Junqueira Duarte Lucas and Allann de Seabra Camargo Paulo
Isabella Marinho
Isadora Poltronieri Vecchi and Diogo de Souza Dutra
João Paulo Siqueira Lopes and Fernando Ticoulat
Juan Eyheremendy
Juliana and Leonardo Gonzalez
Juliana Mamy Suzuki and João Gabriel Pennacchi
Juliana Versolato dos Santos and Raphael de Almeida Fonseca
Leilane Sabatini and Felipe Sabatini
Lia and Ricardo Pedro Guazzelli Rosario
Lucas Danicek Borges
Lucas Marques Pessôa
Luis Eduardo Sanchez Maluf
Luiz Augusto de Souza Campos Junior and Caio Rocha Correa
Marcela Levy Zilberberg and Eduardo Zilberberg
Marcelo Padua Lima
Maria Carolina Gattaz Caneiro and Caio Galli Caneiro
Maria Rita Drummond and Rodolfo Barreto
Mariana Schmidt de Oliveira Iacomo
Nathalie Felsberg
Paula Paes Batista da Silva and Fernando Cezar Cunha Spnola Junior
Regina Civolani da Cruz and Renzo Pasquale Zeglio Agresta
Renata Alice Lobo Lisboa
Ricardo Von Brusky and Flavia Waiswol Reitzfeld
Rodrigo Hsu Ngai Leite
Stephanie Schultz Wenk and Gabriel Sauer
Susanna Crestani and Marco Kheirallah
Thais Abujamra Nader and Luiz Starace Fonseca Ayres Pimentel
Thomas Ondracek Lemouche and André Donato Mathias
Valentina Circe Vettori and Rafael Vettori
Victoria Zuffo and Paulo Kassab Jr.
Vinicius Veloso
Vittoria Meneghel Ferraz de Camargo Van Den Berg and Pedro Henrique Buffara Van Den Berg

*List of international donors: Friends of MASP and International Council.

MASP ENDOWMENT

CHARITABLE
Fernão Carlos Botelho Bracher (*in memoriam*)
Geyze Diniz
Rose and Alfredo Setubal

DIAMOND
Ana Eliza and Paulo Setubal
Luciana and Ronaldo Cezar Coelho
Luis Stuhlberger
Roberto Egydio Setubal

GOLD
Amália Spinardi and Roberto Thompson Motta
Família Repucci
Gabriela and Antonio Quintela
Helio Seibel
Marisa and Salo Davi Seibel

SILVER
Carolina and Patrice Etlin
Israel Vainboim
Maria Alice Setubal
Marjore and Geraldo Carbone
Martha and André De Vivo
Mônica and Eduardo Vassimon
Nádia and Olavo Setubal
Neide Helena de Moraes
Paulo Proushan (*in memoriam*)
Sandra and José Luiz Setubal
Sonia and Luis Terepins

PATRONS
Lais Zogbi and Telmo G. Porto (*in memoriam*)
TVML Foundation

STRATEGIC PARTNER
Itaú

MASTER SPONSORS
Nubank
AkzoNobel
B3
Bradesco
Citi Brasil
Klabin
Mckinsey & Company
Renner
Vivo

SPONSORS
Banco Pan
Biolab Farmacêutica
Bloomberg
Deloitte
EMS
Goodyear
Grupo Ultra
Ticket
Unilever
Unipar

SUPPORTERS
BNDES
banco BV
Chanel
Farfetch
Goldman Sachs
Grupo Comolatti
JP Morgan
Lefosse
MasterCard
Mattos Filho
Origem Energia
Sotheby´s
Tallento Gerenciadora
Terra Foundation of American Art
Too Seguros
UBS
Vinícola Guaspari
VR

PARTNER COMPANIES
Banco Alfa
Bye Cupim
Comerc Energia
Kaspersky
Iochpe
Safra
Singulare

MEDIA PARTNERS
Buzzmonitor
Canal Arte1
Cult
Estadão
Harper´s Bazaar
JCDecaux
Revista 451
Revista Piauí
Zanzar

Every effort has been made for the mentions of our sponsors, board members, patrons, young patrons, and members of the International Council to be published correctly. If there is any error, please inform us, and we promise to correct it in future editions.

ARTISTIC BOARD
Adriano Pedrosa
ARTISTIC DIRECTOR

COLLECTIONS AND CONSERVATION
Regina Teixeira de Barros
Alejandra Orellana
Aline Assumpção
Juliana Batista
Juliana Peixoto
Marina Pelegrini
Millena Benício
Nalú Maria de Medeiros
Paula Coelho Lima
Taynara Lima
Tereza Moura

CURATORS

Julia Bryan-Wilson
CURATOR-AT-LARGE OF MODERN AND CONTEMPORARY ART

Marcia Arcuri
CURATOR-AT-LARGE OF PRE-COLUMBIAN ART

Regina Teixeira de Barros
COORDINATING CURATOR AND CURATOR OF COLLECTIONS

Amanda Carneiro
CURATOR

Fernando Oliva
CURATOR

Isabella Rjeille
CURATOR

Guilherme Giufrida
ASSISTANT CURATOR

Laura Cosendey
ASSISTANT CURATOR

Leandro Muniz
ASSISTANT CURATOR

Isabela Loures
ASSISTANT CURATOR

Matheus de Andrade
ASSISTANT CURATOR

Teo Teotonio
ASSISTANT CURATOR

Danilo Cavalcante
RESEARCH ASSISTANT

Ana Beatriz Sugahara
CURATORIAL INTERNSHIP

David Queiroz
CURATORIAL INTERNSHIP

EXECUTIVE PRODUCTION
Marina Moura
Ana Laura e Silva
Gabriel Belvis
Isaque Vieira
Maicon Ferreira
Maria Rosalem
Marília Amorim
Marina Rebouças
Matheus Gumerato
Pedro Henrique Lopes
Steffânia Prata
Victória Dirotildes

EXHIBITION DESIGN
Flora Gurgel
Melissa dos Santos

MEDIATION AND PUBLIC PROGRAMS

André Mesquita
CURATOR

Glaucea Helena de Britto
ASSISTANT CURATOR

Ana Flavia Amaral
Carlos Henrique Martins
Daniela Rodrigues
David Ribeiro
Iliriana Rodrigues
Isart Silva
João Victor Bomfim
Karolina Vargem
Rafael Figueiredo
Vitória Machado

PUBLISHING
Carol Ribas
Ana Canellas
Carolina Menegatti
Felipe de Souza
Mariana Trevas
Marina Marcondes
Renier Vasconcelos
Tulio Costa

RESEARCH CENTER

Adriana Villela
Beatriz Yoshito
Bruno Mesquita
Emily Pinheiro
Maycon Richard
Miller Sereno
Pamella Mazucatto
Raquel Brito
Sara Jesus

FINANCE AND OPERATIONS BOARD

Marcelo Ribeiro
FINANCIAL AND OPERATIONAL DIRECTOR

ENGAGEMENT AND DIGITAL

Beto Gonçalves
Daniela Nunes
Davison Cruz
Gabriel Soares
Gabriela Rabelo
Gustavo Correia
Isabela Marques
Jefferson Sousa
Joan Guedes
Mariana Castro
Patrick Matias
Paulo Cesar Mafra de Matos
Ryan Eloy
Xarlys Souza

HUMAN RESOURCES

Karina Alonso
Henrique Rodrigues
Kátia Gomes
Luiz Fernandes

LEGAL

Mariana Luvizutti
Larissa Neves
Letícia Cobiak
Nicole El Murr

MASP STORE

Adélia Borges
MASP STORE CURATOR-AT-LARGE

Milton Schubert
Abraão Rangel
Larissa Brito
Maíra Carvalho
Paulo Javurek
Raphael Ottoni
Roberta Lopes
Tobias Nunnes
Viviane Lacerda
William Ferreira

OPERATIONS

Karina Del Papa
Adeilton dos Santos Gomes
Alejandra Novaes
Allan Lafitte
Ana Cecília Souza
Andrelito Souza
Andressa Silva
Antônio de Souza Matos
Antônio José dos Santos
Beatriz Pereira
Bianca Ferrari
Bianca Mariano
Bruno Orsini
Charles Reis
Christiane Flores
Clayton Gonçalves Andrade
Cosmes Magalhães
Cristiano Jesus
Damião Barreto da Silva
Danielle Rocha
Dionísio Ortiz
Domingos de Jesus dos Santos
Edson Lima
Elaine Matias
Elaine Neris
Elis Fabro Barreira
Everton Silva
Fábio Silva
Fabiula Lima
Fernanda dos Santos
Flavia Giaconto
Flávia Rosa
Francisco Soares Silva
Gabriela Rodrigues
Geovanna Brandão
Gilberto de Sousa Bezerra
Gustavo Alves
Henrique Gomes
Hilderlane Oliveira
Jéssica Coutinho
José Wesley Silva
Lara Duarte
Larissa de Araújo
Liliane Matos
Luan de Alencar
Lucas Modaneze
Luciano Oliveira
Maquipha Silva
Marcello Israel
Marcelo Nascimento
Márcia Batista
Marcos Pimentel
Marion Novais
Mateus Freitas
Matheus Ferreira
Mikaele Oliveira
Mirian Rodrigues
Myrella Marques
Natanael Oliveira
Nicolle Vieira
Rik Castilho
Robinson Xavier Barbosa
Rodolfo Toledo Nogueira
Rodrigo Ferreira
Rômulo Alberto de Oliveira
Sandra Soares
Severino Cassiano Lopes
Sidiclei dos Santos
Silvano Ferreira
Susana da Silva Morales
Thais Domingues
Thatielly Vidal
Valter Silva
Victor Phols
Vinícius Flauaus
Wanda Mirabile

PROJECTS AND ARCHITECTURE

Miriam Elwing
Joana Elito
Joaquim Oliveira
Leonardo Andrade
Lúcia Furlan
Marco Scriboni

STRATEGIC PLANNING, FINANCE, AND ACCOUNTING

Fernanda Ferraz Bonini
Alife Cardoso
Ana Carolina Silva
Ana Paula Moreira
Anna Beatriz dos Santos
Bruno Araújo
Carla Silva
Clara Alves
Franciele Cruz
Gabrielly Dal Pozzo
Iago Miguel da Silva
Izaias Candido
João Paulo Gonçalves
Letícia Lisboa
Marina Kolm Sgnotto
Patrícia Martinez
Tânia Aparecida Souza
Victor Serra Lima

SECRETARIAL OFFICE

Paula Zoppello
Débora Ferreira
Gustavo Salla

DEVELOPMENT BOARD

Carolina Rossetti
DEVELOPMENT DIRECTOR

Beatriz Bettiol
Marina Piedade

COMMUNICATION AND MARKETING

Priscila Asche
Julia Bastos
Laura Jabur
Pablo Mazzucco
Ticiana Gavioli

EVENTS, SPONSORSHIPS, AND TAX INCENTIVE PROJECTS

Gabriel Di Pietro de Camillo
Ana Beatriz Brayner
Brenda Koschel de Farias
Joana Bomfim
Júlia Weckelmann
Juliana Mara
Noemia Braz

NATURAL PERSON PROJECTS

Jussara Nascimento
Carolina Johansen
Cintia Guimarães
Darlan Lopes
Heloísa Lucas

NEW PROJECTS

Manuela Errera

LEONILSON

NOW AND OPPOR TUNI TIES

MASP, 8.23–11.17.2024

EXHIBITION

ACESSIBILITY
Ana Flávia Amaral
Daniela Rodrigues
Isart Silva

ACESSIBILITY CONSULTING
Mais diferenças

ART HANDLING
Elias Joaquim
Helio Iwasa
Juan Castro
Mauro Nagase
Rafael Filipe
Renato Bomfin

AUDIOVISUAL
CABREL | Escritório de Imagem

COLLECTIONS AND CONSERVATION
Alejandra Orellana
Aline Assumpção
Camila Marchiori
Carla Sousa
Elton Hipolito
Fabiana Oda
Gil Chaves
Giulia Alcântara
Juliana Batista
Juliana Peixoto
Marina Pelegrini
Millena Benício
Nalú Maria de Medeiros
Paula Coelho Lima
Regina Teixeira de Barros
Taynara Lima
Tereza Moura

COMMUNICATION
Julia Bastos
Laura Jabur
Priscila Asche
Ticiana Gavioli

COPYEDITING, PROOFREADING AND TRANSLATION
Ivan Sousa Rocha

CURATOR
Adriano Pedrosa
With the assistance of
Teo Teotonio

EXECUTIVE PRODUCTION
Ana Laura e Silva
Gabriel Belvis
Isaque Vieira
Maicon Ferreira
Maria Rosalem
Marília Amorim
Marina Moura
Marina Rebouças
Matheus Gumerato
Pedro Henrique Lopes
Steffânia Prata
Victória Dirotildes

EXHIBITION DESIGN
Flora Gurgel
Melissa dos Santos

GRAPHIC DESIGN
Pablo Mazzucco

LIGHTING DESIGN
Fernanda Carvalho

RESEARCH CENTER
Adriana Villela
Beatriz Yoshito
Bruno Mesquita
Emily Pinheiro
Maycon Richard
Miller Sereno
Pamella Mazucatto
Raquel Brito
Sara Jesus

CATALOG

COPYEDITING AND PROOFREADING
floresta
Ivan Sousa Rocha
Mór Madden
Lara Rivetti
Rafaela Biff Cera

EDITORS
Adriano Pedrosa
With the assistance of
Teo Teotonio

EDITORIAL CONSULTING
Karen Marta Editorial Consulting

EDITORIAL COORDINATION
Ana Canellas
Carol Ribas
Felipe de Souza
Mariana Trevas
Renier Vasconcelos

EDITORIAL PRODUCTION
Carolina Menegatti
Marina Marcondes
Tulio Costa

GRAPHIC DESIGN
Rara Dias
Alexsandro Souza

PRINTING CONSULTANT
Lilia Góes

IMAGE PROCESSING AND PRINTING
Ipsis Gráfica and Editora

TRANSLATION
Adriano Pedrosa
Daniel Lühmann
Jess Oliveira
Lara Rivetti
Sarah Poppel

FONTS
Avenir LT Std
Fayon Pro

PAPERS
Cover: Masterblank Linho 135g
Text Block: Munken Lynx Rough 120g and Eurobulk 150g

IMAGES CREDITS
© Andreas Sterzing Courtesy of the artist and P·P·O·W Gallery, New York 18
© Centre Pompidou, MNAM-CCI, Dist. GrandPalaisRmn/Bertrand Prévost 160
© Centre Pompidou, MNAM-CCI, Dist. GrandPalaisRmn/Georges Meguerditchian 150
© Centre Pompidou, MNAM-CCI, Dist. GrandPalaisRmn/Philippe Migeat 9
© Pepe Espaliú, VEGAP/AUTVIS; Rocco Ricci 19
Ana Paula Latorre Ceccato/Projeto Leonilson 60, 351
Courtesy of Anelie Schinaider and Felipe Félix 4
Courtesy of Blanton Museum of Art, The University of Texas at Austin, United States 34
Courtesy of Nora Fisch Gallery, Buenos Aires, Argentina 31
Courtesy of Contemporary Arts Museum Houston; Emily Peacock 22
Cris Bierrenbach/Projeto Leonilson 235
David Bonet/Projeto Leonilson 6, 357
Edouard Fraipont/Courtesy of Luisa Strina 188
Edouard Fraipont/Projeto Leonilson 8, 10, 12, 14, 36, 37, 43, 44, 46, 48, 65, 69, 72, 79, 101, 102, 113, 114, 121, 132, 139, 140, 143, 154, 157, 163, 164, 169, 183, 191, 194, 216, 218, 223, 229-231, 233, 236, 237, 356, 376
Eduardo Brandão/Projeto Leonilson 125, 238, 239, 368, 369
Eduardo Ortega cover, 152, 377, 378
Eduardo Ortega/Projeto Leonilson 5, 27, 40, 56, 57, 103, 109, 112, 116-118, 136-138, 141, 142, 146, 148, 149, 155, 165, 198, 212, 234, 240, 242, 244-252, 254, 256-282, 284-297, 299, 301, 303-307, 309-328, 331, 332, 334-345
Falcão Jr./Projeto Leonilson 35, 122, 232, 243, 350, 355
Fernando Aurélio Silveira/Projeto Leonilson 375
Frank Steve Moss/Projeto Leonilson 373
Gabriella Pampillon 41
Isabela Matheus/Projeto Leonilson 358
Jaime Acioli/Projeto Leonilson 38, 210
Jéssica Mangaba 186, 227
Job Janssen/Projeto Leonilson 361
J. W. Boerrigter/Projeto Leonilson 147
Kunstmuseum Basel, Switzerland 39
Letícia Parente 21
Marcel Miranda 25
MASP Research Center 2, 3
Miguel A. López 28, 29
Nacho Iasparra, Courtesy MALBA 23
Naná Cola 365
Paul Salveson 24
Philipp Schönborn 353
Philipp Schönborn/Projeto Leonilson 370
Projeto Leonilson 7, 26, 47, 61, 224, 253, 255, 283, 298, 300, 302, 308, 329, 346, 347, 360, 364, 371, 372
Projeto Leonilson/Courtesy The Museum of Modern Art, New York 52, 354
Renato Parada 200
Renato Parada/Projeto Leonilson 11
Rômulo Fialdini/Projeto Leonilson 1, 17, 51, 58, 63, 71, 73, 75, 85, 100, 128-130, 144, 192, 196, 213, 215, 222
Ronaldo Miranda/Projeto Leonilson 366, 367
Rubens Chiri/Projeto Leonilson back cover, 13, 15, 32, 42, 45, 49, 50, 53-55, 59, 64, 66-68, 70, 77, 81-84, 87, 89, 99, 104-107, 110, 111, 115,

119, 120, 123, 124, 126, 127, 131, 133-135, 145, 151, 153, 156, 158, 159, 161, 162, 167, 168, 170-182, 184, 187, 189, 190, 193, 195, 199, 201-209, 211, 214, 217, 219-221, 225, 226, 228, 333, 349, 352, 362, 363, 374
Sergio Guerini/Projeto Leonilson 16, 30, 62, 74, 108, 185, 330
Tate Images 241
The Philadelphia Museum of Art/Art Resource, New York 20
Tom Van Eynde/Projeto Leonilson 197
Unknown Authorship 359
Vicente de Mello/Projeto Leonilson 76, 78, 80, 86, 88, 90-98, 348
Vitor Butkus/Projeto Leonilson 166
Wolfgang Fuhrmannek, Hessisches Landesmuseum Darmstadt 33

ADDITIONAL CAPTIONS
Cover
Leonilson
Agora e as oportunidades
[Now and Opportunities], 1991
[img. 152]

Back cover
Leonilson
Príncipe [Prince], from the series
Os dedicados [The Dedicated], 1991
[img. 170]

On the next page

377. Leonilson
Untitled, 1980

Watercolor on paper
16.5 × 28 cm
Museu de Arte de São Paulo Assis Chateaubriand, gift família Bezerra Dias/ Sociedade Amigos do Projeto Leonilson, 2021,
MASP.11153
PL.0176.0/00

378. Leonilson
Untitled, 1980

Permanent ink on paper
14 × 16 cm
Museu de Arte de São Paulo Assis Chateaubriand, gift família Bezerra Dias/ Sociedade Amigos do Projeto Leonilson, 2021,
MASP.11154
PL.0183.0/00

Edition 2024

1.0 - 2.5/2.5

Dados Internacionais de Catalogação na Publicação (CIP)

M986Le
Museu de Arte de São Paulo Assis Chateaubriand
Leonilson : now and opportunities / curated and edited by Adriano Pedrosa ; with assistance of Teo Teotonio ; texts by Adriano Pedrosa… [et al.] ; designer by Rara Dias and Alexsandro Souza. – São Paulo: MASP, 2024.
426 p., 378 ilus. color.

ISBN: 978-65-5777-060-3
Catalog of the exhibition held in São Paulo, at MASP, from August 23 to November 17, 2024

Leonilson (1954-1993). 2. Brazilian Art. 3. Generation 80. 4. LGBTQIA+ Artists. I. Pedrosa, Adriano (curad., org. e text.) II. Teotonio, Teo (curad. and ed.). III. Riccioppo, Carlos Eduardo (text.). IV. Small, Irene V. Bryan-Wilson, Julia (text.). VI. Lopez, Miguel (text.). VII. Lafuente, Pablo (text.). VIII. Dias, Rara (designer). IX. Souza, Alexsandro (designer). X. Title: Leonilson: now and opportunities.

CDD (20. ed.): 709.81

Librarian: Sara Ferreira, CRB8-9366

MASP MUSEU DE ARTE DE SÃO PAULO ASSIS CHATEAUBRIAND
Avenida Paulista, 1578
01310-200 São Paulo, Brazil
www.masp.org.br
info@masp.org.br

ISBN 978-65-5777-060-3

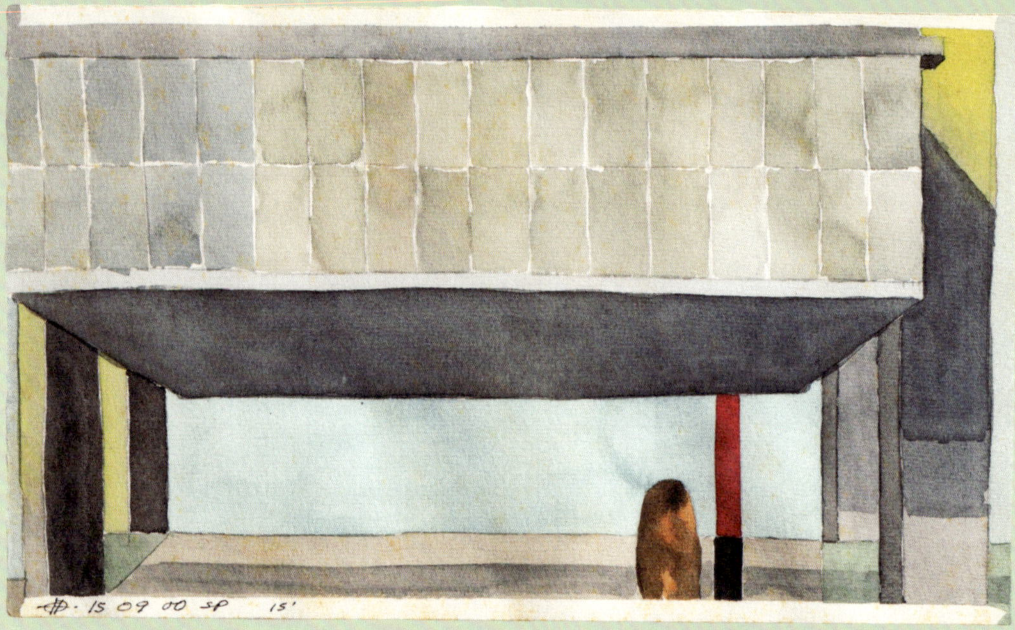

377

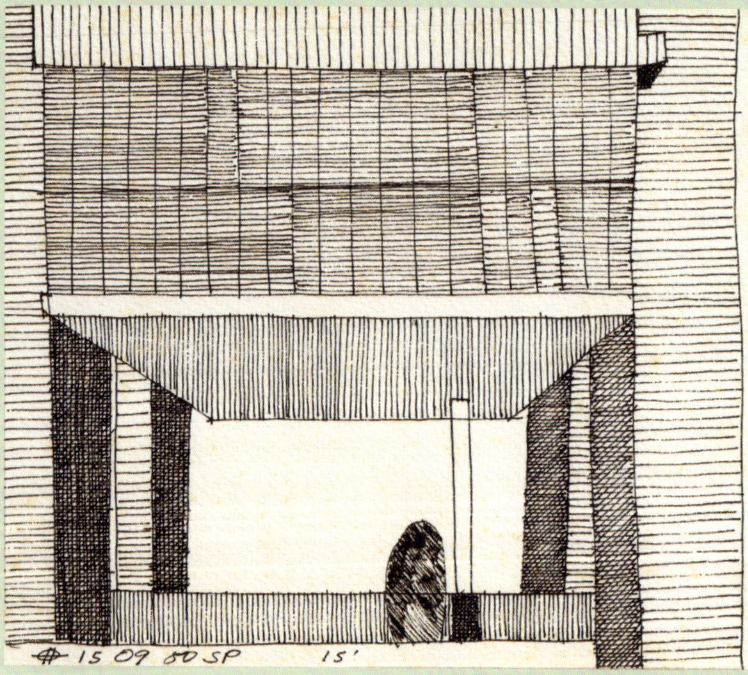

378

MASP, a diverse, inclusive, and plural museum, has the mission to establish, in a critical and creative way, dialogues between past and present, cultures, and territories, through the visual arts. To this end, it should enlarge, conserve, research, and disseminate its collection, while also promoting the encounter between its various publics and art through transformative and welcoming experiences.